China's Economy: Towards 2049

Chenyi Yu

China's Economy: Towards 2049

厦门大学出版社
XIAMEN UNIVERSITY PRESS
国家一级出版社
全国百佳图书出版单位

Springer

Chenyi Yu
Foreign Languages College
Zhejiang Wanli University
Ningbo, Zhejiang, China

ISBN 978-981-15-9226-3 ISBN 978-981-15-9227-0 (eBook)
https://doi.org/10.1007/978-981-15-9227-0

Jointly published with Xiamen University Press
The print edition is not for sale in China Mainland. Customers from China Mainland please order the print book from: Xiamen University Press.

This Springer imprint is published by the registered company Springer Nature Singapore Pte Ltd.
The registered company address is: 152 Beach Road, #21-01/04 Gateway East, Singapore 189721, Singapore

Foreword

While studying the history of the world, we would often feel amazed at the various miracles accomplished by mankind. To a large extent, it is these miracles that have accelerated the progress of civilization. In the global economic arena, although the emergence of China as an important player is believed by many of its counterparts a miracle, by taking a step back in the time tunnel, it can be noticed that this is not a pure emergence; rather, it is a re-emergence because until the late nineteenth century, despite the irreversible decline under the Qing Dynasty's reign, China's total GDP still surpassed most countries by a considerable margin.

Although it is true that there is nothing new under the sun, the world today is full of much more opportunities and challenges, through which China has managed to realize an unprecedented pace of growth. Over the past decades, the robust momentum of development has not only enabled its people to reap tremendous benefits, such as a materially better quality of life, exposure to fresh ways of thinking, and enhanced freedom of choice, it has also contributed to the stability of the global economy. However, to have these achievements consolidated, it is equally crucial to identify the costs behind. In particular, given the widened gap between the rich and the poor, the deteriorating ecological environment in both the urban and rural areas, the precarious food security situation, etc., if no major improvements could be made within a reasonable length of time, they would sooner or later become stumbling blocks that restrain China from attaining higher goals.

From the year the People's Republic of China was established, the country would very soon approach its 70th anniversary. According to the Chinese philosopher and sage Confucius, seventy is an age when a person could follow his heart's desire without transgressing the norm (from *The Analects of Confucius* translated by A. Charles Muller). If utilizing the same rationale on China, this should be a stage at which it is capable of harmonizing diverse affairs, either domestic or international, with wisdom and foresight. Apparently, for the acquisition of such an ability, reflections over the past are indispensable prerequisites, especially those episodes intertwined with twists and turns. To portray in a systematic way what have taken place in China's economic scene since 1949, the book uses a chronological order and the entire period is divided into four separate phases, i.e. pre–1978, 1978–1988, 1989–1999, and the post-WTO era. Generally, the focus in the earlier sections is laid on the internal side and highlights the fluctuations impacted by the political vicissitudes from the 1950s to the 1970s. With a view to depicting how the economy has been transformed after the adoption of the opening-up policy, chapter four and five elaborate more on the external sectors like foreign trade, foreign direct investment, in addition to the numerous moves that would prepare China for a deeper integration with the world.

Admittedly, China's ongoing transition into socialist market economy is a rather complicated and arduous task which necessitates the mobilization of all the resources at home. Besides, borrowing experiences from the outside with an open and humble heart may help smooth out the process. Anyhow, irrespective of the path that is chosen, the ultimate ideal of increasing people's wellbeing should be common across the universe and from this point of view, all the barriers (especially the prejudices and doubts) impeding its materialization should be broken down. Whereas competition is inevitable in the short run; over the long term, it is via collaboration that we can expect to secure a truly abundant future. What's more, being a member of the international community, the fate of China is already closely linked with that of the whole world. Therefore, mapping the economy is no longer just a "domestic" business, but a matter incorporating concerns about the cross-border repercussions.

Looking ahead, what await the Chinese leadership to tackle are no less stressful as compared to the eve of the 1978 reform, because after almost 40 years of speed- and quantity-oriented pattern of growth, the timing is now appropriate to shift to another model which is quality-centered and efficiency-driven. The days are gone for its annual GDP to shoot up at a double-digit rate, in its place, the "new normal" state ('*xin chang tai*') characterized by a slowdown to 7-8PCT has taken shape. In fact, this is a reminder calling for further structural adjustment and adaptation. Is China in a position to tune itself finely? There is no easy answer for the time being and if the same question had been raised in 1978, it would have been very likely unanswered too. Nevertheless, having gone through the first round, the country is now more experienced and thus confident. Most significantly, it has a clearer understanding of what is meant by a globalized economy. Based on its initiation of free trade agreements with multiple foreign partners, the "Belt and Road" scheme, and the Asian Infrastructure Investment Bank (AIIB), etc., China is indeed getting itself ready for the next round of transformation. On the one hand, the endeavor is similar to the building of the miraculous Great Wall which zigzags thousands of miles and involves the collective efforts of generations; on the other hand, unlike the Great Wall whose erection has led to self-imposed isolation, China is increasingly tolerant of national disparities and willing to embrace imported practices. In case such a trend is to continue, the road for the accomplishment of its objectives would be better paved. Above all, with a vision set for tomorrow, China today is in need of fulfilling all the preconditions to turn it into reality.

Ningbo, China Chenyi Yu

Acknowledgements

The initial idea of publishing a book on the Chinese economy is from Prof. Dong Junfeng, a respectable colleague of mine at the Foreign Languages College of Zhejiang Wanli University. However, it soon turned out that taking a decision is much easier than the process of writing itself, which not only involved huge amount of preparatory works on sourcing, reading, and thinking, but also the challenge of furnishing authentic data for different time periods, especially those of the earlier stage. In order to get myself better prepared, I went to the United States in the first half of 2015 as a visiting scholar at the University of North Carolina, Chapel Hill. The library there offered me a good opportunity to access the materials and publications which are related to the subject project. Also at Chapel Hill, I met Prof. Steven Rosefielde who enlightened me with valuable advice on the writing. Being a specialist of the Soviet economy, his lifetime devotion to academic study is equally a great inspiration to me. During my stay, I also got to know Prof. Edward Tower of Duke University. He shared with me his insight about today's foreign trade and similar to Prof. Rosefielde, he also offered to read my first draft and give me suggestions when it is finished. Moreover, from their efficient and supportive working style, I see important qualities a true scholar should possess, which is beyond the realm of knowledge and the level of expertise.

Due to the necessity to allocate a big chunk of time to teaching, as well as the complexities involved in the project, I did not have much energy left for the housework. Fortunately, my parents are both healthy and understanding. As always, they looked after my life with relentless care and love, which I could hardly repay. By bringing me into this world, they direct me to the right way I should walk, the only way that leads to truth and light.

In addition, I would like to express my gratitude to a bigger family of mine, i.e. the faculty of the Foreign Languages College. By working with these nice colleagues for some 16 years, I feel rather blessed for they are so cooperative and nice whenever I am in need of encouragements. It is their smile and soothing words that have enabled me to see the beauty of life.

Contents

1 Introduction 1
References 3

2 China from 1949 to 1977 5
1 Restoration of the National Economy (1949–1952) 5
1.1 A Pressing Need of Restoration 5
1.2 Adoption of a Four-Pronged Approach 6
1.3 Impact on Prices: From Fluctuation to Stabilization 15
2 The First Five-Year Plan (1953–1957) 19
2.1 Agriculture: From MATs to Higher APCs 19
2.2 Industry: A Heavy-Industry-Centered Model from the Soviet 21
3 The Great Leap Forward of the Second Five Year Plan (1958–1962) 25
3.1 People's Commune, a Step Further to Collectivized Farming 25
3.2 The Iron and Steel Campaign for Industrial Modernization 27
3.3 The Great Famine and Economic Adjustment 28
3.4 An Episode Worthy of Contemplation 31
4 Retrenchment and Readjustment (1963–1965) 32
4.1 Corrective Measures Underway 32
4.2 The "Third Front" and Its Impact 33
5 The Cultural Revolution (1966–1976) 35
5.1 Urban Industrial Enterprises in the Movement 35
5.2 Rural Policy Changes and Their Effects 40
5.3 Lessons from the "Cultural Revolution" 42
6 A Window to the Outside World: Foreign Trade 45

6.1 A Policy Consistent with the Heavy-Industry-Centered Model . . . 45
6.2 A State-Monopolized Sector . . . 47
6.3 A Centrally-Planned System . . . 49
6.4 A Uniform Pricing Mechanism . . . 50
6.5 Stringent Control Over Foreign Exchange . . . 52
6.6 Mirror of the Macro Environment . . . 53
References . . . 56

3 Economic Reform, the 1st Phase . . . 61
1 The Great Leap Outward . . . 62
1.1 One More Ambitious Yet Unrealistic Plan . . . 62
1.2 Obstacles Challenging Its Fulfillment . . . 63
2 Initial Reforms Kicked off (1978–1983) . . . 65
2.1 The Guiding Ideology . . . 67
2.2 De-collectivization of Agriculture via HRS . . . 68
2.3 From CBEs to TVEs . . . 74
2.4 De-centralization in Industry . . . 77
2.5 Rationalization of the Banking Sector . . . 83
2.6 Centralization-Decentralization Cycle of the Fiscal System . . . 89
2.7 Internationalization via SEZs . . . 95
2.8 Dual-Track System of Managing the Exchange Rates . . . 99
3 New Wave of Reform (1984–1988) . . . 102
3.1 The Price-Formation Mechanism . . . 103
3.2 Urban Area: CRS of the SOEs . . . 106
3.3 Rural Area: TVEs . . . 109
4 Summary of the 1st-Phase Reform: 1978–1988 . . . 114
4.1 GDP Growth . . . 115
4.2 FDI and Export Increase . . . 116
4.3 Inflation Under an Overheated Economy . . . 117
References . . . 118

4 Eve of Socialist Market Economy: The 2nd-Phase Reform . . . 123
1 Systemic Change . . . 123
2 The Southern Tour Amid Ideological Clashes . . . 124
3 Retrenchment Efforts and the Tradeoffs (1989–1991) . . . 125
4 Monetary Instrument for Economic Cool Down . . . 127
5 Tax Assignment System, the 2nd Round of Fiscal Reform . . . 129
5.1 Establishment of the System and Its Administrative Organs . . . 130
5.2 Arrangements to Stimulate the Local Governments . . . 131
5.3 Restructuring of the Turnover Tax System . . . 132
5.4 Unification of Nominal Tax Rates on Enterprise Income . . . 134

5.5 Positive Effects of the Reformed Scheme 135
5.6 Problems Behind the Unsatisfactory Performances 135
6 Restructuring of the SOEs 137
6.1 The Ailing SOEs 139
6.2 Transforming the LMSOEs via Modern Enterprise System 142
6.3 Privatization of Small SOEs 149
7 Banking Sector Reform 158
7.1 Central and Commercial Banks 159
7.2 Foreign-Funded Banks 166
8 The Foreign Exchange Regime 174
8.1 The Tale of Multiple Currencies Under the Kuomintang Regime 174
8.2 The Post-1949 Mechanism of Forming the RMB Exchange Rates 176
8.3 Stagnant Foreign Trade Under the Rigid Exchange Regime 178
8.4 Retention Scheme for Export Earnings 181
8.5 The Short-Lived IRTS and Initiation of the Swap 182
8.6 The Booming Foreign Exchange Adjustment Centers 184
8.7 A Unified Managed Floating Regime 188
8.8 The Inter-Bank Foreign Exchange Market 189
8.9 Free Convertibility of RMB Under Current Account Transactions 191
8.10 A Tight Control of the Capital Account 192
8.11 Rationales to Keep RMB Intact Under the Asian Financial Crisis 196
8.12 Necessity to Liberalize the Capital Account 198
9 The Securities Market 199
9.1 A Retrospect of the Days Long Ago 199
9.2 Post-1949 Decades, A Transition Stage 205
9.3 Resurgence of Securities Exchanges Since the 1990s 205
10 Foreign Trade, A More Decentralized External Sector 217
10.1 Composition of Imports and Exports 218
10.2 Relaxation of Trading Rights 219
10.3 Coexistence of Command and Guidance Plans 220
10.4 Losses of FTCs 221
10.5 Implementation of Contract Responsibility System 223
10.6 Correlation Between Export and the Rebate Mechanism 224
10.7 Another Round of Reform 226
10.8 Accession to the WTO 227

11 Foreign Direct Investment, a Critical Engine of the Economy 228
11.1 From Closeness to Openness 230
11.2 Enlargement of the "Laboratories" 232
12 Evolution of Outward-Looking Policies 237
12.1 Phase One: 1979–1986 237
12.2 Phase Two: 1992–1999 239
References 240

5 New Century, New Economy 249
1 Accession to the WTO, a Fresh Beginning 250
2 Capital Market 251
2.1 Convertible Bond, a Hybrid Security 252
2.2 Split-Share Structure Reform 253
2.3 Delisting of Underperforming Stocks 257
2.4 Multi-Tiered Stock Exchange 258
2.5 Private Equity 261
2.6 Bond Market 268
3 Foreign Trade in the New Era 276
3.1 Revision of the Foreign Trade Law 276
3.2 Reduction on Import Tariffs 277
3.3 Restructuring of the State FTCs 279
3.4 Trade in Services: A Growth Engine for the Future 281
3.5 Trial of Free Trade Zones 285
4 RMB Exchange Rates and Capital Account Liberalization 289
4.1 Initial Adjustment of the Mechanism, a Gradual Approach 289
4.2 Conditions Prepared for the Next Stage of Reform 292
4.3 New Exchange Rate Regime in 2005 293
4.4 Establishment of Market Maker System 296
4.5 Launch of Foreign Exchange Derivatives 298
4.6 Capital Account Convertibility 300
5 Outward Foreign Direct Investment 319
5.1 Ready for Takeoff 320
5.2 Growing Presence on the Global Stage 320
5.3 Accelerated Pace of OFDI 322
5.4 The Belt and Road Initiative 324
6 Agriculture, the Lifeline of the Nation 326
6.1 Situations During the Pre-reform Stage 326
6.2 The Critical Move of Relaxing Grain Circulation 328
6.3 Endeavors of Structural Adjustment 330
6.4 Growing Reliance on the External Supply 333
6.5 Concerns Over Food Security 336
6.6 Means to a Sustainable Development 339
6.7 From "Bringing in" to "Going Out" 341

7 Urbanization and the Fate of Migrant Workers 343
7.1 "Hukou" System, a Constraint on Labor Mobility 344
7.2 ID Card: "Passport" to Liberalized Migration 345
7.3 Headaches Following the Designation of New Towns and Cities 346
7.4 "Secrets" Behind Export Miracle 348
7.5 Citizenization of Migrant Workers 349
7.6 Relationship Between the Service Sector and Urbanization 352
7.7 Key to Sustainable Urbanization 355
References 359

6 Conclusion 369
References 373

Abbreviations and Acronyms

ABC	Agricultural Bank of China
ADB	Asian Development Bank
AIIB	Asian Infrastructure Investment Bank
AMC	Asset Management Company
APC	Agricultural producers' cooperative
BECZ	Border economic cooperation zone
BOC	Bank of China
BOP	Balance of payments
CAR	Capital adequacy ratio
CBC	Construction Bank of China
CBE	Commune and brigade enterprise
CBRC	China Banking Regulatory Commission
CCCPC	Central Committee of the Communist Party of China
CDB	China Development Bank
CFETS	China Foreign Exchange Trading System
CGSDTC	China Government Securities Depository Trust & Clearing Co., Ltd.
CHIBOR	China Inter-bank Offered Rate
CIT	Corporate income tax
CPC	Communist Party of China
CPI	Consumer price index
CRS	Contract responsibility system
CSRC	China Securities Regulatory Commission
ETDZ	Economic and technological development zone
FCS	Fiscal contracting system
FDI	Foreign direct investment
FEAC	Foreign exchange adjustment center
FIE	Foreign-invested enterprise
FTA	Free trade area
FTC	Foreign trade corporation
GATT	General Agreement on Tariffs and Trade

GDP	Gross domestic product
GLF	Great Leap Forward
GNI	Gross national income
GNP	Gross national product
HRS	Household responsibility system
ICBC	Industrial and Commercial Bank of China
IFC	International Finance Corporation
IIP	International investment position
IMF	International Monetary Fund
IPO	Initial public offering
IRTS	Internal rate for trade settlements
ISR	Internal settlement rate
LIBOR	London Inter-bank Offered Rate
LMSOE	Large and medium-sized state-owned enterprise
MAT	Mutual aid team
MBO	Management buyout
MOC	Ministry of Commerce
MOF	Ministry of Finance
NASDAQ	National Association of Securities Dealers Automatic Quotation System
NBS	National Bureau of Statistics
NBTT	Net barter terms of trade
NDRC	National Development and Reform Commission
NEEQ	National Equities Exchange and Quotations
NEOs	Net errors and omissions
NPL	Non-performing loan
NTS	Non-tradable share
OBOR	One Belt and One Road
ODA	Official development assistance
OFDI	Outbound (outward) foreign direct investment
OMO	Open market operation
OTC	Over the counter
PBoC	People's Bank of China
PE	Private equity
QDII	Qualified domestic institutional investor
QFII	Qualified foreign institutional investor
RCC	Rural credit cooperative
ROC	Return on capital
RPI	Retail price index
RQFII	Renminbi qualified foreign institutional investor
SAC	Securities Association of China
SAFE	State Administration of Foreign Exchange
SAT	State Administration of Taxation
SEZ	Special economic zone
SHIBOR	Shanghai Interbank Offered Rate

SMC	Supply and marketing cooperative
SME	Small and medium-sized enterprise
SOE	State-owned enterprise
SRF	Silk Road Fund
SSE	Shanghai Stock Exchange
STRI	Service Trade Restrictiveness Index
SZSE	Shenzhen Stock Exchange
TIC	Trust and investment company
TS	Tradable share
TVE	Township and village enterprise
UNCTAD	United Nations Conference on Trade and Development
UNFAO	Food and Agriculture Organization of the United Nations
VAT	Value-added tax
VC	Venture capital
WPI	Wholesale price index
WTO	World Trade Organization

List of Graphs and Photos

Chapter 2

Photo 1 The family of Gao Caiguan, a peasant from Jiaxing, Zhejiang Province, was apportioned land in the agrarian reform of 1950. They are quite happy to receive the newly-issued land certificate. By the spring of 1953, this nationwide reform was basically accomplished. *Source* https://paper.people.com.cn/rmrbhwb/html/2011-10/28/content_949221.htm 7

Photo 2 In 1957, Kushkin, a 65-year-old Soviet expert shared his experience with Chinese workers at Jilin Fertilizer Plant. *Source* Song, 2015 23

Graph 1 Changes in the WPI and RPI of Shanghai. *Source* Zhu, 2005 12

Graph 2 Changes in the National Wholesale Price Index. *Source* Zhong, 1992 16

Graph 3 Spending on Economy and National Defense in the Total Fiscal Expenditure, RMB Billion. *Source* Dong, 2001 18

Graph 4 Value of Agricultural and Industrial Output (at current prices), RMB100 Million. *Note* value of agricultural and industrial output (A&I) calculated by the author. Source: value of agricultural output (A) and value of industrial output (I) from NBS, 1999 42

Chapter 3

Graph 1 TVEs' export versus China's total, RMB100 million. *Source* Total export: NBS (2001); direct export by TVEs: NBS (2004); PCT share of TVEs in the total is calculated by the author 113

Chapter 4

Photo 1 Office building of Xiamen International Bank, the first joint venture bank of China opened on November 28th, 1985 in Xiamen Special Economic Zone. *Source* https://www.xmnn.cn/dzbk/xmrb/20111226/201112/t20111226_2118801.htm 169
Photo 2 Foreign exchange quotations board of Shenzhen FEAC on November 5th, 1988, Saturday. On that date, the average prices for USD100 and HKD100 were offered at RMB649.21 and RMB82.55 respectively, with the price of the retention quota set at RMB2.5405 per US dollar. *Source* Tan (2010). . . . 186
Photo 3 The 1st stock certificate (sample) of China, issued by China Merchants Steam Navigation Company (CMSNC) in 1872, i.e. the 11th year of Emperor Tongzhi's reign and priced at 500 taels of silver each share. *Source* China Merchants Group at https://www.cmhk.com/main/a/2015/k08/a231_286.shtml. . . . 200
Photo 4 News report on the agreement reached between China and the Soviet Union to set up a jointstock airline by the Southern Daily ('Nanfang ribao') on April 2nd, 1950. Named Sino-Soviet Civil Airline, it officially went into operation on July 1st, 1950. *Source* https://www.caac.gov.cn/website/old/D1/60years/jkcy/zsmh/ 229

Graph 1 Financial performance of the industrial SOEs, RMB billion. *Source* NBS (2012) 141
Graph 2 Export of FIEs in China's total, USD100 million. *Source* MOC (2013). 156
Graph 3 Investment income (debit) under the balance of payments, USD100 million. *Source* SAFE (2015) 156
Graph 4 Export and foreign exchange reserves, USD billion. *Source* NBS (2001) 196
Graph 5 Issuance of three types of bonds, RMB100 million. *Source* Gui (2003) 215
Graph 6 Losses of the FTCs financed by central government budget, RMB100 million. *Source* losses of FTCs and total losses of SOEs: World Bank (1993); total export volume: NBS (2000) 222
Graph 7 Export rebate versus central government's expenditure, RMB100 million. *Source* export rebate: Ministry of Finance, from https://www.mof.gov.cn/zhuantihuigu/2006ysbgjd/tjsj/200805/t20080519_23380.html; central government's total expenditure: NBS (2005); PCT share of export rebate in the total expenditure: calculated by the author 225

Graph 8 FDI actually used by the four SEZs, USD Million. *Source* FDI of Shenzhen SEZ: Shenzhen Statistical Yearbook 2014, Shenzhen Bureau of Statistics, from https://www.sztj.gov.cn/xxgk/tjsj/tjnj/201503/t20150331_2836397.htm; FDI of Zhuhai SEZ: Zhuhai Statistical Yearbook 2014, Zhuhai Bureau of Statistics, from http://www.stats-zh.gov.cn/tjsj/tjnj/201504/t20150401_204496.htm; FDI of Shantou SEZ: Shantou Statistical Yearbook 2014, Shantou Bureau of Statistics, from http://sttj.shantou.gov.cn/tjsj/tjnj/tjnj2014/; FDI of Xiamen SEZ: Yearbook of Xiamen Special Economic Zone 2014, Xiamen Bureau of Statistics, from http://www.stats-xm.gov.cn/2014/ 231
Graph 9 FDI actually utilized by Hainan SEZ and its export, USD Million. *Source* Hainan Statistical Yearbook 1998, from https://www.hnszw.org.cn/data/news/2012/09/54459/ 233
Graph 10 Distribution of FDI and other foreign investments in three areas, PCT. *Source* Wei (2001) 238

Chapter 5

Photo 1 Distribution of the four free trade zones in China, from the north to the south, they are Tianjin FTZ, Shanghai FTZ, Fujian FTZ, and Guangdong FTZ. *Source* https://www.chinadaily.com.cn/business/2015-04/21/content_20493185_2.htm 288

Graph 1 Market capitalization of tradable shares versus total market capaitalization, RMB100 million. *Source* monthly report of China's securities market for selected years, China Securities Regulatory Commission. https://www.csrc.gov.cn/pub/newsite/sjtj/zqscyb/index_5.html. 256
Graph 2 Comparison of PE-Backed IPOs and the Aggregate PE-Backed Exits. *Source* Number of PE-backed exits: 中国股权投资市场2015全年回顾与展望. Zero2IPO Research Center, 2016. Number of PE-backed IPOs: 中国私募股权投资年度研究报告 of the selected years, Zero2IPO Research Center. . . . 265
Graph 3 Composition of Different Benchmark Interest Rates for RMB Interest Rate Swap Transactions, PCT. *Source* 中国人民银行 (PBoC). 金融市场运行情况 of selected years, from https://www.pbc.gov.cn/jinrongshichangsi/147160/147171/147173/22578/index4.html 273
Graph 4 Tariff Reduction of the Pre- and Post-WTO Periods, PCT. *Source* 1951 & 1985: Ma & Li, 2007; 1996: Long, 1996; 2001–2010: MOF, 2012 278

Graph 5 Composition of the Gross Domestic Product, PCT. *Note* 1985 marks the end of the 6th Five Year Plan (FYP), 1990 is the end of the 7th FYP, 1995 is the end of the 8th FYP, so on and so forth and until 2015, it is the end of the 12th FYP. *Source* 1978–2010: NBS, 2016. 2015: NBS. 2015 年国民经济和社会发展统计公报, 2016 282
Graph 6 Export Growth Rate, PCT. *Note* calculated by the author based on the export volume of selected years. *Source* NBS, 2016 286
Graph 7 Comparison of Foreign Exchange Reserves and Balance of Payments Performance, USD Billion. *Source* NBS, 2003, 2004, 2005 and 2006 292
Graph 8 Average Daily Foreign Exchange Market Turnover of Selected Countries, USD Billion. *Note* China's daily turnover for 1998 is calculated by the author by dividing the annual turnover of USD51.96 billion by 252 trading days; for 2001, it is calculated by dividing the annual turnover of USD75.03 billion by 252 trading days; for 2004, it is calculated by dividing the annual turnover of USD209.04 billion by 252 trading days. For China, the volume is based on the entire year and pertains only to inter-bank spot transactions. For markets outside China, daily averages are for the month of April and cover spot, forward and swap transactions. *Source* China: SAFE, 1999, 2002 & 2005; Countries outside China: BIS, 2013 296
Graph 9 Time-Series Data of International Investment Position, USD Billion. *Note* from the first quarter of 2015, the IIP of China was compiled according to the standard of BPM6 of the IMF. Apart from 2014, those of the previous years were not adjusted. *Source* SAFE, 2016. 316
Graph 10 OFDI Flows of China and the World, USD Million. *Source* Foreign direct investment: inward and outward flows and stock, annual, 1970–2015, at current prices, UNCTAD, from https://unctadstat.unctad.org/wds/TableViewer/tableView.aspx?ReportId=96740. 323
Graph 11 Composition of the Gross Output Value of Agriculture, PCT. *Source* calculated by the author on the basis of China Statistical Yearbook 2015, NBS 333
Graph 12 Export and Import of Wheat, Tons. *Source* UN Comtrade database from https://comtrade.un.org/data/ 336
Graph 13 Agricultural Water Withdrawal in Total Water Withdrawal, 100 Million Cubic Meters Per Year. *Note* Agricultural withdrawl as PCT of the total is calculated by the author by dividing agricultural water withdrawl by the total water withdrawl. *Source* NBS, 2016 339

Graph 14 Per Capita Income of Urban and Rural Households, RMB/Month. *Note* figures for rural households are the per capita net income whereas those for urban households are the per capita disposable income. *Source* NBS, 2001 347
Graph 15 Budgetary appropriation for recurrent expenditure per student of elementary schools, RMB. *Source* MOE, 1998, 1999, 2000 & 2001 348
Graph 16 Comparison of Average Salaries between Urban and Migrant Workers, RMB/Month. *Source* Salary of urban workers is calculated by the author on the basis of the average annual salaries of employees working in China's cities and towns. NBS, 2010. Salary of migrant workers: Lu, 2012 349
Graph 17 Proportion of Migrant Workers Participating in Social Insurance Program, PCT. *Source* NBS, 2014 & 2015 351
Graph 18 Urbanization Rate of Jiangsu Province in 2013 and Targets for 2017 & 2020, PCT. *Source* 江苏省国家新型城镇化综合试点工作方案要点, 2014. From https://www.gov.cn/xinwen/site1/20150204/40201423027629790.pdf 356
Graph 19 Regional Comparison of Urbanization Rate, 2008–2014, PCT. *Note* According to the National Bureau of Statistics, the three parts of China are divided as follows: East China include 11 provinces (including municipalities directly under the central government), i.e. Beijing, Tianjin, Hebei, Liaoning, Shanghai, Jiangsu, Zhejiang, Fujian, Shandong, Guangdong, and Hainan; Central China include 8 provinces, i.e. Shanxi, Jilin, Heilongjiang, Anhui, Jiangxi, Henan, Hubei, and Hunan; West China include 12 provinces (including municipalities directly under the central government, autonomous regions), i.e. Inner Mongolia, Guangxi, Chongqing, Sichuan, Guizhou, Yunnan, Tibet, Shaanxi, Gansu, Qinghai, Ningxia, and Xinjiang. Source: classification of the three parts of China: https://www.stats.gov.cn/tjsj/zxfb/201604/t20160428_1349713.html; 2008 & 2010: http://www.gov.cn/zhengce/2014-03/13/content_2637871.htm; 2012: http://www.chinacity.org.cn/cstj/zxgg/125672.html; 2014: http://chinareform.org.cn/area/city/Practice/201604/t20160414_246899.htm 357

Chapter 6

Graph 1 Per Capita GDP of China, Asia and the World, 1990 International Geary-Khamis Dollars. *Source*. Maddison, 2010 371

List of Tables

Chapter 1

Table 1 Comparison of China's Per Capita GDP with selected countries and the world, 1–1950 AD (1990 International Geary-Khamis Dollars) 2

Chapter 2

Table 1 Growth in the total and per capita output of grain, 1949–1952 8
Table 2 Fiscal (Im)balance: revenues and expenditures, 1949–1952 10
Table 3 Overall price indices, 1951–1952 (preceding year = 100) 18
Table 4 Output of major industrial products, 1952–1957 22
Table 5 Composition of the gross industrial output value, 1952–1957 24
Table 6 Comparison of GDP, population and grain output, 1958–1962 29
Table 7 Investment in industrial infrastructures, 1952–1978 46
Table 8 Growth of foreign trade, 1952–1978 47
Table 9 Composition of the main exports, 1950 48
Table 10 Composition of the main imports, 1950 49
Table 11 Trade volume between China and the Soviet Union, 1958–1967 51
Table 12 Comparison of foreign trade and gross industrial & agricultural output, 1952–1978 54
Table 13 Shifts in Foreign Trade and GDP, 1953–1977 55

Chapter 3

Table 1 Growth in grain yield per unit area and output, 1977–1983 72
Table 2 Division of the central and local revenues, 1980–1989 94
Table 3 FDI, export and GDP of Shenzhen, 1979–1983 99

Table 4 Growth of the TVEs, 1978–1988 110
Table 5 GDP growth and per capita GDP, 1978–1988 115
Table 6 Foreign direct investment actually utilized, 1979–1988. 116
Table 7 Foreign trade and export growth, 1978–1988 117

Chapter 4

Table 1 A comparison of growth in GDP, CPI and money supply, 1994–1998 129
Table 2 Composition of industrial SOEs, 1995 139
Table 3 Gross industrial output contributed by different types of enterprises, 1994–1998 153
Table 4 Four AMCs and transfer of NPLs from corresponding banks by mid-2001 161
Table 5 Growth in M2 and its impact on consumer price index, 1990–2000 165
Table 6 Financial performance of the Bank of Shanghai, 1999–2011 . . . 172
Table 7 Foreign exchange reserves and exchange rates, 1950–1978 177
Table 8 Losses in RMB for earning one US dollar, 1975–1979. 179
Table 9 Coexistence of three exchange rates, 1981–1985 184
Table 10 Changes in official exchange rates and its impact, 1993–1995 189
Table 11 Comparison of the NEOs and the volume of commodity trade, 1996–1999 193
Table 12 Dominant Asian markets for Chinese exports and their share in the total, 1997–1998. 195
Table 13 Summary of the stock market performance, 1991–2000 207
Table 14 Composition of import commodities in selected years, 1980–1990 218
Table 15 Composition of export commodities in selected years, 1980–1990 219
Table 16 Leading investors of Shenzhen SEZ and their Investment, 1986–1989 232
Table 17 FDI actually utilized by the 171 National ETDZs in 2012 235
Table 18 Shifts in the general net barter terms of trade, 1981–1993 239

Chapter 5

Table 1 Tradable & non-tradable shares of domestically-listed companies, 1993–2005 254
Table 2 Transaction of shares at the new third board, 2006–2015 260
Table 3 Raised capital and newly-established private equity funds, 2006–2014 264
Table 4 Comparison of VC & PE attractiveness among the BRICs, 2016 268

Table 5 Forward transactions of the inter-bank bond market, 2006–2016 . . . 271
Table 6 RMB interest rate swap transactions, 2006–2014 . . . 271
Table 7 Proportion of direct financing as a share of total social financing, 2002–2014 . . . 275
Table 8 Comparison of foreign trade between 1978 and 2001 . . . 276
Table 9 Composition of export by diverse foreign trade entities, 2002 and 2015 . . . 279
Table 10 Sectoral composition of import and export in services, 2000–2014 . . . 282
Table 11 Export of services by industries, 2000–2014 . . . 283
Table 12 Country comparison of service trade restrictiveness index (STRI) and export . . . 284
Table 13 Selected indicators of the economy after the 1997 Asian financial crisis, 1998–2000 . . . 290
Table 14 Movements in RMB exchange rates against selected currencies, 2005 . . . 295
Table 15 RMB foreign exchange forward and swap transactions, 2006–2007 . . . 298
Table 16 Four-stage movement of USD/RMB exchange rates, 1994–2014 . . . 300
Table 17 Composition of financing instruments by non-financial sectors, 2003–2005 . . . 303
Table 18 Current account surplus and foreign exchange reserves, 2005–2010 . . . 305
Table 19 Time of capital account openness of selected economies . . . 306
Table 20 Status of capital account liberalization, 2011 . . . 307
Table 21 List of the QFIIs approved before the end of 2003 . . . 310
Table 22 QDIIs approved by January 30th, 2015 . . . 312
Table 23 RQFIIs approved by March 26th, 2015 . . . 315
Table 24 Direct investment and portfolio positions (in USD Billion), 2005–2015 . . . 317
Table 25 International comparison of portfolio investment position against GDP, December 2015 . . . 318
Table 26 Outward FDI flows and stocks, 1985–2002 . . . 321
Table 27 Comparison of OFDI flows and stocks with selected countries and the world, 2000 . . . 322
Table 28 Land-population balance, 1949–1978 . . . 327
Table 29 State budgetary expenditure for agriculture, 1950–1980 . . . 327
Table 30 Grain purchasing price index and the annual output, 1978–1995 . . . 329
Table 31 Soybean production and trade volume, 1992–2012 . . . 334
Table 32 Cereal import dependency ratio of selected countries and the world, 2001–2011 . . . 337

Table 33 Fertilizer consumption of Arable land, 2010–2014 338
Table 34 Average annual growth of selected time periods. 340
Table 35 Distribution of population in urban and rural China, 1950–1978 341
Table 36 Comparison of urbanization rate and the level of industrialization, 2000–2010 353
Table 37 Comparison of China's service sector with selected countries and income groups, 2010 354
Table 38 Employment elasticity of Beijing municipality, 2001–2010 355

Chapter 6

Table 1 GDP of China and the World, 1–1950 AD (Million 1990 International Geary-Khamis Dollars). 370

Chapter 1
Introduction

Economy, a social domain related to activities ranging from production to distribution, fabricates a network through which individuals and institutions interact with each other. Usually, how a country structures its economic system has a direct impact on the way resources are allocated and wealth is accumulated. Further, it may also affect its foreign relations, as well as international status. Although economy does not display a society in a panoramic way, what it mirrors is of no doubt multi-dimensional, including the embedded ideologies, values, and beliefs, etc. Additionally, once a major shift occurs, either in strategies or policies, the effect is often contagious because not only the sectors involved, relevant industries, markets, and even the livelihood of people would also undergo changes. Therefore, to gain insight into any nation in the world, especially from a historical point of view, economy serves as a window through which the past and the present can be portrayed.

Before exploring China's economy in the post-1949 era, it is essential to have some knowledge about where it stood internationally over the previous centuries. Given the fact that early in the first year of the Christian era, i.e. 1 AD, China's population already hit 59.6 million, accounting for over 26 PCT of the World's total which registered 225.8 million (Maddison, 2010), per capita GDP as an indicator of people's standard of living can better illustrate the relative performance of China's economy against that of others. Moreover, behind the ups and downs in these numbers, it is actually the political and societal revolutions that caused the shifts to take place in each particular stage of the history.

The table below (Table 1) shows the per capita GDP of China as compared with a number of selected countries from Europe, North America, and Asia. Till 1600 AD, i.e. under the reign of emperor Wanli during the Ming Dynasty, China in general outperformed the world average as well as most of the chosen counterparts. Then over the following two centuries (mainly the rule of the Qing Dynasty), China stood almost unchanged whereas other nations caught up, with the exception of India. The year 1870 under emperor Tongzhi's reign should be taken as a turning point because China ranked the lowest among the five countries. Later on, despite some minor recoveries, the gap continued to expand at an accelerated pace, which manifests how

C. Yu, *China's Economy: Towards 2049*,
https://doi.org/10.1007/978-981-15-9227-0_1

Table 1 Comparison of China's Per Capita GDP with selected countries and the world, 1–1950 AD (1990 International Geary-Khamis Dollars)

Year	1	1000	1600	1700	1820	1870	1900	1913	1950
China	450	466	600	600	600	530	545	552	448
United Kingdom	400	400	974	1,250	1,706	3,190	4,492	4,921	6,939
United States	400	400	400	527	1,257	2,445	4,091	5,301	9,561
Japan	400	425	520	570	669	737	1,180	1,387	1,921
India	450	450	550	550	533	533	599	673	619
World average	**467**	**453**	**596**	**615**	**666**	**870**	**1,261**	**1,524**	**2,111**

Source Maddison (2010)

drastic the collapse of the Qing Dynasty was. Unfortunately, this downward spiral did not end when there was a transfer of power in 1912. After almost four decades of constant upheavals, the per capita GDP of China by 1950 was merely one fifth of the world average, leaving it among the poorest countries across the globe.

On the basis of the track record of most countries, modernization can be roughly divided into four types, i.e. pacemakers who always take the leadership and enjoy first-mover advantage over others, imitators who are risk averse and prefer to copy proven experiences, borrowers to begin with but catch up later with independent innovations, and advocates of autarky who stick to their obsolete models of development and thus are way behind the rest of the world. Several large economies today have followed the route of the third category, which also is described as the catch-up-and-overtake pattern. The first one is the United States, as a superpower, it quickened its pace of modernization and surpassed the GDP of the United Kingdom in the early 1870s, a period which is also named the Gilded Age following the rapid expansion of industrilization. The second example is Japan whose industrialization kicked off after the successful Meiji Restoration (the Meiji era of 1868–1912). In spite of the Second World War which devastated its economy, Japan outperformed the United Kingdom by the mid-1960s. Besides, the "Four Asian Tigers" including Hong Kong, Singapore, South Korea, and Taiwan also fit this catch-up-and-overtake pattern. From 1965 to 1990, they maintained extraordinarily high GDP growth rate, which averaged over 8 PCT (Rao, Tamazian, & Singh, 2009), and transformed themselves into advanced economies.

Different from the above-mentioned cases, China demonstrates a rather complicated picture. Once a closed economy and firmly unwilling to rely on any external assistance, China reformed and opened to foreign products, capital, and technologies, etc. in 1978. Ever since, dramatic changes have been taking place across the board, which not only pushed up China's domestic output, but people's standard of living as well. Together with China's various phenomenal achievements, there were also costly failures and setbacks. An ancient Chinese proverb states "Remembrance of the past is the teacher of the future" ('*qianshi buwang, houshi zhishi*', from *Strategies of the Warring States* or '*Zhan Guo Ce*', a renowned historic work of the Warring States Period between the fifth and third centuries BC), to avoid stumbling over the same stone again, it is meaningful to have an in-depth review of the past, especially the harsh lessons that should be drawn. Besides, in order to better deal with the challenges to come, a profound reflection is necessary so that in the future, the transformation of China will continue to benefit both itself and the entire world.

References

Maddison, A. (2010). Historical statistics of the world economy, 1–2008 AD. Retrieved May 25, 2014, from https://www.ggdc.net/maddison/oriindex.htm.

Rao, B. B. et al. (2009). What is the long run growth rate of the East Asian tigers? MPRA paper No. 12668. Retrieved May 20, 2014, from https://mpra.ub.uni-muenchen.de/12668/index.html.

Chapter 2
China from 1949 to 1977

China during the pre-reform stage did not follow a consistent path of growth; instead, its path involved major strategic adjustments, some of which brought staggering consequences for its people. Until today, many Chinese still have vivid memories about the pre-reform years. In their eyes, it is a period which makes them understand how closely an individual's destiny could be tied up with that of a country. Although any efforts to periodize this 28 years is somewhat artificial, divisions are still needed to highlight the hallmark events of this unforgettable era.

1 Restoration of the National Economy (1949–1952)

On Oct. 1st, 1949, the People's Republic of China (PRC, hereafter referred to as China) was established. With the capital city located in Beijing, its foundation symbolized a complete change in the country's political elite and mode of governance. At that time, given the poor state of the economy, there is no exaggeration to say that almost every single facet was in urgent need of restructuring.

1.1 A Pressing Need of Restoration

Several occurrences took place one after another prior to 1949, which, by working in tandem, became a vicious cycle. Among these incidents, the most destructive ones were the long-standing political turmoil under the Kuomintang regime before and after it consolidated its power nationwide in 1927, eight years of fighting with the Japanese invading troops from 1937 to 1945, as well as the civil war between 1945 and 1949, etc. Because of these incessant armed conflicts, a huge number of mines and factories were bombarded, causing industrial output to fall. After 1942 in particular, the decline was rather steep (Kubo, 2005). Besides, owing to the disruption

C. Yu, *China's Economy: Towards 2049*,
https://doi.org/10.1007/978-981-15-9227-0_2

of basic infrastructures such as transport and telecommunications, internal trade was severely curtailed and this further multiplied difficulties in domestic supply. Regarding agriculture, since North China was the principal battlefield, productivity and output were both adversely affected. Even as late as 1950, some areas in North China had not yet returned to their peak pre-war output levels due to the shortage of manpower and draught animal. Although in contrast, the south and the west were relatively unscathed, manpower and grain requisitions by the military undermined the supply of foodstuffs. In those locations, as a result, the vast majority of Chinese suffered from starvation and malnutrition.

In 1949, China had a population of over 540 million (NBS, 1999), accounting for approximately one-fifth of the world total, which was 2.5 billion. With just 3 million workers engaged in industrial production, the country at that time produced less than one-tenth of one percent of the world's steel (Chen & Huang, 2009). In terms of electricity, its annual generation was merely 4.3 TWh (Yang & Yang, 2012), a rather insignificant level which ranked 25th in the world. Apart from that, unemployment and disguised unemployment were common while runaway inflation made the currency virtually worthless and plagued all the spheres of the economy.

1.2 Adoption of a Four-Pronged Approach

Confronting the imminent task of restoring order and stability, a four-pronged approach to recovery and rehabilitation was adopted. Specifically, it included socializing unprotected assets, enacting the Agrarian Reform Law, establishing the central government's authority over economic administration, and revitalizing the productive forces of a near-bankrupt economy.

1.2.1 Redistribution of Assets and the Land Reform

First of all, socializing unprotected assets means the confiscation of industrial enterprises previously owned by the Nationalist government under the dominion of Kuomintang or its high-ranking officials. To be specific, they were largely capital and fixed assets of industry, transportation, and communication at that time. As a matter of fact, in the 1947 "Manifesto of the Chinese People's Liberation Army" drafted by Mao Tse-tung (the founding father of the PRC and chairman of the People's Communist Party of China from 1949 to 1976), which is also known as the "October 10th Manifesto" ('*Shuangshi xuanyan*'), confiscating the property of the big four families of Chiang Kai-shek, Soong Tse-ven, Kung Hsiang-hsi, and Chen Li-fu brothers (with his elder brother Chen Guo-fu), of the chief war criminals, and confiscating bureaucratic capital were listed among the eight basic policies of the Army. By the end of 1949, of the enterprises taken over from the Kuomintang regime, there included 2,400 banks, 2,858 industrial and mining ventures, 10 monopolistic trading firms, and 30 rail vehicle factories and shipyards, etc. With regard to the original value of the fixed assets confiscated, it was estimated to be around RMB15 billion in total (Bai, 1999). Following the establishment of the PRC, another important directive calling for the confiscation of the property of war criminals, traitors, bureaucratic capitalists, and counter revolutionaries was released by the central government in 1951. One year later, most of the work had been accomplished. On the basis of these acquired assets, the country was in a position to set up what would turn out to be the dominant state sector of the economy.

Concerning the agrarian reform (or the land reform), it took place in 1950 and aimed at dismantling China's long-standing feudal agrarian system. The reform was significant in that it was a rather egalitarian apportionment of farmland among peasants. After two years, more than 300 million landless peasants and former sharecroppers (representing nearly 60PCT of the rural population, which was over 503 million in 1952) received 700 million mu (or about 46.7 million hectares) of land and other means of production, e.g. farm implements, drought animals, and rooms for accommodation (Photo 1), etc. Besides, the once heavy land rents, i.e. 35 billion kilos of grains which peasants used to pay to landlords annually were abolished (Niu & Chen, 1992).

Indeed, the distribution of land and other means of production was a prerequisite for peasants to generate more sources of income. As a consequence, their enthusiasm was greatly inspired and this led to an immediate rehabilitation of agriculture. Take grain as an example, there were consecutive year-on-year growth in both the total and per capita output from 1949 to 1952 (Table 1). An equally positive trend was recorded for other products like cotton, oil-bearing crops, and tobacco, etc. Together

Photo 1 The family of Gao Caiguan, a peasant from Jiaxing, Zhejiang Province, was apportioned land in the agrarian reform of 1950. They are quite happy to receive the newly-issued land certificate. By the spring of 1953, this nationwide reform was basically accomplished. *Source* https://paper.people.com.cn/rmrbhwb/html/2011-10/28/content_949221.htm

Table 1 Growth in the total and per capita output of grain, 1949–1952

Year	Grain output[1] (Million Tons)	Population[2] (Million)	Per capita output[3] (Kilograms)
1949	113.18	541.67	208.95
1950	132.13	551.96	239.38
1951	143.69	563	255.22
1952	163.92	574.82	285.17

Source [1,2]NBS, 1999; 3: Calculated by the author by dividing 1 by 2

with the upward movement of production, peasants could earn more. If compared to 1949, their per capita net monetary income witnessed an increase of 111.5PCT by 1953, an indicator linked directly to stronger purchasing power (Hu, 2014).

Despite the initial achievements, however, what should not be ignored is that given the vast population in rural China, each household could only possess limited acreage and insufficient farm tools, a situation which not only prohibited the further expansion of production, but also the enhancement of efficiency. Out of concern over productivity, the government encouraged peasants to help one another by pooling their resources, which enabled them to retain title to the land while handling more agricultural tasks, from plowing, seeding, to harvesting, etc. Inspired by the instant benefits, different kinds of "mutual aid teams" ('*huzhu zu*') were formed around the country and by the end of 1952, the number exceeded 8.3 million, with their participants accounting for 40PCT of farm households (Cao, 2010). Not long later, another form of joint farming called "lower-level agricultural producers' cooperatives" ('*nongye shengchan hezuoshe chujishe*') were introduced on a trial basis in certain regions. Since these cooperatives required a contribution of land, tools and animals, half of the payment would be based on the number of hours worked for the cooperative and the other half according to the land, equipment and animals contributed. The downside of the scheme was that the quality of labor input was not taken into account; with all peasants deemed to be able to perform any kind of activity, everyone was treated as skill-neutral. Under such a flawed approach which failed to recognize the economies of specialization, it is not hard to explain why efforts to promote productivity were not as fruitful as expected.

1.2.2 Three Balances in the Economy

Prior to 1949 when political uncertainty was still a matter of concern across the country, administration of economic affairs in conquered areas was largely assigned to the local administrators. Once the military conquest was over, there was an immediate shift in the priorities of the newly-established central government. On its agenda, tasks listed at the top were centralizing revenue and expenditure authorities, controling flows of strategic supplies, curtailing the money supply, and drafting the state budget, etc. Among them, the most critical need was to harness inflation, which had been rampant following the collapse of the previous regime's monetary system.

As the first step, the multiple denominations in circulation had to be exchanged for the renminbi currency (RMB, or literally the people's currency) issued by the People's Bank of China (PBoC, which later became the central bank of the People's Republic of China). While in the east region like Shanghai, the conversion rate was fixed at RMB1 = 10,000 gold yuan, it varied elsewhere from place to place (Wu, 1995). At the same time, the trading of gold, silver and foreign exchange was strictly prohibited. Nonetheless, private holding of precious metals was still allowable with the provision that they could be sold at any time to the Bank of China (designated as the foreign exchange bank for the national banking system) only. Foreign exchange, on the other hand, had to be turned in either for RMB or for foreign exchange deposit certificates. Since at that time, people were gripped by the fear of heavy penalties and a shortage of cash, implementation of these stringent regulations did not encounter much resistance. As a result, both foreign exchange and gold reserves at the disposal of the succeeding regime were considerably augmented.

However, in its attempt to stabilize the RMB, the government chose not to back the new currency with these reserves. In fact, the RMB was not even remotely linked to gold, but instead tied to a limited commodity standard. To be specific, the stabilization experiment was based on a government guarantee against loss of purchasing power, at least for vital daily necessities (Burdekin, 2004). Thereby, wage payments, bank deposits, certain government expenditures, and bond issues were expressed in terms of wage, parity deposit, and victory bond units respectively. By and large, this device was designed to restore the faith of the public in the monetary medium, discourage the flight from money into goods, and foster the accumulation of savings and bank deposits. Yet above all else, the regime understood clearly that complete control of the inflationary spiral would be impossible if without fiscal and financial stability. To have the condition satisfied, its plan to control inflation involved "three balances", i.e. balancing the revenues and expenditures, balancing the flow of bank receipts and payments, and balancing the purchasing power and supply of goods without resort to inflationary adjustments (Li, 1991).

Fiscal Policy

For most of 1949, China was in a state of power vacuum and things like a national budget simply did not exist. When it comes to government spending and revenue collections, they were largely decentralized and on a more or less ad hoc basis. With tax morale and tax collecting mechanism being thoroughly disrupted in the urban areas, agricultural taxes for quite some time constituted the major source of government income. In order to tackle chronic fiscal instability, a draft resolution on the budget for 1950 was announced (at the fourth session of the Central People's Government Committee of China on Dec. 2nd, 1949 by the then finance minister Bo Yibo in his "Report on the National Draft Budget Estimates for 1950") and according to the plan, the government revenue base was to be greatly extended. Furthermore, the expenditures covered by deficit financing were to be limited to only 19PCT, of which no more than 62PCT was to be based on new note issue. In case government

Table 2 Fiscal (Im)balance: revenues and expenditures, 1949–1952

Year	Fiscal revenues (RMB billion)	Fiscal expenditures (RMB billion)	Balance (RMB billion)
1949	30.3 billion catties[1] of millet	56.7 billion catties of millet	−26.4 billion catties of millet
1950	6.52	6.81	−0.29
1951	13.31	12.25	1.06
1952	18.37	17.6	0.77

Note [1]Catty, or '*Jin*', is a traditional Chinese unit of mass, one catty is rounded to 500 g. *Source* Zhao, 2009

deficit incurred, it should be financed through the launching of the "People Victory Bond" campaign. On the same day, the "Decisions on the Issuance of People Victory Bond" was passed at the conference. Projected to sell 200 million '*fen*' (Victory Bond units), this campaign was designed not only as a means of raising revenues, it was also expected to help boost the flat purchasing power.

Together with the above measures, there was the promulgation of decrees on the "unification of finance" in 1950 (on March 3rd, 1950, the "Decisions on the Unification of the National Financial and Economic Works" was released by the Government Administrative Council of China), which called for a rigorous scrutiny of government expenditure, reshuffling of the tax structure, and the establishment of a highly-centralized fiscal regime. As supplementary methods for the fulfillment of these goals, salaries of public officials were kept at a low level; and a central treasury management system was formed to monitor the cash position of the state. Local government fiscal operations were, without exception, curtailed and placed under the tight supervision of Beijing. Actually, the top-down approach adopted in the early 1950s to ease the financial predicament was based on a hierarchical relationship which would be considered rigid and obsolete today. Nonetheless, given the special circumstances of that special age, it produced some encouraging effects. For instance, after two straight years of fiscal imbalances (Table 2), China in 1951 and 1952 realized a net revenue of RMB1.06 billion and RMB0.77 billion respectively. Moreover, efforts to drain excess liquidity and attack commodity speculation also paid off for order and confidence were gradually restored to the market.

Monetary Policy

Similar to its concern over fiscal affairs, the leadership at the very outset was anxious to institute a centralized system of monetary management, with which it could expect to enforce financial stability around the country in an efficient manner. Accordingly, several important moves were initiated toward that end, such as consolidating the functions of government banking, unifying the regional currencies still in circulation, cutting back credit lines, and encouraging savings by offering attractive interest rates, etc. In the execution of these policies, the PBoC, as the central bank, was assigned the key responsibilities, many of which should belong to the role of commercial banks. Therefore, competition between the PBoC and private banks became inevitable.

In the end of May 1950, the PBoC had established branches in just 219 localities. By October 1951, it was operating 5,300 offices with a branch in almost every county on the mainland (Bell & Feng, 2013). With the rapid expansion of the state banking system, private banking was shrinking simultaneously. For instance, at the time the People's Republic of China was founded in 1949, the country had 1,032 private financial institutions, including banks, money shops, and trust companies, etc. By the end of the same year, the number of those remained was 833. Following a series of transformation and reorganization, only 387 stayed in business after March 1950 (Chen & Chen, 2013). Besides, private financial institutions were integrated into the state banking system at the urging of the PBoC, with each member subscribing part of the capital and participating in the management (called '*gong si he ying*', this form of operation based on joint state-private ownership was rather common in China during the 1950s). Gradually, private banks all became part of a collectivized system; in other words, they were nationalized.

In accord with a highly-centralized banking system, the PBoC began to pursue a credit planning mechanism which was both unified and comprehensive. Because of the skyrocketing prices, as well as the subsequent chaos in the market, a tight and deflationary policy was adopted. Together with other anti-inflationary devices, i.e. reduction of public spending, upward adjustment of urban taxation, especially the industrial and commercial tax, the issuance of People Victory Bonds, and the withdrawal of currency from circulation, etc., the PBoC finally succeeded in combating speculation and underground credit while managed to stabilize interest rates. Take Shanghai's interbank lending as an example, the highest monthly rate of 1949 hit 2,400‰; by the end of the year, it fell to 390‰ (Hong, 2005). After China's unification of its financial management system in March 1950, the downward trend continued. By June 1952, monthly rates charged to Shanghai's institutional borrowers was recorded at 6–11.1‰ whereas for private borrowers, the range was 10.5–19.5‰.

By and large, the above described policies were effective in that they successfully brought about a decline in price. According to the *Chronicles of Shanghai*, the city went through four rounds of price increase from June 1949 to February 1950. With monthly price (wholesale price) increases averaged 46.3PCT, its wholesale price index (WPI) registered a stunning 20-fold rise. As the country's financial hub and industrial center, what took place in Shanghai soon spread elsewhere, resulting in rampant inflation throughout China. Obviously, if the government wanted to pacify the panicked populace and bring the money back on track, it should first and foremost deal with the situation in Shanghai. Indeed, the city itself also was aware of the pressing need to secure a sound environment. By holding in hand the supply of key commodities (like grain, cotton, and coal, etc.), restricting the money in circulation, and using important policy instruments, Shanghai's inflation was under better control. From 1951 to 1952, both its wholesale price index (WPI) and retail price index (RPI) became more stabilized and were no longer soaring so sharply as the 1950–1951 period (Graph 1). Simultaneously, similar changes also happened in other parts of

Graph 1 Changes in the WPI and RPI of Shanghai. *Source* Zhu, 2005

the country which was quite encouraging. Whereas China's retail price index (RPI) stood at 112.2 in 1951 (preceding year = 100), it dropped to 99.6 in 1952. In terms of the consumer price index (CPI), it fell from 112.5 of 1951 to 102.7 in 1952 (NBS, 1999).

Like a double-edged sword, however, measures to counter inflation unavoidably caused a contractionary drag on the economy, which was characterized by symptoms like bank closures, business failures, accumulation of unsold inventories in cities, and widespread unemployment, etc. In order to prevent the downward spiral from escalating into a deeper recession, the government made up its mind to apply state capitalism before transforming the country into full-fledged socialism. Most notably, purchase orders were placed in a direct way with private industrial enterprises so as to enable them to thrive. In 1950, the products procured by the state accounted for 27PCT of total output value; the share climbed to almost 82PCT by 1955 (Tian, 2011). What's more, to alleviate the burden on private enterprises, other incentives such as tax reduction and loans were made available, especially to those engaged in the supply of scarce materials and daily necessities.

For state-owned enterprises, credit was of no less importance. Ever since the early 1950s, administration of state enterprises in China was placed under a broader framework of cash and currency control. Via the scheme, the central bank in effect acted like a national clearing center for all the deals of the state enterprises. Accordingly, government enterprises and agencies of other kinds were without exception mandated to have their accounts opened with the PBoC only. Every day, their cash receipts, if any, should be saved in the account; when settling payment, the funds still had to be transferred between accounts at the PBoC. Furthermore, they were no longer permitted to extend any credits to each other, not even short-term merchandise loans (Zhao, 2006). Besides, once every month or every quarter, these enterprises would submit to the PBoC statements of cash receipts and expenditures so as to facilitate supervision by the latter.

The motives behind the "cash control" scheme were to reduce the excess supply of money, realize economies in the utilization of financial resources, and enable Beijing to have a bigger say in the management of economic activities, etc. Unfortunately, the PBoC's capabilities were inadequate for the task of handling such an immense amount of transactions, thus resulting in considerable incompetence in both accounting and governance. Later, the headaches were relieved with the imposition of a floor on the value of transactions to be cleared through the Bank. Moreover, the institution of the "cash and currency control plan" had another obvious flaw, i.e. it seriously strained the administrative resources of the state banking system. By overloading it with responsibilities that should be assigned to commercial banks, efficiency plummeted and cost soared.

Distribution Policy

Despite the anxiety to eliminate the runaway inflation, policy-makers in the beginning were clear in their mind that outright price fixing would not be a pragmatic solution. The series of wars and the subsequent repercussions, especially via altering social psychology through incessant turbulences, had created panic which dominated people's thinking. Usually, panicing people tend to purchase and hoard which, if coupled with other factors like "abnormal" money printing or speculation, may result in inflation. Although outright price fixing can temporarily stop inflation, once the ceiling is abolished, the rebound effect would exacerbate inflation to a degree that is irreversible. By contrast, an indirect price control can be implemented through state trading, a manipulative device applied in combination with fiscal and/or monetary instruments. For a centrally-planned regime like China, this type of control should prove more feasible and better suited to its special stage of economic and bureaucratic development, as well as promote a more rapid growth over the long run. Yet considering that satisfactory performance of the domestic trading mechanism was possible only if the volume of goods entering distributive channels could be greatly expanded and the share of state trading in the total grow, two tasks remained to be done to satisfy these prerequisites, i.e. restoration of the badly disrupted transport network and resumption of the severely curtailed farm and industrial production.

In 1949, of the 21,800 km of railway lines possessed by China, only 11,000 km were still in service because of the unending wars. Referring to the total length of roads open to traffic, it just measured 80,700 km, with a density of 0.8 km per 100 square kilometers. For the rehabilitation of transport, a large proportion of government investment was directed to this priority in the three years starting from 1950 (Fang, 2008). By the end of 1952, all the pre-war rail lines were restored and the intensity of transport utilization was greatly increased. At the same time, a railway linking Chengdu and Chongqing, two important cities in southwest China, was completed. It was the first railway line to be built in the history of the People's Republic of China. As to roadways, they more than tripled to 254,000 km by 1957 (Wang, 2009).

While focus was laid on the improvement of the transport network, there were other endeavors to activate the sluggish economy of both the urban and rural areas.

Fortunately, in its efforts to recover production, the country was blessed by a bumper harvest in 1950. With the annual growth rate of grain output exceeding 16.7PCT, the harvest provided foodstuffs for the nation's distributive pipelines at a time when they were badly needed to ease the stress from the mounting inflation. In the short run, the regime was anxious to increase its stabilization reserves. From a longer-term perspective, it also perceived the necessity to loosen the bonds of the rural subsistence economy and draw it gradually into the commercialized sector. Indeed, this recognition was essential because in a subsistence-oriented economy, the scope for resource mobilization, allocation and planning was very much restrained. Therefore, emphasis on the promotion of rural–urban interchange, especially the swap of key commodities like grain, raw cotton, and textiles, etc., became fundamental. With the opening up of new trading channels, the chronic supply–demand imbalance that had existed between the two sides was better resolved. During the early 1950s, the bazaars, exhibitions and fairs that were held around different parts of China contributed tremendously to the production and marketing of both agricultural and industrial goods, which in turn also made the once-stagnant commerce thrive.

1.2.3 Formation of Cooperatives to Stimulate Production

The booming production which happened in those early years was partially due to a growing interest in probing institutional alternatives to maintain the efficiency of exchange. At that time, the United Federation of All-China Cooperatives ('*Zhonghua quanguo hezuoshe lianhe zongshe*', set up in 1950 and renamed All-China Federation of Supply and Marketing Cooperatives since 1954) as an organization responsible for the development of the nation's cooperatives was formed. Under its guidance, an increasing number of rural supply and marketing cooperatives (SMCs) began to emerge. By the end of 1952, over 32,000 SMCs were present across the countryside, with their members accounting for more than 90PCT of total rural households (Jia, 2012). As an important component of the rural economy, SMCs played a critical role in stimulating the interflow of goods between cities and countryside, ensuring adequate market supplies, accelerating the industrialized management of agriculture, and providing services to peasants to assist them in their production activities (Guo, Henehan & Schmit, 2007).

These various moves, accompanied by a gradual restoration of transport and production, did result in a rather marked boom of internal trade. For the period 1950–1952, increase in the national retail sales of commodities was recorded to be up to 44.7PCT and the procurement value of agricultural and sideline products registered an increase of 62.1PCT (PHRC, 2011). Without a well-established system of distribution, it would not have been possible for China to attain comparative price stability by 1952, nor the gradual narrowing of price disparities between diverse regions and major market centers.

As to the dominant participants of the booming domestic trade, they included not only cooperatives in cities and the countryside, but also state-owned commercial entities. In 1952, more than 60.5PCT of wholesale trade was carried on by state-owned businesses, a portion enabling them to control the circulation of a vast majority of commodities (PHRC, 2011). Overall, policy during that particular period was geared to the gradual displacement of private trade through competition from state counterparts. Actually, the influence of the latter upon the pattern of distribution and prices was much more profound than would appear from its overall share in the total domestic trade. This was due to the fact that since 1952, these companies, together with the rural cooperatives, had virtually monopolized the procurement and wholesale of the most essential daily necessities and industrial raw materials, ranging from grain, salt, to raw cotton, cotton textiles and coal, etc. As a result, they could use their unchallenged position in the market to regulate prices. Usually, commodity prices for major market centers at which the state enterprises would trade were determined by the Ministry of Trade; but for smaller markets located within each of the regional trading areas, the prices were fixed by the provincial or local department of trade (Wan, Lan & Liu, 2014).

Apart from the aforesaid indicators which can testify the active transactions conducted at that stage, there is yet another measure of China's flourishing businesses and it is the state revenues. In terms of the tax levied on the commercial sector, it more than tripled from RMB1.07 billion in 1950 to RMB4.17 billion in 1952. Over the same three-year period, income under the category of industrial and commercial tax augmented to RMB6.15 billion, an impressive jump of over 160PCT (PHRC, 2011). To enhance the role of state enterprises in the national economy, some incentives were provided during the early 1950s to encourage them to raise profit margins. Through arrangements such as a special fund to award top performers, and an above-target profit-sharing scheme, etc., policymakers appropriated resources in a way that greatly favored the privileged sector (Sha & Yang, 1981). Viewed in this light, it is not surprising that before the 1978 reform, state enterprises as a whole remained indisputably the largest single source of government revenues.

1.3 Impact on Prices: From Fluctuation to Stabilization

Irrespective of the diverse approaches introduced for the restoration of order, China from 1949 through 1952 focused intensely on curbing inflation and restoring confidence in the medium of exchange. Not only was attainment of price stability considered a prerequisite for the pursuit of other economic ambitions; more fundamentally, it was also a precondition for the maintenance of social stability, without which any strategy would prove to be futile. In the preceding sections, the measures and means employed to accomplish price stabilization have been analyzed. In this section, the price behavior between 1950 and 1952 is surveyed so as to ascertain the extent to which the goal of price stability was actually fulfilled.

Before the new regime took power in 1949, the arduousness of combating persistent inflation was already self-evident. In dealing with this vicious "tiger", the government first centered on mitigating its destructive effects. For example, in cities like

Graph 2 Changes in the National Wholesale Price Index. *Source* Zhong, 1992

Beijing, Tianjin and Shijiazhuang (Hebei Province), etc., the PBoC launched on a trial basis a special form of deposit named '*zheshi chuxu*', or the RMB value of parity deposit units. By denominating bank deposits in basic commodities like rice, wheat flour, vegetable oil, cotton cloth and coal, etc., losses from currency devaluation could be offset. When the saving product became available in Shanghai, it gained immediate popularity among local residents. Between November 1949 and February 1950, sales rocketed from 11.2 million units to 46.61 million units (Hong, 2009). Over the three-year period from 1950 to 1952, fluctuations which had persisted for decades began to show signs of stabilization, with the index of wholesale prices moving downward to 92.6 in December 1952 (Base: March 1950 = 100, Graph 2). In the meantime, the country's retail price index (RPI) demonstrated the same encouraging trend. Using 1950 as a base year (RPI equal to 100 in 1950), the index declined slightly from 112.2 of 1951 to 111.8 in 1952 (Tang, 2001).

The price readjustment of the spring and summer of 1950 bore the characteristics of deflation which, from the standpoint of the regime, had both disturbing and salutary effects. On the one hand, it led to an acute, even though temporary, depression in the private sector. At the country level, openings of private industrial and commercial businesses in the first two months of 1950 outnumbered their closings; yet starting from March, the latter began to overtake the former. In particular, regarding the performance of 10 major cities including Shanghai, Beijing, Tianjin, Wuhan, and Guangzhou, etc., the second quarter was even worse for they together witnessed 6,847 more closings than openings (Tang, 2001). Quite naturally, following the occurrence of large-scale shutdowns, there was remarkable shrinkage in both output and trade, which greatly aggravated the urban unemployment problem. In March and April of 1950 alone, the nation's newly laid-off workers reached 100,000 and this resulted in an approximated 380,000 to 400,000 total job losses in cities. Another record high of unemployment happened two years later. Among the cities and municipalities under the jurisdiction of the provincial government, registered job applicants rocketed to

387,000 within a matter of just four months, from September to December, 1952 (Song, 2010).

On the other side of the coin, however, there were also benefits delivered by the same rehabilitation initiatives. In view of the fact that inflation had been partially exacerbated by actions such as hoarding and profiteering, fiscal retrenchment to a large extent cut back the funds available to many black market operators, speculators, and small private banks, whose bankruptcy made it easier for the central government to consolidate its control over commerce and banking. Regretfully, as wholesale and retail prices began to resume stability, the outbreak of the Korean War (from June 25th, 1950 to July 27th, 1953) provided a renewed opportunity for speculation. Taking advantage of the short supply of industrial raw materials, some greedy merchants once again stockpiled commodities in huge quantities, which drove prices beyond their fair value. To tame the fluctuating market, the central government in June and November issued two directives, both of which emphasized the necessity to prohibit manipulative and disruptive trading activities (one was the "Directives on the Stabilization of Finance and Prices" released by the Central Finance and Economics Committee of the Government Administration Council on June 29th, 1950; the other was the "Directives to Outlaw Speculative Commercial Behaviors" by the Ministry of Trade on November 14th, 1950). Prices by the end of the year were back to a relatively normal level.

The situation changed in the following year because of a number of reasons. In 1951, two positive signs emerged. First, as a result of the steady recovery of agricultural and industrial production, their gross value of output recorded an annual increase of 19PCT. Second, despite the projected budget deficit due to the stress of ballooning military expenditures and resource diversion to Korea, the country realized a government budget surplus of RMB1.06 billion (Zhao, 2009), an outcome derived from the enhanced fiscal, monetary, and trade control. Yet, given the stubborn inflationary pressures, prices continued to move up, but at a decelerated pace. Furthermore, due to its involvement in the Korean War, China had to cope with the consequences of trade embargoes, especially a plunge of imports. At the same time, against the soaring demand for gauze pads, bandages, and military uniforms, the domestic supply of raw cotton was running short. To prevent prices from rising too fast, production and sales of cotton-related goods were orchestrated by the state from early 1951 (Chen, 2008). Given the special status of cotton in China, it is indeed not uncommon for the leadership to act in such a way.

In 1952, open inflation was beginning to be replaced by suppressed inflation characteristic of all full-employment economies operating within a framework of state controls. If compared to 1951, there emerged a fall in retail price index whereas for the consumer price index (CPI), the growth fell back into the normal range (Table 3).

Despite these improvements, the impact of the Korean War, especially its huge costs, should not be ignored. By getting involved in the war, China's direct military spending totaled RMB6.2 billion (Xu, 2010), almost at the same level as its fiscal revenues of 1950 which were RMB6.52 billion. Inevitably, the three-year war pushed up the country's defense expenditures. In 1951, it accounted for 43PCT of its fiscal

Table 3 Overall price indices, 1951–1952 (preceding year = 100)

Year	1951	1952
General Retail Price Index	112.2	99.6
General Price Index of Living Expenses of Residents[1]	112.5	102.7
General Purchasing Price Index of Farm Products	119.6	101.7
General Rural Retail Price Index of Industrial Products	110.2	99.5

Note [1]after 1985, it was renamed general consumer price index. *Source* NBS, 1999

outlays (Graph 3), i.e. 14PCT higher than the portion claimed by the economy (Dong, 2001). From 1951 to 1952, the amount spent on national defense rose by almost 10PCT and hit RMB5.78 billion. Since supplies for the front took priority over those for the satisfaction of domestic demand, consequently, imbalance occurred between the rising national income and the supply of consumer goods. Therefore, bond or bond-type campaigns were launched in later years not just to raise state revenues, but to mop up the liquid purchasing power as well.

Fairly speaking, the period from 1949 to 1952 should be considered as a crucial stage of recovery and rehabilitation for China. All the initiatives by the government were designed to serve the overriding goal of creating a sound environment in which more comprehensive economic transformation could be carried out smoothly. By 1952, with the establishment of price stability, restoration of commerce, and revitalization of industrial and agricultural production, the basic objectives set for the post-civil war period had been fulfilled. In other words, the ground was prepared for long-term growth and stability that would later direct the country toward a socialist model with centralized planning.

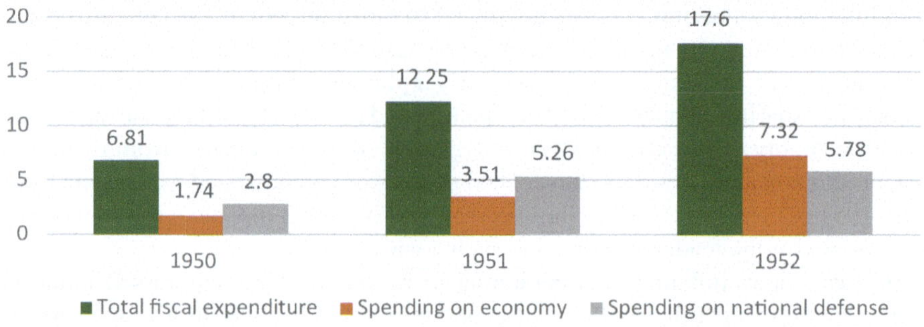

Graph 3 Spending on Economy and National Defense in the Total Fiscal Expenditure, RMB Billion. *Source* Dong, 2001

2 The First Five-Year Plan (1953–1957)

Having restored a viable economic base, the leadership was ready to embark on an intensive program of industrial growth and socialization. For this purpose, the administration imported the Soviet economic model which was chiefly based on centralized planning, state ownership of the industrial sector, and large collective units in agriculture. As a typical manifestation of this borrowed approach, the first Five-Year Plan (1953–1957, also the first national economic and social development plan in China's history) was formally adopted at the Second Session of the 1st National People's Congress of 1955. The process of implementing the plan had started two years earlier when it was first announced.

In a typical Soviet economy, the main pursuit is a high rate of growth, especially of the industrial sector, in which the development of heavy industry and capital-intensive technologies are emphasized the most. Likewise, China during the first Five-Year Plan period followed a similar policy of prioritizing heavy industry. For lack of experience in the management of large-scale industrial projects, Soviet experts were brought in to help. In addition, large numbers of Soviet engineers, technicians, as well as scientists assisted in the installation and operation of new heavy industrial facilities, including entire plants and separate pieces of equipment purchased from the Soviet Union. Since socialist transformation meant abolishing private ownership over means of production, this process involved the socialization of properties along three frontiers: agriculture, rural handicraft, and industry.

2.1 Agriculture: From MATs to Higher APCs

For quite a long time, rural governance in China remained rather loose. On most occasions, it was the wealthy gentry and big families that influenced or even manipulated local affairs. According to Sun Yat-sen, the founding father of the Republic of China in 1912, it was the absence of a well-structured Chinese society, especially rural society, which accounted for the nation's failure to defend itself against foreign invasions. To facilitate the mobilization of agricultural resources, improve the efficiency of farming, and increase government access to agricultural products, the authorities continued to organize peasants into increasingly large and socialized collective units. Collectivization was, at that time, taken as the best way to overcome the backwardness and reduce the vulnerability of the rural economy. Additionally, behind the collectivized approach to managing agriculture, a more fundamental motive was the pursuit of large-scale development of the national industry. To have the aim fulfilled, it was considered imperative to have an abundant supply of diverse raw materials, including grain, cotton, oil-bearing crops, and sugar, etc. However, this was absolutely beyond the capabilities of a disintegrated and small peasant economy. As a quick fix to deal with the contradiction, collectives were organized.

Prior to the initiation of the first Five Year Plan, campaigns for mutual aid and cooperation had already been launched in agricultural production around China. At that time, both mutual aid teams (MAT) and lower-level agricultural producers' cooperatives (APC) were based on private ownership of land and farming materials. But by comparison, MATs were simpler and temporary establishments organized chiefly during busy seasons (Zhao, 2015); but for cooperatives, they had a more formal structure which enabled all members to manage. Later, when collective ownership of the land replaced the system of pooling land, the evolvement of lower-level APCs into advanced APCs became common. In 1951, there was only one advanced APC among the 130 cooperatives in China. By 1954, the total number of cooperatives soared to more than 114,000 and 200 of them were advanced cooperatives. Beginning with the second half of 1955, the country entered a period in which most elementary cooperatives, as well as MATs, were transformed into the advanced form. Thus, towards the end of 1956, 750,000 cooperatives existed in China, with 210,000 of them being lower level and 540,000 of them being higher level (Chen, 2011).

To a large extent, the change in these figures is a reflection of the mindset of peasants. Before volunteering to participate, they had to be convinced that the cooperatives could really bring better harvests than individual farms. It was their gradual understanding and recognition that led to a rapid expansion of the cooperatives in the mid-1950s. After private ownership of land and means of production was discarded, member households began to demonstrate greater concerns about the interest of the cooperatives. By entering into cooperatives, it became easier for them to reach agreements over issues like improvement of farming techniques, cultivation of crops, and allocation of funds, etc. In turn, with a higher efficiency in the utilization of agricultural resources, advanced cooperatives could plan production in a way that not only suited the land, but also guaranteed the supply of a given level of output and income.

Through the evolutionary process from mutual-aid groups, to elementary cooperatives, and to advanced cooperatives, rural society was restructured. As a fundamental type of agricultural organization, mutual-aid groups were firstly formed on the basis of voluntary participation and reciprocity. Then step by step, elementary agricultural cooperatives were developed for the purpose of promoting production. At that stage, it was largely the land size and labor input of each household that determined income distribution. Compared to the "semi-socialism" of primary cooperatives, advanced cooperatives were completely socialist organizations where farming materials were all public and income distribution was commensurate with the labor input of each individual. During the initial six years of the 1950s, the rural economy transitioned from private ownership to public ownership, which helped absorb individual peasants into collective production. Moreover, it also changed their relationship with the state. Although the collectivization process began slowly, its pace accelerated in 1955 and 1956. By the end of 1956, over 96PCT of farm households in China had joined advanced cooperatives and one year after, each cooperative on average consisted of 158.6 household members (Wang, Liu & Bai, 2012).

Despite the lack of state investment in agriculture during the first Five-Year-Plan period, the gross value of production for 1957 reached RMB44.39 billion, an increase of 12PCT over that of 1952. Grain output rose by 19PCT and hit 195.05

million tons in 1957 (NBS, 1999). To analyze the reasons behind the double-digit growth, gains in efficiency should be counted as the key, a result of the nationwide collectivization movement. However, seeing that sectors like industry and transport registered a much more impressive pace of growth than agriculture, Chinese leaders had to direct greater attention to the relatively sluggish performance of agriculture, as peasants felt somewhat discouraged by losing ownership of their land and profit. If China expected to maintain long-term growth in its agricultural output, peasants should first and foremost be motivated with appropriate incentives.

In rural China, handicraft producers were equally important to the agriculture sector. In the mid-1950s, they totaled more than 10 million, including both full-timers and part-timers. As an indispensable force in agriculture, they supplied inexpensive farm implements, produced crude inputs such as bricks and tiles for construction works, and provided menial services which rural communities needed. For an agrarian economy that lacked modern industries, the crucial role of these craftsmen was self-evident.

Considering that rural handicraft producers were widely dispersed and independent in operations, which was unfavorable for overall rural administration and productivity increase, the scheme of collectivization was applied too. Similar to the process of collectivizing farm works, handicraft cooperatives also followed three steps. The first was the grouping of handicraft workers into mutual aid teams; although they were united to engage in production and marketing, each member still had decision-making prerogative and ownership of tools that they used. Then, the small-scale mutual aid teams gradually gave way to the enlarged purchasing and marketing cooperatives. In this phase, members would leave factor procurement and product distribution decisions to the cooperatives while each individual would focus almost exclusively on productive activities. When public ownership of means of production was established and members became salary workers, the third stage of forming rural handicraft cooperatives was completed. In general, the process of grouping rural handicraft people into cooperatives didn't take long, which happened chiefly from 1953 to 1957. Despite the lack of specific information about how fast their expansion occurred, statistics show that in 1957, China's handicraft cooperatives and mutual assistance teams numbered 106,400 and the gross output value of the rural handicraft industry reached RMB13.76 billion, an annual increase of 17.6PCT, or accounting for over 19.5PCT of the nation's total industrial output (Wang, 2009).

2.2 *Industry: A Heavy-Industry-Centered Model from the Soviet*

For a vast country like China, particularly given its huge population and rich natural resources, building a comprehensive industrial system was absolutely essential for the consolidation of its development. On the one hand, an industrial system is needed to produce various types of capital goods (such as machine tools, steel, and equipment) that can furnish basic means of economic expansion. What's more, such a system can also supply a wide selection of consumer goods so as to ensure steady growth in the people's standard of living.

As reiterated earlier, when China was newly founded in 1949, the entire economy was in urgent need of restoration. By then, the industrial system was not only rudimentary but also extremely unbalanced. For instance, gross industrial output was only RMB14 billion in 1949 and the ratio between the contributions of the coastal and those of the hinterland was 67.3:32.7. In other words, more than two thirds of the output was generated by the coastal area (Su, 2001). Further, the same phenomenon appeared within the coastal region itself. In 1949, Liaoning Province, Shanghai, and Tianjin together produced over 55PCT of its total industrial output. In the west which covered 68PCT of China's land area, and especially the remote frontiers inhabited by ethnic minorities, industry was almost nonexistent (Zhu & Gong, 2008).

With a view to rectifying the imbalance, the government intentionally directed more investment to inland China while drafting the first Five Year Plan. Of the 150 key projects that were actually carried out (originally, the Plan had 156 projects, including those aided by the Soviet Union), 83 of them were based in the interior, i.e. equivalent to a share of 55PCT (Chen, 2001). Simultaneously, heavy industries like iron and steel manufacturing, coal mining, cement production, power generation, and machine building, etc. were targeted as being in need of major reform. Therefore, apart from the erection of new industrial plants, existing units were strengthened, transformed, expanded and/or technologically equipped in order to boost productivity and output. From 1953 to 1957, China's industrial and manufacturing sector expanded at an accelerating pace: annual growth in this sector averaged 18PCT by value and there were thousands of new factories, mines and infrastructure projects initiated (PHRC, 2011). As the table below shows (Table 4), while coal production in 1957 hit 131 million tons, almost double that of the year 1952, production of iron and steel more than tripled. By and large, production of most industrial goods exceeded the targets set by the state at the end of the first Five-Year Plan.

However, due to insufficient technicians and inadequate technical knowledge, China at the beginning of the first Five Year Plan confronted great difficulties. Therefore, Soviet industrial technologies and organizational designs were transplanted. In particular, the 150 large industrial projects built chiefly in the inland regions and the

Table 4 Output of major industrial products, 1952–1957

Product	1952 (million tons)	1957 (million tons)
Coal	66	131
Pig iron	1.93	5.94
Steel	1.35	5.35
Cruid Oil	0.44	1.46
Cement	2.86	6.86
Chemical Fertilizer	0.04	0.15

Source NBS, 1999

Photo 2 In 1957, Kushkin, a 65-year-old Soviet expert shared his experience with Chinese workers at Jilin Fertilizer Plant. *Source* Song, 2015

Northeast were imported from the Soviet Union or from Eastern Europe. Since the Russian machinery embodied fairly advanced industrial technology as compared to that of the Chinese, blueprints and technical specifications were provided as well. By sending experts to China, the Soviets offered enormous training and technical assistance. From 1954 to 1957, approximately 5,000 Soviet advisers came to China (Photo 2). By the end of 1956, the number of Soviet specialists working in China peaked at 3,113, with 2,213 of them providing technical support (Shen, 2002). At the same time, more Chinese were sent for training and study at the Soviet Union's various famous academies. Among them, technical workers from key industries, students, college teachers, and researchers, etc. were the major participants of the movement to learn in the Soviet Union.

Due to Soviet assistance, the number of Chinese technicians multiplied in many fields of industry, including prospecting, designing, civil engineering and installation, etc. Studying and training in workplaces further improved Chinese professional competencies. With enhanced skills and knowledge, China during the first Five-Year-Plan period accomplished the design and building of its own industrial units, railways and water conservancy projects, like the integrated iron and steel works of Anshan (Liaoning Province) and Baotou (Inner Mongolia), coal mines of Fushun and Fuxin (both in Liaoning Province), chemical plants of Jilin (Jilin Province), Taiyuan (Shanxi Province) and Lanzhou (Gansu Province), hydro-electric power stations of Shangyou (Ganzhou, Jiangxi Province) and Gutianxi (Gutian, Fujian Province), to name just a few. Except for cases which involved special geological conditions or technical barriers of great complexity, China no longer had to rely on external support. In the manufacturing of products like jet aircrafts, automobiles, seamless steel tubes, and precision instruments in particular, China's increasing independence began to prepare the country for the forthcoming industrialization process.

As a matter of fact, China's engagement in large-scale industrial construction and its pursuit of rapid development of state-run industries happened soon after the socialist transformation of private enterprises. In early 1956, almost all capitalist

Table 5 Composition of the gross industrial output value, 1952–1957

Year	Gross industrial output value (RMB billion)	By state-owned enterprises (RMB billion)	By collectively-owned enterprises (RMB billion)	By heavy industry (RMB billion)	By light industry (RMB billion)
1952	34.9	14.5	1.14	12.4	22.5
1957	70.4	37.85	13.4	31.7	38.7

Source NBS, 1999

industries had come under joint state-private operations, which marked a fundamental change in the structure of China's industrial economy. By 1957, the value of industrial production (including that of the handicrafts industry) had surged to 56.7PCT of the total production of industry and agriculture, as compared to 43.1PCT in 1952 (NBS, 1999). Also in the same year, of the total industrial output that reached RMB70.4 billion, state-owned industry claimed 53.8PCT whereas collectively-owned firms contributed 19PCT (Table 5). With regard to the private sector, it was losing ground quickly. In addition, when the first Five Year Plan was over, the share of heavy industry had risen from 35.5PCT of the total in 1952 to more than 45PCT. Given the dynamic growth of the heavy industry, it is not surprising that light industry lagged behind after 1958.

To a large extent, it was China's awareness of its weak economic base, especially the industrial backwardness that pushed the country to draft the first Five-Year-Plan so as to better enhance the strength. In terms of per capita industrial production for example, the performance in 1952 was rather insignificant if compared to other countries. In that year, China's per capita steel stayed at 2.37 kg, but that of the Soviet Union and the US already hit 164.1 kg and 538.3 kg respecively. Besides, its per capita electricity generation was just 2.76 kilowatt hour (kWh) whereas in the Soviet Union and the US, the number was 553.5kWh and 2,949kWh respectively (Liu, 1999). With an aim to combat backwardness in a more efficient way, implementation of the plan involved massive investment in fixed assets, which amounted to RMB46 billion over the five years, or 1.9 times larger than what China had possessed at the end of 1952 (Pei, 1986). Unavoidably, this rapid pace of industrialization exerted a major impact on how the Chinese people lived; some were relocated to other areas to work while others worked outside of their experience and training. What the future would hold, very few people could prophesy, but at least by 1957, most indicators suggested that China had laid down a preliminary foundation for her socialist industrialization, a sound basis for its advance toward the next stage.

3 The Great Leap Forward of the Second Five Year Plan (1958–1962)

At the 8th National Congress of the Communist Party of China in 1956, Premier Zhou Enlai made a report on the proposal for the second Five Year Plan (1958–1962). One year later, the government was no longer content with the momentum of growth and aspired to move forward at a much faster pace. At the same time, China's relationship with the Soviet Union began to get intense and these two allies even lost trust in each other. As a result of the deepening hostility, China no longer wanted to imitate the Soviet industrialization pattern; instead, China replaced it with a new initiative called the Great Leap Forward (GLP, '*da yue jin*'), which is considered today to be a miscalculated attempt to resolve contradictions by doing everything in a rush simultaneously, irrespective of the actual constraints of resources.

The official approval of *the new goal of the "Great Leap" took place in* 1958 at the second session of the 8th *Central Committee of the Communist Party of China. By taking the decision,* the leadership expected to achieve a quantum leap in production across all sectors of the economy. Unwilling to use historical trends of output as a planning criterion to modernize industry, agriculture and science, the 2nd session called for an immediate construction of socialism with a forced pace of development. For the achievement of a drastic transformation, targets were even raised to unbelievable heights. Ambitions to increase production by 100PCT or more were deemed fairly common.

3.1 People's Commune, a Step Further to Collectivized Farming

By 1957, agriculture could hardly satisfy the demand from industry and other non-farming sectors whose growth was more vigorous. In fact, the problem had already existed in the early 1950s and to have it resolved, the government in 1953 began to adopt a centralized and unified procurement-and-sales policy on grain, cotton, and vegetable oils in order to address the shortage of farm produce. However, when the second Five Year Plan was to be carried out in 1958, the situation did not change much. Once again, collectivization was taken as an effective measure to mobilize the rural population and expand the workforce. Rather notably, a number of methods were adopted to deal with the acute labor shortage. For female adults who had beforehand worked most of their hours at home, they were encouraged to participate in farming. Besides, both males and females were required to work longer than before (Zhang, 2010). With a view to increasing productivity, collectives in many places started to organize communal canteens in the fields. By offering free meals to peasants, a lot more time could be allocated to serving the paramount goal of modernizing agriculture.

In addition to the above, mergers of cooperatives were promoted by policy-makers in the spring of 1958 to help ensure efficient irrigation and mechanization of cultivation. Not long later, experiments conducted in several parts of the country were reported by newspapers. On April 12th, *People's Daily* (an official newspaper providing direct information on the policies and viewpoints of the government) in its headline introduced Minhou County (Fujian Province), which integrated 23 cooperatives into a single one within three months. Similarly, another eye-catching example was Liaoning Province. Using just one month, it managed to consolidate 9,600 cooperatives into 1,461, with each one having about 2,000 farm households (PHRC, 2011). Indeed, formation of larger-scale agricultural producers' cooperatives represented a major shift in the countryside, it symbolized the replacement of private ownership with collective ownership in the management of agricultural activities. In a sense, enlargement of cooperatives was beneficial because it enabled peasants to access a greater amount of resources, with which they could more easily attain their goals on output and productivity. But from another perspective, the enlargement in size would become a burden if the internal mechanism failed to adapt itself to the change. Unfortunately, this was the case of China. At a time when its people were preoccupied with the dream of making a "leap" to overtake developed countries of the West, little attention was attached to the chance of achieving the ambition. In their eyes, the bigger the better. Even though these cooperatives were not perfect, the drawbacks could be eliminated as long as they became larger. Therefore, guided by the mindset of turning cooperatives into a more advanced and comprehensive rural organization, people's communes came into being in 1958. In that July, Chayashan Commune, China's first commune, was set up in Suiping County, Henan Province (Duan, 2012).

One month later, at an enlarged session held by the Political Bureau of the Central Committee of the CPC in Beidaihe (a summer resort in Hebei Province), resolutions were reached to establish people's communes throughout rural China. The subsequent pace of communization was incredibly fast, in the end of October, communes totaled 26,576, with their members consisting of 99PCT of the peasant households of the nation (Ji, 2012). If compared to the 8,730 communes of August, the increase exceeded 200PCT.

To ensure that its operations across the country would be consistent and well under control, the CPC Central Committee promulgated the "Decision on Several Issues Concerning People's Communes" in December 1958, which gave a detailed account of the hierarchical structure within the organization. In general, a people's commune should include three levels of administration and they were the "commune" ('*gong she*'), the "production brigade" ('*shengchan dadui*'), and the "production team" ('*shengchan dui*'). Among them, the production brigade was the basic accounting unit. While the production team was to arrange routine activities like plowing, planting and harvesting, etc., it was still the commune which was held responsible for profits and losses (Chen, 1959). In March 1959, to better look after the interest of peasants who had been somewhat discouraged by the existing institution, power was delegated downward and with the production team acting as the basic accounting unit, it began to enjoy certain autonomy in taking decisions and allocating revenues. With regard to the incentive scheme of people's communes, it was modelled after the practice of Chayashan Commune from Henan. Specifically, this was a package which integrated two types of reward, one was named "performance-based wages" (*'gong zi zhi'*) and like the name suggests, the appraisal focused a lot on the contribution of *labor. In other words, the more he worked, the higher the pay he would receive. Referring to the other one, it was "need-based provision of grain" ('liangshi gonji zhi'), a system that provided free grain to all the commune members in accordance with their needs (*Deng, 2004*).*

Apparently, the second method of remuneration was flawed given the fact that by then, China's was still a subsistence economy. For the vast majority of its rural population, their primary task was to combat poverty and hunger. Even if the country were already affluent enough, such an unrealistic ideal would only exhaust the resources and drag it into bankruptcy. But anyhow, since the "Great Leap Forward" itself was a miscalculated movement in which objectives were blindly set and numbers were randomly inflated, what happened to the people's communes were not incomprehensible. However, it was only following the release of the "Regulations for the Work of Rural People's Communes (Amended Draft)" in 1961 that the "need-based provision of grain" was abolished, and together with it the communal dining hall. To a large extent, the promotion of the integrated compensation system in China's countryside from 1958 to 1961 has exacerbated the three-year great famine. In complete disregard of the actual situation and based on a kind of egalitarian utopia, no wonder the people's commune as an institution was restructured in the early 1980s, shortly after the country began to reform and open up.

3.2 The Iron and Steel Campaign for Industrial Modernization

In addition to increasing agricultural output, the second Five Year Plan aimed at building a comprehensive industrial system in both rural and urban areas. At the very core of this giant mission stands heavy industry which consumed the lion's share of the resources. Almost every citizen, skilled or not, was involved in this unprecedented movement, some directly and some indirectly. In particular, given the prominent role of iron and steel, it was not uncommon to see schools and hospitals participate in the production. Males, both old and young, were commanded to source raw materials and attend melting furnaces in either rural communes or urban neighborhoods. Since at the same time, a lot of routine farm works, especially those for the busy sowing and reaping seasons, had to be attended by male labor, even women and children were required to join in the mass steel campaign.

Unfortunately, the reality soon turned out bleak. In spite of an immeasurable amount of inputs, much of the iron and steel made by these primitive blast furnaces were useless. Furthermore, the prospect of attaining the forecasted rapid speed of growth was overshadowed by the threat of grain shortage, which could be explained by two major sets of factors. One factor was the diversion of productive resources away from agriculture, including capital and labor. In 1958 for example, seeing some positive signs that may lead to a bumper harvest, the government was inclined to accept excessively magnified estimates of grain production. Misguided by the false belief that China had almost resolved its grain problem, a "three-three system" ('*san san zhi*') for the utilization of agricultural land was introduced in 1959 under the principle of "sowing less and harvesting more" ('*shaozhong duoshou*'). According to the system, one-third of arable land was to be used for grain crops, one-third for cash crops, and the remaining one third for rotation (Lin & Yang, 1998). Within just one year after the implementation of these policies, the sown area for grain crops dropped from 127.6 million hectares in 1958 to 116 million hectares in 1959, a 9PCT fall. Referring to grain output, it fell by 15PCT to 170 million tons only (NBS, 1999).

In addition, since the steel campaign was in need of a huge amount of labor, millions of workers from the people's communes (usually the best workers) were diverted from agricultural activities to mine coal or produce iron in backyard blast furnaces that were often poorly built. In addition, as a result of the massive expansion of industrial construction, urban employers had a stronger demand for labor, which led to a relaxation of central control over recruitment. Therefore, rural-to-urban migration became prevalent in the early years of the Great Leap Forward. In 1958 alone, of the 20 million jobs newly created in cities, more than 10 million of them were performed by temporary and contract workers coming from the countryside (Lin, 2014). As a result, the rural labor force that remained in the fields fell, not just in absolute numbers, but also in the quality of performance for many of the workers that stayed were either inexperienced or physically fragile. Besides, what made things worse were the natural calamities during 1959–1961, which further reduced grain production (Lin & Yang, 1998). Still an agrarian society with backward farming technologies, the impact of climate on food availability was severe. In this regard, Chinese historical records do not lack descriptions on how natural disasters continually afflicted the country and its people over the past centuries. From 1959 to 1961, natural disasters like prolonged drought, heavy flooding, and some other calamities hampered normal agricultural production. Nevertheless, despite the harms that have occurred, the impact of natural disasters on grain production during the Great Leap Forward should not be overstated because bad weather of similar magnitude also happened in 1962 and 1963, without producing such serious contractions. Instead of collapsing, annual grain output managed to grow by 8.5PCT in 1962 and by 6.3PCT in 1963, hitting 160 million and 170 million tons respectively (NBS, 1999).

3.3 The Great Famine and Economic Adjustment

Due to the interplay of man-made and natural factors, the worst famine in China's modern history took place in 1959 and persisted until 1961. While the number of direct casualties has been debated and no single source is authoritative enough to convince others;according to *The History of the CPC* (Volume 2),the great famine has caused an abnormal population decline of approximately 10 millions in China in 1960,a compared to that of 1959. The table below (Table 6) shows that China's GDP, which had climbed to RMB145.7 billion in 1960, dropped sharply to RMB114.9 billion by 1962, a shrinkage of almost RMB31 billion within a couple of years. Moreover, from 1959 to 1961, the population of China plunged by 13.5 million and apparently, starvation was the key reason for that drop. In terms of grain production, it had equally gone through a downward trend since 1959. Although 1962 witnessed a slight recovery, the output was still well below the pre-famine level. In 1962, the population size was larger than that of 1958; however, grain output was significantly lower.

Indeed, the radical policies imiplemented during the second Five-Year-Plan period made China even more unbalanced. First of all, as compared to 1957, industrial output in 1960 was up by over 130PCT, reaching RMB163.7 billion. But agriculture suffered a 15PCT decline to RMB45.7 billion. Second, in the industrial sector, the share of light and heavy industry was 55PCT vs. 45PCT in 1957; yet in 1960, it became 33.4PCT vs. 66.6PCT (NBS, 1999). Apparently, the over-rapid development of industry, especially heavy industry, was achieved at the expense of agriculture and light industry, which worsened the tension between supply and demand, enlarged the fiscal deficit, and increased inflation expectations, etc.

Confronted with such a problematic situation, the government was not unaware of its grave consequences. Rather, it understood the pressing need to alter the misplaced emphasis and rebalance the economy. Starting from the second half of 1960, a series of adjustment programs were initiated and their purpose was to reduce problems through institutional changes. Among them, stringent measures included the cancellation of large-scale industrial and water conservation projects, downsizing the urban workforce, slashing the government's grain procurement quota, and importing large amounts of grains, etc. During the initial phase of the Great Leap, many rural workers migrated to cities where they got construction jobs. However, China's rebalancing initive cut the need for urban workers while the demand for rural workers increased. Thus many of these migrants were sent back to where they came from. Of the over 18 million dismissals which happened from 1961 to 1963, 67PCT of them were reported to have returned to the countrywide (Jiang, 2011). As an immediate effect, the backflow pushed up the number of frontline workers available for agricultural production, thus enabling the country to boost the output of major farm crops by the end of 1963.

Table 6 Comparison of GDP, population and grain output, 1958–1962

Year	1958	1959	1960	1961	1962
GDP (RMB billion)	130.7	143.9	145.7	122	114.9
Population (million)	659.9	672.1	662.1	658.6	673
Grain output (million tons)	200	170	143.5	147.5	160

Source NBS, 1999

In dealing with the devastating famine which cost millions of lives, central planners equally had to modify the established practices, one of which was the procurement quota. Back in the early 1950s, to ensure adequate supplies of grain and edible oil to urban residents without a substantial increase in prices, the "unified purchase and unified sales" system ('*tonggou tongxiao*') for grain and oil-bearing crops was introduced. Under this system, peasants were required to sell a certain portion of their output to the state at a fixed but low price before being allowed to retain some for their own consumption. By doing so, the state was in a position to monopolize the distribution of agricultural output, a privilege that no private dealers could expect to enjoy. Later, during the nationwide campaign of building a heavy-industry-oriented economy, food demand in cities surged quickly. On the other hand, fueled by the falsified and exaggerated report on the real agricultural output, the actual quota imposed on peasants shot up also. In 1958, the net proportion of government procurement was recorded at 20.9PCT (i.e. the share of the amount purchased by the government in the total output after deducting what was later sold back in the rural area); a year after, the figure moved up to 28PCT. Ironically, the grain output for the same one-year period declined by 15PCT to 170 million tons. In dealing with the mass starvation, it became apparent that maintaining the quota was no longer pragmatic; thus, it was lowered to 21.5PCT in 1960 before being further slashed to 17.5PCT the next year (Chen, 2004).

In order to reserve the meagre foreign-exchange deposits to purchase more capital goods and technologies from abroad, China had pursued a strategy of grain self-sufficiency, which also made it a net exporter throughout the 1950s. Even when the domestic production crisis caused unbearable hunger in 1959 and 1960, China still chose not to import grain. Only after 1961, did the government decide to resort to the overseas market to fill the supply gap. For the entire 1960s, China's overseas purchase of food averaged 4.4 million tons per annum, making it a net food importer (Qu, 2006). Concerning the countries which supplied food to China, they included its traditional allies like the Soviet Union and Mongolia, and those from the "Western" world such as Canada, the US, France, Germany, and Australia, etc.

Accompanied by institutional shifts, the urban population and the labor force employed by the state were greatly reduced. Within the rural people's communes, the public dining halls were shut down in 1961 and one year later, the basic accounting unit was transferred from the production brigade down to the production team (Luo, 2009). However, no direct large-scale famine relief operation was undertaken since the disaster had been so widespread that relief would have put tremendous strain on the already over-exhausted resources. Instead, the government since 1961 removed barriers to agricultural production and allowed peasants to keep some private plots at their own disposal. From a demographic point of view, this measure worked well. Although agricultural production picked up slowly and grain output did not recover to its 1958-level until 1966, mortality dropped back to normal soon after its implementation and an unprecedented fertility boom followed in 1963, which peaked at 43.37PCT (NBS, 1999). In summary, all these post-crisis events imply that the demographic crisis during the Great Leap period was mainly due to erroneous government policy decisions (on top of natural disasters), as well as hastily introduced institutional changes and innovations for which China was ill prepared.

3.4 An Episode Worthy of Contemplation

In addition to the above discussed negative effects, the Great Leap Forward produced some positive effects on agriculture. In particular, the construction of water conservancy and irrigation facilities relieved drought and allowed for sustained increases in production, the erection of flood defenses and the application of techniques like terrace farming enhanced the ability of peasants to cope with adverse climate conditions while increasing the amount of cultivated areas.

Regarding the Great Leap Forward in industrial policies, it included "walking on two legs" ('*liangtiaotui zoulu*'), which implies the side by side development of both small and medium-sized rural industry along with heavy industry. Unlike the backyard steel furnaces, many other successful workshops and plants were set up in rural areas, based on the idea that rural industry should meet the needs of the local people. These entities, by providing various production inputs like fertilizers, cement (for water conservation schemes), implements and equipment, etc., helped communes to more effectively manage their agricultural work. Being labor-intensive businesses whose primary goal was to satisfy local demand, they did not have to rely on the provision of a nationwide infrastructure of road and rail to transport the goods, which was good. However, if viewed from a national perspective, such a model failed to realize economies of scale for it ignored the gains from the division of labor. In other words, the comparative advantages that existed between different localities were not fully used, which led to incalculable depletion of resources.

As stated above, the Great Leap Forward was a movement centered on the establishment of modern heavy industry, especially iron and steel. Accordingly, massive amounts of materials, manpower and funds flowed in that direction. Many workers in light industries were shifted to steel factories and, in some cases, light industries were even transformed into steel makers. Consequently, for lack of enough skilled workers, consumer goods like clothes and edible oils, etc. were in short supply. Thus the imbalance between heavy industry, on the one hand, and light industry and agriculture on the other was even worse. By probing more deeply, it can be found that the imbalance existed between two kinds of social production, i.e. the reproduction of the means of production and the production of goods for consumption purposes. The bias that was excessively in favor of steel and heavy industry prevented new state investment from flowing into agriculture. As a result, the rural sector fell into a disadvantaged position whose growth was overshadowed by the nationwide drive for rapid industrialization.

Haste makes waste. The Great Leap Forward, a movement seriously disconnected from reality and contradictory to the law of economic development, pushed the Chinese economy backward by at least one decade. It distorted the relationships between industry and agriculture, between heavy industry and light industry, and between the raw materials industry and the processing industry. Moreover, the efficiency of industrial production dropped by a large margin. Until today, the period from 1959 to 1961 is a nightmare which most of the Chinese living at that time are unwilling to recall. Due to the introduction of many irrational policies, the campaign ended with a great human tragedy. Except for those already mentioned, others included the implementation of egalitarian distribution schemes in both industry and agriculture, and the curtailing of private plots and rural markets, etc. Although the motive behind these policies was to promote production, they resulted in an opposite effect which markedly decelerated productivity by dampening enthusiasm with fewer incentives. The policy implications of this time period are that China must have flexible strategies and tactics for modernization and should not try to make its development fit into a rigidly-set pattern. Instead of letting radical social change pave the way for economic growth, the development of economy itself is to determine what sorts of changes are necessary and appropriate in such spheres as management, ownership, and distribution.

4 Retrenchment and Readjustment (1963–1965)

In January 1961, the Ninth Session of the 8th Central Committee of the Chinese Communist Party agreed on a general principle to direct the national economy, and it is "adjustment, consolidation, enrichment and improvement" ('*tiaozheng, gonggu, chongshi, tigao*'). By carrying out this eight-character guideline, the government intended to straighten out the proportional relationships between different sectors so that China might quickly extricate itself from the quandary. While attempts were made to balance the uneven development of agriculture, light industry, and heavy industry, feeding and clothing the population was considered another pressing issue to address.

4.1 Corrective Measures Underway

Rather notably, the pace of building heavy industry was slowed down. Except for some key complexes, the construction of many projects was either canceled or postponed. By June 1963, 20 million new urban immigrants were sent back to the countryside to resume farming activities (Liu, 2010). Also in the rural area, with the abandonment of the mass organization of production, communes were drastically restructured and greater responsibility was laid on smaller production teams or even households. Economic incentives were reintroduced following the application of a set of four policies throughout the country. Known as "Three Freedoms and One Responsibility" ('*sanzi yibao*'), these policies included the freedom to increase the size of private plots for individual household to cultivate ('*zi liu di*'); freedom to develop small enterprises with sole responsibility for profits and losses ('*zi fu ying kui*'); and freedom to develop an open market ('*ziyou shichang*'). The one responsibility was to fix output quotas based on the household ('*baochan daohu*') (Pan, 2010). Although the collectivized model was maintained for certain works like water control, promotion of mechanization, and supply of chemical fertilizers, etc.; in general, the '*sanzi yibao*' system stimulated the growth of private enterprises and weakened the collective spirit of peasants.

To implement the eight-character principle in the industrial sector, an important document released in 1961 was reintroduced. Entitled the "Seventy Clauses of the Directive for State-Owned Industries" (also known as '*gongye qishitiao*'), it stressed the responsibility of management, as well as the technical authority of professionals and experts. By laying emphasis on rules, regulations and material rewards, the Seventy Clauses severely tightened the discipline of labor force. Moreover, piece-rate systems and bonuses were used to boost productivity. By the end of 1963, production workers of state-owned enterprises who were compensated on a piece-rate basis rose to 19.9PCT, up from less than 5PCT in 1960 (Lin & Zhu, 2015). Poor-performing factories were simply shut down by the thousands in order to channel resources to plants with higher efficiency and profitability. For example, the number of farm machinery manufacturers shrank to 1,301 by the end of 1963, a decrease of 50.42PCT over that of 1960 (Zhang & Li, 2012).

Ration coupons were used to allocate scarce necessities since as compared to the much larger demand, it was impossible to make production catch up within a short time period. In fact, this was by no means the first time that China used rationing, it had been used in the early 1950s, i.e. shortly after the establishment of the "unified purchase and unified sales" system for grains. From then on, urban families were given grain coupons with which they could buy a fixed amount of grain at a lower state-subsidized price. Given the occurrence of the great famine and its disastrous aftermaths, it is understandable to see a greater reliance on coupons. Virtually, almost all basic goods were rationed and coupons, by playing the role of a second currency, became irreplaceable for the purchase of a wide assortment of items, from foods, clothes, bicycles, to furniture and kerosene, to name but a few (Zhang, 2003). Although this institutional arrangement provided a temporary solution to inadequate supply, the government as a result was fiscally stressed. Moreover, this approach did not identify or address the root cause of the imbalance, which was China's command economy. In an effort to lessen the burden of scarcity, urban free markets which had been closed during the Great Leap Forward, were reopened starting from the early 1960s. While benefiting the residents of cities, these markets gave peasants an additional channel to sell their surplus produce.

4.2 The "Third Front" and Its Impact

In 1963, as China was in the process of recovery, increasing attention was shifted towards the elaboration of a set of long-term strategies. Because much of China's industry was still clustered along the east coast, the leaders endorsed a massive investment plan to build new facilities in remote and mountainous inland regions, including the provinces of Guizhou, Sichuan, and Yunnan in the southwest, Shaanxi, Gansu, and Qinghai in the northwest, and parts of the provinces of Shanxi, Hubei, and Hunan, etc. Known as the "Third Front" ('*san xian*') strategy, its objective was to create an entire industrial base that would grant China strategic independence when it was under military threat by external "foes". In a broader sense, the strategy also was consistent with the economic policies implemented during the 1950s, through which the government had unremittingly transferred resources, including plants, capital, and personnel, etc., to the inland and northeast provinces in order to narrow down their gap with the east. From the first Five-Year Plan (1953–1957) to the Great Leap Forward (1958–1960), these same areas continued to be the most favored destinations of the state investment (Su, 2001).

Beginning in the second half of 1964, a new tide of production was initiated, with its focus laid on the construction of factories and railroad lines in China's southwestern provinces, particularly Sichuan and Guizhou. By relocating factories of the coastal regions to establish complete industrial systems in interior locations, the Third Front program absorbed a fairly big portion of China's new investment. For instance, in 1965 alone, of the country's infrastructure investment that reached RMB13.39 billion, RMB4.2 billion went to the Third Front, accounting for about one third of the total (Chen, 2003). Although the most intense period of investment and construction was not very long, which spanned from 1964 to 1971, the program lasted until 1978. In contrast with other attempts to develop inland industries, this particular scheme delivered little benefit to the national economy. Since a lot of projects were based in the most inaccessible areas, many were aborted before completion. As to those which materialized, their lack of geographical advantage and feasibility prevented them from fostering the development of industries supplying inputs to the immediate neighborhood. It is estimated that throughout the period 1966–1972, direct and indirect losses thus sustained exceeded RMB30 billion, over 18PCT of the total investment in the Third Front for the same six years (Su, 2000). As a typical example, the 1967's groundbreaking ceremony of the Second Automotive Works was held in Lu Zi Gou (Shiyan, northwestern Hubei Province), a barren gully deep in the mountains. Without railway lines to bring in the construction equipment, the setting up of a car factory was extremely slow. By the time it went into full operation, it was already 1975. Instead of spawning a whole string of support industries for the province, the carmaker suffered huge financial losses in the following two years, plus major quality problems. Until 1978, the situation began to turn for the better and the venture became profit-making (Wu, 2009). However, given its remote location, the original plan of serving as an engine for regional industrialization couldn't be easily fulfilled.

The expansion of rail service to the vast unreachable hinterland is perhaps one of the few positive legacies of this massive project. Yet given China's limited resources and low level of productivity, it was still found difficult to satisfy the gigantic inputs required. Therefore, following the chaos and violence of the Cultural Revolution (which started in 1966), the pace of investment decelerated before being finally halted in 1978. Through these years of readjustment, there was a reversal of fiscal deficit and rising price indexes were under better control, which suggested improvements in market supply. However, since the overriding policy of developing a heavy-industry-driven economy was virtually unchanged, rationalization of the sectoral structure and growth pattern failed to make a real breakthrough.

5 The Cultural Revolution (1966–1976)

Culture, representative of people's way of life, is also a reflection of people's way of thinking, including their value, faith, and ideologies, etc. Over thousands of years, the Chinese people have always been quite proud of their own culture and to a large extent, it is culture which enables them to possess a unique identity in the world. In May 1966, a movement named the "Great Proletarian Cultural Revolution" (or the "Cultural Revolution") was officially launched around China. Like the name suggests, its aim was to challenge the traditional Chinese culture and replace the dictatorship of the bourgeoisie with that of the proletariat. Before initiating the campaign, Beijing's plan was to proceed in phases and have it confined to education, culture, and the party & government organs. However, the subsequent development was like fire burning because very soon, it became out of control, a situation which had not been fully anticipated by the central leaders.

5.1 Urban Industrial Enterprises in the Movement

After three years of readjustment and retrenchment, China began to witness signs of improvement on multiple fronts. According to the third Five-Year Plan (1966–1970), the industrial output set for 1966 was RMB151.2 billion, an increase of 12PCT over the previous year (Ma, 1998). By that June, its actual production exceeded 50PCT of the plan and registered RMB79.4 billion, a 20.3PCT rise as compared to the same period of 1965. Besides, due to the growth in productivity and reduction in cost, earnings of enterprises reached a level that was almost 21PCT higher than that of 1965. Fairly speaking, if such a positive trend could persist, then China should be able to fulfill its five-year plan by the end of the term. Contrary to what had been expected, however, when more and more schools were closed down in response to the call of Beijing to "rebel", students (as well as some teachers) of both middle schools and universities moved around different parts of the country shouting slogans and propagating revolutionary ideas. Since there was often a red armband on their sleeves, these fanatic youths were vividly called the "Red Guards" ('*hong wei bing*', implying their loyalty to the dogma of the CCP). From August to November, 1966, the Red Guards received by Chairman Mao at Tiananmen Square were estimated to be over 13 million (Yu, 2005). Although it is hard to tell precisely how many Red Guards travelled in China during the 10-year Revolution, given the vastness of its territory, the number should be rather immense.

5.1.1 Organization and Management

When these zealous boys and girls were present in cities and towns where most of the country's enterprises were located, it is unlikely that the effect would be insignificant. First and foremost, the large influx of Red Guards added much burden to rail and water transport. For lack of sufficient capacity, delivery of important raw materials like coal, cement, steel, and timber, etc. had to be put off, which severely disrupted production. In addition, agitated by the movement of the Red Guards, these enterprises also formed similar rebel groups to attack authorities, chiefly the cadres, in order to demonstrate their pro-Revolution stance. As a result of all these disturbances, not only production, all the routine activities were more or less influenced. In certain regions and sectors, many enterprises were simply in a state of paralysis. Understandably, when the external environment was turbulent, an individual business would be vulnerable to greater uncertainties.

In 1965, of all the 157,700 industrial enterprises in China, 29PCT of them were state-owned whereas those of the collectively-owned accounted for 71PCT (NBS, 2012). Yet in terms of their output, it is the former which claimed the majority 90PCT. Given the dominant position of the state sector, it is necessary to make some analysis of its management so as to better understand how it contributed to the national economy. Prior to the Cultural Revolution, each state-owned enterprise was under the leadership of a party committee and very often, a director (or manager) was held responsible for its daily operations (Zhang, 2006). Instead of being elected by workers, the director was generally appointed by the superior authorities in charge, either a ministry in Beijing or a provincial/regional bureau. Although in principle, it was the party members of the enterprise who could decide on the composition of the party committee; in fact, the decision-making power was in the hands of higher-ranking party officials. Modelled after the Soviet Union's way of management, the director was the master who did not have to consult workers before taking actions; regarding the latter, they should just obey and observe the instructions from the above. Needless to say, such kind of arrangement was unfavorable to the motivation of workers, nor could it contribute positively to the enhancement of their performance. Sometimes, they even felt hostile to the director for his manipulation of almost everything.

Anshan Iron & Steel Company ('*An Gang*', located in Liaoning Province), the earliest-established iron and steel complex of China, formed its unique pattern of management which provided a solution to the aforesaid problems among the SOEs. Later referred to as the "Angang Constitution" ('*Angang xianfa*'), the core ideas of the company were synthesized into "two participations, one reform and three-in-one unity" ('*liangcan, yigai, sanjiehe*'). Specifically, it means the participation of cadres in labor and workers in management; reform of inappropriate rules & regulations; and unity between cadres, workers, and technicians. In recognition of Angang's practice and with a view to having them promoted to other parts of the country, the central government in 1961 released the "Regulations on the Work of State-Owned Industrial Enterprises", which totally included 70 articles (Dai, 1999). As a key document guiding SOEs' development for many years, it laid great emphasis on the mobilization of the masses, including workers, engineers, and other staff, so that they could exert more influence over the operations of their business. Although the former system of full responsibility by director under the leadership of party committee remained unchanged, cadres were required to do jobs on the basis of closer linkage and solidarity with the masses. In particular, when major problems concerning production or technology arose, the principle of "three-in-one unity" invented by Angang should be applied in their settlement.

Fairly speaking, involvement of workers in management was quite beneficial to the technological innovation of these SOEs. Familiar with the manufacturing process and facilities, workers could point out precisely the flaws that existed. Sometimes, they would also furnish constructive ideas that enabled the "three-in-one" group to come up with quicker solutions. In addition, when their voices were heard on more occasions, they had a stronger sense of belonging and this in turn boosted the morale of the entire enterprise. Nonetheless, after the outbreak of the Cultural Revolution, the 1961 Regulations was denounced as an attempt to restore capitalism because in support of using material incentives (like bonus) and paying workers according to their performances, the Regulations was considered a denial of the socialist concept of egalitarian income distribution. By 1978, in an effort to rebuild economic order which had been disrupted by the Cultural Revolution, the Central Committee of the CPC promulgated the "Decisions on the Acceleration of Industrial Development (Draft)". If to compare it with the 1961 Regulations, they shared many similarities (Zhang, 2015) and rather notably, soon after the implementation of the Decisions, the once quite sensitive bonuses and piece-rate wages were again prevalent among more and more enterprises.

Although in terms of output, it was the state enterprises which claimed the biggest proportion of the nation's total, their number was much smaller once taking into account the collectively-owned entities. Distributed in both urban and rual China, the latter was equally an important contributor to the nation's industry. In the 1960s and 1970s, many of those located in urban areas were called street factories ('*jiedao qiye*') because the formation was in general initiated voluntarily by the residents of a particular neighborhood. Like their state counterparts whose administration was placed under a revolutionary committee (a special group composed of the officials from the People's Liberation Army, cadres and masses of the enterprise, and subordinate to the party committee) during the 10-year Revolution, all the street factories were subject to the leadership of a street-level revolutionary committee based in the same locality. Given the fact that they were not funded by the government, most street factories were either small or medium-sized. Besides, the activities they engaged in were chiefly to meet local demand, such as sewing, mending, and laundry, etc. For some of them which were larger, their business scope would cover processing and manufacturing, with products being sold to more remote markets. Since the recruitment threshold of street factories was lower than that of the SOEs, a lot of females (including housewives) got the opportunity to find a full-time job, which helped ease the pressure on urban employment.

5.1.2 Two Rounds of Unsuccessful Restoration

With the continual escalation of the movement, the whole country was involved in a state of hysteria and chaos. Under such circumstances, industrial production became an immediate victim whose decline in 1967 and 1968 caused big concerns among the central leaders. Furthermore, based on a survey of over 20,000 enterprises around China, 25PCT of them incurred losses in the first half of 1971; for several provinces, the unprofitable SOEs even exceeded 50PCT (Ma, 1998). In order to halt the downward spiral and get the increasingly anarchic industry back on the right track, the first round of rehabilitation kicked off in 1972 at the urging of Premier Zhou Enlai (Chen, 1994). By laying stress on the application of seven criteria to evaluate enterprises, i.e. output, product variety, consumption of raw materials, fuel & power, quality, productivity, cost, and profit, etc., he also called for the reinforcement of their governance, especially concerning issues like job responsibilities, employee attendance, quality inspection, equipment maintenance, and safety management in production, etc. Besides, with regard to the reward scheme, "pay for performance" was once again recognized as an important principle to eliminate the negative effect of egalitarianism. Despite all the measures that aimed to rectify the industrial sector, their implementation was by no means a smooth one due to the more powerful forces in the party that supported left-wing ideologies. Consequently, with the industrial output in 1974 reaching RMB279.6 billion, China only accomplished 93.2PCT of its plan. At the same time, due to the failure to hit other targets like fixed assets investment and their rate of utilization, decline in state revenues resulted in a fiscal deficit which registered RMB770 million.

After going through eight years of Cultural Revolution, China was indeed thirsty for a pacified environment that could enable its economy to develop in a stable way. Perhaps it was based on the same consideration that Deng Xiaoping, a pro-reform figure who had been purged during that special era, was reappointed the vice-premier in 1974 to support the work of the ailing Zhou Enlai. Quickly, his resumption of power was followed by the launch of a series of endeavors. Since these endeavors were both related to the industrial sector, they were referred to as the second round of industrial rehabilitation. First and foremost, to bring order to the nearly-paralyzed transport system, the "Decisions of the CPC Central Committee on the Improvement of the Railway Work" was released in March 1975. While placing the nationwide rail network under the uniform administration of the Ministry of Railways, leadership by the party committee at different levels was consolidated to ensure efficient execution of both the state plan and local priorities. Within just one month, all the 20 railway bureaus in China (except for Nanchang) fulfilled their plan on wagon loading, making the total number of loads reach 53,700 per day, the record high in history. In turn, improvement in rail transport greatly facilitated industrial production, which from January to April rose 19.4PCT if compared to the same period of the previous year.

In China's blueprint for the building of a well-established system for its heavy industry, steel has always remained in a paramount position. Seeing that industrial production had been affected by the shortfall in steel output in the initial four months of 1975, Deng Xiaoping provided several concrete approaches to ameliorate the situation. Apart from strengthening the leadership of the Ministry of Metallurgy Industry (i.e. the ministry in charge of the sector), and stricter enforcement of regulations; motivation of employees, especially experienced cadres, skilled workers and technicians, etc., was treated with equal importance in his program (Mao, 2013). Similar to the positive changes which happened in the rail transport system, progress in the steel sector was also quite promising. In that June, for example, China produced 72,400 tons of steel per day, higher than the planned average for the whole year. Meanwhile, the adjustment of the rail and metallurgy industry mobilized many other sectors and as a result, monthly production of crude oil, coal, chemical fertilizer, electricity, and cement, etc. peaked in May and June. By the end of 1975, China's gross industrial output registered RMB320.7 billion, a 15PCT rise over that of 1974 (NBS, 1999).

Indeed, the impressive effects of the second round of industrial rehabilitation were a reflection of the eagerness of the general public to return to normal life. Bearing witness to the tragedies and destructions of the unprecedented campaign, they wanted to grasp every single chance available to recover the lost time. With the same mindset, they responded actively to the initiative of Beijing to repair the derailed economy. Nonetheless, at a time when the political scene was still characterized by incessant frictions and conflicts, it was impossible for the country to move toward the same direction in a cohesive way. Once again, despite the commitment of several like-minded central leaders and the support of the grassroots, pressure from the fanatical opponents had been too immense to resist. Finally, the second rehabilitation was terminated in the end of 1975. To gain a better understanding of the impact of this aborted attempt, it is necessary to make a comparison between 1975 and 1976. Although in 1975, there was an increase of industrial output over the previous year, the rate was 6.9–7.7PCT lower than expected. Besides, production of several major industrial goods in 1975 both recorded a double-digit annual growth, with steel at 13.2PCT, coal at 16.7PCT, crude oil at 18.8PCT, and cotton yarns at 16.9PCT, etc.; but the performance in 1976 was no longer so optimistic. While the output of coal was equivalent to 100.6PCT of the plan, that of steel and cotton yarns accounted for just 79PCT and 88PCT of the plan respectively.

Anyhow, if to view it from another perspective, the significance of the unsuccessful trial in 1975 should not be underestimated. Its recognition that to have a well-developed economy, attention should be directed to factors like productivity, institutional construction, and absorption of foreign technologies, etc. was rather farsighted. Additionally, by advocating incentive-based pay, it challenged the deep-rooted egalitarian approach of compensation and provided a feasible alternative that helped foster employee motivation. To a high degree, this round of rehabilitation paved the way for China's reform and opening up in 1978. Based on the experiences accumulated three years before, the country was in a position to carry out its grand scheme more effectively without incurring much unbearable risks and losses. For instance, from the practice of initiating restoration in the rail and steel sector before having it promoted to other economic sectors, China in the early 1980s learned to first open 4 special economic zones instead of granting the same treatment to the whole country (Zhao & Zhang, 2004). By doing so, the feasibility of the policy could be tested on a small scale and after some adjustments, its implementation in a larger number of areas may proceed more smoothly and fruitfully, thus resulting in a lower opportunity cost.

5.2 Rural Policy Changes and Their Effects

In the very beginning, cities and towns were at the epicenter of China's "Cultural Revolution". But gradually, as more and more "educated youths" ('*zhishi qingnian*') were involved in the movement of "up to the mountains and down to the villages" ('*shangshan xiaxiang*'), the countryside could no longer stay immune. As a matter of fact, the initiation of the movement could be traced back to the early 1950s when elementary and middle school graduates coming from rural areas were called by the central government to return to participate in agricultural production. Later, to deal with the increasing number of urban graduates who could not further their education nor find jobs because of the fall in enrollment and recruitment, sending them to work in the fields was also taken as an effective way out. When the outbreak of the "Cultural Revolution" led to the closure of more schools and a full-fledged recession of the economy, the approach naturally became the primary solution to ease the headache of millions of urban surplus labor. By the end of 1968, the number of educated youths (also called "rusticated youths") being sent down reached 2 million, higher than the sum of that of the 5 years before the Revolution (Liu, Ding, Shi & He, 1995). If taking into consideration the entire 10-year period from 1966 to 1976, then over 14 million youths had been mobilized and this represented 8.6PCT of the country's urban population in 1976. In fact, such a phenomenon is only comparable to the rural exodus of China since the late 1980s, although the latter was in the opposite direction.

When these young people settled down in the countryside, what they brought to the local peasants were not all that favorable as expected. Most prominently, given the limited supply of arable land, the surge in rural population not only caused the per capita cultivated area to drop, it also pushed up the amount of surplus labor force, which further exacerbated the imbalance between people and land. Usually, such kind of problems was rather common in regions nearby Shanghai and Beijing because with a higher standard of living, they were much more attractive destinations to the educated youths. Therefore, peasants in these places tended to express greater discontent than those of the remote and backward locations. In addition, to make sure that the sent-down youths would not suffer from hunger, some underdeveloped provinces even allowed these urbanites to receive rationed grains without having to work as hard as peasants. In view of the aforementioned reasons, plus the additional tasks of looking after the incoming youths, it is understandable that the movement was not welcomed by all peasants.

In essence, Cultural Revolution is an ideological campaign that aims to consolidate the dictatorship of the proletariat through nationwide thought reforms, very few Chinese could be an outsider and escape its influence. Referring to the 612 million rural population in China in 1966, they were not exceptional either. Although at the outset, Beijing had released several directives trying to ensure that agricultural production would not be disturbed by the turmoil, the situation changed in the end of 1966 when the central policy demanded the formation of revolutionary committees and Red Guard groups among the poor and lower-middle peasants (*'pinxiazhong nong'*). As a result, escalation of violence and conflicts made the countryside more chaotic; due to the misplaced focus, some regions even fell into a state of anarchy. While in 1967, agricultural output increased by 1.5PCT over the previous year, there was a decline of 2.45PCT in 1968 (Zheng, 1998). Also for the same year, grain output registered 209 million tons only, which was 8.76 million tons lower than that of 1967.

With a renewed emphasis on political consciousness and collective effort, activities like sideline production, private ownership of plots and exchange in free markets, etc. were completely banned because they would lead China down the "capitalist road". Besides, in compliance with the principle "take grain as the key link" (*'yiliang weigang'*), some extreme measures were adopted to boost grain production. For example, in order to acquire more land, lakes were filled up and forests were destroyed, which resulted in ecological imbalances that could not be easily rectified (Zou, 2010). People's communes, a major rural institution, were urged to pursue self-reliance by building small-scale industry and becoming self-sufficient in grain. It was under such circumstances that Dazhai, a rocky and backward village of Xiyang County (Shanxi Province), became a renowned name during the Cultural Revolution. In fact, the slogan of "In agriculture, learn from Dazhai" had been coined together with "In industry, learn from Daqing" in 1964 to promote the two models across the nation. Until today, Dazhai spirit is still considered as a symbol of unswerving courage and tenacity when confronting hardships. Located in a mountainous region about 1,000 m above the sea level, Dazhai lacked the basic conditions to develop agriculture, especially in view of its water shortage and barren soil. However, by relying on the most primitive tools like pickaxes and shovels, its people still managed to convert the mountains into terraced fields where sorghum and corn were cultivated. From the mid-1960s to the late 1970s, in response to the call to learn the Dazhai spirit, 9.6 million people visited the model county (Li, 2011). Meanwhile, thousands of foreigners also made trips there, including the heads of states like Mali, Ethiopia, Senegal, Albania, Mexico, the Netherlands, and East Germany, etc.

Nonetheless, no matter how encouraging the Dazhai spirit was for rural China, its impact was still a limited one in comparison with the much more profound repercussions of the Cultural Revolution. In particular, with the intensification of the movement, the incentives necessary to motivate peasants were diminishing quickly. For instance, according to the "Regulations on the Work of the Rural People's Communes (Draft)" passed in 1962, a clear dividing line was set between reward and punishment. Specifically, it stipulated that remuneration of commune members (peasants) should be based on the quality and quantity of the work performed. If they failed to accomplish their due responsibilities, then either the pay would be lowered or other punitive measures would apply. But after the Revolution began, the practice of Dazhai which advocated selfless devotion to the collective was greatly valued and introduced to different parts of the country. Since its way of distribution showed little concern over the gap in efforts, skills, and outcome, etc., the enthusiasm of high-performing peasants was severely dampened (Zheng, 1998). Besides, with the existing '*hukou*' system which rigidly prohibited free movement of labor, these peasants were bound to the land without any possibility of seeking a better alternative elsewhere. In the absence of choice, motivation, and an assured future, fluctuations in agricultural production were by no means rare and apart from the downward shift in 1968, the same happened in 1972 and the 1976–1977 period respectively. Nevertheless, at a time of extreme volatility in almost all facets of life, what the agriculture sector has displayed is pretty normal.

5.3 Lessons from the "Cultural Revolution"

To measure the disturbing effects of this decade-long revolution on the Chinese economy, especially the twists and turns it has undergone, some statistics might be worth noting. In terms of the total value of agricultural and industrial output, it dropped by 9PCT and 4PCT respectively over the initial years of 1967 and 1968 (Graph 4), with gross industrial output in these two years falling more steeply, by 15PCT and 7PCT.

In the following years, as political stability was gradually restored, a renewed drive for coordinated and balanced development was set in motion. In particular, to

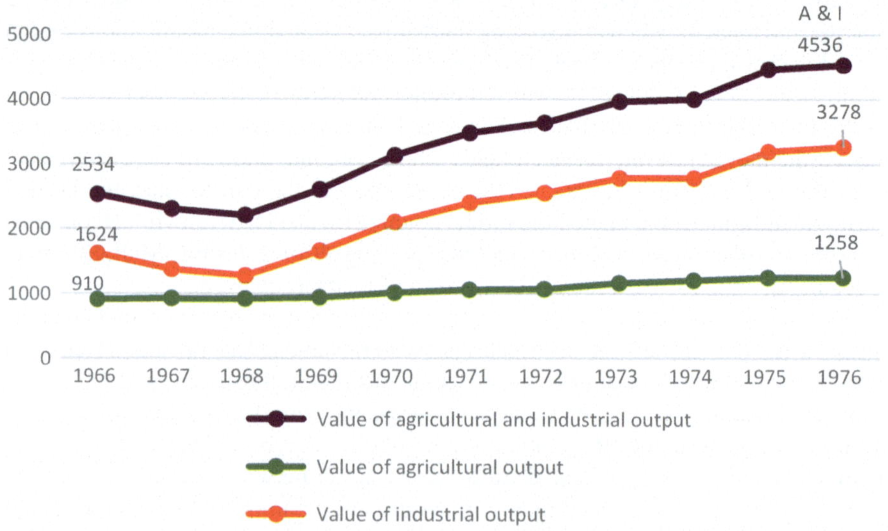

Graph 4 Value of Agricultural and Industrial Output (at current prices), RMB100 Million. *Note* value of agricultural and industrial output (A&I) calculated by the author. *Source* value of agricultural output (A) and value of industrial output (I) from NBS, 1999

revive efficiency in industry, a campaign was carried out beginning in 1968 to return workers, including the skilled and highly-educated personnel to the jobs from which they had been displaced during the Cultural Revolution (On July 3rd and July 24th, 1968, two bulletins were released by the central government to command workers to go back; in July 1974, another notice was issued with similar demands). In addition, aware of the necessity to import key equipment and technologies, a program worth USD4.3 billion was approved in early 1973, through which 26 industrial projects were to be imported. Later, the total value was increased to USD5.18 billion and the investment was directed to the construction of major facilities for the production of chemical fertilizers, chemical fibers, steel plates, and oil extraction & refining, etc. (Hua, 2012).

Although the period from 1969 to 1973 was by no means peaceful for China, at least, the economic environment was improving, which enabled industrial output to realize steady growth. Nonetheless, during the first half of the 1970s when the whole country was devoted to the restoration of the economy, a radical group known as the "Gang of Four" ('*si ren bang*') vehemently attacked the policies of Zhou Enlai (the Premier) and Deng Xiaoping (a communist leader and reformer who was purged *twice* during the Cultural Revolution) in order to dominate the power center. As a result of these disturbances, gross agricultural and industrial output in 1974 and 1976 fell well short of targets, although they did slightly increase. Between these two years, 1975 is notable because of the reappointment of Deng Xiaoping. After he was brought back into politics as the First Vice-Premier in January 1975 (in 1976, he was once again removed from all his posts), Deng quickly launched a series of rectification measures to repair structural deformities within the system and this effectively boosted industrial output by the end of the year.

Increased state investment in agriculture is the main reason agricultural output picked up. In the first and second Five Year Plan, government funding for agriculture merely posted 7.1PCT and 11.3PCT of the total. Through the adjustment period of 1963–1965, as one of the remedies to save the recessing economy, the share allocated to agriculture rose to 17.7PCT, and 1963 peaked at 23PCT. Later on, agriculture's proportion stayed at around 10PCT till the end of the 1970s (Dong, 2008). Backed by stable fiscal support, which went chiefly to the building of infrastructural facilities and the promotion of mechanized farming, the value of agricultural output did not suffer steep declines despite interruptions from the Cultural Revolution. Additionally, to encourage grain production, a decision was made in 1966 to increase state procurement prices of six types of grains, i.e. wheat, rice, millet, corn, sorghum and soybeans, by 17.1PCT, over 4PCT higher than the rate of growth for the unified selling price of the state, which was 13.07PCT (Zhao, 2016). The adoption of these policies, plus the practice of rewarding above-quota purchases with certain markups in 1967, not only helped maintain the stability of grain yield; they also enabled the nation's agricultural output to expand at a modest pace of 3.3PCT per annum over the 1967–1976 decade (Luo, Lu & Zhao, 2013).

GDP, a chief indicator representing overall economic performance, increased. In most of these 10 years, China's GDP grew with exceptions being 1967, 1968 and 1976. Anyhow, figures alone cannot mirror the whole picture during the Cultural

Revolution. Given all the chaos and political turmoil, the country was very much like a vessel devoid of radar, clueless about its destination port. In 1976, there emerged a political vacuum following the loss of three top leaders, and they were Zhou Enlai in January, Zhu De (general and principal founder of China) in July, and Mao Zedong in September. Also in the same year, a devastating earthquake hit Tangshan (Hebei province), a coal-mining city not far from Beijing. According to the official broadcast, this earthquake killed 242,000 people and severely injured some 164,000.

It is hard to put a monetary value to the cost of the Cultural Revolution, however, we should not forget the following lessons from this tragic time period. First, state policy which excessively prioritized the development of a socialist economy under public ownership suppressed the dynamic and indispensable non-state sector. Besides, emphasizing heavy industry does not mean that the significance of light industry should be underestimated. In light of China's huge population, if basic needs are not satisfied, it is impossible for the country to maintain lasting stability. However, records show that China's average share of investment in heavy industry increased from 36.1PCT during the first Five Year Plan (1953–1957) to 49.6PCT in the fourth Five Year Plan (1971–1975), while the share of investment for light industry fell from 6.4PCT to 5.8PCT (Dong, 2012). Consequently, it is not difficult to understand why the chronic shortages of consumer goods that have plagued China since the 1950s were not alleviated in the Revolution.

Regarding the agricultural sector, the guideline of '*yiliang weigang*' (grain first) was applied across the whole nation with no regard to local agricultural variation in endowments. In Beijing, for example, multiple grain-cropping was rigorously expanded at all costs, despite increasing financial losses (Zeng, 1981). In a similar way, many regions substituted grain for cotton, peanuts and other oil-bearing crops, entirely ignoring the law of comparative advantage in sown area allocation. For quite a long time, the "grain first" practice was carried to such an extent that the country had to rely more and more on imports to feed China's population. For instance, already a net importer of cotton since 1949, the failure of China's cotton yield to catch up with ballooning consumption only made the trade deficit even larger. Over the 1950s-1960s period, due to its limited volume of trade, the fluctuations were narrow and mostly below zero, implying more imports and less exports. Although the movements after the 1970s turned out to be more dramatic, China's trade position as a net cotton importer remained unchanged for most years, with the only notable exception being in the second half of the 1980s (Lu, 2000).

At a time when China was in desperate need of foreign exchange, the hard currency spent on cotton imports could have been saved if the structure of China's farming industry had been reasonably organized. The fact that China is now among the world's largest cotton producing countries tells clearly where its advantage truly lies. Put in a broader perspective, although the motive of the "grain first" strategy was for the achievement of self-sufficiency in main food grains, its implementation throughout the Cultural Revolution era led to numerous negative consequences that were significant. By suppressing the production of cash crops, it hindered the diversification of rural economic activity and curbed the transfer of surplus labor. Given the country's endowment in agricultural resources, it would have made more sense to import land-extensive crops such as wheat and rice and to preserve precious arable land for high-value export products like fruits, nuts, or vegetables.

Last but not the least, another lesson to learn is that during the Cultural Revolution, the blind pursuit of high-speed growth was not a sustainable goal. Since growth was achieved at the cost of efficiency, the resulting abuse of resources would hurt the macro economy in the long run. From this perspective, if China expected to catch up with the rest of the world, a critical move was to abandon the closed-door policy and replace it with openness to multilateral cooperation, which is the key to the prosperity of the nation. When the Cultural Revolution was winding down, Premier Zhou Enlai set in motion China's blueprint for the future. Speaking in 1975 before the National People's Congress, the top legislative body, Zhou restated that it was imperative for the nation to focus on economic development by modernizing four key areas, i.e. agriculture, industry, national defense, and science & technology, before the end of the twentieth century. These "Four Modernizations" ('*sige xiandaihua*'), as they would be called, formed part of the foundation of the economic policies of Deng Xiaoping, who became China's paramount leader by the early 1980s. Included in this foundation was '*duiwai kaifang zhengce*', or the "policy of opening up to the outside world".

6 A Window to the Outside World: Foreign Trade

Historically, nations around the globe have different ways of establishing and strengthening relationships with their foreign counterparts; among them, the exchange of goods and services is a dominant conduit. In the case of China, the Silk Road is perhaps the most well-known bridge through which this ancient oriental civilization connected itself with the rest of the world. Ironically, however, when it comes to the Qing Dynasty, the rulers' lack of interest in trade with Westerners clashed with the latter's eagerness to tap this lucrative market. After being defeated in two opium wars, the Chinese court was forced to bow its haughty head. Although with a great deal of reluctance, the mysterious eastern giant widened its door to embrace more overseas merchants to bring in and ship out commodities.

6.1 A Policy Consistent with the Heavy-Industry-Centered Model

The period between Qing's fall and the founding of the People's Republic of China covers about four decades, the characteristics of this particular stage in Chinese history was anything but stable and peaceful. After going through one chaotic scene after another, prosperity was nowhere to be found. Naturally, the most pressing task of the new regime after 1949 was to clean up messes while putting the economy back onto the right track. Copying the model of the Soviet Union, a command system was soon established, with priorities overwhelmingly emphasizing heavy industry. To ensure that production would proceed in an unhindered manner, all other sectors were ranked secondary to serve the paramount goal of socialist industrialization. Economic policy throughout the 1950s and 60 s could be characterised as import substitution, whose ultimate goal was the achievement of self-sufficiency. By introducing equipment, technologies and even whole plants from the Soviet Union, China's chief trading partner, the country sought industrial independence, hoping that it would soon no longer have to rely on importing from the outside. This autarky, a Utopian ideal that can only be found in literary or economics works, was then pursued with irrational enthusiasm.

For many years, especially since the implementation of the first Five Year Plan (1953–1957), foreign trade functioned as a channel for resources to be transferred from agriculture to industry, and from consumption to investment. Together with the transfer, agricultural, mineral and industrial exports were dispatched in exchange for raw materials and capital goods that were scarce at home. Moreover, within the framework of a command system, the state investment plan influenced the flow of foreign trade. Once an industrial project was officially established, imports would take place if considered necessary to improve the facilities or the technological level of the new project. Every time the country's foreign exchange reserves were found inadequate, goods would be allocated accordingly for export in order to fulfill the target program. Domestic sales were often cut to increase exports so that all the foreign supplies needed for industrial construction would be available (Li, 2011). Table 7 shows that during the 1952–1978 period, the government favored heavy industry over light industry whose weight kept declining until 1965. Although there was a slight adjustment in the proportion of each segment by 1978, the overall picture remained unchanged. Further, total investment during the two stages of 1952–1957 and 1965–1978 rose by a large margin, reaching 329PCT and 207PCT respectively. Given the enormous fiscal stress to accomplish the post-1949 aim of restoration, the

Table 7 Investment in industrial infrastructures, 1952–1978

Year	Total investment (RMB100 million)	Light industry		Heavy industry	
		Amount (RMB100 million)	Share[1] (PCT)	Amount (RMB100 million)	Share[2] (PCT)
1952	16.89	4.06	24.04	12.83	75.96
1957	72.4	11.04	15.25	61.36	84.75
1965	88.96	7.01	7.88	81.95	92.12
1978	273.16	29.3	10.73	243.86	89.27

Note [1,2]are calculated by the author by dividing the amount of investment in the light and heavy industry by the total investment. *Source* NBS, 1985

Table 8 Growth of foreign trade, 1952–1978

Year	Total trade volume (USD100 million)	Export		Import	
		Volume (USD100 million)	Growth rate[1] (PCT)	Volume (USD100 million)	Growth rate[2] (PCT)
1952	19.4	8.2	-	11.2	-
1957	31	16	95.12	15	33.93
1965	42.5	22.3	39.38	20.2	34.67
1975	147.5	72.6	225.56	74.9	270.79
1978	206.4	97.5	34.30	108.9	45.39

Note [1,2]are calculated by the author. *Source* NBS, 2000

significant expansion of heavy industry investment shows clearly how devoted the state was to the building of its own industrial system.

The rapid increase in the scale of investment caused a simultaneous increase in the demand for foreign machinery and know-how, which pushed up the aggregate volume of foreign trade from USD1.94 billion of 1952 to USD20.64 billion in 1978 (Table 8). In addition, with the extremely small size of foreign exchange reserves, it is understandable that exports outpaced imports in most of these years so as to accumulate more hard currencies. In fact, it was not until the mid-1970s that imports began to overtake exports. Due to the accelerated growth of imports, the deficit in 1978 was enlarged to an unprecedented USD1.14 billion.

6.2 A State-Monopolized Sector

As a result of the movement in the early 1950s to transform private commercial and industrial entities into either nationalized or collectivized businesses, foreign trade became a completely state-controlled sector by 1956. Beforehand, the Government Administrative Council ('*zhengwu yuan*', the predecessor of the State Council) issued a decision in 1950 that a dozen national corporations would be charged with conducting trade at home and abroad. Among them, there were several specialized foreign trade corporations (FTCs) which handled products ranging from silk, minerals, to tea and grease, etc. In addition, these FTCs were also authorized to establish regional corporations in each of the six major administrative regions (namely, Huabei area or North China, Dongbei area or Northeast China, Huadong area or East China, Zhongnan area or Central & South China, Xibei area or Northwest China, and Xinan area or Southwest China) to assist in and direct the business of their branch offices in various provinces and municipalities. In 1950, import and export volume by these state FTCs accounted for 68.4PCT of the nation's total; two years later, the share soared to 92.8PCT (Huang & Song, 2002).

The Ministry of Foreign Trade (MFT), established in 1952 after being split from the former Ministry of Trade, functioned as the executive agency responsible not only for China's foreign trade, but also for its economic relations, including technical cooperation with other nations. Before the reform of the late 1970s, several adjustments were made to the structure and business scope of these FTCs, which caused their number to shift; however, they generally remained between twelve and fifteen. The earliest established one was China National Import Company (today's Sinochem Group engaged in chemical and energy-related activities) which came into being on March 10th, 1950. To open up more distribution channels to import scarce materials, a representative office was set up in East Berlin in the summer of 1952. From this platform, closer trade relationships with Western European countries gradually emerged.

Based on a snapshot of China's exports for the year 1950 (Table 9), it can be inferred that most of China's exports were food-related agricultural products and raw materials for industries, a composition rather normal for an agrarian economy.

With regard to imports, the breakdown of 1950 (Table 10) shows that China was in need of buying various industrial raw materials and equipment to cope with the national campaign of economic reconstruction and rehabilitation. Apparently, the country was not yet capable of producing these commodities by itself. Moreover, with its increased spending on heavy industry, most of these supplies continued to flow in over the next few years.

Table 9 Composition of the main exports, 1950

Export items	Share of total exports (PCT)
Soybeans	14.4
Tung Oil	7
Hog Bristle	6.7
Edible Oil	5.4
Groundnut Oil	4.7
Egg and Egg Products	4.7
Wool	4.1
Tea	3.3
Colored Metals	3
Live Pig	2.2
Crude Oil	2
Silk	1.9
Coal	1.2
Sum	**60.6**

Source Hsin, 1954

Table 10 Composition of the main imports, 1950

Import items	Share of total imports (PCT)
Cotton	18
Rubber	11.5
Steel Materials	11.3
Machinery	8.3
Petroleum	6.3
Pharmaceuticals	4
Cars and Steam Boats	3.2
Gunny Bags	2.9
Chemical Materials	2.3
Lubricating Oil	2.2
Dyestuff	2
Red Sugar	2
Fertilizer	1.9
Copper	1.7
Steel Rope	1.5
Newsprint	1.3
Bitumen	1.1
Rice	1
Sum	**82.5**

Source Hsin, 1954

6.3 A Centrally-Planned System

Ideally, a planned economy creates consistency, with supply and demand anticipated irrespective of potential fluctuations in the market, either at home or abroad. As a consequence, the whole state is like a well-tuned machine operating strictly in line with projections orchestrated by a centralized regime. Given the fact that the emphasis of China was predominantly laid on heavy industry, imports were used to a great extent to make up for the limited capacity of domestic production. Exports, instead of being a profit-maximizing instrument as it is for most companies in the world, was taken merely as a means to finance imports. Prices were not market-based either. Prefixed by planners, prices would be automatically written into the contract when FTCs purchased from domestic producers for export. In the eyes of these producers, each item had only one price tag and thus, it didn't make much difference as to where their supplies would be sold later (Feng, Zhang & Wang, 1989). From the government's point of view, it was favorable to have a pricing mechanism that was insulated from movements in the international market. On the one hand, this ensured a tight control of the national economy, which was characteristic of a command system; on the other hand, such a separation could also help achieve the government's ultimate goal of being self-sufficient and independent of the outside world. However, the tradeoff is that important considerations like the country's comparative advantage and efficiency in resource allocation were downplayed or even simply cast aside, thus resulting in substantial losses.

As to the pricing of import products, it was designed specifically to match the state strategy of import substitution. During the 1950s and the early 1960s, the country did not have a unified method to price imports, and this caused the adoption of multiple approaches, with some taking domestic wholesale prices as their reference, and some based on the total import costs, etc. (Zhao, 1992). Concerning the domestic prices of imported producer goods like machinery, equipment, intermediate products and raw materials, etc., they were in general determined by first converting the import prices (on CIF basis including cost, freight, and insurance premium) into RMB using the official exchange rates; then the FTCs, as import agents, would charge a certain percentage of commission, usually 1-3PCT, in order to cover their transaction expenses before selling to the domestic buyers. At that time, the value of the yuan was intentionally set at a high level (Li & Lin, 2011) and this benefited Chinese producers because the price they paid for imports was much lower than it would have been if the exchange rate were not that artificially inflated. By doing so, the government was actually subsidizing domestic enterprises, a step deemed necessary to lower down the cost of production.

Toward the mid-1960s, however, the same pricing policy could not be sustained because after 10 years of implicit subsidies, both quantitative and qualitative progress had been achieved among Chinese producers. They were now in a position to furnish the same products at home, which implies that those former overseas suppliers had become their competitors. Thus, confronting an imminent conflict of interests, it was no longer sensible to keep import prices artifically low. At the same time, China's foreign trade was facing unprecedented difficulties following the deterioration of its bilateral relationship with the Soviet Union, a long-term strategic ally. In terms of Sino-Soviet trade, the volume plunged from USD1.54 billion in 1958 to USD111 million by 1967 (Table 11). Over this decade, 1960 can be taken as a watershed year because from then on, the downward trend persisted until the end of the period. As a consequence, the Soviet share of China's total trade volume shrank from the peak of almost 48PCT in 1959 to less than 3PCT in 1967. Already vigilant of what the tension would lead to, China since 1960 shifted its focus onto two other foreign markets, i.e. Japan and Western Europe while at the same time reviving its trading activities with Canada through wheat imports. By 1965, China's import and export volume with the West accounted for 52.8PCT of the total, up from 17.9PCT in 1957 (Dong, 2005).

6.4 A Uniform Pricing Mechanism

Internally, the extreme financial hardship produced by the Great Leap Forward and the three-year great famine no longer allowed the government to handle foreign trade in the same way as before. On the one hand, the provision of import subsidies had

Table 11 Trade volume between China and the Soviet Union, 1958–1967

Year	Trade volume (USD billion)	Export volume (USD billion)	Import volume (USD billion)	Trade balance[1] (USD billion)	Share in China's total trade volume (PCT)[2]
1958	1.539	0.899	0.64	0.259	39.8
1959	2.097	1.118	0.979	0.139	47.9
1960	1.664	0.819	0.845	-0.026	43.7
1961	0.828	0.536	0.292	0.244	28.2
1962	0.702	0.491	0.211	0.28	26.4
1963	0.601	0.407	0.194	0.213	20.6
1964	0.445	0.312	0.133	0.179	12.8
1965	0.407	0.222	0.186	0.036	9.6
1966	0.305	0.14	0.165	-0.025	6.6
1967	0.111	0.055	0.056	-0.001	2.7

Note [1]calculated by the author by subtracting import from export, and minus means trade deficit; [2]calculated by the author by dividing the trade volume by that of China's total
Source export, import and trade volume between China and the Soviet Union: EBACFERT, 1984; China's total trade volume: NBS, 1999

already denied any likelihood of profits generated from that source; on the other hand, the artificially overvalued yuan pushed up export prices, which resulted in declining net revenues. Without the blow of Sino-Soviet split, perhaps the situation would not have been that bad. Anyhow, facing the downward spiral of the macro-environment, China had to lessen the losses from foreign trade by setting up a separate and devalued rate of exchange for the yuan.

In December 1963, the State Council issued the "Provisional Regulations on Implementing the Uniform Price Formation Methods for Imported Commodities", which stipulated that starting from 1964, most imports should be priced according to the level of similar domestically-made goods. For other imports that could not fit into that category, like those not yet available at home or with irregular production, their prices would still be based on the import costs, i.e. the CIF value plus tariffs, industrial and commercial tax, as well as some relevant import expenses. When the FTCs were to settle payment with their domestic buyers, the RMB cost of the CIF value would not be calculated simply against the official exchange rate as before; instead, a specified markup of 103PCT would be added to it. This implied that at the prevailing official rate of RMB2.46 per US dollar, the real exchange rate for the settlement of imports would be doubled to almost RMB5 per US dollar (2.4618×2.03). The intention of the state was to use the additional earnings from the sale of imported goods to offset the losses incurred in exports (Yang, 2005). In case the foreign currency was Soviet rubles, the premium was set at 7PCT (one ruble was equivalent to RMB4.5). In 1975, with a view of severing the link between international and domestic markets so that the impact of price fluctuations from the outside could be minimized, the State Council further expanded the scope of imports priced comparable to homogeneous domestic products. The other decision it made in the same year was the adjustment of the original 103PCT markup down to 60PCT, which in 1977 was raised to 80PCT (Liu, 2009). The measure to double import prices through an explicitly devalued yuan was favorable to the import-competing producers in China; in particular, those of the emerging producer goods sector. Under the shield of such a significant price gap, their advantage bacame self-evident and hard to challenge.

In 1965, the State Council promulgated the "Interim Regulations on the Uniform Price Formation Methods for Commodities Supplied for Export". As a general principle, the benchmark that was laid out for export products was their domestic selling prices. Specifically, if industrial goods were supplied directly by enterprises, then the ex-works price would be taken as the reference for export. For agricultural materials, the prices set by the commercial departments that allocated them became the basis of the prices offered by the Chinese FTCs. By and large, the tone of this document was flexible, with emphasis laid on the necessity to make adjustments based on the actual conditions of each deal, such as quality, quantity, and the target market, etc. Indeed, this was an approach which should have been adopted years ago, especially considering that the rising domestic costs of export products had already exceeded the pace of the devaluation of the official RMB exchange rates.

In China, one indicator which has often been used to measure the profitability of exporting is the domestic currency cost of earning one unit of foreign exchange. Take the US dollar as an example, in 1952, while the official quotation was still at one US dollar for RMB2.227, the yuan cost in return for one US dollar of export revenue stood on average at RMB3.08, implying that behind each US dollar, Chinese exporters or FTCs would suffer a net loss of RMB0.853. Ten years later, i.e. in 1962, when the official rate declined to RMB2.4618 per US dollar, the cost that was paid for one US dollar through export had soared to RMB6.65, thus widening the gap to a shocking RMB4.1882 (Chen, 1984). As a result, the vicious cycle is that the more the country exported, the greater the losses it incurred. Rather than contributing to the coffer of a cash-strapped government, exporting, as well as importing, drained the country financially. Although the practice of using markups to devalue the yuan could to some degree allow the country to extract some profits from importing to improve the bottom line of its export account, it was at its best a quick fix which could not cure the root of the problem. As long as supply and demand remained under the tight control of central planners, no measure would deliver lasting benefits.

6.5 Stringent Control Over Foreign Exchange

Unlike a market economy in which the currency value floats due to shifts in supply and demand, the Chinese yuan was not allowed to move flexibly. Indeed, at a time when almost all aspects of economic life were subject to central plans, it is impossible that the pricing of legal tender would be an exception.Trading companies did not worry about the value of the yuan because profits and losses were not taken as a measure of their performance. They knew that even if they operated in the red, the Ministry of

Foreign Trade would help them reverse the imbalance by getting money from those which were financially sound (Wang, 1990). This method was not uncommon prior to 1978 and, consequently, for FTCs that could generate profits, they did not take it as their own earnings because sooner or later, it would be transferred to make up for losses elsewhere.

As stated in the above, during the initial decades when China was very much reliant on imported machinery and intermediate goods like steel to rebuild the nation's heavy industry, foreign exchange was a precious instrument without which the grand program could not be accomplished. Quite naturally, the export sector served the role of bringing in the needed foreign currencies. To ensure that all revenues from abroad, including export, remittances from overseas Chinese, and tourism, etc. would not be used outside the framework designated by the state, stringent foreign exchange controls were put in place shortly after the founding of the PRC. While the People's Bank of China, the central bank, was charged with the responsibility of general administration, the Bank of China (BOC, still a department of the PBoC before being separated in 1979) was authorized in 1953 as the only specialized foreign exchange bank handling transactions for the FTCs. Since these transactions were absolutely mandatory, little autonomy was extended to either sellers or buyers of foreign exchange. As soon as China's exporters were paid by foreign customers, they had to surrender unconditionally all the receipts to the BOC in return for the corresponding amount of RMB. Similarly, importers, or buyers, were required to apply to the BOC for foreign exchange when payment was due (Xue & Zhou, 2009). Instead of functioning like a modern commercial bank, as it is today, the BOC before the late 1970s was simply an extended arm of the state bureaucracy which enjoyed the privilege of directing the limited foreign exchange reserves to the uses deemed critical by the central regime.

6.6 *Mirror of the Macro Environment*

Following the implementation of a heavy-industry-centered development strategy in 1952, resources nationwide were mobilized for that single yet paramount objective. In turn, this caused a dual effect which was not necessarily tangible within the short run. On the one hand, the increasing output of capital goods by domestic manufacturers gradually reduced the need for imports, thus leading to a steady decline in the ratio between the capital goods acquired from the international market and the country's overall demand. At the same time, although it was universally clear that China, being the most populous country in the world, was endowed with a comparative advantage in labor-intensive products, with resources allocated primarily to heavy industry, there was little left to cultivate the advantage into global competitiveness.

Therefore, in the pre-reform period, no matter how much China was actually in need of imports and exports to lift its economy, the continuation of the "self-reliance" policy greatly constrained the development of both. In fact, even though the situation became improved after the 1970s, which accelerated the growth of foreign trade,

Table 12 Comparison of foreign trade and gross industrial & agricultural output, 1952–1978

Year	Total import and export volume[1] (RMB100 million)	Gross industrial and agricultural output[2] (RMB100 million)	Ratio of 1 to 2 (PCT)
1952–1954	230.2	2,820	8.16
1976–1978	891.6	15,148	5.89

Source Lin, Cai & Li, 1994

the dependency ratio, i.e. the trade-to-GDP ratio, remained still at 9.8PCT in 1978, almost the same as in 1953, i.e. the beginning of the first Five Year Plan (NBS, 1999). Also in 1978, with the total trade volume reaching USD20.64 billion, China's share of world trade was merely 0.78PCT (Lü & Yu, 2006). During 1952–1954, the country's trade volume still registered 8.16PCT of its total industrial and agricultural output; but by 1976–1978, the portion contracted to 5.89PCT (Table 12). Besides, it can also be shown that as industrial and agricultural output expanded more than four fold and exceeded RMB1.5 trillion by 1976–1978; the pace of trade growth was less than three fold within the same span of time. Obviously, the latter had fallen behind and this indicates that prior to China's reform and opening up, the degree of China's interaction with the outside world had been falling.

As two closely-connected links that shape the foundation of a society, politics and economics always influence each other and mirror the circumstances that are characteristic of a given historical stage. Since foreign trade is an integral part of the economy, its ups and downs are also reflective of the political scene, especially when it is full of turbulences. If there is a word that can vividly describe the political situation of China before the late 1970s, it would be "volatile". With diverse rounds of events coming forward one after another, the country became economically vulnerable; moreover, the effect was further transmitted to the foreign trade sector, whose fluctuation provides a faithful reflection of all these upheavals. For example, 1953–1957 belongs to the first Five-Year-Plan period during which China modelled itself after the Soviet Union and laid the framework of industrialization. When the whole country was taking a concerted effort toward the same goal, the accomplishments were rather impressive. While gross domestic output (GDP) increased by almost 30PCT (Table 13) and reached RMB106.8 billion in 1957, China's foreign trade, especially exports, grew at a similarly dynamic pace. Nevertheless, referring to the second Five Year Plan that spans from 1958 to 1962, the statistics, without exception, display a recession.

Due to the initiation of the Great Leap Forward, a movement with blind boasting and exaggeration of output, people became victimized and suffered from an unprecedented famine. Consequently, not only GDP fell by about 12PCT to RMB114.93 billion in 1962; foreign trade, including both imports and exports, all turned backward. Then, before the launch of the Cultural Revolution in 1966, China's overall development was relatively stable and this enabled its foreign trade to be restored together with domestic output. However, that did not last long and the disruption of the 10-year Cultural Revolution once again left its footprint on the economy, especially in

Table 13 Shifts in Foreign Trade and GDP, 1953–1977

Year	GDP (RMB100 million)	Foreign trade volume (USD100 million)	Export volume (USD100 million)	Import volume (USD100 million)
1953	824	23.7	10.2	13.5
1957	1,068	31	16	15
1958	1,307	38.7	19.8	18.9
1962	1,149.3	26.6	14.9	11.7
1966	1,868	46.2	23.7	22.5
1967	1,773.9	41.6	21.4	20.2
1968	1,723.1	40.5	21	19.5
1969	1,937.9	40.3	22	18.3
1970	2,252.7	45.9	22.6	23.3
1977	3,201.9	148	75.9	72.1

Source NBS, 1999

the initial years of 1967 and 1968. If compared to GDP, foreign trade dropped steeply by almost 13PCT, from USD4.62 billion in 1966 to USD4.03 billion by 1969. In the later stage of the Revolution, although there was still chaos and social unrest, several critical adjustments to economic strategies halted the downward spiral, resulting in a steady process of rehabilitation. In 1977, i.e. one year prior to the reform, China's foreign trade more than tripled from USD4.59 billion in 1970 and hit USD14.8 billion.

At a time when foreign investment, either inbound or outbound, was prohibited, foreign trade was the only major channel through which China maintained its contact with the rest of the world. Ironically, under an ideology that firmly believed in the necessity of gaining absolute independence, this channel was opened for the ultimate purpose of having it closed for good. Fortunately, this is a mindset that did not prevail all the time. When approaching the end of the 1970s, some wise leaders started to notice the need to open China more widely. They recognized that due to the uneven distribution of resources, every country was in possession of some unique advantages. At the same time, however, in view of the undeniable fact of limitedness, an autarkic model would prove to be self-defeating with the loss of efficiency and vitality. For the sustainment of a healthy economy, assimilating fresh inputs from the outside is necessary. China, in its drive to achieve the goal of "Four Modernizations", equally had to use an open mindset to pave its way to a promising future.

References

Bai, S. Y. (1999). *Modern general history of China (1919–1949)* (Vol. 1). Shanghai: Shanghai People's Publishing House.

Bell, S., & Feng, H. (2013). *The rise of the People's Bank of China*. Cambridge, MA: Harvard University Press.

Burdekin, R. C. K. (2004). Nontraditional monetary policy options: Is commodity-based stabilization policy worth another look? Retrieved July 26, 2014, from https://www.econstor.eu/bitstream/10419/23392/1/2004-05.pdf.

Cao, G. Y. (2010). Analysis of the development process of China's rural cooperative economic organization after the founding of the P.R.C. *Century Bridge, 3,* 28–29.

Chen, D. L. (1959). Unified leadership and hierarchical management in the economic organization of the Pople's Commune. *Economic Research, 4,* 6–8.

Chen, D. L. (2001). The three generations of the Communist Party of China leading group's western development thought and practice. *Contemporary Chinese History Research, 4,* 76–86.

Chen, D. L. (2003). *The Third Front construction: Western development during the war preparation period*. Beijing: CPC Central School Press.

Chen, D. L. (2004). An investigation of the "three-year natural disaster" period from the perspective of disaster economics. *Contemporary Chinese History Research, 1,* 83–93.

Chen, D. L. (2008). Chen Yun's strategy to resolve the 1951 cotton "embargo" crisis. *Contemporary Chinese History Research, 5,* 65–72.

Chen, H., & Chen, K. (2013). The central committee of the CPC's "instruction" in 1948 and the changes of the banking sector before and after the founding of the P.R.C. *Journal of the Party School of CPC Tianjin Municipal Committee, 1,* 89–92.

Chen, J. G., et al. (2009). *Blue book of industrialization: Annual report on China's industrialization (2009)*. Beijing: Social Sciences Academic Press.

Chen, L. X. (1994). On Zhou Enlai's rectification in 1972. *Party History and Literature, 6,* 17–19.

Chen, Q. L. (2011). Minority girls in cooperatives. Retrieved September 2, 2014, from https://dangshi.people.com.cn/GB/15974466.html.

Chen, Q. G. (1984). The historical evolution of RMB exchange rates and the direction of reform. *Financial Research, 12,* 19–21.

Dai, M. L. (1999). Research on Angang Constitution. *Research on the History of the CPC, 6,* 38–43.

Deng, Z. W. (2004). The implementation of the supply system of the People's Commune. *Hubei Archives, 12,* 26–27.

Dong, Z. K. (2001). The Korean War and economy of the P.R.C. *Contemporary Chinese History Research, 5,* 24–32.

Dong, Z. K. (2005). Historical experience of economic adjustment in the 1960s. Zhang X. X. (Ed.). (2005). *Historical experience of contemporary China's successful development: Proceedings of the fifth annual conference of national history*. Retrieved June 4, 2014, from https://www.hprc.org.cn/gsyj/yjjg/zggsyjxh_1/gsnhlw_1/wuguoshixslwj/200906/t20090629_13006.html.

Dong, Z. K. (2008). Changes in the rural infrastructure investment of China (1950–2006). *Contemporary Chinese History Research, 3,* 29–37.

Dong, Z. K. (2012). Retrospect and prospect of investment structure adjustment and economic structure change: With consideration of growth pattern transformation (1950–2010). *Chinese Economic History Research, 1,* 7–18.

Duan, X. Z. (2012). Wasted years of the first People's Commune. *Century Bridge, 10,* 55–59.

Editorial Board of the Almanac of China's Foreign Economic Relations and Trade (EBACFERT). (1984). *China's foreign economic and trade yearbook 1984*. Beijing: China Foreign Economic and Trade Press.

Fang, H. X. (2008). Restoration of the railway before and after the founding of the P.R.C. *Tianfu New Views, 3,* 116–120.

Feng, Z. W., et al. (1989). Review of the ten-year foreign trade system reform and its development trend. *Decision Exploration, 6,* 21–23.

Guo, X. Y. et al. (2007). Rural supply and marketing cooperatives in China: Historical development, problems and reform. Retrieved January 4, 2015, from https://ncera.aae.wisc.edu/Events/2007meeting/china_paper.pdf.
Hong, J. G. (2005). *Shanghai Tongzhi* (Volume 25). Shanghai: Shanghai People's Publishing House, Shanghai Academy of Social Sciences Press. Retrieved June 3, 2015, from https://shtong.gov.cn/node2/node2247/node4578/node79500/node79509/userobject1ai103927.html.
Hong, J. G. (2009). Sixty years of changes in China's finance. *China Finance, 19,* 109–112.
Hu, A. G. (2014). Taking the road of agricultural modernization with Chinese characteristics (1949–2012). *Contemporary Chinese History Research, 3,* 24–37.
Hsin, Y. (1954). *The foreign trade of communist China.* Hong Kong: Union Research Institute.
Hua, X. (2012). The "43 program" opens the door to the introduction of new technologies from the West. *Party and Government Forum: Cadre Digest, 7,* 42–43.
Huang, X. L., & Song, P. (2002). *China's foreign trade* (2nd ed.). Beijing: University of International Business and Economics Press.
Ji, N. W. (2012). The establishment of rural public canteens during the period of the People's Commune: Based on Jiangsu province. *Journal of Liaoning Administration College, 9,* 170–176.
Jia, M. S. (2012). Strengthening the cultural construction of cooperatives requires consolidation of lower-level cooperatives. *China Cooperative Times.* Retrieved July 2, 2015, from https://www.ccfc.zju.edu.cn/a/hezuozatan/2012/0723/11881.html.
Jiang, C. Q. (2011). A probe of the impact of streamlining urban population in the early 1960s on the Chinese economy. *Ancient and Modern Agriculture, 3,* 1–10.
Kubo, T. (2005). Industrial development in Republican China, newly revised index: 1912–1948. Hitotsubashi University. Retrieved May 5, 2015, from https://hi-stat.ier.hit-u.ac.jp/information/schedule/schedulelog/S050/TK.pdf.
Li, C. Q. (1959). On the distribution system combining the wage system and the supply system: From the distribution system of a People's Commune. *Academic Monthly, 2,* 32–35.
Li, G. H. (2011). On the principle of domestic sales being subject to foreign sales in the history of China's foreign trade. *Research on the History of the CPC, 1,* 70–81.
Li, H. (1991). Formation of Chen Yun's "three balances" thought. *Financial Research, 7,* 52–57.
Li, H., & Lin, Q. (2011). Evolution and evaluation of RMB exchange rate system and export rebate policy. *Economics and Management, 7,* 69–73.
Lin, J. Y. F. & Dennis T. Y. (1998). On the causes of China's agricultural crisis and the Great Leap famine. *China Economic Review, 9,* 125–140. Retrieved May 3, 2015, from https://public.wsu.edu/~hallagan/EconS391/weeks/week3/greatleapcause.pdf.
Li, Q. S. (2011). Unlocking the farmer "vice premier" Chen Yonggui and his years in Dazhai. *Beijing Daily.* Retrieved May 3, 2015, from https://dangshi.people.com.cn/GB/85039/15856376.html.
Lin, C. C. (2014). Overcapacity after the Great Leap Forward and reform on efficiency enhancement of the urban industry. *Historical Review, 3,* 133–145.
Lin, P., & Zhu, Y. (2015). The political concept of economic policies: Abolition of the piece-rate wage system in the 1950s. *Research on the History of the CPC, 5,* 46–55.
Lin, Y. F., et al. (1994). *The China miracle: Development strategy and economic reform.* Shanghai: Shanghai Sanlian Bookstore, Shanghai People's Publishing House.
Liu, Q. M. (1999). The first five-year plan and 156 construction projects. *the Essence of Literature and History, 11,* 4–8.
Liu, S. (2010). A study and review of national economic adjustment from 1961 to 1965. *Beijing Party History, 1,* 29–35.
Liu, S. Y. (2009). *History of Hainan province: Price management history.* Haikou: Nanhai Publishing Company.
Liu, X. M., et al. (1995). *Story of Chinese educated urban youths.* Chengdu: Sichuan People's Publishing House.
Lu, F. (2000). A study on the phenomenon of "cheap selling and expensive buying" of China's cotton international trade. *Economic Research, 2,* 3–9.

Lü, H. F., & Yu, X. P. (2006). Changing the growth pattern to achieve sustainable development of foreign trade. *Northern Economy, 6,* 32–33.
Luo, P. H. (2009). Decentralization of the basic accounting unit of People's Commune in 1961. *Historical Data of the CPC, 1,* 126–135.
Luo, P. H., et al. (2013). Was the national economy on the verge of collapse during the Cultural Revolution? *China Newsweek, 45,* 84–86.
Ma, Q. S. (1998). *History of China's industrial economy: 1966–1978.* Beijing: Economic Management Press.
Mao, Z. R. (2013). Deng Xiaoping's comprehensive rectification in the later period of the Cultural Revolution. *Party History Review, 9,* 12–16.
Meisner, M. (2003). Mao Zedong's China and beyond: History of the People's Republic of China (Third Edition). Retrieved June 6, 2015, from https://marxists.anu.edu.au/chinese/reference-books/meisner/mao_china_and_after_21.htm.
National Bureau of Statistics (NBS). (1985). *China industrial economic statistics (1949–1984).* Beijing: China Statistics Press.
NBS. (1999). *Compilation of 50-year statistical data of the P.R.C.* Beijing: China Statistics Press.
NBS. (2000). *China statistical yearbook 1999.* Beijing: China Statistics Press. Retrieved April 20, 2015, from https://www.stats.gov.cn/tjsj/ndsj/.
NBS. (2001). *China statistical yearbook 2000.* Beijing: China Statistics Press. Retrieved April 20, 2015, from https://www.stats.gov.cn/tjsj/ndsj/.
NBS. (2012). *China industrial economic statistics yearbook.* Beijing: China Statistics Press.
Niu, R. F. & Chen J. Y. "Small farmers" in China and their development. Sustainable agricultural development: The role of international cooperation. Peters, G. H. & Stanton, B. F. (Eds.). (1992). *Proceedings of the 21st international conference of agricultural economists.* Association of International Agricultural Economists. Retrieved May 12, 2015, from https://ageconsearch.umn.edu/bitstream/183351/2/IAAE-CONF-363.pdf.
Pan, S. C. (2010). Three freedoms and one guarantee. *Archive World, 11,* 14–20.
Party History Research Center (PHRC). (2011). Active market expands urban-rural exchange. *History of the CPC (1949–1978)* (Volume 2 of Book One). Beijing: Central Party History Press.
Pei, Y. X. (1986). Strengthening the technological transformation of enterprises to improve economic efficiency. *Economic Review, 4,* 50–53.
PHRC. (2011). Comprehensive recovery and initial growth of the national economy. *History of the CPC (1949–1978)* (Volume 2 of Book One). Beijing: Central Party History Press.
PHRC. (2011). Historical experience and remaining issues of socialist transformation. *History of the CPC (1949–1978)* (Volume 2 of Book One). Beijing: Central Party History Press.
PHRC. (2011). The rise of the People's Commune movement. *History of the CPC (1949–1978)* (Volume 2 of Book One). Beijing: Central Party History Press.
Qu, S. (2006). A historical analysis of the international trade of China's grain and its nature. *Research on China's Economic History, 3,* 20–28.
Sha, N. A., & Yang, M. (1981). Evolution of profit retention system for enterprise funds by state-owned enterprises (Part 1). *Financial Research, 5,* 77–81.
Shen, Z. H. (2002). A historical survey of the problems of Soviet experts in China: Basic conditions and policy changes. *Contemporary Chinese History Research, 1,* 24–37.
Song, L. (2015). Shen Zhihua deciphers historical details of Soviet experts' aid to China: The salary of Soviet experts far exceeds that of Chinese ministers. *Changjiang Daily.* Retrieved May 21, 2015, from https://cjrb.cjn.cn/html/2015-05/26/content_5445068.htm.
Song, Y. J. (2010). Adjustment and response of China's employment policy during the period of national economic recovery. *Journal of Fuyang Teachers College (Social Science Edition), 4,* 80–83.
Su, S. Z. (2001). A study on the gap between China's coastal and inland economic development in the 1950s and 1970s. *Journal of Zhongnan University of Finance and Economics., 1,* 6–12.
Su, X. (2000). Historical experience of western development. *Research on the History of the CPC, 4,* 8–11.

Tang, Y. Y. (2001). Relationship analysis of the complementarity and contradiction of China's public and private economies from 1949 to 1954. *Studies of Chinese Economic History, 3,* 23–32.
Tian, J. J. (2011). Socialist transformation: Successful initiative by Mao Zedong's leadership of China's economic construction. *Party Literature, 4,* 59–65.
Wan, D. W., et al. (2014). Changes and reflections on the establishment of commercial administrative institutions. *Business Times, 32,* 142–145.
Wang, F. L. (2009). The non-negligible role of urban cooperative economy: Review and reflection on the development of urban cooperative economy in 60 years since the founding of the P.R.C. *China Collective Economy, 14,* 4–7.
Wang, H., et al. (2012). Vicissitudes of China's rural land system. *Journal of Sichuan Education College, 7,* 38–43.
Wang, L. S. (1990). Review and reflection on foreign trade system reform. *Science and Technology Review, 1,* 34–38.
Wang, J. Q. (2009). Way forward. *China Daily.* Retrieved April 21, 2015, from https://www.chinadaily.com.cn/60th/2009-09/30/content_8752263.htm.
Wu, L. (1995). Monetary unification before and after the founding of the P.R.C. *Contemporary Chinese History Research, 4,* 1–12.
Wu, W. Q. (2009). The story of the Second Auto: A paradigm for the tough breakthrough of the Chinese auto industry. *China Youth Daily.* Retrieved April 16, 2015, from https://zqb.cyol.com/content/2009-09/24 /content_2867161.htm.
Xu, Y. (2010). Impact of the Korean war on China and other parties. *History Reference, 12,* 118–123.
Xue, H. F., & Zhou, Y. C. (2009). China's exchange rate formation mechanism and market supply and demand decisions. *Economic Research Guide, 4,* 50–51.
Yang, F. (2005). A historical review of RMB exchange rate system. *a Study of the History of the Chinese Economy, 4,* 59–64.
Yang, M., & Yang, F. (2012). *Negotiation in decentralization: Case study of China's carbon trading in the power sector.* London: Springer-Verlag.
Yu, J. Z. (2005). Witnessing Mao Zedong's meeting with the red guards. *Literature and History Monthly, 4,* 4–7.
Zang, Y. S., & Dong, S. L. (2009). "Do when conditions are available and when unavailable, create conditions to do": Interview at the 50th anniversary of the discovery of Daqing Oil Field. *Research on the History of the CPC, 10,* 12–18.
Zeng, X. G. (1981). A technical and economic analysis of the agricultural multiple cropping index in the suburbs of Beijing. *Agricultural Economic Problems, 6,* 50–53.
Zhang, J. C. (2015). Deng Xiaoping and the formulation and trial implementation of the Seventy Articles on Industrial Work. Retrieved May 1, 2015, from https://www.hprc.org.cn/gsyj/rws/lsqy/201501/t20150104_310680.html.
Zhang, M. C. (2006). Establishment of the system of responsibility by the factory director under the leadership of the party committee by the 8th National Congress of the CPC. *News on Shanghai Authorities, 11,* 35–36.
Zhang, X. B. (2003). Establishment of ticket system in China. *Journal of Capital Normal University (Social Science Edition), S1,* 68–75.
Zhang, Y. Q., & Li, Q. (2012). The development of agricultural mechanization in the first 30 years of China and its contemporary enlightenment. *Theory Research of Mao Zedong and Deng Xiaoping, 4,* 53–59.
Zhang, Z. Y. (2010). Emancipation of dislocation: A review of rural women participating in production in North China during the Great Leap Forward. *Jiangxi Social Sciences, 4,* 51–55.
Zhao, D. Y. (2016). Formulation and benefits of China's unified grain purchasing and marketing policy from 1966 to 1976. *South China Agricultural University Journal (Social Science Edition)., 2,* 1–11.
Zhao, J. Y. (1992). *Annals of Shaanxi province* (Vol. 42). Beijing: China Prices Press.
Zhao, L. Y., & Zhang, J. Q. (2004). The historical position of economic rectification in the history of the party's economic works in 1975. *Research and Teaching of Party History, 5,* 14–19.

Zhao, S. (2015). On the rural mutual aid group system in the early period of the founding of the P.R.C. *Agricultural Archaeology, 3,* 68–72.

Zhao, X. J. (2006). A brief discussion on commercial credit in the 1950s' China. *Research on Contemporary Chinese History, 3,* 60–67.

Zhao, Y. Q. (2009). From "centralization" to "decentralization": The trajectory of the reform and development of the fiscal system in 60 years since the founding of the P.R.C. *Zhejiang Finance and Taxation, 10,* 56–60.

Zheng, Y. G. (1998). An analysis of the fluctuations of agricultural production and its causes during the Cultural Revolution. *Research on the History of the CPC, 3,* 71–77.

Zhong, T. H. (1992). On the issue of market prices during the period of national economic recovery. *Research on the History of the CPC, 2,* 38–44.

Zhu, J. C., & Gong, J. (2008). The evolution and effect evaluation of China's regional economic policies. *Theoretical Journal, 12,* 58–60.

Zhu, X. X. (2005). *Shanghai general annals* (Vol. 16). Shanghai: Shanghai People's Publishing House.

Zou, H. B. (2010). Mao Zedong and the proposal of "taking grain as core" and its role. *Party History Research and Teaching, 6,* 46–52.

Chapter 3
Economic Reform, the 1st Phase

To be sure, China in 1976 had some notable economic accomplishments to its credit, despite the political instability created by the Cultural Revolution. In general, China had realized moderate rates of growth, especially in the industrial sector. However, the chronic economic difficulties that China faced in that same year should not be ignored despite these achievements. To a large degree, China's problems were the result of the inefficiencies inherent in a Soviet-style planned economy, including irrational prices, isolation from foreign competition, lack of contact between supplier and consumer, and a pervasive emphasis on quantity rather than the quality of output, etc. Among these problems, many were later exacerbated by the government-influenced biases against material incentives, markets, and the division of labor. Besides, another dilemma that China confronted by then concerned technology. Due to the country's relative technological autarky after its break from the Soviet Union in the late 1950s, particularly its minimal program of sending students and scholars abroad for training and refusal to absorb foreign investment, there were few opportunities other than the purchase of complete plants to introduce technologies from abroad. At the same time, the work of China's scientists and technicians, except for those in the national defense industry, had been seriously disrupted by the anti-intellectual climate of the Cultural Revolution (Gao, 2002). Consequently, despite some impressive progress in certain high-priority areas like nuclear power and spacecraft, China's overall competitiveness in technologies lagged far behind the world level by the mid-1970s, with a gap of three to four decades on several fronts. Regarding the technological base provided by the Soviet Union and Eastern Europe in the mid-1950s, they were already decaying yet not upgraded timely by indigenous inventions.

These various internal problems, while challenging to the leadership, were also powerful forces that pushed them to change. In fact, the stress was not merely coming from within. According to the statistics released by The *United Nations Conference on Trade and Development* (UNCTAD), between 1971 and 1980, many developing countries in Asia registered quite remarkable momentum in their average annual growth of GDP, like South Korea (9.29 PCT), Singapore (9.09 PCT) and Malaysia (9.59 PCT), etc. (UNCTAD, 2016). When it comes to China which had traditionally

C. Yu, *China's Economy: Towards 2049*,
https://doi.org/10.1007/978-981-15-9227-0_3

regarded itself as the most advanced country in Eastern Asia, its less significant performance of 6.28 PCT relative to that of the aforementioned counterparts was particularly disturbing, thus intensifying the need to take quick actions and make up for what had been lost in the past decade.

1 The Great Leap Outward

Held in Beijing from August 12th to 18th, 1977, the 11th National Party Congress officially proclaimed the ending of the Cultural Revolution. Besides, it reiterated that "the fundamental task of the party in the new historical period is to build China into a modern, powerful socialist country by the end of the twentieth century". During this congress, Deng Xiaoping, a critical figure, restored his power and set a new policy that directed the future of China. It was largely because of his opposition to the Great Leap Forward and the Cultural Revolution that had led to his removal from all his positions in 1967 and 1976; in other words, he was sidelined twice (Gong & Shi, 1995). In general, his style was both bold and cautious, especially when concerning economic issues. In his eyes, China is blessed with a vast territory and rich natural resources, but due to almost two decades of isolation and extreme self-reliance, the majority of these resources could not be converted into actual means of production. Thereby, to better coordinate its development and enhance the country's international status, opening to the outside world should be taken as an unswerving and fundamental national policy.

1.1 One More Ambitious Yet Unrealistic Plan

However, many contradictions persisted and until the 5th National People's Congress of February and March 1978, differences between two competing factions: dogmatists headed by Hua Guofeng (successor of Mao Zedong and Chairman of the Communist Party of China Central Committee) and anti-dogmatists represented by Deng Xiaoping, became increasingly apparent. In his address to the Congress, Hua Guofeng presented the "Ten Year National Economic Plan", or the Ten-Year Plan (covering the 1976–1985 time frame), with specific targets of the first phase of the Four Modernizations Program assigned to the various sectors and industries. In order to complete this initial stage of development by 1985, the Plan called for massive investment push in large-scale projects. Formally launched at the end of 1977, this crash program in essence was a Great Leap Forward-style attempt to catch up with and overtake the world's advanced economies in as short a time as possible. The strategy of Hua assumed that higher rates of growth could be realized by political stability, more investment, and greater incentives without any structural reforms in either the urban or rural economies. Once again, great emphasis was laid on heavy industry, with a package of 120 brand-new projects consisting of 10 iron and steel complexes, 9 non-ferrous metals facilities, 8 coal combines, 10 oil and natural gas fields, 30 hydroelectric stations, 6 trunk rail lines, and 5 key harbors (Liu, 2005).

Actually, what lied behind this fancy plan was a firm yet unrealistic belief that China was capable of achieving faster growth once the focus was reoriented to economic undertakings. Yet the fact was crystal clear, i.e. all of these schemes were to be backed by substantial financial input, which was far beyond the capabilities of the country. What's more, it would inevitably keep other sectors thirsty for funds as did before. Regarding the major targets outlined by the Ten-Year Plan, it included an increase of steel production to 60 million tons and crude oil to 250 million tons by 1985. In terms of gross industrial output, the 10-year growth rate was set at a pace which averaged 10 PCT each year. Differing from its 1958 predecessor, the 1978 leap discarded the principle of self-dependence. Rather than relying on native methods like the backyard steel furnace, advanced technologies were to be imported from the very countries China was aiming to surpass. Vendors and banks from those countries were expected to provide the financing in many cases. Besides, there would also be contracts with foreign companies for capital goods including complete steel plants, textile machinery, and oil rigs and mining equipment, etc. (Fang, 2016). Because of its support of openness to the outside world, the plan was later sarcastically referred to as the "Great Leap Outward" ('*yang yue jin*').

For the fulfillment of these projections, the Plan would require a substantial rise in capital accumulation and investment in the capital goods sector, which was estimated to be around RMB70 billion per annum over the 1978–1985 period. Since this figure roughly equals China's total investment in infrastructure through the entire twenty-eight years of its prior existence, it was actually an incredible amount. Nevertheless, in their forecasts for the Plan, Hua Guofeng and his economic team dramatically overestimated China's potential export revenues from raw materials, particularly petroleum, and underestimated the difficulty of raising money on the global capital market, the two primary sources of funding for the Plan. At home, they also tried several ways. Considering that China was still a predominantly agrarian society, the government wanted to rely upon the revenues gained by requiring the sale of agricultural products to the state at artificially lower prices before selling them at a higher price. But this policy failed to encourage productivity and quite naturally, agricultural development stagnated. As to the state enterprises, instead of being a source of profit, they still relied upon huge subsidies in order to survive. Therefore, due to the failure in raising enough funds, the whole program quickly ran into financial difficulties.

1.2 Obstacles Challenging Its Fulfillment

It did not take long before the capital scarcity began to hamper the execution of the Plan. In 1978, China signed contracts for twenty-two large imported projects and they totally were worth USD13 billion (Liu, 2005). As a result of payment for these expensive deals, the country's net foreign exchange reserves dropped to a negative

USD1.3 billion by 1980, which had rarely happened since 1949. More importantly, the whole reform program focused almost exclusively on the hardware side of industrialization, such as equipment and production facilities whereas little attention was paid to the management of these establishments, or to the domestic capacity to absorb all the imported technologies. Similarly, consideration was seldom given to the links between the new industrial complexes, like their upstream suppliers and downstream customers. As a result, even those successfully finished projects were severely underutilized. What's more, being isolated from the rest of the economy, these industrial complexes also failed to generate any significant technological spillover.

In addition to the above, China in 1978 suffered yet another serious shortage, i.e. the shortage of technical personnel. During the Cultural Revolution, the theory that "knowledge is useless" had excerted a profound impact on the Chinese society. Many specialists were thereby compelled to abandon their occupations, with most training and educational schemes came to a complete halt. Referring to the higher education, it was unavoidably victimized. After the closure of universities, students joined the Red Guards and professors became the main *targets of* incessant attacks, even humiliations. Although in 1970, many *universities began to resume classes,* they could hardly steer clear of the noises outside. As a result, when the 10-year disorder was over and the country was mobilized for a restoration, the number of skilled personnel was too small to satisfy the demand (Feng, 2006), which seriously obstructed the application of imported modern technologies and independent innovation of manufacturing processes that were compatible with these technologies. What's more, given the way resources were allocated during the Cultural Revolution years, the regime was not yet capable of dealing with the subsequent challenges like management of the massive resource flows, selection of sites and detailed project planning, etc. (Naughton, 2007), especially when confronting regional disparities. Thus, for lack of intellectual inputs and hands-on experiences, it was even more impossible for the ambitious undertaking to proceed in a fruitful way.

By and large, the thirst for capital and well-trained labor force not only exemplifies what China was really like in 1978, it also revealed that the Ten-Year Plan of Hua Guofeng was but a loosely and hastily drafted program. Many projects were deployed without prudent evaluations, nor any serious calculation of the actual needs of the economy. In many cases, plants were designed, sited, and contracted in great haste without adequate consideration of their technical feasibility, infrastructure requirements or cost effectiveness. If valued positively, the Plan did yield certain high rates of growth. For example, one year after its implementation, total industrial and agricultural output of 1978 rose by 12.3 PCT, with agriculture increasing by 8.9 PCT and industry 13.5 PCT (NBS, 1979). Nonetheless, since the targets had been far too impractical, the cost of these achievements was considerably high, which led to the creation of external as well as internal imbalances. Externally, the 41 PCT growth of import in 1978 was not fully matched by the increase of exports, which was 20 PCT, China ran a trade deficit of USD1.14 billion. Since the Chinese leadership did not want to incur too much external debt, it was obliged to use part of its foreign exchange reserves to offset the unfavorable balance. However, the USD167 million left in its reserves of that year was apparently far from enough to settle all the import payments.

In fact, there were two reasons to explain the trade deficit. To begin with, the absence of supervision in the planning system plus the overconfidence of the central planners had resulted in an unchecked spending spree. Secondly, the 10 additional oil fields necessary to expand petroleum export never materialized. In fact, China had been too dependent on Daqing Oil Field, which alone contributed over 40 PCT to the nation's annual output during the 1960s and 1970s. This was by no means sustainable since it would easily cause reckless exploration and the danger of depletion. On the other hand, in 1978, while China's oil production reached 104 million tons, its own consumption hit 91.3 million tons (Lin, 2010), suggesting that without much excess capacity, it was very hard for the nation to rely on oil to generate the needed foreign currencies to tackle the problem of trade deficit. Domestically, if China had a well-developed light industry, then it would still be able to reverse the negative balance in the short run without having to halt the contracted imports of foreign equipment and technologies. However, the economic situation of China did not allow a rapid surge in the export of light industrial goods since by launching the Four Modernizations Initiative, almost all free resources were directed to the heavy industry sector, thus leaving only a minor portion for the light industry and agriculture. As long as the sectoral imbalance in the domestic economy remained, the goal of increasing exports to pay for imports seemed unlikely to fulfill.

The impending imbalances arising from the enforcement of the Ten-Year Plan soon put it on the brink of collapse. In addition to the criticisms by economists like Xue Muqiao, high-ranking government officials including Chen Yun, Deng Xiaoping, and Li Xiannian, etc. were also aware of the potential crisis hidden behind the irrational pursuit of a high speed of growth, they equally acknowledged that the initial phase of the Ten-Year Plan was seriously flawed by a lack of proper preparation, which had already led to enormous wastes (Jiang, 2013). At this moment, down-sizing the macroeconomic targets and introducing some microeconomic reforms were found to be imperative. On June 18th, 1979, the Second Session of the 5th National People's Congress passed the resolution to postpone the Ten-Year Plan and introduce a three-year period of "adjustment ('*tiao zheng*'), restructuring ('*gai ge*'), rectification ('*zheng dun*'), and improvement ('*ti gao*')" of the national economy during 1979–1981. The retreat from the unrealistic Ten-Year Plan caused the suspension or even cancellation of some of the large industrial projects, particularly the production of steel, equipment and chemicals. At the same time, priorities began to shift away from heavy industry toward agriculture and light industry, with decision-making power decentralized and material incentives resumed (Xiao, 2015).

2 Initial Reforms Kicked Off (1978–1983)

In China's modern history, a decisive event that turned the country from a poor and stagnant socialist economy into one of the world's most vibrant economies happened in December, 1978 when the Third Plenary Session of the 11th Central Committee of the Communist *Party* of China was held. At this session, the commitment of building a modern China was highlighted and economic progress for the first time, became paramount to all other objectives. It was also by then that Deng Xiaoping ultimately consolidated his position as the *core of* the second generation leader. In his eyes, reform was both necessary and pressing if to make China a modernized country. His pragmatic style can be reflected by two of his famous quotations, i.e. "seeking truth from facts" ('*shishi qiushi*') and "development is the absolute principle" ('*fazhan caishi yingdaoli*'). He believes that the success of China lies in the harmony and convergence between theory and practice, which cannot be divorced from each other. Different from his predecessors, he no longer downplayed personal wealth; instead, he argued that to get rich was something glorious. In general, the core of Deng Xiaoping's philosophy was based on pragmatism and success, which should be measured by common sense rather than by rigid ideologies. Once, he dramatized this philosophy by insisting: "It does not matter whether a cat is black or white; so long as it catches mice, it is a good cat".

About four decades ago, China's was indeed a very backward economy. When the average GDP per capita of the world in 1978 was already more than USD1,969, that of China stood at only USD156 (current US dollars, the World Bank data, from https://data.worldbank.org/indicator/NY.GDP.PCAP.CD?locations=CN). As explained in the previous part, after years of self-imposed isolation from the rest of the world, the country faced enormous constraints, mainly financial and technological. Therefore, recognizing that to modernize China was by no means an easy task, the sentiment rather prevalent at that particular stage could be described as "look, before you leap" ('*sansi erxing*'). Behind it, there lied some uncertainties over two key issues, i.e. the response of western investors and banks toward China's decision to develop economy in a market-oriented way; and the potential capabilities of the Chinese to deal with the upcoming challenges. Later, by sending several delegations to the West, it was found that enterprises there all welcomed China's decision to open up (He, 2008).

Besides, given the fact that the world economy was afflicted with a recession caused by the energy crisis during 1979–1980, these western companies were eagerly looking for new source of revenues and China's announcement of the plan to open up was of course thrilling. They could sell almost everything in this huge and virtually untapped market, and generate lucrative profits. For the Chinese leaders, they were of course greatly encouraged by the positive response abroad. This time, however, they were determined to act in a prudent manner. Although recognizing the pressing need to narrow the gap with the west, they did not want to repeat the lessons of the past. In fact, because of the recklessness in planning the economy under campaigns like the Great Leap Forward and the Great Leap Outward, the entire country was far from fully recovered. Therefore, to avoid taking the wrong path once again, a gradualist approach was considered more pragmatic and applicable to China.

2.1 The Guiding Ideology

If looking up the dictionary, the Chinese equivalent for "ideology" is '*yishi xingtai*'. More specifically, '*yishi*' is translated into "consciousness" while '*xingtai*' means "shape" or "form". According to the context involved, the "shape of consciousness" can be social, cultural or political. On certain occasions, there are some other words that might serve as synonyms or simply reflect close relationships with the concept of '*yishi xingtai*', like '*si xiang*' (thought), '*xin tiao*' (doctrine), and '*li lun*' (theory), to name but a few (Zhou, 2011). Universally, "ideology" is perhaps the realm which incurs the most debates and arguments. Due to this reason, people are often divided into diverse camps based on where they stand. Furthermore, under the influence of their respective convictions and attitudes, the concrete approaches they would adopt in dealing with the same issue may vary from one to another, thus leading to a multi-faceted world. Concerning the Communist Party of China (CPC), its terminology of '*yishi xingtai*' has always been interpreted as a kind of "political thought" or "theory" directing not only its "thought work" ('*sixiang gongzuo*'), but also the enforcement of policies. In turn, the development strategies covering almost all the spheres of the society are without exception reflective of the same '*yishi xingtai*'. In other words, it is the latter which sets the tone for the whole population to follow. From the perspective of the political leaders, the necessity to ensure an unswerving implementation of the given ideology is paramount above everything else, it is a fundamental basis to fulfill the goals outlined for various undertakings.

In view of the political scene of China since 1949, it is apparent that ideology has remained firmly at its centerpiece. Identifed 100 PCT with the tenets and the ultimate ideals of Marxism, the way in which the ideologies of the CPC are shaped is of no much difference. At the operational level, such kind of commitment is not hard to identify either, from the code of conduct to the practice guidelines, etc. Although among the state-level policymakers, there do exist disagreements or sometimes even conflicts; by nature, their vision for the future is common, i.e. building a socialist country before attaining the stage of absolutely egalitarian communism. Besides, in response to the constant shifts of the environment, the leadership of each generation (a group based on the collective leadership system) has its distinct extension of the Party ideology. Seemingly, this may cause a departure from the authodox doctrine of Marxism; in fact, however, the cornerstone is never changed and after several rounds of evolvement, it has just become more flexible and institutionalized, bearing the characteristics of the time and the personal style of the core leaders.

As a prominent figure and chief architect of the reform and opening-up in 1978, Deng Xiaoping's ideas (collectively called the Deng Xiaoping Theory) were undoubtedly embodied in the diverse policies initiated in China as the Party's overriding ideology, along with the thoughts of his predecessors. Recognizing that history has to follow certain phases of development, Deng's Theory is centered on the building of "Socialism with Chinese Characteristics" ('*zhongguo tese de shehui zhuyi*'), i.e. to take advantage of some positive aspects of capitalism while heading on the road of socialism. In the blueprint of Deng Xiaoping, socialism is regarded as a separate "mode of production" which is featured by three major attributes: public ownership of the means of production, distribution on the basis of labor, and observation of the law of value (Yong, 2005). In addition, considering the three stages from capitalism to communism, i.e. a transitional stage from capitalism to socialism, a developed socialist stage, and the communist stage, China's socialism was just at the beginning given its low level of productivity, education, and per capita GDP. Thereby, to ensure that the aim of communism could be achieved in due course, the focus of the country at that particular stage was identified as "socialist modernization". Specifically speaking, by the mid-twenty-first century, China as a modernized nation could expect to go beyond the initial phase of socialism (Chen, 2014). When talking about the critical task of establishing socialist market economy in this process, Deng once said that "developing a market economy does not mean practicing capitalism", even if some typical practices of a capitalist market economy overlapped with those of a socialist country.

Together with the pursuit of "Socialism with Chinese Characteristics", Deng Xiaoping also highlighted in a speech of March 1979 the "Four Cardinal Principles" ('*sixiang jiben yuanze*') as the basic prerequisite for achieving modernization. These four principles include: keeping to the socialist road, *upholding* the dictatorship of the proletariat, *upholding* the leadership of the Communist Party, and *upholding* Marxism-Leninism and Mao Zedong Thought. Unlike the decision to shift from the former centrally-control*l*ed economy toward a dual-track approach which allowed market forces to function alongside the planned economy, Deng's emphasis of the above Four Principles symbolizes explicitly his endorsement and unquestionable fidelity to the official ideology of the CPC. With regard to the dual-track approach, on the one hand, economic agents were assigned rights to, and obligations for, fixed quantities of goods at fixed planned prices as specified in the state plan. On the other hand, a market track was introduced under which economic agents could participate in the market at free market prices, yet on the condition that they should first fulfill their obligations under the plan (Lau, Qian, & Roland, 2000). Through such an arrangement, prices were liberalized on a limited scale while planned prices and quotas were still maintained for some time before being completely abolished. In the same sense, all the reform measures that were to be introduced should be subject to a managed market economy before being ultimately replaced by a full market economy. With the guidance of this fundamental ideology, the initial phase of the reform that roughly covered ten years from 1978 to 1988 included a number of key endeavors and they were agricultural de-collectivization, industrial decentralization, and promotion of the external sector via special economic zones, etc.

2.2 De-collectivization of Agriculture Via HRS

One of the most far-reaching economic changes in the rural area should be taken as the de-collectivization of agriculture, the weakest sector of the Chinese economy.

During the Great Leap Forward and the Cultural Revolution period, Chinese agriculture suffered a lot when state investment overwhelmingly favored industry, leaving the sector chronically underfunded. Besides, what made it even worse was that profits derived from agriculture followed the investment to subsidize the nationwide industrialization. As a result, *250 million* people lived in absolute poverty in *rural* China by *1978* (Hu, Hu & Chang, 2005). In that same year, the country's rural population totaled 7*90 million, which means that in every three people, one was below the poverty line,* a rather horrible situation. To boost output and *alleviate hunger*, the Chinese government since 1979 has significantly increased the prices paid for major agricultural products like grains, cotton and hogs, etc. and subsidized the use of chemical fertilizers (Ma, 1992). But real fundamental reforms took place only when de-collectivization and the household responsibility system (HRS) were developed from the bottom upward.

2.2.1 Collectivized Farming, a Disincentive to Output Growth

Collective farming began in China in 1955 and one year later, almost all farm households were included in cooperatives, which were later transformed into several other forms like communes, production teams and brigades. Meanwhile, the state's unified procurement and marketing system replaced private agricultural purchasing and distribution networks. Accordingly, agricultural output was sold under a rationing scheme to urban consumers and industries at subsidized prices. If counting the most severe problem with collective farming, it should be the low efficiency. Since individual effort was not rewarded adequately, the collective income-distribution system provided little incentive to peasants. In fact, collective farming didn't discern between hardworking and lazy peasants, both were paid in an equal way irrespective of their actual contributions or performances. It is therefore not difficult to understand why shirking became a widely observed phenomenon, with an increasing number of peasants going to the field simply to obtain work points ('*gong fen*', the basis on which the contribution of each labor was measured under the collective system) but did not want to make a serious effort (Wang, 2008).

Besides, the planning system in collective farming is a flawed one because it ignored regional comparative advantage within China. To support industrialization, local self-sufficiency in grain production was taken as an overriding goal. In other words, what mattered was simply quantity; but with regard to quality and variety, they did not receive much attention. Further, collective farming was intrinsically defective because efficient production was possible only under the condition that someone had personal responsibility for the utilization of agricultural inputs, but when peasants were deprived of their ownership of land and other means of production, a higher productivity and output appeared a mere fantasy.

2.2.2 Contract Farming: Trials Initiated

In 1977, some of China's pragmatic leaders recognized that if without a closer linkage between the job performed and the remuneration received, peasants would not work hard and then agriculture may continue to grow at a sluggish pace. In fact, there was no fundamental change in the per capita grain output between 1956 and 1977, which remained at around 300 kilos. Following the rehabilitation of Deng Xiaoping in July and the 11th National Congress of the Communist Party of China of August, more voices were heard that unanimously called for the reintroduction of material incentives in rural areas. They not only came from provincial agricultural departments and experts; *People's Daily*, a flagship newspaper of the Communist Party, equally expressed its support of these changes. Indeed, with a system that relied so heavily on the administrative orders from the above and left no room for local initiatives, discontent was easy to accumulate. In 1978, some provinces (mainly Sichuan and Anhui) that had extensive regions of low yields and consequent low standards of living began experimenting with new forms of production (Zhou, 1987). Known as the "output contract system" ('*bao chan zhi*'), it included "household contracting" ('*baochan daohu*') and "group contracting" ('*baochan daozu*'), etc. Referring to the former initiative, production team would contract with individual households, especially those with special expertise to produce certain sideline items. Then, these households were to sell the contracted goods back to the production team, who would resell at higher prices. The profits thus made would be distributed among all the team members. With regard to the second alternative, it is essentially a rudimentary endeavor of contracting production to individual groups, with each one composed of six to ten households. Every group was responsible for supplying a fixed quota to the state and the collective; if there was surplus production, group members could keep as their own. Although the history of these practices was rather short, peasants' motivation had an impressive increase, and together with it their productivity. Partially, it is because that they can now take major decisions for themselves; partially, it lies in the system itself which prohibited egalitarian redistribution of people's outputs. At the same time, with the declining wastes of labor and other resources, more peasants began to value every single hour since if they overproduced the quota, they could earn more.

Since 1980, the household contract system has taken precedence in most of China's rural areas and it was by then a simple yet bolder form of responsibility system came into being. Called "all-round contracting" ('*da bao gan*'), it was synonymous with independent farming (Wang, 1998). Based on the system, the production team maintained collective ownership of the land and would divide the land and other means of production (such as farm tools and draft animals) among individual households. Once signing the contract, each household was obliged to pay tax and meet the minimal compulsory sales. As long as these obligations were fulfilled, they may grow whatever they would like and dispose of the rest of the surplus output in any way they found suitable. Owing to its immediate positive effect on output and hence on household income, and more importantly, because it was de facto privatization, '*da bao gan*' was soon adopted throughout the country. After three years of practice, especially between the autumn of 1981 and the autumn of 1982, the household contract system became the nation's most recognized operating model. By the end of 1982, more than 92 PCT of China's agricultural production teams had de-collectivized into the family-operated modes of farming (Huang, 1987).

2.2.3 Official Launch of the Household Responsibility System

With the growing popularity of the contract system in rural China, the central government also showed its full support through the issuance of a series of agricultural policy directives during 1982 and 1986. Since both were released by the Central Committee of the Communist Party of China (CPC) at the beginning of these five years, the directives were also known as "Central Document No. One". In 1983, the second "Central Document No. One" gave the all-round contract system an official name, i.e. the household responsibility system (HRS). Being the first document to sanction the HRS officially as a legitimate rural production arrangement, it permitted individual farm households to hire labor; buy and own trucks, tractors, and farm machinery; and sell their surplus goods in free markets, etc. In 1984, explicit party endorsement of the household responsibility system was reinforced with the third "Central Document No. One", and its main contribution to the reform was to extend minimum leases from the former two to three years to fifteen years (Ma & Li, 2013), with an intention to encourage peasants to increase their investment so as to foster the fertility of soil and practice intensive operation. In summary, within the first ten years following the Cultural Revolution, the collective system, a predominant feature of the agricultural sector for a number of decades, was largely replaced by the household responsibility system, which established a closer link between effort and reward for individual peasants.

In fact, taking household as the basic unit of management to engage in diversified economic activities is by no means new in China. Back to the feudal societies, it was rather common for landowners to rent their land to peasant households in small plots. However, the household agriculture practiced in the 1980s was fundamentally different from its predecessor. Based on the premise that the land belonged to the collective, it was more a combination of a unified collective economy with scattered household production. In general, the collective would look after water conservation facilities, irrigation, repair of machinery, supply of seeds and fertilizers, forecast of crop diseases, etc. With regard to individual households, they were responsible for crop cultivation and field management (Feng, 2008). Since the purchase of major agricultural products was organized by the collectives, peasants did not have to worry about the marketing of their produce. While they had to perform specific obligations such as paying taxes, fulfilling the state mandatory procurement quotas, and contributing to collective undertakings, they were entitled to all that was left, which granted them a fair degree of financial flexibility. As a result, there was an increase in privately-owned means of production such as small farm machines, plowing oxen, etc. Accordingly, the Chinese rural economy has changed from a system prohibiting peasants from owning any means of production, other than a few simple tools like sickles and hoes, to a mixed economy in which power was more decentralized to the grassroots. The people's commune, which had played a fundamental role from the late 1950s to the 1960s to assist the industrial development of urban areas, lost their basis for existence. In Oct. 1983, the Central Committee of the CPC and the State Council together promulgated "The Notice on Separation of Government Administration from Commune Management and Establishment of Township Government". Based on this notice, township government became the lowest level of government fulfilling various functions and people's communes were thus turned into units of production only, or simply disappeared in many places.

At the same time, a major phenomenon accompanying the nationwide spread of household contract system was the growing number of specialized households ('*zhuan ye hu*'). They first emerged in 1981 and after two years of swift development, they shared 13.6 PCT, or totaled 24.82 million of all the rural households in the country (Cai, 1985). Equipped with diverse skills in activities like raising livestock, firing tiles, casting iron, weaving, or embroidering, etc., these people could not fully utilize their abilities during those days when grain production was taken as the "key link" in agriculture. But right now, with the loosening policy and relaxed control, they got a good chance to do something which can not only bring qualitative change to their lives, but transform the natural economy of rural China into a commodity economy as well. From the social point of view, their existence helped increase division of labor in agricultural production and enhanced the awareness of economic efficiency among peasants.

These rural reforms, coupled with sharp increase in procurement prices and stringent curb over input costs, had a significant impact on yield per unit and agricultural production (Table 1). First, average grain yield rose by almost 50 PCT from 2,487 kg/hectare in 1977 to 3,716 kg/hectare in 1983. Second, as a result of increases in the yield, the growth rate in grain output was equally significant. By 1983, the amount was 43 PCT higher than that of 1977. As a result, the per capita net income of rural household rose from RMB133.6 in 1978 to RMB309.8 in 1983 (Li, 1984). Increasing income not only lifted the absolute living standards of rural people, it also narrowed

Table 1 Growth in grain yield per unit area and output, 1977–1983

Year	Grain yield[1] (kilograms per hectare)	Grain output[2] (million metric tons)
1977	2,486.9	239.83
1978	2,791.8	269.82
1979	3,032.5	289.52
1980	2,937.3	277.19
1981	3,081.6	283.33
1982	3,456	312.09
1983	3,716.1	342.27

Source The World Bank, [1]https://data.worldbank.org/indicator/AG.YLD.CREL.KG?locations=CN; [2]https://data.worldbank.org/indicator/AG.PRD.CREL.MT?locations=CN.

down the urban–rural income gap. In 1978, the per capita disposable income of urban households reached RMB343.4, i.e. 157 PCT above the per capita net income of the rural household; but by 1983, the disparity was lowered to 82 PCT when the former registered RMB564.6 whereas the latter hit RMB309.8 (NBS, 2013).

2.2.4 A System with Undeniable Flaws

As an institutional innovation, the household responsibility system did provide certain economic incentives for peasants to work harder and has thereby enabled China to raise its agricultural production as well as improve the standard of living of the rural people to some degree. More significantly, the fundamental problem of feeding the giant population, which had been a great pressure for several centuries, was basically resolved. Nonetheless, despite these positive effects, it would be naive to expect the system to address everything, especially given the fact that after several years of practice, a number of inherent limitations and weaknesses were exposed. First of all, de-collectivization of farmland, as the central plank of HRS, contained some fundamental defects that could easily lead to fragmentation in land cultivation. Put in a specific way, since farmland in a village was collectively owned by all of its members and the norm for distributing land was based on the size of the peasant family, every member as a result had equal claim on land property rights. But given the unbalanced population-to-land ratio, the amount distributed to each household was very small. In 1984, for example, the arable land available to each peasant averaged only 1.5 mu (equivalent to 0.1 hectares) (Jiang, 2002). Moreover, considering that farmland differed from parcel to parcel in terms of soil fertility, irrigation conditions, and location, etc., it was divided into several different grades and each household thereby would obtain a portion of land in each of these grades. As a consequence, the total land under the name of these households was usually fragmented and scattered around villages, which wasted a lot of their time and labor. Under this condition, it was no longer realistic to expect peasants to use advanced mechanical equipment to modernize their farming methods.

Second, under the household responsibility system, egalitarianism was generally the leading principle in land distribution, with little consideration given to inter-family differences like labor capabilities, education levels, and personal preferences. Due to the existence of this flaw, some large households whose labor force was limited might have too much land to till while other smaller households, including those specialized in agriculture, could have insufficient land for full employment. In particular, concerning regions which were going through rapid rural industrialization and urbanization, there was a general deterioration in the quality of agricultural labor force as the most able workers tended to leave the villages to hunt higher-paid off-farm works. Therefore, the already scarce resources were underutilized. Third, although the state policy had extended in 1984 the validity time of contracted land for farm households to 15 years, most of the peasants preferred much longer use rights than they possessed. Deep in their heart, they were still fearful of the sudden change of the system and this unavoidably made them reluctant to improve the quality of land or engage in long-term conservation works. Rather, they preferred to engage in activities that could generate more short-term profits. In summary, the household responsibility system did not fully resolve the problem of efficiency, which in turn would become a stumbling block to the further development of China's agriculture. In this consideration, China was once again confronting a challenge.

2.3 *From CBEs to TVEs*

Township and village enterprises (TVEs), if defined in a broader sense according to the *Statistical Yearbook of China 1986*, should refer to all rural non-agricultural enterprises consisting of four categories: township enterprises ('*xiangban qiye*'), village enterprises ('*cunban qiye*'), joint household enterprises ('*lianhu qiye*'), and privately-owned enterprises ('*geti qiye*'). But in a narrower sense, they represent business entities collectively owned by residents of a rural community (at either town or village levels) and controlled by the local government. In this book, the term "TVEs" stands for the first two categories of rural enterprises.

2.3.1 The Rise and Fall of Commune and Brigade Enterprises

Referring to the development of TVEs in China, it was of no doubt the fruit of rural economic reform started in 1978. To gain a comprehensive knowledge of how they came into being, it is necessary to look back at those campaigns that had led at great cost to two vast waves of decentralization, i.e. the Great Leap Forward in the late 1950s and the Cultural Revolution of the 1960s. In the first wave, people's communes were established across all the rural areas of China where they played a dual role: they were both the lowest government apparatus and the highest level of the rural collective system. Inside the commune, its organization was hierarchical, with brigades being its immediate subordinate units and production teams at the bottom level of the collective hierarchy. During the Great Leap Forward period of 1958–59, consistent with the heavy industry development strategy and in response to the central government's campaign to "run industry by the masses" ('*quanmin bangongye*'), large-scale commune and brigade enterprises (CBEs or '*shedui qiye*') were established, many of which were engaged in the production of steel with rudimentary technologies, as well as cement, farm tools, hydroelectric power, and foodstuffs, etc. Based on the statistics for 1959, there were around 700,000 CBEs in rural China and the total employment reached 18 million, with the gross value of industrial production hitting RMB10 billion (Huang, 2015).

Behind the mass movements, however, there was no market, nor rigorous bureaucratic rules to support the circulation. In addition, with the widespread poverty and immobility of resources, many of their products were useless. Following the failure of the Great Leap Forward campaign and confronting the extremely severe shortages of raw materials, the central government decided to shut down most CBEs.

Within just four years, their number plummeted and by 1963, the value of industrial output registered merely RMB410 million (Yan, 2007). Then came the second wave in the early 1970s, a period when a huge amount of resources were decentralized, the central government emphasized agricultural mechanization and called its people to strive for "self-reliance". In order to diversify their revenue streams, many rural areas tried once again to set up commune and brigade enterprises manufacturing agricultural machinery, repairing tools, or supplying construction materials, etc. In 1976, i.e. the end of the Cultural Revolution, China had nearly 1.12 million CBEs and their gross industrial output hit RMB24.35 billion (Guo, 1999), over 7.4 PCT of the nation's total which was RMB327.8 billion.

2.3.2 Official Recognition of the Township-Village Enterprises

The later spurt of TVEs which happened since the mid-1980s was not designed nor even guided by the state, it was more like a spontaneous evolution in response to the changes in China's political and economic landscape. After the Third Plenum of the 11th Central Committee in 1978, in particular, restrictions on peasants' non-agricultural activities were greatly relaxed. Moreover, the nationwide introduction of the household responsibility system further enhanced the enthusiasm of peasants and increased their income, which provided surplus capital for the development of the rural industry. Before the economic reform, CBEs had been completely subordinated to the people's commune system, which means that they were not autonomous business entities with their own balance sheets and therefore, assets could be moved in and out at the will of the commune authorities. In the early 1980s, following the adoption of HRS, the commune structure was gradually dissolved and replaced by townships that had existed prior to 1958.

Consequently, when the governmental functions of nearly all communes were converted to townships ('*xiang*') and most of the production brigades became villages ('*cun*'), all the CBEs were officially reclassified as township-village enterprises, or TVEs (On March 1st, 1984, the State Council's Document No. 4 formalized the political and legal status of TVEs, which gave them access to government support of diverse forms like bank loans or the exemption of value-added tax, business tax and income tax, etc.). By then, most TVEs were collectively-owned enterprises and their properties belonged to all the residents of the township or village. A township government, regarded as the "representative" of the people, was the de facto executive owner (or the principal) of the TVEs (Zang, 2000). As to the daily operations, they were partly delegated to managers (or the agents of the principal) through a contract with the executive owner, the township government. Thus, it is these two groups of actors who jointly take decisions concerning the TVEs.

Because of China's vast territory, local circumstances vary sharply across different regions, so did the TVE model, which was an organizational response to both the macroeconomic environment and the local conditions. Generally, regions with outstanding TVE performance often have a long history of entrepreneurship and a favorable climate benefiting business activities. In this regard, the role local government plays is always essential and as the de facto owners, local governments had a strong incentive to promote their development, although the method of involvement was not necessarily the same. As a result, there emerged in China a variety of regional models of TVE development and among them, the most prominent included the '*Su nan*' (Southern Jiangsu Province) model, the '*Wen zhou*' (Zhejiang province) model, and the '*Zhu jiang*' (Pearl River, Guangdong Province) model, etc. (Chen, 2005).

Representing three typical ownership structures and management approaches, these three models have drawn a lot of interest among researchers and media since the mid-1980s. With regard to the Sunan model, it relied primarily on collectively-owned TVEs managed by local/community government officials. Indeed, this model was not just restricted to Southern Jiangsu, it was often applied to other parts of the country where local government played a dominant role in corporate decisions. By contrast, the Wenzhou model should be taken as a reaction of the local government to the spontaneous development of private businesses. Therefore, it is characterized by family-run TVEs, with most of them engaged in the processing of goods for export. Referring to the Zhujiang model, its TVEs received massive overseas investment (in particular from Hong Kong and Taiwan) thanks to the special economic zones established in Shenzhen, Zhuhai, and Shantou in the early 1980s. Thus many of them were in fact joint ventures located around the Pearl River Delta area. Despite the above differences, they together shared some common features, e.g. they were all led by entrepreneurs, and they all had intimate relationship with the local governments, etc.

In summary, the diversity of organizational forms taken by rural enterprises enabled them to adapt more resiliently to a wide variety of economic conditions. In most cases, TVEs were owned by local governments and this certainly had its pros and cons. In terms of the latter, inadequately specified property rights, frequent government interventions, and inappropriately defined incentives were perhaps the major disadvantages. But at the same time, it should not be denied that when China's command economy remained its dominion over the allocation of production factors and important materials such as steel, coal, wood, etc. were still strictly controlled and rationed because of severe shortages, TVEs did not have much problem accessing these resources. The reason behind was that in the rural area, it was the local government who enjoyed the privilege in allocating these materials. In addition, when TVEs were in need of funds, "local government officials often acted as intermediaries or even guarantors reassuring the local agents of the banking system that their loans would be repaid" on time (Naughton, 2007). With local government helping with fund raising, these rural enterprises were in a position to utilize China's relatively abundant household savings, which soared by almost 12 times during the 1980s and resulted in a dramatic expansion of fund supply at local Rural Credit Cooperatives (RCCs). Quite naturally, these RCCs became the major source for TVEs to finance their business activities. If without the sponsorship of local government, it would be unlikely for TVEs to survive and prosper in such a smooth way. According to the National Bureau of Statistics, from 1978 to 1983, the gross output value of CBEs (predecessor of TVEs) rose from RMB49.3 billion to RMB101.7 billion, representing an annual growth rate of 21 PCT. In terms of employment, these CBEs totally recruited 32.35 million workers by 1983, an increase of 14.4 PCT over that of 1978 (NBS, 1999).

2.4 *De-centralization in Industry*

After the Third Plenum of the 11th Central Committee of CPC, the Chinese leaders regarded enterprise reform as a key component to the revitalization of the socialist economy. Similar to the agricultural sector, de-centralization was also applied as a preferred tool to reform industry, which was at that time chiefly dominated by state-owned enterprises (SOEs). An editorial in the *People's Daily* on February 19th, 1979 could represent faithfully the official position of the Chinese government at that time, it stressed that "the most urgent task for the current economic reform is to expand the autonomy of enterprises" (People's Daily, 1979). In the following years, enterprise reform became a nationwide campaign highlighting two key aspects, i.e. expansion of enterprise autonomy and increased use of economic levers.

2.4.1 Delegation of Greater Power

Prior to 1978, most Chinese enterprises were state-owned, with their management characterized by a unified and collective pattern of governance. In general, production of these SOEs was planned by the state and inputs like raw materials and equipment were furnished through an administrative allocation system. Enterprises basically did not have any autonomy over employment of workers, use of profits, plan of production, and sale of their products. For lack of a market-based adjustment mechanism, managerial discretion was potentially a serious problem and losses, if any, would be borne by the state. Hence, the over-centralized control by the state and weak incentives to managers and workers made SOEs in China notoriously inefficient and inflexible. In recognition of these problems, enterprise reform efforts were described as "administrative decentralization" (*'jianzheng fangquan'*), in which there was a *devolution of* decision-making power from the central government to the *government* at a sub-national level, such as a regional or local level. However, it was soon discovered that de*l*egation of power simply from central to local government was far from enough; to make the reform truly fruitful, power should be further decentralized from the government to enterprises themselves.

The experiment of SOE reform was initiated in Sichuan Province in October 1978. First introduced to six SOEs, the program aimed to expand the autonomy of enterprises (Chen, 2015), which was a good starting point to tinker with the system because it was relatively less controversial. Even the most conservative planner might agree that a management system would perform better with more autonomy at the base level. After fulfilling state plans, these SOEs could have certain decision flexibility in production, marketing, employment, and technological innovation, etc. Besides, they may also share some profits according to the prespecified retention rates. By April

1979, the number of the industrial SOEs participating in Sichuan's experiment had increased to one hundred. Based on the experiences of Sichuan, the central government in May 1979 carried out its own pilot reform in eight large SOEs including Beijing Shougang (Capital Steel Factory), Shanghai Diesel Engine Plant, and Tianjin Bicycle Factory, etc., followed by five State Council circulars in that July spelling out policy instruments to further enlarge managerial autonomy of the SOEs. These five documents included: "Regulations on the Expansion of Operational Management Autonomy for State-Owned Industrial Enterprises"; "Regulations on Retention of Profits by State-Owned Enterprises"; "Provisional Regulations on Levying Fixed Assets Tax in State-Owned Industrial Enterprises"; "Provisional Regulations on Accelerating the Depreciation of Fixed Assets for State-Owned Industrial Enterprises and Improvement of the Usage of the Depreciation Fee"; and "Provisional Regulations on the Adoption of Loan and Credit Methods for the Floating Capital in State-Owned Industrial Enterprises".

2.4.2 Retained Profit and Bank Loans: New Sources of Financing

Referring to the profit retention scheme, in particular, the amount of profit retained by a firm was based on the total funds it had been granted in 1978 for workers' welfare, bonus, enterprise funds, new product research and development, and training, etc. Then its total profit in the same year would be linked to that sum and the percentage thus calculated was to become the firm's profit sharing ratio, or its retention rate. According to the requirement, the retained profit should be split into three separate funds, i.e. "production development fund" for reinvestment purposes, "employee welfare fund" for the housing, health care and education of employees, and "employee reward fund" for bonus and piece-rate compensation. Moreover, based on these five documents, the selected SOEs could enjoy accelerated depreciation and have the right to sell above-plan output, etc. This step marks the beginning of China's nationwide urban reform. Although the program as initially proposed was for a small number of experimental enterprises; it proved to be so popular that in the end of 1980, of the total 42,000 factories under the state budget, over 6,000 enterprises had taken part in and obtained some limited autonomy. Together, they accounted for 60 PCT of the gross output and 70 PCT of the total profit (Wang, 2005).

Together with the institution of profit retention, the financing structure underwent some changes too. Before the initiation of the reform, investment capital of SOEs came primarily from the state budget, with the remaining reliant upon enterprise funds, chiefly depreciation funds. Even though lending from domestic banks was still available, the amount was insignificant and usually allocated at the instruction of the government. By and large, the reform program of 1978 prompted decentralized investment financing in two ways. On the one hand, retained profit was taken as the major source of enterprise funds in the early 1980s (Zheng, 1983). At the same time, there was a steady growth in bank lending, which made up for the decline in government funds. For instance, bank loans to industrial SOEs was RMB48.7 billion in 1981; two years later, it rose to RMB59.7 billion (Song & Qu, 1997), an increase of over 22 PCT.

2.4.3 Tax-for-Profit Scheme

In fact, decentralization not only happened in the state enterprises, it is a trend that characterized the reform of other sectors as well. On the basis of the initial reform in expanding the decision-making power of enterprises, further experiment was introduced in 1981 in order to improve the fiscal performance of the SOEs. Named "economic responsibility system" ('*jingji zeren zhi*' or '*yingkui baogan zeren zhi*'), it was implemented on a trial basis during that spring in Shandong Province. Very soon, it spread nationwide and by the end of 1981, 42,000 industrial enterprises (Huang, 2008), i.e. almost 50 PCT of the total 84,200 industrial SOEs in the country, had implemented the scheme. With the profit retention remaining at the core, these ventures were held responsible for their own profits and losses.

By enabling enterprises to understand clearly their objectives in raising revenues from the outset, they could draft plans for the whole contractual period before having them carried out in a systematic way. Concerning the down side, since the targets were set against the performance record of the previous year, the bargaining between government and enterprises often ended in "punishing" the best-performing ones with an even higher quota to accomplish. But for those who had failed to fulfill the quota, they were not penalized and the state would continue to help them cover losses. With a view to resolving the imbalance between reward and punishment, as well as various other problems in execution, the government decided to suspend the system and replaced it with a "tax for profit" ('*li gai shui*') scheme in 1983, implying that the SOEs should pay taxes instead of turning in profits as they originally did, thus intensifying their budget constraint and increasing motivation.

Besides, by replacing profits with taxes, policy makers wanted to standardize the revenues turned over to the government by enterprises, strengthen their responsibilities, and equalize the competition conditions among enterprises. Obviously, the central idea behind the scheme was to take the large undifferentiated mass of accounting profits and reclassify it into several economically more meaningful categories, most of which could be labeled as taxes. In addition, by redefining some profit as tax, a legally instituted financial obligation of enterprises, they could have substantially greater autonomy in the disposition of the part of profit that was not included in tax. Indeed, through this arrangement, the government intended to combine the financial reform with the conversion of enterprises into independent economic entities, and limit their responsibilities to the state to tax payments. Considering that the price system was seriously distorted, the tax-for-profit scheme was carried out in two stages and the first stage started in April 1983 when the State Council promulgated the "Implementation Rules on Converting State-Owned Enterprise Profit Submission into Taxation". Based on the rules, large and medium-sized enterprises were required to pay a uniform tax rate, which was 55 PCT of their profits. For smaller enterprises, eight progressive tax rates were applied (Han, 1992).

As indicated in the above, profit remittance until 1983 was still determined on an annual basis through negotiations between the government and the enterprise. The problems with this practice were the revenue instability faced by the government and uncertainties faced by firms over their future obligations. With the new tax-for-profit system, a clearer financial relationship was established and both sides could better concentrate on their own duties. As to the initial results of the first stage, they were rather encouraging. By the end of 1983, a total number of 26,500 industrial enterprises were involved and this represented 94.2 PCT of the profit-making SOEs in the country (Wang, 2005). At the same time, the profit generated by all the participating state enterprises (including industrial, commercial, and transport, etc.) rose by 11.1 PCT and hit RMB63.3 billion in 1983. Of the additional profit realized, the share retained within the business reached RMB12.1 billion, an increase of 28.2 PCT over the previous year (Lu, 2008).

2.4.4 Relaxed Grip of the Central Planners

Nevertheless, enterprise reform by itself cannot achieve much unless there is an adequately functioning market environment which could enable them to run with greater autonomy. In the case of China, the concern that divided policy makers was how to harmonize plan with the market. The relatively conservative camp, on the one side, saw the market as a concession to the Chinese reality. Considering that planning could hardly be comprehensive enough to cover all spheres of the economy, the market should be allowed to govern on a smaller scale those unimportant decisions. For the more radical reformers, on the other hand, the entire economy should operate according to market principles based upon the condition that the market would be shaped and guided by a state plan, with economic levers such as tax, interest rates, and price, etc. being the highest form of planning to monitor macroeconomic development. Despite the theoretical debates, the reality remained that plans were still necessary for China but had to be adapted to the rapidly changing economic environment. Take the machinery industry as an example, during 1979–1981 when the central strategy tended to slash machinery investment and cut demand to cope with the rising inflation, planners (i.e. eight separate ministries of machine building) responded quickly by giving machinery enterprises more flexibility and encouraged them to look for new customers themselves. Under the pressure of inventory accumulation, these enterprises were often in a position to set up their own distribution networks at home and abroad, like Shanghai Machine Tool Works (Yang, 1981). Moreover, by taking advantage of the decentralized financing sources, they effectively buffered the impact of policy shifts.

Simultaneously, a similar trend also happened to the sector of consumer goods, in which the distribution had been monopolized by the state commerce system prior to 1978. Like what had happened elsewhere, the tight grip could not bring much positive effects but severe shortages of basic commodities, with many of the key items rationed and inconvenient access to the goods that were available only via official channels, etc., which too plagued the Chinese economy. Confronting the circumstances, if the country wanted to get out of the predicament, reorientation should be taken as a pressing issue to address. Prompted by an increasing demand of consumers for a wider range of choice and the need of enterprises for more freedom, as well as the necessity to reduce urban unemployment rate, the rules that once tied factories to the state commercial system for distribution were gradually loosened in 1979. By the early 1980s, multiple supply channels characterized by different ownership forms came into being. Among them, a larger number of collective and private enterprises steadily developed into a non-negligible presence in both urban and rural China. With the shrinking share of the state commerce, the portion claimed by the collective and private picked up quickly. Within eight years, it rose from 7.5 PCT of 1978 to over 35 PCT in 1986 (Du, 1987). To some degree, it is the very existence of these new rivals that pushed state enterprises to learn how to maintain a strong foothold in the market when the central plans could no longer provide them an absolute level of assurance as before.

2.4.5 Constraints Not Yet Removed

By and large, SOE reform with the main theme of profit-sharing and power-delegating did achieve certain positive effects. As part of the grander economic reform program in China, these measures gradually disengaged SOEs from a tightly-controlled economy and allowed them to participate in and adapt to market competition with non-state counterparts. In terms of the incentive mechanism, since both the management team and workers of SOEs could actually share profits with the state, they were no longer content with nothing more than the accomplishment of the state plans. Rather, they became infused with a strong profit motive knowing that if they worked harder, they would be able to acquire even bigger reward. Referring to the delegation of greater decision-making power, this not only means expanded managerial autonomy for these enterprises, it also represents less administrative interference from the above. Anyhow, while recognizing the advantages of the reform, it cannot be denied that the impact was quite limited because it failed to change the basic institutional framework of the SOEs. Under the existing factory system, SOEs had a closed structure of ownership that was not easily accessible by investors from the outside. Therefore, the director still remained subject to the joint supervision of the party committee, the workers, and the superior party and government institutions. Due to the inevitable conflict of power and ambiguous division of responsibilities, such kind of governance system often fell into a paralytic state, which resulted in an immeasurable loss of efficiency.

In addition, although the state-owned enterprises were granted more decision-making powers, some crushing constraints remained, especially the fragmented industrial structure. Due to repeated attempts by the pre-reform regime to make each locality (from counties to provinces) as self-sufficient as possible, the vast majority of the SOEs were without exception small in scale yet vast in number, and were in general completely isolated. Even upstream and downstream firms of the same industry rarely interacted with each other in a direct way, but would communicate through the government bureaucracy. As a result, it was rather common to see a cluster of enterprises in a single region, even though many of them were already redundant and did not possess any advantage. To address this structural problem, the State Council in July 1980 issued the "Provisional Rules for Promoting Economic Association", which called for horizontal integration and consolidation among the state-owned enterprises. Thus, some of the inefficient enterprises were closed down and some consolidated or merged with more successful ones. At the same time, subsidies to those failing to achieve profit targets were being cut off. To raise technical levels and operational efficiency, the government also decided to set up specialized companies at both national and regional levels, with an intention that these firms would better steer clear of political interference (Xing, 1982a, 1982b). Fairly speaking, their establishment reflected a new emphasis on the need for greater specialization and division of labor throughout the economy.

Normally, state enterprises should be charged even when receiving investment from the government. However, China's SOEs had always enjoyed a special privilege because they were never required to pay any monetary cost for the incoming funds, either used on fixed assets or as working capital (only a minor proportion of the bank loans was interest-bearing). Following the reform of the SOEs, the government was determined that the process should be accompanied by financial rationalization. In July 1979, the State Council issued several regulations (stated in the above) concerning the first stage of China's enterprise reform and among other things, the regulations stipulated that the SOEs should pay a charge (tax) on their fixed assets. Besides, working capital would be 100 PCT transformed to bank loans (provided by the People's Bank of China) rather than previously granted from the state budget by the Ministry of Finance and local Financial Bureaus. Later, more government directives were issued demanding the SOEs to pay a certain percentage of fees on all the future state investment. But, when it comes to the physical implementation, few enterprises were under serious pressure to use funds in an efficient way since supervision was rather loose. To a large extent, bank loans would be easily available as long as they apply (Zou, 1987). By 1983, when retained funds and bank lending substituted state investment and became the chief source of financing for the SOEs, the role of the budgetary system was no longer that significant.

The limited success of initial enterprise reforms demonstrates how deep-rooted the problems were among the state firms. Employing 76.8 PCT (i.e. 80.19 million) of the workforce in 1980 (Liu, 2011), they dominated the key sectors of China's industrial economy and provided essential raw materials like power, steel, chemicals, and machinery, etc. In services and infrastructure, the SOEs were largely protected from competition and thus could use their unchallengeable market positions to prevent entry of new rivals, in most cases aided and backed by government and party officials. While it is true that each element of reform since 1979 introduced a bit more flexibility into decision-making at the enterprise level, the shadow of the past did not as a result go away and the SOEs continued to be bound by the overlapping control mechanisms that restrained them from functioning better. In fact, many of them remained so submissive to the bureaucratic apparatus that they were more like mere extensions of government bodies instead of market-oriented firms.

2.5 Rationalization of the Banking Sector

As a general principle, financial development is positively related to a country's economy. In particular, the efficiency of financial intermediaries (chiefly banks) is key to technological innovation, capital accumulation and increased productivity. Conversely, a repressed or underdeveloped financial system may lead to misallocation of resources and thus retard the sound growth of the real economy. With regard to the reforms in China's financial sector, they were introduced in the context of the overall economic reform program initiated in the late 1970s. Similar to what happened in other sectors of the Chinese economy, financial reform equally took a "crossing the river by groping the pebbles beneath" ('*mozhe shitou guohe*', a metaphor coined by Deng Xiaoping and means to be modest and prudent when trying something novel) approach and was carried out largely on an experimental basis. Although at the outset, there was no ready-made blueprint to refer to, at least two objectives were explicitly highlighted. The first was to mobilize more savings and facilitate an efficient allocation of credit so as to quicken economic growth. Secondly, reforms should improve macroeconomic management and enhance stability in a decentralized economy. Ever since the beginning of the reform, it has become increasingly clear that the Chinese authorities wished to put in place a financial system modeled after the Western type with diversified financial intermediaries, a competitive financial market structure, and an effective regulatory and supervisory framework (Ding, 2013). It is believed that backed by such a system, efficient allocation of resources and healthier economic performance would be more readily achieved.

Being a critical pillar of China's financial system and primary financier of the real economy, the banking sector had always been overburdened with policy loans throughout the pre- and post-reform decades, a direct result of the nationwide strategy to prioritize the development of the state-controlled industrial sector. Furthermore, in order to support the smooth and gradual restructuring of the SOEs, banks had to furnish sufficient capital to them whenever requested; but as to the repayment, it was seldom strictly enforced. In most cases, they did not enjoy the autonomy to base their lending decisions on profitability until very recently. To a large extent, it is this institutional feature which weakened the ability of banks to discern in which conditions their apportionment of loans would be beneficial (Song, 2009). Therefore, when preference was heavily weighted towards funding the feeble SOEs instead of profitable business entities which had a greater potential, the impact on these banks was not merely reflected in their disappointing balance sheet, but lost efficiency as well. From a long-term perspective, such a situation could not last and the Chinese banking sector was in need of reform so as to resume its vibrancy. More significantly, a well-functioning banking institution could also strengthen the authorities' ability to exercise macroeconomic governance. To comprehensively understand the reformed financial system, a brief review of the banking sector prior to 1978 would be helpful.

2.5.1 A Retrospect of the Pre-1978 Period

As one of the fundamental tenets of socialism, every sector of the economy should be brought under direct government control through a central planning mechanism. Along with the centralization of all financial undertakings into a single institution, financial operations were made as simple as possible so that they could accommodate the central strategy for the entire economy. As China's ultimate decision-making body, the State Council was (and still is) responsible for orchestrating the nation's economic plans. Usually, after taking into consideration the regional and industrial priorities, the plan would outline output targets for different sectors, the allotment of resources to enterprises, and the evaluation of performance against the projected targets, etc. Then based on that, the Ministry of Finance (MOF) would draft a complementary yet unified national credit plan ('*tongshou tongzhi*') in which the credit funds to be allocated to regions and industries were detailed (Liu, 1981). By comparison, the credit plan was largely accommodating so as to make sure that the output targets of the broader economic plan would be ultimately fulfilled.

During the whole process, the banking sector had its own roles to play and as a matter of fact, after the foundation of the PRC in 1949, especially during the Cultural Revolution era (1966–1976), all financial institutions were either shut down or nationalized. The result was that between 1953 and 1978, the People's Bank of China (PBoC), which was government-owned and subordinate to the Ministry of Finance, served as the central as well as the sole commercial bank in charge of a wide scope of business, like the conduct of drafting monetary policies and exchange rate policies, managing foreign exchange reserves, taking deposits, as well as the financing of development projects, etc. Despite the existence of multiple other banks at the beginning of the 1950s, such as the Bank of China, the Bank of Communications, the Agricultural Bank of China, and various rural credit cooperatives, etc., they were all merged into the PBoC system and functioned merely as its branches before the end of the 1950s. Besides, in the execution of the national credit plan, what the PBoC did was to monitor enterprises and extend credit only when needed for the desired working capital and investments determined by the superior authorities. In other words, if enterprises and other economic entities wanted to receive grants and loans directly from the PBoC, it was not allowed. Although such kind of arrangement was supposed to make the supervision of enterprises' use of credit by the banking sector efficient and effective; in reality, the incentive for bank branches to encourage enterprises to economize on the use of loans, for example by speeding up the turnover of their loans, was rather weak or even virtually absent.

In addition, since decisions on capital allocation were taken without exception within the planning system, banking by nature was just to carry out the authorities' plans and responsible for the collection of savings from both households and enterprises. Under certain occasions, credit from the banking sector had to be expanded in case the physical targets in the central plan was set too high. Behind it, a general belief was that banking as a part of the service sector existed simply to serve the financial needs of enterprises. As long as a credit application could result in higher levels of production, the banking sector should not turn it down. Little attention was paid to whether such an increase in production, even though achievable, was necessary for the country or not. Under the centrally-planned financial system, enterprises (mainly the SOEs) at that time relied on two sources of funds: the state budget and the PBoC, with the former providing most of their needs (such as investment in fixed assets) and the latter the remainder, primarily in the form of low-interest working capital according to the national credit plan prepared by the State Planning Commission of the State Council (Fang, 1999). In turn, these enterprises would have their transactions settled through accounts with the Bank where they also had cash savings. It is fair to say that within a rigidly-operated framework, the PBoC did not have any degree of freedom in its lending business, all were set via administrative orders. In 1969, even the head office of the PBoC was merged with the MOF as its subordinate agency, making it a de facto comptroller and cashier for the government rather than a bank. Although the PBoC did issue bank notes (i.e. RMB), its chief function was to distribute funds according to government directives. In most cases, even this function was just supplementary because collection and distribution of funds were already included and handled by the central plans.

Obviously, the simplicity of the Chinese financial system before 1979 was conditioned by the fact that its banking activities were just a passive undertaking attached to central planning, and there were no such things as the money market or the capital market in operation. Furthermore, at the microeconomic level, few instruments were available with which banks could effectively exercise their supervisory functions. Indeed, even if they detected some inappropriate conduct of financial management on the part of enterprises, they couldn't do much except to alert the relevant authorities. At a time when allocation of funds and other financial resources were strictly subject to the mandatory plans of the central authorities, the conventional functions of the banking and financial system could not be brought into full play.

2.5.2 Formation of a Two-Tier Banking System

Calls for restoring the roles of the financial system emerged when the historical conference deciding on China's massive economic reform was held in the end of 1978, both the CPC and the central government decided to abolish the Soviet style mono-banking system. Generally, it is believed that the financial system should undertake two main functions. The first is to provide a medium of exchange and a store of value, or simply a payment mechanism, for the country. While currency can serve these purposes, when the size and the structure of an economy gets increasingly greater and more sophisticated, the financial system should satisfy the needs for other more complex means of payment so as to make economic transactions easier. Regarding the second function of the financial system, it is to mobilize savings from surplus units and channel the funds to productive investment. Here between savers and investors, the financial system acts like an intermediary using its professional skills and unparalleled access to information to manage assets for both parties in a more efficient manner. As a major move of China's financial reform, restructuring of the banking sector was placed high on the agenda. To ensure that the sector would be able to run in an effective way, banks themselves had to operate autonomously and independently. Similar to other enterprises or economic units, they should be held responsible for their own profits and losses.

With a view to transforming the PBoC from an all-inclusive state bank into a genuine central bank, actions started in 1979 when some of its commercial banking business was taken over by three independent and state-owned banks. First of all, the Agricultural Bank of China (ABC) was reestablished in February to serve the rural sector while at the same time to watch over a network of rural credit cooperatives. Then in March, the Bank of China (BOC) was separated from the PBoC and given the mandate to specialize in foreign exchange and settlement of cross-border transactions. Due to historical reasons, the BOC is until today still the dominant foreign-exchange bank and has the leading position in foreign-trade settlement and other relevant business in China, despite the ending of its exclusive rights to handle foreign exchange in 1984 when other specialized banks were granted the same rights (for example, Shenzhen Branch of the ICBC was the first bank receiving the permit in June that year). In fact, none of the specialized banks today are confined to their originally designated range of activities. In August 1979, the third bank, i.e. the People's Construction Bank of China (PCBC, renamed the Construction Bank of China in 1996) was separated from the MOF to finance manufacturing and infrastructure projects. In September 1983, with the approval of the State Council, the PBoC formally departed the Ministry of Finance and became a separate entity engaging in the functions of a central bank only. As to the fourth state-owned commercial bank, i.e. the Industrial and Commercial Bank of China (ICBC), it was set up in 1984 to handle urban deposit and lending business for both individual and institutional customers. Later on, given their prominence in China's banking sector, these four national commercial banks are collectively nicknamed the "Big Four".

Since this organizational change separated the operation of loaning from that of the control of credit and issue of currency, the banks which enterprises dealt with no longer had the power to print money. Thus, the ability of specialized banks to meet whatever demands enterprises placed upon them was somewhat limited if compared to the previous system. But despite the limitation, since the "Big Four" were also permitted to branch out into non-traditional areas of service such as housing loans, consumer credit and trust business, etc., they were in a better position to meet the needs of both individual and institutional customers. Following the removal of commercial functions from the PBoC, an elaborate and more sophisticated two-tier banking structure came into being, which could be taken as the first milestone in the modernization of the Chinese financial system (Song, 2009). This two-tier banking structure did allow some competition on the liabilities side, since banks were entitled to raise deposits from the public. From the perspective of the PBoC, by divesting its non-core business, it could focus on the functions associated with a genuine (but not independent) central bank, like setting the national credit plan, managing currency issues, and fixing interest rates, etc. In addition, it could also play a supervisory role overseeing the entire financial system as well as institutions operating in the economy, and act as the lender of the last resort.

While changes were taking place within the *central bureaucracy, local governments were on the move as well. From 1979 onward, more and more non-deposit taking financial institutions, primarily trust and investment companies (TICs), were established in diverse localities.* In general, they consisted of two broad types. One was international-oriented known as the ITICs, of which the best known is China International Trust and Investment Corporation (CITIC). Formed under the direct supervision of the State Council in October 1979, it quickly assumed its major role as a type of merchant and investment banking institution in China's endeavor of opening to the outside world. Through identifying relevant projects and potential investors, it helped with fund raising in the international capital markets. Modeled after CITIC, more ITICs have been founded by both provincial governments (like *Jiangsu*, Hubei, Hebei, and Guangdong, etc.) and municipalities (such as Guangzhou, Shanghai and Tianjin) since 1980. Referring to the second type, it was domestically oriented specializing in long-term investments financed by shareholders' funds or from the sale of bonds. In the beginning, they were mostly affiliated to the state-owned banks, but later they asserted independence in handling trust business under the sponsorship of either provincial or local governments. Within just three years of development, the number of TICs in China exceeded 620 in the end of 1982 (Geng, 2001). Their rapid expansion was partly due to the fact that by comparing to the interest rates of the state-owned banks, the PBoC in 1982 allowed TICs to add a 20 PCT floating band on the authorized rates when absorbing funds or granting loans (Shao, 1994). More importantly, with the privilege of channeling funds from foreign sources, they enabled domestic enterprises to more easily access capital which would otherwise be hardly available from the state-controlled banking system. In this capacity, no wonder ITICs were taken as the primary source for most international bond borrowings of China during the 1980s. Along with the trust and investment companies, there was also a spread of rural and urban credit cooperatives servicing households and small-scale enterprises, they in general operated under the supervision of ABC and ICBC respectively.

Before 1978 when China's SOEs relied almost exclusively on budgetary financing, it is the Ministry of Finance which was charged with the responsibility of allocating investment and operating capital to these ventures. Between the two sides, the People's Bank of China acted like an intermediary for the transfer of funds. Since in most cases, direct disbursement by the state did not have to be paid back, enterprises only had to calculate the opportunity cost when they used the funds to purchase assets. But as China's economic reform gradually gained momentum, the leadership intended to establish a positive price for capital by requiring that enterprises pay a fixed percentage of capital charge on the value of the state-supplied assets they possessed (Wu, 1981), and that future state investments would be made in the form of interest-bearing loans. Based on a 1979 directive by the State Council, the provision of investment funds started to shift away from the government budget toward loans via the banking system, subject to interest rates and repayment of the principal.

Named '*bo gai dai*' (replacing budgets with loans), the scheme was experimented in the initial two years in Beijing, Shanghai and Guangdong Province before entering into a *full-fledged implementation.* Accordingly, both the PBoC and specialized banks gained the permit to extend medium or even long-term loans (five to ten years). For enterprises, it implies that from then on, the major portion of capital would come in the form of credit rather than direct grant. On the one hand, this new policy increased government revenues since it would no longer invest for free; however, it added to the burden of enterprises, some of them even faced severe shortage of cash flow and thereby were unable to carry out production in a smooth way.

2.5.3 Progress and Problems

The first five years (1979–1983) of China's financial reform can be characterized by the formation of the two-tier banking system, with the establishment of the central bank and specialized banks, plus a major development in the non-banking sector, i.e. the emergence of numerous financial institutions including trust and investment corporations and rural and urban credit cooperatives. It is a period which witnessed a massive dispersion of financial resources away from the direct control of the central planners and financial authorities into the hands of local governments, enterprises, and households. In particular, the system became more diversified with the introduction of certain commercial practices, like the more flexible use of interest rates, more systematic accounting procedures, and some limited competition for deposits, especially among the non-bank institutions, etc.

Despite these encouraging changes, however, the undeniable fact is that the financial system remained, directly or indirectly, a state monopoly managed within an administrative framework. Whereas it is true that interest rates were used in a more flexible way, they were still set primarily by the central financial planners instead of the market forces. Regarding the banking sector, it continued to serve as an arm of the economic planning system and was thus expected to implement sectoral plan objectives through policy loans at preferential rates (the same could be said of the mushrooming TICs sponsored by local governments). Even though the increase in the number of banks did trigger certain competition for deposits, lending business remained relatively intact since each specialized bank was supposed to operate within its own sectoral terrain ('*hang ye*'). Indeed, for a planned economy to shift into a market-oriented economy, tremendous tasks were involved, not only in changing the ways of doing things, but in altering the styles of thinking as well. In most cases, the latter is much more challenging and crucial. Back to the financial reform of China, a top-down ideological renewal of mind was of course imperative; simultaneously, issues like commercialization of state banks, opening the financial sector for foreign competition, and development of financial markets should also be addressed seriously so as to guarantee macroeconomic stability and efficiency.

2.6 Centralization-Decentralization Cycle of the Fiscal System

Fiscal policies, which include both revenue collection and spending by the government, can exercise a profound impact on economic development. In general, it has three major functions. To begin with, it determines the way taxes are raised and the direction in which funds are allocated. As to the latter, it often takes the form of a national budget specifying how much is to be set aside for which purpose(s). Besides, given the cyclical nature of the market, good times are often succeeded by bad times. Therefore, to avoid instability and recession, unrestrained growth can be effectively suppressed using contractionary or austerity measures. Thirdly, by selecting and funding the key projects of diverse sectors, engines that fuel the economy could remain constantly powerful.

2.6.1 The Necessity to Initiate the Reform

Looking back at the evolution of China's fiscal policy since 1949, it has been intertwined with the theme of centralization and decentralization. In the very beginning, the newly constituted regime viewed the rehabilitation of the war-torn economy and rapid industrial development as its primary objectives. Throughout the first Five-Year Plan (1953–1957) in particular, the establishment of a comprehensive range of heavy industries was put in a paramount position, with its investment accounted for 85 PCT of the sum of industrial infrastructure and 72.9 PCT of the overall investment in agricultural and industrial infrastructure (Chen & Wu, 2009). As a matter of fact, the resolve to prioritize heavy industries was rather incompatible with China's endowment structure, which was characterized by an absolute scarcity in capital. Additionally, being a closed economy unwilling to receive financial assistance from the outside world (with the exception of Soviet Union and a number of socialist countries in Europe), it became even harder for the policymakers to materialize their ambitions.

Therefore, it is not hard to understand that in order to carry out the capital-intensive industrialization, a highly centralized fiscal system named "unified revenue and unified expenditure" (*'tongshou tongzhi'*) was established in 1950. Under this system, it is the Ministry of Finance which claimed the absolute authority in determining local revenue and expenditure plans on an annual basis. While revenues were collected by the local governments, they should all be accrued to the center (Xing, 1982a, 1982b). Apparently, this consolidated budget system denied the discretionary spending power of local governments, they even did not have independent budgets because their budgets were formulated and monitored item by item by the central government. Considering that local finance came from the central budget, intergovernmental transfers were set to finance the balance between locally collected revenues and permitted local expenditures. In case of a regional surplus income after covering the expenses due, it should still be submitted to the central government so that the gaps incurred elsewhere could be made up accordingly (Shen, 2012).

To a certain degree, such a top-down approach to policy decisions had its own merits. By ensuring that capital mobilization and allocation could happen in an uninterruptible way, it facilitated the building of a large industrial base and the ultimate accomplishment of the first Five Year Plan. Nonetheless, in a country whose scale of production was expanding quickly, the tasks to formulate, implement and coordinate the plans were extremely strenuous for the central planning and finance organs. Furthermore, in the absence of sufficient incentives and flexibility, it was rather impractical to expect the local governments to fully cooperate in the management of these industrial projects. As a major initiative to improve the situation, the unified fiscal management system was altered in 1953 into a three-level managed fiscal system consisting of a central budget, provincial/municipal budget, and county budget, with each one having its own revenues and expenditures (Jiang, 2011). To some degree, the first round of decentralization enlarged the decision-making power of local governments, but their share in the total fiscal revenues was rather small, which implies that the room left for them to maneuver their own revenues and expenditures was still limited (Jiang, 2015).

2.6.2 The Second Round: A Broadened Sharing Scheme

By 1956 when there was a critical reassessment of the performance of Soviet economic model during the first Five-Year Plan (in preparation for the 8th National Congress of the Communist Party of China which would take place later that year), a consensus was reached among the central leaders that the Soviet model had been somewhat over-centralized and could not provide effective incentives to motivate the local governments, nor enterprises (Wu, 1996). Therefore, something should be done about it. This time, the fiscal reform (the second round) was coordinated with the reform of both industrial and commercial systems according to the three inter-related directives issued by the State Council in November 1957, they were: the "Regulations on the Improvement of the Fiscal Management System", the "Regulations on the Improvement of Industrial Management", and the "Regulations on the Improvement of Commercial Management". What these three circulars had in common is the enlargement of decision-making power of the local governments; in particular, they were delegated the jurisdiction of nearly all the SOEs (only except for some special central enterprises). Since beforehand, enterprise finance had been closely tied to public finance under a command economy, transfer of control to the lower level implies a major increase in the weight of the local budgets.

Additionally, there was also a decrease in the tax collected by the central government and a broadened revenue-sharing scheme that covered three years (extended to five years from 1958). As compared to the former system in which revenues retained by each province/municipality were determined by the level of expenditures to underwrite the centrally-approved provincial/municipal economic plan ('*yizhi dingshou*') and in which revenue-sharing rates were adjusted annually; the new one adopted a reversed principle, i.e. expenditures were to be determined by revenues, and the revenue-sharing rates would remain valid for five years once fixed (‘*yishou dingzhi, wunian bubian*’). This meant that each province/municipality no longer had to bargain with the center for annual expenditure increases. As long as revenues grew over time, they would automatically receive a proportionate share of increase.

With the encouragement of these decentralizing measures, lower-level governments demonstrated tremendous enthusiasm in setting up enterprises since the profits generated would go straight to their revenues. Indeed, by weakening the control of the central government, the reform enhanced the authority that the local governments could possess, which led to an accelerated pace of the economy. As an immediate effect of this round of decentralization, the sub-national fiscal revenue to the nation’s total soared from 19.6 PCT in 1958 to 75.6 PCT in 1959, suggesting that the proportional share of the center experienced a plunge, from 80.4 PCT to 24.4 PCT over the same period. Nevertheless, this seemingly positive effect also caused an over-rapid pace of investment by different regions. Consequently, inefficient duplication of construction dragged the country into a budget deficit amounting to almost RMB14.82 billion in total from 1958 to 1961. Coupled with the failure of the Great Leap Forward (1958–1961), leaders in Beijing adopted a series of recentralization measures covering finance, enterprise administration, and credit, etc. Starting from 1961, all the large and medium-sized industrial enterprises were once again subordinated to the central authority, and the move pushed up the share of central revenue from 21.5 PCT of the country’s total to 35.2 PCT by 1966. Yet very soon, the outbreak of the Cultural Revolution disrupted all realms of social life, which remained in a state of chaos, particularly from 1967 to 1969.

2.6.3 Reflections on the Third Round Reform

Aware of the disastrous effect the Cultural Revolution had brought to the nation, including the contraction in the national revenue from RMB55.9 billion of 1966 to RMB36.1 billion in 1968, the leadership decided to take immediate actions to make up for the huge losses. It was under these circumstances that the third round of fiscal decentralization began, it started in 1970 and had some similar features like the previous one. For example, most large-scale SOEs were again delegated to the provincial and municipal governments (Xu, 2009); together with this, there was also a shift of most revenue sources and expenditure categories. As long as the lower-level governments had transferred a lump sum to the center according to the annual sharing agreement, all the remaining revenues were at their disposal. Unfortunately, because of the strengthened budgetary authority and broadened sources of funds, the same investment fever reemerged, resulting in an irrational industrial structure and continuous fiscal deficit totaling RMB4.2 billion from 1974 to 1976. For lack of a better solution, the central government had to recall the power, signaling that the cycle of re-centralization was under way. Thus, due to its failure to learn from the past lessons, China was stuck into a constant dizzy cycle, i.e. relaxation of control would almost without exception be accompanied by disorder; then recentralization, although to some degree helpful to the restoration of stability, could easily turn into another state of indifference. Between revenue and expenditure, power and responsibility, there was no institutionalized link that can balance the two.

By and large, China's development strategy prior to 1978 was very much oriented to the heavy industry, but given the incompatibility between the capital-intensive undertaking and the country's weaknesses in endowment, a highly-centralized allocation of resources, especially fiscal, was perhaps the only feasible alternative since the latter was the major financial channel for China to fund its industrialization. However, to tackle the subsequent headache of low efficiency, the government resorted to both fiscal and administrative decentralization without changing its development strategy and the planned system. In other words, only the symptom was treated, not the disease itself. Inevitably, this gave rise to more complicated problems like the building of redundant projects, imbalance in industrial structure, and widened capital gap, etc., which compelled the planners to turn back and centralize powers. This dilemma of centralization and decentralization indicates that if the design of a country's development strategy could not match its comparative advantages, no approach would fundamentally resolve the challenges that are set to arise.

2.6.4 "Eating from Separate Stoves"

Throughout the period when the command system dominated the economic landscape of China, there was almost no interplay of market forces and therefore no self-correcting mechanism to prevent things from getting worse. Revenues and expenditures were adopted simply as instruments of control to help implement the central policies. However, towards the end of the 1970s, there were signs of change indicating that such a rigid regime could no longer work well. In fact, more and more commercial activities were already in the forefront of being market-oriented, a trend which would soon permeate other spheres of the economy. Obviously, the once effective plan coordination was neither adequate nor consistent with the movement, which prompted a deeper reform in the fiscal domain. During 1976 and 1977, the proposal of revenue-sharing arrangements was put forward by several provinces to further expand their fiscal autonomy and Jiangsu, an economically developed coastal province, was selected to carry out the experiment. Under the so-called "fixed-rate responsibility system" ('*guding bili baogan*'), total provincial revenues were split between the center and the province, with Jiangsu's share set at 42PCT when the scheme started in 1977 (from 1978, it was adjusted to 39PCT). Regarding the expenditures, it was no longer the Ministry of Finance, but the province itself which would take decisions. The pilot turned out to be a success in that by 1980, Jiangsu's fiscal revenues hit aomost RMB6.25 billion, an increase of 42 PCT over that of 1976, which registered RMB4.4 billion (Jiang, 2010).

The experiment of Jiangsu province was soon echoed by a path-breaking move in February 1980 when the State Council issued the "Provisional Regulations on Implementing the Financial Management System of Apportioning Revenues and Expenditures while Contracting Responsibility at Multiple Levels". Picturesquely described as “division of the stove from which people eat” (‘*fenzao chifan*’), the new tax system involved three major categories of revenue: fixed revenue (the tax of centrally-controlled enterprises and customs duties belonged to the central fixed revenue whereas the tax of locally-controlled enterprises, *salt tax*, *agriculture tax*, *animal husbandry tax*, and other minor taxes were classified as local fixed revenues), fixed proportional revenue (the tax of local enterprises under direct central administration, with a shared ratio of 80/20 between the central and local governments), and adjustment revenue (local industrial and commercial tax). If local fixed revenue and fixed proportional revenue exceeded local expenditures, then a certain proportion of the surplus would be handed over to the central government; otherwise, adjustment revenue could be used by the local governments to offset the deficit. In case adjustment revenue still failed to cover expenditures, the center would provide subsidies.

In principle, this fiscal contracting system (FCS or tax-sharing system) required each level of government to contract with the next level up in order to meet certain revenue and expenditure targets; and ultimately, it was subject to the approval of the Ministry of Finance and the State Council. Once an agreement was finalized, especially concerning the sharing rate and the amount of subsidies, it would remain unchanged for five years. Considering that from then on, sub-national governments had to finance their own expenditures through self-generated and shared revenues, the FCS marked a step in the direction of hardening the budget constraint on local governments. In addition, the strategy of laying more weight on the financial interest of localities boosted the construction of nonproductive infrastructures, such as telecommunication, transport, and housing, etc., which had long been ignored due to the preference to the nationwide industrial expansion and could more immediately benefit the general public. Undoubtedly, the new fiscal formula did provide the local governments with greater incentives to collect tax revenues and develop local economies. Sometimes, there were even conflicts when Beijing tried to restrict the production of certain items by increasing the tax rates, local officials did the opposite because this would enable them to amass more earnings. Indeed, it is not hard to understand their behaviors, especially given the fact that China was at that time still a shortage economy, having more money was considered equivalent to a greater chance to access the needed materials and resources.

Simultaneously, other policies like enlargement of enterprise autonomy and promotion of export triggered the expansionary trend, resulting in a surge of gross industrial output by 16.3 PCT in 1984 and 21.4 PCT in 1985 (NBS, 1999). Over these two years, the total investment in fixed assets by the state sector displayed a more explosive growth, which hit 24.5 PCT and 41.8 PCT respectively. No matter where, such a phenomenon could not be taken for granted, it warned that inflation and overheated economy were right around the corner (in 1985, China’s retail price rose by 8.8 PCT, as compared to 2.8 PCT in 1984). What’s more, now that local officials had a direct stake in the local industry, to make sure that profits would not be squeezed by rivals from outside, competition was inhibited as a result of rampant protectionism and regional favoritism, resulting in increasing fragmentation of the domestic market, high level of redundant input, and unbalanced industrial distribution, etc. (Chen, 1997).

In addition to the above, there was yet another negative effect of the tax-sharing scheme. With the dispersal of fiscal power downwards, some local officials arbitrarily cut tax rates for enterprises or simply granted them exemption so as to lower down the revenues to the central budget; then they would apportion some government expenditures to these enterprises to draw the money back (Zhao, 2009). Or on certain occasions, with a view to attracting foreign direct investment, the local tax rates were slashed. The center was not unaware of these misconduct, in fact, various instruments had been adopted to ensure that the revenues due could be remitted without hindrance from the local authorities. But, these instruments often led to more tricky and perverse reactions from the lower since with the power of tax collection in hand, sub-national governments knew how to strategically evade sharing revenues with the center. As listed in Table 2 below, over a 10-year period from 1980 to 1989, the share of the central government revenues in China's total kept increasing against that of the local in the initial period. But ever since 1985, there has been a steady decline in its portion vis-à-vis that of the local in total revenues, implying at least partially that the central government lacked effective supervision of tax collections and remittances by the local governments, which in turn left loopholes for the system to be abused.

With the adoption of the fiscal contracting system, the Chinese policymakers aimed to replace the old practice of "eating from one single stove" ('*chi daguofan*'). Behind it, their motive is very clear, i.e. by offering the local governments sufficient incentives to maximize revenues, the national fiscal cake could become bigger, which would automatically enlarge the size of the center's own slice. In this consideration,

Table 2 Division of the central and local revenues, 1980–1989

Year	Total revenues (RMB 100 million)	Central revenues and share in the total		Local revenues and share in the total	
		(RMB 100 million)	(PCT)[1]	(RMB 100 million)	(PCT)[2]
1980	1,159.93	284.45	24.5	875.48	75.5
1981	1,175.79	311.07	26.5	864.72	73.5
1982	1,212.33	346.84	28.6	865.49	71.4
1983	1,366.95	490.01	35.8	876.94	64.2
1984	1,642.86	665.47	40.5	977.39	59.5
1985	2,004.82	769.63	38.4	1,235.19	61.6
1986	2,122.01	778.42	36.7	1,343.59	63.3
1987	2,199.35	736.29	33.5	1,463.06	66.5
1988	2,357.24	774.76	32.9	1,582.48	67.1
1989	2,664.9	822.52	30.9	1,842.38	69.1

Note [1] and [2]Calculated by the author
Source NBS (2000)

decentralization should not be taken as a free gift from the central government; rather, it was a trade-off between obligations and rewards for both the state and the local. Under certain conditions, it was even inclusive of some conflict of interests. Most prominently, with the local governments being devolved more fiscal power, the share of resources directly controlled by the central government declined. Thereby, unlike the previous decades, it could no longer monopolize investment, which is also the most important macro-economic mechanism they could employ. Similar to a chain reaction, its capacity to promote the development of particular regions or industries was weakened as well. Confronting the dilemma in the second half of the 1980s, the challenge for the state was how to balance power and authority productively so that the reformed fiscal regime could better assist subordinate governments and business entities to develop economy in a more harmonious manner. Obviously, the way ahead is still long.

2.7 Internationalization via SEZs

The economic renovation conducted by China in the years of 1979–1983 was a presentation of the ability as well as the determination of the country to re-orient its development strategies. By looking at the history of other nations which have passed the transition stage, it may be noticed that foreign capital is without exception adopted as an important catalyst to propel a more robust momentum of growth. The rationale behind is not just because that foreign investors could provide the much needed funds; in addition, they often bring in advanced technologies and efficient management models through which the host countries may facilitate the progress of industrialization. Then through a series of push and pull effect, influence from the outside would ultimately give birth to a more dynamic economy.

China followed a similar path. Before 1978, the Chinese economy was virtually an autarky since by then, the overriding philosophy firmly held by its leadership was self-reliance and self-sufficiency. After Deng Xiaoping returned to power in July 1977, he demonstrated a fundamentally different way of thinking. Contrary to the majority of his predecessors, he valued the role of the market and favored the opportunities that would arise once the country was open to the outside. In fact, the concept of Deng was not totally new, but was based on the program of "Four Modernizations" by Premier Zhou Enlai. Early in 1964 when Zhou gave a report on government work to the Third National People's Congress, he for the first time called for the modernization of agriculture, industry, national defense, and science and technology by the end of the twentieth century. In addition, to bring China to the forefront of the world economy, Zhou also advocated the use of foreign technologies. Similar to Zhou Enlai, Deng Xiaoping believed that the opening up of China, especially to the West and other developed countries, was a necessary move to speed up its economic growth and stimulate the advancement in science and technologies. Thus ever since 1978, with a view to increasing its foreign trade, attracting direct investment, and soliciting assistance from international organizations, China has become more and more active in the global market.

2.7.1 Emergence and Materialization of the Idea

In general, a special economic zone (SEZ) can be described as a particular geographic area within a nation where certain economic activities are encouraged by a series of preferential measures not equally applied to the rest of the country. Institutionally, the existence of SEZs is reflective of the fact that the government conducts its economic policies in a manner that enables certain regions of the country to enjoy greater advantages over others. For China, the initiative to set up SEZs was an incremental process which could only happen on the condition that it was determined to reform economically. Otherwise, it would be unimaginable for a socialist country to even think about using SEZs as a "window" to widely absorb technologies and investment from capitalist countries. Moreover, taking the decision of opening up as a national policy is one thing, having it carried out successfully is another. Much effort is to be devoted in shaping the overall agenda and in this regard, no readily available prescription could be 100PCT transplanted. On the internal side, China's own experiences could hardly offer much help to the policy-makers either. In fact, the kind of economic reform envisioned at the turn of the decade required them to move with daring steps instead of making minor adjustment of the existing mechanisms like before. Obviously, what they needed were those unconventional yet outward-looking practices that could bring about the desired effects in an efficient way without incurring unbearable political, economic and social costs. From this perspective, conducting some experiments by extending the *privilege* to *certain areas* in the country and see how they would work out appeared more pragmatic to the Chinese leaders. But given China's vast territory, where should the laboratory be located?

In terms of geographical locations, Guangdong enjoys a special superiority as compared to other provinces because it is adjacent to Hong Kong and Macao. Referring to its residents, quite many of their family members or relatives are living overseas. Aware of Guangdong's closest, widest and the most convenient connections with the outside world, and encouraged by the Third Plenum's strategy focusing on the reform and acceleration of economic construction, its provincial Party Committee made a decision in January 1979 to raise the administrative status of Bao-an (officially renamed Shenzhen in that March) and Zhuhai from county to municipality in order to establish assembly-and-processing bases and promote foreign trade (Cui, 2016).

While Guangdong's leaders were contemplating how to map an export-driven economy, there were also some other people who shared a similar concern. Yuan Geng, the standing vice chairman of China Merchants Group (CMG, founded in 1872 with China Merchants Steam Navigation Company being its predecessor, is the first Chinese-owned shipping company headquartered in Hong Kong, a direct subsidiary of the Transport Ministry), had been seeking the possibility of building an industrial zone in Bao-an (Yuan Geng's hometown) to branch out into activities beyond the traditional business scope of CMG. In December 1978, Yuan talked over his idea with Ye Fei, the Minister of Transport, who was in Hong Kong on his investigation trip back from Western Europe and obtained full support from Ye (Tu, 2009). Very soon, the proposal that CMG was to set up an industrial zone in Bao-an was echoed by the leaders of Guangdong Province. After several rounds of meetings and field surveys, the two sides (Guangdong authority and the Ministry of Transport) jointly submitted a report to the State Council on Jan. 10th, 1979, which formally put forward a request to establish an industrial zone in Shekou, an area at the tip of Nantou Peninsula in Bao-an (Shenzhen). Not long after, an important meeting to discuss the joint report was held on Jan. 31st in Zhong Nanhai (the central headquarters of the Communist Party of China and the State Council in Beijing). It was presided over by the vice Chairman Li Xiannian and joined by Gu Mu (the Deputy Premier in charge of economy and foreign trade), Peng Deqing (the Deputy Minister of Transport) and Yuan Geng. When Yuan Geng finished his introduction about the plan and asked Li Xiannian to grant a small piece of land for the construction of the zone, Li not only confirmed the necessity; to the surprise of Yuan, he agreed to give the whole peninsula of Nantou to CMG for its industrial project and it covered 30 square kilometers. In fact, on the mind of pro-reform leaders like Li Xiannian and Deng Xiaoping, not only Guangdong, the entire coastal region of China including Fujian Province and Shanghai should also consider the same strategy of marking off certain areas to develop outward-oriented economy. Therefore, they regarded Bao-an county as just a beginning, a breakthrough.

2.7.2 Formation of the Four SEZs and Its Effects

On July 15th, 1979, as part of China's commitment to the policy of opening-up, the State Council and the Central Committee of the CPC jointly issued a directive allowing two southern provinces of Guangdong and Fujian to practice special policies and employ flexible measures in foreign economic and trade issues. This was the well-known Central Document No. 50, which also signaled the rising of China's SEZs. While delegating the local authorities greater autonomy to enable them to move one step ahead and strive for a more remarkable pattern of economic development, the directive approved an experiment of special economic zones in four cities, with Shenzhen and Zhuhai (both belong to Guangdong Province) taking the initiative before expanding to Shantou (Guangdong Province) and Xiamen (Fujian Province). Only five days later, i.e. on July 20th, 1979, Shekou (in Shenzhen) Industrial Zone formally started its construction and not longer after, it was integrated into Shenzhen SEZ. By November 1981, with Shantou SEZ breaking ground, all the SEZs in the initial batch were fully under way.

While both functionally diverse in activities and services, the four SEZs can still be roughly grouped into two categories in terms of their initial situations. With regard to Xiamen and Shantou, since they were relatively better developed cities with their own industrial base, only a part of the city area was transformed into an SEZ. By contrast, considering that Zhuhai and Shenzhen were just small towns when the SEZs were established, they were planned as comprehensive zones so that all the facilities and characteristics of a modern city could be developed. Although in other parts of the world, SEZs and its variants such as export-processing zones, industrial parks, and free trade areas, etc. are not uncommon, the segregation of specific regions to attract foreign direct investment with preferential treatments was indeed an unprecedented trial in China's history. Located along the South China coast which is remote from Beijing the power center and can thus circumvent a lot of political interferences, these four economic zones are also in close proximity to the much more advanced Hong Kong, Macau, and Taiwan, thus enabling them to have an easier access to the resources from these neighbors, like capital, information, technology, and management know-how, etc. As indicated earlier, launching these four SEZs was by no means a onetime plan of policy makers; instead, via the four specially designated zones, they tried to test some bold and controversial approaches on administrative system, entrepreneurship, finance and employment matters which, if proved fruitful, would be applied further to other parts of the country.

Serving as a "bridge" through which the domestic economy can be linked with the rest of the world, a variety of industries in the SEZs were open to foreign investors, including processing and manufacturing, services (banking, real estate, hospitality and tourism), agriculture, as well as infrastructural facilities, etc. (Li, 1990). Besides, domestic enterprises, either state-owned or non-state-owned, were allowed to do business there alongside firms funded by foreign capital. Moreover, all the ventures in the zones were encouraged to set up connections with their domestic counterparts in order to foster technology transfers and promote growth through expanded economic links. In order to develop an outward-oriented economy, boosting foreign trade has always been a central task of the SEZs, which necessitated the absorption of foreign investment, a dominant source of the capital and technologies in need. As part of the incentive packages, the corporate income tax levied on foreign-funded firms was set at 15 PCT, far below the 30 PCT rate imposed on joint ventures outside the zones. For those manufacturing enterprises whose operations in the zone were over 10 years, beginning in the first year in which profits were earned, there was an extra benefit of "2 + 3 years", meaning zero tax for year one and year two, then tax at a low rate of 7.5 PCT from the third to the fifth year (Zhu, 2006). Similar tax exemptions were also available to firms in the service sector, especially in the initial years before profit could be realized. Moreover, since most of these firms were engaged in foreign trade, tariffs on import and export goods were generally slashed or even exempted. Apart from various tax concessions, the organizational structure in the SEZs was leaner, with bureaucratic procedures simplified to ensure efficient administration and effective governance.

These approaches, plus the relatively cheaper rental rates of land and production facilities, as well as some flexible employment arrangements, have resulted in a number of immediate gains. On the one hand, China witnessed an increased inflow of foreign capital which was often accompanied by the establishment of new ventures; besides, there was also a boom in the country's export and import. Take Shenzhen, the largest SEZ, as an example. Prior to the reform of 1978, it was just an obscure and

Table 3 FDI, export and GDP of Shenzhen, 1979–1983

Year	Foreign capital actually used (USD million)	Export (USD million)	GDP (RMB100 million)
1979	5.48	9.3	1.96
1980	27.55	11.24	2.7
1981	86.18	17.45	4.96
1982	57.71	15.97	8.26
1983	113.16	62.3	13.12

Source SMBS (2010)

technologically-backward border county, with no industrial base nor encouraging potential for impressive economic development. At that time, the only attractiveness Shenzhen had in possession was perhaps its geographical location, including the closeness to Hong Kong and direct link to the international trading routes. However, after being granted the green light to set up SEZ, absorption of overseas funds was accorded its top priority. Based on the statistics below (Table 3), from 1979 to 1983, the city totally received more than USD290 million in foreign direct investment, through which it benefited a lot from the innovation spillover effect across boundaries. By gradually transforming its comparative advantage from low-cost labor to advanced technologies, Shenzhen was in a stronger position to promote its export, which in turn led to a GDP growth of almost six times over this five-year period.

While Shenzhen was moving forward with leaps and bounds, dramatic changes were simultaneously taking place in the other three SEZs. These chosen places, as a result, became the showcase of rapid transition in China's controlled economy. While it couldn't be denied that such selective approach to opening up inevitably created regional disparities, or creeping inequalities, given the vastness of Chinese territory and the enormousness of the Chinese population, having some regions or provinces that went ahead of others is perhaps a stage the country had to go through in order to propel the overall economic growth more efficiently.

2.8 Dual-Track System of Managing the Exchange Rates

In China, *Renminbi* (RMB, or the people's money) acts as the official *currency* and legal tender while the *yuan* is taken as the base *accounting unit*. Unlike other currencies which can respond quickly to the changes in market supply and demand, the yuan had remained rather static in a country virtually closed to the outside world since 1949. By the time the comprehensive scheme of economic reform kicked off in 1978, the dominant portion of China's economy was operated by using the yuan exclusively. This is in fact associated with the state monopoly over foreign trade, under which all the contracts with foreign firms could only be signed by a limited number (within the range of twelve and fifteen) of authorized import and export corporations. Furthermore, in pursuit of the goal of self-sufficiency, export was simply undertaken to earn foreign money to pay for imports, and imports in turn, were to serve the broader scheme of industrialization.

2.8.1 A Once Rigidly-Controlled Regime

As a result of the obsession with independence, the yuan was intentionally overvalued since this could enable the government to provide strategic imports (such as steel, machinery, and equipment, etc.) at a relatively lower cost than otherwise would have been possible. However, the overvalued yuan had also led to an excess demand for foreign exchange, and intractable losses for Chinese exports. In 1953, the year when nationalization of the financial sector was almost completed, the Bank of China (BOC, by then a department of the People's Bank of China) was mandated to act as a specialized bank representing the government to exercise foreign exchange control (Mu, 2011). In principle, all foreign exchange earnings by exporters were to be sold to the bank unless prior approval had been obtained. Additionally, when they were in need of foreign exchange, they still had to purchase from the BOC, which would allocate strictly according to the priorities set by the state plan. If these enterprises suffered losses in currency swap, the government would have it covered through national budget; but in case profits arose, they had to surrender to the government in tax. With such a centralized accounting mechanism, fluctuations in official exchange rates had become almost meaningless in the sense that they would simply redistribute financial profits and losses among different import and export companies and thus would not affect the overall balance of trade.

Starting from 1955, a fixed exchange rate regime was adopted in China and for about sixteen years until 1971, the exchange rate of RMB to USD was fundamentally fixed at RMB2.4618 each dollar. Amid the collapse of the Bretton Woods System, the rate revalued to RMB2.2673 on Dec. 18th, 1971 when the dollar fell by 7.89 PCT against gold (Han, 2009). After then, with the floating exchange rate adopted by most countries, China began to implement a relatively more flexible rate pricing system in order to fence off the exchange risks of its export income. Beginning from 1973, China pegged the RMB exchange rate to a basket of currencies, thus making it more closely reflective of the ups and downs in the international financial market.

2.8.2 Foreign Exchange Retention Scheme

Since 1979, the evolution of China's exchange rate regime has demonstrated a higher degree of flexibility when basket pegging gradually gave way to managed flotation. In this regard, the most important move to a market-determined exchange rate was the relaxed control over foreign trade. In 1979, following the establishment of the State Administration of Foreign Exchange (SAFE, an agency associated initially with the Bank of China and tasked with supervising the flow of foreign exchange), some industrial ministries were allowed to set up their own companies to directly import and export the goods produced by a network of factories under their jurisdictions. For instance, China National Aero-Technology Import and Export Corporation (CATIC) was founded in that year by the Ministry of Aviation Industry as a state-authorized dealer of aviation products and technologies (Zong, 1998). Meanwhile, the same permit was equally given to provinces and municipalities to establish trading companies to handle foreign trade in their respective regions. Ever since, the breakup of the state's monopoly became a positive act that injected new vitality into China's foreign trade system.

Apart from the decentralization of trading rights, the government in the same year introduced a foreign exchange retention scheme that enabled exporters, their provincial or local government owners, as well as industrial ministries to retain the privilege of buying back a certain proportion of foreign exchange revenues from the central authorities, of course on the condition that the actual foreign exchange had been sold to the latter at the official rate in the first place (Chen, 1990). Once they wanted to use their retained quota, they could spend the RMB to buy according to the prevailing rates, as long as the use fell within the confines of the regulation. As a matter of fact, the retention scheme adopted in 1979 was rather complex and on the basis of the sources of foreign exchange income, types of the goods exported, and the authorities in charge of export, etc., the government would assign different retention rates to the relevant parties, including the government agencies, trading companies and production entities. In 1979, the retention rate for exports handled by ministerial departments was 20 PCT of the earnings above the domestic procurement level achieved in 1978. Concerning the rate for exports under the jurisdiction of local governments, it was set at 40 PCT. As to the different types of trade, the retention rates also varied. For instance, if the exports contained imported material inputs, the retention ratio was 15 PCT of the net foreign exchange earnings; for fees received from processing and assembly of foreign components, 30 PCT could be retained, with 15 PCT distributed to the enterprises and the other half to the local governments.

2.8.3 Internal Settlement Rate, One More Export Incentive

Besides, the other major instrument used by the state to stimulate foreign trade was devaluation of the RMB. Given the overvalued official exchange rates and central government's reluctance to provide subsidies, many foreign trade companies found it difficult to sustain their export. Take 1979 as an example, the national average cost of earning one unit of foreign exchange was RMB2.41 each US dollar while the official exchange rate stayed at RMB1.555 per dollar (Yang, 2005). Given the gap between the two, the cost of many export goods could not be covered by the official rate, thus generating losses for exporters. Under general circumstances, it means that the more they sold, the greater losses they had to endure.

To alleviate the negative effects of currency overvaluation on exports, a dual-track system consisting of an official exchange rate (pegged to a basket of currencies) and an internal settlement rate (ISR, pegged to the US dollar) for foreign trade-related transactions was introduced from January 1st, 1981. The ISR was initially set at

RMB2.8 to one dollar, based on the average cost of generating one US dollar of foreign exchange earnings of 1978, which was RMB2.53, plus a 10 PCT profit margin. Then in line with the rising average cost of generating foreign exchange earnings, the exchange rates would be gradually adjusted downward so as to make export profitable. Therefore, the new rate, which was chiefly applied to foreign trade transactions, represented a depreciation of almost 100 PCT against the official rate of RMB1.5 to one dollar. The reason it was regarded a dual track system is because by then, non-trade deals such as overseas Chinese remittances, tourism, foreign investment, and foreign trade transport and insurance charges, etc. still had to use the official rate. Fairly speaking, since the introduction of the dual exchange rate system exhibited enhanced incentives for exporters, it increased the possibility of more flexible pricing for above-plan exports. Consequently, encouraged by a favorable swap rate, they were no longer that reluctant to sell goods in the international market.

During the initial phase (1978–1983) of economic reform, another sector was simultaneously going through changes and it was education. In particular, young people were encouraged to go abroad to renew their skills and knowledge, and to pursue higher degrees in various scientific and technical fields. This is a phenomenon rather critical to the success of the second-stage reform which may follow soon in the upcoming years. If compared to other countries undergoing transition from a planned economy, China had the luxury of initiating its reforms at a time when it faced no macroeconomic nor serious political crisis. As a result, fundamental changes reshaped the Chinese economic landscape, although many of them had not been foreseen by the government leaders nor reformist economists. By and large, the easing of central control over diverse business activities created a benign environment that enabled both the state and non-state sectors to grow and prosper. In other respects, however, certain conservative forces from the bureaucratic apparatus remained rather stubborn and hostile, which made the undertaking hard to proceed smoothly. Conflicts seemed inevitable, but the ongoing movement was set to continue.

3 New Wave of Reform (1984–1988)

Between 1978 and 1983, the Chinese economy experienced a period of rapid change. Most notably, there was a remarkable growth in agriculture and a steady development of industrial and non-agricultural production in rural areas. In terms of foreign trade, although the momentum of expansion was much less significant, it still managed to reverse from a deficit of USD1.14 billion in 1978 to a surplus totaled USD840 million in 1983. Regarding its fiscal revenues and expenditures, after going through five r*oller-coaster years,* a gap persisted at RMB4.26 billion by 1983, which imposed a rather immense burden on the economy (NBS, 1999). Bearing in mind the overa*ll* picture that combined both success and problems not yet fully addressed, the year 1984 marked a new starting point for the Chinese *l*eaders. On the one hand, the part of the economy subject to central planning remained to be further reduced; on the other hand, deeper reform of the industrial and urban sectors was compelling and should proceed more and more steadfastly.

3.1 The Price-Formation Mechanism

The most crucial component of the economic reform in China during the second half of the 1980s was its price reform. Ratified in October 1984, the "Decision of the Central Committee of the Communist Party of China on the Reform of the Economic Structure" gave a high priority to the establishment of a rational price system. If referring to those countries with a full market economy, it is price which plays a central role in guiding efficient distribution of commodities and ensuring optimized allocation of factors of production. Yet in terms of China, since price and quantity were both fixed by the state during the entire period of central planning between 1949 and 1978, they did not bear any particular relationship to the market equilibrium. Therefore, the price could be either below or above the market level without major shifts in supply and demand.

3.1.1 Price-Setting Regime in Early Times

After the PRC was established in 1949, the country's development strategy was very much heavy-industry biased. Given the fact that heavy industries were in general capital intensive whereas China at that time was still an agrarian society thirsty for capital, prices of agricultural products were suppressed at a low level and procurement was made mandatory; at the same time, industrial products were priced artificially high (Zhao, 1998). The net effect of these "price scissors" ('*jian dao cha*') was to squeeze funds out of agriculture so as to subsidize the urban industry. Besides, requisitioning surplus agricultural production at low prices enabled China to supply inexpensive foods to the urban residents. In turn, low food prices led to low wages, thus facilitating capital accumulation for re-investment of industries. In real practice, the central planners set two prices for each of the controlled farm product, i.e. a quota procurement price and an above-quota procurement price. The latter was higher than the former, with an intention of providing extra production incentives beyond the fulfillment of the quota. Nonetheless, both prices were much lower than potential market levels. After harvests, state agencies would purchase various products at quota or above-quota prices, transport them to cities before state-owned grain or grocery stores managed final sales, of course still at controlled prices. By then, neither individuals nor private agencies were permitted to deal in food commerce, which made it possible for the government to have everything planned happen.

Inevitably, such a regime distorted prices, which caused supply to fall due to a lack of incentives for peasants; in turn, the consequential shortage made consumers equally suffered. Until today, a vivid memory remains with most Chinese who lived in urban areas at that time. It was quite normal that they often had to get up very early in the morning to queue several hours for the necessities that were rationed, like rice, edible oils, meat, *and* sugar, etc. Even by doing so, there is no 100 PCT guarantee that they could finally get what they wanted to buy.

3.1.2 Introduction of Market Mechanism in Pricing

Realizing that the pervasive scale of unsatisfied demand for food could not sustain the economy, a package of measures was initiated first in the agricultural sector in 1979. By launching the Household Responsibility System, the state not only raised the overall procurement prices for major agricultural and sideline products (in order to alleviate the urban-industrial bias in the pre-reform economy), it also managed to lower the prices of agricultural machinery, fertilizers and pesticides, etc., which greatly induced peasants to increase cropping intensity and purchase more productive inputs. Despite its positive effect, the adjustment was only limited to relative prices and failed to involve the creation of a market pricing mechanism. In fact, what the government had actually done was by no means complicated, through a price increase of the goods in shortage and a price decrease of the goods in surplus, it narrowed the gap between the planned and market equilibrium prices. Referring to the industrial sector, enterprises of machinery products from 1979 were allowed to sell their extra, outside-plan output at higher floating or negotiated prices. At the initial stage, the negotiated prices were regulated and not allowed to exceed plan prices by more than 20 PCT (Wu & Xiao, 2009). This move was later considered as the start of a dual-track price system, although it was only on trial and far from being fully implemented.

Fairly speaking, when the necessity for a price reform was widely acknowledged, most Chinese officials preferred that the best way was to keep the existing planned mechanism, and gradually supplement it with a market-oriented one. Such a gradualist approach was to a large extent due to the reluctance of these decision makers to bear big costs and risks. They thought that if carried out step by step over a longer period, it would be less likely for them to make irreversible errors. Based on this mindset, policies until 1983 had been chiefly concentrated on coordinating agricultural prices relative to industrial prices. But not long later, it was found that by procuring from peasants at inflated prices, the state had to appropriate much more revenues to subsidize the urban residents, which was apparently unaffordable over the long run. With mounting budgetary pressures, the government was compelled to introduce market mechanism into its price formation process and thus planted the seed of the dual-track policies.

Theoretically, the dual-track system is a hybrid economic system under which the plan track and the market track coexisted as instruments of resource allocation. Under the system, one single commodity would often be allocated at state-set planned price which was much *l*ower and a market price typica*ll*y higher. For China, it is on January 1st, 1985 when the government removed the limit on outside-plan pricing that the dual-track system was officially ushered in (Li, 2002). In fact, this change was important for the country. Based on the premise that price as a barometer is reflective of market demand, when a product is in high demand, the price would go up, which in turn may raise the profits of production and eventually increase supply. By allowing prices to swing with the market, the imbalance between production and consumption or between supply and demand could be automatically minimized. Nevertheless, relaxing state control over prices would not bring fundamental changes unless enterprises were also permitted to respond in line with the market ups and downs. Very likely, this causal relationship has also been recognized by the Chinese leaders, who ever since 1978 started to orient the planned economy toward the market.

The new mechanism covered both the industrial and agricultural sector, with the central concerns shifting gradually from production for *production's sake* to people's actual needs. In industry, essential raw materials like petroleum, coal, iron and steel, etc. remained under the control of the government. For the state-owned enterprises (SOEs) engaged in the manufacture of these materials, they still had to fulfill the compulsory quota at the plan price. Once the plan obligations were accomplished, they would be allowed to produce more (outside-plan output) and sell at a higher price in open markets. In other words, SOEs could develop a dual-track production system, with one being state-centered and the other market-centered. Like what had happened before, the plan prices continued to be fixed centrally and were often substantially lower than the market levels. In terms of agriculture, the government abandoned mandatory procurement quotas for basic commodities such as grain, edible oils, and cotton, and replaced it with the contract-procurement system (Wu & Xiao, 2009). Like the name suggests, purchase contracts were to be negotiated between the state and peasants prior to the planting season before being executed at stipulated prices. Referring to the quantity that exceeded the contracted output, peasants could sell at market-determined prices via two channels. One was voluntary above-quota deliveries to the state at negotiated prices not controlled by central directives, but to be mutually agreed in response to market forces based on regional, seasonal, and quality factors. The other channel was the free market like seasonal rural market fairs and grain wholesale markets. Although this dual-track mechanism was not a full de-control of agricultural prices, it signifies an increasing reliance on the market to provide economic incentives to boost efficiency.

In the entire price reform process, apart from the dual-track approach, the number of commodities whose prices were subject to state control was simultaneously reduced. Most radically of all, the prices of non-staple consumer goods including vegetables, fish, and meat were significantly increased, which prompted peasants to diversify their agricultural activities so as to better meet the rising consumer demand. Undoubtedly, the emergence of this dual-track system in both city and countryside demonstrated a fresh way of thinking among the Chinese leaders, from the initial principle that only granted the market a supplementary role, they were more in favor of an economy that was not dominated by rigid state plans. Though far too early to be called a free market, China's developmental landscape in the second half of the 1980s was already not the same.

3.2 Urban Area: CRS of the SOEs

State-owned enterprises, employing the majority of urban work force, dominated the Chinese economy throughout the centrally-planned period from 1949 to 1978, as well as in the initial stage of the reform. Since whenever they were in need of inputs like capital, labor and materials, they would enjoy the privilege of putting forward the demand directly to the state. To a large extent, profits and losses did not make much difference to them. In essence, they were somewhat like a subsidiary of the administrative authorities, but not an independent commodity producer. For lack of pressure and motivation, however, they became structurally weak and *operationally inefficient, with the creativity of both the enterprise and the employees seriously oppressed*. Even with the experimental policy thrust like decentralization of power in the *l*ate 1970s, they were not totally autonomous, but restrained within the overall framework of control that covered almost all the dimensions of industrial management, from procurement of raw materials, production, pricing, distribution, to marketing, etc. So naturally, it is inappropriate to say that these SOEs were the decision-makers for themselves; rather, they did not have enough authority necessary to run in a dynamic and efficient manner. In one word, something was still missing to fully stimulate their potential.

3.2.1 Major Moves Toward the Contract Responsibility System

Following the first step of "tax-for-profit" scheme which was launched in 1983, the State Council promulgated the "Second Stage Provisional Rules of Converting State-Owned Enterprises' Profit Submission into Taxation" in 1984 (Tian, 1984). As a part of the restructuring package of the urban economic system, this reform aimed to change the method of making a combined payment of profits and taxes to the state into one in which enterprises pay taxes according to a list of 11 stipulated types of taxes. Moreover, in case the post-tax profits of large and medium-sized SOEs exceeded that of the previous year, they would be remitted to the government in the form of adjustment tax. Determined on a firm-by-firm basis against the 1983 profit levels, the adjustment tax was levied in order to eliminate unequal opportunities caused by factors such as different pricing structures or subsidies. Regarding those small SOEs, 8 new progressive tax rates were applied. After paying taxes, they could allocate profits according to their own needs. In general, the after-tax profits retained were to be divided into five parts; namely, new product development fund, production fund, reserve fund, employee welfare fund, and employee bonus fund. Through the implementation of this second step reform, state revenues which had been previously generated from both profits and taxes remitted by the SOEs were merged into one single tax resource. From the standpoint of enterprises, as long as they have paid the taxes due, they could enjoy greater power in the management of their own properties and finances. Thereby, the preliminary conditions to truly separate the functions of administrative organs from those of entrepreneurial entities were created.

In May 1984, the State Council issued the "Provisional Regulations on Further Expanding the Autonomy of State-Owned Industrial Enterprises". Known as "Ten Articles" ('*kuoquan shitiao*'), it granted ten autonomous rights to these SOEs and they covered aspects like production planning, selling, pricing, allocation of funds, and disposal of assets, etc. Take pricing as an example, after fulfilling the state plan, enterprises could sell their surplus industrial materials at a price below or above 20 PCT of the state level (this 20 PCT limit was abolished in January 1985 and succeeded by a dual-track price system, with state-controlled in-plan and market-oriented out-plan prices coexisted). By October of the same year, the Third Plenum of the 12th Party Congress passed the "Resolution on Economic System Reforms", which explicitly pointed out that boosting the vigor and vitality of enterprises, especially the SOEs, should be taken as the central piece of the reform. As one more concrete step, the State Council in 1985 approved the "Provisional Regulations on Strengthening the Vitality of Large and Medium-Sized State-Owned Industrial Enterprises". By illustrating the key barriers that still hampered the growth of SOEs, the directive urged governments and supervisory administrative organs of all levels to *cut red tape* and delegate more power to enterprises. All in all, these series of decisions suggested that while the market mechanism was gaining a stronger foothold in the industrial sector, it was imperative that China's SOEs should assert their due responsibilities and be really independent in making decisions and taking actions.

From the mid-1980s onward, it became increasingly clear that although the SOEs had started to enjoy more autonomy and incentives, responsibilities were still not adequately outlined. To a certain degree, it is due to the recognition of various deficiencies that prompted radical reform proposals calling for a tightened link between enterprise performance and personal reward. At that time, debate was most intense between proponents of the contract system and those of the shareholding system (Yang, 1988). Referring to the former, they argued that while maintaining state ownership, SOEs could still perform in an efficient way with responsibilities, rights and benefits of both the state and themselves clearly stipulated in the contract. As to the latter, they held that only the shareholding system could resolve in a complete way the problem of inseparability between government administration and enterprise business and thus can promote optimal allocation of resources. In practice, however, SOEs' reform in the second half of the 1980s was dominated by the contract system, although other proposals were also experimented on a smaller scale. The reasons that made the contract system more popular were because on the one hand, there was no pressing need to alter state ownership; on the other hand, similar trials in agriculture had proved to be quite successful. On Dec. 5th, 1986, the State Council issued the "Regulations on Intensifying the Enterprise Reform and Revitalizing Enterprises", which put forward two approaches for the reform of the SOEs. For large and medium-sized SOEs, they may carry out diverse forms of responsibility systems and in case conditions were favorable, some may implement pilot programs of the shareholding system. With regard to the small SOEs, leasing or contractual operations could be applied. In 1987, the *Fifth Session* of the *6th National* People's *Congress clarified for the first time the necessity to promote contract responsibility system (CRS) among the SOEs nationwide. By the end of that year, 78 PCT of the SOEs covered by the state budget had implemented the contract system, among which 80 PCT were of large and medium-scale* (Zhou, 1988*).*

3.2.2 Operations of the CRS and Its Effects

According to the "Provisional Regulations Concerning the Contract Responsibility System of State-owned Industrial Enterprises" issued in 1988, the essential feature of CRS is that a contract should be negotiated and signed between a state agency (or its representative bureau) and a manager (or a group of managers) of an SOE. Via the contract, the latter was expected to engage in various economic and technical undertakings such as profit earning, quality control, product innovation, loan repayment, and equipment utilization, etc. Besides, the contract also provided that the enterprise could enjoy complete rights to possess, use, and benefit from its property. Then based on the actual performance, if the realized profit exceeded the target, the manager would be allowed to share the above-target part with the state at a rate stipulated in the contract. However, if the target was not met, then the manager would have to pay a penalty either fixed or proportional to the difference between the target and the realized profit, or the performance bond would be forfeited. As to the profit retained inside the enterprise, it was usually used for three purposes, i.e. re-investment, employee welfare, and bonus. In fact, the autonomy to award bonus to employees should be taken as a breakthrough since before hand, employees were only paid a fixed salary, which gave no consideration to individual efforts. But under the new system, the amount of the bonus to be paid was largely dependent on how well the individual could meet his/her job requirements. Quite naturally, everyone wanted to work harder and outperform others since this would bring them a higher income.

On the basis of public ownership, the contract responsibility system attempted to separate property rights from managerial rights. By reducing government intervention, enterprises acquired some financial independence through which they could focus more on efficiency and profitability rather than merely on plan fulfillment. Combined with the dual-track price system which permitted the SOEs to sell their products above the planned quota at higher market prices, this measure provided them one more incentive and consequently, their performance was improved. Fairly speaking, from the perspective of mobilizing enterprises to hit specific profit targets within a certain time period, the contract system was rather effective. Nevertheless, it also gave rise to some concerns. For instance, since most contracts ran for only three to five years, in order to maximize short-term benefits within the contracted period, there was a tendency among managers to concentrate primarily on the basic quantitative targets set out in the contract; and in turn, to neglect the long-term development strategy and actual needs of the enterprise itself (Luo, 1989). In particular, the very existence of a widespread neglect of technological innovation unless it could quickly bring about increased production or profit was perhaps the most disappointing by-product of the CRS, since this had traditionally been the weakest point of the state sector of China and thereby should have been put at the top of its reform agenda.

In addition, from the viewpoint of enterprise property rights, there are also questions to be raised. Once China embarked on the course of economic reform, and especially the reform of the SOEs, separation of management from ownership was soon considered a major obstacle to deal with. Although the CRS was originally intended as a new institutional arrangement to facilitate the division, what really happened is that due to the insufficiently distinguished property rights between the state and enterprises, their distributional and control relations over retained profits remained rather ambiguous (Lee & Jin, 2009). If the provisions of the contract were applicable, i.e. the profit retained belonged to the enterprise, then the ownership of the assets produced through reinvestment of the retained profit should also go to the same enterprise. But, the result of such a practice is that the whole assets of the enterprise, many years later, will be divided into two parts: state-owned and the enterprise's collectively owned. Furthermore, the percentage of the latter will be increasing with the continuous expansion of production. Evidently, such an outcome will in the end change the basic nature of the ownership and conflict with the fundamental requirements of China's system of socialist public ownership. In this regard, as long as the issue of property rights is not clarified, then the reform of the SOEs could hardly claim a real success.

3.3 Rural Area: TVEs

The TVE (township and village enterprises) phenomenon of China is rather unique in the sense that the emergence of rural entrepreneurs and enterprises has not been experienced in any other country on such a large scale and at such a rapid pace. Even the central government had not fully anticipated that the seemingly insignificant force from the countryside could expand so dynamically within a short time period. Fairly speaking, in relieving employment pressure and improving the living standard of rural China, TVEs should without any dispute take credit for their contributions. More importantly, the absorption of surplus labor force, a headache which had confronted the government of all levels, did not require much state investment. Instead of flocking into cities, these peasants were reshaping towns and villages with their own wisdom and diligence.

In order to encourage more people to work at rural enterprises so as to further alleviate the burden of unemployment, central policy toward TVEs was getting more favorable in the early 1980s. Together with the relaxation of state monopoly over industry, government of diverse rural areas had strong motives to nurture new economic engines other than relying solely on traditional farming. Therefore, in the pursuit of common interests, a close partnership linking TVEs and governments came into being, which greatly invigorated the former and benefited the latter. Also, of special significance was the decentralization of foreign trade to provincial and local levels, a measure that enabled TVEs to penetrate overseas markets and quicken their pace of expansion. Further, at a time when the vast majority of the Chinese peasants were not yet in a position to remove and find jobs freely in urban areas, working in rural collective industries should be an attractive alternative for them to better utilize their abilities and get more earnings.

3.3.1 Policy-Backed Impressive Growth

In 1984, the Central Committee of the Communist Party of China (CCCPC) issued the "Notice of Rural Work Document No. 1" (referred to as Central Document No. 1 of 1984), in which individual land use right was set apart from collective land ownership. Besides, it also stipulated that collective land could be contracted to households for a term of fifteen or more years. As a matter of fact, starting from the end of 1983, some 97 PCT of the country's arable land had already been allocated to rural households (Huang, 2009), which not only stimulated the growth of agricultural production, it also furnished a possibility for individual capital accumulation in the rural sector. Consequently, a new investment mechanism that transferred the surplus of the agricultural sector into the non-agricultural sector was formed. Private enterprises, in addition to the existing joint-household and cooperative TVEs, were set up in fast growing numbers, which pushed the government to amend its property rights policy immediately.

In March 1984, the CCCPC approved the "Report on the Exploration of New Prospects for Commune and Brigade Enterprises" by the Ministry of Agriculture, Animal Husbandry and Fish Farming (also referred to as Central Document No. 4). This document on the one hand officially re-named the commune and brigade-owned enterprises as township and village enterprises; at the same time, it also broadened the concept of TVEs to include other forms of property rights such as enterprises owned by single (self-employed) or joint households. This change of name and definition was very symbolic since it represented a formal recognition of the rural enterprises organized by individual and joint capital. By taking advantage of the central policies that were gradually shifting from mere tolerance to encouragement, TVEs underwent a dramatic and sustained growth between 1984 and 1988, during which the most remarkable surge happened in the initial two years before entering into a steady path of development (Table 4). In 1988, the total number of TVEs hit

Table 4 Growth of the TVEs, 1978–1988

Year	Number (million)		Output value (RMB billion)
1978	1.52	28.27	51.44
1984	1.65	38.48	142.08
1985	12.23	69.79	272.84
1986	15.15	79.37	371.7
1987	17.5	88.05	505.5
1988	18.88	95.45	750.24

Source NBS (2004)

18.88 million, a scale that was absolutely unimaginable just four years ago. At the same time, these enterprises had created an immense number of job opportunities for the abundant rural surplus labor. In terms of the workers employed by the TVEs, they more than doubled from 38.48 million of 1984 to 95.45 million in 1988. Additionally, what accompanied the expansion of rural industry during this period was a substantial increase in the gross output, which by the year 1988 exceeded RMB750 billion, more than fivefold if compared to that of the 1984 level.

Based on the above, it is fair to say that the speedy development of the TVEs during 1984–1988 should be attributed primarily to the favorable policy environment. In this consideration, it is necessary to direct some special attention to the new fiscal relationship between central and local governments, especially at township levels. Before the reform era, revenues had been collected by the local governments and then turned over to the center where expenditures would also be determined. With the central government setting spending priorities and approving budgets according to local needs, this consolidated system in fact deprived sub-national governments of basic autonomy in drafting independent budgets and allocating discretionary outlays. But at a time when the economic fundamentals were still shaky and infrastructures remained inadequate, the highly-centralized planning was deemed a necessary alternative.

As Chinese leaders embarked on the journey towards market economy from 1978, the flaw with the fiscal system became increasingly manifested in that for lack of much incentives, it was hard to make local governments fully committed to the promotion of regional economies. Thereby, numerous regimes were introduced in the early 1980s and they were collectively called the "fiscal contract" ('*caizheng baogan*') system. Under this system, government of each level was to sign a revenue-sharing contract with the subordinate (for example: central with provincial, provincial with municipal, municipal with prefectural, prefectural with county, and county with township), in which the amount or rate of fiscal revenues to be remitted was specified (Xiao, 2008). Since the contract allowed local governments to retain some revenues if they could outperform the required target, they had a stronger incentive to develop the local economy so as to enlarge their tax bases. Consequently, government at township and village levels demonstrated unprecedented enthusiasm to support TVEs. Having in their hands broader powers and in particular, access to resources like bank loans from rural credit cooperatives (RCCs, chief financial institutions serving the rural areas), they often acted as sponsors and guarantors when TVEs were in need of financing.

3.3.2 FDI, Catalyst to Trigger Expansion

Anyhow, as compared to the state enterprises (or the SOEs), it was still much more difficult for TVEs to secure bank loans, even if they had the warrant issued by the local governments. Besides, a successful loan application was generally accompanied by strict commercial clauses demanding repayment without delay. Facing the pressure of hard budget constraints, TVEs understood clearly that unlike the SOEs whose financing was covered by public budget and not bound by these harsh conditions, they could not keep borrowing if they failed to pay back or suffered net losses; once bankrupt, nobody would come to their rescue. Nonetheless, like a double-edged sword, the very threat of failure was simultaneously one of the main stimulants that prompted these TVEs to act more cautiously and engage in efficient and innovative behaviors to stay solvent. In order to raise more external capital, several other means were used, including foreign direct investment (FDI).

Geographically, the TVEs which flourished the most were in general found among coastal provinces like Jiangsu, Zhejiang, Guangdong, and Fujian whereas in history, it was also these same regions which had already established close business relations with Hong Kong, Taiwan, Macao, and Singapore, etc. Long-term cooperation has enabled both parties to know about each other fairly well and in terms of the advantages of investing in the TVEs alongside coastal China, they were quite prominent and the most attractive ones included abundant cheaper labor, less stringent approval procedures, preferential treatment in tax and profit repatriation, and location proximity, etc. Therefore, it is not hard to understand why foreign investment played an essential role in the rapid boom of TVEs during the second half of the 1980s. Together with capital, the most needed input, it was rather common for a package of other resources to be transferred as well, like production technologies, management expertise, and overseas sales networks, etc., which not only enhanced the competitiveness of TVEs themselves, but also spurred local industrial development through the positive spillover occurrence.

3.3.3 Easier Access into Two Markets

Apart from the support of the government and the absorption of FDI, one more contributing factor that should not be ignored was the liberalization of the commodity markets. Due to the removal of mandatory procurement and sales by the state, TVEs of China were granted the opportunity to have their products distributed in both the urban and rural areas. In addition, due to the biases in the pre-reform system that over-prioritized the heavy industry, light industrial products, household items and services were in short supply around the country. For TVEs, this represented an opportunity that whoever could manage to grasp would be guaranteed immediate profits, which is important for them to survive. In this consideration, a major benefit for TVEs was that without much interference from the senior government officials, they enjoyed a higher degree of operational autonomy than the SOEs (Liu, 1994). Quite naturally, they started to engage in all kinds of non-agricultural production, especially consumer goods, provided that they were not prohibited by the state. That was indeed a golden time since the market was underserved, which enabled these TVEs to sell easily whatever they had produced, and some of them even reaped monopoly profits from the "first mover advantage". As a result, it did not take long before the TVEs started to pose a threat to the state enterprises. In particular, by offering better salaries and perks, they attracted from the latter many skilled workers and even experienced managers, thus improving the overall quality of the labor force. Furthermore, with the right to retain all the profits, they often invested heavily in upgrading technologies and know-how, another critical approach to the consolidation of their competitive advantage.

Together with the opening of the domestic market, the vast overseas market also became accessible to the TVEs. At the 13th National Congress of the Chinese Communist Party in 1987, the new general secretary of the Party Zhao Ziyang publicly advocated what was referred to as the "coastal economic development strategy". The strategy called for a strengthening and broadening of integration into the world market for the coastal region as a whole, and in particular emphasized the export potential of the fast growing TVEs in the regions of the Yangtze River Delta and Pearl River Delta (Gao, 2005). Specifically, it advocated the use of rural labor in these areas to produce labor-intensive light industrial products for export. Encouraged by the new policy, as well as some favorable treatments like preferential tax rates, low-interest loans, retention of partial foreign exchange earnings and profits, etc., export rapidly became a major catalyst strengthening the rural industries, especially those in the east coast.

By and large, TVEs exported their products via three channels, among which the first was also the dominant one, i.e. they relied on the state-owned foreign trade companies because at that time, they were not yet granted the privilege to handle international business directly. So what they did was to sign sales contract with these firms before their products were shipped abroad for sale. The second one was that by establishing joint ventures with foreign investors, they automatically obtained the permit to export without having to rely on an intermediary. The third alternative was rather rare and it was adopted when these TVEs themselves had the "license", so they were in a position to negotiate with foreign buyers and exported under their own names. Powered largely by the outstanding performance of the coastal TVEs, their overall direct export (excluding export via trading companies) rose from RMB11.9 billion in 1987 to RMB141.7 billion in 1993 (Graph 1), representing an increased share of the country's total from 8.1 PCT to almost 27 PCT, a dynamic trend which was set to continue in the years to come.

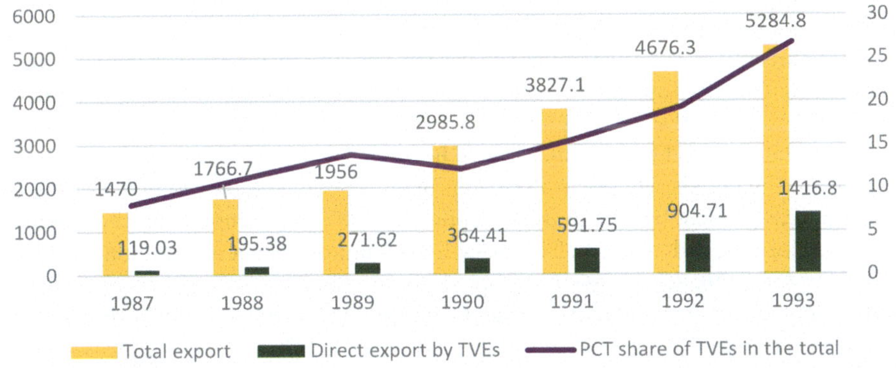

Graph 1 TVEs' export versus China's total, RMB100 million. *Source* Total export: NBS (2001); direct export by TVEs: NBS (2004); PCT share of TVEs in the total is calculated by the author

The rapid development of township and village enterprises over the period of 1984–1988 dramatically restructured China's rural economy. With the majority of them engaged in manufacturing and a growing number in the tertiary sector (i.e. construction, transport, retail, and tourism, etc.), the expansionary pace of those staying in agriculture has been less aggressive. Of the contributions they have made to the rural non-agricultural (material products) department, the most notable ones should include the creation of jobs, generation of revenues, innovation of technologies, and improvement of living standards, etc. Therefore, it is by no means an exaggeration to say that TVEs drove much of China's growth in the 1980s. Besides, capable of responding quickly to market demand, they challenged state-owned enterprises to act in kind. From then on, the Chinese industry was not entirely monopolized by the SOEs anymore. In a long-term perspective, moreover, the impact of TVEs on the country was positive and far-reaching since by introducing competition into the market, the transformation that has been taking place would go much deeper, more comprehensive, and consistent.

4 Summary of the 1st-Phase Reform: 1978–1988

While the period covering 1978 and 1988 recorded for China one of the most dynamic growth performances in its modern history, by the time the government decided on the policy of reform and opening up, there was no concrete roadmap as to how the giant scheme should be carried out. Therefore, every single step made thereafter was experimental and prudent. Considering that China was still a low-income country with almost one billion people to feed (its population hit nearly 963 million in 1978), it is not hard to understand why upgrading the agricultural sector was chosen as the primary target by the central planners. With a view to minimizing potential risks connected with domestic food security, and resource constraints that may curb the overall pace of development, the policymakers increased prices for farm produce and substituted "household responsibility system" for collective farming, which allowed the sale of above-quota output at higher market prices.

These incentives greatly stimulated peasants and as a result of more inputs, especially in machinery, further efficiency was gained. According to the data compiled by the USDA (i.e. the US Department of Agriculture), China's agricultural total factor productivity (TFP, a key measure of how efficiently inputs such as land, labor, capital, and materials, etc. are utilized) during 1978–1988 demonstrated a positive year-on-year growth, only with the exception of 1987. By comparison, if checking the pre-reform period, negative TFP growth per annum was not uncommon (USDA, 2016). In turn, this achievement prompted the re-allocation of labor from agricultural to non-agricultural activities, thus facilitating the structural transformation of the whole country.

While engaged in rural reforms, the Chinese government also moved forward to adjust the non-agricultural sector. At the outset, a dual-track system was introduced under which state-owned enterprises were equally granted the autonomy to buy and sell beyond quota at market prices. Besides, through the "fiscal contract system", the central government delegated greater powers to the lower government at provincial, municipal, and county levels, which led to a tremendous expansion of township and village enterprises. In terms of their number, it skyrocketed from 1.52 million of 1978 to 18.88 million in 1988 (NBS, 2004), an amazing increase that exceeded 11-fold. Similar to what happened in the agricultural sector, the total factor productivity in industry picked up as well. By comparison, since the non-state enterprises were more market-oriented than those owned by the state, their speed of development was much faster.

4.1 GDP Growth

In summary, from 1978 to 1988, China's GDP more than quadrupled to almost RMB1.5 trillion, an annual increase that averaged a double-digit growth momentum (Table 5). What accompanied this dynamic trend was the per capita GDP, which went up from USD156 to USD284, signifying a steady improvement in the living standards of the Chinese people. The following are some detailed statistics through these years.

Here, one more thing to point out is that in 1981, the country's population began to cross the one billion mark whereas that of the whole world was 4.52 billion (the United Nations Department of Economic and Social Affairs, Population Division. From https://esa.un.org/unpd/wpp/DataQuery/). Quite naturally, how to promote the quality of life for nearly one fifth of the global population remained a question that challenged the Chinese government. At that stage, people were no longer content with the provision of basic necessities; further, they were in need of a much wider variety of choice and expected to enjoy what modernization could really bring.

Table 5 GDP growth and per capita GDP, 1978–1988

Year	Total GDP[1] (RMB100 million)	GDP indices[2] (preceding year = 100)	Per capita GDP[3] (USD)
1978	3,624.1	111.7	156.4
1980	4,517.8	107.8	194.81
1982	5,294.7	109.1	203.34
1984	7,171	115.2	250.71
1986	10,202.2	108.8	281.93
1988	14,928.3	111.3	283.54

Note Data in this table are calculated at current prices
Source [1] and [2]NBS (2001); [3]https://data.worldbank.org/indicator/NY.GDP.PCAP.CD?locations=CN

4.2 FDI and Export Increase

Apart from GDP, the opening-up policy of China also recouped an exhilarating harvest in foreign direct investment (FDI) and foreign trade, two key indicators reflecting how this *long-closed* country was gradually integrating itself with the rest of the world. To absorb more foreign capital, diverse policies aimed to favor overseas investors were adopted, like tax holidays, easier access to loans, special privilege in using foreign exchange and profit retention, etc. If referring to the most critical steps, they should include the experiment of setting up four Special Economic Zones (SEZs) in the southeast provinces of Guangdong and Fujian, adjacent to Hong Kong, Taiwan and Macao. In addition, fourteen coastal cities received special incentive programs for FDI in 1984. Four years later, when Hainan Island officially became the youngest province of China, it was simultaneously turned into the biggest SEZ on the mainland.

Statistically, the momentum with which China opened these areas can be displayed by the amount of direct investment that were attracted into the country. Based on the table below (Table 6), the entire period may be divided into two phases. The first one spanned four years from 1979 to 1982 when the total FDI actually realized was only less than USD1.8 billion. But at the second stage ended in 1988, the amount of each year kept rising at a much more rapid rate, hitting almost 30 PCT per annum, with most of the projects located in the coastal regions.

Similar to many developing countries in the world, China in its initial years of the reform valued FDI very much because it can boost trade and help accumulate foreign exchange reserves. Due to the fact that most foreign-funded enterprises were engaged in cross-border business activities, the country's volume of foreign trade demonstrated an upward trend of movement throughout the 1978–1988 period. In terms of export, it climbed from USD9.75 billion of 1978 to USD47.5 billion in 1988 (Table 7). Behind the growth, one major contributor was the devaluation of yuan against the US dollar, which dropped from RMB1.5771 each dollar in 1978 to RMB3.7221 in 1988, granting its products greater price advantage in the international market. Nevertheless, it should also be noted that due to the even stronger demand

Table 6 Foreign direct investment actually utilized, 1979–1988

Year	Actually utilized FDI (USD100 million)	Growth rate (PCT)
1979–1982	17.7	–
1983	9.2	–
1984	14.2	54.9
1985	19.6	37.8
1986	22.4	14.7
1987	23.1	3.1
1988	31.9	38

Source MOC (2004a, 2004b)

Table 7 Foreign trade and export growth, 1978–1988

Year	Total trade volume (USD100 million)	Export volume (USD100 million)	Year-on-year export growth[1] (PCT)
1978	206.4	97.5	–
1980	378.2	182.7	33.7
1985	696	273.5	4.6
1986	738.5	309.4	13.1
1987	826.5	394.4	27.5
1988	1,027.8	475.2	20.5

Note [1]Calculated by the author
Source MOC (2004)

for imports, the nation's current account recorded a deficit for most of the years and in particular, it peaked at USD14.9 billion in 1985. Under the direct impact of the unfavorable balance of trade, the foreign exchange reserves declined sharply and registered almost USD3.4 billion by 1988 (NBS, 1999).

With a view to further promoting foreign trade and aligning the domestic economy with the rest of the world, China in 1986 officially presented an application to the General Agreement on Tariffs and Trade (GATT) to resume its contracting party status. After the formation of the Working Party on China, negotiations on bilateral levels got started in 1987 and were still in full swing till the end of the 1980s.

4.3 *Inflation Under an Overheated Economy*

By and large, the economic reforms of 1978–1988 were primarily incentive-driven, with subsidies taken as the dominant means to fund the process. Besides, one more feature of the reforms during this period is that strong efforts were directed to the production side so as to put the economy on a fast-growth track. With an attempt to enable market forces to play a bigger role in resource allocation, prices for a gradually widened scope of products were allowed to fluctuate more freely than ever before. Thus, in anticipation of new opportunities and profits, there was an unprecedented enthusiasm among rural and urban enterprises to invest in infrastructure and expand capacity. Starting from the fourth quarter of 1984 in particular, the growth rate became abnormally high when subsidized loans, unblinking government support and a rush to make quick money led to a surge in demand, which in turn caused prices to soar across the board (Jiang & Zhang, 1986).

Besides, as the size of business entities was enlarged, they began to recruit more employees; but given the rising cost of food and other necessities, workers claimed higher pays. In 1980, for instance, the average money wage of China was RMB762; five years later, it jumped over 50 PCT to RMB1,148. In the subsequent years, the level continued to climb by more than 10PCT per year before reaching RMB1,747 in 1988 (NBS, 2001). Eventually, the money supply (M0) in the market stayed high, which hit RMB213.4 billion toward the end of 1988, an average annual increase of 26 PCT if compared to RMB21.2 billion of 1978. However, considering that the gross social product for the same time period only rose at a pace of 11 PCT, too much money had been put into circulation (Liu, 1989). As a consequence, the consumer price index (CPI, a key indicator of inflation) skyrocketed to 118.8 in 1988 (preceding year = 100). Due to the widespread panic over inflation, as well as expectations of further price rises, a massive bank run and the largest spending spree since 1949 were reported in the summer of 1988, when countless consumers rushed to the local grocery or department stores scrambling for whatever were available, from daily necessities like salt, soaps to electrical appliances like black-and-white televisions, washing machines, and tape recorders, etc., all without exception driven by the fear of shortage (Zhang, 1994).

Obviously, these phenomena together pointed to the same fact that by the end of the 1980s, the Chinese economy was over-heated and austerity measures should be taken quickly in order to cool it down. As a key approach to dampen inflation, the government slashed its fixed investment in 1988 by cutting back on the construction of multiple collectively-owned and privately-owned projects. Till that November, the number of those halted or postponed amounted to 10,200, representing a scale of RMB33.4 billion that were underway (Wang & Jiang, 1989). Moreover, it also kept a tighter rein on the credit that was granted to enterprises. After two years' adoption of these soft-landing approaches, the situation was gradually back to normal. Among the most immediate effects, China's GDP growth rate dropped to 4.1 PCT in 1989 whereas that of the previous year had been 11.3 PCT. In addition, inflation was back under control and by 1990, the CPI was down to 103.1 (preceding year = 100). Anyhow, irrespective of the diverse problems that arose during the initial reform, the government remained firmly convicted that the overall gains far outweighed the losses. Therefore, instead of being hesitant as to where to go in the future, China was thinking about new forms of decentralization so as to get ready for the next phase of reform, as well as the challenges that would follow.

References

Cai, Y. E. (1985). Supply and marketing cooperatives should actively support the development of rural commodity production. *Research on Financial Problems, 1,* 26–30.

Chen, Z. H. (1990). Problems and reform ideas in the current foreign exchange retention system. *International Trade Issues, 9,* 45–47.

Chen, H. (1997). Analysis of the reasons for regional industrial structure convergence in China and some policy recommendations. *Economic Management, 5,* 28–30.

Chen, W. L. (2005). Institutional innovation of the local government management model and its role: comparison of the Pearl River Delta model, the Sunan model and the Wenzhou model. *Journal of Wuhan University (Humanities Edition), 1,* 87–92.

Chen, Z. H. (2014). Four elements beyond the primary stage of socialism. *Journal of the Central Institute of Socialism, 5,* 104–107.

Chen, Z. M. (2015). On the formation of the basic economic system of socialism with Chinese characteristics. *Beijing Party History, 1,* 16–22.
Chen, J. H., & Wu, Y. H. (2009). Correlation analysis of industrial structure changes and economic growth in 60 years since the founding of the P.R.C. *Journal of Guizhou Commercial College, 4,* 22–25.
Cui, X. S. (2016). An interpretation of the history of administrative divisions in Shenzhen. *Special Zone Practice and Theory, 4,* 71–74.
Ding, Y. F. (2013). Reform and development of China's financial system. *Marxism and Reality, 2,* 15–21.
Du, Y. (1987). China's circulation system reform has made a breakthrough. *China Reform, 9,* 26–27.
Fang, X. X. (1999). *China's corporate financing: Institutional change and behavior analysis.* Beijing: Peking University Press.
Fang, M. (2016). Hua Guofeng and opening to the outside world. *Annals of the Yellow Emperor, 5,* 9–15.
Feng, J. H. (2006). *Destiny and mission: a centurial retrospect of Chinese intellectual issues.* Beijing: Chinese Press.
Feng, Y. K. (2008). Reform and innovation of centralization-and-decentralization combination and the two-tier management system. *Journal of Xiangfan University, 7,* 5–8.
NBS. (1979). Communiqué of the National Bureau of Statistics of the P.R.C. on the implementation results of the national economic plan 1978. Retrieved January 20, 2016, from https://www.stats.gov.cn/tjsj/tjgb/ndtjgb/qgndtjgb/200203/t20020331_29991.html.
Gao, J. (2002). The scientific and technological strategic thinking of the party's three generations of leaders. *Contemporary Chinese History Research, 3,* 4–12.
Gao, B. W. (2005). Choice and effect of the economic development strategy of coastal areas in the 1980s. *Contemporary Chinese History Research, 4,* 92–100.
Geng, L. X. (2001). Analysis of the impact of external environment on the financial trust industry. *Southern Finance, 12,* 52–53.
Gong, Y. Z., & Shi, Z. Q. (1995). The heavy trust of the time & the choice of history: the origin of Deng Xiaoping's becoming the core of the second generation of central leadership. *Theory and the Contemporary, 2,* 45–48.
Guo, S. T. (1999). Rural China: labor force differentiation and social structure changes. *Science and Technology Review, 1,* 6–9.
Han, J. Q. (1992). On the reform of profit and tax diversion. *Journal of Liaoning University (Philosophy and Social Sciences Edition), 3,* 18–20.
Han, S. (2009). A textual research on the evolution of RMB exchange rate system in 60 years since the founding of the P.R.C. *Legal System and Economics Bulletin, 12,* 139–140.
He, L. B. (2008). The five-country tour of western Europe before the reform and opening up. *Prosecutorial Review, 24,* 66–68.
Hu, A. G. et al. (2005). China's economic growth and poverty reduction (1978–2002). In W. Tseng & D. Cowen (Eds.), *India's and China's recent experience with reform and growth.* London: Palgrave Macmillan.
Huang, J. Z. (1987). The third wave of agricultural revolution in China and its prospects. *Journal of Liaoning University (Philosophy and Social Sciences Edition), 5,* 50–52.
Huang, S. J. (2008). Practical evolution and empirical analysis of the reform of state-owned enterprises. *Economics and Management Research, 10,* 20–31.
Huang, Z. H. (2009). How to break through rural land transfer? Revelation from reverse contracting in the Pearl River Delta. *China Rural Discovery, 2,* 50–53.
Huang, X. H. (2015). Research on establishing a unified urban and rural construction land market. *Shanghai Land and Resources, 2,* 1–8.
Jiang, C. Y. (2002). Social security of rural land and farmers. *Comparison of Economic and Social Systems, 1,* 49–55.

Jiang, C. Q. (2010). The financial system of Jiangsu province and the development of township and village enterprises in the early days of reform and opening up. *China Economic History Research, 2*, 92–97.

Jiang, C. Q. (2011). The establishment of county-level finance in the early days of the founding of the P.R.C. *Local Finance Research, 6*, 74–80.

Jiang, Y. Q. (2013). Brief description of the two decisions on national economic adjustment from 1977 to 1982. Document Research Office of the Central Committee of the CPC (Ed.), *A collection of personal research results of the document research office of the central committee of the CPC 2012* (Book 2). Beijing: Central Literature Press.

Jiang, C. Q. (2015). Research on central and local fiscal decentralization and economic performance (1953–1957). *Chinese Economic History Research, 6*, 111–116.

Jiang, W., & Zhang, J. J. (1986). Basic situation of China's macro control and regulation in 1985. *Macroeconomic Research, 4*, 34–38.

Lau, L. J., et al. (2000). Reform without losers: an interpretation of China's dual-track approach to transition. *Journal of Political Economy, 1*, 120–143.

Lee, K., & Jin, X. H. (2009). The origins of business groups in China: an empirical testing of the three paths and the three theories. *Business History, 1*, 77–99.

Li, B. H. (1984). The annual net income growth of farmers in China (Yuan) from 1978 to 1983. *Journal of Theory Research, 2*, 10.

Li, W. S. (1990). Summing up experience and speeding up the introduction of foreign capital: ten-year review and reflection on the Shenzhen special economic zone. *International Economic Cooperation, 11*, 20–22.

Li, W. (2002). Corruption during the economic transition in China. In D. D. Porta & S. R. Ackerman (Eds.), *Corrupt exchanges: Empirical themes in the politics and political economy of corruption.* Karlsruhe: Nomos Verlag. Retrieved March 28, 2015, from https://faculty.darden.virginia.edu/liw/papers/zif-c3.pdf.

Lin, C. P. (2010). Analysis of the development prospect of China's coal-to-liquid chemical industry. *China Petroleum and Chemical Industry, 4*, 22–28.

Liu, C. S. (1981). Some views on the reform of national economic management system. *Journal of Northwest University (Philosophy and Social Sciences Edition), 4*, 89–97.

Liu, R. X. (1989). The key to curbing inflation: Implementation of a tight monetary policy. *China Economic and Trade Guide, 10*, 27–28.

Liu, K. B. (1994). The operating mechanism of township and village enterprises and the development of China's market economy. *Exploring, 3*, 29–32.

Liu, R. G. (2005). A historical review of the import of 22 complete equipment projects in 1978. *Research on the History of the CPC, 5*, 85–92.

Liu, R. X. (2011). Several questions about the reform of state-owned enterprises. *State-Owned Enterprises, 7*, 114–117.

Lu, Y. (2008). Evolution of China's taxation system in 30 years of reform and opening up. *Public Economic Review, 9*, 7–21.

Luo, X. M. (1989). Dilemma and way out of contracting management of enterprises. *Jiangxi Social Sciences, 4*, 45–47.

Ma, K. (1992). Further deepening the reform of agricultural product prices. *China Price, 11*, 5–8.

Ma, J. W., & Li, L. (2013). Research on the implementation effect of rural land contracting policy: taking Xilizhuang village, Dingtao county, Shandong province as an example. *Enterprise Herald, 10*, 20–21.

Ministry of Commerce (MOC). (2004a). Foreign direct investment since 1979. Retrieved August 2, 2015, from https://zhs.mofcom.gov.cn/article/Nocategory/200405/20040500218171.shtml.

MOC. (2004b). Import and export volume since 1978. Retrieved August 2, 2015, from https://zhs.mofcom.gov.cn/article/Nocategory/200405/20040500218163.shtml.

Mu, K. Y. (2011). Research on issues related to foreign exchange management in China. *Managers, 6*, 16.

NBS. (2000). *China statistical yearbook 1999*. Beijing: China Statistics Press. Retrieved April 20, 2015, from https://www.stats.gov.cn/tjsj/ndsj/.
NBS. (2001). *China statistical yearbook 2000*. Beijing: China Statistics Press. Retrieved April 20, 2015, from https://www.stats.gov.cn/tjsj/ndsj/.
NBS. (2004). *Statistics of Chinese townships and villages 2003*. Beijing: China Statistics Press.
NBS. (2013). *China statistical abstract 2013*. Beijing: China Statistics Press.
Naughton, B. (2007). *The Chinese economy: transitions and growth*. Cambridge: The MIT Press.
NBS. (1999). Sixth series of analysis report on China's 50 years: the emergence of rual township and village enterprises. Retrieved October 5, 2015, from https://www.stats.gov.cn/ztjc/ztfx/xzg50nxlfxbg/200206/t20020605_35964.html.
People's Daily. (1979). The power of enterprises must be expanded. Retrieved January 25, 2016, from https://sdc.wenming.cn/sdc/content/2008-09/30/content_2860.htm.
Shenzhen Municipal Bureau of Statistics (SMBS). (2010). *Shenzhen statistical yearbook 2010*. Beijing: China Statistics Press.
Shao, L. H. (1994). Current situation and way out of China's interest rate management system. *Wuhan Finance, 2*, 30–31.
Shen, C. L. (2012). Bridging fiscal divergence in China. The University of Maryland. Retrieved April 3, 2016, from https://drum.lib.umd.edu/bitstream/handle/1903/12539/Shen_umd_0117E_12912.pdf?sequence=1&isAllowed=y.
Song, S. Y. (2009). The beginning of market-oriented reform of China's banking sector: 1979–1984. *Journal of Liaocheng University (Social Science Edition), 1*, 87–94.
Song, G. M., & Qu H. L. (1997). Reform of China's state-owned enterprises and the banking sector. Retrieved May 25, 2016, from https://www.neri.org.cn/document/20120402110205511 03.pdf.
Tian, Z. G. (1984). Explanation on some specific issues concerning the second-step profit-to-tax reform of state-owned enterprises. *Accounting Monthly, S1*, 12–16.
Tu, Q. (2009). Yuan Geng and the frontier of the construction of China's special economic zone: Shekou. *Chinese and Foreign Book Digest, 2*, 32–36.
UNCTAD. (2016). Gross domestic product: total and per capita, growth rates, annual, 1970–2015. Retrieved July 12, 2016, from https://unctadstat.unctad.org/wds/ReportFolders/reportFolders.aspx.
United States Department of Agriculture (USDA). (2016). Agricultural total factor productivity growth indices for individual countries, 1961–2013. Retrieved July 12, 2016, from https://www.ers.usda.gov/data-products/international-agricultural-productivity/.
Wang, Y. Z. (1998). All-around contracting is the conscious choice of hundreds of millions of farmers: commemorating the 20th anniversary of China's rural reform. *Party Literature, 6*, 38–43.
Wang, H. B. (2005). The practical process of the reform of Chinese state-owned enterprises (1979–2003). *Research on Chinese Economic History, 3*, 106–107.
Wang, B. (2008). Recalling earning work points in rural areas. *Financial Economy, 4*, 68–69.
Wang, C. Z., & Jiang, Z. G. (1989). Recognizing the economic situation & improving governance. *Macroeconomic Management, 2*, 5–7.
Wu, C. L. (1981). Several issues on paid use of funds. *Finance and Accounting, 4*, 7–9.
Wu, L. (1996). The party's understanding of the Soviet Union's economic construction model and its limitations before and after the Eighth National Congress of the CPC. *Studies in Contemporary Chinese History, 5*, 19–21.
Wu, L., & Xiao, X. (2009). A brief discussion on the evolution of the commodity price formation mechanism in 60 years since the founding of the P.R.C. *Finance and Trade Economics, 9*, 47–58.
Xiao, P. (2008). The experience and enlightenment of the fiscal reform of "dividing tax types, verifying revenue and expenditure, and grading contracting." *Financial Supervision, 5*, 16–18.
Xiao, D. L. (2015). A study of economic adjustment from 1979 to 1981. *Research on the History of the CPC, 9*, 65–79.
Xing, H. H. (1982). Two questions about the implementation of cross-regional and cross-sectoral economic unions of state-owned enterprises. *Journal of Hubei University (Philosophy and Social Sciences Edition), 5*, 65–68.

Xing, H. (1982). A highly centralized fiscal system with unified collection and distribution in 1950. *China Finance, 11,* 37–39.

Xu, B. L. (2009). Reform of the state-owned assets management system. *State-Owned Assets Management, 10,* 56–61.

Yan, G. P. (2007). A historical investigation and reflection on the development of commune and brigade enterprises before 1984. *Research on Contemporary Chinese History, 2,* 60–69.

Yang, G. P. (1981). Several issues in the adjustment of the machinery industry. *Finance and Economics Research, 4,* 19–24.

Yang, G. (1988). A series of investigations on the reform process of large and medium-sized state-owned enterprises: primary contracting system advanced contracting system shareholding system. *Tianfu New Theory, 2,* 9–12.

Yang, F. (2005). A historical review of RMB exchange rate system. *Research on Chinese Economic History, 4,* 59–64.

Yong, T. (2005). Deng Xiaoping's main contribution to the sinicization of Marxism. *Marxist Philosophical Research, 5,* 611–620.

Zang, N. K. (2000). Positioning of government functions after the clarification of property rights of township and village enterprises. *Research on Township and Village Enterprises, 2,* 27–29.

Zhang, L. H. (1994). On inflation and bank run. *Economist, 7,* 19–21.

Zhao, J. W. (1998). Some new insights into the price scissors between industrial and agricultural products. *Price Monthly, 10,* 7–9.

Zhao, Z. R. (2009). China's fiscal reform and the imbalance of provincial fiscal capacity: review, analysis and recommendations. *Public Administration Review, 2,* 73–100.

Zheng, J. H. (1983). The nature of company's own funds and related issues. *Jianghan Forum, 1,* 1–5.

Zhou, Q. R. (1987). Farmers, markets, and institutional innovations: deeper reforms facing rural development 8 years after contracting production to households. *Economic Research, 1,* 3–16.

Zhou, S. L. (1988). Contract management responsibility system of enterprises has a strong vitality. *Economic Management, 5,* 4–8.

Zhou, S. D. (2011). Changes in the official ideology in contemporary China. The Griffith Asia Institute. Retrieved October 20, 2016, from https://www.griffith.edu.au/__data/assets/pdf_file/0011/333749/Zhou-Regional-Outlook-Paper-29.pdf.

Zhu, Y. W. (2006). Combination of the two taxes should select the "high merger" plan. *China Economic Weekly, 22,* 30–31.

Zong, H. (1998). Foreign trade business of China's aviation industry in pace with reform and opening up. *China Foreign Trade, 1,* 19.

Zou, X. Q. (1987). On the reform of liquidity management system. *Financial Research, 10,* 30–31.

Chapter 4
Eve of Socialist Market Economy: The 2nd-Phase Reform

By far, the 10-year evolutionary reform has enabled China to experience the power of the "invisible hand" in the marketization of a planned economy which consisted of diverse interest groups, both individuals and institutions. When all the parties involved were chasing their own interests, not only did clashes emerge, the demand for a better system grew even stronger, a system in which both public and private assets could be under legal protection and loopholes that may encourage the *embezzlement of those belonging to others are non-existent*. Although until today, such an ideal is still not fully realized, the expectation itself reflects that when a country is going through a transition stage, attention should not be solely attached to the speed; rather, effective regulation of the activities in the process should be given a greater priority. Otherwise, an elusive prosperity is only synonymous with erosion of resources in a more lavish degree, and foreshadows but a misfortune that is irreversible.

1 Systemic Change

Toward the end of the 1980s, a more radical reform was found necessary not only for the well-being of the people and a more balanced development of the economy, but also to pave the way for the country's resumption of the contracting party status in GATT (following the establishment of the World Trade Organization in 1995, the ambition was replaced by a new application for the WTO accession). To ensure that these objectives could be achieved in due course, a higher governmental efficiency was found both critical and indispensable. Just like the fact that adults would no longer wear the clothes of their childhood, transformation of government functions becomes a must when the macro-environment is no longer the same. Therefore, from 1988 onward, massive administrative reforms were unveiled and they covered a more comprehensive scope of engagements such as the innovation of government roles, simplification of bureaucratic procedures, and staff reduction, etc. Meanwhile, regulatory functions were to be transferred to the market so that there would be a

C. Yu, *China's Economy: Towards 2049*,
https://doi.org/10.1007/978-981-15-9227-0_4

greater efficiency in the allocation of resources. With regard to enterprises, their operations would be separated from the jurisdiction of the government, thus making them autonomous entities acting in accordance with market principles. Furthermore, by overhauling the internal management system, this round of reforms aimed to create for the government a fresh image which was less manipulative, yet more supportive in the building of the socialist economy.

Referring to the concept of "socialist market economy", its first official recognition happened at the 14th National *Party*'s *Congress* of 1992. Simultaneously, it was also endorsed as the reform goal of China, implying that the establishment of a market economy was no longer a contentious issue, as long as the path was moving in a socialist direction. Symbolic of an "emancipation of the mind" ('*jiefang sixiang*'), this move was followed in November 1993 by a more concrete strategy put forward in the "Decision on Issues Concerning the Establishment of a Socialist Market Economic Structure". As the first major document encompassing various aspects of transition, the Decision highlighted two major priorities, i.e. the building of a uniform and open market system, and development of market-supporting mechanisms. Specifically, the former one was a non-discriminatory market system in which all participants could play by the same rules of the game and there was no external interference to obstruct fairness. As to the latter, it was not merely related to the improvement of the existing macroeconomic instruments (from fiscal, financial, to monetary, etc.) so that they may better serve the increasingly decentralized economy; moreover, it also called for a greater role of intermediary organizations like accounting firms, quality certification bureaus, consultancies and asset evaluation institutions, etc. In addition, a plan was included to unify tax rates among enterprises of different ownership structures. By clarifying these numerous tasks, China was in fact attempting to align its domestic policies and practices with international norms, which was equally a prerequisite for the successful membership of the WTO.

In summary, the November 1993 document was a milestone in China's history of reform because for the first time, China decided to abandon the central-planning system and set up a modern market system by assimilating both the fruits and lessons of other countries. This is not just a learning process, it also means self-negation in certain respects. Around the world, there was no precedent for a socialist country to make a fundamental transition into market economy, nor was there any established theory that could prophesy if what had been happening in China would lead to a sure success or failure. However, with the clock ticking, China did not have the luxury to wait for a definite answer. To make sure that the next stage of the "long march" would yield some satisfactory results, the country first and foremost had to be well-prepared in its ideological and institutional spheres.

2 The Southern Tour Amid Ideological Clashes

Before the consensus to establish a socialist market economy in mainland China was reached in 1992, there had existed a lot of confrontations and conflicts within the

CPC to cast off some obsolete ideological bonds. Since all reforms involve some change in the rules of the game and what happened in China was no exception, it would equally shake the economic base as well as some other aspects of the superstructure. Concerning the interest groups representing the old regime, they were largely government officials at various levels, for fear of losing power and prestige, they were among the most obstructive forces aiming to resist the change. Therefore, instead of complying with the laws of the market, they preferred to keep the status quo, i.e. to make central planning stay at the heart of the economy and exert its control over capital investment, labor movement and product circulation, etc. But contrary to these conservatives, the radical reformers on the other hand wanted to remove central plan to the secondary position so that the market could gain dominance and play a much bigger role.

At that time, China was already governed by its "third generation leaders", with Jiang Zemin as the core (Mao Zedong is taken as the "first generation" leader and Deng Xiaoping being the "second generation"). Jiang became the General Secretary of the Communist Party of China in 1989 and like Deng Xiaoping, he was equally keen on modernizing the Chinese economy. Nevertheless, 1989 was a year when many reform efforts were halted due to the interferences of the conservative. Simultaneously, hot ideological debates persisted within the Party over the magnitude, pace and direction of the reform. At this critical juncture, to prevent an abortion of what had been achieved in the previous decade and confirm China's commitment to economic liberalization by pushing forward the implementation of radical free market methods, Deng Xiaoping embarked on a trip to the south, which was popularly known as '*nan xun*' (southern tour) from January 18th to February 21st, 1992. Although Deng was already 88 years old and had retired from all his party and government positions, he was still the most revered political figure in China.

During his visit of cities like Wuchang (Hubei Province), Shenzhen, Shanghai and Zhuhai, the former Chinese leader made several speeches which boldly dismissed the leftist ideology and conservative thinking that prohibited continued reform. With a famous remark "development is of overriding importance" ('*fazhan shi yingdaoli*'), he explicitly asserted that reform was the only path of the country and that whoever was opposed to it should step down. The symbolic meaning of Deng's tour was immense in that it helped secure China's second phase of reform and opening up. As a result, the country was able to effectively avoid the return of old planned patterns. Moreover, it also allowed China to confidently join the WTO, a step without which it would never expect to usher in a golden period of development in the first decade of the twenty-first century.

3 Retrenchment Efforts and the Tradeoffs (1989–1991)

Beginning in the second half of the 1980s, China's economy demonstrated a mixed picture that was both encouraging and worrying. On the one hand, industrial output kept growing at a double-digit pace for several consecutive years; at the same time, nominal wage rates rose at an average level of almost 15 PCT and reached RMB1, 935 in 1989. Consequently, the increased supply and disposable income encouraged consumption, which made nationwide retail sales of consumer goods nearly doubled from RMB430.5 billion of 1985 to RMB810.14 billion in 1989 (NBS, 2001). However, since economically, a speed too fast is often symbolic of an abnormal state of development, the seemingly positive phenomena in China was soon accompanied by an accelerating inflation rate, suggesting that the economy had been severely overheated. Retail price index, another measure of the general level of inflation reflected in the retail price of a basket of goods and services, surged from 128.1 in 1985 to 203.4 in 1989 (1978 = 100). Fairly speaking, the reasons were largely institutional and rooted above all in the expansionary fiscal and monetary policies adopted by China, in addition to other structural imbalances which weakened its economic foundations.

Obviously, if the runaway situation could not be harnessed in an efficient manner, real crisis may soon arrive and endanger the stability of the whole country. Although in anticipation of even higher prices, hoarding had been taken by both households and enterprises as the best option to save money, it undoubtedly put more pressure on inflation. In the summer of 1988, with an aim to curtail the rampant inflation and end the wave of mass panic buying, an emergency austerity scheme was released. Under the program, the key measures included squeezing bank credit and money supply, and withholding or even rolling back some reform policies, especially those related to the private sector. Within a couple of years, by cutting inflation rate to a fairly low level of 3.1 PCT (CPI) in 1990, the drive successfully tamed the hot economy. Nonetheless, no pains no gains.

Together with the tightened belt, costs gradually incurred too. For example, since the adjustment aimed particularly at restricting bank loans to the rural industry, township and village enterprises (TVEs) were denied new credit and compelled to raise funds from within, i.e. from among the peasants themselves (Hu, 2008). Besides, supply of raw materials and energy were also limited, making them unable to continue with normal production. What's more, a campaign to increase administrative control over the private sector was launched around China in August 1989 to crack down the rampant tax evasion and illegal wholesale profits (Zhou, 1990). As a consequence, with the number of TVEs falling down by over 195,000 to 18.69 million in 1989, contraction of the workforce exceeded 1.78 million and 1.02 million in 1989 and 1990 respectively. Meanwhile, the shrinking rural industry increased the relative attractiveness of agriculture, which was subjective to fewer restrictions. By absorbing more resources, the grain output of 1990 rose over 13PCT to 446.24 million tons, as compared to 1988. Obviously, this was achieved at the expense of TVEs. For the country as a whole, the lowered inflation had yet one more trade-off. With the intervention of the government and tightened control over fixed-asset investment, GDP grew at 4.1 PCT only in 1989 before further declining to 3.8 PCT in 1990; yet prior to 1988, the pace had been much more impressive.

4 Monetary Instrument for Economic Cool Down

In many countries, especially the developed ones, monetary policy has always been treated as an important instrument for the government to intervene and overhaul economy at the macro level. As to China, it is only after the establishment of the central banking system in the early 1980s that its monetary policy began to exercise the proper role in macroeconomic management. Gradually, with the deepening of the reform, the system introduced some international practices like reserve requirements, refinancing, rediscount, etc., which further enhanced its functions. Actually, what happened during the late 1980s is a typical example of its growing influence. On the one hand, the central bank (the People's Bank of China) announced an increment in the reserve ratio of commercial banks from the original 10 PCT to 12 PCT and 13 PCT in 1987 and 1988 respectively (Sun, 2013). On the other hand, it also raised the interest rate on one-year time deposit from a low of 8.64 PCT to a high of 11.34 PCT in February 1989; for one-year working capital loans, the rate went up from 9 PCT to 11.34 PCT at the same time (based on the "Notice of the People's Bank of China on the Adjustment of the Deposit and Loan Interest Rates" issued in January 1989). Consequently, the tightened spending and expensive credit resulted in a hard landing for the Chinese economy. Although hard landing is not without its adverse impact, a temporary modification of the pace or even slowdown is definitely necessary to mobilize all the resources on a new growth track which is healthier and more sustainable over the long run.

Simultaneously, there emerged a misinterpretation of the relationship between economic reform and the availability of financial resources, in which the latter was taken as a determinant of how fast the reform should proceed. Once there was a shift in the monetary policy, be it contractionary or expansionary, the signal perceived by the public would automatically change. When inflation decelerated (the consumer price index stayed at 103.1 and 103.4 in 1990 and 1991 respectively, preceding year = 100) after the economic cool down, access to financial resources was once more widened, with the one-year time deposit rates slashed from 10.08 PCT to 8.64 PCT in August 1990 before being further reduced to 7.56 PCT in April 1991. In terms of the one-year working capital loans, it also underwent a downward adjustment from 10.08 PCT to 9.36 PCT in August 1990 before reaching 8.64 PCT in April 1991 (according to the "Notice of the People's Bank of China on the Adjustment of the Deposit and Loan Interest Rates" issued in August 1990 and March 1991).

For enterprises and institutions, the message they received from these cuts was the government readiness for another round of growth and expansion. Encouraged by the loosening of monetary policy, investment in fixed assets underwent a dramatic increase of 23.9 PCT in 1991. Over the next two years, encouraged by Deng Xiaoping's visit to the south, the figure kept soaring and in 1993, a record high 61.8 PCT was registered (NBS, 2000). Till then, history repeated itself because the economy was once more overheating; in fact, the symptom had already emerged since the second half of 1992. As the most direct measure, China's GDP from 1992 to 1994 grew at double-digit rates. Meanwhile, the CPI which had been held in check since 1990, ballooned once again to 114.7 and 124.1 in 1993 and 1994 respectively (preceding year = 100). Together, these conditions suggested that the monetary policy of the country had been too lax and was in need of immediate restrictions. Otherwise, greater wastes and stronger turbulences would very likely make the situation beyond control.

To tell the truth, the central government had already claimed on numerous occasions that economic growth should not be achieved at the expense of high inflation. Nevertheless, given the fact that irrational pursuit of fast expansion persisted stubbornly in many regions, it was very difficult to restrain excessive investment financed via bank credit. Further, it should also be acknowledged that the current monetary policy was by no means flawless and thereby created inflationary pressures. Improvement of the system, as a result, was not just necessary, but also demanded consistent effort, especially in the building of an effective supervisory mechanism compatible with a transition economy. Subsequently, in June 1993, CCCPC and the State Council jointly issued the "Opinions on Strengthening Macroeconomic Control under the Current Economic Situation" (or known as the Austerity Plan). Consisted of 16 concrete measures, it focused chiefly on the regulation of the financial order which was rather chaotic at that time. In general, these measures included withdrawal of the loans extended outside the credit plan, halt to all forms of irregular interbank borrowing, ban of unwarranted fund-raising, and clearance of disorganized investment activities, etc.

Aware of the weaknesses of the country's monetary watchdog, i.e. the People's Bank of China, in dealing with local pressures and regulating the financial system, the then vice Premier Zhu Rongji took over the governorship of the PBoC himself from July 1993 to June 1995, which greatly elevated the status of the Bank in the central government. By centralizing the power of drafting monetary policies in the PBoC's headquarters, Zhu's governorship facilitated the modernization of the monetary policy framework. Besides, it also consolidated the Bank's authority in currency issuance, credit control, and interest rate adjustment, etc. As a major instrument to counter inflation, interest rates were raised in May and July 1993. Considering the weak financial position of many state-owned enterprises, the PBoC raised lending rates by much more modest amounts as compared to the rise in the savings rates. For example, on May 15th 1993, the one-year time deposit rate grew by 1.62PCT (from 7.56 PCT to 9.18 PCT) while the rate for one-year working capital loans only floated by 0.72 PCT (from 8.64 PCT to 9.36 PCT) (based on the "Notice of the People's Bank of China on the Adjustment of the Deposit and Loan Interest Rates" issued in May 1993). Inevitably, the imbalance between the conspicuous growth of deposit rates and the fractional hike of lending rates during a time of accelerated inflation squeezed the interest margins of commercial banks. However, these Chinese banks did not have much choice since they knew clearly that if they charged higher rates, more enterprises would become insolvent. By July 1993, the two rates were made the same, both at 10.98 PCT on one-year basis (as per the "Notice of the People's Bank of China on the Adjustment of the Deposit and Loan Interest Rates" issued in July 1993).

Table 1 A comparison of growth in GDP, CPI and money supply, 1994–1998

Year	GDP growth rate (PCT)	Consumer price index (preceding year = 100)	M0 growth rate (cash in circulation/PCT)	M1 growth rate (narrow money/PCT)	M2 growth rate (broad money/PCT)
1994	13.1	124.1	24.3	26.2	34.5
1995	10.9	117.1	8.2	16.8	29.5
1996	10	108.3	11.6	18.9	25.3
1997	9.3	102.8	15.6	16.5	17.3
1998	7.8	99.2	10.1	11.9	14.8

Source NBS (2011)

Indeed, from this round of austerity, it can be found that the role of monetary measures had been quite essential. In a broader sense, with a slowdown in the growth of money supply and rekindled desire of savers to put money at banks, the rapidly soaring inflation was tamed at a low sacrifice ratio of GDP. Usually, there is a close relationship between money-supply growth and long-term price inflation. If there is a rapid increase in money supply, then the overall price level of a country will also pick up. Broad money (M2), which includes cash in circulation (M0), savings by residents, and time deposits by enterprises, etc., is a key economic indicator used to forecast inflation. As indicated in Table 1 below, although the growth rates of M2 stayed at a double-digit level from 1994 to 1998, the pace has been obviously moving down. At the same time, inflation too kept declining in a rapid way. During 1996–1998 in particular, the downward trend became rather remarkable. By comparison, China's GDP maintained at a fairly stable momentum of growth, implying that the country did not suffer too much from the austerity as before and the economy has thus realized a soft landing.

5 Tax Assignment System, the 2nd Round of Fiscal Reform

The fiscal reform that took place in the 1980s was very similar to the reforms of agriculture and industry during the same period because both were predominantly oriented to the devolving of power from central to lower-level governments and enterprises. As had already happened beforehand, the process of this well-intended decentralization was also mixed with an undesirable loss of order and even chaos, which later compelled the state to re-centralize. Perhaps it is not history itself that moves in a cyclical pattern, it is the failure to reflect over the past lessons that has caused repeated adoption of the same approach to get out of the trouble. But sadly, the root of the problem remained unresolved. If a nation's economy can be likened to a jumbo machine, then all the components should be finely tuned so that it can run well. Otherwise, a partial adjustment may only lead to incompatibility and thus a lack of synergy, which would sooner or later undermine the performance of the whole.

For China, its mega economic reform was not inherently consistent nor complete. For lack of a well-developed market system, especially major price reform and significant changes in the way commodities circulate, fiscal decentralization alone could hardly bring about lasting positive impact. For some twenty years, despite the shifts in productivity and cost, the mechanism applied to determine prices was scarcely altered. Therefore, it is impractical for enterprises to take actions that really make economic sense. The same holds true for the local governments, when delegation of greater fiscal authorities was not accompanied by simultaneous relaxation of constraints, especially on price, then misleading price signals would easily mobilize resources toward the wrong direction. No wonder out of narrow-minded protectionism to favor local interests, duplication of investment projects gave rise to fever and imbalance in the national economy, a situation which could only be countered by passive intervention from the center.

5.1 Establishment of the System and Its Administrative Organs

Following the trend in the second half of the 1980s, the share of the central government revenues in the country's total continued to shrink rapidly after 1990, which fell from 33.8 PCT to 22 PCT in 1993. At the same time, another disturbing decrease was in the ratio of government revenue against GDP, which showed a straight downward slope after 1978. By comparison, the proportion between the two was still 31.2 PCT in 1978; yet by 1993, it dropped to only 12.6 PCT (NBS, 2001). Concerned about the potential political and economic consequences of its weakened fiscal power, as well as the unsatisfactory contribution of the revenue to national development, the central decision-makers were determined to introduce a new fiscal reform. This time, they understood clearly that minor modifications of the existing revenue-sharing formula could not help them raise the two ratios; instead, they were in need of a bolder plan of institutional restructuring.

After some experiments in four provincial areas (i.e. Liaoning, Zhejiang, Tianjin and Xinjiang) and five municipal regions (i.e. Chongqing, Wuhan, Shenyang, Dalian and Qingdao), the State Council in the end of 1993 promulgated the "Decision on Implementing Tax Assignment Management System", a replacement of the former negotiation-based system (Wang, 1994a,1994b). Named in Chinese '*fen shui zhi*', it laid the foundation for today's intergovernmental fiscal framework. With an attempt to consolidate the central control of national revenues and highlight the role of public finance in macroeconomic management, revenue sources and expenditure responsibilities were divided between the center and local governments in a concrete way. For example, no longer based on a negotiated lump-sum revenues remitted to the center, the new revenue-sharing system classified strictly three categories of revenues: fixed central revenue (import tariffs, consumption tax, import-related consumption and value-added tax collected by the customs, income tax of centrally-owned enterprises, etc.), fixed local revenue (business tax, income tax of local enterprises, personal income tax, house property tax, and arable land use tax, etc.), and shared revenue (value-added tax with a 75/25 ratio between the center and local, securities exchange stamp tax with a ratio of 50/50, etc.). Referring to the expenditure items, they were also clearly separated between the two sides, while the center was to look after investment in national defense, foreign aid, technological upgrading of centrally-owned enterprises, and infrastructures under its jurisdiction; the local governments should bear the outlays of urban maintenance and construction, subsidies, science, education, cultural and health undertakings, to name just a few.

As a major move to straighten out the intergovernmental fiscal relations and enhance the re-distributive function of the center, separate state and local tax administration systems were officially formed by the State Administration of Taxation (SAT) in 1994 (Zeng, 1994). SAT on the one hand had its own branch bureaus and operated from the provincial down to the county level; simultaneously, there was an independent local tax service acting as a part of the local finance department and funded also by local resources. The setup of this parallel structure means that ever since, local tax bureaus were no longer entrusted the task of collecting virtually all the taxes. Instead, their job became simpler, i.e. to levy those assigned in the category of local revenues only. Under the same rule, the newly-established state taxation organs were responsible for imposing central revenues and shared revenues. Apart from tax collection, the SAT also represented the highest authority to oversee the national taxation system, particularly the policy making of different localities.

Considering that in the 1980s, a lack of effective supervision had caused many subordinate officials to alter their tax rates arbitrarily (in the form of tax exemptions or tax holiday), which favored their own interests but endangered the macroeconomic stability, a tightened control and regulation were considered to be absolutely necessary to a balanced development of the entire nation (Liu, 2009). From 1994, the once rather common interference of the local governments in tax administration was substantially restrained. Moreover, tax concessions and exemptions, if any, should be first approved by the center before they were executed. From this single perspective, it is found that the 1994 fiscal reform was coupled with tremendous efforts in adjusting the subtle relationships among powerful parties of vested interests. Though by no means easy to cope with, they were prerequisites for China's fiscal system to become truly transparent and unbiased so as to better serve the requirements of a market economy.

5.2 *Arrangements to Stimulate the Local Governments*

Despite certain measures to limit the authorities of local officials, the central leaders understood clearly that if without their full cooperation, the goals of implementing tax assignment system could not be fulfilled. While it was inevitable to touch their interests, the center had to reaffirm that it would not happen too adversely. Therefore, to make sure that the transition from the old fiscal contracting system to the new one could take place in a smooth way, a number of concessions to the sub-national governments were included in the reform package of 1994. Since no one was willing to see a decline in revenue income, a transfer mechanism named "tax refunding system" ('*shuishou fanhuan zhidu*') was established and in a sense, it was more like a promise of the central government that the revenue retained by sub-national governments would not be lower than what they had received in 1993.

Under this mechanism, the retained revenue of 1993 would be taken as the "base" ('*ji shu*') for the calculation of the amount of the revenues returned from the center to the local. As far as the year 1993 was concerned, the center would guarantee a 100 PCT compensation in case net revenue losses incurred in any locality. Then starting from 1994, the total amount of rebate funds would be calculated in connection with the growth of consumption tax and value-added tax. If local revenues arising from these two items could rise by 1 PCT, then the central government would return up to 0.3 PCT on top of the base amount (Zhao, 2005). Acting like a buffer, the rebate scheme helped ease resistance from sub-national officials, especially at the outset of the reform. It offered them an assurance that increased tax flowing to the central government would only be derived from the additional part of the revenues, chiefly the VAT.

Here, regarding tax refund by the state, something that had happened beforehand is worth noting. In 1993, Beijing's decision to use 1993 (instead of 1992) as the base year for the new tax-assignment system was revealed prematurely to the lower-level governments, which soon prompted a collection fever. It has been reported that a variety of methods were used around the country, with some collected taxes in arrears or pushed local banks to lend to enterprises so that they could pay outstanding taxes, and others levied in advance the tax due in 1994. As a result, local revenues surged to RMB339.14 billion by the end of 1993, an increase of more than 35 PCT over that of 1992, which was RMB250.39 billion. If to compare the pace of growth with the preceding 10–20 years, this record was obviously abnormal yet understandable at that particular time period, for these officials had one common objective on mind, i.e. to collect as much as possible to maximize their base revenues for 1993 and once the new regime came into effect, they could expect to receive a larger refund from the center. Anyhow, from the point of view of the latter, the positive aspect is that it could utilize this occasion to test the real taxable capabilities of its subordinate governments; but the price was also huge: it had to pay a lot more in rebate in 1994, which actually reduced its revenues.

5.3 Restructuring of the Turnover Tax System

As noted, the radical fiscal reform launched in 1994 was triggered mainly by the low ratio of budgetary revenue to GDP, which reflected a weak tax intake and low efficiency in revenue collection. Therefore, the centerpiece of the reform involved an effort to increase the revenue elasticity of the tax system so that in the long run, the rate of revenue growth could match the development of the economy. Early in November 1993, Beijing's resolution to engage in the undertaking had already been included in its circular entitled the "Decision of the CCCPC on Various Issues Concerning the Building of a Socialist Market Economic Mechanism". Of the various critical tasks outlined, clause 18 focuses on the reform of the existing fiscal mechanism. While stressing the necessity to transform into tax assignment system and establish state and sub-state tax agencies, the Decision also laid out a number of principles governing the improvement of taxation work, e.g. equalization of tax burdens, simplification of tax structure, and rationalization of central and local powers, etc.

Regarding the concrete steps, the reorientation of turnover taxes ('*liuzhuan shui*', an indirect tax) towards VAT was also highlighted in the Decision. Before 1994, China's turnover taxes included product tax ('*chanpin shui*'), value-added tax ('*zengzhi shui*'), and business tax ('*yingye shui*') (Mo, 1994). In general, product tax as the dominant one was imposed on the total sales value of a good (either domestically manufactured or imported), whereas VAT was levied chiefly on the production process of certain industrial products (covering 31 taxable items from 1988 onward). In terms of business tax, it was applied to services rather than goods. The problem with the triple indirect taxes was the employment of over-complicated rates and calculation bases; as a result, disparities in treatment could not provide a level playing field for all enterprises, nor could it meet the goal of the government to create a fair environment to optimize the allocation of resources.

With a view to unifying the existing system and making it simpler, the State Council in December 1993 promulgated three important directives to guide the execution of three new types of indirect tax and they were the "Provisional Regulations of the PRC on Value-Added Tax", the "Provisional Regulations of the PRC on Business Tax", and the "Provisional Regulations of the PRC on Consumption Tax" (Li, 1994). Both the three laws went into effect on Jan. 1st, 1994 and from then on, VAT became the largest contributor to the nation's annual tax revenues, with a significantly broadened coverage ranging from all industrial products (either made at home or imported), wholesale and retail commodities, to services directly related to the processing and preparation of goods. For most of these products, the VAT rate was set at 17PCT, which was also the highest; referring to those agricultural goods like grains, edible vegetable oils and fertilizers, as well as water, gas for household use, the rate was 13 PCT. The lowest zero-percent rate applied only to exports, or as otherwise provided by the State Council. Together with the enlargement of products subject to VAT, taxpayers were no longer just limited to domestic enterprises, all foreign-invested businesses were involved (prior to 1994, they paid consolidated industrial and commercial tax instead of VAT), either joint ventures or wholly foreign-owned subsidiaries.

Similar to VAT, business tax in the new structure of turnover taxes also had a widened scope of payers covering both the domestic and foreign ventures operating in China. With tax rates adjusted from 3 to 20 PCT instead of the former 3 PCT to 15 PCT, it was applied not only to the provision of labor services (like entertainment, food, financial, and transport services) as before; it covered the transfer of tangible and intangible assets, especially real estate sales as well. Besides, the most prominent change in 1994 is that by introducing the new consumption tax, product tax and consolidated industrial & commercial tax were simultaneously abolished. Moreover, based on the regulation by the State Council, consumption tax targeted 11 categories of consumer goods, such as cigarettes, alcohol, cosmetics, jewels, gasoline, motorcycles, and cars, etc., with the rates varying from 3 to 45 PCT. By assigning consumption tax as a turnover tax, it is very likely that enterprises were discouraged from producing these goods.

5.4 Unification of Nominal Tax Rates on Enterprise Income

Before 1994, another reflection of the tax burden being unequally distributed across enterprises was the enterprise income tax. By then, Chinese large and medium-sized SOEs were subject to 55 PCT income tax rate whereas for small SOEs and collectively-owned enterprises, eight level progressive rates of excess profit from the lowest 10 PCT to the highest 55 PCT were applied. In terms of private enterprises, they were taxed 35 PCT. Fairly speaking, foreign-funded enterprises at that time were better off because their rate was on average 33 PCT (i.e. 30 PCT national tax plus 3 PCT local surcharge). In case they were located in special economic zones, it was an even more favorable 15 PCT. Additionally, for manufacturing ventures which had been operated in China for ten years, in the initial two years after they began to generate profit, they could be exempted from taxation; after that, they could still enjoy a 50 PCT tax reduction for another three years.

Apparently, it was for the attraction of more overseas capital and advanced technologies that the Chinese government offered preferential tax rates to foreign-invested enterprises. But in contrast, large and medium-sized SOEs had to bear a heavier tax burden and became the most disadvantaged group under the unfair taxation scheme, which partially explains why their after-tax profitability had remained lower than that of the non-state entities since the late 1980s. On certain occasions, they preferred to cut the amount of taxable profit by increasing the wages and benefits of workers even to the point of reporting losses for there was little threat of bankruptcy to unprofitable enterprises. Fortunately, this situation did not last very long before deeper-level macroeconomic reforms were carried out in the early 1990s, particularly on taxation. Based on the "Provisional Regulations of the PRC on Enterprise Income Tax" by the State Council in November 1993, China from 1994 started to adopt a uniform tax rate of 33 PCT not only for large and medium-sized SOEs, but also for all types of enterprises regardless of their ownership structures. While it is true that the new rate enabled domestic enterprises to gain the same treatment as their foreign counterparts; to avoid dampening the enthusiasm of investors from abroad, the 15 PCT rate levied on foreign enterprises in special economic zones remained, and if they chose coastal regions, then what they had to pay was 24 PCT (Zhu, 2006).

5.5 *Positive Effects of the Reformed Scheme*

In any sense, the 1994 fiscal reform should not be merely considered as a slight modification that did not touch the very basic of the old system, it was rather comprehensive in reshuffling almost all the key aspects of the institution, from the legal framework, division of power, to the tax structure and collection management, etc. Regarding the chief accomplishment of this endeavor, it was manifested mainly in the adjustment of two pairs of relationship, i.e. government and enterprise, central and local governments. As to the former, what had happened beforehand is that there was no fixed rules which required both parties to observe strictly; and in this regard, even the binding force of the contract responsibility system was quite limited. Since everything was up to negotiation, too much flexibility caused a lack of respect for the mechanism, which unavoidably undermined the quality of performance. But after 1994, their relationship was more guided by norms and regulations; in particular, the previous 32 taxes on industries and commerce were simplified into the current 18 (Ma, 1996) and enterprises, no matter state or non-state, were charged with a uniform income tax rate of 33 PCT. As a result, instead of spending a lot of time bargaining with each other, both could better concentrate on their own duties.

Simultaneously, China's intergovernmental fiscal relations also went through a fundamental change. Prior to 1994 when contract-based revenue sharing system was adopted, emphasis was laid on local interests and growth. Thereby, the center had to rely on the local governments to collect most taxes; in terms of the allocation of revenues, it was shared between the local and the center based on a formula negotiated separately. Indeed, tax administration at that time was ruled by negotiation rather than by law, which delegated local officials too much discretionary power to make up their own policies as long as they thought appropriate to the circumstances. To some degree, these multiple arrangements only fostered self-centeredness and widened the gap among regions, especially between the coastal and the interior (Lu, 1998). By shifting toward tax-assignment system which highlighted discipline, standardized laws became the foundation of a more transparent and stable relationship. With a clarified division of revenues and responsibilities, the two sides were better aware of their roles and benefits. Different from the practices beforehand, the autonomy of local governments was curtailed and the center would not step into local taxation affairs either. Besides, the establishment of a restraint mechanism enabled the latter to reclaim its power of setting rates and defining tax bases, which was quite essential to facilitate the adjustment of industrial structure and optimize the allocation of resources across the country.

5.6 *Problems Behind the Unsatisfactory Performances*

Nevertheless, apart from the achievements, problems could not be ignored. Most prominently, the fiscal reform of 1994 did not raise the share of central revenues in the nation's total as expected. Apart from that very year when an impressive growth was realized from 22 PCT of 1993 to 55.7 PCT, there had been a steady decline over the next three years before it slightly rebounded to 49.5PCT in 1998. By coincidence, similar phenomenon occurred to the revenue-to-GDP ratio as well, which witnessed a fall from 11.2 PCT of 1994 to 10.9 PCT in 1996; until 1997, it showed only a sluggish recovery when hitting 11.6 PCT (NBS, 2001). Actually, there are numerous reasons to explain why the performance turned out to be unsatisfactory and among them, the most prominent factor is perhaps that some local taxes, such as personal income tax and business tax, rose very sharply; but for certain central revenues like value-added tax and import tariffs, the pace of growth was not equally dynamic. For example, the local business tax in 1995 totaled RMB82.82 billion, representing a 28 PCT growth over that of 1994, which was RMB64.74 billion (Anonym, 2013). In contrast, concerning the VAT collected by the center, it climbed from RMB172.84 billion to RMB194.79 billion over the same period, an increase of just 12.7 PCT (Bai & Wu, 2010).

Besides, on Dec. 31st, 1993, in order to enhance the transparency of foreign trade system, China once more slashed its import tariff rates on 2,898 tariff lines with an average rate of 8.8 PCT (Zhang, 1996a, 1996b). Consequently, its tariff revenue registered RMB29.18 billion in 1995, a rise of only 7 PCT over the previous year. In addition, the low profitability of state-owned enterprises should be one more important factor for China's weak revenue performance throughout the post-reform years. In 1993, the income tax of SOEs still contributed 13.7 PCT to the nation's total tax revenues; but later, the share was no longer exceeded and dropped straight to 8 PCT by 1998 (NBS, 2001).

Further, an important issue not fully addressed in the tax assignment reform was the extra-budgetary funds. As the name suggests, these are revenues not included in the official budget system but belonged to the fees charged by sub-national government agencies according to the relevant rules and regulations. In 1994, while the center pushed down expenditure responsibilities to subordinate governments, it failed to provide adequate financial support at the same time. Although there was a transfer program for redistribution purposes, it did not look after the regional disparities in income level and fiscal capacity, thus widening the gap between the rich and the poor. Consequently, core public services such as education and health care were under-funded in those less-developed rural areas. Under the mounting pressure of tightened budgetary situation and the growing spending needs, what local officials did was to resort to extra-budgetary funds, causing a significant portion of their expenditure circumvent the formal budgetary channels (Gao, 2007).

In fact, such a phenomenon had already existed under the fiscal contracting system before 1994, when many localities shifted revenues to these funds to avoid sharing revenues with the center. After 1994, they continued to utilize the same approach to deal with central restrictions on the use of funds. With enormous amount of revenues wandering outside the budgetary system, the control of fiscal authorities over the allocation of resources, together with their re-distributive power was weakened. In the long run, their potential to proliferate equally posed a big threat to the soundness of fiscal control and the overall quality of public financial management. Given the severity of its impact, an independent public sector auditing system covering extra-budgetary revenues and expenditures should be developed. In addition, the central leaders also need to establish strong gate-keeping mechanisms to reduce the probability that unjustified funds would escape the supervision and eventually damage the integrity of the budgeting system (Zhou, 1997). Of course, administrative measures to mend the loopholes and leakages should be accompanied by appropriate separation of fiscal powers between diverse levels of government, particularly considering the vastness of China's territory and sharp distinctions from one area to another.

Therefore, instead of having the central government fix the rules for all taxes, the local governments should be allowed flexible ranges within which the rates could float, provided that certain conditions required by the law were met. If local officials wanted to introduce new taxes, they ought to seek the approval from the above. Similarly, legislation should also demarcate expenditure responsibilities so as to ensure that localities enjoy the autonomy in customizing the levels and kinds of local services according to the needs of their residents. The advantage for doing so is that it can protect the local governments from arbitrary burden-sharing requirements that might otherwise have been imposed by the central bureaucracy. With a view to balancing the fiscal deficit of poor regions and meeting the minimum quality of services, central transfer of funds should be backed by a well-designed formula including key measures and data that can genuinely reflect local conditions.

From the above analysis, it could be found that the tasks facing the Chinese fiscal authorities in the late 1990s were still quite arduous and among them, the most pressing one is perhaps legislation. Fundamentally, since both the central and local governments are executors and defenders of the law, the defects that remained in China's fiscal system, like arbitrary policy changes, high-rising transaction costs, lack of transparency in fiscal management, and a mismatch between fiscal power and accountability, etc., were largely due to their misplaced roles. However, a full market economy demands law-binding behaviors and before the law, no single party could enjoy any special privilege. Fairly speaking, as an attempt to replace the former discretion-based system with a rule-oriented one, the 1994 fiscal reform was preceded and followed by the passage of a dozen of laws and regulations, which demonstrated a move in the right direction. With the deepening of the reform, it is inevitable that more obstacles would emerge, especially when there is a clash of interests between certain groups. Yet if the central government could exert the leadership by restraining its own powers and strictly abiding by the established rules, officials at the lower level would be willing to follow suit, thus ensuring a sound institutional foundation for the ultimate fulfillment of goals.

6 Restructuring of the SOEs

As a universal principle, transition into market economy would not be genuinely successful unless enterprises, which serve as the cornerstone, become independent players whose operation is no longer manipulated by the *government*, but subject chiefly to the laws of *supply and demand*. In the case of China, this criterion is equally applicable. By the year 1993, the economy had become increasingly fragmented, with the corporate world divided into four parts: SOEs dominating heavy industry and utilities, collectively-owned TVEs focusing on labor-intensive products and export assembly, foreign-funded enterprises mainly confined to export, and private companies of generally very small size. Moreover, they were put under distinct and often different legal and regulatory frameworks. But no matter how, the SOEs remained indisputably a dominant force driving China's industry. In 1994, for example, their share exceeded 37 PCT of the gross output value of the industry. In terms of employment, some 112 million workers were recruited by the SOEs, accounting for 66.7 PCT of the urban employment (Chen, 1996). Referring to fixed-asset investment, the state sector claimed RMB961.5 billion, or over 56 PCT of the nation's total.

However, behind their large scale, a harsh reality was that in 1994 alone, a total number of 4,220, or 29.7 PCT of the large and medium-sized SOEs suffered losses that amounted to RMB32.21 billion (Wang, 2011). When it comes to those industrial SOEs, the performance was even worse. In the same year, their overall losses reached RMB48.26 billion whereas the profit made was merely RMB82.9 billion. To put it in a more concrete way, the magnitude of the losses was in excess of 1 PCT of the GDP recorded for 1994. In 1995, the situation further deteriorated, with losses surging to RMB63.96 billion and profit shrinking to RMB66.56 billion (NBS, 2012). The government, while collecting less and less revenues from the SOEs, had to provide more subsidies to *prevent them from collapsing* and the subsequent massive redundancies. Obviously, it was just a temporary solution, especially when coupled with the huge drain on state assets through bank loans, these subsidies threatened to cause macroeconomic instabilities like high inflation. Provided that effective remedies could be adopted immediately to cure the ills of the SOEs, China's overall pace of development would be severely undermined.

In fact, what persisted behind the mounting losses of profit was a shockingly low efficiency and this should be attributed first and foremost to the governance structure of the SOEs. Under the premise of public ownership, most of them displayed a number of common characteristics, e.g. insider control, soft budget constraint, and managerial incompetence, etc. (Zhang & Wang, 2006). Despite the fact that by then, incentives like profit-sharing, two-tier pricing schemes, as well as provision of certain autonomy to managers were still available to unleash efficiency and boost output, fundamental issues like property rights and organizational governance did not gain sufficient attention, especially when considering from the perspective of the small and medium-sized SOEs. In 1995, of the 87,905 industrial SOEs in China (Table 2), those small and medium-sized together accounted for nearly 95PCT; but once it comes to the output value, theirs was a disproportionate share of less than 40 PCT.

Faced with the arduous tasks of enhancing efficiency and reversing the downward trend of profit, the Chinese policymakers in the mid-1990s began to shift its focus of SOE reforms from piecemeal approaches to more comprehensive packages. Considering the irreplaceable role these enterprises had played in the national economy and their social responsibilities, it would be impractical to denationalize all

Table 2 Composition of industrial SOEs, 1995

Industrial SOEs	Number and share in the total		Value of output and share in the total	
	(Unit)	(PCT)	(RMB billion)	(PCT)
Large	4,685	5.33	1,590.73	61.44
Medium	10,983	12.49	530.24	20.48
Small	72,237	82.18	468.03	18.08
Total	**87,905**	**100**	**2,589**	**100**

Note It is hard to use a uniform measure to generalize the size of SOEs since they are from different industries. According to the National Bureau of Statistics, large industrial enterprises have 1,000 or more employees and RMB400 million in annual turnover; medium-sized industrial enterprises have 300–1,000 employees and RMB20-400 million in annual turnover; and small industrial enterprises should have 20–300 employees and RMB3-20 million in annual turnover
Source NBS (1997)
Definition based on 统计上大中小微型企业划分办法, NBS (2011). From https://www.stats.gov.cn/statsinfo/auto2073/201310/t20131031_450691.html

of them. Instead, corporatization of the large and medium-sized and privatization of the small ones appeared to be a pragmatic solution to breathe fresh air into the ailing state sector. As to the former, it could help clarify the property rights of the SOEs and make them separate legal entities independent of the state in decision-making. With regard to the latter, the government wanted to encourage individuals to become entrepreneurs holding their personal stake in firms, which would make them better positioned to avoid many of the pitfalls in governance that had beset the SOEs at the initial stage of the reform.

6.1 *The Ailing SOEs*

Before the 1990s, reform of China's SOEs had been channeled primarily through incentives, subsidies, and growing autonomy to individual enterprises. Unfortunately, these measures just stayed on a superficial level and did to move deeper to touch the core of the problems. Since they neither streamlined corporate governance nor overhauled the structure of ownership, the vast majority of the SOEs as a result remained intrinsically the same, with no fundamental changes in their *operational mechanisms*. To better comprehend the nature of these problems, it is necessary to first have a brief overview of the regulatory and legislative forms upon which modern management systems of the Chinese SOEs were based, as well as their impact.

In July 1992, the State Council released the landmark "Regulations on Transforming the Operating Mechanisms of the State-Owned Industrial Enterprises", which specified concretely 14 autonomous rights they could enjoy. Among them, the rights to make decisions on the disposal of assets and matters related to personnel management were perhaps the most difficult to carry out in real practice. For lack of a clear identification of the relationship between management autonomy and the property ownership of the state, debate was protracted concerning the extent to which the state, as an owner of the SOEs' properties, should reserve control over such issues. In order to clarify state ownership of the properties, the State Council issued in 1994 the "Regulations Governing the Monitoring and Management of SOEs' Properties". As a regulatory foundation for state asset management in China, the regulation declared through Article Five that "SOEs' properties should belong to the whole people of the nation, i.e. they are owned by the State. The State Council representing the State should exercise ownership rights over the SOEs' properties in a unified way". Importantly, this regulation created a Board of Supervisors (*'jian shi hui'*) for each SOE, which consisted of representatives from the enterprise's official supervisory departments, managers and workers of the enterprise invited by the supervisory departments, etc. Moreover, the Board of Supervisors should not intervene with the enterprise's managerial autonomy; it is the director who could represent the legal person and exercise the property rights on behalf of the owner, the State. Despite the attempts at clarification, the concept of enterprise property rights remained a confusing one in terms of the management autonomy of the SOEs (Yang & Liu, 1995). In other words, these documents failed to point out who really was in control of the SOEs' assets as an "acting" owner for the State. Based on the institutional settings of China, the real acting owners of the state assets were somewhere in the government hierarchy and distributed among various departments to ensure adequate checks and balances. Very likely, they would impose non-contractual obligations and privileges on both enterprises and their stakeholders. As long as such intervention remains, the property rights extended to the SOEs themselves would continue to be a limited one. Consequentially, instead of protecting asset value for the long-term development of enterprises, more short-sighted behaviors would emerge to take advantage of the institutional weaknesses and maximize private gains.

While in the early 1990s, the government was already determined to deepen the reform of the SOEs, the prevailing ideological orthodoxy did not allow any major experiment to promote a mixed-ownership economy by diversifying their shareholding structures (mainly through corporatization and privatization). Thus most SOEs were still under the administrative authority of their supervisory agencies, either central or local, which in turn led to a number of serious problems. To begin with, since bureaucratic interference in day-to-day operations was rather common, the so-called management autonomy did not wholly belong to these enterprises. On many occasions, before taking decisions on personnel appointment and removal, they still had to listen to the officials from the above (Pan & Zhang, 2001). Second, when the separation of government and enterprise was incomplete, their roles were often blurred, with the latter acting like state institutions whose primary job was to guarantee to their workers social services such as employment, health care and education, etc. (Zhang, 2003). Sometimes, even knowing that these undertakings would cost them efficiency and economies of scale, they would rather maintain the status quo instead of casting away the misplaced responsibilities. Quite naturally, the vast majority of the Chinese SOEs became overstaffed; due to the lack of competence in technology, quality of labor, and managerial skills, etc., they could hardly compete with the much more nimble township and village enterprises (TVEs) for the latter were not burdened with the same non-productive tasks. Already losing ground to the aggressive TVEs, during the high inflation years of the late 1980s and early 1990s, SOEs were further pressured by the government to not only promise the "*iron rice bowl*" ('*tie fan wan*', meaning lifetime employment) to employees, but also hire more so as to maintain social stability. As a result, underemployment reemerged, together with cash flow gaps and contracting profits, which deteriorated the situation of the SOEs.

As noted already, China's SOE sector was in real trouble by the mid-1990s. Standing on the verge of insolvency, it would sooner or later drag the national economy down if the government was to adopt a *laissez-faire approach.* From another perspective, it is just because of the persistent financial underperformance of the SOEs that made the need for drastic reform imminent. Still taking the industrial SOEs as its representatives, Graph 1 indicates that from 1993 to 1998, total losses of the loss-making enterprises more than doubled from RMB45.26 billion to RMB115.07 billion. During the same period, profit plunged by over one third, from RMB81.73 billion to RMB52.51 billion. In terms of all the SOEs in China, official record of the same started only from 1998. In that year, the overall losses of the loss-making SOEs hit RMB306.65 billion whereas the profit generated by profit-making firms was RMB328.02 billion (Deng, 2014), implying that the net profit of China's SOE sector was merely RMB21.37 billion.

This low profit margin of public enterprises was of course a reflection of their own weaknesses, as analyzed in the above; however, it should also be recognized that ever since the mid-1990s, the business environment has also become increasingly harsh, such as the intensified competition with the non-state counterparts, especially those private and foreign-funded companies; the unfavorable sales price due to excess supply, an effect of blind investment and redundant construction during 1992–1994, etc. Therefore, considering both the internal deficiencies and external challenges, another round of SOE reforms kicked off following the opening of the Fifth Plenary Session *of the 14th Central Committee of the CPC* in September 1995. As part of the session's "Proposal on the Ninth Five-Year Plan on National Economy and Social

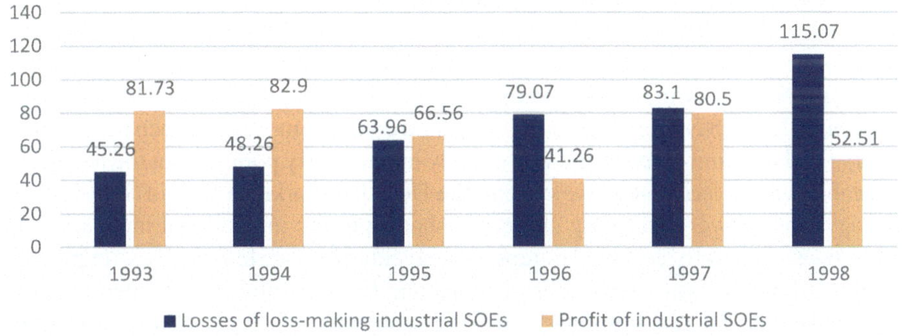

Graph 1 Financial performance of the industrial SOEs, RMB billion. *Source* NBS (2012)

Development and Long-Range Objectives to the Year 2010", the major strategy of this new wave of reforms could be synthesized as "grasping the larger and releasing the smaller" ('*zhuada fangxiao*'), which laid out two different guidelines for the SOEs to observe (Chen, 1999). The former one concentrated on the corporatization ('*gongsi zhi*') of large and medium-sized SOEs (LMSOEs) which until today dominate chiefly in monopoly industries such as petroleum, telecommunications, electricity, air/rail transport, and banking, etc. Regarding the small SOEs, they were mostly under the supervision of municipal and county governments, by permitting them to go through another process called "transformation of ownership" ('*zhuan zhi*'), policymakers expected these enterprises to develop into other hybrid ownership forms through selling, auctioning, and merging, etc. In certain conditions, they were even allowed to go into bankruptcy.

6.2 *Transforming the LMSOEs Via Modern Enterprise System*

Corporatization, a process of establishing governance by restructuring the SOEs into joint stock companies with limited liabilities, is a useful step in enterprise reform. It does not necessarily involve significant ownership changes because in principle, it holds directors responsible for the assets of the company and could prevent further asset erosion. Besides, it also provides a mechanism for information flows, setting the stage for selling shares, and separating the state from the enterprise. Ever since the inception of one more round of SOE reforms, corporatization has been taken as an important means of converting large and medium-sized state enterprises into modern corporate entities with commercial objectives. While initiating a diversified ownership structure and introducing governance mechanism of a shareholding system, it established accountability of the management to the enterprises' owners, i.e. the state.

6.2.1 Enactment of the Company Law in 1994

Early in November 1993, through the passage of the "Decision on Issues Concerning the Establishment of a Socialist Market Economic Structure" at the Third Plenary Session of the 14th National Party's Congress, a concrete move to deepen the reforms of large and medium-sized SOEs was already included. By pointing out the necessity to establish a modern enterprise system, the Decision marked a shift in SOE reform strategy from power-delegating and profit-sharing to the institutional innovation of enterprises. Generally accepted to represent an enterprise system that has "explicitly clarified property rights, well-defined rights and responsibilities, separated government and enterprise functions, and scientific management", the institution was often characterized by a slogan of four groups of Chinese equivalents, i.e. '*chanquan mingxi, quanze fenming, zhengqi fenkai, guanli kexue*' (Wang, 1998a,1998b). Since the march toward a modern enterprise system should start with the incorporation of the LMSOEs into either limited liability companies or shareholding firms, the "Company Law of the People's Republic of China" went into effect in July 1994. To a large extent, it is this law that laid the legal groundwork for China's endeavor to organizationally restructure the SOEs. In view of the irreplaceable role of these LMSOEs, the majority or complete ownership still belonged to the government (including its agencies in charge of specific sectors such as machinery or textiles). As to private capital and foreign investment, they were allowed to hold a minor stake.

Along with the transition into mixed-ownership enterprises, the supervisory authorities were required to put themselves in the right position when dealing with the SOEs. Specifically, they had to strike a balance between the bureaucratic role of managing the macro-economy and the corporate function of owning state assets. Indeed, such a requirement coincided with the characteristics of modern enterprise system under which the ownership and managerial control of state assets should be set apart. Equally in July 1994, with a view to promoting the state sector of the economy, a three-tier hierarchy concerning the management of state-owned assets in enterprises was laid out (via the directive named the "Regulations Governing the Monitoring and Management of SOEs' Properties" by the State Council). At the top was the State Council, which represented the central government to exercise proprietary right over all state assets. The second level included those institutions or departments authorized by the State Council, they acted as supervisory organs overseeing the management of state assets. Referring to the third tier, it consisted of the SOEs which had been incorporated into large conglomerates, group companies or share holding companies; they could enter into contractual relationship with either governmental or non-government entities in relation to the use and operation of these assets. By and large, the setup of the three-level model clarified ownership of state assets, thus creating the necessary condition for management functions to be decentralized smoothly to enterprises themselves.

6.2.2 The 100 Enterprise Pilot Program

Similar to other economic reforms at the forefront, the introduction of modern enterprise system has taken a gradualist approach, with an experiment started in certain enterprises before being executed in full swing across the entire country. In November 1994, 100 LMSOEs were chosen by the State Council to pilot corporatization according to the criteria of modern enterprise system. Called "the one hundred enterprise pilot program" ('*baihu xiandai qiye zhidu shidian*'), it covered firms coming from major industrial and commercial sectors located in diverse geographic areas of the country (Zhang, 2002a, 2002b). Inside these enterprises, government agencies or other non-state institutions that had made investment were granted shareholders' rights proportional to the stakes they held. Treated as independent economic entities, these enterprises enjoyed a high level of autonomy which enabled them to make quick response against market changes. What's more, their rights and obligations were explicitly defined and *mutually conditional*, thus leading to a greater sense of responsibility in business operations.

With regard to corporate governance, it was mainly managed by *four* constituent decision-making *bodies*, i.e. the general *shareholders meeting*, the board of directors, the supervisory committee and the management (Zhao, 2001). Among these four parties, the supervisory committee was obligated to oversee the board of directors. Specifically, in order to protect the legal interest of shareholders, its primary concerns were over issues like *financial* reporting and *accounting*, legitimacy of managerial behaviors, etc. Beforehand, board of directors in China had faced a serious "insider control" problem since most directors were themselves managers inside the firms. Although there were rules that overhauled insider-controlled boards, majority power remained largely concentrated.

In addition, the problem of information asymmetry had made it even more difficult, if not impossible, to monitor board and management performance. Now with the supervisory committee to restrain the abuse of power, the Chinese SOEs could expect to run in a more transparent and healthier manner. According to the government's original plan, a period of two years, i.e. 1995–1996, would be spent to lay the foundation of the grand and arduous task. But due to the lack of emphasis on using diversification of share ownership to restructure the existing SOEs into real enterprises, many participants of the experiment simply converted themselves to wholly state-owned companies that were similar to modern corporations only in form (Yin, 1997). Therefore, the pre-scheduled evaluation at the end of 1996 showed that very few experimental enterprises had truly achieved the standards of a modern corporation. Thereby, the project had to be further extended by one more year.

6.2.3 Drawbacks that Necessitated the Corporatization Reform

It was until the Fourth Plenary Session of the 15th Central Committee of the CPC in 1999 that the corporatization reform of large and medium-sized SOEs entered the period of establishing modern corporations on the basis of internationally prevalent norms. In particular, the "Decision on Several Important Issues Regarding Reform and Development of State-Owned Enterprises", which was adopted at the Fourth Plenary Session, put forward some new requirements for the corporatization of the LMSOEs. To begin with, it emphasized corporate governance by pointing out that "corporate governance structure, which can establish checks and balances between the owner and the manager, is the core of the corporate system" and required that all the corporatized SOEs establish effective corporate governance. Second, it stated that except for a minority of enterprises which should be monopolized by the state, the rest may "actively develop into corporations with multiple equity-holding entities", including non-state equity investment. Further, it mandated that large and medium-sized SOEs, especially well-performing ones suitable for the shareholding system, be converted into shareholding enterprises through initial public offerings, establishment of Sino-foreign joint ventures, and use of cross-sharing among enterprises.

These steps, in turn, would help develop a sector of mixed ownership, with the state holding a controlling interest in important enterprises.

The introduction of a modern enterprise system automatically replaced the former contract responsibility system (CRS). Fairly speaking, CRS had its own merits because it enabled SOE managers to possess a certain degree of autonomy. For instance, by retaining more profits, they could reinvest in *existing facilities* and raise the payroll of workers, which in turn enhanced productivity and optimized the allocation of production factors. Nevertheless, the downside is that the autonomy was a highly restricted one, with the state reluctant to give up its influence over the SOEs. In this regard, the state was still the de facto boss. While exercising macroeconomic functions of regulation and supervision, it was simultaneously involved in a broad range of microeconomic activities like financing, divesting of surplus labor, etc.

Needless to say, such a phenomenon is in violation of the law that the referee and the player cannot be the same person since these two roles are inherently contradictory. On the one hand, the former macro-economic role meant that the state should concern itself with the overall performance of all enterprises; yet the latter microeconomic role required that it should only look after how individual enterprises have been functioning, which is a task impossible to accomplish. By then, a rather common practice was that the manager of a state enterprise was appointed by the government and thus had no authority to run the business independently (Yang, 1996). What's more, in case of losses or failures, he would not be held accountable, which greatly undermined the responsibilities that such an important position should be entrusted with. No wonder throughout almost the entire 1990s, China's SOE sector had been so financially fragile. To turn around the downward spiral and create market-driven enterprises, disintegration of these two conflicting roles is essential and should even precede all the other initiatives.

6.2.4 Shougang, a Forerunner in the Pilot Scheme

Concerning the one hundred SOEs involved in the trial transformation, it was inevitable for them to encounter setbacks. In fact, even the policymakers themselves were yet probing for pragmatic solutions. From another perspective, however, if without these lessons and mistakes, they could hardly step onto the right track. Here, the story of Shougang (also known as Capital Steel) is representative of what many Chinese state enterprises have gone through in those early years of exploration, which was a mixture of success and failure. Established in 1919, Shougang Group (initially Shijingshan Iron and Steel Plant before being renamed Shougang Corporation in 1992; in 1996 when Shougang Group was founded, Shougang Corporation became its parent company) was already a large-scale integrated iron and steel plant by the 1950s. In 1979 when the decision was taken to initiate the contract responsibility system (CRS) experiment as part of China's economic reform program, Shougang, one of the country's largest and best-known state enterprises, was selected to lead the trial.

As indicated in the above, one of the major problems with the CRS is the disparities in contractual terms, which were subject to the negotiations between individual SOEs and the state authorities (Chen, 1989a, 1989b). In other words, the precise terms of the contract varied according to factors like the nature of the enterprise, the industrial sector and geographical area to which it belonged, plus the pre-CRS levels of investment, and so on. In the case of Shougang, it was granted very generous conditions because of its size and significance in the regional and national economy. When most state-enterprise contracts ran for three to five years, Shougang's was a much longer period of fifteen years (i.e. 1981–1995). Besides, other than turning over a certain percentage of profits each year to the state during the course of the contract, Shougang gained the permission to pay the state in 1981 a sum totalling RMB270 million, which was 9.3 PCT more than the profit handed over in the previous year; and based on this figure to rise at an annual rate of 6 PCT (it was adjusted voluntarily by Shougang to 7.2 PCT from 1983) throughout the rest of the term (Yao, 1991). This turned out to be very favorable because from 1979 to 1988, its actual profit increased at an annual rate of 20 PCT, but its remittance to the state only grew at a much lower pace each year. From this perspective, Shougang was undoubtedly one of the few which "got rich first".

Apart from the unusually long contract and retention of a bigger share of profits, other special treatments included favorable depreciation rates, the right to exclude bonuses from normal wage costs, and the freedom to sell a given proportion of steel products at market prices, etc. In the early and middle stage of the contracting period, Shougang achieved incredible performances. However, while approaching the end of the term, problems started to emerge since 1992 and in particular, the enhanced autonomy and higher profit margins had led to an over-rapid expansion. From April 1985 to December 1994, it was reported to have invested into 96 projects of fifteen industries outside of Shougang, which amounted to RMB2.89 billion (Zhang, 2007).

Unfortunately, Shougang at that time was ill-prepared to cope with such a large scale of business activities. Due to management deficiencies, outdated facilities, and a heavy debt burden, its pace of development slowed down. By coincidence, since 1995 was also a year when the modern enterprise system was put on a trial basis, Shougang took advantage of this opportunity and initiated the same experiment, which enabled itself to get out of the predicament and enter a new stage of adjustment and transformation. After the establishment of Shougang Group in 1996, Shougang Corporation as the parent company was authorized by the Beijing municipal government to enforce its shareholder's rights upon the second-tier companies within the group. At the same time, measures like labor downsizing, technological upgrading of steel production, and *sell*ing off *unprofitable non-core businesses,* etc. were adopted to reshuffle the internal organization. Three years later, Shougang Corporation selected its high-quality assets and formed them into Beijing Shougang Company Limited. Its initial public offering was launched in December 1999 at Shenzhen Stock Exchange and of all the shares issued, the state share (held by Shougang Corporation) was 84.85 PCT. In 2001, its net profit increased by over 20.6 PCT to RMB709.34 million, as compared to that of the previous year which registered RMB588.09 million (Annual Report of Shougang 2001).

In addition, through corporate restructuring, a hierarchical managerial system with the board of directors, managers and a monitoring committee came into being. Before 1998, Shougang Group was under two-tiered administrative control of both the Ministry of Metallurgical Industries (MMI, abolished in 1998) and the Beijing municipal government, with the former mainly in charge of Shougang's production and investment, and the latter taking control of its employment and finance. In view of the rapidly growing role of the market forces from the 1980s, the planning function exercised by the MMI was transferred to individual steel enterprises in a gradual manner. Undoubtedly, this was rather favorable to Shougang; by freeing itself from the thick bureaucratic red tape and making full use of the expanded autonomy, the Group could be better prepared to meet the challenges of the shifting environment and fierce competition.

6.2.5 Noticeable Yet Limited Improvements

Not long after, with more enterprises being picked out by the State Council to participate in the project, their number reached 2,343 in 1996 and covered thirty one provinces, autonomous regions and *municipalities directly under the central government*. What's more, investigations showed that among these restructured firms, 71 PCT had their own board of directors, 63 PCT set up supervisory committees, and 33 PCT held shareholders' annual general meetings (Hu, 2000). In the fo*ll*owing years, the reform continued with its in-depth development and a mechanism for state-owned enterprises to exit was gradually taking shape. If to check the theoretical basis for China to implement the modern enterprise system, it can be found that certain mechanisms and elements were derived from the Western corporate system, which are also considered as factors that have enabled Western companies to successfully fend off government interferences. For example, the corporate structure with board of directors and shareholders, and less reliance on the state in daily operations, etc. Apart from this, the system in real practice was still endowed with Chinese characteristics, especially given the fact that the state continued to maintain its complete or majority ownership when the internal governance was being reshaped. Anyhow, as the reform proceeded, some decision-making power that had belonged to the government was delegated to the SOEs and consequently, the once frequent administrative intervention was reduced in a gradual way.

While the endeavor to set up the modern enterprise system brought marked improvements in the entrepreneurship and performance of the LMSOEs, problems still persisted. In particular, the *overlapping* functions between the government and enterprises were not completely eliminated. Apart from interfering with business operations, the hand of the government was also visible in its authority to hire or fire managers, to approve or disapprove major decisions of enterprises, and to regulate their activities via macroeconomic and industrial policies. Although with the development of the capital market in China and the announcement of the central government that the capital market should serve SOE reforms, state-owned stocks which accounted for about two-thirds of the total equity of all the listed companies could not be circulated (Yang, Zhang, & Duan, 2000). Therefore, it is fair to say that the governance structure of the listed companies whose controlling interest was held by the state was in essence of no much difference from that of the typical SOEs. Moreover, because of the highly centralized equity, the chance for minority shareholders to have a say in the operational decisions became rather slim. Inevitably, they lost motivation and means to monitor management, thus leaving enterprises exposed to even greater risks and costs.

In March 1998, premier Zhu Rongji at a press conference declared the government's ambition to spend three years to enable the majority loss-making LMSOEs to turn around and introduce the modern enterprise system via reorganization, transformation and improved management. Consequently, through a series of corporatization reform according to the demands of the modern enterprise system, 430, or some 83 PCT of the 520 key state enterprises had been restructured into corporations by 2000, with 282 of them wholly or partially transformed into limited liability companies or joint-stock companies (Zheng, 2004). Besides, in November 2000, the number of the loss-making LMSOEs was reduced by 4,391, a fall that accounted for over 66.5 PCT of that of 1997, which had stayed at 6,599 (Song, 2004).

Fairly speaking, these achievements were hard earned. Not only the state, all localities, institutions and enterprises were mobilized to revive the state sector of the economy. In this process, intensified efforts were directed to increasing the efficiency of the LMSOEs, like the exit mechanism for insolvent and uncompetitive businesses, r*edundancy* and redeployment *arrangements for the surplus staff*, etc. Referring to those enterprises which were incurring heavy losses, they were to retreat from the market through merger or bankruptcy. In addition, under the program of establishing a "modern enterprise system", corporatization was not just taken as a major modality by the government to transform the large and medium-sized SOEs into commercially viable entities while retaining state control; it also became a necessary step to introduce diversified ownership of the SOEs via ways like listing them on the domestic and even foreign stock exchanges.

6.2.6 Trials with Large Enterprise Groups

Together with corporatization, there was yet another complementary approach which was applied, i.e. the formation of large enterprise groups. Beginning in December 1991, motivated by the increasing competition that state enterprises were facing in the domestic market, especially from firms funded by foreign multinationals, the State Council kicked off the trial reform of building large enterprise groups and in the first batch of this nationwide experimentation, 55 groups (later increased to 57) were chosen (Zang, 1998), with each one formed by integrating a selected number of enterprise units under an existing central industrial ministry (including forestry, metallurgy, chemicals, construction materials, machinery and electronics, energy, aviation & aerospace, and pharmaceuticals, etc.). In terms of the organizational structure, each enterprise group was to possess a strong group core acting as the investment center, and it also had to develop a multilayer structure within which every member enterprise maintained its independent legal person status.

For instance, in July 1992, under the jurisdiction of the Ministry of Machinery and Electronics Industry, Jiefang Automotive Company was selected as one of the first batch and reorganized into a large enterprise group named the First Automotive Works (FAW) Group, with the First Automotive Works as the core of the group. To ensure that the enterprise group was an integrated and cohesive whole, the group core was commissioned to set up linkage between member enterprises and coordinate cooperation in production as well as other activities. In particular, the FAW was encouraged to hold the shares of other member enterprises so as to install the parent-and-subsidiary corporate structure within the group. As to the scale and scope of business, these enterprise groups were generally cross-regional covering diverse sectors and capable of competing with foreign multinationals. Moreover, they were all bestowed with significant managerial autonomy in financing, investment, and employment, etc.

Seeing that the trial work of the first batch of 57 groups had successfully achieved its goals, the State Council in April 1997 issued the "Opinions on Deepening the Trial Work of Large Enterprise Groups" to further consolidate the strengths of backbone state enterprises. In the notice, a list of the second batch consisting 63 trial groups were attached, thus making the total number of large enterprise groups under the central government rise to 120. However, being bigger is not a sure guarantee of enhanced competitiveness. Referring to the economic performance of these enterprise groups, it was a rather mixed picture: while many have reaped a higher return with the penetration of new markets at home and abroad, some still failed to meet their objectives. By exploring the reasons, it can be found that they were either in blind pursuit of diversitication, or lacked professional knowledge in maintaining effenciency over the course of expansion (Li, 2001). To summarize, modern enterprise system had major implications not only for the SOEs, but for the government as well. From the perspective of enterprises, they were better motivated to transform into a corporate entity so that management could be separated from the state's bureaucracy. For the government authorities, they learned how to re-position themselves and function more like a supervisor and supporter when dealing with the SOEs.

6.3 Privatization of Small SOEs

Ever since the mid-1990s, private and foreign-funded companies have entered into a fast lane of development as China maintained its momentum of transition into a market-oriented economy. Following the compromise in the once *unshakable insistence that assets of all the state enterprises should be under tight and absolute control of the government, restrictions against the ownership reform of the SOEs began to ease. Consequently, privatization as a political taboo for almost five decades began to receive serious attention of the Chinese leadership. Indeed, for industries connected with national defense, supply of public goods and basic energy materials,* etc., *it is understandable for the state capital to continue with its dominance. But referring to other non-strategic areas, divestiture and even complete withdrawal of state-owned assets should be a feasible alternative, especially when the small SOEs are concerned.*

According to the willingness and ability of the local governments to cope with the impact of restructuring, China introduced diverse approaches to privatize the small SOEs and they mainly included leasing, contract operations, joint ventures with foreign investors, formation of business alliances with other firms, and acquisition by outsiders, etc. (Zhao & Duan, 1998). However, since in most cases, both the enterprises and employees would prefer to have the existing management retained, conversion of these SOEs into shareholding co-operative enterprises has been the most prevalent option, especially in the industrial sector.

6.3.1 Stakes That Lied Behind the Reform

When the policy of "grasping the larger and letting go the smaller" was firstly announced in 1995, the intention of the leadership was already crystal clear, i.e. to retain government control of the large and medium-sized SOEs that operated in the strategic sectors and retreat from the small SOEs that engaged in highly competitive markets. Here, what should be noted is that instead of using the term "privatization", the Chinese prefer several other expressions such as "restructuring" ('*zhuan zhi*'), "readjustment of ownership structure" ('*suoyouzhi jiegou tiaozheng*'), or "transformation of ownership to a joint stock/share-holding system" ('*gufenzhi gaizao*'), etc. Similarly, they often use "non-public ownership" ('*fei gong you*') as a substitute for "private ownership" ('*si you*') (Cao, Qian, & Weingast, 1999). While it is true that by the early 1990s, the large and medium-sized SOEs contributed the vast majority of China's industrial output, it is the small SOEs whose number dominated the state sector. In other words, privatization of the latter was at least equally, if not more, challenging as the corporatization of the LMSOEs. Besides, unlike their larger counterparts, these enterprises did not enjoy the same level of protection from the government, plus the fact that they were equally often subject to the administrative interventions from the above, they became less flexible and thus more vulnerable to the competition from those non-state rivals.

After all, it is always easier said than done. Privatization is not merely a transfer of ownership from the state to private hands, it unavoidably involves a change of fate to millions of families accustomed already to the security provided by the socialist "iron rice bowl". SOEs, which had been the best career option for their guarantee of lifelong employment and admirable perks such as pensions, near-free health care and housing, etc., would no longer be the same. Large-scale layoffs posed a real challenge not only to the government, but to the workers as well. By then, a nationwide social security system encompassing low-income family allowances, unemployment insurance and supplementary *schemes were still immature and could hardly stand any major test. But considering the huge losses these deteriorating SOEs had incurred year on year, the subsequent non-performing loans, and the massive subsidies that never got paid off, money couldn't be thrown into this bottomless pit anymore. Instead of giving them fish, it makes far greater sense to teach them how to fish for themselves.*

In order to make sure that the upcoming painful restructuring would not lead to social chaos, different localities unveiled their own policies to pacify losers, such as early retirement or buyout offers, free reemployment training programs, etc. Under certain conditions, microcredit with low-interest rates was offered to encourage start-ups by the self-employed. To smooth the way for labor reorganization, the State Council issued in 1997 the "Supplementary Notice on Some Issues Related to the Trial Implementation of Merger and Bankruptcy for the SOEs and Reemployment of Workers in Selected Cities", a circular that echoed the report by the Ministry of Labor concerning the "Implementation of the Reemployment Project" presented two years before. With a view to helping the redundant SOE workers find new jobs, the Project had been launched first on a trial basis in 30 cities (e.g. Shanghai, Shenyang, Qingdao, Chengdu and Hangzhou, etc.) since 1994 before being promoted around the whole country.

6.3.2 The Hardening of Budget Constraint, a Key Motive

Officially, it was the *15th National Congress* of the *CPC* in 1997 which endorsed the transformation of the SOEs through total or partial privatization. As compared to the LMSOEs which were mostly under the supervision of the central and provincial government, the small SOEs were by and large administered by local authorities at municipal, county and township levels. Although individually, they could not match the LMSOEs in size and significance, when counted in a collective sense, their function and influence should hardly be underestimated. As a matter of fact, the experiment of privatization started as early as 1992 at municipal and county levels, among which the three prominent pioneers were Yibin, Sichuan Province; Shunde, Guandong Province; and Zhucheng, Shandong Province (Song & Liu, 2014). Since 1994, the campaign has become more widespread.

Take Zhucheng as an example, in October 1992, Zhucheng Electric Motor Factory, a producer of generators established in 1970, was in the first batch of the five local SOEs to carry out the trial reform. With its 277 workers voting in favor of 100PCT buy-out for RMB2.7 million, the factory was incorporated into Kaiyuan Electric Motor Co., Ltd., a joint-stock cooperative enterprise. Within only four months' time, both its output and profits more than doubled (Xie, 1995). By July 1994, a total number of 282 local enterprises, including both state and collectively-owned, had been restructured and following the model of Zhucheng Electric Motor, 90PCT of them also had their assets sold to employees (Shi, 2008). The overall reported results of privatization in Zhucheng County have been rather positive, in terms of the records concerning profits made by the reformed SOEs, return on capital (ROC), government revenues, and the income of employees, they both registered rapid growth within the initial three years of privatization.

As indicated in the above, the vast majority of the small SOEs were within the jurisdiction of local governments. Thereby, if privatization were expected to proceed smoothly, support of these authorities should be an indispensable condition. Actually, their response was not without calculation between costs and benefits. During that specific time period, there existed two factors that compelled them to think favorably about privatization, i.e. hard budget constraints and competition pressure from the non-state sector. The first determinant has something to do with the reform in China's taxation system. In the 1980s, the policy was named '*li gai shui*', i.e. substitution of tax payment for profit delivery, which required all the taxable SOEs to pay income taxes instead of turning over profits to the state, and this made it possible for enterprises to have their after-tax profits 100 PCT retained. From 1988 to 1993, the "fiscal contracting system" ('*caizheng baogan zhi*') was implemented under which almost all the revenues were collected by the local authorities and they were allowed to keep a certain part of the revenues to finance local expenditures. Referring to the sharing rates, each province had to bargain individually with the central government and then to remit according to the agreed percentages. Since this practice granted the local governments greater control over their own tax revenues, while negotiating for higher retention rates, they even began to hide some revenues so as to more quickly develop their own economies. With the gradual dissolution of the central power, its share in budgetary revenue dropped from 40.5 PCT of 1984 to merely 22 PCT by 1993 (NBS, 2001), which not only weakened its role in bridging regional fiscal disparities, its provision of basic public services was also constrained. Given the fact that the contracting system could hardly reverse the trend of falling fiscal revenues, the "tax sharing system" ('*fenshui zhi*') was enacted in 1994 with an aim to recentralize control on fiscal instruments. By simplifying taxes into three categories, i.e. central, local, and shared, the new system specified clearly how revenues were to be allocated between the central and local. After its implementation, the central share of national budgetary revenue rose to 55.7 PCT in 1994 and remained at around 50 PCT over the following years.

Beforehand, when all taxes were collected by the local governments, they could try a variety of means to reduce or even exempt themselves from the taxes that should be handed over to the central coffer. However, the 1994 reform plugged that loophole with the establishment of the state and local tax bureaus, with the former held responsible for levying both central and shared taxes and had offices at all levels of government. Besides, as a rule-based system of revenue-sharing that replaced the old bargaining one, it also made the country's budget structure more transparent and standardized. For example, the value-added tax (VAT, 17 PCT) being the most important tax was shared between the central and *local* at the ratio of 75:25. This ratio was no longer subject to negotiation and applied to all the provinces, a method that reduced much transaction costs. Referring to the corporate income tax (CIT, 33 PCT) which became unified too covering all the domestic enterprises, the central treasury could claim 60 PCT whereas the remaining 40 PCT belonged to the local.

For all transition economies including China, one of the main arduous challenges has been the problem of soft budget constraint. Usually, it happens when the strict relationship between earnings and expenditure is relaxed because overspending could be covered by some other government institutions. The downside is that if an enterprise or a government can always expect to be bailed out once in the red, it would be unlikely to strive for greater efficiency so as to maintain a balanced budget. Considering the sheer size of China, such a phenomenon was definitely unsustainable and in the long run, only a hardened budget constraint can enable the country to allocate its resources in a more cost-saving way. Through the new tax assignment scheme introduced in 1994, a more rigorous budget constraint was imposed on the local governments, which was fairly tough for them to adapt to at the outset. But it was also from the seemingly unacceptable shift in the tax regime that affirmed their commitment to reorganizing the ailing state enterprises. Although privatization of the SOEs would leave them many thorny problems to tackle, especially concerning the sacking and re-employment of redundant workers, the potential gains were self-evident as well. Instead of being a fiscal burden, they would contribute to local economies through tax payment, job creation, and technological innovation, etc. Therefore, by comparing the costs and benefits, it is not hard to understand why in the late 1990s, local governments of China were among the major forces that facilitated the privatization of the small SOEs.

6.3.3 Pressure from the Thriving Non-State Sector

Apart from the hard budget constraints, the other reason that prompted the local governments to endorse privatization was the growingly fierce competition from the non-state sector. In terms of the value of gross industrial output, the statistics below (Table 3) indicate that since 1994, the share of state enterprises has been shrinking steadily, which suggests that during the same period, non-state firms were expanding in a vibrant way, accounting for over 60 PCT of China's total. By 1998, the contribution of the former reached its 5-year low whereas the weight of the latter began to exceed the 70 PCT mark. Here, what is necessary to point out is that while state enterprises as a whole were facing the challenge, the LMSOEs *affiliated* to the *central government* were relatively safer since many of them enjoyed a *monopolistic*

Table 3 Gross industrial output contributed by different types of enterprises, 1994–1998

Year	SOEs and share in the total		Collectively-owned enterprises (RMB100 million)	Private enterprises (RMB100 million)	Others (RMB100 million)
	(RMB100 million)	(PCT)			
1994	26,200.84	37.34	26,473	7,082	10,421.35
1995	31,220	33.97	33,623	11,821	15,231
1996	36,173	36.32	39,232.2	15,419.8	16,582.3
1997	35,968	31.62	43,347.18	20,376.13	20,982.01
1998	33,621	28.24	45,730	20,372	27,270

Note SOEs represent those owned or controlled by the state; collectively-owned enterprises mainly refer to the township and village enterprises; private enterprises are located in both urban and rural China; and others include foreign-funded enterprises
Source NBS (2012)

advantage unattainable to other rivals; but with regard to the small SOEs, their industries in general had a low entry threshold and thus were exposed to a much higher level of threat.

By and large, the rapid boom of the non-state sector in the 1990s was chiefly driven by three forces and they were township and village enterprises (TVEs), private enterprises and foreign-invested firms. In particular, the emergence of TVEs was largely in response to the relaxed state monopoly over the economy, especially over production and investment, in order to ease the tight supply of basic consumer goods, a situation that had already affected the normal life of the Chinese grassroots. Although by comparing with the SOEs which had the support of favorable government policies, TVEs were weak in areas such as research and development of new technologies, educational and skill levels of the workforce, and *availability of financial* resources, etc.; they still possessed certain advantages that were missing among most SOEs, chiefly in the flexibility of ownership and governance. Concerning the latter, it enabled them to diversify their business scope, boost employee morale, and turn decisions quickly into actions without having to go through a complicated hierarchical procedure to obtain the approval. Obviously, these advantages far outweighed the deficiencies and in a country whose role of the market was becoming more decisive, it is not surprising that the TVEs could manage to outperform their state counterparts while successfully invigorating the local economies.

As the most vibrant portion of the Chinese economy, the private sector witnessed its fastest pace of expansion during the 1990s. In 1990, for example, the value of its industrial output stood at merely RMB129 billion; but within a matter of just five years, it jumped by over eight fold to more than RMB1.18 trillion in 1995. Till 1999, the number rose further by over 90 PCT and exceeded RMB2.29 trillion. During this entire 10-year period, the share of the private sector in the national industrial output climbed from an insignificant 5.39 PCT to 18.18 PCT (NBS, 2012). Such an explosive way of development was in sharp contrast with the *sluggish* state-owned firms that were decaying day by day. In the late 1970s when the private sector of China began to reemerge in both the rural and urban regions (after 1956, only public and collective economic entities were granted legitimacy), it was confined to self-employed individual or household entrepreneurs known as '*ge ti hu*' (*sole proprietorship*). Due to capital scarcity and policy constraints, they in general operated on a small scale in businesses like farming, handicraft, catering, transportation and retail, etc. Despite the fact that since the very beginning, their momentum of growth had been rather aggressive, official recognition of their status did not come automatically. Instead, it was in the "Amendment of the Constitution" at the 7th National People's Congress of 1988 that permission was formally given to the private sector to exist as a complement to the socialist public economy, with its legal rights and interests protected by the state. Some ten years later, in 1999, the Constitution was once more amended to improve the private sector from a mere complementary status to an important component of the country's market economy, which further optimized its operating environment (Li & Bo, 2002).

These constitutional changes not only allowed '*ge ti hu*' to expand into private enterprises by recruiting more employees (beforehand, they were only allowed to hire fewer than five employees), they also prompted an increasing number of *collectively-owned* TVEs to privatize. Apart from the country's need to provide more job opportunities and *enrich the supply of daily necessities, the major reason that powered the rapid boom of the private sector was in its overall efficiency, which on average was much higher than both the SOEs and TVEs. Without much special treatment to expect from either the central or local governments, they had to depend entirely on themselves to establish a foothold in the market. To some degree, they were under constant exposure to the threat of business failure or bankruptcy because once a wrong move was made, they should bear the consequences alone and no institution would come to their aid. Confronting the enormous stress, the owner of these private firms often worked very hard with the staff, and through effective management and ceaseless innovation, they slashed cost, improved quality and thus gained a competitive edge over their bigger rivals. Some of them performed so well that in the late 1990s, more and more large-scale private enterprises emerged in China, like Huawei* (*solutions provider of information and communications technology*), *Legend* (renamed *Lenovo since 2003, PC maker*), Suning (appliance retailer), etc., and they are still industry leaders today.

During the reform era, China's policy of opening up enabled the country to absorb substantial foreign capital (mainly foreign direct investment or FDI) and this in turn gave rise to the so-called "FIE (foreign-invested enterprises) phenomenon". Inclusive of both wholly foreign-owned enterprises and joint ventures, these entities have become a sizable player in virtually every part of China's economy since the 1990s. Based on the industries in which FIEs had a propensity to concentrate (namely, telecommunications, automobiles, and electronics, etc.), it can be found that they were a more significant competitive force to the SOEs. By contrast, TVEs and private firms were mostly in the marginal business segments where the state capital rarely held a dominant stake. Besides, the FIE phenomenon can be best displayed by their aggressive engagement in export, an evidence proving how FDI has contributed to China's export boom. As shown in Graph 2, during the 1995–2000 period, its share of China's export rose by over 15PCT, claiming almost half of the country's total in 2000.

Fundamentally, the primary motive of China to welcome FDI in the late 1970s was not only because it could bring in foreign capital to fund the country's domestic construction; moreover, the much valued intellectual properties would also be transferred. In other words, enterprises established by foreign investors often enjoyed marked advantage in technological know-how, production expertise, as well as management skills, etc., which in turn enabled them to run in a more efficient and profitable way. To gain some idea about their profitability in China, the item named "investment income" under the current account of the country's balance of payments (BOP) can be referred to as a key measure. Inclusive of the income that accrues to a foreign investor from ownership of direct investment capital in an enterprise based in China, the outflow (debit) that had incurred can demonstrate to a certain extent the profit being paid to foreign investors. In 1995, it first recorded a sharp increase of more than USD15 billion as compared to 1990, before it climbed continuously and hit USD26.5 billion by 2000 (Graph 3). Such an impressive growth momentum was

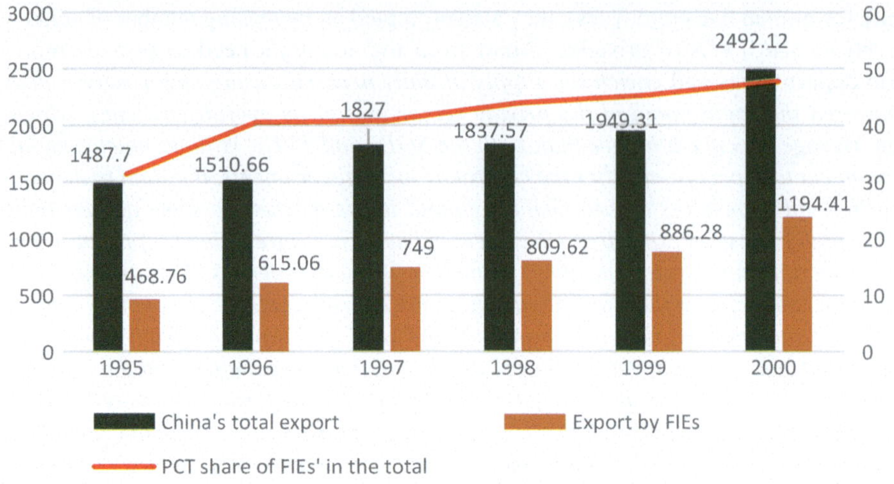

Graph 2 Export of FIEs in China's total, USD100 million. *Source* MOC (2013)

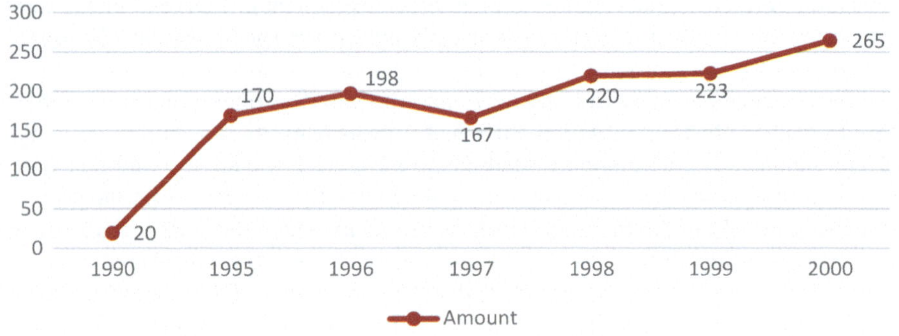

Graph 3 Investment income (debit) under the balance of payments, USD100 million. *Source* SAFE (2015)

actually a sharp contrast against the titanic losses that were eroding China's SOEs during the same time period. In addition, since the late 1990s, with the growing importance of innovation in market competition, FIEs in China have accelerated their pace of research and development, resulting in even higher productivity and better performance than the state firms, which were far less responsive to these changes.

To a large extent, these thriving non-state enterprises greatly intensified the competition of China's business landscape throughout the 1990s, during which profits became more closely linked to the ability of firms to cope with the mounting challenge. Under such circumstances, the inability of the state enterprises to maintain a reasonable profit margin may not only lead to declining bonuses or fringe benefits of employees, it would even shake the foundation of existence. For the local governments, particularly those at county or township levels whose revenues relied heavily on the profit-making of the SOEs subject to their jurisdiction, once these enterprises were incurring losses or suffering bad debt problems, the fiscal threat would be rather imminent. In order to prevent such a dire situation from coming true and ensure that sufficient revenues would flow in to fund the expenditure budget for subordinate regions and institutions, the local governments were no longer willing to blindly rescue the poor-performing state enterprises as they had done before; instead, they were decisive to initiate ownership restructuring to revitalize these entities. From the viewpoint of the whole country, the hardened budget constraints and enhanced competition were both positive incentives that motivated the local governments to privatize the loss-making SOEs. After all, if China were to reap a bumper harvest in the grand reform project, having its enterprises run under the direction of the market and according to the guidance of international norms are both indispensable prerequisites. Besides, as major participants of economic activities, if enterprises could not tackle the stress of competition, it would be unlikely for them to act as a constant power source for the nation's long-term development. Despite the fact that the small SOEs were mostly sold off, privatization is by no means the ultimate goal of their reforms. Rather, financial and operational autonomy, the induction of modern corporate management, etc. should remain the core of their pursuit throughout the entire process.

Toward the end of the twentieth century, there have been important developments that signaled further broadening and deepening of the letting-go process. **In September 1999, for example, an important guideline was adopted following the approval of the "Decision of the CPC Central Committee on Major Issues Concerning the Reform and Development of the State-Owned Enterprises". This decision provided an official sanction** for provincial and local governments to begin transforming their medium-sized SOEs along the lines that had been applied to the small ones. Specifically, most of them would be transformed into joint stock co-operatives or contract management firms (rather than privatized) and the process was expected to be completed within the next five-year plan period (i.e. the 10th Five-Year Plan covering 2001–2005).

As time passes by, the contours of China's reorganization of its state sector has become much clearer. While the ultimate sphere for state ownership to maintain its influence has been shrinking, the extent to which private ownership could exert its role has been enlarged substantially. Based on the experiences of other countries, the contribution of the SOEs to the overall economic performance is likely to be maximized when they are confined to certain industries where extensive public ownership is necessary on both economic and social grounds. In the case of China, it is equally critical to define a narrow scope within which state enterprises would dominate. Simultaneously, there should be a broader withdrawal of the SOEs from competitive industries so that both foreign and private capital could participate more actively in the restructuring of the state sector.

7 Banking Sector Reform

China's financial system, similar to that of many developed countries, consists of various kinds of institutions such as regulatory watchdogs, policy banks, commercial banks, investment firms, and supportive infrastructures like the interbank trading platform and securities market, etc. Being an important component of the economy, its chief responsibility is invariably to promote capital formation necessary to sustain the growth of the whole country. In the first phase of China's financial reform which took place during the 1980s, especially prior to 1985, a two-tier banking system consisting of a central bank (the PBoC) and four state-owned specialized banks (i.e. the ABC, BOC, PCBC, and ICBC) was established. At the same time, the two-tier structure was supplemented by other financial institutions following the proliferation of trust & investment corporations in the urban and resurgence of credit cooperatives in the rural areas (the history of rural credit cooperatives could be traced back to 1923 when the first RCC was set up in Xianghe county, Hebei Province). Besides, unlike the former means of financing channeled chiefly by state appropriations, the SOEs were encouraged to fund the majority of their investment projects with bank loans. However, since China's financial system had been dominated by state-owned banks, they were often obliged to grant policy-loans to the poor-performing SOEs irrespective of their repayment abilities. As a result, the efficiency of capital allocation was seriously undermined. For most state banks, they were overwhelmed by conflicting objectives of policy lending and profit making. Anyhow, despite these dilemmas, the banking sector of China still underwent a rapid expansion in the 1980s. With regard to the deposits (year-end balance) of national banks, the figure increased from RMB457.95 billion in 1985 to RMB1,004.36 billion in 1989. In terms of their credit funds, it equally more than doubled from RMB627.19 billion in 1985 to RMB1,346.95 billion by the end of 1989 (Chen, 1990). Perhaps, such a pace of growth in credit extension was too rapid for the country to cope with and it did not take long before the effect showed up. Most notably, the retail price index (RPI) as a key measure of inflation surged to 117.8 in 1989 as compared to 108.8 of 1985 (preceding year = 100).

To prevent the economy from getting overheated, China entered into a stage of retrenchment to curb inflation and this caused the financial reform to slow down during 1989–1991. As typical signs of a higher level of centralization, the role of government-directed credit regained its significance while control over the non-bank sector was tightened. Trust and investment companies (TICs), whose reemergence since 1979 was chiefly due to the increasing demand of regional enterprises and local governments to provide financing not available from state-owned commercial banks, became the major target. Having a stable source of funding (from deposits by government financial departments, enterprises, pension funds, etc.) and flexibility in setting their own lending rates (variable within a 20 PCT band relative to bank rates), as well as a privilege to raise capital from overseas markets, the TICs had quickly developed into a preferred supplier capable of financing projects sponsored by diverse localities and in particular, the coastal areas. Under a system whose credit was almost exclusively extended via state banks, their contribution to China's regional economy should not be underestimated. Viewing the country as a whole, however, if there were no brakes on the rampant expansion of credit through the TICs, then the inflationary pressure would sooner or later threaten the macroeconomic stability. For fear of cyclical fluctuations of the real economy, the State Council in September 1989 released a directive which called for immediate rectification and consolidation of the TICs. By the end of 1988, there were still 745 PBoC-approved ITCs (rumored to be more than 1,000 if including those not sanctioned by the central bank). Two years later, the number dropped to 339 and they were subject to more stringent supervision (Tang, Lai, & Lin, 1999).

7.1 Central and Commercial Banks

To a great extent, the second wave of financial reform was initiated as a result of one more round of inflationary pressure brought by booming investment in 1992. In particular, the actually used value of foreign direct investment exceeded for the first time the USD10 billion mark and reached USD11 billion, almost 160 PCT higher than that of the previous year (Chu, 1994). Moreover, that same year also witnessed a 14.2 PCT growth rate of the GDP, another indicator suggesting that the economy was moving too fast. Recognizing the unprecedented vitality of market forces, as well as the fact that measures to curb inflation would not be effective if without a modern financial system, the State Council issued in December 1993 the "Resolution on Financial System Reform". Targeting chiefly at the banking business, the decision set forth three major objectives and they were: to transform the People's Bank of China (PBoC) into a modern central bank performing its due obligations such as promulgation and execution of monetary policies, supervision of *subordinate* agencies, etc.; to reposition the state-owned specialized banks so that they would operate as genuine commercial banks independently responsible for losses, profits and risk controls; *and* to establish a well-ordered financial market in which monetary operations and securities transactions may take place openly under strict regulation.

7.1.1 Initial Formation of the Banking System

As part of the government's determination to separate policy lending from commercial lending, three policy banks were set up in 1994 and they included China Development Bank, the Export and Import Bank of China, and the Agricultural Development Bank of China. This is a very significant move because on the one hand, it can help push forward the commercialization of the state-owned banks; at the same time, it would facilitate the implementation of an indirect monetary policy, i.e. liquidity management at the level of the system, rather than at the level of individual banks or simply to meet the targets of the credit plan. In the same year, the four existing specialized banks, i.e. the Agricultural Bank of China (ABC), the Bank of China (BOC), the People's Construction Bank of China (PCBC, renamed the China Construction Bank or CCB in 1996), and the Industrial and Commercial Bank of China (ICBC), became known as state-owned commercial banks. To encourage competition, several joint stock commercial banks came into being during the 1990s as well, like Shanghai Pudong Development Bank and Huaxia Bank in 1992. With regard to the first private shareholding bank of China, i.e. China Minsheng Banking Corporation, it was established in 1996 by the All-China Federation of Industry and Commerce, an association of private enterprises. In addition, with the Hong Kong-based Nanyang Commercial Bank opening a branch in Shenzhen Special Economic Zone in 1982, which was also the first foreign bank operating in mainland China after the reform, more foreign banks were allowed to set up their own subsidiaries or representative offices in this promising market. Undoubtedly, the appearance of all these non-state banks was a positive push that not only facilitated the shift of China's banking operations towards a more market-directed one, its spillover effects would also be permeated into other sectors constructive to the whole economy.

In the early 1990s, the most prominent headache facing the banking sector of China was the huge amount of non-performing loans (NPLs) accumulated by the state-owned banks whose lending practices were both biased and poorly-regulated. These loans had been largely extended as subsidies to the loss-making SOEs and because of their weakening competitiveness, the loans were unlikely to be repaid on or even after maturity. As to the scale of the NPLs, although official statistics are not easily available for that period, the establishment of four government-owned asset management corporations (AMCs) in 1999 could describe to some degree the tip of the iceberg. Each of the four AMCs was originally paired up with one of the four state-owned commercial banks; namely, Cinda (April 20th) with the CCB, Orient (October 15th) with the BOC, Great Wall (October 18th) with the ABC, and Huarong (October 19th) with the ICBC. Together, the AMCs purchased at book value nearly RMB1.4 trillion of NPLs from the Big Four and the China Development Bank. Referring to the distribution of the transfer among the four AMCs, Table 4 can provide a detailed picture. Labeled "doubtful" loans, they were released prior to 1995 and became overdue by the end of 1998. By purchasing these bad debts with bonds and cash, the four AMCs were mandated to recover them as much as possible over ten years, either by collection, debt-equity swaps (DES), or loan repackaging and resale, etc. Speaking at the NPL International Forum in Nov. 2001, the then central bank governor Dai Xianglong announced that the scheme had reduced the banks' combined NPLs by almost 10 PCT. Besides, in terms of the share of the NPLs in the total loan portfolio of the Big Four, it dropped to 25.37 PCT by the end of 2001 (Huang, 2002). Although the ratio was still high if compared to the global average, as a major step of restructuring banks, this highlighted the government's determination to improve their asset quality and balance sheets. While the initial record was impressive, there was definitely a long way ahead before the thorn of NPL could be significantly removed.

Table 4 Four AMCs and transfer of NPLs from corresponding banks by mid-2001

Asset Management Corporations (AMC)	Banks matched	Assets transferred (RMB billion)
Cinda AMC	China Construction Bank	373[1]
Orient AMC	Bank of China	267.4
Great Wall AMC	Agricultural Bank of China	345.8
Huarong AMC	Industrial and Commercial Bank of China	407.7
Total		**1,393.9**

Note [1]Inclusive of RMB100 billion of NPLs from the China Development Bank
Source Chen (2012)

7.1.2 Passage of Two Landmark Laws

Additionally, in an effort to consolidate the legal basis on which the banking sector was to be governed, two important laws were enacted in 1995, one was the Law of the People's Republic of China on the People's Bank of China (or the Central Bank Law) and the other was the Law of the People's Republic of China on Commercial Banks (or the Commercial Bank Law). While the former law strengthened the central bank's authority to determine monetary policies, oversee payment systems and monitor commercial banks, it also had a significant disciplinary effect on the flow of credit in the lending market. Accordingly, the intermediate objective of the PBoC changed from regulating credit quotas to the management of money supply. From the third quarter of 1994, it started to publicize statistical and supervisory index of monetary supply on a quarterly basis, which was divided into four levels: M0 (currency in circulation); M1 (M0 + corporate checking accounts + institutional savings + rural savings + individual credit card savings); M2 (M1 + residential savings + corporate fixed deposits + deposits in foreign currencies + entrusted deposits); and M3 (M2 + financial bonds + commercial bills + large liquid assets, etc.) (Mao, 1996). By comparison, M1 represents money in a narrow sense and has strong liquidity whereas M2 is a broader measure of money supply including less liquid assets.

With regard to the Commercial Bank Law, it was promulgated in order to push commercial banks to follow standard international practices. Very explicitly, the Law stipulated some technical requirements such as capital adequacy ratio (CAR), the ratio of the outstanding balance of loans to that of deposits, and the ratio of the outstanding balance of liquid assets to that of liquid liabilities, etc. (Article 39). Most notably, by stating that no organization or individual may force a commercial bank to extend loans or provide guarantee for loans (Article 41), the once policy-natured lending functions were taken over by the three newly established policy banks; namely, China Development Bank, the Export and Import Bank of

China, and the Agricultural Development Bank of China. Although it was impossible for the commercial banks to absolutely steer clear of interference from the central and local governments, they were given a higher level of autonomy in taking decisions for lending businesses, which enabled them to become more profit-driven and operationally independent.

7.1.3 Relaxed Control of Interest Rates in Inter-Bank Transactions

Prior to 1985, a very common phenomenon in the banking sector was that banks with surplus funds, instead of lending to other banks in need, would just keep it. By then, only vertical allocation of funds was allowed, i.e. from the State Council through the central bank before reaching the four state-owned specialized banks (Xue, 1998). This system worked well in a planned economy because it was the state that controlled the purchase and sale of products, supply and demand as a result could both be anticipated. Accordingly, allocated credit could only be used to purchase the designated quantities of materials at fixed prices. Like a pre-determined plot, what is called surprise rarely happened. Therefore, banks had little motivation to be market-sensitive and profit-seeking. But the situation began to change with the freeing-up of the economy after 1979, plans were no longer that authoritative when more and more industrial and commercial activities shifted away to observe the rules of the market. Obviously, the increased uncertainties were far beyond what the rigid credit plans could cope with. In addition, considering the regional disparities, a mechanism was desperately necessary to be established so that funds could flow not just vertically, but also horizontally from capital-thirsty to capital-rich areas.

In order to tackle the problem with the supply system of finance, the People's Bank of China in 1984 issued the "Rules for the Management of Credit Funds". By turning the relationship between the central bank and specialized banks from the one based on allocation of funds to repayable credits, the Rules stated clearly that lending between banks was permitted. This could be taken as the first official document which approved the formation of inter-bank markets. On Aug. 30th, 1986, the Industrial and Commercial Bank of China, Shanghai Branch set up the first money market which enabled banks to openly engage in short-term borrowing and lending of funds. Within the same year, 140 deals were concluded in the market, with a total transaction value amounting to RMB2.8 billion (Hu, 1987). By the end of 1987, similar markets, either visible (between banks of the same region) or invisible (inter-regional), were spread around the country and the cumulative inter-bank transactions skyrocketed to RMB230 billion; only one year before, the figure was merely RMB30 billion (Peng, 2001). The rapid expansion of inter-bank market during the 1980s was a revolution in China's financial reform, it challenged the old system of rigid credit management and replaced it with a dynamic mechanism which could effectively balance the needs of capital across the nation. Thus, a higher efficiency of funds allocation could be realized.

Interest rates, as a financial instrument of risk management and asset pricing that may ultimately influence the allocation of resources, is used by the monetary authorities worldwide to exercise macroeconomic adjustment. Before the late 1970s when all the price levels were set by the state, there was no need for the Chinese policymakers to use interest rates to regulate the economy. But gradually, with the formation of a more open system, such a manipulated structure was in obvious conflict with the nation's strategy to enhance the role of the market. In addition, from the perspective of increasing the competitiveness of financial institutions, liberalization of interest rates was a sure path to go. At the initial stage, the authorities experimented with increased interest rate flexibility. For instance, in June 1983, the State Council approved the report on the "Unified Management of the State-Owned Enterprises' Working Capital by the PBoC" (or known as Document No. 100), which for the first time authorized the central bank to have its lending rates floated by up to 20PCT above and below the centrally-determined benchmark.

After several years of trials, the PBoC started to move one step further in 1987 by permitting the commercial banks to raise their lending rates for working capital loans by no higher than 20 PCT over the corresponding rate of the state. While this decision stimulated the interest of banks to grant more loans, enterprises faced a heavier burden of repayment and shrinking profit margins (for this reason, the preceding swing of the lending rate was narrowed to ± 10 PCT around the benchmark in 1996) (Gu & Wu, 2008). Efforts to deregulate bank lending and deposit rates went ahead in the following decade. In December 1993, the State Council issued the "Decisions on the Reform of Financial System". This landmark document not only provided a blueprint for China's overall financial reform through the 1990s, it also endorsed the central bank to utilize policy instruments like deposit and loan rates, statutory reserve requirement, and official re-discount rate, etc. in a flexible way so as to maintain monetary and economic stability.

Relaxation of the state's grip on interest rates was not just limited to the lending business between banks and enterprises, the trend equally took place in the inter-bank market, especially after the mid-1990s. Following the trial operation of a unitary inter-bank lending computer network in January 1996, a two-level market was established where banks were in a position to lend funds among themselves for liquidity needs (Chen, 1997a, 1997b). The first level, or called the national level, consisted of the headquarters of 15 commercial banks and 35 financing centers; as to the second level, or the regional level, it included bank branches and other financial institutions of diverse administrative regions, such as trust and investment corporations, urban and rural credit cooperatives, as well as insurance companies, etc. In this new market, the central bank (the PBoC) imposed strict limits on the term of maturity and amount of lending or borrowing for all the participating institutions. Regarding the lending and borrowing among commercial banks, the maximum term should not exceed 4 months and the amount involved should be fixed in proportion to the balance of deposits. As to the lending or borrowing by non-bank financial institutions, the term should be no more than 7 days and the amount was also fixed according to the level of capital. By setting these limits, reckless lending or borrowing could be well harnessed, thus preventing excess liquidity from hurting the economy.

On January 4th, 1996, the China Inter-bank Offered Rate (CHIBOR) was published. Representing the weighted average short-term rate of the market, its calculation was based on the real transactions for each maturity, from one day to no more than 120 days. Although at that time, the interest rate cap was still determined by the PBoC, both the institutional and technical conditions were in fact basically prepared for the liberalization of inter-bank lending rate. On June 1st, 1996, with the issuance of the "Notice of Abolishing Upper Limits on Inter-bank Lending Rate", the PBoC abolished the ceiling and from then on, the lending rate was determined through negotiations between lenders and borrowers according to the supply of and demand for funds in the market (Liu & Wang, 1997). Fairly speaking, since the inter-bank lending market was the foundation for the central bank to carry out its monetary policies, the lifting of controls paved the way for more radical reforms of interest rates in the years to come.

7.1.4 Open Market Operations

In June 1997, another important step was taken through which the PBoC used the existing inter-bank lending market as a platform to deal in inter-bank bond repo transactions and outright cash settlement. Similarly, the interest rates were also opened for negotiation between involved parties (Chen, 2006). Considering the fact that bond market is a critical component of financial market, liberalization of interest rates greatly facilitated its development because financial institutions could better price their products against the ups and downs of the market and adjust asset composition in a more flexible way. At the same time, it also laid a solid foundation for the central bank to conduct its monetary policies via indirect tools including open market operations (OMOs), minimum reserve requirements, relending and rediscount, etc.

Adopted as a major form of sterilized intervention to counter the potentially harmful effects of capital inflows, open market operations was first introduced by the PBoC in 1994 to stabilize the growth of the monetary base which had been rather exponential in those years (Liu & Zhang, 1994). Taking M2 (broad money), a measure of money supply including cash and demand deposits (M1) as well as quasi money (i.e. time savings and foreign currency deposits of resident sectors other than the central government) as an example, statistics in the table below (Table 5) indicate that ever since the beginning of the 1990s, China's M2 had been growing at a rather fast pace. Besides, in terms of the M2/GDP ratio, it had also been rising steadily, hitting 150.46 PCT in 2000. Obviously, such a momentum of monetary expansion was very dangerous and could easily result in rampant inflation (in fact, 1994 was the year when China's inflation soared to its highest ever since its foundation in 1949, with the retail price index and the consumer price index recorded at 121.7 and 124.1 respectively, preceding year = 100) and even collapse of the economy.

Therefore, together with the implementation of a moderately tight monetary policy, the PBoC did a lot of preparatory work for open market operation, a means commonly used to control the liquid reserves of financial institutions. In 1996, it tested the bond market by purchasing from fourteen commercial banks the treasury

Table 5 Growth in M2 and its impact on consumer price index, 1990–2000

Year	M2[1] (RMB100 million)	Year-on-year growth rate[2] (PCT)	M2/GDP ratio[3] (PCT)	CPI[4] preceding year = 100
1990	15,293.4	–	82.45	103.1
1992	25,402.2	31.3	95.36	106.4
1994	46,923.5	34.5	100.35	124.1
1996	76,094.9	25.3	112.09	108.3
1998	104,498.5	14.8	133.38	99.2
2000	134,610.4	12.3	150.46	100.4

Source [1, 2] and [4]NBS (2006); [3]calculated by the author

bills of the Ministry of Finance with a face value of RMB290 million (Tao, 1998). Usually, if the central bank wants to inject liquidity, it may buy back negotiable securities such as government bonds or bills in the open market (called repos); given the huge amount involved, its actions can often stimulate economy with the lowering cost of investment. Conversely, by selling securities (called reverse repos), the central bank can withdraw the money available in the market, and this in turn will curb the credit of commercial banks, thus resulting in a decline of overinvestment and soft landing of an overheated economy. Toward the late 1990s, such operations were more frequently carried out by the PBoC to influence interest rates. In terms of the effects, they were fairly noticeable. On the one hand, the growth rate of M2 kept decreasing from 1994. Referring to the inflation rate (represented by CPI), it realized a parallel movement, particularly between 1996 and 1998 when it declined from 8.3 PCT to −0.8 PCT, a signal of deflationary tendencies. The close relationship between M2 and the inflation rate suggests that by regulating the monetary-supply growth, the PBoC could effectively influence the slope of inflation.

By and large, interest rates liberalization in China was orchestrated in a cautious and sequential manner. It started with short-term wholesale transactions in the interbank market (from overnight to 120 days) before shifting to retail banking operations, allowing banks and financial institutions to price their interest rates, especially those for working capital loans, within a certain floating margin against the benchmarks set by the PBoC. Through the years, the margin had been expanding and in September 1999 for example, the commercial lending rates for small and medium-sized enterprises (SMEs) were allowed to float 1.3 times above the benchmark interest rate, up from the previous 1.1 times whereas the band for large enterprises stayed unchanged at 10PCT above or below the benchmark (based on the "Notice of the PBoC on Issues Concerning Further Expanding the Floating Range of Lending Rates for SMEs" released in 1999). By developing a mechanism to price loans and deposits in a market-oriented way, the PBoC was not simply seeking to regulate the overall monetary and credit aggregates in the economy, it also aimed to improve the risk management and profitability of state-owned commercial banks, especially when in connection with their loan portfolios.

Above all, in view of the weight of the banking sector in the entire financial system, its soundness and well-functioning are undoubtedly crucial to maintaining macroeconomic stability in the long run. Given the transition that happened in China during the 1990s, it was rather positive in that both the central and state-owned commercial banks tended to show more respect for free market principles. They had a clearer idea as to what responsibilities to carry and which instruments to utilize in order to fulfill their part as intermediaries in the national economy. Anyhow, the control-oriented nature of the Chinese planning system remained, although the sphere and extent of its influence was much less significant than before, and this to a large degree prohibited the banking entities from acting more aggressively in the allocation of resources. Moreover, various structural deficiencies, particularly in terms of regulation, supervision, and governance, were not yet 100 PCT addressed. Unless these fundamental problems were resolved, it would be impossible to make deeper financial reforms a fruitful one.

7.2 *Foreign-Funded Banks*

Fairly speaking, it was Marco Polo's Asian travels (1271–1295 AD) that made Cathay (the name he gave to ancient China) known to the Western world. In his famous book *The Travels of Marco Polo*, he described how amazed he was when discovering that China, which was by then part of the Mongol Empire under the great conqueror Kublai Khan, had already possessed the secret of producing paper money known as '*chao*' during the Yuan Dynasty (1271–1368 AD). Already the dominant power in Asia, Cathay believed that it was self-sufficient and superior over other nations, thus there was almost no need to trade with the outside world. Until 1757 when the Qing Dynasty (1644–1911 AD) was reigned by Qianlong Emperor, Westerners coming to China to seek mercantile interests were still regarded as "insignificant barbarians" and their trading was confined to a limited number of ports in Guangdong, Fujian, Jiangsu and Zhejiang Province. Perhaps the huge and lucrative Chinese market was so irresistible to these foreign merchants that for the pursuit of a bigger share of the market, initial pockets of conflict with the regime ultimately escalated into two Opium Wars (the first 1840–1842 and the second 1856–1860), leaving more ports opened to free trade and foreign residence after the failure of the arrogant Qing court.

7.2.1 Early Presence on the Mainland

The opening of more Chinese ports not only benefited Western companies, the rapid expansion in bilateral trade also created fresh demand for credit and transfer facilities, which attracted their banks to conduct business in this ancient oriental country (Xu & Wu, 2003). Regarding the first foreign bank operating in China, it should be '*Liru Yinhang*' (Chinese name) set up as a branch in Shanghai in 1847 by the Bank of Western India headquartered in Bombay, India (in 1845, with the removal of its head office to London, the name was changed to the Oriental Bank Corporation). Very soon, other British or British-Indian banks followed suit, such as '*Huilong Yinhang*' (1851) in Guangzhou by the Commercial Bank of India, '*Ajiala Yinhang*' (1854) in Shanghai by Agra and United Service Bank, and '*Youli Yinhang*' (1854) by the Chartered Mercantile Bank of India, London and China in Shanghai, etc. After 1860, banks from other countries like France, the US, Japan, and Germany, etc. began to establish their presence in China as well and among them, the pioneer is Comptoir d'Escompte de Paris (Discount Bank of Paris) which has been engaged in the discount business of negotiable instruments in Shanghai since 1860.

Backed by the full official support, strong capital base, transnational business links, and modern corporate structures, these foreign banks quickly asserted unquestionable dominance in China's international remittance, foreign exchange transactions, and foreign trade financing, etc. Moreover, due to the inadequacies of Qing's banking legislation and the status of extraterritoriality (i.e. being exempt from the jurisdiction of the local law under the Treaty of Nanjing after the end of the First Opium War), they even issued banknotes for circulation in the territory of China, an exclusive right which should belong to sovereign governments only and no external forces may infringe. In general, notes were denominated either in taels ('*liang*', the Chinese dollar) or dollars ('*yuan*'). For example, '*Liru Yinhang*', though not granted the royal charter until 1851, printed in 1847 Hongkong's first paper money which totaled 56,000 dollars after the opening of its local branch. During the 1860s, it was more common to see banknotes flowing in the market, such as those from '*Maijiali Yinhang*' (the Chartered Bank of India, Australia and China, predecessor of today's Standard Chartered Bank), and '*Huifeng Yinhang*' (the Hongkong and Shanghai Banking Corporation), etc. Issuing banknotes in China not only led to booming business activities, it further enhanced the reputation of foreign banks, which made it easier for them to diversify by offering deposit and loan services to the local residents. However, the first half of the twentieth century was by no means peaceful. Externally, there were two World Wars which devastated the global economy. Internally, incessant uprisings and foreign attacks overshadowed almost every facet of people's life. In order to cover the soaring military expenditure, the Qing court and its succeeding Kuomintang regime (of the Republic of China, 1911–1948) were without exception compelled to borrow from foreign banks, leaving the country more fragile and thus vulnerable in that turbulent era.

7.2.2 Resurgence After 1978

After the founding of the People's Republic of China in 1949, the overall environment for foreign banks became increasingly unfavorable under the policy of nationalization and the resolution to run the economy in a centralized way. Instead of promoting international cooperation, self-reliance was highlighted by the new regime as a decisive factor for its people to reach their full creative potential and attain greater growth. Seeing the mounting constraints and vanishing opportunities, foreign-funded enterprises in China had no choice but to leave. Like a chain reaction, banks withdrew as well since they could not afford the loss of these valued customers. By 1956, while the HSBC, the Chartered Bank of India, Australia and China, the Oversea-Chinese Banking Corporation and Bank of East Asia were the only four that decided to stay, their operations remained just nominal throughout the following thirty years.

When launching the radical program of reform and opening up, the *leadership in Beijing* was already determined to create a competitive environment in which its various economic entities, especially those owned by the state, could learn to operate independently instead of relying on the preferential government policies to survive. Besides, the record-high budget deficit for two consecutive years of 1979 and 1980, which hit RMB17.07 billion and RMB12.75 billion respectively (Xiang, 1983), also pushed the country to give up its decades-long policy of self-reliance and resort to external sources to relieve the fiscal burden. In this regard, the entry of foreign banks could undoubtedly help create a better financial environment for the attraction of funds from the global market. Additionally, with solid capital base and adequate liquidity access, these banks were themselves providers of short- and long-term loans to finance China's economic development. From another perspective, the presence of overseas competitors would add pressure to the domestic banking sector. Modeling the advanced management practices of these foreign counterparts, Chinese banks could more easily identify the gaps and thus expect to catch up with up-to-date techniques and better services. Given the fact that in the international financial industry, there exists a reciprocity principle relating to the establishment of banking institutions in foreign countries. By allowing overseas banks easier access into China, its domestic banks could equally head abroad, not merely for the expansion of business networks, but also for the enhancement of the overall image of the country worldwide.

If counting the first legislative effort that provided a statutory framework for the management of foreign financial institutions operating in China, it should be the "Regulations of the PBoC on the Establishment of Representative Offices by Overseas and Foreign Financial Institutions". Released in 1983, it covered in details the opening, monitoring, and closing procedures that should be observed. Two years later, permission was extended to the opening of branches when the State Council promulgated the "Regulations on the Administration of Foreign Banks and Sino-Foreign Joint Venture Banks in the Special Economic Zones". Although inevitably, both documents involved restrictions on certain activities, especially the provision of local currency business to individual citizens, they delivered to foreign banks a positive message indicating that China's banking strategy was under reform and it wouldn't take too long before reaching a deeper-level of relaxation.

Rather interestingly, the publication of both Regulations were without exception preceded by some trial operations. In December 1979, the Export–Import Bank of Japan, a Japanese government agency, became the first foreign bank approved to open its representative office in Beijing and this marked a prelude to the opening up of the Chinese financial system to the outside. In January 1982, another major progress was achieved when Nanyang Commercial Bank, the first foreign bank incorporated in Hong Kong, set up an operational branch in Shenzhen Special Economic Zone. Encouraged by the proactive attitude of the Chinese regulators toward foreign banks, more liaison offices and branches were established, like the representative office of the Bank of Montreal in Beijing in 1982, HSBC (the Hongkong and Shanghai Banking Corporation) Shenzhen Branch and UOB (United Overseas Bank) Xiamen Branch in 1985, as well as Crédit Lyonnais (acquired by Crédit Agricole in 2003) Xiamen Branch in 1989, etc., in addition to the Standard Chartered Bank, Bank of East Asia, and Oversea-Chinese Banking Corporation which continued to expand elsewhere after having opened their branches earlier.

Here, what is worth noting is that the first Sino-foreign joint venture bank was also formed during the 1980s. It happened in November 1985 when the three domestic shareholders including the Fujian branch of ICBC (Industrial and Commercial Bank of China), Fujian Investment and Enterprise Corporation, and Xiamen Construction and Development Corporation invested together with their overseas partner Panin Group Corporation (from Hong Kong, renamed Min Xin Group in 1988). As a result, with the former three taking 40 PCT stake and the latter 60 PCT (later changed to 51 PCT and 49 PCT respectively), Xiamen International Bank (Photo 1) came into being in Xiamen Special Economic Zone (Zhao, 2008). During that particular period, coastal cities were almost the exclusive destinations for these foreign banks to locate their facilities in China, which to a large degree also reflected the mindset of the government to safeguard the inexperienced commercial banks, especially in non-coastal areas, from foreign competition. But ever since the mid-1990s, the landscape has changed. As more officials became open-minded, an increasing number of inland cities including Chengdu (Sichuan Province), Wuhan (Hubei Province) and Kunming (Yunnan Province), etc. were chosen by overseas investors to host their banking business (Zhao & Yu, 1996).

Photo 1 Office building of Xiamen International Bank, the first joint venture bank of China opened on November 28th, 1985 in Xiamen Special Economic Zone. *Source* https://www.xmnn.cn/dzbk/xmrb/20111226/201112/t20111226_2118801.htm

7.2.3 Gradual Expansion of the Business Scopes

Before the mid-1990s, although foreign banks were allowed to open their branches in China, they just gained a limited access to this huge emerging market. In general, they could only handle foreign currency businesses that chiefly targeted at ventures whose investors were from outside China, such as corporate lending, saving, bill discounting, and international settlement, etc. While it is true that China by then was in need of large sums of money to finance its massive construction projects, foreign banks had few opportunities to carve out niches in the investment programs of the Chinese economy. Particularly, due to the vagueness in regulations, a lack of information transparency, and systemic deficiencies in the credit assessment of borrowers, uncertainties persisted over debt repayment when Chinese enterprises were in default situations. On the other hand, the very fact that these foreign banks were not familiar with the local climate having been there for only a short time also put them in a disadvantageous position when competing with their domestic rivals, chiefly the Bank of China (BOC). Furthermore, Chinese individuals or enterprises by then were not yet permitted to open accounts at foreign banks. If they were in need of foreign currencies, they had to first apply to the State Administration of Foreign Exchange (SAFE, the regulatory and management authority responsible for managing China's foreign exchange reserves). Upon approval, they would almost without exception buy from the BOC, the major state bank specializing in foreign exchange business. Besides, on many occasions, simply for the protection of its own banks, the government would also give them more favor. Thereby, the initial period for these foreign banks upon their entry into China was mixed with difficulties, which could only be overcome through adaptation and self-adjustment.

Nevertheless, to view from the perspective that China during the 1990s was preparing for the WTO accession, deepened reform was an indispensable prerequisite to make itself better qualified, especially concerning the financial sector which was not yet fully opened to foreign competition. In 1996, a gesture was made when the PBoC promulgated the "Provisional Rules Governing the RMB Business Operations of Foreign-Funded Financial Institutions in Shanghai Pudong" and licensed nine foreign banks in the newly-developed Pudong district of Shanghai to conduct RMB business on a trial basis, these banks included the Citibank, HSBC, Standard Chartered Bank, the Bank of Tokyo-Mitsubishi, the Dai-Ichi Kangyo Bank, the Sanwa Bank, the Industrial Bank of Japan, Banque Indosuez, and the International Bank of Paris & Shanghai (a joint venture between Banque Nationale de Paris and the ICBC) (Li, 1999a, 1999b, 1999c). Two years later, Shenzhen followed Shanghai and became the second city that allowed foreign banks to experiment local currency transactions (Liu, 2001).

In addition, ever since 1998, foreign banks have also been allowed to take the lead in arranging syndicated loans denominated in RMB for infrastructure projects. As the name suggests, a syndicated loan is offered by a group of lenders (called syndicate) to a single borrower, either a company, a project, or a sovereign government. Unlike ordinary loans, there should be a lead bank (or sometimes several) known as the "lead lender" which originates the loan, forms the syndicate and processes payments.

In China, the first foreign bank pioneering the domestic-currency syndicated loan was Standard Chartered Bank. Being the lead lender, it worked with a group of six Chinese and foreign banks in December 1998 and extended an RMB80 million one-year short-term loan to Shanghai Tire and Rubber Company, one of China's biggest tire makers (Gong, 1999). Regarding the other two foreign banks that participated in the package, they were Credit Agricole Indosuez and the International Bank of Paris and Shanghai. The conclusion of this deal not only marked the widened scope of business activities for foreign banks operating in China, it was also representative of a significant step in tightening their cooperation with indigenous banks.

Apart from establishing a wholly foreign-owned bank and opening a branch or representative office, foreign strategic investors including industry players, financial and private equity investors could also expect to hold equity stakes in Chinese banks. Although by the mid-1990s, no legal framework was available for foreign entities to acquire stocks in Chinese commercial banks; in practice, it was not impossible and could be approved on a case-by-case basis by the State Council, after consulting the advice of the PBoC, the regulatory and administrative authority in charge of China's commercial banks. The first case happened in 1996 when Asian Development Bank (ADB), a multilateral finance institution based in Manila, spent USD19 million and acquired a 3.29 PCT stake in China Everbright Bank (Ba, 2006). Undeniably, it was just a minority share if using today's standards; but the symbolic meaning was much more far-reaching because through introducing strategic partners, a new page was opened for China's banking sector. With a more diversified ownership structure, risks could be under better control. Besides, the absorption of foreign experiences in corporate governance was also a plus to the improvement of its overall performance. Three years later, International Finance Corporation (IFC), a member of the World Bank Group focusing solely on the private sector in developing countries, bought a 5 PCT stake of the Bank of Shanghai (BOS) for USD22 million (it was increased to 7 PCT in 2001). From then on, more foreign investment flowed into mainland China and this led to the partnership which is taken as a norm of operation in its banking sector today.

7.2.4 Changes Brought by Foreign Stakeholders: A Glimpse of BOS

Indeed, the inroads of these foreign banks should not be taken simply as "wolves" threatening their Chinese counterparts, which for decades had been running in an environment free of external competition. Based on a stereotypical mindset that since the government was there to bear risks and losses, they even had no awareness of the urgency to improve their quality of service and efficiency of management. As a result, despite the fact that some of them were already burdened with immense non-performing loans left by the SOEs, the feeling that they were "too big to fail" outweighed the pressing need for reform. Obviously, such an adverse situation could not sustain and changing the status quo was perhaps the only way out, although it was rather uncomfortable in the beginning. If taking a long-term view, Chinese banks should treat the opening-up of the sector as a good opportunity to internalize the best of the global financial practices and restructure themselves from mere executors of the central plans into rule-abiding and market-responsive players. In this consideration, certain spillover effects should not be ignored. For example, the broader range of products and services, as well as the efficiency gains stemming from advanced techniques and professional expertise may be soon translated into positive welfare implications for both individual and institutional customers. Further, by lending from foreign banks, domestic enterprises, especially the small and medium-sized which had been denied of state loans, had more channels to finance their business at lower expenses. In turn, they could realize higher sales and expand more smoothly. At the macro level, a healthier and well-functioning financial system is a primary driver that fosters the economy to move forward steadily.

Back to the Bank of Shanghai (BOS), founded in 1995 and headquartered in Shanghai, it received equity investment by the IFC in 1999. As an investor holding a 5PCT stake, the IFC not only appointed its director John Langlois to the board of BOS (Ba, Hua, & Niu, 2005), it also helped expedite the transformation of this city commercial bank through multiple advisory services; namely, the introduction of international best practices in banking management, the consolidation of risk control capabilities, and improvement of corporate governance, etc. What's more, with a view to better serving the small and medium-sized enterprises (SMEs) in China's booming private sector, the IFC also shared its idea and framework of microfinance operations with the BOS. In December 2001, a grand signing ceremony was held in the Pudong district of Shanghai at which HSBC acquired an 8PCT stake in Bank of Shanghai for RMB518 million; simultaneously, Shanghai Commercial Bank (SCB, based in Hong Kong) took a share of 3 PCT. After including the additional 2 PCT stake by the IFC, foreign capital totally accounted for 18 PCT of that of BOS (Zhang, 2002a, 2002b).

Overall, ever since its alliance with foreign partners such as the IFC and HSBC, the Bank of Shanghai has been demonstrating greater financial strengths than many other Chinese banks, with considerable expansion in assets, reduction in non-performing loans (NPLs), and improvement in profitability, etc. The table below (Table 6) shows a comparison of several indicators relating to the performance of BOS during and after the investment by the IFC. From around 1999 to 2011, there has been an increase

Table 6 Financial performance of the Bank of Shanghai, 1999–2011

Year	Assets (RMB billion)	Profits (RMB million)	Leverage ratio loan/assets (PCT)	NPLs[2] (PCT)	ROE[3] (PCT)
1999[1]	73	267	–	3	11.1
2007	309	2,934	48.5	2.41	19.9
2011	656	5,807	51	0.98	18

Note [1]the data is for the year IFC invested or the nearest available; [2]non-performing loans; [3]return on equity
Source Chen & Liu (2012)

of almost eight fold in its assets and an even more impressive profit growth of over twenty times, reaching RMB5,807 million by 2011.

With regard to the leverage ratio, it is a measure often used to monitor the vulnerability of financial institutions. Usually, it should be maintained within a certain range for both micro- and macro-prudential purposes. A ratio too low (i.e. less than 4 PCT in China) means the institution is over-conservative and not well capitalized; but once it swings to the other extreme, then a higher risk exposure would emerge and may very likely lead to potential problems when meeting debt obligations. Despite an absence of data for the year when the IFC invested in BOS, the levels of 48.5 PCT in 2007 and 51 PCT of 2011 should be considered prudent, suggesting that the BOS was capable of handling liquidity or systemic risks if any. In addition, the shrinkage of its NPLs from 3 PCT to less than 1 PCT could be taken as a sign of improved oversight of credit risks and safer balance sheet of BOS. In terms of return on equity (ROE), a financial ratio that evaluates the return on stockholders' equity, it is reflective of the profitability of business entities and shows how well a company uses investment funds to achieve earnings growth. The increase in the ROE of the Bank of Shanghai was actually in line with its pace of profit rise over the same period. After taking all these statistics into consideration, it is evident that the performance of BOS cannot be so encouraging if without the continual technical assistance and direct participation of foreign partners such as the IFC, HSBC and SCB in its daily operations. By and large, the case of BOS is not to be isolated from the overall landscape of China's banking sector. While in pursuit of management efficiency through internal restructuring, assimilation of valuable experiences from overseas players is an indispensable alternative that facilitated the transformation. Although competition is set to cause some Chinese banks to lose or even fail, if skipping this process, there would be no way for them to cope with the challenges once they were to access the international financial market.

Of course, by recognizing the positive role of the incoming foreign banks or organizations, it would be naïve to expect that they can resolve all the existing problems of China's banks or of its banking sector at large; instead, they should be viewed as a pushing force stimulating the Chinese players to aim high and attain excellent banking performance through enhanced strategic capabilities and better management of risks. Additionally, concerning the issue of financial innovation, it was merely a concept in China since the products and services offered by its own banks were largely homogeneous, irrespective of their different locations, advantages and target customers. On the one hand, this created unnecessary competition and squeezed their profit margins; at the same time, it also caused certain niche markets to remain underserved. In the short run, such a business model was still workable given the country's huge customer base and their strong propensity to save at local banks. But with the deepening of the nationwide reform and opening up, as well as the growing reliance on imported know-how, foreign investors had more incentives to penetrate this lucrative market. Their provision of diversified products and customer-oriented services are hardly resistible to the Chinese people. With regard to this phenomenon, if domestic banks were still content with the status quo and couldn't respond with multiple business lines tailored for specific market segments, the future would be doomed. Conversely, if the mounting pressure from the outside is utilized in an effective way, banks in China could expect to function as integrated financial corporations handling a wide range of activities like banking, insurance and securities, etc. By the end of 2001, the year when China gained its membership of the WTO, foreign banks had established 158 branches and 214 representative offices, the total assets of these foreign banks reached USD45.2 billion, accounting for about 2 PCT of that of China's banking industry (Zheng, 2003).

8 The Foreign Exchange Regime

The reform that has taken place in the banking sector, especially the policy that permitted foreign investors to access this area of business, was made possible partially because of the changes in the country's foreign exchange regime, which is used to govern the value of one currency (legal tender) against that of other currencies. Literally translated as the "people's currency" and also known as the Chinese yuan (CNY), the first series of renminbi (RMB) banknotes was issued on Dec. 1st, 1948 by the People's Bank of China, about one year before the founding of the PRC. By then, the ongoing civil war had seriously disrupted normal financial order and hyperinflation was an everyday nightmare, with *the peak period lasting from 1946 to 1949*. Consequently, circulation of the RMB not only unified multiple currencies of different regions (including '*Fabi*', which literally means legal tender and the gold yuan issued by the Kuomintang regime), it also helped stabilize the turbulent situation. In the end of 1951, the RMB has become the only legal tender in China except for Tibet, Taiwan, Hong Kong, and Macau. Later, considering that the denominations of the first series of RMB were too big (as high as RMB50,000) for people's daily life, plus the fact that the design did not show much unity due to the technology limitations, the second series of RMB was launched on March 1st, 1955 (at a rate of one new RMB to 10,000 old RMB), and with it the first series ceased to circulate on May 10th of that year.

8.1 The Tale of Multiple Currencies Under the Kuomintang Regime

Indeed, it is from the lessons of the former Kuomintang government that the new Chinese leaders learned how to handle the renminbi, especially in the initial stage of takeover. When '*Fabi*', the national currency of the Republic of China (ROC) was issued in 1935, it could be freely traded to US dollars and British pounds. Based on the Sino-American Silver Agreement reached in 1936, the rate was fixed at 1 *Fabi* yuan to 0.2975 US dollars (or 1 US dollar to 3.36 Fabi yuan). At the same time, 1 *Fabi yuan could be* exchanged on average for *1 shilling* and 2.5 *pennies (*Cheng

& Jin, 2011). By June 1937, just one month before the start of the war with Japan, 3.41 *Fabi* yuan was converted into one US dollar. In order to pay for the colossal expenditures and acquire more military materials, the Japanese started to counterfeit *Fabi* from December 1938, a policy they named "sustaining the war by means of war" ('*yi zhan yang zhan*', with the latter referring to the non-shooting economic war). Special organizations were established in both Japan and Shanghai for that purpose. According to historical records, the total amount of fake *Fabi* printed by the Japanese during the war (ended in 1945) was an astonishing 4 billion yuan (Feng, 2008), which destroyed ruthlessly the credibility of the already shaking monetary system of the ROC.

Coupled with people's lost confidence due to the worsening inflation, a black market of foreign currencies flourished quickly, in which 18.93 *Fabi* yuan were sold for one US dollar in December 1941. Four years later, i.e. after the end of the Second World War and Japan's surrender, the value of *Fabi* had fallen to 1,222 yuan to the dollar before further diving to 23,280,000 yuan by May 1949 (Ebeling, 2004). Facing the runaway inflation, especially the fact that hoarding of gold and foreign money had become so common for individual households, the regime introduced a series of measures to stabilize the monetary situation while trying to put an end to these headaches. On August 19th, 1948, the Central Bank of China (the policy bank of Kuomintang government established in 1928 and headquartered in Shanghai) replaced the existing *Fabi* with the gold yuan ('*jin yuan*') notes at the rate of one gold yuan against three million *Fabi* yuan (Wang, 2010). From that day on, all private holdings of gold, silver and foreign currencies were no longer allowed and should be sold to the central bank in exchange for gold yuan notes by September 30th. In case of failure to meet the requirements, these possessions would all be confiscated.

Actually, this did not help much given the perilous budget deficit hitting 370 million (in gold yuan notes) during September and October of that year. In December 1948, it further galloped to 2.2 billion yuan (Li, 1999a, 1999b, 1999c). More critically, people's skepticism continued to prevail over order and harmony; in their eyes, future was still overshadowed by the bleakness of the past and uncertainty of the present. Therefore, although the authorities in the very beginning had planned to curb the issuance of gold yuan notes under a two billion limit; within less than three months, i.e. on November 11th, the ceiling was removed. Until June 1949, the aggregate volume of gold yuan notes in circulation exceeded 130 trillion yuan, over 240,000 times as compared to that of the end August, 1948.

Additionally, the widespread fear of inflation led to heavy disinvestment of capital to Hong Kong, Taiwan, or even the United States in the form of gold bars or US dollars. As a consequence, it didn't take long for the massive outflow to exhaust China's reserves of gold and foreign exchange. In the end of 1945, there were still around USD858 million worth of deposits (Wang, 1999); but by March 1949, it declined to the equivalent of USD275 million, a shrinkage of almost 68 PCT. During that period, what the Kuomintang government did to restrain the outward movement of foreign money was a tightened control of foreign trade, a major activity that was in need of currency transactions. Specifically, it demanded that only banks (chiefly the Bank of China and the Bank of Communications) appointed by the Central Bank of China could deal in the exchange and besides, all the earnings from export should be sold to the Central Bank at fixed rates. In case of purchasing foreign exchange, it could only take place with appointed banks for authorized imports and other payment purposes (Wang, 2013a,2013b).

Nonetheless, at a time of extreme chaos, restrictions did little to ameliorate the problem; rather, it only ensued greater panic and an acceleration of capital flight. After the central government was removed from Nanjing to the provisional capital of Guangzhou due to its defeat in the civil war, it made one more desperate attempt in July 1949 by replacing the gold yuan notes with the silver yuan notes (with one silver yuan worth 500 million gold yuan), dreaming that it may help save the hyper-inflated situation. Quite as expected, however, the value of the new currency again dropped sharply together with the doomed destiny of the Kuomintang regime. Very soon, it was no longer in circulation after the change of power in October 1949.

8.2 The Post-1949 Mechanism of Forming the RMB Exchange Rates

Although it was not long after the first issuance of the renminbi that it became the only home currency of the People's Republic of China, taming the inflationary spiral was by no means an outcome that should be taken for granted. Throughout over two decades of the civil war (starting from 1927), the Chinese leaders had witnessed how disastrous it would be once prices were out of control. They of course wanted to put brakes on it before carrying out various economic activities. Two days ahead of the founding of the PRC, i.e. on Sept. 29th, 1949, a provisional constitution was passed by the First Plenary Session of the Chinese People's Political Consultative Conference in Beijing. Entitled the "Common Program" ('*gongtong gangling*'), it specifically cited in clause 39 that domestic circulation of foreign currencies was prohibited. Moreover, like the approaches adopted by the former Kuomintang government, trading of foreign exchange, foreign currencies, gold and silver was restricted to the state banks only. At that time, it was the People's Bank of China which functioned as the nation's exclusive body for administering foreign exchange and regarding the Bank of China, it was placed under its leadership. Then, with the supervision of the BOC, 53 designated banks got the license to engage in the buying and selling of foreign currencies and they included 35 local banks, 3 overseas Chinese banks, and 15 foreign banks (Zhao, 2002).

Four years later, the BOC was officially authorized as a specialized foreign exchange bank under the "*China Banking Ordinance*" issued by the Central People's Government Administration Council ('*zheng wu yuan*') in 1953. Since the system of gold standard was no longer in practice, the theory of purchasing power parity (PPP) was taken as the basis for the determination of exchange rates. Accordingly, the price ratios of tradable goods became the determinants behind the ups and downs of the RMB. To be more specific, the formula included two major variables: one was the weighted average cost of 75–80 PCT major Chinese export commodities to earn one unit of foreign currency, plus the profit margin of 5–15 PCT (Chen, 1984a, 1984b). Besides, other factors such as the weighted average price of imports and relative price changes in the international market would be used as references for the modification of the RMB rates. This approach of calculation was helpful because on the one hand, it ensured exporters that their activities could safely bring them a reasonable return; on the other hand, relatives of overseas Chinese would not suffer unfavorable rates when converting foreign exchange remittance into the RMB. After all, the war-torn agrarian country was extremely thirsty for money, especially foreign money, to import materials urgently needed in the rehabilitation.

Considering that the overall domestic price level was still fluctuating from time to time, and the scarcity of foreign exchange reserves (merely USD157 million in 1950), China operated a flexible exchange regime, with the RMB being depreciated many times from 1949 to 1950 in order to promote export and restrain import. It was on Jan. 18th, 1949 that the RMB was first quoted against foreign currencies by the PBoC in Tianjin (Xie, 2004); on that date, one US dollar was worth RMB80 (the old RMB). Due to the disparities of commodity prices across the country, other regions like East China, Central China and South China fixed their own rates against the offer of Tianjin. But with the gradual stability of the national economic order and the establishment of financial systems, the headquarters of the PBoC (in Beijing) began to publish unified quotations from July 8th, 1950. Since 1953, apart from several occasional movements, the RMB rate has remained rather stable until 1971, with a total revaluation of RMB0.14, or around 5.5 PCT. Later, the upward trend continued to the end of that decade. By looking at the changes in China's foreign exchange reserves over the same 29-year period, its performance was perhaps not that satisfactory. Almost without exception, a minor increase would always be succeeded by a decrease (Table 7), a picture representing from a broader perspective the country's political and economic vicissitudes. If just calculating the difference between 1950 and 1978,

Table 7 Foreign exchange reserves and exchange rates, 1950–1978

Year	Foreign exchange reserves[1] (in USD100 million)	Exchange rates per USD[2] (annual average)
1950	1.57	RMB2.75
1955	1.8	RMB2.604
1960	0.46	RMB2.617
1965	1.05	RMB2.4618
1970	0.88	RMB2.4618
1975	1.83	RMB1.97
1978	1.67	RMB1.72

Source [1]the State Administration of Foreign Exchange via https://www.safe.gov.cn/wps/portal/sy/tjsj; [2]the People's Bank of China from https://intl.ce.cn/specials/zxxx/201308/08/t20130808_24645854.shtml

it seems that China returned to its starting point after nearly three decades of "long march".

8.3 Stagnant Foreign Trade Under the Rigid Exchange Regime

In the initial period after its foundation, the PRC still maintained its relationship with foreign countries, although the vast majority of them were of the socialist regime. From the late 1950s, however, particularly under the national policy stressing independence and self-sufficiency, China became more and more isolated from the outside world. Following the passage of the first Five Year Plan (1953–1957) in 1955, China's socialist command economy was officially established (in fact, the original draft of the Plan had been drawn in the spring of 1951, but was later amended several times until its final approval). With little attention directed to its comparative advantages and the overall strategy oriented to the heavy industry, both the allocation of capital and decisions on production were absolutely manipulated by the central leaders. In terms of the legal tender RMB, it functioned chiefly as an accounting tool that served the planned distribution of resources. Thus, the transmission effect from the movement of international market could hardly be reflected in the value of yuan, making domestic price levels immune to external influences as well. At that time, foreign trade was the dominant if not the only sector that was in need of currency exchange for the settlement of cross-border transactions. Unlike the earlier period when private enterprises were quite active in conducting commercial dealings, the four-year socialist transformation (1953–1956) resulted in a large portion of the private economy under state control. The Ministry of Foreign Trade (predecessor of today's Ministry of Commerce), representative of the central government in regulating China's import and export, was the only authority to issue "trade license", a means through which the country's flow of foreign exchange could be well supervised.

In 1953, the Ministry reorganized all the existing state-owned foreign trade corporations (FTCs) into a dozen specialized firms (Pei, 2013), with the scope of business covering machinery, chemicals, metals and minerals, cereals, oil and foodstuffs, native produce and animal by-products, and light industrial products, etc. The number varied many times in the following years and by the end of 1978, if excluding their regional branches, national specialized FTCs which enjoyed the rights of transacting with customers worldwide remained less than fifteen. Besides, trading ports were also restricted to Guangzhou (Guangdong Province), Dalian (Liaoning Province), Shanghai, Qingdao (Shandong Province) and Tianjin prior to 1974. Later that year, together with the Ministry's trial of devolving autonomous trading rights to more localities, a broadened opening was extended to four more provinces and they were Jiangsu, Hebei, Zhejiang, and Guangxi. Given the fact that import and export deals were just an execution of the mandatory state plan, these corporations had little discretion in setting export procurement prices or domestic selling prices for imports. To

Table 8 Losses in RMB for earning one US dollar, 1975–1979

Year	Exchange rates per USD (annual average)[1]	Average cost of earning USD1 via export[2]	Losses per USD1 of export earnings[3]
1975	RMB1.97	RMB2.96	RMB0.99
1976	RMB1.97	RMB3.27	RMB1.3
1977	RMB1.84	RMB2.78	RMB0.94
1978	RMB1.72	RMB2.53	RMB0.81
1979	RMB1.55	RMB2.41	RMB0.86

Source [1]the People's Bank of China, from https://intl.ce.cn/specials/zxxx/201308/08/t20130808_24645854.shtml; [2]Yang (2005); [3]calculated by the author by subtracting corresponding numbers in column 1 from those in column 2

them, profits and losses did not have much difference because they would either be submitted to or subsidized by the Ministry of Finance.

As noted already, the long-standing disconnection between domestic and international markets had already made the RMB immune to external impact. Ever since 1973, while most of the world's currencies have demonstrated a higher frequency of fluctuation with the advent of the floating exchange regime and the rising commodity prices, China resumed the quoting of its RMB rates by pegging them to a basket of foreign currencies instead of fixing to the US dollars alone. Due to the adjustment of the component currencies and their weight, the Chinese yuan appreciated year-on-year despite the growing inflation pressure at home. By 1978 when the national average cost of earning one US dollar of exports was already RMB2.53 (Yang, 2005), the official RMB-USD rate still stood at 1.72. Obviously, the great deviation suggested that the RMB had been overvalued and for the FTCs, by surrendering every single US dollar to the Bank of China, they would lose more than RMB0.8 (Table 8). Simultaneously, since the high exchange rate lowered the cost of imports, the government was in a position to use the profits to subsidize the export losses.

Needless to say, such a way of managing foreign trade was absolutely unsustainable, nor should it be even regarded as a quick fix; rather, it only laid a heavier financial burden on the country, making it more difficult to move forward in a dynamic manner. As a result, when China's GDP already registered RMB362.41 billion in 1978, the total volume of export only stayed at RMB16.76 billion (equivalent to USD9.75 billion), a rather minor contribution of less than 5 PCT to the national economy. If taking its performance of the 2000s into consideration, during which the export/GDP ratio of China averaged well above 25 PCT (from https://data.worldbank.org/indicator/NE.EXP.GNFS.ZS?locations=CN), it is not difficult to explain why the figure used to be so low, incentives were too scarce to power the sluggish foreign trade, especially export. After 1978 and beyond, this tightly planned system was injected with greater flexibility when a series of important measures were implemented to allow more companies and even manufacturers to engage in foreign trade. Anyhow, relaxation alone could not boost the vitality of the whole sector if the exchange rate mechanism stayed rigidly intact; to a large degree, its development is very much reliant on how well-functioning and adaptive the system is.

If giving a retrospective review of China's exchange regime before the 1978 reforms, it was an evolutionary process consisting of three stages. From 1949 to 1953, with an effort to promote export and overseas inward remittance, China adopted a managed floating system under which the value of the yuan was adjusted against the ratio between domestic and foreign prices (Chen, 1989a, 1989b). Starting in 1953, a fixed exchange rate regime took its place and the yuan from then on was less frequently altered. While nominally pegged to the pound sterling, it actually moved in line with the US dollar under the Bretton Woods System. During that period, because of the close relationship with the Soviet Union and several other socialist countries, the RMB was once pegged to the ruble (the legal tender of the Soviet Union) for settling bilateral trade transactions (Zheng & Li, 2005). Eighteen years later, the collapse of the Bretton Woods System in 1971 ended the unified fixed exchange rate regime and the world financial system entered the era of general floating currencies. To maintain the stability of the yuan and reduce exchange risks, China in 1973 delinked its currency from the US dollar and made it pegged to a basket of international currencies. Through all these shifts in the regime, the real value of the RMB was intentionally overestimated for the entire period. This was in fact consistent with the goal of the government to import the needed materials, in particular capital goods and technologies, less expensively using the export proceeds in foreign exchange.

Similar to what had happened in other spheres of the economy, little attention was directed to the lost efficiency and the shockingly high opportunity cost. The practice of overvaluing the domestic currency to subsidize import and using the profits from import to cover the losses of export, a typical feature of China's centralized foreign trade sector for over two decades, nullified the role of exchange rates as a means of current account adjustment. It was a time when determination of RMB's value was neither based on supply and demand, nor was it linked to other economic variables. Once the plan was formulated, all resources should be unconditionally mobilized in that direction, no matter how unbearable the cost would be. After all, since the performance of the Ministry of Foreign Trade and the FTCs was not evaluated on the profit they could create, but on whether they had accomplished the state plan; thereby, the exchange rates were just numbers unworthy of their concern. In a sense, export losses in the 1960s and 1970s were still manageable because all the prices were tightly planned and the volume of export was rather insignificant as compared to the GDP. But toward the end of the 1970s, the relaxation of central planning and gradual liberalization of market activities made production more sensitive to the state procurement prices. In other words, it became rather difficult to keep the actual prices in line with the government-set levels. Under this scenario, it would be unlikely for export to circumvent a harsh "winter" if its autonomy was not enhanced and the arbitrary approach of fixing the exchange rates maintained. Moreover, as a contagious effect, the fiscal budget which had already been a big headache to the central leaders would suffer. Take the period of 1976–1980 as an example, the total deficit exceeded RMB19.28 billion, a situation impossible to allow further financial remedies to repair the export sector. Fortunately, 1978 turned out to be a watershed year in history. From then on, the scene was reversed when the leadership felt the imperative to switch to an intensive growth model that could enable resources to be allocated in a less blind and more efficient manner.

8.4 Retention Scheme for Export Earnings

At the initial phase of the reform and opening up, the authorities did not have the intention to completely transform the old foreign exchange regime; instead, they just tried to improve the existing system without casting away the central planning framework. In March 1979, the State Administration of Foreign Exchange (SAFE) was established as a special institution to assume the function of foreign exchange control (beforehand, the role had been carried out by the People's Bank of China). By August of the same year, with the State Council releasing the "Regulations on Several Issues Concerning Greater Promotion of Foreign Trade and Increasing Foreign Exchange Revenues", a new scheme named "foreign exchange retention" ('*waihui liucun zhidu*') was launched as an incentive to stimulate export. Accordingly, local authorities, departments and enterprises were permitted to retain the rights to buy back a certain proportion of their foreign exchange earnings from the central authorities. Then, these retained earnings would be used primarily on the import of advanced technologies and key equipment for the modernization and upgrading of small and medium-sized enterprises. The formula to calculate the retention of export earnings was based on the value of the export goods procured domestically in the previous year. If the foreign exchange earnings exceeded that of the previous year and the commodities fell under the central administration, the retention ratio was set at 20 PCT, which would be divided equally among the ministry in charge, the local authorities and the enterprises. In case the merchandise was managed by sub-national governments, the retention ratio became 40 PCT and would also be shared evenly by the provincial authorities, the local bureaucracy (at either city or county level), and the enterprises. Regarding those items processed with import materials, the exporters would be eligible to claim 15 PCT of the net foreign exchange earnings. In terms of receipts arising from the processing and assembly of foreign components, the ratio was 30 PCT (Based on the "Trial Measures on the Foreign Exchange Retention for Export Commodities" issued in 1979).

Fairly speaking, the implementation of the foreign exchange retention scheme should be regarded as an important step for China to break through the foreign exchange control. Instead of surrendering all the export proceeds, enterprises were granted some limited autonomy over the utilization of their income, which also helped increase the efficiency of allocating foreign exchange resources. Moreover, the 1979 retention system symbolized a major shift of China's foreign trade strategy from import substitution to export-oriented development. Different from the planning era when export was just secondary and supplementary to import, it was entrusted for the first time with an irreplaceable responsibility to channel foreign exchange and power the economy of the whole nation. Representing another official clarification of the same scheme, the "Provisional Regulations for Foreign Exchange Control of the Peoples Republic of China" was released in the end of 1980, in which the State Council declared that all foreign exchange retained by domestic organizations with SAFE's approval must be deposited with the Bank of China, and the usage in turn should also be jointly supervised by the two institutions.

After the mid-1980s, there were some policy changes to the practice of retaining foreign exchange revenues, among which the most notable amendment was released in 1985 by the State Council in the "Notice on Foreign Exchange Retention Arrangements for Export Commodities". No longer based on the amount of domestic procurement for export in the previous year, the retention ratio is linked to the actual income of overseas sales. Besides, apart from the export of general commodities which could qualify for 25 PCT retention, four categories of products with higher ratios were separately listed and they were 50 PCT for machinery and electrical products, as well as complete sets of equipment; 100 PCT for military products; 30 PCT for exports using or processed with imported materials; 3 PCT for crude oil and refined oil under the state plan and 100 PCT if exported on commission basis above the plan. Furthermore, another major difference from the 1979 version could be found in the division of shared portion, with preferences apparently tilted toward the localities. For instance, 80 PCT of the retained earnings for centrally-managed exports would go to the provincial, municipal governments and enterprises whereas the balance 20 PCT belonged to the corresponding ministry in Beijing. In case the goods were within the scope of local governance, the retention would be kept entirely in the local account, with 50 PCT for enterprises and the rest distributed among the provincial, municipal and county authorities. In 1988, to ensure that the contract responsibility system could be launched smoothly in the foreign trade sector and particularly, with a view to boosting export, the retention ratios were once more increased. While for foreign exchange earnings below the contractual targets, the ratio for the local remained at 25 PCT; once the goal was outperformed, 80 PCT could stay and be divided by the local governments and exporters (Chen, 1988).

8.5 The Short-Lived IRTS and Initiation of the Swap

In 1978, another reason that pushed the central leaders to restructure the foreign exchange regime was the mounting pressure to devalue yuan. Even with the existing retention arrangement, exporters would not be really motivated if they were still losing money. Of course, it is crystal clear that if lowering the value of yuan, Chinese exports would be more competitive in the global market; but as a trade-off, the cheaper yuan would simultaneously enhance the purchasing power of foreign currencies, with which overseas buyers may take advantage of the subsidized domestic prices. Ultimately, a solution that could look after both concerns was laid out on January 1st, 1981 and it was known as the "internal rate for trade settlements" (IRTS, or '*maoyi neibu jiesuan jia*'). By nature, what China established was a dual-track exchange rate system under which the internal rate was applied only to the settlement of foreign trade transactions; referring to the official rate, it remained valid for non-trade transactions. Fixed at RMB2.8 each US dollar, the IRTS was based on the average domestic cost of earning one US dollar in export (i.e. RMB2.53 in 1978), plus a 10 PCT premium as profit margin for exporters (Bai, 2008). In contrast with the official rate of RMB1.53 per US dollar on the same date, the IRTS rate represented a de facto devaluation of the yuan by over 80 PCT.

While it should be recognized that the adoption of this dual exchange rate system was an attempt of the government to set the price right, it was very soon found out that the rate of RMB2.8 each US dollar could hardly cope with the constant changes that were taking place in the cost of earning one unit of foreign exchange. In other words, using RMB2.53 as the basis to calculate the internal exchange rate failed to reflect the actual cost of the following years, which kept rising quickly. Considering that China's export by then was dominated by primary goods, especially food and agricultural products, suppose the general purchasing price index of farm produce for 1978 was 100, then it quickly rose to 122.1 in 1979 before climbing to 130.8 and 138.5 for 1980 and 1981 respectively (NBS, 2001). If in the beginning, the IRTS did provide certain incentives to the Chinese exporters; their enthusiasm was diminishing as time went by.

Ironically, from 1981 onward when the official exchange rate was continually headed down, the IRTS was comparatively intact, which caused the two rates to merge and by January 1st, 1985, the IRTS was abandoned when both rates were at par, namely RMB2.8 per dollar (in the end of 1984, the official rate was USD1 = RMB2.7963). Nevertheless, the problem remained unsettled as long as the regime could not enable the exchange rates to adjust flexibly according to the market forces. At least, an objective parameter that may guide the policy makers in valuing the yuan against other currencies was still missing. In the past, they had been preoccupied with the central plan and ignored the fact that since economy has its own laws, any violation would only bring about severe and even irreversible consequences. To avoid that from happening, a sensible choice was to usher in a swap market in which currency transactions could be conducted in a more, if not completely, liberalized way.

Concerning the origin of such a market, it should be attributed to the introduction of the retention scheme in 1979. As indicated earlier, the scheme granted exporters a quota proportional to the foreign exchange earnings which they had surrendered to the government in return for the home currency. With this quota in hand, they were entitled to purchase the corresponding amount of foreign exchange at the official rate to pay for imports. But with the steady growth of retention ratios, an unexpected situation emerged: some holders (mainly foreign trade companies) got more than enough retained foreign exchange but lacked RMB funds to buy them back. At the same time, others (officially approved domestic enterprises) had sufficient RMB in pocket yet were in need of more entitlements to fulfill the growing import requirements. Quite naturally, the best method to deal with the excess supply on the one end and the unsatisfied demand on the other was to set up an exchange platform where both sides could get their problems resolved.

Table 9 Coexistence of three exchange rates, 1981–1985

Year	Official exchange rate per USD[1] (middle rate)	Internal rate for trade settlements[2] (per USD)	Swapping rate[3] (per USD)
1981	RMB1.7051	RMB2.8	RMB3.08
1982	RMB1.8926	RMB2.8	RMB3.08
1983	RMB1.9757	RMB2.8	RMB3.08
1984	RMB2.327	RMB2.8	RMB3.08
1985	RMB2.9367	Abolished on Jan. 1st	RMB3.08

Source [1]NBS, 2001; [2]Jin (1989); [3]calculated by the author by multiplying RMB2.8 by the 10 PCT floating band

In October 1980, the Bank of China experimented the business of trading retention quotas in twelve cities (Zhang, 1990) and they were Beijing, Shanghai, Tianjin, Guangzhou (Guangdong Province), Qingdao (Shandong Province), Dalian (Liaoning Province), Fuzhou (Fujian Province), Nanning (Guangxi Province), Hangzhou (Zhejiang Province), Nanjing (Jiangsu Province), Hankou (Hubei Province), and Shijiazhuang (Hebei Province). At the outset, the price was fixed on the IRTS of RMB2.8 per US dollar plus a floating band of 10 PCT (added or deducted), thus setting RMB3.08 as the ceiling of exchange rate. But by 1984, the over-rapid expansion of investment in fixed assets caused the nation's economy to get overheated, which directly led to the depreciation of the yuan and a soaring black-market exchange rate. Within a matter of just one year, the official rate of the yuan dropped by over 26 PCT, from RMB2.327 to RMB2.9367 each US dollar in 1985 (Table 9). But in the black market (also called the underground market), the yuan's decline was much steeper and each US dollar was already speculated up to a double-digit level, as high as RMB12-15 in 1984 (Yu, 2010). For traders, they knew clearly what the sharp gap meant if they continued to transact via the BOC. Gradually, the once strong enthusiasm gave place to the fear of shrinking profits, which made the bank's swap business hard to sustain.

8.6 The Booming Foreign Exchange Adjustment Centers

In November 1985, the establishment of the first official foreign exchange adjustment center (FEAC) in Shenzhen Special Economic Zone marked the termination of the swap business at the BOC. With its formal operations commenced in December that year, management of this new FEAC was more flexible and the price of the retention quota was set at RMB1 per US dollar, with a ceiling of RMB4.2 to exchange for each US dollar (Ba, 1999). Originally, access to the swap market was only granted to the Shenzhen-based Chinese enterprises, and swaps involving foreign-invested enterprises (FIEs) were not allowed. In October 1986, the State Council promulgated the "Provisions on the Encouragement of Foreign Investment", through which FIEs got the permission to buy and sell foreign exchange according to their needs at prices more favorable than the official rates. As one further step toward a relaxed control, the People's Bank of China issued in March 1988 the "*Notice* on Provision*s* for the *Foreign Exchange Adjustment* Business". Based on Clause Four, the cap imposed on the swap rate was lifted for special economic zones (SEZs) and Hainan Island (the limit on the swap price of other regions in China remained, but was increased to RMB5.7 per US dollar). Thereby, negotiating parties, both domestic and foreign, could enjoy the privilege to fix the price among themselves freely.

Encouraged by these favorable policies, the exchange prospered nationwide. While the transaction volume recorded during the 2nd–4th quarters of 1986 was USD1.89 billion; in 1987, USD4.2 billion worth of deals was concluded throughout the whole year (Ba, 1999). Together with the rapid growth in swap business, FEACs expanded with an equally impressive pace around China, especially in SEZs and coastal cities where foreign trade accounted for a large portion of the local economy. Till the end of 1988, the aggregate turnover of the country's 90 FEACs amounted to USD6.26 billion. The boom of foreign exchange swap market since 1986 represented the reemergence of a de facto dual exchange rate system in China, with the coexistence of both official rate governing the in-plan trade and swap rate for transactions outside the plan. By allowing traders to swap at more liberalized prices, the market provided a regulatory mechanism to help counter the distortionary effects of the overvalued yuan, and this in turn also promoted the organic growth of the export sector.

Through a closer analysis, it could be found that the existence of the swap market enabled participants, both buyers and sellers, to realize economic benefits. For most buyers at FEACs, they were importers who before the mid-1980s had little chance to obtain foreign exchange outside government channels, which severely hampered their development. Right now, although it was still impossible to transact at the even lower official rate, the market at least offered them an option. As long as the import business could bring some profits, they would still be willing to pay a higher price for foreign exchange at the swap centers to finance their procurement from abroad. From the perspective of sellers, at a time when foreign exchange was rather scarce in China, they had irresistible incentives to participate in the swap market. After receiving payment from foreign customers, they would prefer to convert their foreign exchange earnings into the home currency at a swap rate more favorable than the official quotations. Even though the latter had been depreciating, the margin could not be compared with that of the market. For example, according to the quotation of Shenzhen FEAC on November 5th, 1988 (Photo 2), USD100 could be exchanged for RMB649.21; but in that same year, the official rate (middle rate) was RMB372.21 per USD100. Through a simple calculation, it can be found that the swap market would generate for exporters almost 75 PCT more revenues over the official rate, if they chose to convert there. No wonder by then, the success story of Shenzhen soon caught the attention of different parts of China and after the PBoC allowed all provinces to set up their FEACs in 1988 (based on the "Notice on Provisions for the Foreign Exchange Adjustment Business" released in that March), swap transactions around the country flourished by leaps and bounds.

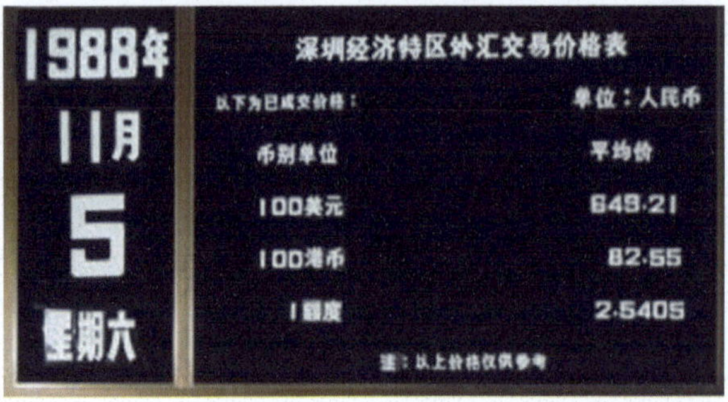

Photo 2 Foreign exchange quotations board of Shenzhen FEAC on November 5th, 1988, Saturday. On that date, the average prices for USD100 and HKD100 were offered at RMB649.21 and RMB82.55 respectively, with the price of the retention quota set at RMB2.5405 per US dollar. *Source* Tan (2010)

It should be admitted that to a certain degree, the thriving adjustment centers curbed the demand source of the black market from enterprises, which squeezed the black market premium (Huang, 1993). However, the introduction of the contract responsibility program in the foreign trade sector in 1988, which granted enterprises a more favorable profit-sharing scheme, powerfully fueled the national import and export. Thereby, the resurgence in the premium again triggered speculative behaviors, signifying that the imbalance between the constrained supply of and skyrocketing demand for foreign exchange has not been fully adjusted. Even today, it is not hard to imagine the messes almost three decades ago when three exchange rates functioned together in China, i.e. the official rate (often-adjusted and pegged to the US dollar), the swap rate (unofficial rate floating against the market but subject to the occasional intervention of the central bank), and the black market rate (more compatible with the pulse of the market). Deviations between these rates allured rent-seekers to utilize the unevenly-distributed opportunities as well as the loopholes in administrative surveillance to garner windfall profits.

In the early 1990s, although decentralization of foreign trade had already been listed on the agenda of the central government, it was still those mega producers, trading corporations and foreign-funded enterprises (the supply side) which manipulated the most, if not all, of the activities. Quite naturally, this position of unchallengeable supremacy furnished them a golden chance to reap greater benefits from the swap market. But as to the dominant players of the black market, they were generally individuals and private enterprises (the demand side) because as compared to the large organizations, they did not possess the same advantage to access foreign exchange freely via official channels. If the official and adjustment center rates were not that favorable, they would resort to the black market to have foreign currencies bought. Anyway, aware of the fact that whenever the official rate was distorted unreasonably beyond a certain margin, transactions would be more active on the swap market and the black market; the Chinese authorities were gradually compelled to take the exchange rates of these two markets into consideration when it was time for them to determine to what extent the official rate was to be modified.

Further, the disorder during that period was not merely the differentials among these three rates; in fact, the real situation was much more complicated. As a principle, the exchange rate at swap centers should be determined on the basis of the supply and demand conditions through a bidding process. But due to regional protectionism, it was fairly common for the local governments to block foreign exchange from moving out of their jurisdictions, especially when supply was tight. Consequently, the rates of the same day among swap centers differed from each other and this in turn created room for arbitrage opportunities (Guan, 1994). In theory, once a company bought foreign exchange from the swap center, it could only use for the purposes stated in its application to the local office of the SAFE, the authority in charge of foreign exchange control. In other words, it would be prohibited if the firm took advantage of the price gap and sold the foreign exchange in another center at a higher level. Nevertheless, the possibility was by no means nonexistent when the company in question had presence across regions. By comparison, since the sale of foreign exchange was much less tightly controlled than the purchase, it is very likely that the business would choose to sell its foreign exchange at one FEAC which offered more favorable prices and went to another to buy at a lower rate. Thus, the larger the amount transacted, the greater the profits it could expect. After all, as far as interest is concerned, very few companies would fail to miss every single moment to maximize their returns.

On certain occasions, some even had a tendency to hoard their retention quotas, which was considered as another typical form of speculation. It happened during 1992–1993 when the Chinese economy experienced a new round of overheating. As chief barometers, its GDP rose by 14.2 PCT and 13.5 PCT respectively; and the growth in fixed-asset investment also stayed high, hitting 44.4 PCT in 1992 before rising further to 61.8 PCT in 1993. As to the producer price index (PPI), it surged from 106.8 to 124 over these two years (preceding year = 100) whereas the consumer price index (CPI) more than doubled to 114.7 by 1993 (NBS, 2001, 2006). In response to these abnormal signs, many sensitive foreign trade companies unanimously decided to withhold their swap transactions for they were anticipating devaluation of the yuan and this led to a sudden shortage of supply. At Shanghai FEAC (opened on September 28th, 1988) for instance, the rate for exchanging each US dollar hovered around RMB5-7 from 1988 to early 1992; but from April 1992, it began to soar and the trend lasted until June 21st, 1993 when the closing rate reached its record high, at RMB10.922 each US dollar. By July 4th, 1993 when the price stood at RMB10.344, the central bank intervened for the first time by pumping huge amounts of US dollars for three consecutive days, i.e. from July 5th to 7th. Seeing the massive injection of dollars, these companies could no longer keep calm, they started to worry that its value would weaken soon. With the closing prices quoted at RMB9.557, RMB8.44 and RMB8.51 on these three days respectively, the change of their mindset helped the yuan to recover. Later on, the yuan became stabilized and remained at around RMB8.7 for quite some time (Wu, 2008). During the same period, the official rate of the yuan was devalued from RMB5.5149 per US dollar of 1992 to RMB5.7619 per US dollar in 1993.

Originated from the foreign exchange retention schemes, the very idea of establishing swap centers granted Chinese exporters more autonomy over their earnings, which made it possible for them to import the products they were really in need of. Apart from these immediate benefits, one more contribution that had a far-reaching impact on China's exchange rate reform is that by providing a platform for supply and demand to interact with each other, the basic elements necessary to the formation of a market-directed exchange regime were being incubated. Nevertheless, considering that a comprehensive and unbiased discernment should not merely include a recognition of the plus side, the deleterious effects equally deserve a fair appraisal. In the long run, the existence of multiple rates not only disrupted the order of economic activities; more seriously, it also harmed the international credibility of the yuan, a fundamental instrument through which all foreign investors and business partners were to carry out their undertakings in China. If without a sound mechanism to price its value, there is no way to maintain the stability of the macro economy; nor would it be possible for other nations to commit themselves to this emerging market with genuine confidence. Both internally and externally, the pressing need was for the government to take drastic actions so as to end the chaos that had been prevailing in China's foreign exchange market.

8.7 A Unified Managed Floating Regime

In the end of 1993, a comprehensive reform package entitled the "Decision of the CPC Central Committee on Several Matters Concerning the Establishment of a Socialist Market Economic System" was unveiled. In this document, by declaring explicitly the necessity to reform the foreign exchange control system, set up a market-based managed floating regime, and to establish a unified and regulated foreign exchange market so that the Renminbi would gradually become a convertible currency, the resolution highlighted two priorities that the central planners intended to address, i.e. the unification of exchange rates and convertibility of the yuan. To make the road map more concrete, the State Council followed up with the "Notice of Further Reform of Foreign Exchange System" in that December. Based on the Notice, a number of new policies were to be implemented from January 1st, 1994 and they included: unification of the official and the swap market rates into a single, managed floating rate reflective of the actual supply and demand; removal of the retention quota system and replacement of swap centers with an inter-bank market in which all foreign exchange transactions, most typically sale of export earnings and purchase for import payment, were to be conducted via designated banks; and abolition of the approval procedure for using foreign exchange and realization of conditional convertibility of the RMB with respect to current account deals, etc.

The fact that by the end of 1993, over 80 PCT of China's trade-related foreign exchange transactions were settled at the swap market rate of RMB8.7 each US dollar provided appropriate timing and foundation for a regime change (Long, 1994). In accordance with the central plan, the official and swap market rate were unified in 1994. From then on, the former dual exchange regime of China was replaced by a single and managed floating regime based on market supply and demand (in practice, this management turned out to be a de facto peg of the RMB to the US dollar until July 2005). The RMB official rate, which was still at RMB5.8 per US dollar on

Table 10 Changes in official exchange rates and its impact, 1993–1995

Year	Official exchange rates per USD (middle price)	Export volume (USD billion)	FDI actually utilized (USD billion)	Foreign exchange reserves (USD billion)
1993	RMB5.7619	91.74	27.52	21.2
1994	RMB8.6187	121.01	33.77	51.62
1995	RMB8.3507	148.78	37.52	73.6

Source NBS (2001)

December 31st 1993, merged with the swap market rate at RMB8.7 on January 1st 1994 and this represented a substantial devaluation of 50 PCT overnight.

The table below (Table 10) can clearly reflect the dramatic changes brought by the reform in China's foreign exchange regime. Due to the RMB's devaluation, the growing transparency, and restored order in the foreign exchange market, export rose rapidly by 32 PCT in 1994 and 23 PCT in 1995. Within just one year, the country managed to reverse its current account deficit totaling USD12.22 billion to a surplus of USD5.4 billion in 1994. At the same time, the actually utilized foreign direct investment (FDI) picked up as well, a phenomenon which was rather understandable since most foreign-funded enterprises were export-oriented. As a result of the expansion in both export and FDI, the foreign exchange reserves of the country rose by almost 250 PCT over these two years.

8.8 The Inter-Bank Foreign Exchange Market

As part of the measures to centralize the allocation of foreign exchange, a compulsory foreign exchange settlement and surrender system ('*qiangzhi jieshouhui zhidu*') was at the same time initiated by the PBoC. Under the arrangement, all domestic enterprises (as well as individuals) were mandated to sell their foreign exchange holdings only to the designated banks; for imports or non-trade payments, they also had to purchase the needed foreign exchange through the designated banks on the spot. In addition, to operate unified foreign exchange transactions smoothly and in particular, to avoid the situation in which some banks had excess foreign exchange while others ran short of it, an inter-bank computerized market went into operation in April 1994. Named China Foreign Exchange Trading System (CFETS, or '*zhongguo waihui jiaoyi zhongxin*'), or the National Inter-bank Funding Center ('*quanguo yinhangjian tongye chaijie zhongxin*'), its head office is located in Shanghai, with 18 sub-centers in major commercial cities (i.e. Guangzhou, Shenzhen, Tianjin, Jinan, Dalian, Nanjing, Xiamen, Qingdao, Wuhan, Chongqing, Chengdu, Zhuhai, Shantou, Fuzhou, Ningbo, Xi'an, Shenyang, and Haikou).

Following its foundation, the regional and segmented swap business of the FEACs around the country were abolished; referring to these adjustment centers, they were transformed into the local branches of the CFETS and became linked with each other via a national integrated electronic network. Unlike the former scene in which participants were chiefly non-financial institutions like trading companies or manufacturing entities, the dominant players included foreign exchange banks, foreign-funded banks and non-bank financial institutions approved by the SAFE. Nonetheless, in the absence of a price-shaping mechanism for the RMB exchange rates, the inter-bank market at the initial stage had to rely on the central bank to set the benchmark. To ensure timely adjustment of the unified rate, the PBoC would fix and publish every day the RMB-US dollar middle rate (or called reference rate) in light of the previous day's weighted-average price on the inter-bank foreign exchange market. At the same time, it would also announce the base rates between the yuan and other foreign currencies according to the ups and downs in the international foreign exchange market (Sun, 1995). Against these offerings, designated banks could, within a specified range, quote buying and selling prices freely. Concerning the swing of exchange rates, it was strictly regulated. On the one hand, the daily fluctuations of the yuan against the US dollar was tuned to a narrow band of ±0.3 PCT around the benchmark rate announced by the PBoC for inter-bank transactions; but for retail transactions between banks and their customers (enterprises), the range was ±0.25 PCT. With regard to the buying and selling rates of the yuan against the Hong Kong dollar and the Japanese yen, they were not permitted to deviate from more than 1 PCT on either side of the base rates.

While the swap system was no longer open to domestic companies for they were demanded to trade foreign exchange only with the designated banks, foreign-invested enterprises could continue to use the same way to buy and sell foreign exchange. By doing so, the government wanted to maintain the consistency of its policies so as to absorb more direct investment from abroad. However, since there were no more FEACs, the operation was integrated into the inter-bank trading system and the pricing was based on the quotations (usually the middle rate) of the PBoC each day plus a 0.15 PCT service charge (Huang, 1996). Since the movement of China's exchange rates was largely made in line with that of the US dollar against third currencies, the yuan's de-facto dollar peg stayed intact under the new managed floating regime. Therefore, it is not difficult to understand why for the 1994–1997 period, the dollar appreciation resulted in a stronger yuan, which revalued by about 4 PCT to RMB8.2898 per US dollar in 1997.

To a certain degree, although the compulsory foreign exchange settlement and surrender system has made it easier for the government to control the country's foreign exchange reserves, domestic enterprises on the other hand did not feel better. For exporters, even if they could reasonably expect to sell foreign exchange at a higher price within a certain time period, they still had to surrender their earnings to the designated banks on the spot. When it comes to the purchase of foreign exchange, various documents such as the covering contract, invoice and payment notice issued by financial institutions abroad, etc. should be submitted for the banks to check, which was often time-consuming to importers. Considering that for foreign-invested enterprises, it was until July 1st, 1996 that they were incorporated into the same settlement and sale system, the policy vacuum still enabled some domestic companies to take advantage. For instance, they obtained foreign exchange secretively from FIEs or even established false joint ventures so as to enjoy the privilege of keeping their export earnings (from October 9th, 1989, FIEs were permitted by the State Administration of Foreign Exchange to open foreign exchange account in China). Besides, referring to those designated banks, they didn't get much authorities either. In fact, the PBoC also had relevant rules to oversee their activities. For each bank, a proportional limit was set based on its assets and international settlement volume; then accordingly, the amount of foreign exchange revolving funds possessed by the bank should not fall short of nor exceed that limit. Otherwise, the gap or the surplus should be balanced through the inter-bank market (Based on the "Announcement of the PBoC on Further Reforming the Foreign Exchange Management System" issued in 1993). Although in principle, these banks could price foreign exchange somewhat flexibly against the reference rate quoted by the central bank; in practice, the rates offered by different banks were generally the same. In other words, they were just acting as a counter of the PBoC to sell and buy foreign exchange without real autonomy.

8.9 Free Convertibility of RMB Under Current Account Transactions

In view of the above problems, especially given the fact that China was at a critical stage of negotiation for its WTO membership, if the country wanted to adapt its foreign exchange regime to the international standard, full convertibility of the RMB under current account transactions should be taken as a prerequisite condition. On November 27th, 1996, an important letter was delivered by Dai Xianglong, the then-governor of the PBoC, to the International Monetary Fund (IMF) (Chen, 1997a, 1997b). In the letter, China pledged that starting from December 1st, 1996, it would accept the obligations stipulated in Article VIII of the Fund's Articles of Agreement (beforehand, China remained under IMF's Article XIV—Transitional Arrangements and was thus allowed to maintain restrictions on payments and transfers for current international transactions). Originally, the year which China had promised to accept Article VIII was 2000 (Ji, 1996). With this commitment, the goal of making the RMB convertible on the current account was attained well ahead of the officially proclaimed timetable.

Within less than one year, seeing that the overall environment had become mature and stable, the central bank made one further step toward a more equitable treatment of enterprises at home. Through a notice unveiled in 1997, it announced that from October 15th, Chinese enterprises (chiefly trading corporations and manufacturers with foreign trade operating rights) could be eligible to keep a given percentage of their foreign exchange income at designated banks as long as certain requirements were satisfied. Specifically, for foreign trade corporations whose annual import and export turnover was more than USD30 million and had over RMB10 million of registered capital; and manufacturers with USD10 million of yearly trade volume and RMB30 million of registered capital, they may retain up to 15 PCT of their current account foreign exchange revenues.

8.10 A Tight Control of the Capital Account

However, despite this encouraging progress, there was no sign of easing control over China's capital account, which is deemed far more complex and demands a sound financial system with highly-developed market infrastructures, multi-functional institutions and macro-prudential internal surveillance well-coordinated among each other. Still in the course of transition, China understood clearly that it was not yet prepared to meet these demanding criteria. As a matter of fact, the screws were even tightened at the outbreak of the Asian financial crisis in the summer of 1997. Contrary to its neighboring states such as Thailand, Indonesia and South Korea which had prematurely opened up their international capital transactions in order to attract foreign loans and investments, China was firmly resolved to shut the door to deter hot money. The rationale behind is that when the currency was not yet allowed to float freely and its financial sector was insufficiently equipped, the inflow of speculative capital would only shake the country's economic fundamentals and cause social turmoil that may even jeopardize people's lives. However, despite the fact that the Chinese yuan remained rather stable (at RMB8.2898 per US dollar in 1997 and RMB8.2791 each US dollar in 1998), the steep and drastic crash of currencies like Thai baht, Korean won, Indonesian rupiah, and Philippine peso, etc. still heightened expectations that the RMB would fall with the same magnitude.

Due to the widespread panic and anxiety, disguised capital flight through illegal conduct such as under-invoicing of exports, over-invoicing of imports, and fake transactions, etc. began to emerge among domestic enterprises while foreign investors were more hesitant in directing their capital into China. It didn't take long before the phenomenon was confirmed by one item of the country's balance of payments (BOPs), i.e. net errors and omissions (NEOs). Since few nations in the world can have absolutely accurate data for reported components (mainly the current account, capital and financial account), NEOs is thereby used as a residual category to ensure that all the credit and debit entries equal to zero. By saying so, however, it does not mean that the size of the NEOs matters not. In fact, it matters a lot and say, if a country's net errors and omissions for several consecutive years stayed unreasonably high, then it not only means that the quality of its BOP statistics is doubtful; it also suggests that private capital was flowing either in or out of the territory beyond the knowledge of its authorities, sometimes in the form of smuggled imports and exports.

Generally, positive net errors and ommisions implies that the sum of current account balance and capital and financial account balance is understated. If negative, the opposite is true. Based on IMF's *Balance of Payments Manual*, a country's NEOs should not exceed ±5 PCT of the gross sum of its merchandise imports and exports; otherwise, the government has to take it as a serious concern (Liu, 2007). By

Table 11 Comparison of the NEOs and the volume of commodity trade, 1996–1999

Year	Net errors and omissions[1] (USD billion)	Gross sum of commodity import and export[2] (USD billion)	Ratio between 1 and 2[3] (PCT)
1996	−15.5	282.6	−5.48
1997	−22.3	319.1	−6.99
1998	−18.7	320.4	−5.84
1999	−17.8	353.4	−5.04

Source [1] and [2]SAFE (2015); [3]calculated by the author

comparing the recorded figures from 1996 to 1999 (Table 11), it can be noticed that China's NEOs throughout these years remained above that security line, with 1997 reaching the peak of almost 7 PCT (negative). Although net errors and omissions is not necessarily equivalent to the amount of capital flight, it can at least indicate the scale of capital exodus over that particular time period. According to a survey conducted by the SAFE, the capital flight from 1997 to 1999 amounted to USD53 billion, which on average was around USD17.7 billion each year, representing 5.5 PCT of the country's gross national product (GNP) for 1998 (Tong, 2003). Moreover, in 1998 alone, the smuggling cases uncovered by the customs reached 7,382, with a total value hitting RMB13.7 billion. In the following year, the number skyrocketed to RMB80 billion, or an increase of RMB71 billion in the tariff income of the customs (Hu, 2004).

Despite the above, given the inability of official statistics to capture all the particulars of illicit commerce, it would be impossible for the Chinese foreign exchange authorities to quantify exactly the depth of the "black hole". But what remains crystal clear is the fact that these flows has been growing at a steady pace, especially following the emergence of the black market that created some convenience for these secretive movements. To crack down on deceitful activities, the SAFE in 1998 fixed a deadline (i.e. October 30th) for offenders to turn themselves in so as to get more lenient treatment. Besides, certain measures were also targeted at foreign-funded enterprises (FFEs). By the time the CFETS went into operation in Shanghai, it was a computer-based network provided predominantly for domestic enterprises to deal in foreign exchange. In other words, their transfer from the swap center to this inter-bank market was mandatory. But with regard to the FFEs, to maintain continuity in the policies toward FDI, China from April 1994 to June 1996 continued to let them balance their foreign exchange needs in the swap market and keep foreign exchange revenues in designated accounts instead of selling them to a bank, on the condition that all the deals of the swap center had to be concluded at the inter-bank market rate. Although at that time, the FEACs were already an integral part of the newly-opened CFETS, the very existence of double rules governing domestic and foreign enterprises in China still brought a lot of inconvenience. In particular, when comparing the settlement efficiency of the two, the advantage of CFETS was much more obvious.

At the strong request of the FFEs, the PBoC in March 1996 authorized the SAFE to initiate an experiment enabling these enterprises to buy and sell foreign exchange through designated banks located in four places, i.e. Jiangsu Province, Dalian, Shanghai and Shenzhen. Here, it is necessary to point out that in order to reinforce the supervision of capital account transactions, each FFE in the chosen areas was required to open a "settlement account" for current account receipts and payments and a "specialized account" for capital account receipts and payments (Du & Wang, 1996). With these two separate bank accounts, illicit foreign exchange in-and-outflows disguised in the name of current account settlement could be substantially curtailed. Therefore, this arrangement was considered as an effective way to tackle unauthorized capital flight, which was accelerating in the late 1990s amid market expectations of a weaker yuan. Seeing that the outcome was expectedly satisfactory after three months' trial, the practice was promoted nationwide on July 1st 1996. Although simultaneously, the swap centers remained functional for the FFEs to trade, the shrinkage in the volume of transactions was so drastic that two years later, the central bank announced the transformation of all the existing 36 swap markets into the sub-centers of CFETS on December 1st 1998, thus marking the termination of the once active foreign exchange swap business (Based on the "Notice Concerning the Closure of the Foreign Exchange Swap Business Activities" promulgated in October 1998). In fact, the closure of swap centers was more than a positive response to the appeal of FFEs; the government wanted to take this opportunity to block the route through which foreign exchange might be channeled unnoticeably to destinations outside China.

With regard to domestic enterprises, the authorities was equally aware of the necessity to regulate their behaviors. On the one hand, with a view to clarifying the authenticity of import payments, the PBoC and the SAFE joined hands with other state departments and scrutinized the import declaration forms dated in the first half of 1998, especially those valued USD200,000 and above. This nationwide campaign started on July 10th, 1998 and ultimately, more than 13,800 fake documents were confiscated, involving over USD11 billion of fraud via that channel (Cao, 2005).

Besides, the negative impact of the 1997 Asian financial crisis was also displayed in the export sector, which witnessed a worsening of the terms of trade when repatriation of export proceeds slowed down. To facilitate the collection and guard against intentionally deferred payment, the SAFE in 1999 announced through its circular the "Interim Measures on Examination of Export Receipts of Foreign Exchange" that all exporters in China, including foreign trade corporations, manufacturers, and research institutions, etc., would be assessed of their revenues both quarterly and annually. Being the key indicator, the ratio between the verified amounts of foreign exchange income against the proceeds due within the testing period would be calculated. If the result turned out to be less than 70 PCT, the business would be graded "risky" and once lower than 50 PCT, a profound investigation was to be initiated to dig out the reasons behind. In case criminal undertakings were discovered, punitive measures would follow to prohibit further transgressions of the law.

History proves that China's decision not to liberalize its capital account as quickly as other Asian nations was farsighted in that it made the country insulated from the immediate attack of external capital flows conditioned chiefly for quick profit. However, the contagious effect from the outside was so strong that as the largest economy in the region, it inevitably got involved in the aftermaths of the Asian financial crisis. When the currencies of neighboring countries plunged sharply due to the massive withdrawal of foreign investment and an overwhelmingly pessimistic forecast of a severe recession, China actually confronted two choices: either to let its currency match the downward spiral or to keep it stable. There were tradeoffs for both alternatives and if China devalued its yuan, the export sector could maintain its competitiveness; but this would very likely trigger another round of depreciation among Asian countries, which may ultimately result in a vicious cycle benefiting none at all.

With regard to the other option, the weakened Asian currencies would only make Chinese products more expensive and quite naturally, they would purchase less to cope with the tightening budget. If based on the statistics of 1997, the weight of their imports from China was by no means negligible. In that year, Asia accounted for almost 60 PCT of China's overall export (Table 12) and if taking into consideration its export volume to the seven selected countries, which totaled USD51.89 billion, their share was over 47.6 PCT of all the Asian markets. At a stage when China's economy was increasingly reliant on export, with an export-to-GDP ratio that exceeded 20 PCT in 1997, decline in the import of these major trading partners would become a drag on its robust development. Actually, figures for 1998 turned out that Asia was the only continent to which China's export decreased and among the seven nations, Philippines was exceptional in that it did not cut imports from China. Although the one percent fall in China's GDP growth rate from 1997 (8.8 PCT) to 1998 (7.8 PCT) could not be absolutely attributed to the shrinking demand of Asian countries, the impact should at least be acknowledged.

Table 12 Dominant Asian markets for Chinese exports and their share in the total, 1997–1998

Export market	Export volume in 1997 (USD billion)	Share in the total[1] (PCT)	Export volume in 1998 (USD billion)
World	182.79	100	183.76
Asia	108.97	59.61	98.18
Japan	31.84	17.42	29.69
South Korea	9.13	4.99	6.27
Singapore	4.32	2.36	3.93
Malaysia	1.92	1.05	1.6
Indonesia	1.84	1	1.17
Thailand	1.5	0.82	1.15
Philippines	1.34	0.73	1.5

Note [1]Calculated by the author
Source NBS (2000)

8.11 Rationales to Keep RMB Intact Under the Asian Financial Crisis

Even before the emergence of the above impact from the financial crisis, China had already been aware of the severity in case it chose not to intervene to lower the currency rates amid the rampant devaluation that was sweeping many Asian countries; yet it did not fail to recognize that the yuan was still locked to the US dollar, thus any signal of devaluation could have led to a disastrous loss of confidence among foreign investors, as had been afflicted by some of its Asian neighbors. Besides, making the yuan weaker to offset losses of export competitiveness was at its best a quick fix which could hardly serve the long-term goal of the country, i.e. internationalization of the RMB so that one day, it can circulate freely in the global market as a settlement currency, investment currency, and reserve currency. In this regard, if losing the firm confidence of the global community, recovery in export wouldn't last long enough to power the macroeconomic growth of the country.

Moreover, based on a practical point of view, the pressure from China's current account wasn't so immense as before and in fact, from 1996 to 1997, it continued to generate huge surplus thanks to the soaring demand from markets outside Asia, such as Africa (an increase of almost 25 PCT), Latin America (47.7 PCT, the best-performing one), and North America (more than 22 PCT), etc. As displayed in the graph below (Graph 4), when China's export climbed by 21 PCT and registered USD182.79 billion at the end of 1997, trade surplus realized a more phenomenal increase, which exceeded 230 PCT. Like a chain reaction, after becoming the second largest holder of foreign exchange reserves in the world (after Japan) by passing the USD100 billion mark in 1996, the figure amounted to nearly USD140 billion within just one year. Taking into consideration the fact that back in 1993, China's foreign exchange reserves was merely USD21.2 billion, if the contribution of export were not that significant, it would be impossible for the country to accumulate abundant

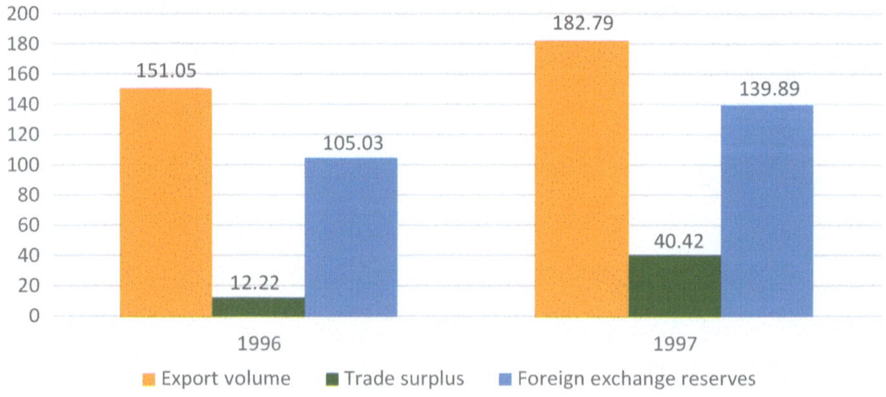

Graph 4 Export and foreign exchange reserves, USD billion. *Source* NBS (2001)

foreign exchange within several years. Strategically, maintaining sufficient levels of foreign exchange reserves is crucial since it could enable a country to weather the turmoil brought by exterior factors (like the 1997 Asian financial crisis) and intervene in a time-efficient way to stabilize the fluctuations of exchange rates. In addition, an enhanced external payment capacity would also lower its cost of financing when domestic enterprises set their sights on overseas markets. Above all, for a country at transition stage, building up more reserves could strengthen its credibility while dealing with various global partners and thereby may further push forward the process of reform and opening-up.

The whole world was watching. Given the tremendous pressure that massive devaluation in neighboring countries had started to exert on China's exports, there was almost no doubt that in sympathy with these Asian currencies, China would surely respond with a more aggressive race of depreciation for the bottom. Nonetheless, Chinese leaders since the late 1997 have vowed on many different occasions that they would not devalue the yuan. For example, speaking on March 19th, 1998 at a press conference, Premier Zhu Rongji said that instead of devaluing the yuan to spur exports, China would prefer a number of new initiatives to turn around the underwhelming, crisis-ridden economy (Wen & Zhang, 1998). The initiatives outlined by the premier included restructuring the loss-making large and medium-sized state-owned enterprises (SOEs), overhauling the financial system to enhance the supervisory and regulatory authority of the central bank and increase the autonomy of commercial banks, etc. Besides, he also emphasized the necessity to streamline and reorganize government institutions at both central and local levels within three years.

What's more, in order to achieve a GDP growth rate of 8 PCT and limit inflation to no higher than 3 PCT in 1998 without resorting to currency plunge, the main focus would be shifted to expanding domestic demand through heavier government spending (projected to be USD750 billion over a three-year period) in infrastructures like railways, highways, agricultural water conservancy facilities, municipal and environmental protection facilities; in addition to greater inputs for high-technology industries, technical upgrading of enterprises, and residential construction, etc. (Yu, 1998). Very quickly, China's resolute commitment received warm welcome by its foreign counterparts and was celebrated as an important contribution not only to the regional, but global economic and financial stability as well. Prior to July 2005 when the next round of exchange rate reform took place, the yuan stood firmly at around RMB8.28 each US dollar with its de-facto dollar peg against third currencies.

In the midst of the Asian financial crisis, especially from June 1998 to March 1999, China adopted a series of practices to tighten its control of foreign exchange, including verification of export receipts, and supervision of import payments, etc. As to the purchase of foreign exchange under capital account, it had equally been strengthened to combat illegal conduct such as fraud, arbitrage or unauthorized flight of capital. Along with the diminishing turmoil triggered by the crisis, these restrictions were relaxed step by step. Particularly, the PBoC and the SAFE in September 2001 issued together the "Notice on Amendments to Some Provisions for the Purchase of Foreign Exchange under Capital Account", which removed the ban on transactions for purposes like repayment of loans overdue, advance repayment of external debts, and outbound investment of projects approved by the State Council, etc. Yet despite all the loosening measures, no specific timetable was provided as to when the country would liberalize the capital account, especially those deals that would lead to an outward movement of foreign exchange. To some degree, China became even more conservative after witnessing how those nations had been plagued by the turmoil when they prematurely granted market access to foreign investors. Anyhow, although being prudent is a sensible strategy to safeguard the achievements after more than two decades of reform, it is imperative for the decision makers in Beijing to realize that opening the capital account itself should not be the result, but an integral part, of the whole restructuring process of the financial sector. Instead of putting it off to reduce risk exposure and maintain stability at home, allowing qualified overseas institutions to operate domestically can accelerate the establishment of a sound financial system which is capable of dealing with various external shocks.

8.12 Necessity to Liberalize the Capital Account

By and large, the exchange rate reform in China since the late 1970s was mainly driven by the reform of foreign trade. At the outset when foreign exchange market was not yet formed, import and export were regulated by the central planners through manipulation of the official exchange rates. In that special period which was characterized by severe shortage of both industrial and consumer goods, earning foreign exchange became the overriding priority of export so as to fund the import of materials and technologies desperately needed at home. Inevitably, the yuan was overvalued and to make up for the losses in export, the authorities introduced a number of remedies such as internal rate for trade settlements (IRTS), foreign exchange retention scheme, and subsidies (in the form of rebate), etc., which not only distorted the allocation of resources, but also laid additional fiscal burden on the government. Thus, the launch of foreign exchange adjustment center (FEAC) in the mid-1980s should be considered as a landmark endeavor in that it greatly facilitated the convertibility of the RMB and directly led to the reform of 1994 when the official and the swap market rates were merged into a single, managed floating rate that could respond more closely in line with the actual supply and demand. In that same year, following the kickoff of the nationwide unified foreign exchange market (named China Foreign Exchange Trading System, or CFETS) in Shanghai, the country was eligible to abandon the transitional status commenced in 1980 under Article XIV of the IMF and obligated itself to Article VIII.

Like a turning point, this shift symbolized that after some sixteen years of assiduous efforts, its current account liberalization was ultimately accomplished. But with regard to the capital account, the progress had been rather uneven and asymmetrical since until the end of the 1990s, it remained subject to the stringent approval procedures set by the state. Yet given its commitment to the WTO of opening the domestic financial markets to foreign investment, as well as the undeniable lack of efficiency that existed in the sector, both the external and internal conditions were pushing China to address its institutional weaknesses with bolder actions while lifting the barriers to capital inflow and outflow in a well-calculated manner. As far as the foreign exchange regime is concerned, the policing and shaping mechanisms of exchange rates between the yuan and other currencies should be treated as an important target of reform. In particular, to address the question of how to strike a fine balance between government intervention and market adjustment, the tasks involved were already quite strenuous and thus required enduring dedication and unwavering commitment in the upcoming years.

9 The Securities Market

As an important component of economic infrastructure, financial market undertakes the responsibility of providing liquidity for a wide range of entities such as banks and investors to engage in business activities. Across the whole world, almost every nation has its own forms of financial markets. Generally, based on the assets traded, they include money market which is chiefly for banks to lend to each other with very short maturities, from several days to just under one year; capital market for institutions of both the public and private sectors to raise funds; derivatives market where instruments change hands together with credit risks; as well as foreign exchange market and commodity market, etc. From the perspective of the vast majority of non-financial corporations, capital market is their primary source of borrowing when bank loans are too costly or unavailable. At the same time, investors with surplus cash would also expect to reap gains there, either through equity or debt. Accordingly, securities, i.e. stocks and bonds, are bought and sold in the market to meet the needs of the two parties.

9.1 A Retrospect of the Days Long Ago

Regarding the history of securities in China, it could be traced to ancient times, as early as the West Zhou dynasty (1046–771 BC). By then, the noble ruling class was already lending to the state on the basis of contracts engraved in bamboo tablets. Named '*fu bie*' (contract of loans), it can be taken as the most primitive form of bonds (Miao, 2011). Toward the second half of the nineteenth century, the Qing Empire was already sliding downhill, especially when threatened by the Taiping peasant rebellion (1851–1864) and the Anglo-French invasion during the Second Opium War (1856–1860). In order to catch up with the West in technologies and infrastructure and to retrieve the loss of national dignity, the regime was compelled to initiate a massive "Self-Strengthening Movement" (1861–1895) through which huge investment was pumped into its defense and civilian industries.

9.1.1 Issuance of the First Batch of Stocks

Considering that the country's shipping business had almost completely fallen into foreign hands, China Merchants Steam Navigation Company (CMSNC, '*Lunchuan zhaoshang ju*'), a shipping firm, was established in 1872 in Shanghai to compete for the shipping routes against overseas vessels along the mainland coastline. However, since the operating capital in need went far beyond the capabilities of the government and a handful of barons, shares were offered to the public to raise funds shortly after its foundation (Photo 3). Thereby, CMSNC became the first joint stock venture in China and this new approach to corporate finance quickly attracted private capital to flow toward enterprises of this modern corporate form (Li, 2013). Among those which also issued shares in the following years, notable examples included Kaiping Mining Bureau ('*Kaiping kuangwu ju*' of Hebei Province, 1876), Shanghai Mechanical Textile Bureau ('*Shanghai jiqi zhibu ju*', 1880), Pingquan Copper Mining ('*Pingquan tongkuang*' of Hebei Province, 1881), and Imperial Chinese Telegraph Administration ('*Zhongguo dianbao zongju*' of Tianjin, 1882), etc.

While these firms were funded in part by the issuance of shares to Chinese merchants, they still bore a close relationship with the government's agenda to reduce the country's dependence upon foreigners. Therefore, although it is true that these new industrial enterprises imitated the western-style business practices, they continued to carry in their names the character '*ju*' for governmental bureau instead of the characters like '*chang*' for factory or '*gongsi*' for company, which would have indicated a private business concern. In essence, by taking the form of '*guandu shangban*' (state-supervised and merchant-managed), these enterprises

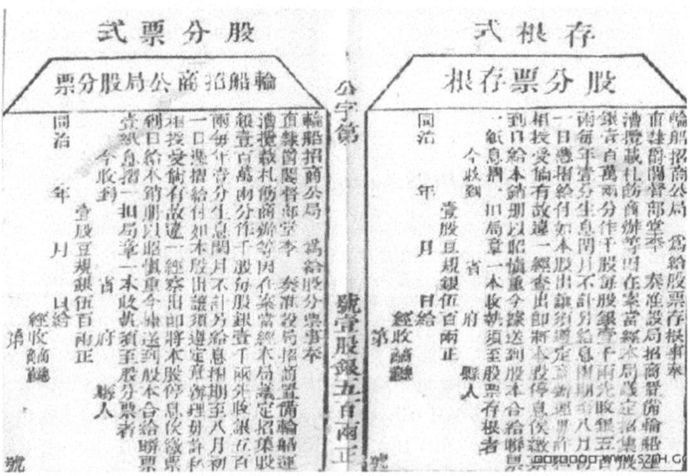

Photo 3 The 1st stock certificate (sample) of China, issued by China Merchants Steam Navigation Company (CMSNC) in 1872, i.e. the 11th year of Emperor Tongzhi's reign and priced at 500 taels of silver each share. *Source* China Merchants Group at https://www.cmhk.com/main/a/2015/k08/a231_286.shtml

were in part sponsored by government loans. However, it was to a great extent up to private investors, mostly merchants, to put up the needed start-up capital. In terms of management, while it was superficially looked after by these merchant investors; officials sent by the state could exercise real control (Li & Ding, 2014). These '*guandu shangban*' enterprises, from their first appearance in the 1870s to their boom in the 1880s and 1890s, had on the one hand enabled the late Qing to restrain foreign involvement in the imperial economy. Simultaneously, they provided officials, particularly at the provincial level, with alternative revenue streams to run the government. Here, what should be clarified is that although called joint stock companies, they were not yet floated on a public equity market since by then, such a market did not exist in China.

9.1.2 Emergence of the Shanghai Stock Exchange

Together with the increase in the number of securities, especially the mining industry which from June 1882 to the end of 1883 alone accounted for over one third of all the 29 joint stock companies (Zhu, 2001), transactions also began to boom. Shanghai, as one of the major commercial ports opened officially to Western colonists in 1843 after the First Opium War (five port cities were opened under the Treaty of Nanking and besides Shanghai, the other four were Guangzhou, Xiamen, Fuzhou and Ningbo), became very active when foreign firms flooded in to tap the Chinese market. In 1869, J. P. Bisset & Co. ('*Changli yanghang*') was established by the British and it was the first brokerage in China that specialized in the buying and selling of securities. With a view to diversifying investments, foreign businessmen founded the Shanghai Sharebrokers' Association ('*Shanghai zhengquan qianke gonghui*', or '*Shanghai gufen gongsuo*') in 1891 in which securities of foreign-registered companies were transacted (Zhang, 2001a, 2001b, 2001c). In 1904, the Association applied for registration in Hong Kong under the provisions of the Companies Ordinance. Renamed Shanghai Stock Exchange (SSE, '*Shanghai zhengquan jiaoyisuo*'), it was taken as the embryo of China's stock bourse.

By the 1930s, Shanghai has become the financial hub of the Far East and SSE was trading a wider range of stocks, shares, government bonds, and futures, etc. At that time, rubber was the prime stock and foreign companies, especially those of the British nationality, enjoyed a predominant position. However, due to the Japanese occupation of Shanghai International Settlement on December 8th, 1941 after the outbreak of the Pacific War (1941–1945), the operation of SSE was abruptly halted. After China resumed full control of Shanghai toward the end of the war, the once unchallengeable privilege and means of enforcing financial contracts for foreign businessmen had gone for good. In other words, the Shanghai Stock Exchange as an association for foreign share brokers was never reopened again.

9.1.3 The First Company Law Enacted

If counting from 1872 in which the CMSNC shares were floated till the fall of the Qing Dynasty in 1911, China has gained almost 40 years of experience in the public trading of stocks. The opening of the stock market in Shanghai in 1891 enabled businesses from a diverse range of industries, such as textile, banking, mining, rail transport, and electric power, etc., to benefit from this new approach of financing. Since it was largely a period of learning through experimentation, there was no lack of twists and turns. In particular, with the emergence of problems such as the expropriation of corporate assets by the state in absence of an independent judiciary, blind speculation of investors due to incomplete disclosure of important information, and fraudulent conduct by issuers under unduly lenient penalties, etc., there arose an urgent need for a legal framework within which officialdom could be separated from commerce and transactional behaviors were under strict regulation.

At the dawn of the twentieth century, in order to satisfy the stronger appeal for constitutional reform while maintaining the political status quo of a conservative imperial monarchy, the Qing court (or more precisely '*shang bu*', i.e. the Ministry of Commerce) promulgated China's first Company Law (named '*gongsi lü*') in January 1904 ('*gongsi lü*' was released together with '*shangren tongli*', or General Rules for Merchants in '*Qinding daqing shanglü*', i.e. the Great Qing Commercial Code) (Jin, 1999). Based on Japanese and English company laws, but in a much abbreviated form, the Law contained 131 provisions in eleven sections and stipulated issues such as forms of organization, shareholder rights, auditing requirements, and board meetings, etc. Above all, the biggest innovation in the code was that by recognizing limited company as one of the four major categories of companies, it offered for the first time a legal basis for firms with limited liabilities to get registered and put into operation.

Despite the fact that the enactment of the Company Law brought China closer in line with the prevailing global norms and encouraged more private enterprises to be incorporated as legal entities with limited liability; in terms of their organizational hierarchy and managerial structure, however, there was still no fundamental change (Wei, 2013). For example, the new financial accounting system was rarely observed in actual operation. Moreover, due to the practice of selecting auditors from among board members rather than using those who were external and independent, shareholders became the disadvantaged group whose interests were at stake. Apparently, the unbalanced distribution of power necessitated an open capital market for enhanced corporate discipline and governance.

In addition, from the perspective of entrepreneurs as well as managers, having a liquid market to diversify their investment holdings may induce them to more willingly abide by the rules that protect shareholders, who in turn would no longer refrain from putting up cash into equities for lack of confidence. On the other hand, the 1870s and 1880s were an era when the whole world was going through a transportation boom in the wake of the invention of internal combustion engine powered by energy-dense fuels such as gasoline and coal gas. Consequently, almost every sovereign nation was confronted with the challenge of financing the construction of large-scale transportation networks to catch up in the Industrial Revolution. China was not exceptional amid the wave, but given its considerable economic potential, if without a functioning domestic capital market to fund these mega projects, it would be impossible for the country to tap the resources while retaining control of its own technological development, a major motive behind the massive "Self-Strengthening Movement".

9.1.4 Rise and Fall of Exchanges

Although China's first stock exchange, the Shanghai Sharebrokers' Association, began its operation in 1891, the traded shares were chiefly for foreign companies to diversify their portfolio investment. As to the extent to which it served the needs and interests of domestic corporations, what the exchange could do was very limited, thus leaving them undercapitalized even with the provision of official subsidies. Nonetheless, until the overthrow of the monarchy in 1911, such a market was nonexistent. In 1918, i.e. the seventh year after the founding of the Republic of China (the ROC), the first Chinese stock exchange, i.e. Beijing Securities Exchange (named '*Zhongyuan zhengquan jiaoyisuo*'), was established. Later, the years 1920 and 1921 witnessed the opening of Shanghai Securities and Commodities Exchange (named '*Shanghai zhengquan wupin jiaoyisuo*') and Shanghai Chinese Merchant Exchange (named '*Shanghai huashang zhengquan jiaoyisuo*' as opposed to the Shanghai Stock Exchange organized and managed by foreign businessmen and for foreign registered corporations) respectively (Zhu, 2014).

Not long after, their lucrative business gave rise to a rash of new exchanges being set up in and outside Shanghai. Take Shanghai for example, in September 1921, there were 70 exchanges dealing in stocks, bonds and commodities; but within just two months, the number rocketed to 112 (Ding, 2007). Since what lied behind the abnormal speed of growth was nothing but a speculative mania, it is by no means surprising that after the bursting of the bubble (described as the "trust and exchange storm"), only 6 remained by March 1922.

9.1.5 Circulation of Bonds

While the irrational fever in China's stock market history was cooling down swiftly, corporate bonds as another funding instrument began to emerge at the same time. In 1921, by entrusting a consortium of 24 banks and money unions, 5 companies under Tongtai Salt Conglomerate ('*Tongtai yanken wugongsi*'), i.e. '*Da feng*', '*Da you jin*', '*Da yu*', '*Da lai*', and '*Hua cheng*', raised 5 million silver dollars by selling a 5-year tenure bond at a coupon of 0.8 PCT (Zhu, 2016). This started the practice among Chinese enterprises to resort to debt financing as a supplementary method when they were in need of capitalizing their businesses (Wan, 2012). For instance, the bonds issued equally in the 1920s included Huaxin Weihui Yarn Mill ('*Huaxin weihui shachang*', in Tianjin), Beiping Electric Tram Company ('*Beiping dianche gongsi*', in Beijing), and Meiya Silk Mill ('*Meiya zhichou chang*', in Shanghai), etc.

In an effort to improve the legal infrastructure of securities trading, especially concerning that of limited liability companies, the ROC government revised the Securities Exchange Act and promulgated the Company Law in 1929 (Yin, 2012). Besides, as a sign of enhanced supervision of the securities market, all the activities were put under the administration of the Ministry of Industry & Commerce in the same year. Following the merging of the securities trading division of the Shanghai Securities and Commodities Exchange into the Shanghai Chinese Merchant Exchange in 1933, the latter soon became the largest and most advanced securities exchange center of the Far East. At the same time, the treaty port Shanghai grew into one of the most influential capital markets in Asia, with a vibrant domestic and international banking sector and a dynamic environment for dealings of domestic and foreign stocks and bonds. Outside the city, stock exchanges could also be found in Beijing, Ningbo, Qingdao, Hankou, and Chongqing, etc. (Zhang, 2001a, 2001b, 2001c). Smaller in scale, they mainly traded local government bonds, in addition to the central government bonds and the stocks of some well-known corporations. However, due to the occupation of the Japanese troops and constant warfare that broke out in large parts of China throughout the 1930s and the early 1940s, normal transactions were often disrupted and even halted for several times, accompanied by sharp fluctuations in prices, a typical phenomenon suggesting that the psychology of speculation had dominated the market when peace was nowhere to find.

Although the Japanese withdrew from China after their surrender to the Allies of the Second World War in 1945, internal peace was still overshadowed by political uncertainties and military tensions. In the next year, the country was involved in the Civil War which lasted until 1949. During this turbulent period, Shanghai Securities Exchange Co., Ltd. ('*Shanghai zhengquan jiaoyisuo gufen youxian gongsi*') was set up in September 1946 on the basis of Shanghai Chinese Merchant Exchange (Zhang, 2001a, 2001b, 2001c). At its opening, 20 stocks were listed, with 225 brokers being admitted to handle the trading of shares, debentures, and government bonds, etc. To boost the sluggish transactions, the Exchange introduced stock futures and carried out experimental operation of the more profitable arbitrage. Very soon, the number of shares traded daily soared to 800 million. By 1947, there were 32 stocks listed and the total market capitalization amounted to 7,078.3 billion yuan (denominated in '*fabi*', or legal tender). Unfortunately, the boom turned out to be rather short-lived and to cope with the rampant hyperinflation, the regime had no better solution but to reform the monetary system. Following the replacement of '*fabi*' with '*jinyuan quan*' (gold yuan note), the Exchange was once again halted in August 1948. Despite the resumption of business in March 1949, it was closed two months later when the troops led by the CPC marched into Shanghai.

On the date of closure, nobody had anticipated that it would take another four decades for the market to be back in full operation. This particular part of the history shows that the post-1927 Republican era was afflicted with incessant wars and financial crunches. As a result, there was no way for the country to create a sustainable equity culture in which investors would be willing to engage in the capital market on a long-term basis and companies, with stable inflow of funds, could concentrate more intensely on boosting their economic performances so as to engender shareholder loyalty. For lack of such a virtuous cycle, no wonder the system of market capitalization at that time was so vulnerable to the persistent economic crises.

9.2 Post-1949 Decades, A Transition Stage

After the Communist Party took over mainland China in 1949, it re-opened the Tianjin Stock Exchange (June 1949) and Beijing Stock Exchange (January 1950) for financing purposes. Nevertheless, having gone through decades of political chaos, individual investors were uncertain about the policies of the new regime, especially whether private assets were to be partially or totally nationalized. Such feelings of insecurity were rather contagious and driven by a gambling motive, many of them became addicted to irregular trading so as to chase quick gains. The subsequent sharp swings in stock prices made the market excessively volatile and speculative, which diametrically contradicted the principles governing the socialist economic system (Zhang, 2001a, 2001b, 2001c). In particular, the system during the pre-reform period was uncompromisingly based on the premise of public ownership and relied on central planning rather than market forces to allocate means of production, including capital. Therefore, with the achievement of fiscal balance and steady increase in government revenues, both exchanges were shut down in 1952 before the nationwide expropriation of private properties, including those of share-holding companies, which kicked off one year later.

From the 1950s to the late 1970s, the development of the Chinese socialist economy was interrupted by constant movements and campaigns which aimed to remold the ideology and traditional values of the society. Even though agricultural and industrial production proceeded like before, the efficiency in the utilization of resources did not receive its due attention. After all, considering that the vast majority of the enterprises were either state-owned or collectively-owned, there was little incentive to establish a corporate governance structure to ensure that whatever actions were to be taken, they would serve the best interest of the ultimate shareholders, i.e. the citizens at large. Therefore, despite the promotion of responsibility system among rural and urban enterprises since the 1980s, fundamental issues like the separation of ownership and control remained incompletely addressed. To a large degree, this also explains why sustainable results were often unattainable after the campaign.

9.3 Resurgence of Securities Exchanges Since the 1990s

Toward the end of the 1980s when a growing number of firms around the country were reorganized into joint-stock corporations, the government began to think about re-launching stock exchanges. In tandem with the ongoing economic reform and opening up, the Shanghai Stock Exchange (SSE) went into full operation on December 19th, 1990. Around half a year later, the Shenzhen Stock Exchange (SZSE) started trading on July 3rd, 1991. As to the release of the Shenzhen Composite Index, it had started earlier on April 4th by taking the previous day as the base of 100 points. On July 15th, 1991, the SSE launched the Shanghai Composite Index, with December 19th, 1990 being its base of 100 points. By the end of that year, the SSE had eight listed stocks while the number of the SZSE was six (Ma, 2009).

9.3.1 "August 10th Incident", the Growing Pain

In early 1992, Deng Xiaoping's southern tour of China and his speech acknowledging the experiments with Shanghai and Shenzhen stock exchanges greatly facilitated their development. Moreover, the passion of the Chinese to make investment in securities was also kindled, they viewed it as a golden opportunity to get rich quickly. On August 7th, 1992, Shenzhen announced that it would distribute 5 million stock subscription forms (or '*xingu rengou chouqianbiao*', which would qualify investors to take part in a lottery for shares at initial public offerings, or IPOs) amounting to RMB500 million at face value (Chen, 2007). Besides, it required that every single person could hold no more than ten identification cards (ID cards) to buy 10 forms. In order to grasp this unprecedented chance, about 1.2 million people from across the country flocked to Shenzhen to buy the forms. On August 9th, all the forms were sold out. Very soon, it was found that due to a severe shortage of subscription forms, as well as the poor organization and some fraudulent practices, a lot of potential investors queued in vain. Filled with extreme anger, many of them marched onto the street on the night of August 10th to protest, an event later called the "August 10th Incident".

In the wake of the incident, the government not only suspended IPOs for one year; more importantly, it began to recognize that the securities market was not without its pitfalls. To better regulate the industry and provide a well-ordered trading environment, the China Securities Regulatory Commission (CSRC) was established in that October. As an institution of the State Council, the CSRC enjoys the authority to oversee the nationwide operation of securities by formulating policies and enforcing laws. Ever since, with the country's capital market being aligned under a better unified supervisory framework, a new chapter has begun.

9.3.2 The Booming Transactions

In order to solidify the legal basis of the framework, especially with a view to dealing with the short-term volatility and steep correction that were occurring in the stock market, the State Council in 1992 also issued the "Notice on Further Strengthening the Macro-administration of the Securities Market". Taken as the first official document which comprehensively outlined the key issues in regulating the stock market, like the enhancement of supervision, standardization of the listing procedures, identification of management functions, and consolidation of the infrastructures, etc., the Circular offered a clear guidance for the future direction of movement. In the following years, considering that building a fair and competitive securities market should be accompanied by a series of institutional reforms, more decrees and rules were enacted by the state, including the "*Interim* Provisions *on the* Management *of the* Issuing and Trading *of* Stocks" (1993), "Measures for the Administration of Stock Exchanges" (1996), "Interim Measures for the Administration of Securities Investment Funds" (1997), and "Securities Law of the People's Republic of China" (1998), etc., to name but a few.

If without these initiatives to lay a solid legal groundwork for China's capital markets, it would be impossible for the country to achieve an explosive growth in the subsequent transactions of stocks, bonds, and other financial derivatives at the turn of the new century. Table 13 is a snapshot of how China's stock markets have evolved throughout the first decade of their emergence. By the year 2000, the SSE and SZSE together had issued over 51.2 billion shares and the capital raised exceeded RMB210.3 billion in total. This represented a phenomenal increase from 1991 when the total shares issued and capital raised were just 500 million and RMB500 million respectively. Besides, the table also displays some information about the number of listed companies, which rose from just 14 in 1991 to 1,088 by 2000. If calculated from 1992, market capitalization of these firms underwent an expansion of almost 45 times when hitting over RMB4.8 trillion in 2000. During this nine-year period, i.e. from 1992–2000, both the Shanghai Stock Exchange Composite Index and the Shenzhen Stock Exchange Composite Index (close) more than doubled, with the former raised from 780.39 to 2,073.48 and the latter from 241.2 to 635.73.

Table 13 Summary of the stock market performance, 1991–2000

Year	No. of listed companies (SSE and SZSE)	Issued shares (100 million)	Market capitalization (RMB100 million)	Raised capital (RMB100 million)
1991	14	5	–	5
1992	53	20.75	1,048	94.09
1993	183	95.79	3,531	375.47
1994	291	91.26	3,691	326.78
1995	323	31.6	3,474	150.32
1996	530	86.11	9,842	425.08
1997	745	267.63	17,529	1,293.82
1998	851	105.56	19,506	841.52
1999	949	122.93	26,471	944.56
2000	1,088	512.03	48,091	2,103.08

Source NBS (2000, 2002)

9.3.3 Bonds in Funding the National Construction

While the equity (stocks) market was thriving rapidly, the debt (bonds) market too witnessed an impressive resurgence of interest. In China, there are mainly three types of bonds, i.e. government bonds (or treasury bonds known as T-bonds), financial bonds, and enterprise bonds. By comparison, government bonds are ranked as the safest investments because they are backed by the credit of the government, either central or local. Universally recognized as the foundation for broader domestic debt markets, government bond market not only offers pricing benchmarks for other kinds of debt instruments, it also serves as a platform for open market operations (OMO) by the central bank. Generally, having an efficient and well-established government bond market is crucial to the smooth functioning of the entire debt markets since the creditworthiness and liquidity of such a market have a stabilizing effect that helps prevent turmoil caused by economic downturns. From this point of view, a logical review of China's emerging domestic debt market should start with a glimpse of the market for government bonds.

In the beginning, the major purpose of issuing government bonds was to tackle budgetary shortfall and the first bond—People's Victory Bond launched in 1950 greatly alleviated the pressure of mounting monetary demand. Later on, to fulfill the first Five Year Plan set out for the period of 1953–1957 and in particular, to resolve the problem of insufficient revenues, National Economic Construction Bond was released for five consecutive times from 1954 to 1958 (Gao & Chi, 2008). Once again, with the easing of budget constraints, the government was in a position to carry out various industrial projects smoothly. **After all the debt principal and interest were paid off by 1968, bond issuance was suspended.**

It was till thirteen years later that the government once again resorted to the bonds to balance its budgetary deficit and this time, it started with the passage of an ordinance named the "Regulations on the State Treasury Securities of the People's Republic of China" in January 1981, which stipulated clearly that they could neither be transferred nor resold. Unlike the way bonds are distributed today, sales at that time was by no means voluntary (Qian, 1994). Instead, it was by nature a form of compulsory taxation on a pre-specified quota share basis. On many occasions, payment for the bonds was often deducted straightly from the payrolls of individual subscribers or simply withdrawn from the bank accounts of institutional subscribers like state or collectively-owned enterprises. Therefore, it is no exaggeration to liken it to a kind of administrative allotment.

9.3.4 Underwriting Mechanism Introduced

In financial jargon, the market where issuers and investors (or intermediaries) transact with each other is called the primary market; referring to the market which involves swaps among investors or between investors and intermediaries, it is the secondary market. The existence of both markets is important for the smooth flow of liquidity and generation of sufficient funds. Conversely, if these two markets could not function well, then the efficiency in the distribution of bonds would be undermined. In particular, investors might be discouraged since they have no way to liquidate their bond holdings when in need. However, this was exactly the case in China prior to 1990; to be more specific, it was only until 1988 that trials to establish a secondary market for treasury bonds were initiated among 61 cities (Wang, 1998a,1998b). Through administrative placement, banks were obliged to accept specified quantities of bonds at rates determined already by the Ministry of Finance. Under this top-down sales model, the need for a market was virtually nonexistent. While it is true that by offering a coupon rate which was one to two percent higher than the interest rate for bank deposits of the same term, the initial issuance of treasury bonds was rather successful, especially among individual investors. But gradually, holders began to feel inconvenient because these bonds had a maturity of five to ten years and during this period, they were not permitted to get the principal back. As a result, their discontent about liquidity outweighed the attractiveness of the yield, and this in turn made the distribution of more bonds difficult.

To regain public confidence, the State Council decided to introduce bond discount procedure from 1985, which enabled individual buyers to have their holdings discounted at banks. For enterprise buyers, they could also use treasury bonds as collateral when borrowing from the four specialized state commercial banks (Zhang, 1985). These measures, although still primitive, prompted the need of establishing a market for treasury bonds trading. Besides, to cope with the strong liquidity demand of investors, 7 cities including Shenyang, Harbin, Shanghai, Chongqing, Wuhan, Guangzhou, and Shenzhen were selected by the Ministry of Finance in April 1988 to lead a pilot program (Zhang, 1988). By that June when 54 more cities were added to the list, China's secondary bond market began to take its shape. Referring to the primary market for treasury bonds, its emergence happened only after 1991 following an innovation in issuance via the underwriting mechanism. In April that year, the Ministry of Finance reached a deal with a syndicate consisting of 58 financial institutions, chiefly commercial banks, securities companies, and insurance firms across the country, to sell RMB2.5 billion of treasury bonds (Jin, 1991). Later, greatly encouraged by the success of this experimental subscription, the Ministry started to distribute more bonds on a voluntary rather than mandatory basis.

From 1988 to 1994, although issues increased in a rapid way, treasury bonds were still used primarily to make up the shortfalls resulting from the overdrafts of the Ministry of Finance from the central bank to fund government operations (Yang, 1998). As a result, the internal forces at play in the government bond market remained rudimentary. After 1994, the State Council formally ruled that the Ministry of Finance could no longer overdraw from the central bank to offset the fiscal deficit; instead, it should rely on bonds to tackle the problem. Obviously, this major policy change brought new opportunities for the development of the bond market in China and very soon, the issuance of government bond expanded from RMB38.1 billion of 1993 to RMB102.8 billion in 1994, an increase of almost 170PCT within just one year (Jia & Wang, 2011).

9.3.5 Structure of the Bond-Dealing System

The accumulation of experiences was simultaneously accompanied by the launch of fresh trials. To facilitate distribution and increase the volume sold by the underwriting syndicates, a primary dealer system was established in 1993 (Zhang, 1995). According to the "Regulations on the Management of Primary Dealers in Government Securities" promulgated in December, 19 qualified institutions were chosen as primary dealers and they were eligible to enjoy certain privileges as compensation once the placement was accomplished. From then on, with a larger number of dealers being approved, they became a dominant force in the primary market of treasury bonds. Moreover, their participation also demonstrated that marketization of T-bond issuance in China has been virtually realized. Before 1997, China had two secondary bond markets (Wang, 1998a,1998b), one was called exchange bond market (or internal market) and the other was known as the bank over-the-counter market (OTC or external market). Referring to the former, it was mainly represented by the Shanghai Stock Exchange and Shenzhen Stock Exchange. After their foundation in the early 1990s, the trading of government bonds started.

By comparison, transactions were more concentrated at the Shanghai Stock Exchange where individuals and institutions participated through brokers. With regard to the bank OTC market, its appearance took place after the release of the "Provisional Regulations on OTC Trading of Securities" by the Shanghai Branch of the PBoC in 1987. For the first time, it allowed government bonds, as well as other forms of securities to be traded over the counter between approved financial institutions and investors, who were either firms or individuals. Not long after, it was found that commercial banks had become heavy traders in the bond market and, sometimes, indirectly in the stock market despite regulations against such activities. In 1997 in particular, an enormous amount of bank-owned cash flowed in and out of the exchange bond market and caused huge volatility in bond prices without fundamental reasons. To prevent the stock market from getting overheated by the illegal movement of bank capital, the PBoC mandated in June that all commercial banks completely withdraw their bond repo (short for repurchase agreement) and cash trading out of the Shanghai and Shenzhen stock exchanges (CGSDTC, 1998). At the same time, their business was moved into the newly-established national inter-bank bond market, a quote-driven OTC market operating through an electronic trading system outside the exchanges, where deals were struck based on bid and ask prices negotiated between the two trading counterparties. From then on, China had one more secondary bond market which consisted of institutional investors such as commercial banks, insurance companies, securities firms, and fund management companies, etc.

At the outset, the inter-bank bond market only had 18 domestic banks (16 commercial banks plus 2 urban cooperative banks). However, by the end of 2015, the number of home-based participants registered 9,642. Besides, those overseas institutions which had been granted accession hit 308. Additionally, of the nation's total outstanding bond which stood at RMB47.9 trillion, the volume of trades under custody in the inter-bank bond market amounted to RMB43.9 trillion. Therefore, by sharing over 90 PCT of the gross domestic bonds, the inter-bank market has already become the dominant player (PBoC, 2016).

9.3.6 T-Bond Derivatives

Apart from the structuring of the market framework, proliferation of bond varieties is of equal importance to its long-term development. Since the early 1990s, derivatives of government bonds have begun to emerge, especially after the establishment of the Shanghai Stock Exchange and the Securities Trading Automated Quotation System (STAQ system or '*zhengquan jiaoyi zidong baojia xitong*'). Referring to the latter, it was modeled after the NASDAQ (acronym of National Association of Securities Dealers Automatic Quotation System, which has evolved from a mere quotation system to the world's first electronic stock exchange) of the US and served as a nationwide computer-based securities trading platform. Considering that by then, trans-regional, well-organized and standardized bond trading was still at its rudimentary stage, circulation of treasury bonds was encountering some difficulties due to their lack of liquidity. Apparently, the launch of the STAQ system in the end of 1990 helped promote transactions and made it easier for investors across the country to strike deals.

In September 1991, i.e. two months after the announcement of the STAQ system to pilot the government bond repo business, the first deal was concluded between two of its member companies (Zhao, 2006). Since in a repurchase agreement, the borrower of money (the repo seller) would provide bond as collateral to the lender (the repo buyer), the credit risks involved could be greatly reduced. Because of this reason, investors are willing to put surplus money into the market, which enhances liquidity while at the same time enables them to manage capital in a safer and more efficient way. From the perspective of borrowers, the repo rate is usually lower than the cost of getting loans from a bank, thus they could equally gain by optimizing their funding sources. In a broader sense, considering that the repo rate is the result of bargaining between lenders and borrowers, it can more accurately mirror the short-term supply and demand of the money market. Therefore, carrying out the repo business of government bond may exercise a positive impact on the marketization of interest rates. The trial that was conducted through the STAQ system soon reversed the sluggish sale of T-bonds. In the following years, the same product became available with a number of other securities exchanges as well, like those in Wuhan and Tianjin, etc. However, the transactions largely remained local until December 1993 when Shanghai Stock Exchange set up bond repo products with maturities spanning from 3 to *182 days, a nationwide repo market came into being (*Liu, 2012*).*

Apart from repos, the other major derivative instrument that dominated the transactions of China's T-bond market during the same period was T-bond futures. In December 1992, an experiment was carried out by the Shanghai Stock Exchange, with 12 different contract types offered to institutional investors. However, the timing was not right for the product because in that year, the economy was already showing signs of overheating and this increased the danger of rising inflation. To ease the inflationary pressure and cool down the economy, the central bank adjusted interest rates on both deposit and loans upward in May and July of 1993 (Liu, 1993). At the same time, for the protection of bond investors whose enthusiasm was diminishing quickly due to their shrinking gains, the government decided to offer subsidies in addition to the coupon. In view of the fact that China's interest rates were not yet market determined, holders of treasury bonds started to bet on the subsidy level rather than the bond yield because it was the subsidy that would affect their ultimate returns. Inevitably, such a speculative mentality permeated the futures market as well, which was turned into a battlefield for players to amass greater profits (Qiao, 1997). Seeing that the futures trading had lost its due functions and become a mere object of speculation, China Securities Regulatory Commission (CSRC) as the administrative organ ordered a suspension of the business in May 1995.

The tasks following the suspension were enormous and in order to get better prepared for the resumption of transactions, the authorities chiefly *strengthened* the *regulation* and supervision of market activities. In particular, the legal vacuum that had existed in the futures trading was filled step by step with the promulgation of a series of statutes, such as the "Provisional Regulations on the Administration of Futures Trading" (1999), the "Measures for the Administration of Futures Exchanges" (2007), the "Administrative Measures for Futures Companies" (2007), and the "Administrative Provisions on Opening Accounts for Investors in the Futures Market" (2009), etc. Finally, when the CSRC announced that the trading of T-bond futures would be resumed on the Shanghai-based China Financial Futures Exchange (CFFEX) in 2013, the 18-year halt was put to an end (Liu & Li, 2013). Although it is not fair to describe these eighteen years as a lost period, the cost was undeniably huge. If in the first place, the country had devoted itself to the consolidation of the above basics instead of rushing into the business prematurely, it wouldn't have had to spend that much time to fix the loopholes. Anyhow, what's done cannot be undone, the lesson is still worthy if the same stumbling block is no longer the cause to fall. Furthermore, from the experience of mature western markets, T-bond futures are not only used as a tool for hedging the uncertainties of investment; their yield is often taken as a benchmark to set interest rates. Because of this, countries like the US and Japan even realized their interest rate reforms by launching T-bond futures. Thereby, it is believed that a healthy growth of T-bond derivatives market for futures and repos is crucial to China, for it can not only channel excess capital to fund the construction of mega state projects; additionally, it will also facilitate the interest rate liberalization as well as the integration of the country into the world financial system.

With the rapid expansion of the Chinese economy, its financing need has also been growing by leaps and bounds, which highlighted the necessity of having a sound treasury market to sustain the momentum. In view of what the market has gone through over decades of development, both the disorders and chaos disclosed the weaknesses in its foundation. But as compared to the very beginning when transactions had been subject to various stringent restrictions, the gradual easing of these trading setbacks enabled bondholders to cash in the principal more conveniently, a major incentive that greatly promoted the circulation and thus issuance of a larger quantity of treasury bonds. Undeniably, this is consistent with the goal of the government, i.e. to mobilize a part of the sizable household savings and direct it to finance public expenditure or the development of the national economy. Nevertheless, after absorbing the needed funds, an even tougher challenge is how to utilize them in an optimal way. In other words, the efficiency of utilization becomes the primary concern. Regretfully, given the track record of China, its performance in this respect was not that satisfactory. Due to the unbalanced role between the government and the market, plus the absence of an effective supervisory mechanism, a vicious cycle of raising new debt to offset the former has been rather common. To get the situation ameliorated, the government of course has to plan, monitor and adjust the whole procedure conscientiously. In particular, from a long-term point of view, an appraisal system evaluating the efficiency of fund usage should be established. This is not only necessary to the state, it is also essential for the protection of investors' interests and in this consideration, ensuring transparency in information disclosure is equally an indispensable part of future efforts.

9.3.7 Financial Bonds: Means of Supplementary Funding

With regard to financial bonds, it is classified as corporate bonds in western countries. But in China, the issuance is separate and generally for the purpose of achieving three major objectives, i.e. recapitalization of the state-owned banks, enhancement of risk control, and management of the mismatch between assets and liabilities in the banking sector. As the name suggests, the issuers of financial bonds mainly include policy banks, commercial banks and other financial institutions. Among them, policy banks take the biggest share and China Development Bank (CDB) as a key player, is perhaps the dominant financing source for national infrastructure, emerging industries, and state-level priority projects. Together with the CDB, the other two policy banks are more specialized, with the Export–Import Bank of China (China Exim Bank) mandated to facilitate the export and import of Chinese mechanical & electronic products, complete sets of equipment, and high-tech products, etc. and the Agricultural Development Bank of China (ADBC) undertaking the mission of supporting agriculture through funds allocation. In general, bonds issued by these policy banks are named policy financial/bank bonds, they are rated as quasi government bonds because of the sovereign credit behind. It was in April 1994 that the first policy bank bonds were launched by the CDB (Hou & Xiang, 2014); after the formation of the inter-bank bond market in 1997, most of these bonds were traded in this market instead of the stock exchanges.

Apart from the policy banks, the role of commercial banks equally deserves attention because they pioneered the issuance of financial bonds in China. It happened in 1985 when the central bank adopted a tight monetary policy to cope with the high-rising inflation; but simultaneously, to ensure that certain key projects with high potential returns would not be halted due to the shortage of capital supply, it released a circular jointly with the Industrial and Commercial Bank of China (ICBC), and the Agricultural Bank of China (ABC) in July demanding that financial bonds would be issued by the ICBC and the ABC (Wan, 1986). Besides, the circular stipulated in a concrete way that the fund raised would be used as special loans for qualified enterprises only. Later in that year, the two state banks together launched RMB820 million worth of bonds (with RMB352 million by the ICBC and RMB468 million by the ABC), the major beneficiaries were collectively-owned enterprises in the urban areas and township enterprises of the rural regions. Since the 9 PCT yield was higher than the deposit interest rate for the same one-year maturity, which stayed at 6.84–7.2 PCT in 1985, they were favored by investors after the release. From then on, several other commercial banks and trust investment corporations also followed suit.

9.3.8 Twists and Turns in Enterprise Bonds Issuance

Over decades, Chinese enterprises, especially the state-owned, had been relying on bank loans for their financing purposes and this in turn laid a huge pressure on banks because of the sharp increase in outstanding debts. With a view to mitigating risks concentrated in the banking system, the government has long been supportive of fund raising via issuance of enterprise bonds. When China started its reform in the late 1970s, demand for bank loans far exceeded supply and this made many enterprises unable to acquire the needed capital, which compelled some of them to try other means to get the problem resolved. For instance, in 1982, China International Trust and Investment Corporation (CITIC), a company whose mission is to promote technology transfer and cross-border investment, issued 10 billion yen bonds in Japan and this was China's first issuance of bonds on the international market (Lü & Song, 1983). Also named samurai bond, 80 PCT of the funds was allocated to build a large-scale chemical fiber plant in Yizheng (Jiangsu Province). If without this timely injection of money from bond issuance, it was very likely for the project to be aborted.

Apart from relying on financial institutions, enterprises themselves began to obtain financing by borrowing from their own employees through a primitive and informal type of enterprise bonds. In 1984 for example, after failing to get bank loans to proceed with technological upgrading, several collectively-owned enterprises in Shenyang (Liaoning Province) resorted to issuing bonds internally to deal with the shortage (Jiang, 1992). As to the earliest recorded enterprise bond, it was by Shenyang Property Development Company in May 1985 with a maturity of five years. Issuance on a larger scale commenced in 1987 when Shanghai Jinshan General Petrochemical Plant (predecessor of today's SINOPEC Shanghai Petrochemical Company) issued bonds amounting to RMB138 million for its 300,000-ton ethylene project (An & Gu, 2008). Under the encouragement of the government, the growth trend continued throughout the rest of the 1980s and the early 1990s. Particularly, as can be found by the graph below (Graph 5), from about RMB25 billion of 1991 to almost RMB68.4 billion in 1992, the pace of increase within one year exceeded a phenomenal 170 PCT. Usually, such an over-rapid pace of expansion is not a purely positive sign; it is more an indicator of potential problems. And indeed, what happened later proved that the linkage is justified. While China's GDP grew at 14.2 PCT in 1992, the consumer

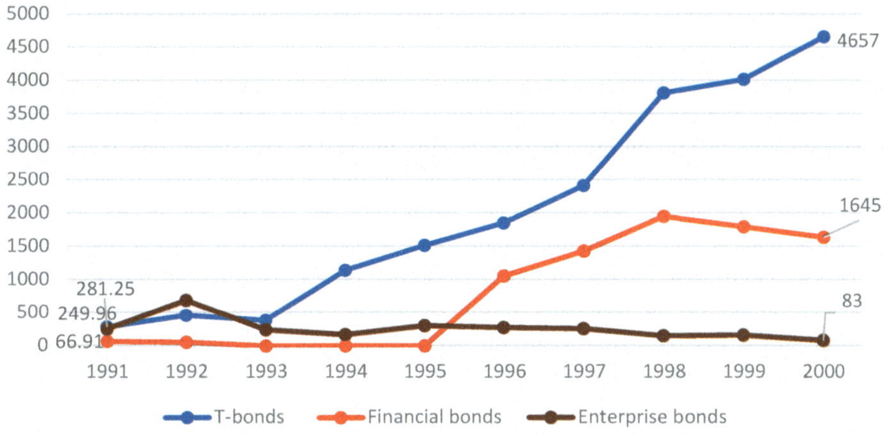

Graph 5 Issuance of three types of bonds, RMB100 million. *Source* Gui (2003)

price index registered a rise of 6.4 PCT, both pointed to the same fact that bubbles had begun to emerge and certain measures should be immediately adopted to restrain the unhealthy momentum.

Although in 1990, the State Planning Commission and the People's Bank of China had already regulated explicitly that the issuance of enterprise bonds, as a major source to sponsor fixed assets construction, should fall under a uniform quota administration (An & Gu, 2008). Nonetheless, the mandate was not strictly observed by the lower-level governments. To boost economy, they encouraged investment and this in turn resulted in the unchecked growth of enterprise bonds. Moreover, in a situation of growing irregularity and disorder, some enterprises which were already on the brink of bankruptcy even used bonds to exchange for payroll funds. By 1993, the deteriorating trend continued and pushed inflation further up to 14.7 PCT. As a consequence, circulation of government bonds encountered extreme difficulties. In an effort to remove the barriers that may impede the issuance of government bonds, the State Council ordered in April a suspension of all the enterprise bonds until the sale of government bonds were accomplished. At the same time, it required that the coupon rate offered by enterprises should not exceed that of the newly issued government bonds. Originally, the annual quota for enterprise bond was set at RMB49 billion in the beginning of 1993 (Wu, 2004), but because of the tightening policies against the unfavorable macro environment, the actual release by the end of the year was merely RMB23.58 billion.

Aware of the necessity to strengthen the management of the enterprise bond market and restore the order of fund raising, the "Administrative Rules for Enterprise Bonds" was published in August 1993. As an amendment replacing the existing interim regulations (released in 1987), it emphasized the uncompromising principle of strict compliance with the annual issuance scale in all localities and in particular, by clarifying the qualifications of underwriters and proposing the introduction of bond rating, the new law marked a step forward in risk control and protection of investors' interest. Based on the experience of mature economies, a well-developed domestic bond market is crucial to the financing of business entities. But given the issuers' likelihood of default, which remains the dominant concern of investors, only a high-quality and independent credit rating system may harmonize the relationship of the two sides. At its initial stage, i.e. during the end of the 1980s, credit rating in China was performed by the provincial branches of the PBoC (Song, 2014). Gradually, these departments were separated from the central bank and developed into independent firms. In 1997, an important notice was promulgated by the PBoC which on the one hand made credit rating a mandatory prerequisite for all the issuers of enterprise bonds; on the other hand, nine domestic institutions were nominated as qualified rating agencies to provide the service and they included China Chengxin International, Dagong Global, and Shanghai Far East, etc. (Li, 2012). Undoubtedly, this attempt was very constructive to the steady growth of the enterprise bond market in China, which was by then nascent and in need of much consolidation work before it could function well. What's more, the connection of credit rating and issuance of enterprise bonds motivated enterprises to pay closer attention to self-discipline and governance, thus preparing them to become responsible corporate citizens in the future.

Since 1993, the amount of enterprise bonds in circulation has been much lower due to the limited scale of issuance and the situation persisted until 2001. This formed a sharp contrast with the launch of other bonds during the same period, especially treasury bonds which kept rising quickly throughout the 1990s. As a result of the widening gap, in 2001, the enterprise bonds issued was only 3.7 PCT of the treasury bonds, which recorded RMB488.35 billion (Gui, 2003). But back to 1991, their difference was by no means so significant. Anyhow, given the reasons explained in the above, especially the privileged status of the treasury bonds, this phenomenon is not hard to understand. It was until 2003 that the policy toward enterprise bonds began to show signs of relaxation. In that October, there was a call for promoting direct financing through the establishment of a multi-tier capital market system. Shortly after that, the State Council released "Some Opinions on Promoting the Reform, Opening and Steady Growth of the Capital Market" in 2004. On the premise of rationalizing the structure of capital markets, it encouraged qualified enterprises to fund themselves by issuing bonds so as to reverse the sluggish activities in bond financing.

9.3.9 Multiple Drawbacks to Deal With

By and large, China's capital market consists of two pillars: the stock market and the bond market. While the stock market was officially formed in the early 1990s when the Shanghai Stock Exchange and Shenzhen Stock Exchange started their operations, the bond market came into being with the resumption of government bond issuance in 1981. Serving as a cause as well as a result of the economic reform over these two decades, they together provided the financial resources that enabled the country to smoothly carry out various construction works, from infrastructure building to the adjustment of industrial structure. Similar to what had happened in other sectors during the transition, their evolution was also under the strong influence of administrative intervention and centralized planning. Because of this, state-owned enterprises (SOEs) have enjoyed much more advantage than non-state entities. In the stock market, for instance, most listed companies were either the SOEs or with a state background. By May 2000, among the 981 listed companies, 664 were state-controlled listed companies (SCLCs, a type of domestically-listed companies whose voting shares were over 50 PCT held by the government agencies or their wholly-owned companies), accounting for 68 PCT of the total (Ju, 2006). When it comes to the issuance of enterprise bonds, preference was equally extended to the SOEs, which left very little opportunity for other business entities (the privately-owned in particular) to access funds via this channel.

However, as compared to the increasingly greater contribution of these non-state ventures to the national economy, the disproportionate relationship was indeed a reflection showing that a large part of the demand for direct financing had not been duly looked after, and this would inevitably restrain the development of the bond market. Besides, since it is impossible for a capital market to function well if without the active participation of investors, protecting their interest should be taken as another important task facing the Chinese policymakers. Given the situation by the end of the 1990s, it was comparatively easier for firms to raise capital than for investors to reap returns. Although the system of credit rating had been introduced, the fairness and independence of the 9 specialized agencies named by the PBoC remained to be tested. In addition, concerning the problem of supervision, the existence of multiple authorities has made the bond market rather fragmented. With the Ministry of Finance (MOF) and China Securities Regulatory Commission (CSRC) regulating the primary and secondary market (in stock exchanges) of government bonds, the National Development and Reform Commission (NDRC) was in charge of the review and approval of enterprise bonds. Moreover, in terms of the issuance of financial bonds, it was jointly handled by the China Banking Regulatory Commission (CBRC) and the PBoC. Seemingly, their responsibilities have been laid out in an explicit way; yet in real practice, jurisdictional overlaps often made conflicts inevitable and thus impeded the formation of a unified and efficient market. Under certain circumstances, there were even loopholes because of the cumbersome bureaucracy. Thereby, if China's capital market were expected to contribute more to the economic development in the new century, all the above-mentioned setbacks should be dealt with effectively.

10 Foreign Trade, A More Decentralized External Sector

With regard to China's foreign trade before the late 1970s, it was indeed a highly centralized system similar to multiple other sectors of the economy. Import, export, as well the allocation of foreign exchange were without exception planned and controlled. Although the principle that backed this mechanism was to export goods in abundant supply and import when there was a short supply, since the development policy had been overwhelmingly biased in favor of producer goods, acute shortages in consumer goods were often ignored. Behind it, the purpose was to serve a higher goal of transforming the country into a heavy industrialized society.

10.1 Composition of Imports and Exports

If taking a look at the composition of China's imports and exports during that period, preferences of the central planners were easily detectable. As far as imports are concerned, the vast majority of them were producer goods since the initiation of the first Five Year Plan (1953–1957). But after 1961, threatened by the food scarcity that had cost the life of millions of Chinese, massive quantities of grain (mostly wheat) were brought in from Australia, Canada and France, etc. to feed the starving population (Shang, 2009). Despite this temporary adjustment, as the priority had always been extended to industrial goods, especially transportation equipment, machinery, and intermediate materials, etc., import of consumer products like foodstuffs and durables hardly claimed an impressive amount throughout the 1970s. In 1980, while primary goods including food and non-edible materials reached a higher level of almost 35PCT among all the nation's imports (Table 14), its volume was still around 47PCT lower than that of the manufactured goods. Over the following decade, the situation turned out to be less favorable as the proportion of primary goods contracted to 18.47PCT by 1990.

Regarding the Chinese exports in the 1950s, they were chiefly primary commodities and as an agrarian country, raw and processed agricultural products like food and vegetable oils, etc. remained as a whole the mainstay of its export trade. Toward the latter half of the 1970s, with the growing export of industrial manufactured goods,

Table 14 Composition of import commodities in selected years, 1980–1990

Commodity Type	1980		1985		1990	
	Volume (USD100 million)	Share[3] (PCT)	Volume (USD100 million)	Share[4] (PCT)	Volume (USD100 million)	Share[5] (PCT)
Total Import	200.17	100	422.52	100	533.45	100
Primary Goods[1]	69.59	34.77	52.89	12.52	98.53	18.47
Manufactured Goods[2]	130.58	65.23	369.63	87.48	434.92	81.53

Note [1]include food and live animals used mainly for food, beverage and tobacco, and non-edible raw materials, etc.; [2]include chemicals and related products, light textile industrial products, rubber products, minerals and metallurgical products, machinery and transport equipment, etc.; [3–5]calculated by the author

Source NBS (2001)

Table 15 Composition of export commodities in selected years, 1980–1990

Commodity Type	1980		1985		1990	
	Volume (USD100 million)	Share[3] (PCT)	Volume (USD100 million)	Share[4] (PCT)	Volume (USD100 million)	Share[5] (PCT)
Total Export	181.19	100	273.5	100	620.91	100
Primary Goods[1]	91.14	50.3	138.28	50.56	158.86	25.59
Manufactured Goods[2]	90.05	49.7	135.22	49.44	462.05	74.41

Note [1]include food and live animals used mainly for food, beverage and tobacco, non-edible raw materials, mineral fuels, lubricants and related materials, etc.
[2]include chemicals and related products, light textile industrial products, rubber products, minerals and metallurgical products, machinery and transport equipment, etc.
[3–5]calculated by the author
Source NBS (2001)

their proportion started to fall. In 1980, the share of these two categories was almost the same (Table 15) and this lasted until 1985. After then, the divergence became increasingly explicit and by 1990, manufactured goods dominated the exports with an unbeatable ratio of almost 75 PCT. From then on, China's position as a manufacturing hub of the world was taking shape.

10.2 Relaxation of Trading Rights

The opening-up policy initiated in 1978 was undoubtedly a great boost to the country's foreign trade. Nevertheless, with regard to the unique circumstances of China, especially its planned economic regime which had been so deeply rooted for almost three decades, it is not hard to imagine the difficulties involved behind any attempt to minimize the importance of the central plan and introduce instead a brand-new system that is based on the market. Not everyone was in favor of a change of the status quo, but by looking at the dynamic momentum of development that had been taking place around the world; in particular, the extraordinary growth rate of the Four Asian Tigers (i.e. Singapore, South Korea, Hong Kong, and Taiwan) during the 1970s, reform was no longer just optional, but obligatory. Most impressively, the export-driven economic structure of these four neighbors provided the Chinese leadership some valuable insight on how to integrate its comparative advantages so that export, instead of being a vehicle for the state to carry out its decisions, would act as an engine to power the whole economy.

At the outset of the grand reform program, China's foreign trade was handled by only a dozen of national foreign trade corporations (FTCs) and their regional branches. Strictly speaking, they were not real corporations in a modern sense, their existence was simply to fulfill all the plans of the government in an unconditional way. While this kind of arrangement was compatible to the command system of the pre-1978 China, it was by no means constructive if the transition to a market-oriented economy was to be realized. In 1984, i.e. two years after the Ministry of Foreign Trade was renamed the Ministry of Foreign Economic Relations and Trade (MOFERT) through a merger with three other institutions (i.e. the Ministry of Economic Relations with Foreign Countries, the State Import & Export Administration Commission, and the State Foreign Investment Administration Commission), the decentralization process was unveiled. In the beginning, provincial branches of the FTCs were allowed to discontinue their affiliation with the head office in Beijing and establish themselves as a legal entity dealing in import and export (Chang, 2005). Later, the MOFERT also granted permission that enabled some large state-owned manufacturing enterprises to engage in foreign trade directly. Beforehand, they had to rely on the state FTCs as an intermediary to enter into contract with overseas customers. Moreover, China at that time already had many foreign-invested enterprises (FIEs). As a basic policy, they would automatically enjoy the trading rights upon registration. Although imports could only be used to meet their demand for production inputs, and exports were equally limited to their own produce, the relaxation of restrictions on trading rights was undeniable. From the second half of 1979 to 1987, the number of newly-approved FTCs surged to more than 2,200, representing a growth of over eleven times if compared to that of 1979 (Song, 2009).

As one major step toward further liberalization, the State Council in 1984 passed the "Report on the Reform of the Foreign Trade System" submitted by the MOFERT. In an effort to draw a line between government functions and business management, the Ministry would no longer be involved in routine transactions; instead, it would look after the general policies and make sure that regulations were observed in due course. For the FTCs, it implies that instead of being subject to the administrative instructions by the Ministry, they could handle day-to-day trading with a higher level of autonomy. In terms of finance, the report also included some reform plans which were designed to turn the FTCs into independent accounting units.

10.3 Coexistence of Command and Guidance Plans

The process of decentralizing the trading authority was accompanied simultaneously by measures that aimed to reduce the role of mandatory planning, which had covered all spheres of foreign trade before the 1980s. Till 1979, for example, the export plan specified more than 3,000 different commodities that were to be procured for sales abroad; in 1982, the number was reduced to 199 and there were some 100 left on the list by 1984 (Liu, 1998). The same progress was equally achieved with the import plan. Prior to the reform, over 90 PCT of the imports were subject to the direction of the State Planning Commission. In 1984, after the MOFERT's release of the "Interim Regulations of the People's Republic of China on the Licensing System for Import Commodities", imports were classified as restricted and unrestricted. Apart from the

28 categories of restricted imports that required license, the Regulations permitted a group of institutions to import unrestricted products without having to go through the Ministry. These designated institutions included national specialized FTCs and their provincial branches, FTCs affiliated with the ministries under the State Council, and the FTCs run directly by the provincial-level governments.

The decline in trade planning was not only reflected by the loosening of control over commodities, the adoption of a dual-track approach to the management of foreign trade since 1984 should equally be taken as a manifestation of this trend. In addition to the existing command plan ('*zhilingxing jihua*'), a guidance plan ('*zhidaoxing jihua*') was introduced in that year. As the name suggests, the command plan was compulsory and set in quantitative terms. To ensure its fulfillment, the state would allocate necessary inputs to the producers of export items. In the case of import, foreign exchange and subsidies would be prepared also in a timely manner. In contrast, the guidance plan was more flexible. Unlike procurement under mandatory plans whose price was fixed and non-negotiable, guidance plan allowed the price to vary depending on how trading corporations of different localities would meet the value targets. Toward the end of the 1980s, the planning system was shifting gradually to a greater reliance on guidance plans and less on command plans. By 1992, the command plans for both import and export were basically abolished (Pei, 2009). As a result, guidance plans (or market regulation) substituted to a significant extent, with an exception of only some commodities which were deemed crucial to the national economy and thus still monitored by quota-based licenses.

10.4 Losses of FTCs

If taking a look at the performance of China's foreign trade in the first half of the 1980s, the growth had been somewhat impressive. In 1980, its trade volume stood at USD38.14 billion, with export reaching USD18.12 billion in total. Within five years, the trade volume rose by more than 80PCT and hit USD69.6 billion in 1985. As to its export, the rise exceeded 50PCT when claiming USD27.35 billion in 1985. Obviously, these improvements should be attributed to the various measures to decentralize the sector, which had long been monopolized by the MOFERT for three decades (named the Ministry of Foreign Trade before 1982). However, there were still hidden problems which deserve special attention. From a macro perspective, reform in foreign trade was not tuned in line with the reform of other sectors, it had outpaced the rest of the economy. In particular, domestic prices remained under control and this acted as a stumbling block which impeded its efficiency as well as profitability. Over years, in order to preclude competition from the outside, the government had kept domestic market prices substantially below the corresponding world prices. As a result, it was not uncommon to see prices of some basic producer inputs such as coal and timber depressed well below their world level. For industries which were users of these materials, they could benefit a lot from the artificially low prices, thus making them competitive when dealing with their foreign counterparts.

Since this kind of advantage was based on a distorted price mechanism, its impact on import and export could hardly be favorable. For instance, when the FTCs were required to purchase products under the import plan, the prices they had to pay were in accordance with the international market. But once the same goods were to be sold in China at the state fixed prices, which were much lower, losses became unavoidable. On the export side, the situation was not better. Because of the exchange rate of the yuan, revenues of the FTCs could not increase as rapidly as it should have been. In fact, starting from the 1980s, the government had steadily devalued the yuan against the US dollar, from RMB1.7051 of 1981 to RMB2.9367 in 1985. Besides, given the financial burden on exporters due to the rising cost of procurement, an internal rate for trade settlements (IRTS) of RMB2.8 to each US dollar was also introduced in 1981 (abolished on Jan. 1st, 1985). Nevertheless, when judged from the demand for foreign exchange and the need for export subsidies, the yuan was still overvalued. As a consequence, export was equally losing money.

As can be noted from the graph below (Graph 6), direct fiscal subsidies for the FTCs to help cover their losses in 1986 alone were RMB24.96 billion; if to put these losses in the perspective of the nation's export volume for the same year, it accounted for over 23 PCT. In the following years, losses continued to mount and hit its highest in 1989 before starting to fall to RMB17.61 billion in 1991. Behind these stunning figures, the lesson to be learned is that reform is not an isolated undertaking; instead, it should be prepared with a well-ordered blueprint. In this regard, it is critical that China's foreign trade reform be preceded with a comprehensive price reform and changes in the way factors of production are allocated. Unfortunately, for lack of these prerequisites, the cost later paid was rather painful.

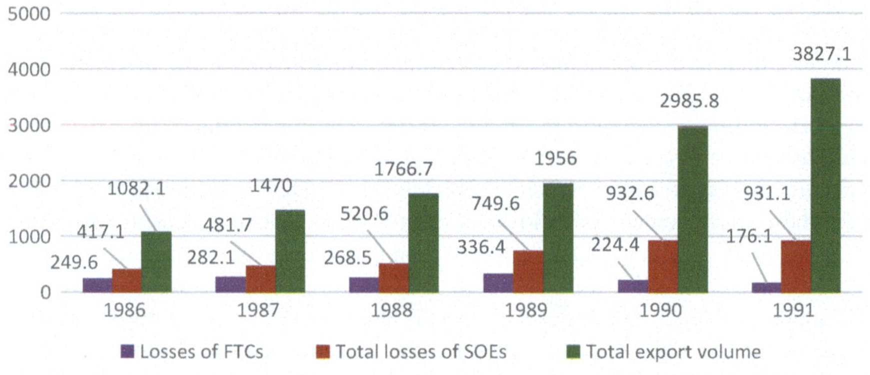

Graph 6 Losses of the FTCs financed by central government budget, RMB100 million. *Source* losses of FTCs and total losses of SOEs: World Bank (1993); total export volume: NBS (2000)

10.5 Implementation of Contract Responsibility System

Confronting the poor sectoral efficiency and the consequential surge in demand for subsidies, the government understood that it could no longer simply use more budget support to tackle the problems. By 1987, the magnitude of the losses incurred in foreign trade, which amounted to RMB28.21 billion, was nearly 60PCT of the total losses of the SOEs (see the graph in the above). The pressure was undeniable and in order to reverse the grim situation, some concrete steps should be taken immediately. In 1988, the State Council released the "Regulations on Several Issues Concerning Accelerating and Deepening the Reform of the Foreign Trade System" and this initiated a new round of reform. By and large, there were two major components in the reform, one was the adoption of foreign trade contract responsibility system and the other was the experiment of greater management autonomy with three chosen sectors; namely, light industrial products, arts and crafts, and garments.

Regarding the contract responsibility system (CRS), it had been firstly introduced on a trial basis in 1987 before its nationwide implementation one year later (Wang, 1990). Based on the system, all the local governments (including those of provincial-level, municipalities directly under the central government, and autonomous regions), specialized national foreign trade corporations, and industrial and trade corporations would enter into a 3-year contract with the central government. In the contract, three major targets were outlined and they were foreign exchange earnings from export; amount of foreign exchange to be surrendered to the central government; and RMB subsidies on export revenues. As to the local branches of the national FTCs, the affiliation was severed and they would fall under the administrative supervision of lower-level governments. Together with this takeover, fiscal subsidies to the export of these former branches would also be linked to the budget of different localities.

Through these arrangements, the motive of the center was rather apparent. On the one hand, the massive expenditure burden could be transferred downward and this helped alleviate the constraints on its own budget. On the other hand, by setting specific targets in the contract, a growing awareness of operational efficiency as well as profitability would be cultivated, which in the long term may transform foreign trade into a financially independent sector that could bring physical contributions to the economy. Besides, as another key element included in the 1988 Regulations to promote the CRS nationwide, three aforementioned industries were selected to conduct a trial which required them to assume full responsibilities for both profits and losses. This implies that they would no longer be subsidized by the government and had to rely on themselves once incurring a negative net income. As a special incentive to encourage these three branches, they were granted a more preferential retention rate of foreign exchange earnings, which was 70 PCT (raised to 80PCT in 1989). At that time, the average retention ratio for exports of other sectors stayed at 50PCT (starting from 1985).

10.6 Correlation Between Export and the Rebate Mechanism

For China, the reform of the external sector is not merely a process of changing its former practices, it is more an endeavor to adapt itself to the international conventions. In Article XVI of GATT 1947, any form of subsidy which operates to increase the export of any product, either primary or non-primary, was limited to given situations because this would cause distortion and unfair competition among the contracting parties. Besides, using subsidies to support export remains a sensitive act that may easily arouse conflicts and undermine the relationship with other trading partners. Apart from these considerations, the mounting state expenditures allocated year on year to cover export losses was already a tremendous pressure on the Chinese government, which should be tackled before the situation turned for the worse.

Export rebate, a kind of refund paid back by tax authorities to exporters for the indirect tax (like sales tax and value-added tax, or VAT) collected beforehand in the production and distribution processes, has been rather common in international trade. According to Article VI of GATT 1994 which centers on anti-dumping and countervailing duties, "no product of the territory of any contracting party imported into the territory of any other contracting party shall be subject to anti-dumping or countervailing duty by reason of the exemption of such product from duties or taxes borne by the like product when destined for consumption in the country of origin or exportation, or by reason of the refund of such duties or taxes". Thus, the exemption of countervailing duties is also a clear confirmation that export rebate should by no means be categorized as subsidies as long as the remission does not exceed the amount of the taxes charged. In 1985, the State Council promulgated the "Notice on Approving and Transmitting the Report of the Ministry of Finance Concerning the Levy and Rebate of the Product Tax and Value-added Tax on Import and Export Commodities". Shortly after that, the export rebate policy went into effect, which was variable according to the sectors and commodities. In 1988, the full rebate principle was introduced (Xu, 1996). As the name suggests, exporters could claim all the input taxes back and obviously, the motive was to encourage them to sell more abroad.

However, with the existence of consolidated industrial & commercial tax ('*gong-shang tongyi shui*'), the problem of overlapping taxes made it difficult to determine how exactly rebate should be computed. In order to better adjust to the changing environment, China carried out the most profound tax reform in 1994, which simplified the tax structure by abolishing both the consolidated industrial and commercial tax and product tax. At the same time, an indirect tax system model was set up, with value-added tax as its basic category, supplemented by consumption tax and business tax (Wang, 1994a,1994b). It was also from then on that VAT became the most important turnover tax covering a much wider scope of products, from agricultural, industrial to daily necessities.

Regarding this new VAT-based tax system, all the Chinese exporters, both domestic and foreign-funded, were subject to its governance. In addition, with the rebate rate set at two basic levels of 13 PCT and 17 PCT respectively, there was also a zero percent rate applicable to certain exports like agricultural products (Li, 1999a,

1999b, 1999c). Therefore, while the nation's VAT revenues soared from RMB108.15 billion of 1993 to RMB230.83 billion in 1994 (NBS, 2001), the country's export rebate also skyrocketed. If compared to 1985 when it was first implemented, there was an increase of over 21 fold, from RMB1.98 billion to about RMB44.8 billion by 1994. Despite this, because of the tight budget, there was still a deferral of RMB30 billion worth of export rebate which could not be paid until the next year (Zhang, 1996a, 1996b). In 1995 when additional rebate claim was added to the bill, the amount that the government was in a position to allocate was just about RMB55 billion, implying that the gap would continue to remain widely open.

For exporters, it means that the more they exported, the more money that was tied up, which caused a big headache concerning the capital turnover. In an effort to ease the mounting fiscal burden, the average actual rebate rate of 16.63 PCT was cut to 12.86 PCT in July 1995, down by 3.77 percentage points. Indeed, the impact was by no means insignificant and the export growth rate, which had registered 44.2 PCT in the first half of the year, quickly fell to 8.8 PCT in the second half (Zhang, 2004a, 2004b). Not long later, the downward trend was further exacerbated by the 1997 Asian financial crisis, which made its export sector among the hardest hit. As a countermeasure, China from January 1998 raised its rebate rates for various products seven times and by July 1999, the average level stood at 15.51 PCT. Fairly speaking, these adjustments were rather effective in that its export grew by 27.8 PCT in 2000, hitting USD249.2 billion.

As a matter of fact, after the 1994 tax reform, export rebate had been shouldered solely by the central government (Liu, 2006) and from Graph 7, it can be noted that the proportion of this particular outlay to the total central expenditure climbed quickly during the next two years and reached 38.47 PCT in 1996. Although there was a steep decline in 1997, the increase in rebate rates over the 1998–1999 period pushed the share upward, which registered 26.8 PCT in 2003. Despite the growth, however, an estimated RMB247.7 billion worth of export rebate remained overdue

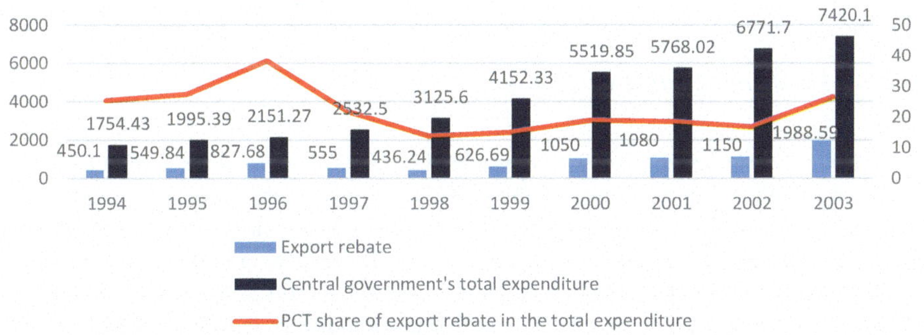

Graph 7 Export rebate versus central government's expenditure, RMB100 million. *Source* export rebate: Ministry of Finance, from https://www.mof.gov.cn/zhuantihuigu/2006ysbgjd/tjsj/200805/t20080519_23380.html; central government's total expenditure: NBS (2005); PCT share of export rebate in the total expenditure: calculated by the author

by the end of 2002 (Zhang, 2004a, 2004b), accounting for 2.36 PCT of the nation's GDP for the same year. Knowing that the limited budget could hardly cope with the mountainous demand for rebate, the State Council in 2003 released the "Decision on the Reform of the Existing Export Rebate Mechanism", which went into effect since 2004. By taking the 2003 export rebate as a benchmark, the amount up to this benchmark would still be borne by the central government. But with regard to any rebates in excess of that benchmark, the local governments had to share 25 PCT of the burden (this ratio was amended to 7.5 PCT in 2005).

Throughout these two decades of implementing the export rebate policy, frequent changes were made to address various economic and fiscal issues. For example, to lift the rates in order to buffer the disruptive impact of the financial crisis; or to trim the rates when found necessary to ease the fiscal pressure. If checking the performance of export that followed these ups and downs, the obvious fact is that it was positively correlated with the rebate rates. In other words, the elasticity of Chinese exports with respect to the rebate rates was statistically significant. As indicated in the above, the 3.77% points of cut that happened in July 1995, which caused the growth of export to plunge, the export elasticity coefficient was as high as 9.39 (Zhang, 2004a, 2004b). Four years later, after a 2.95 PCT of increase in the rebate rates on July 1st, 1999, the originally negative export growth rate of 4.7 PCT during the previous six months was reversed to a positive 15.8 PCT for the rest of the year, and this in turn represented an export elasticity coefficient of 6.95. Indeed, what can be revealed by these numbers is the fact that China's export was somewhat too vulnerable to the movements in rebate rates, which demonstrated a lack of competitiveness and resilience. This is by no means insignificant since once becoming a member of the WTO, China as a developing country had to fulfill multiple commitments and bear the corresponding obligations. In particular, the export sector would be at the forefront to be tested by international standards and rules. If its dependence on government incentives like tax rebate could not be gradually replaced by advantages cultivated from within, then it cannot sustainably fuel the economy as a powerful engine.

10.7 Another Round of Reform

Despite the first-phase promotion of contract responsibility system, which to some degree reduced the dependence of the FTCs on government financial support and increased their awareness of corporate governance, these enterprises were still not fully accountable for their own profits and losses. In other words, if the net revenues turned out to be negative, they could continue to rely on subsidies to offset the imbalances. Moreover, the lack of a uniform standard concerning subsidies and foreign exchange retention ratios resulted in a distorted competitive environment in which some firms could always gain more advantage over others.

For the creation of a level playing field and cultivation of a genuine sense of responsibility that could lead to increased efficiency of the FTCs, the State Council in December 1990 released the "Resolutions on Issues Related to Further Reforming and Improving the Foreign Trade System". As a highlight of the various resolutions, all the FTCs were required to become independent accounting units responsible for their profits and losses. Together with this, the provision of direct financial subsidies for export were to be abolished from January 1st, 1991. Besides, a new and unified foreign exchange retention system was established. No longer based on geographical regions, the division of shares was according to the type of products exported. In general, after remitting 50 PCT of foreign exchange earnings from export to the central government, the remaining half could be distributed among the local governments and the FTCs (Chen, 1991). As compared to the ratio of allocation before 1991, which on average allowed the central government to claim no less than 75 PCT, the rise in permitted retention rates represented a decline in the state monopoly over access to and use of foreign exchange.

10.8 Accession to the WTO

During this period, a major initiative which later brought extensive impact on China's foreign trade as well as the overall economy was undoubtedly the decision to resume its contracting party status to the General Agreement on Tariffs and Trade (GATT), a treaty signed in 1947 to restrict national barriers impeding import, export, and market forces. Considering that China's foreign trade by then had been conducted primarily with GATT nations on the basis of multiple bilateral treaties, membership would enable the country to replace all these agreements with a single and comprehensive GATT accord. Furthermore, by observing the same rules of the game, the bond connecting China and the rest of the world would be further strengthened, which can generate numerous spillover effects in the long run. Additionally, given China's ongoing decentralization of the foreign trade sector, which had long been dominated by the state, resumption of its original status with GATT would exert a push to the reform process. At the same time, the pace of its integration into the international system could also be facilitated, a prerequisite for multilateral cooperation to become truly constructive and fruitful.

It was on July 10th, 1986 that China formally submitted an application for the resumption of its status as a contracting party of GATT. In March 1987, the Working Party on China's status was established by the Council of Representatives under GATT. While being responsible to examine the foreign trade regime of China, the Party was also engaged in the task of drafting a protocol of resumption that would cover both the rights and obligations to be borne by China once the approval was granted. Apart from the first meeting held in that October which made some general arrangements for the upcoming agenda, subsequent meetings centered largely on the review of the Memorandum of China's Foreign Trade Regime, a document lodged not long after China's application. This single task lasted for five full years and till October 1992 when the Party met for the eleventh time, the review was almost completed (Fu, 2002). It was also from then on that China's accession entered into its critical stage of bilateral negotiation over market access.

Nonetheless, due to the failure to conclude these negotiations before the formation of the World Trade Organization (WTO) in 1995, the Working Party on resumption to GATT was converted into the Working Party on China's Accession to the WTO in December, 1995. Afterwards, negotiations with diverse member economies of the WTO proceeded, with China offering a series of new conditions covering not only tariff reduction, but also regulations on the production and distribution activities of foreign companies operating in China. Despite the existence of gaps, progress was still visible. According to the timeline of major agreements China reached with its numerous counterparts, New Zealand was the first western country that concluded talks with China in 1997. About two years later, the most critical Sino-US protocol was reached. Up to May 2000, with the conclusion of EU-China accord, the major obstacles to China's accession to the WTO were virtually removed. On September 13th, 2001, the date when the deal with Mexico was reached, China finalized all the required bilateral negotiations on market access with 37 WTO members.

Back in 1986 when China made up its mind to return to the international trading community, it very likely did not anticipate that the journey would be so long and so tough. By the time the approval of China's entry to the WTO was announced at the fourth WTO Ministerial Conference in Doha on November 10th, 2001, the long march had totally taken the country fifteen years. Nevertheless, considering that China was by then the 143rd member of this big organization, the challenges in dealing with the other 142 parties were enormous. In view of the comprehensive commitment that China had made, which ranged from service trade, foreign direct investment, to the protection of intellectual property rights and market liberalization, etc., not only the foreign trade sector, all the relevant departments of the national economy should be well-prepared to adapt themselves to the new rules, standards and practices. While the reward would be highly attractive, the stake is also unquestionably high.

11 Foreign Direct Investment, a Critical Engine of the Economy

In March 1950, based on the "Treaty of Friendship, Alliance and Mutual Assistance" signed by the Soviet and Chinese governments, the two parties agreed to set up three joint ventures (Dong, 2007). Four months later, Sino-Soviet Civil Airline became the one that was first established (Photo 4). As a 50:50 joint venture, its equity totaled 42 million rubles. Not long later, Sino-Soviet Petroleum Joint Stock Company, Sino-Soviet Non-Ferrous and Rare Metals Company came into being. Both located in Xinjiang Uyghur Autonomous Region, they were the earliest ventures that absorbed foreign investment in the post-1949 China. Unfortunately, due to the emergence of increasing conflicts and the consequential erosion of trust, the seamless cooperation was terminated by the mid-1950s.

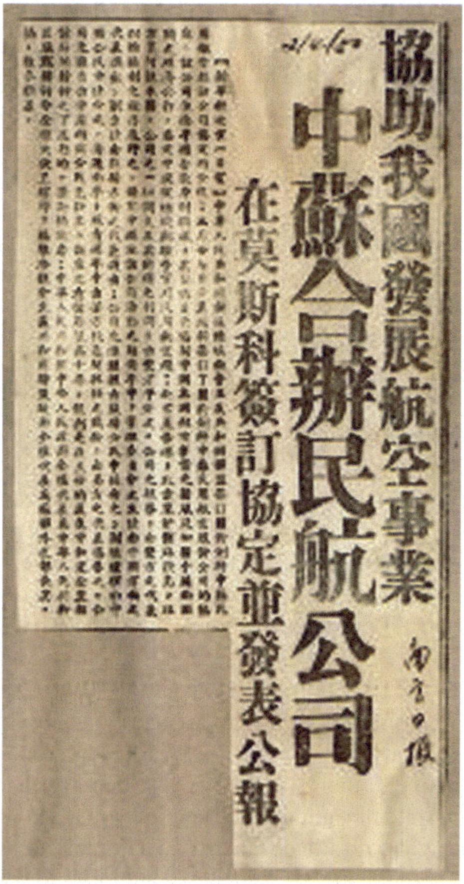
協助我國發展航空事業

中蘇合辦民航公司

在莫斯科簽訂協定並發表公報

Photo 4 News report on the agreement reached between China and the Soviet Union to set up a jointstock airline by the Southern Daily ('Nanfang ribao') on April 2nd, 1950. Named Sino-Soviet Civil Airline, it officially went into operation on July 1st, 1950. *Source* https://www.caac.gov.cn/website/old/D1/60years/jkcy/zsmh/

While these entities failed to stand the test of time, there is yet another foreign-funded company which came into being during the same period but has managed to survive and thrive in today's international market. Also known as Chipolbrok, the establishment of Chinese-Polish Joint Stock Shipping Company was the result of an agreement reached by the two governments in early 1951. When opened to business in June that year, its assets were worth 80 million rubles (equivalent to USD39 million by then, with the business license issued one year after). Right now, after over six decades of expansion, its fleet consisting of 21 multi-purpose vessels (chiefly heavy-lift ships) sail across oceans between Asia, Europe, America and Africa, etc.

11.1 From Closeness to Openness

Ever since the 1950s, China had been isolating itself from the outside world, a policy deliberately designed to lead the country toward a utopia-like ideal called autarky. Under the guidance of this paramount objective, every single industry was striving to be self-sufficient so as to reduce its dependence on imports. If at that time, foreign trade was still occasionally taken as a means to deal with domestic undersupply of food or technological backwardness, the door once open to foreign direct investment was virtually closed. Apart from entering into three more joint shipping companies with Czechoslovakia in 1959, Albania in 1962 and Tanzania in 1967 (Rong, 2012), which were largely out of political considerations, China did not show much interest to be the host country where overseas firms could have a physical presence.

In terms of the reversal of the policy, it did not happen until the late 1970s when the leadership was determined to execute a departure from the centrally-planned economy toward a market-oriented economy. Aware of the hardships in achieving economic parity with the western powers, as well as the inability to overcome all the setbacks on its own, soliciting investment from abroad came up naturally as a pragmatic conduit to channel not only capital, but technological and management resources that were rather scarce in the country. As a rudimentary legal framework to govern the process, the "Law of the People's Republic of China on Joint Ventures Using Chinese and Foreign Investment" (Joint Venture Law) was approved in July 1979 (amended twice in 1990 and 2001 respectively) by the National People's Congress. According to Article Four, foreign participants in general were required to contribute at least 25 PCT to the venture's registered capital. Concerning the ceiling of their stake, however, there was a lack of clear and unequivocal stipulation. Despite the ambiguities and inadequacies with certain provisions, this Joint Venture Law should still be taken as a major institutional undertaking that affirmed the resolution of the highest legislative authority to cooperate with international partners in the development of the economy. Only one month later, two state agencies mandated to administer the capital inflow came into being, and they were the Foreign Investment Commission and the Import–Export Control Commission. While these basic conditions were ready for the country to welcome overseas investors, one more concern remained. For three decades, the link between China and the world had been virtually disconnected, with the exception of Soviet Union and a few Eastern bloc nations. Now that the door would open again, yet nobody had a concrete idea even about how to negotiate with the incoming business partners.

Apparently, instead of a simultaneous invitation of FDI across all regions, it was more sensible to have it initiated in given areas before promoting on a larger scale. In 1980, four special economic zones (or SEZs including Shenzhen, Zhuhai, Shantou, and Xiamen) were officially created in the coastal Guangdong and Fujian Province to absorb foreign investment. By providing favorable tax treatment and other incentives, these four SEZs were by then vividly likened to the windows of China's opening up. Among the early entrants, Chia Tai Group, the largest agricultural company of Thailand, was a pioneer demonstrating strong interest to invest in the mainland market. After two years of preparatory work, it established a 50:50 joint venture with the US-based Continental Grain Company in Shenzhen in 1981. Named Chia Tai Conti Group, the certificate of approval it received from the Shenzhen municipal government bears the number "0001", suggesting that it was the first foreign-funded enterprise in the city.

Of the four special economic zones, Shenzhen took the precedence and resolved to transform itself from an insignificant county whose economy was agriculture-dominated into a modern industrialized city via export processing. Although in early 1979, China had declared to abandon its pre-reform policy of autarky, such a vision was still considered daring at that moment. The endeavor, with its built-in tendency to produce investment opportunities, enabled Shenzhen to quickly outperform its counterparts once the central planners accorded them SEZ status in 1980. In the very beginning of the 1980–1989 decade, the foreign direct investment actually utilized by Shenzhen SEZ had already reached USD27.55 million, way above those of Zhuhai, Shantou and Xiamen (Graph 8). Toward the end of this 10-year period, the gap between them was even larger. Moreover, based on the fact that in 1989, the capital inflow of China through FDI totaled USD3.39 billion, whereas the amount received by the four SEZs alone registered USD635.38 million, or equivalent to almost 19 PCT of the nation's total, it is fair to say that their role in the initial phase of China's openness was rather prominent. On the one hand, for the purpose of developing an export-led economy, they chose FDI as a carrier through which both the management and technological levels could be improved. Simultaneously, they set for the rest of the nation a role model and through their practices and lessons, those non-SEZs could figure out concrete approaches that may equally enable them to reap benefits from FDI.

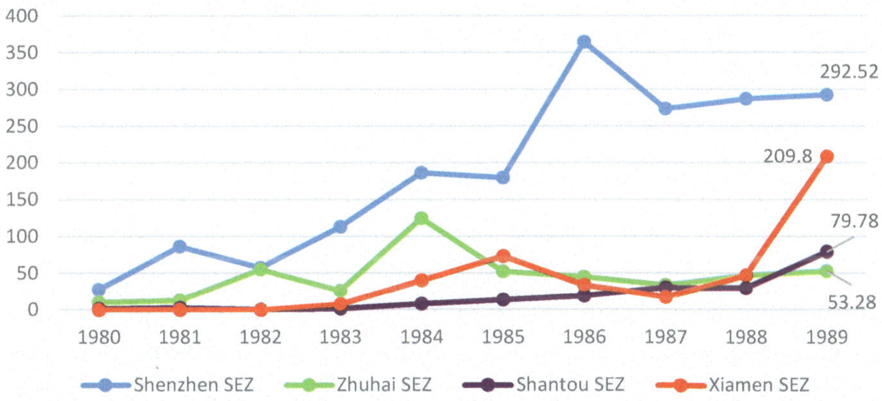

Graph 8 FDI actually used by the four SEZs, USD Million. *Source* FDI of Shenzhen SEZ: Shenzhen Statistical Yearbook 2014, Shenzhen Bureau of Statistics, from https://www.sztj.gov.cn/xxgk/tjsj/tjnj/201503/t20150331_2836397.htm; FDI of Zhuhai SEZ: Zhuhai Statistical Yearbook 2014, Zhuhai Bureau of Statistics, from http://www.stats-zh.gov.cn/tjsj/tjnj/201504/t20150401_204496.htm; FDI of Shantou SEZ: Shantou Statistical Yearbook 2014, Shantou Bureau of Statistics, from http://sttj.shantou.gov.cn/tjsj/tjnj/tjnj2014/; FDI of Xiamen SEZ: Yearbook of Xiamen Special Economic Zone 2014, Xiamen Bureau of Statistics, from http://www.stats-xm.gov.cn/2014/

Table 16 Leading investors of Shenzhen SEZ and their Investment, 1986–1989

Year	Total foreign capital used by Shenzhen SEZ[1] (USD million)	Hong Kong and Macao (USD million)	Japan (USD million)	The US (USD million)	France (USD million)
1986	489.33	385.87	70.09	25.6	4.99
1987	404.49	256.32	92.91	31.01	11.94
1988	444.29	281.98	145.67	2.94	5.01
1989	458.09	287.29	100.04	11.43	33.99

Note [1]includes foreign loans, foreign direct investment, and other foreign investments
Source Shenzhen Statistical Yearbook 2010, Shenzhen Bureau of Statistics. https://www.sztj.gov.cn/xxgk/tjsj/tjnj/201012/t20101224_1620341.htm

Actually, the major reason for Guangdong and Fujian to be designated to host the first batch of China's special economic zones was to a large degree because of their location. Both situated on the east coast and not far away from Hong Kong, which was already a key entreport in Asia–Pacific and notable for its financial services, it was convenient for the two mainland provinces to borrow western ideas and apply them in the development of their local economy. As the famous hometown of a large number of overseas Chinese who have been active in doing business around the world, the preferential policies adopted in the four SEZs would enhance their willingness to catch the opportunity and direct investment to their birthplace. In fact, it didn't take long before the prospect was turned into reality. Of the foreign capital that flowed into Shenzhen SEZ from 1986 to 1989, the biggest chunk was without exception from Hong Kong and Macao, which on average accounted for over 65PCT of the total (Table 16). Similarly, with regard to the source of direct foreign capital absorbed by Zhuhai, Shantou, and Xiamen SEZs, it was still Hong Kong and Macao which contributed the lion's share.

11.2 Enlargement of the "Laboratories"

Although the absorption of FDI at this stage was not limited to the four SEZs, since the autonomy granted to Guangdong and Fujian provinces in approving projects and setting policies was not equally available elsewhere, special economic zones had virtually played the role of a "laboratory" testing what changes could be realized via the inflow of foreign capital. A couple of years after the establishment of Shenzhen, Zhuhai, Shantou, and Xiamen SEZs, the spillover effect exerted by the FDI growth began to be magnified. Together with the giant leaps of GDP, the surge in export was even more dynamic, which greatly enhanced their economic vibrancy.

11.2.1 Opening of 14 Port Cities and the 5th SEZ

As a result of the encouraging experiment, the State Council in May 1984 approved the "Summary of a Forum Attended by Participants from Some Coastal Cities", which recommended the opening of fourteen coastal cities. Although not named SEZs, the authority they could enjoy concerning the approval of FDI projects was equally expanded. In case the ventures were technology-intensive or export-oriented, preferential tax rates would be offered, like a reduced 15 PCT corporate income tax or exemption of import tariffs, etc.

With regard to the largest SEZ, it should be Hainan Island in the southernmost part of China. In 1988, by separating from the jurisdiction of Guangdong Province as its administrative region, it simultaneously became the youngest province as well as the fifth special economic zone ready to embrace foreign investors (He, 2013). At the initial stage, the level of its FDI did not have significant change and stood at the USD100 million mark (Graph 9). But since the early 1990s, it has begun to rise quickly, hitting USD1.06 billion in 1995, which was also the peak of the 10-year period. If compared to its performance of export during the same decade, there appeared a similar pattern of growth. By no means just a coincidence, this picture is a proof of the causal relationship between inward FDI and export.

Of the foreign-invested enterprises established in China during the 1980s, most of them were joint ventures in which the Chinese side held a majority stake. This phenomenon is rather normal since during the initial stage of introducing FDI, both the host country and overseas investors were somewhat cautious; unfamiliar with each other's norms and practices, joint-venture arrangement was a good option that enabled them to test the water before diving in with greater commitment. At the same time, wholly foreign-owned enterprises (WFOEs), another form of business entity that is rather common in today's China, began to emerge. Although not comparable in numbers, they represented the demand of some investors to exercise complete control

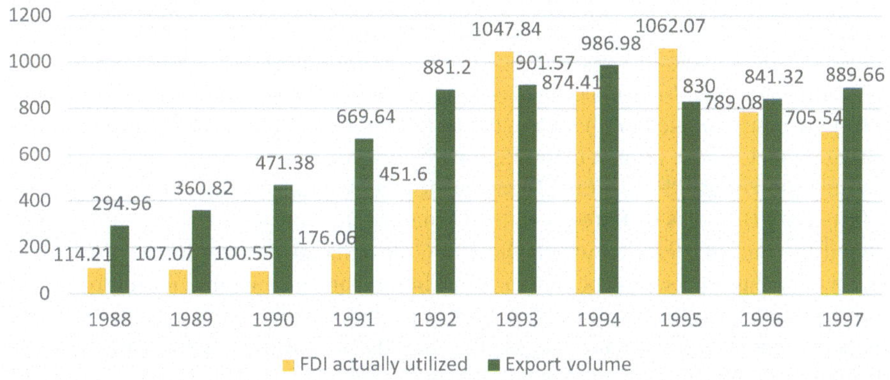

Graph 9 FDI actually utilized by Hainan SEZ and its export, USD Million. *Source* Hainan Statistical Yearbook 1998, from https://www.hnszw.org.cn/data/news/2012/09/54459/

over their operations in this booming market. Sanyo Electric, a Japanese electronics company, was the earliest to set up its wholly-owned subsidiary in Shenzhen in 1983 (Chen, 1984a, 1984b). About one year later when 3 M China Ltd. was registered in Shanghai in November 1984 by its US-based parent company 3 M (originally known as the Minnesota Mining and Manufacturing Company), it became the first WFOE outside the country's SEZs (Jia, 2012). However, even despite the passage of the "Wholly Foreign Owned Enterprise Law of the People's Republic of China" in 1986, which to some degree clarified the institutional uncertainties that had deterred the establishment of WFOEs, it was until the late 1990s that their proportion started to exceed joint ventures (Zhang, 2006).

11.2.2 Pudong, an Emerging Financial Hub

If by far, the vast majority of the FDI projects which had been approved were related to export-oriented manufacturing activities, it was after the decision of the State Council in 1990 to speed up the development and opening of Shanghai Pudong (a district located on the east bank of the Huangpu River) that boosted investment in the financial sector. Known later as the Pudong New Area, it bears certain characteristics of a special economic zone in that preferential treatments were also offered to foreign-funded enterprises engaged in export, such as income tax concessions and exemption of tariffs, etc. Moreover, considering that Shanghai had already been the financial hub of the Far East during the 1930s, it would be impossible for the city to reclaim its status if without the physical presence of the world's leading banks and insurance companies, the PBoC in 1990 released the "Measures on the Administration of Foreign-invested Financial Institutions and Chinese-foreign Equity Joint Financial Institutions in Shanghai Municipality". By stipulating clearly that foreign financial institutions could engage in branch operations in Shanghai, the Central Bank's provisions quickly aroused the interest of multiple qualified investors.

In 1992, American International Assurance Company (AIA), a subsidiary of the New York-based AIG (American International Group) by then, set up its Shanghai branch in Pudong and this opened the door for foreign insurance companies to enter the Chinese market. In terms of the banking sector, by 1995, among the 29 branches of foreign banks located in Shanghai, the Fuji Bank from Japan took the leadership in setting up its Chinese branch in the Pudong New Area (Hong, 2005). Inspired by the promulgation of the "Provisional Measures for the Administration of Pilot Operation of Renminbi Business by Foreign-funded Financial Institutions in Shanghai Pudong" toward the end of 1996, in which the PBoC designated Pudong as the only place where overseas banks could conduct Renminbi business in China, more prominent industry leaders followed suit and moved into this freshly-emerged economic and financial center, like the Citibank, HSBC, Standard Chartered Bank, and the Bank of Tokyo-Mitsubishi, to name but a few (Mei, 1998).

By the end of 1999, the number of foreign banks in Pudong New Area reached 42, with 19 of them obtaining the license to handle Chinese-currency business (Zhang, 2000). As a result of Pudong's favorable investment climate for overseas banking institutions, Shanghai became the immediate beneficiary. One year later, the total assets of foreign-funded banks in Shanghai reached USD18.1 billion, accounting for over 52 PCT of that of the country's total, which registered USD34.6 billion (Fang, Li, & Zhang, 2009).

11.2.3 Formation of ETDZs and BECZs

Generally speaking, following the establishment of special economic zones alongside the east coast, China's opening of its interior and border regions to FDI mainly takes two forms, one is economic and technological development zones (ETDZs), and the other is border economic cooperation zones (BECZs). With regard to the former, the first batch of 14 national ETDZs was approved by the State Council during 1984–1988 and both of them were based in the 12 newly-opened coastal cities, i.e. Dalian, Qinhuangdao, Tianjin, Yantai, Qingdao, Nantong, Lianyungang, Shanghai, Ningbo, Fuzhou, Guangzhou, and Zhanjiang (Chen, 2000). Since the 1990s, their pace of expansion has been accelerating quickly, with more of them situated in inland cities such as Shenyang, Ha'erbin, Beijing, Wuhu, Wuhan, Chongqing, and Urumqi, etc. Till 2012, the number of national ETDZs in the central and western part of the country for the first time exceeded 50PCT of the total, hitting 87 (Table 17). In terms of the foreign capital that flowed into these regions, however, Eastern China still enjoyed a much greater advantage. In that single year, it totally attracted almost USD38.14 billion, which was more than three times the sum absorbed by the other two. Although the gap began to narrow down gradually in 2013 and 2014, the overall landscape remained fundamentally the same.

Referring to the BECZs, like the name suggests, they were set up chiefly in border areas so as to boost the local economy through closer cooperation with the neighboring countries. Since the primary motive was to favor the ethnic minorities, the initial batch of 14 BECZs which gained the green light of the central government in 1992–1993 was without exception found in provinces populated by

Table 17 FDI actually utilized by the 171 National ETDZs in 2012

	84 National ETDZs in Eastern China	49 National ETDZs in Central China	38 National ETDZs in Western China
Number of Newly-Approved Foreign-Funded Enterprises	3,145	272	74
Actually Utilized FDI (USD100 Million)	381.36	93.8	31.4
Accumulated Amount of FDI Actually Used (USD100 Million)	4,069.92	628.97	174.47

Source MOC (2014)

these groups, including Heilongjiang, Jilin, Inner Mongolia Autonomous Region, Liaoning, Xinjiang Uighur Autonomous Region, Yunnan, and Guangxi Zhuang Autonomous Region, etc. (Zhou & Hang, 2011). Take Dandong BECZ of the South-eastern Liaoning Province as an example, due to its geographical proximity to Japan and South Korea, as well as the possession of an ice-free deep-water seaport, the introduction of FDI has been rather prominent if compared to the other counterparts. In 1993, i.e. the first year after its operation, inbound investment was USD7.58 million; when celebrating the 20th anniversary in 2012, the volume registered USD480 million, representing an average year-on-year growth rate of 24.3 PCT (MOC, 2012).

11.2.4 Tertiary Sector: The Ice Broken

Together with the geographical expansion of areas hosting FDI, restrictions against foreign participation in sensitive sectors such as retail and tourism also began to show signs of relaxation after the 1990s. In July 1992, 6 cities including Beijing, Shanghai, Tianjin, Guangzhou, Dalian and Qingdao plus the 5 SEZs were selected by the State Council to experiment with Sino-foreign equity joint ventures or cooperative joint ventures in the retail business (Yu, 1997). Although wholly foreign-owned subsidiaries were not yet allowed, this move marked one step further in the fulfillment of China's commitment to the WTO to open its tertiary industry to foreign investors. In the same year, a Japanese retail group named Yaohan International received the first license to enter into a joint venture with Shanghai No. 1 Department Store in Pudong New Area. On December 20th of 1995, when the No. 1 Yaohan Department Store was officially opened, 1.07 million people entered the shopping mall simultaneously, which set the record of the largest crowd gathering in a single department store within a short amount of time (Chen, 2008). Within the first year of its operation, the sales revenues exceeded RMB600 million. Besides, other retail entities that were established during the same period included Beijing Lufthansa Friendship Shopping Mall, Shanghai Orient Shopping Center, Walmart Supercenter and Sam's Club in Shenzhen, and Qingdao No. 1 Parkson Company, etc.

Regarding another important segment of the tertiary sector opened to foreign investors in the 1990s, it was tourism. While approving 12 national holiday resorts in 1992, the State Council encouraged joint venture operations in diverse activities, from tourist car to cruise companies, etc. In 1998, a Sino-Swiss travel agency was given the permission to set up its presence in Kunming Dianchi National Tourist Resort of Yunnan Province (Wang & Liu, 2000). Prior to China's accession to the WTO, there were totally 11 joint venture tourist companies which had gained the license to run their business, with investors coming from Japan, France, the US, and Singapore, etc. Without exception, their majority shares were all controlled by the domestic firms (Chen, 2002).

12 Evolution of Outward-Looking Policies

Undoubtedly, China's policy of opening up should be considered as the central aspect of its entire reform program. To a large extent, it is via this initiative that has enabled the country to become better aware of its gap with the outside world. As a matter of fact, after decades of self-imposed isolation, the trade/GDP ratio was below 10 PCT by the time it was determined to discard the obsolete ideology and reunite itself with the global community in 1978. Regarding the pre-1978 period, except for the occasional borrowings from the former Soviet Union, China since 1965 had remained in a state of zero external debt (Gao, 1994). Ironically, despite the chronic shortage of funds, such a record was once even taken as something to be proud of. Moreover, because of the rigid allegiance to the ideology of staying independent, foreign companies were simply non-existent, nor was it a member of the major public lenders like the World Bank and the IMF, etc. Nonetheless, as China set its target of transition and modernization after the end of the Cultural Revolution, the policy of opening-up was naturally given a priority in the overall agenda. For the purpose of reviving the underdeveloped economy, external support in the forms of capital, technology, equipment, and human resources, etc. was once again treated as necessary and indispensable. In terms of its first step to the utilization of overseas capital, it happened in 1979 when the Japanese government offered China an official development assistance (ODA) loan worth JPY50 billion (equivalent to around RMB330 million or USD220 million based on the exchange rate at that time) over a term of 30 years (Wang, 2013a, 2013b). Later, it turned out that such an outward-looking policy went through an evolutionary process; in other words, the door was opened up via a number of stages.

12.1 Phase One: 1979–1986

As a matter of fact, even when formulating its strategy of opening up, China did not borrow any idea from foreign experts; instead, they were largely derived from hot internal debates between the pro- and anti-reform camps. Although the former finally got their proposition passed, for lack of experience, the agenda in the beginning was a rather experimental one, it is something that had to be tested and tried. If counting the first phase of opening up, it should be the 1979–1986 period. Apart from witnessing more cross-border exchanges in goods, services, and capital, etc., China in 1980 resumed its membership status at the IMF and the World Bank (Dai, 1980), and started negotiations for the re-entry of the GATT in 1986. Regarded as another critical move, special economic zones (SEZs) were established in 1980 in the four coastal cities of Guangdong and Fujian provinces. Authorized to grant special treatments (like tax holidays, autonomy in management, repatriation of earnings, and land-use incentives, etc.) to foreign investors, plus the coincidence that they were equally the homeland to many overseas Chinese, rapid increase in inbound FDI greatly powered their economic development. With a view to enabling other parts of China to benefit from the spillover effect, similar policies were further extended to 14 coastal cities in 1984, and to the Yangtze River Delta, the Pearl River Delta, and the Minnan delta region in southern Fujian in 1985 (Su, 1988). Subsequently, foreign banks were licensed to open offices in the SEZs as well as in the coastal cities, although not yet permitted to run RMB business.

Besides, China prior to 1980 had no more than 15 national foreign trade corporations (FTCs, excluding their regional branches) which enjoyed the privilege to conduct export and import. Therefore, they were considered as the sole dealers representing the whole country to transact with the rest of the world. Later on, when industrial ministries and provincial-level governments could also establish their own FTCs, state monopoly was gradually broken. By 1984, the number of trading corporations had increased dramatically to over 1,000 (Zhang, 1998). Referring to the absorption of foreign investments, despite the nationwide thirst for capital, China chose to begin with some selected provinces to observe the effects before heading onward, a style which was not uncommon in the reform of the following decades. From the four special economic zones to the three aforementioned delta regions, it is fair to say that China's openness till the mid-1980s was predominantly limited to the areas alongside the east coast. From 1983 to 1986, in particular, the lion's share of foreign investments remained in the east part (Graph 10). Although there was a steady growth in the proportion claimed by central and western China, their weight in the country's total stayed at a level that could hardly pose a challenge to the east.

Normally, with an increase in both export and FDI, a country's foreign exchange reserves should also rise. Indeed, such a causal effect did happen in China over the 1979–1983 period, during which its foreign exchange reserves surged from USD840 million to USD8.9 billion (NBS, 2001). Quite unexpectedly, however, there was a steep decline in the next few years and by 1986, the country only had USD2.07 billion in its deposits. Behind the sharp contraction, the dominant reasons were the over rapid expansion of both the domestic fixed-asset investment and credit, which led to massive spending on imports to meet the soaring demand. As a consequence, while foreign exchange reserves underwent a rapid shrinkage, trade surplus soon

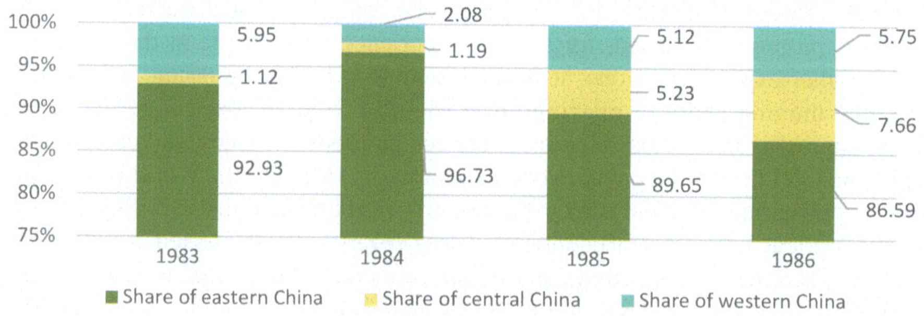

Graph 10 Distribution of FDI and other foreign investments in three areas, PCT. *Source* Wei (2001)

turned into a deficit and from 1984, the negative balance remained unchanged until the end of the 1980s. Not unaware of the widening trade imbalance and worried about the weakened ability to pay, a notice was released in 1985 by the State Council calling for strict quota control on the regional use of their own foreign exchange to import. Ironically, based on the fact that China's import continued with its upward spiral cycle for the rest of the 1980s, the effect turned out to be rather limited.

12.2 Phase Two: 1992–1999

From the end 1980s to the early 1990s, the Chinese government had to introduce various austerity measures in order to cool down the overheated economy. Although these measures did not cover the external sectors like trade and investment, the MOFTEC was still determined to carry out a thorough overhaul of all the domestic FTCs in 1988 and the purpose was to close down the unqualified players (Zhang, 1989). This should be considered a necessary step since by then, due to the vicious competition among the growing number of trading firms, the terms of trade had been worsening since the mid-1980s. Terms of trade (TOT), the ratio of export price index to import price index, is a key measure of the gains from trade. Usually, an improvement in TOT implies that for every unit of export sold by a country, it is in a position to purchase more units of imports. Moreover, since import prices are falling, it could also help ease domestic cost-push inflation. On the other hand, the effect would just be the opposite in case of a deterioration in TOT. As a major form of TOT, net barter terms of trade (NBTT) is often used to demonstrate how the situation goes. Throughout the 1981–1990 decade, the TOT of China experienced two types of shifts (Table 18), with the first half turning in general for the better. However, a notable decrease dominated the scene from 1986, which was caused chiefly by the fall in export price index and rise in import index. If looking at the performance after 1990, there emerged an impressive recovery which brought the terms of trade almost

Table 18 Shifts in the general net barter terms of trade, 1981–1993

Year	Export price index	Import price index	Net barter terms of trade
1981	145	117.5	123.4
1983	135.7	109.7	123.7
1985	75.7	50.8	149
1987	69	49.6	139.2
1989	73.9	63.2	117
1991	76.3	60.3	126.6
1993	68	46.8	145.2

Source Kong & Sun (2007)

back to the 1985 level. At least partially, it is the overhaul which made the positive turn take place.

In 1992, following the famous south China tour of Deng Xiaoping, as well as the reported achievements of the coastal cities, a new wave of external liberalization began. With the opening up of more regions to foreign investment, ownership requirements for FDI were also relaxed. Encouraged by the loosening policies, the wholly foreign-owned subsidiaries that were set up in 1997 outnumbered for the first time the joint ventures established in the same year, with the former totaled 9,604 and the latter 9,046 (Sang & Li, 2006). In addition, the government began to allow FDI on a trial basis in certain service sectors like retail trade, insurance, transport, and civil aviation, etc. With a view to exploring more channels to attract foreign capital, the B-share market was launched in 1992 in both the Shanghai and Shenzhen Stock Exchanges (Lü, 1995). Through this arrangement, domestic companies could issue shares denominated in foreign currencies and therefore, non-resident investors were given an opportunity to buy these shares. Besides, one more significant move toward the liberalization of FDI was that in 1998, foreign investment was allowed to participate in the restructuring of the SOEs through equity purchase or capital injection (Based on the "Interim Regulations on Restructuring State-owned Enterprises with Foreign Investment" issued by the State Economic and Trade Commission).

Additionally, to boost the confidence of foreign investors and reaffirm China's commitment to a socialist market economy, one more important document reflecting its FDI policy during the 1990s should be the "Amendment to the Constitution of the People's Republic of China" (ratified on March 29th, 1993). If compared to the previous editions, what remained unchanged was Article No. 18 which claimed that "lawful rights and interests of all foreign enterprises, other foreign economic organizations as well as Chinese-foreign joint ventures within the Chinese territory are protected by the laws of the People's Republic of China". Although this article was not a newly added one, having it reiterated marked a continuity of the state policy in dealing with foreign investment. As a result of all these measures, foreign capital that flowed into China increased at a robust pace. Over the two-decade period from 1979 to 1999, the value of FDI actually used hit USD306 billion, accounting for 10PCT of the world's total and 30PCT of that of the emerging economies (Chen, 2001).

References

An, G. J., & Gu, S. G. (2008). A review of 30 years of China's bond market. *The Banker, 10,* 20–23.

Anonym. (2013). Revelant situation on national local business tax revenues from 1994 to 2011. *Local Finance Research, 5,* F0003.

Ba, S. S. (1999). Evolution of China's foreign exchange market: theory and policy development. *International Trade Issues, 3,* 30–36.

Ba, S. S., et al. (2005). The best path for urban commercial banks to reform: Shanghai Bank's foreign investment model & Zheshang Bank's equity diversification model. *New Fortune, 11,* 106–123.

Ba, S. S. (2006). Foreign investment in China's banking industry: debate over how to go beyond the bargain sale and differences. *Financial Economics Research, 2,* 7–11.
Bai, X. Y. (2008). The history and logic of RMB exchange rate system reform. *World Economic Research, 12,* 29–34.
Bai, Y. F., & Wu, Z. F. (2010). Research on the sharing proportion of central and local value-added tax. *Finance and Trade Economics, 3,* 39–46.
Cao, Y. Z., et al. (1999). From federalism, Chinese style to privatization, Chinese style. *Economics and Transition, 1,* 103–131.
Cao, Y. (2005). An empirical study of the impact of international capital flows on China's monetary policy. *Journal of Zhongnan University of Economics and Law, 5,* 86–91.
Chang, W. J. (2005). Principles of national treatment and qualifications for foreign trade management: thinking on the new Foreign Trade Law's expansion of the scope of foreign trade operators. *International Trade Issues, 11,* 26–28.
Chen, Q. G. (1984a). Historical evolution of RMB exchange rate and the direction of reform. *Financial Research, 12,* 19–21.
Chen, Y. H. (1984b). Sanyo Electric (Shekou) Co., Ltd., Japan's first wholly-owned enterprise established in China. *International Trade, 4,* 61.
Chen, B. H. (1988). Foreign exchange sharing and retention. *Zhejiang Finance, 6,* 64.
Chen, B. R. (1989a). A preliminary study on the reform of RMB exchange rate. *International Finance Research, 10,* 4–6.
Chen, Y. (1989b). On negotiation between government and enterprise: also on the contracting system. *Economist, 4,* 66–73.
Chen, Y. (Ed.). (1990). *China financial yearbook 1990.* Beijing: China Financial Yearbook Editorial Department.
Chen, Z. H. (1991). Some thoughts on further liberalizing foreign exchange swap market. *International Trade Issues, 12,* 41–44.
Chen, X. H. (1996). The current situation and main problems of state-owned enterprises. *Economic Research Reference, 58,* 144–149.
Chen, J. X. [陈江旭]. (1997a). Several issues concerning China's realization of RMB convertibility under current account. *Policy, 2,* 46–47.
Chen, X. H. (1997b). The significance of developing China's unified interbank lending market. *Wuhan Finance, 1,* 47.
Chen, W. H. (1999). Speeding up the establishment of a modern enterprise system and promoting the reform and development of state-owned enterprises. *Productivity Research, 6,* 111–113.
Chen, Y. S. (2000). Development of economic and technological development zones in China. *Science and Technology Management Research, 6,* 1–4.
Chen, M. (2001). Effectiveness analysis of China's introduction of foreign direct investment. *Guangdong Economy, 3,* 93–103.
Chen, Q. L. (2002). Research on the problems and countermeasures of the joint operation and development of China's travel agency industry after its WTO entry. *Journal of Huaqiao University (Philosophy and Social Sciences Edition), 4,* 19–26.
Chen, X. S. (2006). A comparative analysis of the two national debt repurchase markets between exchanges and banks. *China Securities Futures, 5,* 66–68.
Chen, H. (2007). Unrest of the Shenzhen stock exchange. *City of Coconut, 7,* 39.
Chen, C. F. (2008). Double cherishing "No. 1". *Shanghai Department Store, 22,* 33.
Chen, C. (2012). Research on the transformation of financial asset management companies: international experience and China's current situation. *Reform and Strategy, 11,* 83–86.
Cheng, S. S., & Jin, Z. J. (2011). Observing inflation from the three currency system changes during the Republic of China period. *Journal of Jiangxi University of Finance and Economics, 4,* 80–85.
Chen, Y. N., & Liu, C. Y. (2012). IFC's role in China's financial sector reform. International Finance Corporation. Retrieved October 14, 2016, from https://www.ifc.org/wps/wcm/connect/aba1b70040667532a557b782455ae521/China%20FM%20Evaluation.pdf?MOD=AJPERES.

Chu, X. Y. (1994). Observation and reflection on China's use of foreign direct investment. *Finance and Trade Economics, 3,* 52–55.
Dai, Q. D. (1980). International Monetary Fund and the World Bank. *Financial Research, 1,* 62–63.
Deng, S. L. (2014). Equity analysis of the development of state-owned enterprises. *Southern Economy, 1,* 98–108.
Ding, Y. P. (2007). The 1921 "financial unrest" due to the excess of trust companies and stock exchanges and the modern Shanghai stock market. *Journal of Qinzhou University, 2,* 108–111.
Dong, Z. K. (2007). Sino-foreign joint ventures in the early days of the P.R.C. *China Investment, 11,* 121–123.
Du, Q., & Wang, Y. (1996). Cause analysis of international liquid capital getting mixed with current account settlement and sale of foreign exchange. *International Market, 11,* 3–4.
Ebeling, R. M. (2004). The great Chinese inflation. *the Freeman, 12,* 2–3.
Fang, H., et al. (2009). Research on the influencing factors of FDI utilization in China's financial industry: theory and empirical studies. *Research on Financial Problems, 2,* 67–72.
Feng, D. (2008). The little-known Sino-Japanese financial war. *Literature on Party History, 3,* 47–49.
Fu, S. H. (2002). China's WTO accession: a retrospect of 15 years' history. *Hubei Finance and Taxation, 6,* 18.
Gao, Z. R. (1994). Development trend and strategy of China's external debt. *Economic Research Reference, 3,* 28–42.
Gao, X. W. (2007). Research on the government restraint mechanism under the tax sharing system. *Journal of Liaoning Taxation College, 6,* 21–23.
Gao, X. L., & Chi, W. (2008). Review of the national economic construction public debt from 1954 to 1958. *Research on Contemporary Chinese History, 5,* 41–47.
Gong, X. P. (Ed.). (1999). *Shanghai yearbook 1999*. Shanghai: Shanghai Yearbook Press.
China Government *Securities* Depository Trust & Clearing Co., Ltd. (CGSDTC). (1998). An overview of the inter-bank bond market in 1997. Retrieved October 26, 2016, from https://www.chinabond.com.cn/Info/920520.
Guan, T. (1994). A probe into China's foreign exchange market. *New Finance, 9,* 19–22.
Gui, H. F. (2003). China's bond market: development, opening up and main issues. *International Finance Research, 9,* 62–67.
Gu, M. D., & Wu, P. X. (2008). SHIBOR revolution and its economic significance. *Shanghai Finance, 7,* 5–9.
He, Y. (2013). Stories in the photo: commemorating the 25th anniversary of the establishment of Hainan provincial special economic zone. *Hainan Today, 5,* 10–14.
Hong, J. G. (2005). *Shanghai general annals* (Vol. 25). Shanghai: Shanghai People's Publishing House, Shanghai Academy of Social Sciences Press.
Hou, T., & Xiang, Y. (2014). Analysis of investment strategy for policy financial bonds. *Northern Economy and Trade, 9,* 182.
Hu, J. (1987). Shanghai's financial market develops rapidly. *China Finance, 7,* 21.
Hu, X. K. (2000). Corporate governance structure theory in enterprise reform. *Law Application, 2,* 4–7.
Hu, A. G. (2004). Black hole of corruption: public disclosure of economic losses of various types of corruption. *Democracy and Science, 4,* 15–18.
Hu, M. (2008). History and enlightenment of the development of township and village enterprises in China since the reform and opening up: taking TVEs of Jiangsu province from 1978 to 1992 as an example. *Party Literature, 4,* 24–29.
Huang, X. (1993). Analysis of exchange rates at China's foreign exchange black market. *International Finance Research, 5,* 36–39.
Huang, J. X. (1996). A brief discussion of the realistic effect on the implementation of foreign exchange settlement system in banks by foreign-funded enterprises. *Finance and Economics, 7,* 44–45.

Huang, Z. W. (2002). The Chinese banking industry surpassing the first threshold of the WTO accession. *Discovery, 4,* 59–60.
Ji, C. H. (1996). Realizing RMB current account convertibility and its impact. *China Foreign Trade, 11,* 8.
Jia, C. Y. (2012). 3M takes root in China's three "treasures." *Electrical Appliance Industry, 11,* 52–53.
Jiang, Y. (1992). Ideas for accelerating the reform of enterprise shareholding system in Liaoning province. *Journal of Liaoning University (Philosophy and Social Sciences Edition), 4,* 34–36.
Jin, X. J. (1989). Several views on the adjustment of RMB exchange rate. *International Finance Research, 12,* 18–20.
Jin, Y. F. (1991). Several thoughts on treasury bills underwriting in 1991. *New Finance, 10,* 18–19.
Jin, T. (1999). The earliest commercial law in China. *China Business, 1,* 73.
Ju, J. W. (2006). Historical transformation of China's national capital during the transition period. *Academic Monthly, 8,* 127–130.
Kong, Q. F., & Sun, X. L. (2007). Reasons for the decline of China's terms of trade and countermeasures. *International Trade Issues, 10,* 23–29.
Li, Q. X. (1994). Introduction of several main tax types in the new tax system. *Shaanxi Water Resources, 5,* 17–18.
Li, C. A. [李长爱]. (1999a). Calculation and accounting of VAT-based export rebate. *Hubei Finance and Taxation, 11,* 31–32.
Li, J. Z. (1999b). Evil case of inflation in old China: a probe into the inside story of gold yuan notes issuance. *Studies in Chinese Social and Economic History, 1,* 72–79.
Li, X. D. (1999c). Impact of foreign banks operating RMB business on China's banking industry and countermeasures. *Times Finance, 6,* 15–17.
Li, H. (2001). Problems in the development of Chinese enterprise groups. *Chemical Industry Management, 12,* 29.
Li, X. F. (2012). Exploration of the independence of Chinese credit rating agencies: with the construction of Shanghai international financial center as the background. *Tianjin Law, 3,* 70–75.
Li, Y. (2013). The first stock market unrest in the late Qing dynasty. *Shanxi Youth, 5,* 72–73.
Li, X. P., & Bo, G. H. (2002). Research on the current situation, contribution and external conditions of the development of private economy. *Economics and Management, 11,* 33–34.
Li, T. T., & Ding, W. (2014). On the relationship between government and business in the government-supervised and merchant-managed model during the Westernization movement. *Historical Records of Heilongjiang, 11,* 243.
Liu, X. L. (1993). Causes and countermeasures of weak interest rate leverage. *Southwest Finance, 9,* 16–17.
Liu, Z. Y. (1998). China's foreign trade: development trends, institutional changes and reform orientation. *Teaching and Research, 4,* 5–13.
Liu, Q. (2001). Some inspirations from Shenzhen-based foreign banks operating RMB business. *Practice and Theory of the Special Economic Zone, 4,* 30–33.
Liu, J. Y. (2006). Ideas to further improve China's export rebate mechanism. *Journal of xi'an University of Finance and Economics, 3,* 75–78.
Liu, Y. C. (2007). Analysis of China's balance of payments errors and omissions. *Sunan Science and Technology Development, 7,* 53–55.
Liu, K. G. (2009). Reform of China's fiscal and taxation system before and after 1994. *Historical Data of the CPC, 4,* 4–24.
Liu, D. (2012). Research on the current situation of China's national debt repurchase market. *Financial and Economic Monthly, 3,* 60–62.
Liu, Y. G., & Li, Y. (2013). Treasury futures relisted after 18 years of suspension. *China Economic Weekly, 36,* 57–59.
Liu, Y., & Wang, F. B. (1997). Analysis of the effect of open market operations in China and countermeasures. *Financial Theory and Practice, 12,* 9–12.

Liu, K. Q., & Zhang, F. X. (1994). Open market business: a major reform of the central bank to regulate currency circulation. *Outlook Weekly, 14,* 10–11.

Long, G. Q. (1994). The role of exchange rate unification in foreign trade. *Civilization and Propaganda, 7,* 42–43.

Lü, P. (1995). Shaking off embarrassment and breaking a new path: review and prospect of B shares. *Chinese Market, 2,* 28–30.

Lu, H. Y. (1998). Ten effects of China's tax-sharing taxation system reform. *Economics Trends, 12,* 15–18.

Lü, F. T., & Song, Y. H. (1983). International bonds and introduciton of foreign investment. *World Economy, 7,* 20–25.

Ma, Q. L. (1996). New tax system after reform. *Decision-Making Consultation, 3,* 76–79.

Ma, J. Y. (2009). 60 Years of tremendous economic changes with capital market becoming a powerful engine. *China Securities Journal*. Retrieved November 10, 2016, from https://www.cnstock.com/paper_new/images/2009-09/16/12530372673875952495677720605.pdf.

Mao, Y. B. (1996). China's money supply statistics and financial control. *Exploration of Economic Problems, 11,* 34–35.

Mei, D. P. (1998). Contemplation on the issue of foreign banks operating RMB business. *Hubei Rural Finance Research, 11,* 41–43.

Miao, K. H. (2011). An analysis of the development stage of the history of Chinese credit notes. *Journal of Guizhou University of Finance and Economics, 3,* 76–81.

Mo, T. S. (1994). The main content of China's tax reform. *Open Herald, 5,* 61–64.

MOC. (2012). Dandong border economic cooperation zone: bridgehead of trade with North Korea. Retrieved November 12, 2016, from https://ezone.mofcom.gov.cn/article/joinus/201211/20121108457400.shtml.

MOC. (2013). China's foreign investment statistics in 2012. Retrieved November 12, 2016, from https://www.fdi.gov.cn/1800000121_33_3807_0_7.html.

MOC. (2014). Table of main economic indicators of national economic and technological development zones in 2012 (2). Retrieved November 12, 2016, from https://ezone.mofcom.gov.cn/article/n/201402/20140200498634.shtml.

NBS. (1997). *China statistical yearbook 1996*. Beijing: China Statistics Press. Retrieved November 14, 2016, from https://www.stats.gov.cn/tjsj/ndsj/.

NBS. (2000). *China statistical yearbook 1999*. Beijing: China Statistics Press. Retrieved April 20, 2015, from https://www.stats.gov.cn/tjsj/ndsj/.

NBS. (2001). *China statistical yearbook 2000*. Beijing: China Statistics Press. Retrieved April 20, 2015, from https://www.stats.gov.cn/tjsj/ndsj/.

NBS. (2002). *China statistical yearbook 2001*. Beijing: China Statistics Press. Retrieved November 14, 2016, from https://www.stats.gov.cn/tjsj/ndsj/.

NBS. (2006). *China statistical yearbook 2005*. Beijing: China Statistics Press. Retrieved November 14, 2016, from https://www.stats.gov.cn/tjsj/ndsj/.

NBS. (2011). *China statistical yearbook 2010*. Beijing: China Statistics Press. Retrieved November 14, 2016, from https://www.stats.gov.cn/tjsj/ndsj/.

NBS. (2012). *2012 China industrial economics statistical yearbook*. Beijing: China Statistics Press.

Pan, Q. H., & Zhang, X. L. (2001). Reflections on the reform of the traditional selection mechanism of state-owned enterprises. *Modern Enterprises, 5,* 31.

Pei, C. H. (2009). An empirical analysis of the establishment of China's open economy: summary of 30 years of opening to the outside world. *Research on Financial Problems, 2,* 3–10.

Pei, C. H. (2013). Basic clues of 65 years of China's foreign trade: reform and growth. *Research on Chinese Economic History, 3,* 23–33.

Peng, Y. L. (2001). The deepening process of China's financial reform and its effectiveness. *Social Scientist, 1,* 15–19.

People's Bank of China (PBoC). (2016). Financial market performance in 2015. Retrieved November 14, 2016, from https://www.pbc.gov.cn/goutongjiaoliu/113456/113469/3009101/index.html.

Qian, J. (1994). Review and reflection on the marketization of China's treasury bill issuance. *Economic Trends, 9,* 33–35.

Qiao, L. (1997). 2·23 National debt futures incident review. *China Investment, 2,* 45–47.

Rong, X. C. (2012). On the development and changes of China's shipping industry (1949–2010). *Research on Chinese Economic History, 2,* 127–137.

Sang, B. C., & Li, Y. M. (2006). Sole proprietorship of foreign investment: motivation and impact. *Open Herald, 4,* 52–55.

Shang, C. F. (2009). Research on China's grain import in 1961. *Historical Data of the CPC, 3,* 155–167.

Shi, P. (2008). Chen Guang's Trilogy. *Southwind, 2,* 30–31.

Song, W. W. (2004). A probe of the development barriers of internationalized management of Chinese enterprises. *Enterprise Economy, 2,* 82–83.

Song, C. F. (2009). The direction and impact of China's foreign trade system reform. *Trade Union Overview—Theoretical Research, 7,* 80.

Song, X. (2014). Credit rating, key to national financial security. *Business Week, 10,* 80.

Song, W. G., & Liu, F. D. (2014). *The logic of mixed ownership: State-owned enterprise reform and opportunities of private enterprises under the new normal.* Beijing: China United Industry and Commerce Press.

State Administration of Foreign Exchange (SAFE). (2015). China balance of payments time series data 1982–2014 (BPM5). Retrieved November 16, 2016, from https://www.safe.gov.cn/wps/portal/sy/tjsj_szphb.

Su, D. B. (1988). Contemplations on China's free economic zone. *Reform and Strategy, 5,* 75–77.

Sun, L. J. (1995). Several issues concerning the operating mechanism of RMB exchange rate. *Southern Finance, 8,* 10–11.

Sun, Y. (2013). China's adjustment of deposit reserve ratio and cause analysis. *Times Finance, 8,* 121–122.

Tan, J. W. (2010). Birth approval certificate available only three years after its formation: Shenzhen's pioneering establishment of a foreign exchange swap center being the origin of the national unified foreign exchange market. *Daily Sunshine.* Retrieved November 16, 2016. from https://sztqb.sznews.com/html/2010-11/09/content_1303785.htm.

Tang, S. N., et al. (1999). Problems and prospects of China's trust and investment industry. *Financial Research, 1,* 57–65.

Tao, H. M. (1998). Requirements of open market business for the development of China's national debt market. *Journal of Tongji University (Social Science Edition), 3,* 89–92.

The World Bank. (1993). China foreign trade reform: meeting the challenge of the 1990s. Retrieved November 17, 2016, from https://documents.worldbank.org/curated/en/860931468023354805/China-Foreign-trade-reform-meeting-the-challenge-of-the-1990s.

Tong, D. H. (2003). Capital flight and opening up internally. *Ningbo's Economy: Financial Perspective, 1,* 21.

Wan, C. Z. (1986). Suspicion over banks' issuance of financial bonds. *Wuhan Finance, 10,* 12–13.

Wan, L. M. (2012). On the main characteristics of modern Chinese corporate bonds. *Research on Chinese Economic History, 4,* 112–121.

Wang, S. X. (1990). A probe into perfecting foreign trade contract system. *International Business: Journal of University of International Business and Economics, 1,* 16–20.

Wang, K. (1994). Similarities and differences between China's tax-sharing system and foreign tax-sharing systems. *Study Monthly, 4,* 13–14.

Wang, R. Y. (1994). Analysis of mixed sale and sideline business involving VAT and business tax. *International Taxation, 7,* 35–36.

Wang, Y. (1998a). Re-understanding the establishment of a modern enterprise system. *Economic Survey, 1,* 58–61.

Wang, Y. (1998b). Perfection and improvement of national debt secondary market. *China Finance, 11,* 40–42.

Wang, C. G. (1999). A brief discussion of the "Gold Storm" in 1947. *Research on Chinese Economic History, 4*, 66–74.

Wang, X. P. (2010). Gold yuan notes and inflation in the last years of the Republic of China: looking at the end of the Chiang dynasty from coins. *China Urban Finance, 9*, 66–67.

Wang, J. (2011). Change of state-owned enterprises from arrears to liquidation. *State-Owned Enterprises, 2*, 112–113.

Wang, H. M. (2013). The national government's legal supervision on foreign exchange business in wartime banks. *Lanzhou Academic Journal, 8*, 39–44.

Wang, X. S. (2013). China's reform and opening up and Masayoshi Ohira: centered on the first yen loan. *Nankai Japan Research, 2*, 1–19.

Wang, D. W., & Liu, G. D. (2000). Greenlight to opening a sino-foreign joint venture travel agency and countermeasures of Shanghai. *Academic Quarterly of Shanghai Academy of Social Sciences, 2*, 38–45.

Wei, H. K. (2001). Location characteristics and changes of foreign investment in China. *Economic Review, 6*, 23–28.

Wei, S. J. (2013). Promulgation of the Company Law and its impact on time: the first attempt at legislative level in response to the modernity challenge in the late Qing dynasty. *Shandong Social Sciences, 5*, 92–97.

Wen, Q., & Zhang, J. G. (1998). On currency appreciation and depreciation: domestic analysis of currency fluctuations. *Jiang Hai Academic Journal, 5*, 20–24.

Wu, L. J. (2004). Analysis of the development of China's enterprise bond market. *Journal of Shanghai Administration College, 1*, 40–46.

Wu, Y. X. (2008). Inside story of the formation of Shanghai's foreign exchange adjustment center and China's foreign exchange trading center. *Youth Daily*. Retrieved November 16, 2016, from https://finance.eastday.com/m/20081117/u1a3987049.html.

Xiang, H. C. (1983). On China's fiscal deficit. *Journal of Zhongnan University of Economics and Law, 5*, 55–59.

Xie, L. J. (1995). A successful model for the reform of state-owned small and medium-sized enterprises: a survey report on the reform of state-owned enterprises in Zhucheng, Shandong province. *Qianjin Forum, 8*, 20–23.

Xie, Y. H. (2004). A review of RMB exchange rate and probe into reform ideas. *Journal of Henan Institute of Financial Management Cadres, 5*, 102–103.

Xu, J. G. (1996). A radical solution to stabilize the scale of export rebates. *China Finance, 12*, 47–49.

Xue, W. C. (1998). The development process and prospect of asset-liability ratio management of China's commercial banks. *Finance Forum, 12*, 12–15.

Xu, D. X., & Wu, C. M. (2003). *Development history of Chinese capitalism* (Vol. 2). Beijing: People's Publishing House.

Yang, C. J. (1996). Discussion on the shortcomings of director contract responsibility system of current state-owned and collective enterprises. *Hubei Economy, 12*, 19–20.

Yang, T. (1998). The "crowding-out effect" of national debt and its impact on the national economy. *Journal of Shanghai Finance University, 2*, 39–41.

Yang, B., et al. (2000). Analysis of equity structure and corporate governance mechanism of state-owned companies. *Contemporary Economic Research, 12*, 26–29.

Yang, F. (2005). A review of the history of RMB exchange rate system. *Research on the History of Chinese Economy, 4*, 59–64.

Yang, T. R., & Liu, X. (1995). Terminating administrative relationship & establishing property right relationship to rebuild new enterprise system. *Management World, 2*, 131–136.

Yao, Y. S. (1991). On contracting system from the achievements of Shougang's reform. *Economic and Management Research, 4*, 31–35.

Yin, Z. J. (1997). A new understanding of the pilot of the modern enterprise system. *Zhejiang Social Sciences, 5*, 25–26.

Yin, Z. T. (2012). A historical survey of China's modern securities market supervision: Based on the perspective of legislation and enforcement. *Financial Review, 2,* 104–114.
Yu, S. H. (1997). Current status of foreign businessmen entering China's retail industry. *China's Foreign Trade, 2,* 16.
Yu, Y. J. (1998). Making good use of RMB750 billion. *Chinese Entrepreneurs, 5,* 39.
Yu, Y. J. (2010). The madness of the black market of foreign exchange. *Daily Sunshine*. Retrieved November 20, 2016, from https://jb.sznews.com/html/2010-11/03/content_1293527.htm.
Zang, Y. R. (1998). Several suggestions for the further development of large enterprise groups. *China Industrial Economy, 9,* 31–36.
Zeng, H. B. (1994). On the coordinated operation mechanism of national tax system and local tax system. *Tax Research, 11,* 39–42.
Zhang, H. Y. (1985). An analysis of the treasury bill issuing system. *Shanghai Finance, 5,* 26–28.
Zhang, S. D. (1988). On the formation of tansfer price for treasury bills after the opening of secondary market: also in discussion with comrade Zhao Haikuan. *Financial Research, 7,* 43–46.
Zhang, S. T. (1989). Conscientious rectification of foreign trade companies by the Ministry of Foreign Economic Relations and Trade. *China Economic and Trade Guide, 24,* 23.
Zhang, G. H. (1990). Review and prospect of China's foreign exchange swap market. *Financial Research, 9,* 1–5.
Zhang, H. L. (1995). On the primary dealers of national debt. *China Finance, 3,* 10–11.
Zhang, E. Z. (1996a). On the economic impact of tariff adjustment on China. *World Economic and Political Forum, 3,* 6–9.
Zhang, L. (1996b). Discussion on China's export rebate management methods. *Journal of Fujian Jiangxia University, 4,* 27–28.
Zhang, J. (1998). Liberalization process and trade growth of China's trade sector. *Shanghai Reform, 12,* 15–19.
Zhang, Z. G. (2000). Investment, construction and prospect of Lujiazui financial and trade zone. *Pudong Development, 8,* 35–37.
Zhang, C. T. (2001a). A brief history of the development of China's securities market (the late Qing dynasty). *Securities Market Herald, 4,* 37–40.
Zhang, C. T. (2001b). A brief history of the development of China's securities market (the Republic of China). *Securities Market Herald, 5,* 45–52.
Zhang, C. T. (2001c). A brief history of the development of China's securities market (before reform and opening up). *Securities Market Herald, 6,* 34–36.
Zhang, Q. Z. (2002a). Chinese-funded commercial banks: ways to survive. *the Banker, 2,* 70–73.
Zhang, W. W. (2002b). An empirical study of the corporatization and reform of the modern enterprise system of state-owned enterprises. *Economic Science, 1,* 27–34.
Zhang, G. K. (2003). On the divestiture of social functions of state-owned enterprises. *Economist, 1,* 133–134.
Zhang, J. (2004a). The background, impact and outlook of export rebate policy adjustment. *Taxation and Economy, 4,* 55–57.
Zhang, R. (2004b). Export rebate: finding the way out in trouble. *Economic and Trade World, 2,* 41–44.
Zhang, X. Y. (2006). Analysis of the trend of sole proprietorship of foreign investment in China. *Contemporary Economy, 15,* 80–81.
Zhang, J. (2007). China's state-owned enterprises development under the contracting system: the case of Shougang Group. *Journal of International Management Studies*. Retrieved December 12, 2016, from https://www.jimsjournal.org/13%20Jie%20Zhang.pdf.
Zhang, Y. F., & Wang, C. J. (2006). Insider control and soft budget constraints: a theoretical hypothesis. *Journal of Nanjing University* (Philosophy · Humanities · Social Science Edition), *6,* 127–133.
Zhao, L. F. (2001). Establishment of a standardized corporate governance structure: a system-supporting project. *Theoretical Research on Finance and Economics, 1,* 82–85.

Zhao, X. J. (2002). Foreign exchange control during the period of national economic recovery. *Research on Chinese Economic History, 1,* 91–101.
Zhao, C. B. (2005). A brief discussion on the current fiscal transfer payment system. *Contemporary Rural Finance and Economics, 11,* 27–28.
Zhao, R. (2006). Analysis of China's national debt repurchase market. *Journal of Tianjin Business Vocational College, 2,* 18–19.
Zhao, Z. X. (2008). Recollection of the founding of Xiamen International Bank. *The Chinese People's Political Consultative Conference Daily.* Retrieved December 13, 2016, from https://epaper.rmzxb.com.cn/detail.aspx?id=179070.
Zhao, J. W., & Duan, J. E. (1998). A brief discussion on the reform of joint-stock cooperation system of small state-owned enterprises. *Theoretical Exploration, 3,* 36–37.
Zhao, J. X., & Yu, X. F. (1996). Entry of foreign banks and opening up of China's financial industry. *Management World, 5,* 41–49.
Zheng, D. X. (2003). Exploration on the supervision of foreign banks in China. *Hainan Finance, 5,* 16–21.
Zheng, X. L. (2004). Mixing all shareholding systems as the main form of public ownership. *Party Construction Research, 1,* 7–11.
Zheng, R. P., & Li, M. (2005). The current characteristics and reform ideas of RMB exchange rate system. *Journal of Quanzhou Teachers College, 5,* 67–71.
Zhou, L. F. (1990). Some thoughts on strengthening individual tax collection and management. *Tax Research, 1,* 43–44.
Zhou, T. S. (1997). An analysis of the relationship between tax sharing system and reform of extrabudgetary fund management: also on reform measures of extrabudgetary fund management. *Journal of Hubei College of Finance and Economics, 3,* 22–24.
Zhou, M. L., & . Hang Z. F. . (2011). Facilitating the process of rejuvenating borders and enriching people with construction of border economic cooperative zones. *Development Research, 1,* 10–13.
Zhu, Y. G. (2001). The first batch of joint-stock enterprises in modern China. *Historical Research, 5,* 19–29.
Zhu, Y. W. (2006). Combination of two taxes should select the "high merger" plan. *China Economic Weekly, 22,* 30–31.
Zhu, Y. (2014). "Financial Unrest" due to the excess of trust companies and stock exchanges in 1921. *China Finance, 20,* 92–93.
Zhu, J. (2016). The beginning and end of syndicated bond issuance of Tongtai Yanken Number Five Company. *Archives and Construction, 5,* 42–47.

Chapter 5
New Century, New Economy

At the turn of the century, China had accumulated some twenty years of experience in the orchestration of its economy which was no longer subject to the manipulation of central plans; instead, it became increasingly oriented according to the pulse of the market at home and abroad. Via these interactions, the country began to realize that development, although a seemingly internal affair, could hardly sustain if without support from other parts of the world. Although such an understanding was still primitive by then, it at least reinforced the conviction of the state to proceed with its reform and opening up, two conditions based on which economic vitality would be better maintained. On many occasions, it is up to the latter to set the momentum for the former. What's more, concerning the concrete norms and practices to be introduced, they are equally dependent on the extent of openness. The higher the level, the greater the necessity to adapt oneself to the universal standards. From a long-term perspective, this kind of self-adjustment could help promote the resilience of an economy, especially when confronting unfavorable movements in the macro environment.

Back to the year 1900 when China was still under the reign of the Qing Empire, its per capita GDP was merely 545 international dollars (or 1990 International Geary-Khamis dollars), one of the lowest in the world (Maddison, 2010). While it managed to climb to 3,162 international dollars in 1999, that of the world average already reached 5,833 international dollars, making the country fall behind many of its counterparts. Thus, when history was soon to step into the new century, the tasks waiting for China remained not much lessened. In particular, still in the aftermath of the 1997 Asian financial crisis, the need to further integrate into the global economy to enhance its ability to stand similar shocks was self-evident. At an age which was increasingly hallmarked by globalization, this is also a sensible choice beneficial not only to China's economic development, but to the enrichment of its culture and the advancement of the whole society as well.

C. Yu, *China's Economy: Towards 2049*,
https://doi.org/10.1007/978-981-15-9227-0_5

1 Accession to the WTO, a Fresh Beginning

As mentioned earlier, one of the objectives of the accelerated reform programs during the 1990s was to allow China to be well-prepared for the accession to the WTO. In fact, internal debates about the gains and costs of its entry had been going on for quite some years because to qualify for the membership, a lot of concessions had to be pledged. Nevertheless, considering the numerous potential advantages in both the short and the long-run, China was rather keen about the entry. Namely, it would grant China a permanent trading relationship with all the WTO member countries; plus an automatic access to the most-favored nation (MFN) treatment with these countries. Further, the status would ensure easier penetration into new markets on the basis of national treatment and transparency, which implies tremendous export opportunities. But like a double-edged sword, subordination to multilateral rules and disciplines was at the same time a condition to satisfy. From this point of view, it was more like a "win some, lose some" accommodation arrangement for China. Despite these tradeoffs, accession to the WTO was without doubt a wise step to take for it could earn China the image of a responsible global player willing to conduct trade and investment in manners consistent with the rest of the world. Additionally, in the context of economic globalization, strengthening ties with the mainstream could help the country deepen its reform by using the approaches already proven elsewhere.

Before China finally secured the green light on Dec. 11th, 2001, it had spent a total of fifteen years bargaining with 37 members on issues related to market entry. While these tough negotiations turned out to be fruitful, what lied ahead was by no means easier because to fulfill the commitment it had pledged, a lot of institutional and technical barriers remained to be eliminated, which would certainly involve unpredictable challenges. From the reshuffling of policy priorities and the system of foreign trade administration, to the unification of inspection & quarantine standards, as well as the promotion of "non-discrimination" in dealing with foreign investors, etc., every single promise was a hard nut to crack, plus the opening up of diverse industrial sectors in a phased manner (Sun, 2011).

With regard to the implications of WTO accession to China's economy, they are undoubtedly profound. Put it in a simple way, economic reforms which had been undertaken during the period of 1978–2000 were still far from over. In fact, the transition to a market economy was not yet even half complete and quite a lot spheres were still in need of change. Considering that based on international norms, the Chinese economy in 2000 was not yet a fully liberalized one, further relaxation and opening up were among the most pressing tasks facing the leadership. In particular, two elements would have to go through major restructuring and they were the SOEs and the banking sector. In addition, from the perspective of the government, entry into the WTO meant numerous imperatives of managing the transition and maintaining the equilibrium on several fronts. Above all, despite the complicated nature of the subsequent agenda, 2001 is without doubt a watershed year for China. If 1978 symbolized a somewhat reluctant farewell to the command economy, then 2001 represented a voluntary acceptance of a freer market within which all the agents should unexceptionally observe the inherent laws and the factors of production are allocated under less bureaucratic intervention.

2 Capital Market

Capital market, which bears its distinct function of providing capital to the real sector, plays an equally important role of enhancing governance through a mechanism named information disclosure. As an indicator of how the economy runs at the current stage, the capital that moves in and out of the market simultaneously serves like a wind vane for future economic trends. Similar to what most countries in the world have gone through, the development of China's capital market was a natural process responding to the growing demand for financial resources in the wake of its grand reform. Before the arrival of the twenty-first century, the two-decade long history of the market had witnessed not only thriving business opportunities, but mounting obstacles as well. In particular, the most outstanding problems included the lack of a fair and open financing platform to entities irrespective of their ownership structures, inadequacies in supervision and regulation, information asymmetry between fund-raising institutions and investors, and the primitive nature of its credit rating system, etc. Actually, none of them was easy to tackle and each one required time as well as a firm resolve from the top to make changes happen. From another point of view, however, if without these impediments to overcome, it would be unlikely for the market to become mature enough to support the national economy.

As a landmark regulation acknowledging the status of the capital market in the country, the "Securities Law of the People's Republic of China" was enacted in 1999 (Ding, 1999). If counting from 1993 when the draft was first submitted to the National People's Congress for its review, it totally cost six years of deliberation and debate to gain the final approval. Containing 12 Chapters and 214 Articles, the Law demonstrated a commitment on the part of the government to move closer to a rule-based approach to the management of the securities market. Although not without flaws, it represented a pursuit of greater uniformity amid the rapidly flourishing securities transactions. After China's accession to the World Trade Organization in 2001, the accelerated restructuring of the financial sector further prompted sequential changes in the capital market. To cope with the proliferation of state and non-state firms seeking funds via equity or debt financing, the Securities Law was amended in 2005 together with the Company Law (implemented in 1994), with revisions went into effect in 2006. The simultaneous amendment of these two laws did not happen by coincidence, it was a reflection of their close relationship to the sound operation of the capital market. By supplementing and deleting certain provisions, the new Securities Law had 240 Articles detailing in a more concrete way the issuing, marketing, trading, and settling securities (Wang, 2006). With regard to the Company Law, it was also enriched with stipulations on the organizational structure of listed firms, and protection of the interests of both creditors and shareholders, etc. If compared to their previous versions, both laws were made more compatible and consistent with each other, thus laying a solid foundation for the legal groundwork of the capital market.

2.1 Convertible Bond, a Hybrid Security

Generally, stocks and bonds are considered as two major instruments of investment and each represents a different claim on the issuer. Holders of the former are called shareholders whereas those of the latter are known to be creditors. In the capital market, they are traded under separate rules. With the constant progress in financial innovation, there appeared one more alternative that could link the above two together and it was convertible bond. Like a hybrid security, convertible bond combines a common bond and a call option. For investors who are risk-averse but desire to reap a higher return from stocks, convertible bond enables them to exchange the bonds they hold for a specified amount of shares of common stock. With regard to the listed companies whose credit rating is low but have strong growth potential, convertible bond is a means of financing with reduced cash interest payment.

Originated in the mid-nineteenth century in the US, it began to appear in China in the early 1990s, almost in line with the emergence of the two stock exchanges. However, the trial by Bao'an County United Investment Company (today's China Bao'an Group, Shenzhen) to issue the first A-share convertible bond was a failure. Here, what is necessary to indicate is that the company was also the issuer of the first stock in China after 1949. One year after getting formally listed at the Shenzhen Stock Exchange, in order to fund its investment in real estate and industrial projects, the company in 1992 released the first convertible bond of China with a total value of RMB500 million and 3-year maturity (Li, 1998). Unexpectedly, from the second half of 1993, a series of contractionary policies were initiated by the government to curb the over-rapid growth in investment and economy. As a result of high-rising interest rates and shrinkage in stock trading, the company faced tremendous burden of repayment when approaching 1995. Ultimately, only 2.7PCT of the amount issued was converted into stocks, which was absolutely contrary to the initial plan (Hu, 1997). Although the company managed to pay back by the due date, its launch of convertible bond was by no means a success. From the standpoint of investors, they equally suffered losses because as compared to the 9.5PCT coupon rate of 3-year government bond issued at the same time, their yield was just 3PCT. If calculating the subsidies later offered by the state to counter inflation, the actual rate of that government bond could be much higher.

While the convertible bond market in China became almost dormant for the rest of the 1990s after the unsuccessful pilot, experiments in overseas markets continued. Totally, three bonds were launched during that period and they were B-share (RMB-denominated shares of domestically-listed companies traded in US dollars at the SSE or HK dollars at the SZSE) bonds by China Textile Machinery and China Southern Glass Holding Company in Switzerland in 1993 and 1995 respectively (Xia, 2001), and H-share (shares denominated in HK dollars by mainland Chinese companies listed at the Hong Kong Stock Exchange) bonds by Sinopec Zhenhai Refining and Chemical Company in Hong Kong and London in 1996 (Ren, 2001). In retrospect, these were all useful trials for Chinese enterprises, although the ultimate number of bonds being converted into shares did not match all their set targets, they gained first-hand knowledge with which they could more effectively take advantage of the tool to serve their financing needs in the future.

Apart from direct experiences, policy guidance was equally necessary to better regulate market behaviors. In 2001, China Securities Regulatory Commission released the "Implementation Measures for the Issuance of Convertible Bonds by Listed Companies" before publicizing one more notice in that December for the improvement of the work. In light of these rules, as well as the procedures explicitly drafted by the Shanghai and Shenzhen stock exchanges in November of the following year, the uncertainties that had overshadowed corporate decisions over convertible bonds were greatly reduced. Very soon, there was a boom in the market and from the second half of 2002 to June 2003, the amount of convertible bonds issued at the two exchanges reached RMB9.9 billion, which was higher than the aggregate issuance of the previous twelve years (Chen & Yi, 2004). When the funds raised via convertible bonds exceeded RMB20.9 billion in 2004, it had dominated the refinancing preferences among listed companies (as compared to share allotment and seasoned equity offerings) by claiming a portion of 46.54PCT.

2.2 Split-Share Structure Reform

In the very beginning, the concept of listed companies in China was derived from the reform of state-owned enterprises. In other words, getting them listed was one way to restructure their internal organization and diversify the composition of ownership. But at the same time, to ensure the controlling interest of the state, the shares of listed companies were divided into two categories: tradable and non-tradable. While tradable shares (TS) could be purchased by public investors and traded on the exchanges, non-tradable shares (NTS) belong to state-owned enterprises and could not be bought or sold in the open market. Generally, TS consist of A-shares, B-shares, and H-shares whereas NTS are composed of state shares (held by the state) and legal person shares (held by the SOEs and other non-bank institutions). Despite the above differences, the odd thing was that NTS entitled the owners exactly the same voting rights which should only be assigned to those of tradable shares. The table below (Table 1) is a display of these two types of shares issued in China from 1993 to 2005. Over this 13-year period, despite the expansion in their volumes, the relative weight of each in the country's total did not change much. In 2003, i.e. two years before the major split-share structure reform, NTS still accounted for almost 65PCT of the total number of issued shares, which implies that only about one third of the shares was in circulation and their investors as minority holders could not exercise decisive influence over corporate decisions. Moreover, of the 457.23 billion NTS issued by the end of 2004, the proportion of state shares claimed 60PCT (Qian, Gao & Tong, 2009).

Table 1 Tradable & non-tradable shares of domestically-listed companies, 1993–2005

Year	Tradable shares		Non-Tradable shares	
	Volume[1] (100 Million Shares)	Share in Total[2] (PCT)	Volume[3] (100 Million Shares)	Share in Total[4] (PCT)
1993	107.88	27.82	279.85	72.18
1995	301.46	35.53	546.96	64.47
1997	671.44	34.56	1,271.23	65.44
1999	1,079.65	34.95	2,009.3	65.05
2001	1,813.17	34.75	3,404.84	65.25
2003	2,269.92	35.31	4,158.54	64.69
2005	2,914.77	38.2	4,714.74	61.8

Note [1]CSRC, 2007; [2–4]calculated by the author based on the total shares issued in the selected years
Source CSRC, 2007

Obviously, the existence of this unfair phenomenon could hardly benefit the reform of the SOEs; rather, it caused serious problems concerning corporate governance. In addition, by fostering insider control and curbing the rights of public shareholders, it also impeded the healthy development of China's capital market.

Aware of the negative impact, China Securities Regulatory Commission (CSRC) began the trial of transferring a portion of the state shares of 10 selected companies in the A-share market in November 1999. According to the plan, China Jialing Industrial and Guizhou Tire pioneered the reduction of state-owned shares one month later. However, the non-tradable shares of both companies were sold at 10 times of their respective average earnings per share over the preceding three years (Wang, 2001), which were over-priced and deviated from the market-expected level. Very soon, the offering triggered significant declines in the stock exchange after the announcement of the trial and eventually, the shares were not fully subscribed, with China Jialing Industrial and Guizhou Tire sold 81.99PCT and 75.29PCT of their state-held equity offered to the existing private investors. The unpleasant results showed that the scheme was rashly launched at a time when neither the government nor the market was well-prepared. In particular, an important mechanism that helps balance the interest of TS and NTS holders was absent. Therefore, given the systemic void and various inadequacies in other respects, the original arrangement for the rest 8 companies to execute the same transfer in the following year had to be put on hold. Actually, 2001–2005 was a rather dismal period for China's stock market, despite the strong performance of the macro economy (its annual GDP growth rate was more than 9PCT on average), the benchmark Shanghai Stock Exchange Composite Index (SHCOMP) fell by over 55PCT, from its record high of 2,245 on June 14th, 2001 to 998 on June 6th of 2005 (Wang & Ji, 2005). Unsurprisingly, the key reason behind such an abnormal phenomenon was related to the problem of split-share structure typical of China.

In June 2001, the "Notice of the Interim Measures of the State Council on the Management of Reducing State-held Shares and Raising Social Security Funds" was promulgated, which required that joint stock limited companies with government stakes should sell their state shares amounting to 10PCT of the funds to be raised while proceeding initial public offerings or seasoned equity offerings. Considering that by the end of 2001, of the total 1,160 listed companies in China, 903 or 78PCT of them were state-controlled, which together had an impact on RMB630 billion worth of social capital (Hu, 2003), it was by no means an irrational concern of public investors that once the 10PCT became privatized, the market would be soon flooded with inflated stock volume, a situation leaving them not only vulnerable but victimized. Within a matter of four months, the SHCOMP tumbled over 30PCT to 1,520 on Oct. 22nd, an evaporation of RMB1.7 trillion in market value (Li & Pang, 2005). On that night, the CSRC called for a halt to the regulation while at the same time pledged to solicit public opinions before drafting a more pragmatic blueprint. Anyhow, as long as the price and circulation of state shares were still fixed subjectively instead of guided by the market, no satisfactory solution could be reached. As noted in the above, unless the interest of private shareholders was given due respect, pushing forward any kind of reform on state-held shares would only prove to be futile.

Concerning the real decisive move to turn around the bearish stock market, it was the release of "Some Opinions of the State Council on Promoting the Reform, Opening and Steady Growth of Capital Markets" in 2004. Also known as the "nine-point guide" ('guo jiu tiao'), it laid out a series of systematic principles in establishing a capital market whose operations were to be closely aligned with market mechanisms. With regard to the issue of TS and NTS, the document not only confirmed its existence as a problem, it also stressed the necessity of separating equity in a market-based and investor-friendly (especially public investors) manner. As part of the efforts to substantiate the general guidance into concrete policies, the CSRC followed up in 2005 with the "Notice on the Pilot Reform of the Split Share Structure of Listed Companies", which formally kicked off one more round of trial since the previous failure of 1999. In the following month, four companies were chosen to initiate the experiment and they included Sany Heavy Industry, Tsinghua Tongfang, Shanghai Zijiang Enterprise Group, and Jinniu Energy Resources. Unlike the previous trial, the four companies were required to put forward their reform scheme plus a compensation package for the approval of the existing tradable shareholders (Zhang & Xu, 2005). This can be taken as a typical feature of the 2005 reform, i.e. in return for the right to sell their shares on the stock exchange, tradable shareholders received payment of consideration from non-tradable shareholders, which averaged 3–4 new shares for each ten shares held, a reflection of increased concern over the interest of public investors.

Take Sany Heavy Industry as an example, being a leading manufacturer of construction machinery, 75PCT of its outstanding shares (i.e. 180 million out of the total 240 million) were non-tradable before the trial. Based on its reform scheme which was approved finally in June 2005, the offer was set at 3.5 new shares and RMB8 for each 10 TS held (Chu, 2005). As the first listed company in China which successfully carried out the split share reform, Sany was also the first to realize full circulation of its shares by unlocking all the 560 million NTS on June 17th, 2008.

After the launch of the second batch of trial covering 42 companies in June 2005, the reform project was soon promoted nationwide. To prevent the market from getting too volatile due to a massive future sale of shares, the CSRC unveiled the "Measures for the Administration of the Split Share Structure Reform of Listed Companies" in September. While stating that the program for each company should be tailor-made and approved through a voting process by its shareholders' meetings, the securities watchdog mandated a 12-month lock-up period after the implementation, during which the NTS could neither be traded nor transferred. Moreover, after its expiration, NTS holders owning more than 5PCT of the company's total issued shares were further prohibited from selling over 5PCT of the company's total shares within twelve months and 10PCT within twenty four months on the stock exchange. Toward the end of 2007, among the listed companies which should take part in the restructuring, 98PCT of them or a total of 1,298 had accomplished the process (Xu, 2009). Due to the presence of various lock-up periods which would expire in at least 1–2 more years, visible changes in the free floating did not happen dramatically until 2008 when the balance between TS and NTS was altered. By October 1st, of the aggregate 2,432.55 billion shares in issuance, the volume for TS reached 1,223.37 billion, exceeding 50PCT for the first time (CSRC, 2008). However, in terms of market capitalization, the dividing line appeared in August 2009 when the value for TS amounted to RMB9,458.25 billion, representing 50.6PCT of the total, which registered RMB18,709.54 billion (CSRC, 2009).

After then, the movement of the same trend was fastened greatly and as demonstrated by the graph below (Graph 1), the ratio between market capitalization of tradable shares and the nation's total kept increasing over the decade of 2005–2014. In particular, if compared to 37.25PCT of 2008, the more-than-doubled figure of 84.72PCT by 2014 implies that the once dominant position of NTS has been replaced by TS. Nevertheless, to really match its status of being the second largest stock

Graph 1 Market capitalization of tradable shares versus total market capaitalization, RMB100 million. *Source* monthly report of China's securities market for selected years, China Securities Regulatory Commission. https://www.csrc.gov.cn/pub/newsite/sjtj/zqscyb/index_5.html

market in the world in terms of market capitalization, China has yet to fulfill the goal of converting an even higher portion of non-tradable shares into tradable shares.

2.3 *Delisting of Underperforming Stocks*

Undeniably, by improving the existing shareholding structure, the NTS reform can to a certain degree promote the governance of the Chinese listed companies. From another perspective, however, as long as there was a lack of information disclosure system to timely monitor their performance and safeguard the interest of shareholders, especially minority shareholders, the positive effect it could exercise should not be magnified. Ever since the two mainland stock exchanges went into operation in the early 1990s, the number of listed firms has been growing rapidly; while there were only 14 in 1991, the number reached 1,088 by 2000 (NBS, 2001). Quantitative expansion does not necessarily bring about proportional improvement in quality and this rule equally applies to the stock market of China. Fascinated by its role of providing massive idle funds, companies of different backgrounds were eager to go public so as to benefit from this magic platform. Although there were laws (such as the 1994 Company Law) to restrict their entry, as well as suspension of listing, the initial threshold was by no means high enough. Besides, the insufficient supervision over the post-listing stage gradually gave birth to a variety of immoral behaviors that victimized countless private shareholders.

To prevent these occurrences from becoming uncontrollably rampant, measures to delist poor-performing companies were adopted. Starting from 1998, the Shanghai and Shenzhen stock exchanges announced that for companies with abnormal financial standing such as negative net profits for two consecutive fiscal years, they would receive "special treatment" (ST, 'tebie chuli') and their shares would be set aside separately under the ST category as a warning. On April 28th, the first ST company emerged and it was Shenyang Materials Development Company (today's Shenyang Ingenious Development Company, photo 5–3 below is its stock) which had suffered two years of losses (Wan, 2013). Fortunately, its performance improved later and after the company's return to profitability, the label of ST was removed in April 1999 from its share name.

As an arrangement targeting the listed companies whose financial losses sustained for over three consecutive years, "particular transfer" (PT, 'tebie zhuanrang') was provided by the SSE and SZSE in July 1999 (Leng, 2013). Stocks falling under this particular category were suspended from normal trading except for Fridays. Besides, a daily price fluctuation limit was set at ± 5PCT and from June 2000 on, the price floor was removed whereas the ceiling remained. In the first batch, four companies were marked with PT and they included Shanghai Shuanglu Electric Appliances, Shanghai Urban Argo Business, Jiangsu Sanshan Industry and Commerce, and Chongqing Yugang Titanium Dioxide. In 2001, following the "Implementing Provisions for Suspending and Terminating the Listings of Loss-making Listed Companies" of the CSRC, the practice of PT was abolished. Instead of allowing companies which suffered three-year losses a transition period, the new rule would straightforwardly suspend their trading on the exchange and in case they recorded further negative profits in the initial fiscal year after suspension, they would simply be delisted.

In that April, after going through 10 years of history, China's stock market for the first time had a delisted company and it was Shanghai Narcissus Electric Appliances, which had by then registered losses for four consecutive years. Till November 2014, i.e. prior to the implementation of a harsher delisting system, the stocks of totally 78 firms had been disqualified and withdrawn from the exchange. Against the scale of 2,667 domestically-listed companies at that time, the progress was rather slow and this is partially reflective of the strong power of resistance not only from the companies themselves, but the local governments as well (Wu, 2014).

2.4 *Multi-Tiered Stock Exchange*

While a mature capital market should enable well-established companies to get funds for further growth and expansion, it has another important role to play for those newly-emerged businesses which are equally in need of money to survive. At the dawn of the twenty-first century, the two-decade-old capital market on the Chinese mainland was chiefly dominated by the two exchanges in Shanghai and Shenzhen. In contrast to the rapidly booming industries, especially of the high-tech and service sectors, the chances available for them to obtain financial resources were rather slim. Considering the challenges associated with the forthcoming WTO membership, the situation was definitely unfavorable to the cultivation of competitiveness that could match China's rising status. To cope with the stronger demand of companies that had immense potential for the future but limited by tight budget, trials were conducted by the Shenzhen Stock Exchange in the early 2000s to establish a second board in support of high-tech enterprises to go public. In June 2004, after the official launch of the "small and medium-sized enterprises (SMEs) board" ('zhongxiao qiye ban', or the SME board) at the SZSE, eight companies became the first to make their debut. Over the following years, the SME board flourished quickly and by the end of April 2015, it had channeled RMB914.6 billion in funds for 746 SMEs and in terms of their market capitalization, it hit almost RMB9 trillion (Wang, 2015). Among them, 535 were prominent in innovative capabilities, which accounted for 71.72PCT of the total.

For the creation of a multi-tiered stock market and in particular, with a view to facilitating the fund-raising of startup ventures so that they could more conveniently capitalize on new technologies, patents, trademarks and other intangible assets, ChiNext (China Next, the first enterprise board of the mainland China, 'chuangye ban') was inaugurated in 2009. In fact, the plan to set up a stock exchange for high-tech firms in China emerged in 1999, but due to the burst of the dot-com bubble in 2000 and the lost confidence in Internet and technology stocks, the project was shelved for ten years. The establishment of the SME board during this period was at the outset taken as a pilot although it later stood out in its own right. In the wake of the global financial crisis of 2008, the entire business world was facing an unprecedented challenge. For entrepreneurs of startups, the hardships they had to weather were even greater. Therefore, the decision to roll out ChiNext, a second-board market modeled after the NASDAQ, under the special circumstances was without doubt a timely help. Since the financial requirements of the listing criteria were set lower than the main board, it offered startup technology-oriented companies a good opportunity to attract investment otherwise not available. After the opening ceremony of ChiNext in 2009, the first batch of 28 firms began offering shares and the funds they together raised was nearly RMB15.48 billion, well above the anticipated level of RMB7.08 billion (Jiang & Li, 2010). Both acting as a powerful incubator to accelerate the transformation of China's development mode, the SME board hosts enterprises that are already equipped with well-defined core business; by comparison, the targets of ChiNext are predominantly innovation-driven companies demonstrating high-growth potential.

In general, a healthy capital market is not simply evaluated by its ability to generate liquidity, the track record of investor protection should be treated as another important measure. When Shanghai Narcissus Electric Appliances became the first delisted company of China in 2001, the incidence simultaneously necessitated the establishment of an exit mechanism for the country's securities exchange. Based on the international practice, such a mechanism should include the removal procedures of a listed stock; besides, the route through which investors could have their remaining holdings traded is also to be made available. Known as the "Agency Share Transfer System" ('daiban gufen zhuanrang xitong'), or called the "Third Board" ('san ban'), the Chinese form of the route went into operation in July 2001. Responsible for regulating the Third Board, the Securities Association of China (SAC) appointed six securities companies to handle the transfer services (Gu, 2006). In the beginning, this independent electronic system mainly asserted the function of providing share transfer services for companies delisted from the main board of the SSE and SZSE. The shares of Shanghai Narcissus Electric Appliances, for instance, were traded on the Third Board in that December. Since most of the stocks were of low quality and high risks, and the time set for open transactions was rather limited (in the case of Shanghai Narcissus, it was two hours in the morning and afternoon every other business day), investors could hardly get the deal concluded at satisfactory price levels, the trading remained rather sluggish in the following years.

To activate this over-the-counter (OTC) stock market, its business scope was expanded in 2006 to offer financing for China's non-listed small yet promising high-tech enterprises. Called the "new Third Board" ('xin sanban', to distinguish from the original one), its trial version was conducted at Beijing Zhongguancun Science Park, a famous cluster of semiconductor, computer, and telecommunication firms. On January 23rd, 2006, the new transfer system began to host its first two registered companies and they were Beijing Century Real Technology and Sinosoft. In August 2012, three more science parks (i.e. Tianjin Binhai, Shanghai Zhangjiang, and Wuhan Donghu) were added to the list of the pilot program (Zhang & Guo, 2012). Although unlike the existing main board, the SME board, and the ChiNext board which imposed stringent rules for corporate financing, the new Third Board acted as a relatively quick conduit for unqualified startups to raise funds. However, problems with the

Table 2 Transaction of shares at the new third board, 2006–2015

Year	Trading volume (Million Shares)	Turnover (RMB Million)
2006	15.93	83.41
2008	54.08	295.28
2010	69.51	418.72
2012	114.56	584.32
2013	202.43	813.96
2014	2,282.12	13,035.8
2015	27,890.72	191,062.25

Source NEEQ, 2015

original Third Board did not go away, like low trading volumes and lack of liquidity. Concerning the reasons behind, the demanding investment threshold was perhaps the key. Set at RMB5 million for institutional investors and RMB3 million for individual investors, it has already narrowed the number of the eligible down to a small scale. Moreover, the uncertainties involved in the profit-making ability of these share-issuing companies also deterred investment.

Due to these visible and invisible barriers, the volume of transaction throughout the eight years after the inauguration of the new transfer system had no significant increase (Table 2), from 15.93 million to 202.43 million shares, the total amount stayed at RMB813.96 million by the end of 2013. The real turning point emerged after the new Third Board was officially named the National Equities Exchange and Quotations (NEEQ, 'quanguo zhongxiao qiye gufen zhuanrang xitong') in 2013, no longer limited to certain regions, the NEEQ became a nationwide OTC market designed chiefly for high-tech SMEs to register and trade their shares (Cai, 2013). As a clear directive reflecting the policy of the central government, the "Guiding Opinions on Financial Support for the Adjustment, Transformation and Upgrading of the Economic Structure" was promulgated by the State Council in that July. Inclusive of 10 measures, the Opinions reiterated the importance of building a multi-layered capital market by broadening the financing channels for the SMEs. Together with several other regulations issued in the same year, market response was very positive. By the end of 2012, the number of companies registered with the new Third Board was merely 200; within just three years, the figure soared to 5,129 in 2015. In addition, the value of transactions for 2015 alone far exceeded the sum of the previous nine years. Backed by the favorable environment and the booming private sector, it is expected that the OTC stock market in the future would thrive with an even more dynamic momentum.

2.5 *Private Equity*

At the current stage, China has about 50 million micro, small and medium-sized ventures and for the vast majority of them, the most common headaches are the shortage of working capital and high cost of financing (Wu, 2014). Actually, this is a situation which has persisted for years and in some measure, their unfulfilled thirst shows the failure of the equity and bond markets to develop as rapidly as it should have in order to cope with the needs of the dynamic Chinese economy. Nevertheless, the existence of problems is not all that bad if analyzed from an optimistic point of view. While the mismatch would push China to expedite its internal reform, the financing gap offers high-return opportunities for investors as long as they are smart enough to identify the right target with strong growth potential.

2.5.1 Newbridge Capital, the First Foreign Player

Private equity (PE), a rather fresh concept to the majority Chinese during the 1980s and even 1990s, had already evolved into a mature industry in the US and Europe. Primarily taken as a means to finance young entrepreneurial firms not yet quoted on public stock exchanges, PE in a broader sense also incorporates venture capital (VC) and leveraged buyouts (LBOs). Since most young businesses would inevitably go through a stage of uncertain prospects and even negative earnings, it becomes critical for them to receive capital injection from PE organizations which are willing to risk losses before recouping investment and reaping decent rewards. Unlike many developed economies whose private equity funds are driven by earning lucrative returns, the introduction of broad-based private equity into China in the mid-1980s was prompted as a part of the government's endeavor to boost the development of science and technology, which had fallen way behind the world. Nonetheless, because of the unclear regulatory guidance and dubious policy environment, neither domestic nor foreign PE firms had their operations by then. After the "Proposal for Encouraging the Development of China's Venture Capital Industry" was put forward in 1998 at the Ninth Chinese People's Political Consultative Conference (CPPCC, a political advisory body), the subject began to attract wider attention. Coincided with the Internet boom, it as a result attracted foreign venture capital funds to flow into the country's top portal sites such as Sina, Sohu, and Netease, etc. (Fang & Liu, 2004). Unexpectedly, when the dot-com bubble burst in 2001 and heavy losses occurred to many of these investment firms, it was hard for the still infant PE sector to resist a downward spiral.

Encouraged by China's pledge to open its financial market to foreign competition upon its accession to the WTO, as well as the gradually reviving confidence after the post dot-com recession, many famous global PE funds like Carlyle, Texas Pacific Group (TPG), Kohlberg Kravis Roberts (KKR), and Blackstone, etc. shifted their focus onto this market, which was largely untapped yet promising. In December 2004, Newbridge Capital, the Asian arm of TPG, reached a milestone deal concerning the

Shenzhen Development Bank (SDB, a regional state-owned commercial bank based in Guangdong Province). Before its conclusion, the negotiation had been proceeding for 32 months. With a total investment of RMB1.235 billion (or equivalent to USD150 million), Newbridge not only took over 17.89PCT stake from the local government entities, it also gained the management control of SDB, which was rather unprecedented in China (Xu & Hu, 2014). Regarding the reason why a foreign PE investor was allowed such a privilege at a state bank, it was chiefly due to its expertise and experiences in dealing with non-performing loans (NPLs). By the end of 2004, the NPLs of SDB reached 11.41PCT of its gross loans; two years later, the level was successfully reduced to 7.98PCT. Besides, there were simultaneous improvements in other key indicators such as the return on equity (ROE), current ratio, and capital adequacy ratio (CAR), etc. Undoubtedly, replacement of the bank's management team by the new owner should be the key factor for its enhanced performance. In 2009 when China's leading insurer Ping An announced a buyout of Newbridge's stake at SDB, the bank's NPL ratio was down further to 0.68PCT. In many aspects, this was a win–win situation. By restructuring SDB into an efficient and healthier organization, Newbridge was also in a position to exit its investment with a lucrative stake sale. Instead of accepting cash payment, Newbridge finally chose the share-swap option and was compensated with 299 million Ping An shares (a 4PCT stake) in May 2010. Once more, this turned out to be a wise choice because when these shares were sold four months later, the total earnings of Newbridge was USD2.44 billion. If compared with its initial investment of some USD150 million in SDB six years ago, the return was without any doubt rather lucrative.

2.5.2 Legal Improvement After China Venturetech's Failure

While an increasing number of foreign private equity firms were penetrating into the Chinese market, domestic PE players have also started to exert their influence since 2004. Although in terms of the fund size and average returns, the former enjoy much greater advantage; the latter is subject to fewer and less stringent restrictions from the perspective of regulatory hurdles. For example, there are certain sensitive sectors (like military, telecommunications, education, and energy, etc.) which prohibit controlling stake or even investment by foreign funds whereas the same ruling does not apply to their Chinese counterparts. As noted earlier, since the initial motive of China to introduce venture capital was for the promotion of technological development, the first domestic VC firm was sponsored by the government agencies (i.e. the State Science & Technology Commission and the People's Bank of China). Set up in 1985, China Venturetech Investment Corporation was endowed with the mission of investing in nascent high-technology industries (Wang & Chen, 2002). Gradually, due to the low and uncertain rate of return, the company shifted its interests from providing seed funds to offering loans. In other words, it was no longer a real venture capital firm. Beginning from the 1990s, it acted more like a trust and investment company engaged in some risky projects, which inevitably resulted in big losses. By 1998 when the PBoC announced its closure because of insolvency, the total debt had amounted to RMB6 billion. In fact, the failure of China Venturetech was not purely the result of wrong business decisions; backed by the government, its operations could not steer clear of the interferences from the above. As a consequence, these bureaucratic constraints, either tangible or intangible, not only undermined its managerial autonomy; the ability necessary to develop, expand, and diversify was also weakened.

From a broader perspective, the lessons behind China Venturetech are not uncommon among many other corporate entities with similar background. Regarding the root cause of the problem, it still lies in the role of the government. For the purpose of maintaining stable deal flow and being able to assist investee companies to grow, governmental support is absolutely essential; but the influence should be limited only to the regulatory sphere and based on the condition that the power exerted by the market's invisible hand is not compromised. Fairly speaking, from the mid-1980s when China's private equity market was taking its shape to the investment boom which accelerated circa 2004, legal framework construction for the purpose of better governance failed to proceed at the same pace. In particular, against the new norms and practices that emerged in the course of evolution, amendment to the relevant laws had fallen behind.

For instance, the first national partnership law, i.e. the "Law of the People's Republic of China on Partnership Enterprises" (hereafter the "1997 Partnership Law"), was firstly promulgated in 1997. Unlike the jurisdiction of mature market economies which have specialized act on limited liability partnership, a very common type of business structure, the provisions of the 1997 Partnership Law only allowed general partnership (Xu, 2001). Nevertheless, since most PE funds are invested by private firms, limited partnership is universally taken as the dominant organizational form. Under this institutional arrangement, investors are limited partners (or LPs) whose liabilities do not exceed the amount of their pledged capital and take no part in running the firm. Concerning the professional PE managers, they are called general partners (or GPs) and undertake the responsibility of how to best allocate the funds. For lack of legal recognition of limited partnership in China's 1997 Partnership Law, all investors were expected to carry unlimited liabilities. Although beginning from the 2000s, a number of rules were released to allow the establishment of limited liability companies, such as the "Regulations on the Administration of Foreign-invested Venture Capital Enterprises" (2002) and the "Interim Measures on the Administration of Venture Capital Enterprises" (2005), etc.; as long as the 1997 Partnership Law remained intact, setting up a PE firm strictly based on limited partnership could hardly be a feasible option.

In response to the growing demand of both investors and law experts, the revised Partnership Enterprise Law was finally passed in August 2006. By comparing to the former version, the most significant change was the introduction of limited partnership enterprises which should be composed of both GPs and LPs, a requirement that was consistent with the international practice. Besides, the other revision that was made in line with the mainstream customs of the world was the issue of taxation. Instead of imposing dual income tax on both the partnership and partners, the only taxable income to be charged was on partners, thus greatly alleviating the burden of investors when they join a PE fund structured on partnership basis. Moreover, in terms of partnership with foreign investors, the revision only contained a single article stating that it would be formulated separately by the State Council. Three years later, detailed rules in this respect were available following the release of the "Administrative Measures on the Establishment of Partnership Enterprises in China by Foreign Enterprises and Individuals". The Measures not only gave permission to foreign partnership in China, it especially encouraged investment in the service industry with advanced technologies and managerial skills. Apparently, aware of the urgency to enhance the competitiveness of the financial sector, as well as the necessity to cultivate a diversified equity market, the government would welcome more foreign investors, including experienced PE funds, to bring in capital and intellectual properties to help achieve the goals.

2.5.3 From Entry to Exit, a Path with Ups and Downs

In 2007, Southern Ocean Development Featured Venture Capital Partnership was established in Shenzhen (Lu, 2007). As a domestic PE fund organized by 3 GPs and 45 LPs, the company became the first venture of limited partnership after the implementation of the revised partnership law which took place on June 1st. Greatly encouraged by the policy relaxation, China's PE market began to develop in a rapid way. As depicted by the data below (Table 3), 2008 witnessed a significant increase in both the volume of raised capital and the number of new funds. However, overshadowed by the 2008 global financial crisis and the stagnant real economy at home, fund-raising in the following years encountered a marked plunge and until 2012, despite the larger number of PE funds established, only RMB25.31 billion worth of funds were raised, a decline of almost 59PCT if compared to that of 2008.

Fortunately, the slump was soon reversed after the inauguration of the second board market — ChiNext in Shenzhen in 2009. Not merely an alternative source of financing for small and medium-sized enterprises, ChiNext also provided an effective route for PE investors to recoup their investment and exit profitably from the startups. Due to the resurging confidence as well as the release of more favorable policies by the local governments (chiefly Shanghai, Beijing, Tianjin, Chongqing and Shenzhen, etc.) to attract PE funds, the market has featured a steady growth since 2012 (Lü,

Table 3 Raised capital and newly-established private equity funds, 2006–2014

Year	Fund raised (USD billion)	Number of new PE funds established
2006	14.2	40
2008	61.15	51
2010	27.62	82
2012	25.31	369
2014	63.13	448

Source Zero2IPO, 2015

2010). By 2014, with the size of fund-raising registered USD63.13 billion, a nearly four-fold expansion was realized from its 2009 low of USD12.96 billion. Besides, the number of new PE funds also hit its record high, reaching 448 in total.

For private equity investors around the world, the projects they engage in might vary greatly, but their ultimate objective is always the same, i.e. to realize the expected return on their investment within a given time period, usually between three to five years after the initiation of the deal. In this consideration, no matter how lucrative the investment appears at the outset, if a fund failed to exit in the last stage, all the previous inputs would be futile. In order to avoid such an unpleasant consequence, PE firms are often very much concerned about the availability of exit routes before taking the final investment decisions. In general, major strategies include initial public offering (IPO), merger & acquisition (M&A), and management buyout (MBO), etc. By comparison, IPO is perhaps the most preferred option among investors for its flexibility in time, price, and quantity. What's more, once certain market conditions are satisfied, this approach has the potential to bring about the highest possible return on investment. Actually, for the PE firms operating on mainland China, either domestic or foreign, they are no much different from their international counterparts. In their eyes, having a smooth exit channel matters a lot to their profitability. Apart from the main board, the launch of the SME board (2004), the New Third Board (2006), and the ChiNext board (2009), etc. did provide more opportunities for PE firms to claim back their funds. No wonder over years, IPOs has remained their dominant exit route. Nonetheless, the way out was by no means easy. On the one hand, the relaxed policy environment toward private equity since 2006 had resulted in a surge of new entrants in the following two years. Based on the general 3–5 year cycle of investment, most of them were approaching the "exit phase" during the early 2010s. The graph below (Graph 2) demonstrates that together with the booming PE

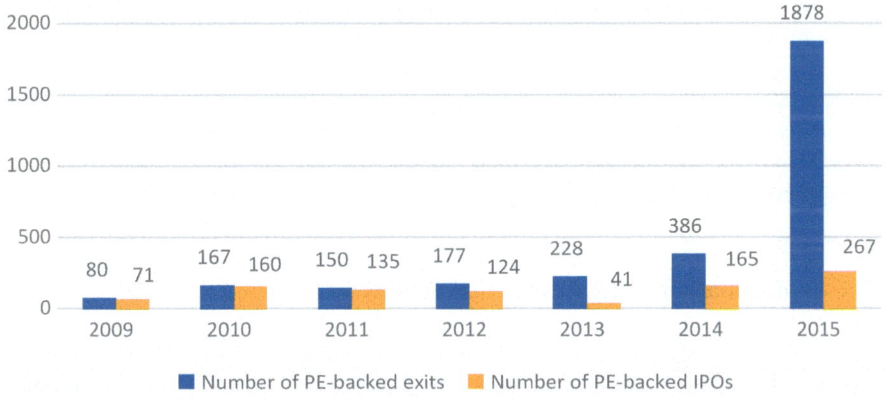

Graph 2 Comparison of PE-Backed IPOs and the Aggregate PE-Backed Exits. *Source* Number of PE-backed exits: 中国股权投资市场2015全年回顾与展望. Zero2IPO Research Center, 2016. Number of PE-backed IPOs: 中国私募股权投资年度研究报告 of the selected years, Zero2IPO Research Center

market over 2007 and 2008, the number of PE-backed exits soared to 167 in 2010 before hitting 177 by 2012, among which the vast majority of them took the form of IPOs to harvest return. Unexpectedly, the trend was discontinued in the next year after China Securities Regulatory Commission (CSRC) called for a suspension on IPOs in November 2012. Concerned about the integrity of the existing share-issuing procedures and fearing that the flood of shares would exhaust liquidity in the market and dampen investors' enthusiasm, the authorities overhauled the system with tougher measures so as to combat collusion and fraud. Later, this turned out to be a 13-month freeze until December 2013 when the reformed mechanism for the issuance of new shares was publicized (Tang, 2013).

- While the temporary halt was necessary to restore order in the securities market, the impact on PE funds was not that equally favorable. For most of them, going public was no longer a feasible outlet; instead, they resorted to merger & acquisition, which totaled 62 cases in 2013. Regarding the number of IPOs, it dropped to 41 only. Rather notably, all of these 41 cases took place on the overseas stock exchanges, with the Hong Kong stock exchange acting as the dominant host. When the securities regulator once again granted approval to new listing applications in the end of 2013, PE-backed IPOs quickly rebounded and reached 267 for the year 2015.

Prior to 2008, China's PE market was largely dominated by foreign giants and the fund raised was rather insignificant if compared to the volume of the world. In 2008, while the capital raised by global PE companies peaked at USD688 billion (Preqin, 2014), the number for China was just USD61.15 billion, less than one tenth of the former. Later on, with domestic institutional investors like the national social security fund (NSSF in April 2008), insurance companies (in September 2010), and securities companies (in October 2012) being allowed to place money with private equity firms, a gradual shift began to occur in the landscape. Due to the active participation of a larger amount of players, market competition became intensified, which was rather positive for the market to get mature. Given the fact that China's economy in the early 2010s was increasingly reliant on the non-state small and medium-sized enterprises, having a vibrant PE sector could help bridge the financing gap left by banks. Moreover, via this process, their capital structure and operational efficiency may also be optimized.

2.5.4 Participation in the Restructuring of SOEs

To sustain the fast growth of both the national economy and the PE business, legal groundwork for the latter was taken as an indispensable part of the government endeavor. Although China had beforehand issued some relevant rules, the guidance promulgated specifically for this sector was available only until 2014 when the "Interim Measures on the Supervision and Administration of Private Investment Funds" was released by the CSRC. While covering a broad range of issues from registration, operation, to the self-discipline of funds, a lot of the routine supervisory functions were delegated to the Asset Management Association of China (AMAC), which from then on began to work side by side with the CSRC to ensure greater transparency and enhance risk prevention of the entire system.

In China, although the role of PE funds in the capital market has been linked primarily to the financing of the private SMEs, their influence goes far beyond to the state sector after decades of development. As a matter of fact, with a view to transforming the state-owned enterprises (SOEs) into modern corporate entities accountable for their own profits and losses, the government had already carried out various rounds of reform which yielded limited improvements. For instance, referring to the idea of "mixed ownership", it was introduced firstly during the 1990s to attract private capital into the SOEs (Li, 2015). But due to the vagueness of its definition and absence of concrete policy directions, the progress remained rather slow. The turning point happened some twenty years later, in the decision document of the Third Plenum of the 18th Central Committee of the CPC released in 2013, the same term was reiterated as part of Beijing's resolute to proceed with the reshuffling of the SOEs. Very soon, vigorous experiment was under way at the local level and of the major trials initiated in different regions, the most well-known took place in Shanghai in 2014. Hony Capital, a PE fund whose fame was mainly from its successful engagement in SOE restructuring, acquired a 10PCT stake at Chengtou, a state-owned holding company for over RMB1.79 billion (Yue, 2014).

Similarly, the authorities at the top were also very decisive and in July, a list of six centrally-controlled enterprises was unveiled by the State-owned Assets Supervision and Administration Commission (SASAC, the country's regulatory body of the SOEs) to participate in its four pilot reform programs (Xin, 2014). Regarding one of the programs which centered on the promotion of hybrid ownership structures, China National Building Materials Group Corp. (CNBM) and China National Pharmaceutical Group Corp. (SINOPHARM) were selected for the trial operation. In their detailed plans later approved by the SASAC, both CNBM and SINOPHARM intended to start with their subsidiaries in which state ownership would be gradually reduced via private equity placements. Later on, similar attempts followed among other central giants as well. In the third quarter of 2014, for example, China Petrochemical Corporation (Sinopec Group), one of the country's leading state-owned oil companies, sold 29.99PCT stake of its Marketing Company to 25 domestic and foreign investors for an aggregate amount of nearly RMB107.1 billion (Sinopec, 2014). Among these investors, major PE funds included HOPU Fund, Qingdao Goldstone Runhui, and RRJ Capital, etc. Given the low efficiency that had long impeded the development of the Chinese SOEs, inviting non-state shareholders could not only improve the quality of their assets; moreover, a diversified structure of ownership may also compel them to be progressively subject to market discipline, without which effective corporate governance can hardly be achieved.

If the foundation of China Venturetech Investment Corporation in 1985 is considered as the initial operation of venture capital funds in the country, then its PE sector has by far evolved for over thirty years, a period blended with both ups and downs.

Table 4 Comparison of VC & PE attractiveness among the BRICs, 2016

Item	Brazil	The Russian federation	India	China
Ranking	54	41	29	24
VC & PE Index (Score)	58.3	63.5	69.9	77.1
1. Economic Activity (Score)	81.1	81.7	103	108.4
2. Depth of Capital Market (Score)	77.5	73.3	79.5	86.7
3. Taxation (Score)	21.3	97.8	84.7	110.6
4. Investor Protection & Corporate Governance (Score)	53.3	53.5	62.7	57.8
5. Human & Social Environment (Score)	33.2	30.9	43.7	50.9
6. Entrepreneurial Culture & Deal Opportunities (Score)	57.9	69.7	62.9	75.9

Source Ranking 2016, IESE Business School from https://blog.iese.edu/vcpeindex/ranking/

Despite its dynamic expansion in the last ten years, the market is still relatively immature if compared with that of the US, whose history could be dated back to the mid-1940s. According to the "Venture Capital and Private Equity Country Attractiveness Index" (developed by the IESE Business School in Spain since 2006), a composite measure showing the attractiveness of a country for limited partners around the globe, the position of China did not change much in the past decade. While it ranked the 25th in 2007 (Groh, Liechtenstein & Lieser, 2011); on the 2016 list, it stayed at the 24th (Groh, Liechtenstein, Lieser & Biesinger, 2016). In addition, of the six key determinants that compose the index (i.e. economic activity; depth of capital market; taxation; investor protection & corporate governance; human & social environment; and entrepreneurial culture & deal opportunities), China scored higher in economic activity, taxation and depth of capital market whereas its performance in the other four criteria were both in need of further improvements.

Although through a comparison of the BRICs (Table 4), an acronym of the four major emerging economies in the world, China led the ranking thanks to its outstanding GDP growth; if to benchmark itself against the top ten of the 2016 list, which were both developed economies, then the gap was much wider. Anyhow, recognizing the disparities is not bad because it may provide China an explicit direction for future efforts. Most notably, if it were to remain one of the world's most active PE markets, an enabling regulatory environment and enhanced accountability should be taken as the two uncompromising imperatives in the years to come.

2.6 Bond Market

In general, a fully-developed capital market should be in a position to provide instruments that contain diverse levels of risks, from stocks characterized by a higher stake to bonds with lower volatility and are thus safer for investors. Referring to the market in which bonds are traded, it not only generates huge liquidity for institutions to raise funds; at the same time, it is also an important carrier that helps transmit the monetary policies of central banks. Usually, the yield curve formed in bond transactions is taken as a benchmark for the pricing of other financial instruments. In line with the rapidly booming activities of the stock exchange, business in China's bond market has been expanding in an equally dynamic way since the beginning of the 2000s. Of its three platforms, the over-the-counter retail market which chiefly offers government bonds by commercial banks to individual investors takes the smallest portion. With regard to the exchange-traded bond market, a wider variety of bonds including treasury bonds, local government bonds, enterprise bonds, and corporate bonds, etc. change hands alongside the stocks on the Shanghai and Shenzhen exchanges. As to the most active segment which claims the lion's share of the deals, it is indisputably the inter-bank bond market (Guo & Yang, 2015).

Comprised of institutional investors like banks, securities companies, and insurance firms, etc., most treasury bonds, policy financial bonds, as well as non-financial corporate bonds are listed and traded via its one-to-one quote-driven system. According to the statistics released by the PBoC for 2015, when the accumulated value of RMB-denominated bonds issued in China reached RMB22.3 trillion, RMB21 trillion were issued through the inter-bank bond market, accounting for over 94PCT of the total. Moreover, by the end of the same year, of its outstanding bonds under custody rising to RMB47.9 trillion, RMB43.9 trillion, or nearly 92PCT were under custody on the country's inter-bank market (PBoC, 2016).

2.6.1 Trading on a Forward Contract

Universally, the development of a country's bond market is measured not only by the range of bond varieties, it is also reflected by the transaction instruments that are available for participants to hedge risks. As far as China is concerned, the progress along these two dimensions since the late 1990s has been rather impressive. On the one hand, the types of bonds have proliferated from the initially limited number of selections (like government and enterprise bonds) to a much wider scope covering policy financial bonds, central bank bills, medium-term notes, as well as general financial bonds, subordinated bonds and hybrid capital bonds of commercial banks, etc. With regard to the transaction instruments, they have equally been diversified. In addition to spot trading and collateral repo (repurchase transaction) which had dominated the market before the 2000s, new options were added in the following years.

In 2004 for example, after the PBoC released the "Administrative Rules on Bond Buyout Repos in the National Inter-bank Bond Market", the business of buyout repurchase was launched and by the end of 2005, its turnover in the inter-bank bond market quickly reached almost RMB219.48 billion, an increase of 72.33PCT over the previous year (CGSDTC, 2006). As a major financial innovation of China's capital market, the buyout repo involves the transfer of bond ownership between the seller (borrower of cash) and the buyer (lender of cash). Since it offers the buyer a short-selling mechanism, profit is still attainable even if the price is expected to move down. From the perspective of the seller, buyout repo is more than just a funding vehicle; what's more, it enables them to hedge a long position when exposed to price increases.

By nature, bond repo belongs to a single transaction that combines a spot sale with a simultaneous forward contract. The benefit of this arrangement is self-evident, especially given the growing volatility of China's interest rates, the uncertainties of future returns have made bond investors more concerned about risk management. Instead of suffering losses passively as before, they were in need of new instruments to balance their portfolios. Based on the international practice, forward trading should be a feasible alternative that can meet the demand. Introduced one year after the inauguration of buyout repo, the first-day transaction on June 15th, 2005 was rather active. Among the participants which were dominated by domestic and foreign commercial banks, Bank of China topped the list by concluding the largest number of deals. However, due to the low level of transparency in information disclosure and poor investor awareness, the trading volume remained flat throughout the rest of the year, which registered RMB17.73 billion (face value) in total (CGSDTC, 2006). The situation was reversed over the next four years, which witnessed dramatic pace of growth and by 2009, the turnover reached its historical high of RMB641 billion, an expansion of more than thirty five times if compared to 2005 (CGSDTC, 2010). Nevertheless, the subsequent decline has been rather steep and during the 2013–2015 period, no single deal was reached.

As a matter of fact, the massive shrinkage was caused by a number of reasons and from the point of view of investors, which were chiefly banks, the contract did not provide them much flexibility. According to the "Administrative Provisions for the Forward Transactions of Bonds in the Inter-bank Bond Market", the governing document issued by the central bank in May 2005, the contractual period should not exceed 365 days. This made it impossible for them to hedge interest rate risks that would more likely occur in the medium and long-term. Besides, settlement on maturity was required to be at a full price calculated by adding the clean price and the accrued interest, which not only increased the liquidity cost of investors, the larger volume of capital flows also undermined the efficiency of the market. Although the regulation put forward a mechanism to guarantee contract performance, it was by no means mandatory and could not really prevent credit risks when default became inevitable. Above all, despite the roller coaster pattern of market performances throughout the 11-year period from 2006 to 2016 (Table 5), the advantages of forward trading should not be annihilated. By locking future returns with a prefixed price, investors may still expect to reduce their exposure to unfavorable movements in interest rates.

2.6.2 Interest Rate Swap

In contrast with the sluggish trading of bond forwards, market response to another derivative has demonstrated a completely opposite picture ever since its appearance.

Table 5 Forward transactions of the inter-bank bond market, 2006–2016

Year	Number of deals	Turnover (RMB billion)
2006	385	65.85
2008	–	498.01
2010	956	310.82
2012	39	14.03
2014	0	0
2016	2	0.02

Source CGSDTC, 债券市场业务总览及中国债券市场年度分析报告of the selected years. https://www.chinabond.com.cn/Channel/19012917?BBND=2005&BBYF=12&sPageType=2#; https://www.chinabond.com.cn/Channel/63390?_tp_il=2

Following the "Notice of the PBoC on Piloting the RMB Interest Rate Swap Transactions" in early 2006, the business was soon carried out in the inter-bank bond market. Designed primarily to cut the financing cost of two parties which have complementary comparative advantages in fixed and floating interest rates, the vehicle allows Chinese banks to better adjust their asset-liability structure while at the same time minimize vulnerability to the volatile interest rates. The first ten-year RMB5 billion deal was finalized between China Development Bank (CDB) and China Everbright Bank (CEB) in February, in which the CEB would pay to the CDB a fixed interest rate of 2.95PCT whereas the latter would pay the former a floating rate linked to the one-year deposit rate (at 2.25PCT at that time) (Zhang, 2006). By entering into this agreement, both the CDB and CEB would reap gains. Additionally, there were other beneficiaries as well. Considering that Chinese banks had long offered floating mortgage rates which added a lot of burden to home buyers, the transaction made it possible for the CEB to be the first fixed mortgage rate provider of the country, thus directly benefiting its customers. In this regard, the deal should also be taken as a successful trial of transferring the risks borne by consumers to the capital market.

As displayed by the statistics below (Table 6), ever since the interest rate swap transactions were initially experimented in 2006, both its number and turnover have maintained a strong momentum of growth year on year. In particular, 2010 was rather remarkable because from then on, the volume exceeded its one trillion mark. Apart from 2013 when there was a decline to about RMB2.72 trillion, the market soon

Table 6 RMB interest rate swap transactions, 2006–2014

Year	Number of deals	Turnover (RMB billion)
2006	103	35.57
2008	4,040	412.15
2010	11,643	1,500.34
2012	20,945	2,902.14
2014	43,019	4,034.72

Source 2006–2012: Zhou, 2014; 2014: PBoC, 2015

recovered aggressively and by 2015, it registered RMB8.23 trillion, an increase of more than 100PCT over the previous year.

2.6.3 SHIBOR, a Benchmark Launched

While it is encouraging to see the thriving swaps of interest rates, the trend could hardly continue if certain problems are not effectively addressed; in particular, the absence of benchmark interest rate. In a full market economy, it is supply and demand that determine the price of money and bonds. As to the benchmark rate, it serves as a reference rate upon which interest swap is based. Around the globe, the most widely-used benchmark interest rates include the inter-bank offered interest rate and bond repurchase rate. For instance, the London Inter-bank Offered Rate (LIBOR) belongs to such kind of benchmark against which many of the world's leading banks charge each other for short-term borrowings. In addition, it is also taken as a reference rate for debt instruments and derivatives. Besides, other benchmark interest rates that bear similar functions include Hongkong Interbank Offered Rate (HIBOR) and Singapore Interbank Offered Rate (SIBOR), etc. In 2006 when bond issuance in China totaled RMB5.68 trillion and the trading volume reached RMB40.19 trillion, with 95.44PCT of the transactions settled via the inter-bank bond market (CGSDTC, 2007), the country's interest rate regime was not yet fully liberalized. On the one hand, a deposit-rate ceiling and a lending-rate floor remained under strict control by the central bank; on the other hand, the money and bond market rates were largely deregulated (Liu, 2013). This is a typical dual-track system which was not uncommon throughout the process of China's reform and opening-up. Moreover, in view of the rapidly expanding bond market, the absence of a benchmark interest rate appeared to be rather incompatible. Without it, investors cannot reasonably estimate their costs and returns, nor would the central bank be in a position to keep its finger on the pulse of the market and exercise influence when found necessary.

To provide a gauge for derivatives such as interest rate swaps, forwards, and short-term interest rate futures, etc., the 7-day fixing repurchase rate (FR007) was launched jointly by China Development Bank (CDB) and the National Interbank Funding Center (NIFC) in 2006, in addition to the daily fixing of overnight repo rate (FR001). After this initial trial, a benchmark interest rate indicator called Shanghai Interbank Offered Rate (SHIBOR) was issued by the NIFC on January 4th, 2007. Averaging the inter-bank RMB lending rates offered by a price quotation group of 18 chosen commercial banks (Wu & Wu, 2014), SHIBOR contains eight maturities, i.e. overnight, 1-week, 2-week, 1-month, 3-month, 6-month, 9-month and 1-year. Shortly after its debut, the first SHIBOR-based interest rate swap was executed in the same month between the Citibank and the Industrial Bank (headquartered in Fujian Province). According to their agreement, the Industrial Bank exchanged a one-year (starting from January 18th, 2007) fixed interest rate of 2.98PCT with the Citibank for a floating rate which was set in line with the SHIBOR of the latest three months (Ren, 2008). Then at each settlement date, i.e. once every three months, the counterparties would exchange with each other the net interest difference. In other words, if within a given period, the fixed rate were lower than the floating rate, the Citibank should pay the difference; but the payer would be the Industrial Bank in case the fixed rate became higher.

With the ongoing process of China's interest rate marketization, the benchmark position of FR007 and SHIBOR has been improving quickly. Take the RMB interest rate swap as an example, the turnover in 2010 based on FR007, SHIBOR (mainly 3 months), and one-year benchmark deposit rate accounted for 54.5PCT, 40.3PCT, and 5.2PCT respectively (Graph 3). Over the following five years, while the importance of each component remained roughly constant, their distribution still underwent certain changes. By far, FR007 as the primary benchmark comprised over 80PCT of the RMB interest rate swap market, an increase of 30PCT if compared with 2010. Regarding the second most popular benchmark, it is SHIBOR which claimed 15PCT. Nevertheless, what should be noted is that its market share has been declining ever since 2012. For the one-year benchmark deposit rate, trading on that basis demonstrated a similar pattern of downward movement. Given its minor proportion of 0.4PCT in 2015, it is very likely that the rate would soon be replaced by the other two.

Apart from RMB interest rate swaps, SHIBOR has a wider application in diverse financial activities of China. Since 2011, it has been increasingly taken as the pricing foundation for the issuance and trading of fixed-interest enterprise bonds, short-term financing bills, and floating-interest bonds, etc. Besides, it is also used in setting interest rates for inter-bank deposits and forward rate agreements, etc. In the context

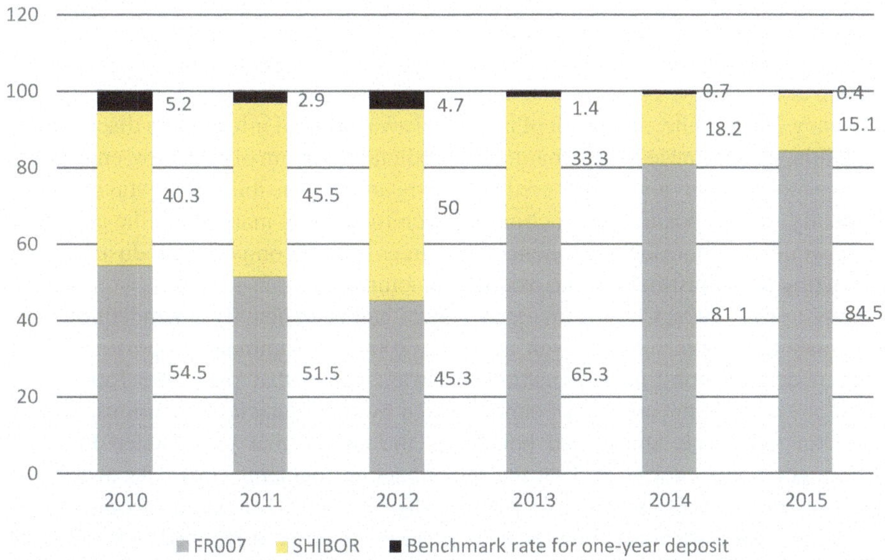

Graph 3 Composition of Different Benchmark Interest Rates for RMB Interest Rate Swap Transactions, PCT. *Source* 中国人民银行 (PBoC). 金融市场运行情况 of selected years, from https://www.pbc.gov.cn/jinrongshichangsi/147160/147171/147173/22578/index4.html

of SHIBOR's growing influence, however, its role as the benchmark for the whole interest rate system still remains to be consolidated, especially in the pricing of medium and longer-term derivatives. In addition, since the transmission of a country's monetary policy is closely linked to the maturity of its bond market, if China could improve the formation mechanism of SHIBOR while at the same time step up with the construction of a bond market which is based on SHIBOR, its regulators would no longer have to maneuver the money supply as they did before; instead, they could exercise macro-control indirectly via adjusting the benchmark interest rate.

2.6.4 Direct Financing Versus Indirect Financing

Fairly speaking, if without the deepened reform of China's economy and the financial sector, it would be impossible for its capital market to go through an impressive growth after the beginning of the new century. In turn, its robust pace of movement has also accelerated the development of the entire nation, at both macro and micro levels. By the end of 2015, the market capitalization of its 2,827 listed companies (the A and B shares listed domestically) hit a record high of RMB53.13 trillion (CSRC, 2016), representing a growth of more than 42PCT over the previous year. Simultaneously, the capital raised by enterprise bonds reached RMB2.94 trillion, accounting for 19.1PCT of China's aggregate financing, a 12PCT rise over that of 2005 (PBoC, 2016). With the expansion of fund-raising capabilities in the capital market, the financing constraints were relaxed to a great extent. Enterprises, instead of relying on fiscal appropriations and bank loans, could have their funding problems resolved via multiple channels and platforms. Additionally, in the process of competing for high-quality financial resources at a lower cost, they were often compelled to introduce a modern corporate governance system, which helped enhance their performance and efficiency. Meanwhile, as a result of improved awareness of information disclosure to the public, plus the necessity to maintain a predictable stream of cash flow, enterprises became more serious about their credit standing and responsibilities for stakeholders. Gradually, such a positive interaction between the capital market and the corporate world would facilitate the movement of resources toward competitive industries, thus optimizing the adjustment of the existing structures.

Prior to the 1990s, China's financial system had been heavily dependent on indirect financing (bank loans). Even after the 2000s, a dominant proportion of the funds raised by non-financial institutions was still in that particular form. Take 2015 for example, the amount of capital raised by non-financial institutions through direct financing (i.e. stocks and bonds) by the end of that year totaled RMB3.7 trillion, accounting for 24PCT of the overall social financing (or total outstanding credit), which stood at RMB15.41 trillion (PBoC, 2016). But when it comes to the outstanding RMB-denominated loans to the real economy, it climbed to RMB11.27 trillion, or over 73PCT of the aggregate value. Although if compared to 2006 when the share of direct and indirect financing were 9PCT (Table 7) and 74PCT respectively, that of the former has managed to hit 24PCT in 2015; the weight of the latter remained little unchanged.

Table 7 Proportion of direct financing as a share of total social financing, 2002–2014

Year	Total social financing[1] (RMB billion)	Enterprise bonds[2] (RMB billion)	Equity financing of non-financial institutions[3] (RMB billion)	Direct financing	
				Amount[4] (RMB billion)	Share[5] (PCT)
2002	2,011.2	36.7	62.8	99.5	4.95
2006	4,269.6	231	153.6	384.6	9.01
2010	14,019.1	1,106.3	578.6	1,684.9	12.02
2011	12,828.6	1,365.8	437.7	1,803.5	14.06
2012	15,763.1	2,255.1	250.8	2,505.9	15.9
2013	17,316.9	1,811.1	221.9	2,033	11.74
2014	16,477.3	2,432.9	435	2,867.9	17.41

Note 4 & 5 are calculated by the author. 4 is the sum of 2 and 3; 5 is 4 divided by 1
Source NBS, 2015

Viewing the fact that among most of the developed countries, an average of 80PCT of the funds raised by non-financial enterprises is backed by securities, China's capital market has obviously fallen behind. From another point of view, such an over-reliance on traditional lending not only laid a huge burden on commercial banks, it also caused their balance sheet to suffer when non-performing loans persisted at a threatening level, reaching RMB1.27 trillion in 2015, an increase of more than 51PCT over the previous year (Zhang, 2016). Therefore, to facilitate the restructuring of the banking sector, an imminent task facing the authorities is to promote direct financing. In the long run, a flourishing bond and equity market is favorable to the reform of the financial sector. Particularly, while alleviating the credit risks borne by banks, it also helps diversify their service offerings through which the profit-making model would be upgraded into a more sustainable one.

Like what happens to various transition economies in the world, China's capital market is rapidly expanding in line with the dynamic growth of other sectors. By comparing to the mature markets of Europe and North America, it is still quite young and faces a lot of challenges ahead. Apart from the need to increase the share of direct financing, it has many other barriers to overcome. From a regulatory perspective, too much administrative control and complex approval procedures only undermine the efficiency of securities issuance. In terms of equities, while most overseas markets have already adopted registration-based systems, which are more standardized and offer greater convenience to participants, China still practices a merit-based approval system that involves higher cost because of considerable bureaucratic influences on the process. As for bonds, the mechanism is even more complicated. Governed by three regulators including the PBoC, the National Development and Reform Commission (NDRC) and China Securities Regulatory Commission (CSRC), multiple standards are applied to different types of bonds, which may easily lead to confusion and even conflicting policies. Furthermore, the segregation of trading platform is another issue to be addressed. With three stock exchanges located in Shanghai, Shenzhen, and Hongkong, transaction of bonds is also split among three markets; namely, the inter-bank bond market, exchange-based market, and commercial bank OTC market. Such a fragmented form of distribution, plus the jurisdiction of separate agencies not only push up the transaction cost, they also create loopholes that might be easily abused by speculators. If China expects to have a globally competitive financial system, not only the market is to be unified, its supervisory regime should also be coordinated in a way that complies with the international norms.

3 Foreign Trade in the New Era

By the time China became a full member of the World Trade Organization, it was already the end of 2001. If compared to 1978 when the external sector was just opened to the outside world, the achievements over the 24-year period should be described as phenomenal. In terms of foreign trade, while the volume exploded in both import and export (Table 8); the once unfavorable balance of trade which had been rather common till the late 1980s was reversed into surplus since the 1990s. By 2001, it totaled USD22.55 billion. Actually, when the chairperson of the Fourth WTO Ministerial Conference announced in November 2001 the decision on China's accession, which was accompanied by a resounding blow of the gavel, the question that had long before dominated the domestic news headlines was "Would WTO membership be the coming wolf?" There was no simple answer to convince all, but what was set to come should be the need to change, both institutionally and operationally.

3.1 *Revision of the Foreign Trade Law*

Back in July 1994 when the Foreign Trade Law (FTL) of China was enacted, it consisted of 44 articles. Although at that time, the foreign trade sector had already been less centralized if compared to the pre-1978 stage, administrative intervention remained rather prevalent, which could also been reflected by this basic law. With greater emphasis laid on the supervisory and management functions performed by the government, directions on the operational side was largely compromised. As

Table 8 Comparison of foreign trade between 1978 and 2001

Year	Total trade volume (USD billion)	Export volume (USD billion)	Import volume (USD billion)	Balance of trade (USD billion)
1978	20.64	9.75	10.89	− 1.14
2001	509.65	266.1	243.55	22.55

Source NBS, 2006

a result of its narrow coverage and lack of practicality, the 1994 FTL later had to be supplemented with multiple regulations, which made the legal dimension of foreign trade rather fragmented. On certain occasions, they even overlapped each other. Moreover, since China by then was not yet a member of the WTO, many of the stipulations were drafted without considering the norms of the international community. But as the negotiation proceeded, especially with regard to the series of commitments made by China to liberalize the regime, amendment to the 1994 FTL became a pressing and obligatory necessity.

On July 1st, 2004, the new Foreign Trade Law went into effect. Inclusive of 70 articles, the revised FTL for the first time permitted individual Chinese to participate in the import and export of goods, technologies, as well as services. In order to obtain the trading rights, approval by the authorized agencies was no longer mandatory; instead, a registration system took its place and this greatly simplified the procedure, thus allowing more interested parties to conduct cross-border activities. Actually, the decrease in the qualification threshold was for the sake of compliance with paragraph 5.1 of the "Protocol on the Accession of the People's Republic of China" (from https://unpan1.un.org/intradoc/groups/public/documents/APCITY/UNPAN002123.pdf) and paragraph 84(a) in the "Report of the Working Party on the Accession of China" (from https://tradeinservices.mofcom.gov.cn/en/b/2001-10-01/24860.shtml), both of which put the liberalization of China's foreign trade rights as a pledge to its WTO membership.

Apart from the above major changes, one more section being added to the new FTL was related to the protection of intellectual property rights, a rather sensitive issue that constitutes one of the three pillars of the WTO legal order; namely, the revised GATT 1994 (covering rules for international trade in goods), the GATS (General Agreement on Trade in Services) and the TRIPS (Trade-related Aspects of Intellectual Property Rights) agreement (Li, 2006). Although safeguarding IPRs is a long-term engagement and China at that moment was just at the very initial stage, incorporating this component into the law demonstrated at least the country's determination to act within the framework of the WTO and assert its due responsibilities that would favor not only itself, but other contracting parties too.

3.2 Reduction on Import Tariffs

Universally, tariffs are perhaps among the most favored means applied by countries to protect their domestic industries or markets. However, as a typical kind of trade barrier, it may easily distort the free movement of products and thus cause frictions across national borders. By joining the WTO in 2001, China immediately confronted a major task of cutting its import tariffs, which covered a process of ten years.

At the outset, it was through the enforcement of the "Customs Import and Export Tariff of the People's Republic of China" in 1951 that the country started to impose duties. Governed by the ideology to prioritize domestic production and safeguard its immature industries from foreign competition, the arithmetic average for tariff rates was set as high as 52.9PCT (Graph 4), with 47.7PCT for industrial products and 92.3PCT for agricultural products. Despite some minor modifications to these rates, the same rule remained effective until 1985, when its amended version named the "Regulations of the People's Republic of China on Import and Export Duties" was promulgated. Taken as the second progressive stage of China's tariff policy, the average rate was cut to 38PCT, also lowered were the rates for industrial and agricultural goods, which slid to 36.9PCT and 43.6PCT respectively. In 1992, to cope with its application to resume the GATT contracting party status, China began to adopt the Harmonized Commodity Description and Coding System (HS), which had been widely used by many countries, as the basis for its domestic tariff classifications. Of the several unilateral reductions that happened afterwards, the sharpest was initiated in April 1996, bringing average tariff from 35.3PCT to 23PCT.

In December 2001, upon its accession to the WTO, China had already committed to having the tariffs on agricultural products decreased to 15PCT. With regard to industrial goods, the average bound tariff level would be brought down to 8.9PCT. Besides, some tariffs would be eliminated while others reduced mostly by the end of 2004, but in no case later than 2010. On January 1st, 2010, with the overall level of China's tariffs averaged 9.8PCT, down from 15.3PCT of 2001, its due obligations concerning all the tariff cuts were accomplished according to the timetable.

Given the causal link that exists between tariff concessions and the expansion of international trade, cutting tariffs becomes an absolute and uncompromisable duty for all nations around the world. In the case of China, if fulfilling the promise to the WTO was a key motive during its initial stage of membership, the long-term engagement in trade liberalization should serve as the ultimate objective. Under this premise, tariffs remain to be further adjusted so that gradually, they may approach the level of those market economies. Although by far, it is still too early to set a schedule for zero tariff on trade, as long as the process moves forward steadily, it is not impossible that China would take the initiative to map out the concrete framework in the foreseeable future.

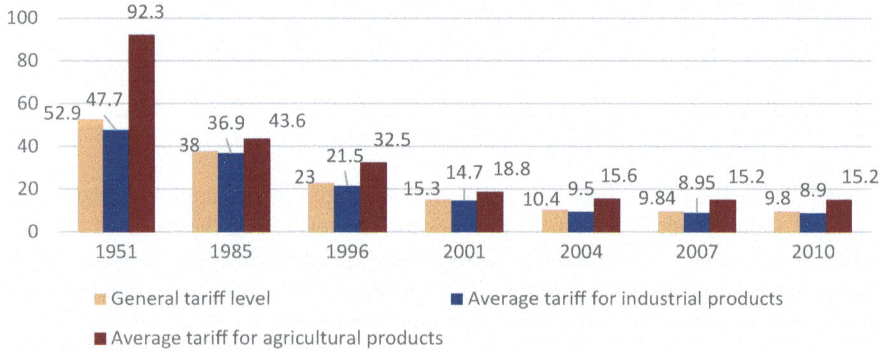

Graph 4 Tariff Reduction of the Pre- and Post-WTO Periods, PCT. *Source* 1951 & 1985: Ma & Li, 2007; 1996: Long, 1996; 2001–2010: MOF, 2012

3.3 Restructuring of the State FTCs

Prior to the 1978 reform, China's foreign trade was almost exclusively monopolized by a dozen of national FTCs (excluding their regional branches). By the year the country joined the WTO, foreign-funded firms as well as private enterprises were already active participants in cross-border exchange. Because of their flexibility in management and quick response to the shifts in the global market, the pace of growth has been rather dynamic, which in turn enabled them to outperform their state counterparts on multiple fronts, especially export. For instance, in 2002, the export volume of foreign-invested firms accounted for over 50PCT of the nation's total (Table 9). Referring to the state-owned FTCs, their share was a bit more than 40PCT. Although in that year, the role of private enterprises was somewhat insignificant, the momentum of expansion was the most impressive among the three. By the year 2015, the contrast became even more obvious. With the contribution of state-run enterprises declining to less than 11PCT, those privately-owned claimed the biggest share which exceeded 45PCT.

Despite the upsurge in the development of China's foreign trade entities, there emerged at the same time a growing concern, especially in view of the competition they were to confront in the international market. To abide by the rules of the WTO, the country could no longer provide incentives freely to these enterprises; rather, they had to rely on themselves to survive and thrive. In this consideration, the challenge was more related to the governance aspect and to stimulate its efficiency, reform of the inner structure was perhaps the most critical point to start with. Fairly speaking, in terms of transformability and adaptability, state-owned FTCs were the weakest. Aware of the necessity to breathe fresh air into these centralized companies, the initial trial had been undertaken early in 1992 with Zhejiang Zhongda Group, which was restructured into a shareholding company (Chen, 2006). Four years later, its shares were listed at Shanghai Stock Exchange and this made the group one of the earliest SOEs that went public in China's foreign trade sector.

Besides, to enable the state FTCs to better cope with the intensifying competitive environment, the Ministry of Foreign Trade and Economic Cooperation (MOFTEC,

Table 9 Composition of export by diverse foreign trade entities, 2002 and 2015

Types of entities	2002		2015	
	Export volume (USD billion)	Share in total[2] (PCT)	Export volume (USD billion)	Share in total[3] (PCT)
State-Owned	122.86	40.07	242.39	10.65
Foreign-Funded	169.94	55.43	1,004.73	44.16
Privately-Owned	13.78	4.5	1,027.83	45.18
Sum[1]	306.58	100	2,274.95	100

Note [1]calculated by the author; [2,3]are calculated by the author by dividing the export volume of each type of entity by the sum of their exports
Source 2002: MOC, 2004; 2015: MOC, 2016

1993–2003, predecessor of today's Ministry of Commerce) also encouraged the establishment of foreign trade conglomerates during the mid-1990s. Similar to Japanese Sogo Shosha or Korean Chaebols, these big firms not only deal in a wide range of products, they are also engaged in diverse activities like finance, logistics, production, as well as intermediary services, etc. Benefiting from the economies of scale, they could take advantage of new commercial opportunities at a lower cost, thus achieving higher efficiency and stable revenue streams. Sinochem (China National Chemicals Import & Export Corp.) Group, a national FTC founded in 1950, gained the approval of the State Council in 1994 to initiate the pilot scheme of converting into a multinational conglomerate integrating a wider range of business scope. On that basis, another major move of restructuring took place in 2009. By setting up a joint stock company under the name of Sinochem Corporation, in which the Group holds 98PCT stake, both the management model and operating mechanism were significantly improved and this to a great extent lowered its exposure to risks when penetrating the overseas markets. In 2015, with the total import and export volume recorded more than USD19.1 billion, Sinochem Group was ranked number nine among the 500 largest foreign trade enterprises of China (Sinochem, 2016).

Following the trial with Sinochem, the experiment of turning the state-owned foreign trade enterprises into transnational trading conglomerates was soon promoted in other parts of the country. At the provincial level, the most notable projects involved entities like Liaoning Animal By-products Import & Export Corporation (in 1994), Shanghai Orient International (in 1995), and Fujian Jiuzhou Group (in 1996), etc. (Lin, 1997). At the same time, for the creation of multiple competitive mechanism so as to facilitate the reform of the state-owned FTCs, the MOFTEC in 1996 issued the "Tentative Measures on the Establishment of Pilot Sino-Foreign Equity Foreign Trade Companies", in which Shanghai Pudong New Area and Shenzhen Special Economic Zone were selected to conduct the program. By 1997, the first three of them had been set up in Pudong, with Mitsubishi (Japan), Cargill (the US), Daewoo (South Korea, photo 5–8), and Sunkyong (SK, South Korea) as the foreign investors. After more than one year of operations, their import and export volume in 1998 totaled USD117.56 million (Gong, 1999).

In 2003, the threshold for foreign companies was lowered when the MOFTEC replaced the 1996 Measures with a revised version. Based on the new rule, they were no longer required to have an annual business turnover exceeding USD5 billion one year prior to their application, nor did they need to have invested over USD30 million in China so as to be eligible. Besides, the registered capital of the joint venture, which had been set at no less than RMB100 million, was cut by half to RMB50 million. In case the registration was in the central or western regions, the limit could be reduced to RMB30 million.

Actually, all these moves were adopted under the condition that when China's foreign trade system was decentralized, the state-owned FTCs could no longer enjoy the same privilege as before. The threat was coming not only from foreign-funded enterprises, but private entities as well. As to the latter, its number soared to 260,000 in 2014, accounting for more than 70PCT of all the businesses engaged in import and export. Although in terms of the experiences in tapping the overseas markets, they still had much to learn. Their strategic approach incorporating both prudence and boldness has enabled them to gain more advantage in the process of development. In the post-WTO era, while efforts to overhaul the inefficient state-run FTCs proceeded, like corporatization, conglomeration, and internalization, etc., the dominant position they had once enjoyed in China's foreign trade could hardly be maintained, as non-state enterprises were rapidly claiming the lion's share. Nevertheless, irrespective of their diverse backgrounds, competing on a level playing field is the only way that can truly demonstrate the strengths of each player.

3.4 Trade in Services: A Growth Engine for the Future

Globally, China is often referred to as the world's manufacturing hub, which on the one hand shows its astonishing scale of production capable of satisfying orders that flood in from almost every corner of the earth. On the other hand, the name also implies the existence of an unbalanced relationship between its trade in goods and trade in services. In 2015, the total volume of its service trade (import and export) was USD713 billion, accounting for only 18PCT of its merchandise trade, which registered USD3.95 trillion (MOC, 2016). Moreover, as a net importer of services, its deficit persisted and stayed at USD136.62 billion, i.e. 14.6PCT lower than the previous year. Regarding the sectors attributable to the deficit, they were mainly tourism, transportation, royalties, license fees, and insurance, etc. In terms of the sources of its surplus, they included processing, telecommunications, computer and information services, consulting, and construction, etc.

3.4.1 Expansion in Service Trade

Despite the persistent gap between export and import, it is still undeniably true that the growth in the service industry has been a steady one. In 1978 when China kicked off its reform and opening-up policy, the tertiary industry contributed less than one fourth to the national economy (Graph 5). By 2012, after over three decades of incessant development, it surpassed for the first time the secondary industry, thus becoming the largest contributor to the country's GDP. In 2015, its share continued to increase and exceeded the sum of the other two sectors.

Under Chapter 51 of the 12th Five-Year Plan (2011–2015), a series of social and economic initiatives which set the course for the next five years, the government highlighted its priorities to develop the tertiary sector. Furthermore, as a concrete roadmap aimed at strengthening the competitiveness of this particular sector, the "Outline of the 12th Five-Year Plan for the Development of Trade in Services" was released six months later in 2011, in which the necessity to optimize the structure of service trade was taken as the most pressing task. For a better understanding of the goals set in this national agenda, a review of the sectoral composition can undoubtedly provide some useful clues. In terms of the import and export value

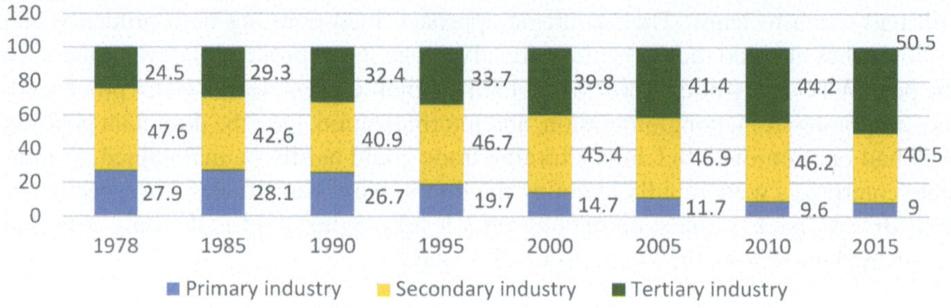

Graph 5 Composition of the Gross Domestic Product, PCT. *Note* 1985 marks the end of the 6th Five Year Plan (FYP), 1990 is the end of the 7th FYP, 1995 is the end of the 8th FYP, so on and so forth and until 2015, it is the end of the 12th FYP. *Source* 1978–2010: NBS, 2016. 2015: NBS. 2015 年国民经济和社会发展统计公报, 2016

contributed by various industries (Table 10), tourism and transportation remained the most important throughout the period of 2000–2014, which together accounted for over 50PCT of the entire sector. At the same time, if counting the one which went through the most noticeable growth, it should be the consulting industry whose share increased most drastically, from 1.5PCT in 2000 to 11.6PCT by 2014, reaching

Table 10 Sectoral composition of import and export in services, 2000–2014

Sector	2000		2010		2014	
	Volume (USD billion)	Share (PCT)	Volume (USD billion)	Share (PCT)	Volume (USD billion)	Share (PCT)
Total	66	100	362.42	100	604.34	100
Transportation	14.07	21.3	97.47	26.9	134.5	22.5
Tourism	29.34	44.5	100.69	27.8	221.71	36.7
Communication	1.59	2.4	2.36	0.7	4.12	0.7
Construction	1.6	2.4	19.57	5.4	20.34	3.4
Insurance	2.58	3.9	17.48	4.8	27.06	4.5
Finance	0.18	0.3	2.72	0.8	10.1	1.7
Computer & Information	0.62	0.9	12.22	3.4	26.86	4.5
Royalties & License Fees	1.36	2.1	13.87	3.8	23.23	3.9
Consulting	1	1.5	37.86	10.4	69.2	11.6
Advertising & Media	0.43	0.6	4.93	1.4	8.8	1.5
Film & Audiovisual	0.05	0.1	0.49	0.1	1.08	0.2
Others	13.2	20	52.76	14.6	57.34	9.6

Source MOC, 2016

Table 11 Export of services by industries, 2000–2014

Sector	2000	2010	2014
	Share (PCT)	Share (PCT)	Share (PCT)
Total	100	100	100
Transportation	12.2	20.1	17.7
Tourism	53.8	26.9	25.6
Communication	4.5	0.7	0.8
Construction	2	8.5	7.1
Insurance	0.4	1	2.1
Finance	0.3	0.8	2.1
Computer & Information	1.2	5.4	8.5
Royalties & License Fees	0.3	0.5	0.3
Consulting	1.2	13.4	19.8
Advertising & Media	0.7	1.7	2.3
Film & Audiovisual	0	0.1	0.1
Others	23.5	20.9	15.5

Source: MOC, 2016

$69.2 billion. Besides, in terms of the trade volume, it is construction, insurance, computer & information, and royalties & license fees which have also witnessed rapid expansion over this fifteen years.

During the same 15-year period, export of services demonstrated some interesting yet similar changes (Table 11). For example, in 2000, the top three exporting industries were tourism, transportation, and communication, which altogether accounted for over 70PCT of the total export volume. In 2014, while tourism maintained its leading position, consulting overtook transportation and became the 2nd largest exporter. By combining the volume of the top three contributing industries, their share of the nation's total export exceeded 60PCT. With regard to import, while insurance and financial services displayed the most dynamic momentum of increase over the past decade, with the booming interest in travelling overseas, tourism stood firmly as the industry that spent the most foreign exchange. In 2014, it claimed 43.1PCT of the total import volume, followed by transportation and consulting.

3.4.2 STRI, a Measure of Market Openness

If comparing to 1982, i.e. the first year when the statistics for China's service trade became officially available, the expansion in its magnitude was rather eye catching, from USD4.4 billion to USD604.3 billion in 2014. However, from its decades-long deficit which reached USD136.62 billion in 2015, it is evident that if the country expects to change its development mode from relying on processing and manufacturing to a new pattern that is service-driven, the road ahead is still full of countless challenges. Since there is always a close relationship between the dynamism of a nation's economy and its openness to the outside world, the future of China's service trade is also to a large extent dependent on how decisive the government is to have it opened to international competition. According to "China's Foreign Trade", a white paper published by the State Council in 2011, all the commitment upon its entry to the WTO had been duly fulfilled, with broad market access offered to foreign players including finance, telecommunications, construction, distribution, logistics, tourism, and education, etc. By and large, of the 160 sub-sectors of service covered by WTO's GATS (General Agreement on Trade in Services), 100 of them had been opened up, approaching the average level of developed countries.

Although this indicator can provide some idea about the breadth of China's openness, it could not tell the depth to which the service sector is actually open. Universally, there is a measure which is often used to evaluate that particular level and it is Service Trade Restrictiveness Index (STRI) of the OECD (Organization for Economic Cooperation and Development). As a special quantitative tool for evaluating the barriers that restrict trade in services (chiefly discriminatory policies or regulations), the STRI indices are valued from 0–100 where 0 is completely open and 100 is completely closed. In 2015, the three leading exporters of commercial services in the world, namely, the US, Great Britain, and Germany, scored the lowest of the selected countries (Table 12). This is not simply a coincidence, it shows that a liberalized regime with fewer artificial constraints is beneficial to the cultivation of international competitiveness. Regarding China, while ranked number five in the services export of the world, the highest among all the developing nations, its STRI

Table 12 Country comparison of service trade restrictiveness index (STRI) and export

Country	Overall STRI score[1]	Export volume of services in 2015[2] (USD Billion)
United States	17.7	690
Great Britain	14.3	341
Germany	17.5	246
France	26.4	239
China	36.6	229
Japan	23.4	158
India	65.7	158
Russia Federation	25.7	49

Note Category of openness STRI scores Completely open: 0 Virtually open but with minor restrictions: 25 Major restrictions: 50 Virtually closed with limited opportunities to enter and operate: 75 Completely closed: 100 From https://iresearch.worldbank.org/servicetrade/aboutData.htm
Source [1]Services Trade Restrictions Index, https://iresearch.worldbank.org/servicetrade/default.htm#; [2]WTO, 2016

scored well above average in all the sub-sectors. In relative terms, retail and transportation were among the least restricted whereas financial, telecommunications and legal services were subject to more stringent controls.

As a transition economy whose comparative advantage is largely derived from its abundant and cheaper labor force, China for more than three decades has reaped a lot from its demographic dividend. Nevertheless, facing the aging population and the rising labor cost, adjustment of the manufacturing sector with more service-oriented strategies remains an imminent need in order to cope with the threat from other emerging markets. Instead of competing at the lower tiers of the supply chain by doing processing and assembling, offering higher value-added services can enable China to move upward and garner a larger share of the profit. Actually, a similar shift is also taking place across the globe, which represents another round of division of labor centered on the service sector. If China can grasp this opportunity and turn its labor-intensive manufacturing economy into a service economy that is knowledge-intensive, its development would be more resource saving and environmentally friendly.

From a primitive agrarian society to an industrial economy, the leap realized by China is by no means an easy one, especially considering its tremendous population. Right now, for another big stride to take place, more strenuous and painstaking efforts are to be made. However, considering the fact that in most developed countries, the tertiary sector already contributes 70-80PCT to the GDP, China does not have much time to waver. Even in case the manufacturing sector is to repeat its success story, as long as the overall services remain backward and underdeveloped, the drag on the growth could hardly be underestimated. As a window connecting China with the outside world, trade in services, chiefly the balance between import and export, offers a benchmark enabling the country to identify not only the obstacles to raising the services share in GDP, but also the reform approaches to the optimization of its structure.

3.5 *Trial of Free Trade Zones*

Around the globe, as a major initiative to promote foreign trade, countries located in a particular geographical region would enter into free trade agreement with each other, the result of which is the establishment of a free trade area (FTA). As the name suggests, barriers that hinder cross-border trade are either minimized or removed, thus enabling member states to boost their import and export. Similar to these multilateral FTAs, there is yet another form which is set up within the territory of a single country, like Shannon Free Zone in Ireland, Colon Free Trade Zone in Panama, and Busan-Jinhae Free Economic Zone of South Korea, etc. Since what they have in common is that all the imported goods are exempted from customs duties, companies buying components from abroad can process them into finished products for export at a much lowered cost, thus acquiring a competitive edge to boost foreign trade. By 2013 when China had already signed free trade agreements with around 20 countries and regions (including Hong Kong, Chile, New Zealand, Singapore, Costa Rica, Iceland, and Switzerland, etc.) (MOC, 2014), it did not have its independent free trade zones (FTZs) yet, which was rather incompatible with the country's position as the world's second largest economy and leading trader of commodities.

For the opening of further domains and in particular, to enable companies of the service sector to operate in a more liberalized environment, the China (Shanghai) Pilot Free Trade Zone (SFTZ) was launched in September 2013 as a platform for the execution of bolder strategies. Based on the "General Plan for the China (Shanghai) Free Trade Zone", a framework that outlined the overall objectives and key measures, six fields of the tertiary sector were chosen to experiment with eased restrictions on foreign investors. Covering totally eighteen industries, these fields were financial; shipping; trade & commerce; professional; cultural; and social services. Besides, for the promotion of transparency, a major institutional innovation that complies with the international norms was the adoption of the "Negative List" ('fumian qingdan'), i.e. the list of sectors which foreign investors could not access inside the zone, thus making it possible for them to extrapolate the activities they may engage in. If comparing to the 2013 version in which 190 items were subject to restrictions and prohibitions, the Negative List for 2014 was shortened to 139 items before being further trimmed to 122 in 2015 (Zhu, 2016).

Although during the post-WTO era, China's export has maintained at an average growth rate of over 28PCT for six consecutive years till 2007 (Graph 6), the momentum slowed down shortly after the advent of the 2008 Financial Crisis and in 2009, a negative rate of 16PCT occurred. Despite a strong rebound in the next two years, the performance afterwards once again displayed a lack of dynamism. Superficially, the sluggish external demand may help explain why China's export failed to sustain a robust increase; however, what the country really had to pay attention

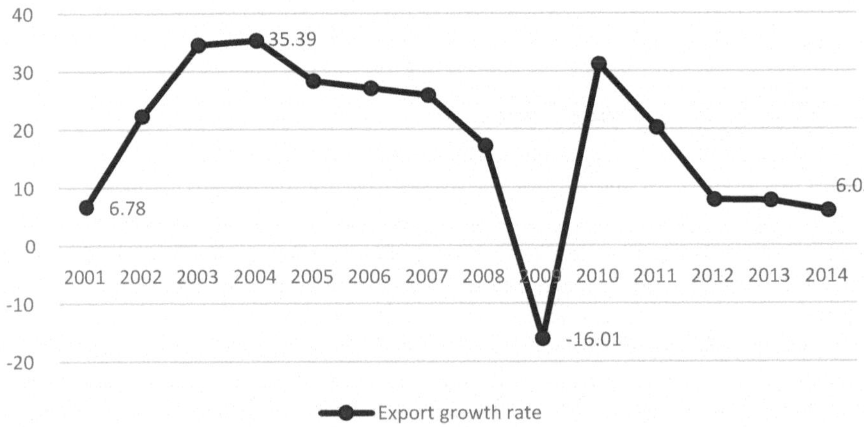

Graph 6 Export Growth Rate, PCT. *Note* calculated by the author based on the export volume of selected years. *Source* NBS, 2016

to was the very fact that its high energy-consuming and resource-intensive development model could no longer match the change in the global trade pattern which is increasingly sensitive to issues like CO2 emissions. In other words, the stagnant export growth was just a mirror of the problem; at the root, the challenge is how to transform into a low-carbon and more ecologically-friendly economy.

Since the endeavor of promoting service trade coheres closely with the prevailing global trend, the formation of the SFTZ is indeed an initiative consistent with that end. With a view to enhancing China's competitiveness and position in the global value chain, various measures have been tested since the opening of the SFTZ. Concerning the supervision of goods and services, for instance, before completing the customs declaration formalities with entry and exit record list, enterprises are allowed to bring goods into the Zone with import manifests, which helps simplify the clearance procedures and reduce the transit time, thus saving them a lot of cost (Wang, 2015). In addition, the tax regime has equally been tailored to support trade. If enterprises based in the free trade zone need to import equipment or machinery for their own use, they would be eligible for tax exemption. According to the customs statistics, the trade volume of the SFTZ in 2014 reached RMB762.38 billion, accounting for 26.6PCT of Shanghai's total, which was RMB2,866.8 billion (MOC, 2015). In April 2015, i.e. nineteen months after the first FTZ was unveiled in the financial hub of China, three more FTZs were set up in Guangdong, Fujian province and Tianjin municipality. Based on their locations (Photo 1), all the free trade zones are without exception situated alongside the coastal region, which to a certain extent reflects that in terms of openness, the interior part of the country has fallen behind.

By far, the experience of both China and the world has confirmed positively the role of free trade zones; in particular, the spillover effects they are in a position to exert. This is extremely significant to China because after almost four decades of reform, the most fundamental task that remains to be tackled is the mechanism through which resources are allocated. For the time being, the intervention of administrative power is still not uncommon and this has greatly undermined the workings of the invisible hand, thus hindering the establishment of a free-market economy. Similar to the special economic zones set up during the 1980s, free trade zones are a testing ground where the thresholds prohibiting fair competition are minimized. As a result, companies, regardless of their background, could operate on a level playing field abiding by the same rules. Simultaneously, by granting national treatment to foreign-controlled enterprises whose offerings are in general higher value-added, indigenous firms would be compelled to respond with more drastic reforms so as to stay competitive. In view of the fact that China's FTZs are dominated by companies of the service sector in which it does not have much advantage, the pressure from the outside may constitute a healthy pushing force that would mobilize the Chinese service providers, especially banks and financial institutions, to come up with lower-cost solutions to better serve the real economy. At the current stage, all the four FTZs are still in the pilot phase. With the promotion of the scheme and participation of more inland localities, the regional gap as well as the sectoral imbalances can expect to be improved in a gradual way. However, given the complexities of China's reform, it is impractical to rely on one single method to deliver the ideal results. In

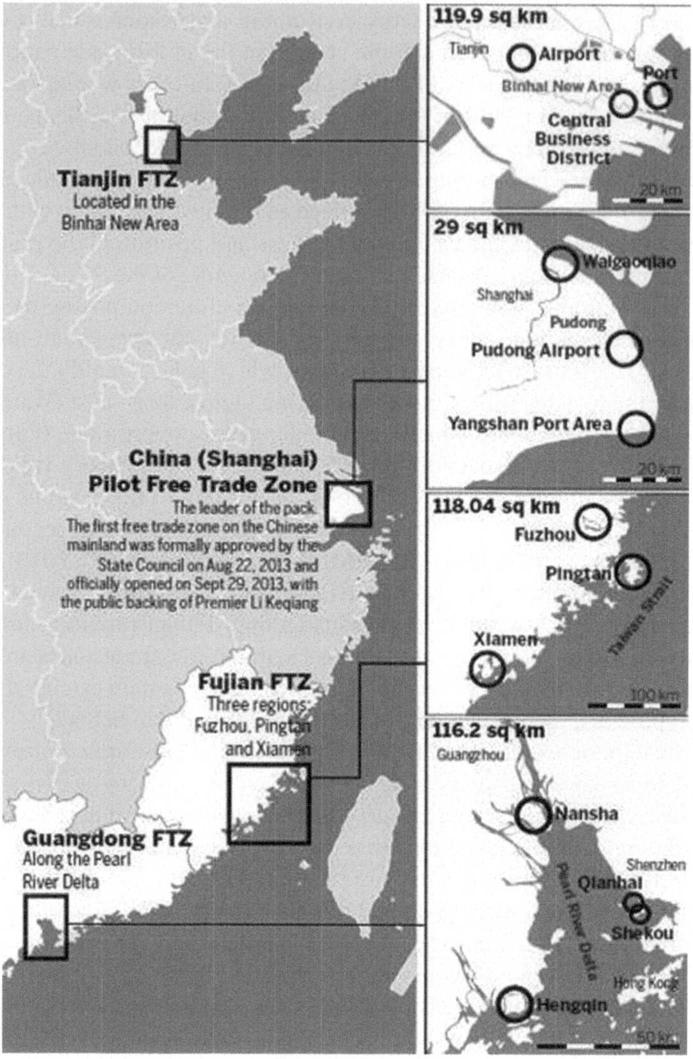

Photo 1 Distribution of the four free trade zones in China, from the north to the south, they are Tianjin FTZ, Shanghai FTZ, Fujian FTZ, and Guangdong FTZ. *Source* https://www.chinadaily.com.cn/business/2015-04/21/content_20493185_2.htm

this consideration, setting up FTZs is at its best part of the economic policy package that would work well only when other supportive strategies are in place.

4 RMB Exchange Rates and Capital Account Liberalization

Every sovereign country has its own legal tender and as long as it is an open economy, it is always necessary to set a price at which its currency can be converted into another. Due to the constant changes in supply and demand, the price, also known as exchange rate, would vary from time to time. In this process, what the government does is to decide on a mechanism through which the value of the currency is to be adjusted. Accordingly, in line with the fluctuations of the exchange rate, not only the performance of current account and capital account, the macroeconomic trends would also be influenced through the profitability of foreign trade and shifts in capital flows.

4.1 Initial Adjustment of the Mechanism, a Gradual Approach

As far as China's exchange rate regime is concerned, it has gone through several stages of reform before the nation gained full membership of the World Trade Organization in the end of 2001. Roughly, the period from 1949 to the late 1970s should be taken as the initial phase during which the state overvalued the yuan in order to serve the national import-substitution industrialization strategy. By pricing the yuan at a higher level and controlling the allocation of foreign exchange reserves, the government was in a position to purchase equipment and machinery from overseas markets at affordable prices in order to support the development of priority sectors, namely the heavy industries. Like a double-edged sword, however, while the overvalued yuan did benefit the import business, export suffered net losses. For more than two decades covering the 1950s-1970s, when the domestic currency cost of earning one US dollar kept rising, the official exchange rate stood firmly, even with an upward movement.

After the late 1970s when export began to play an increasingly predominant role in the national economy, the exchange regime underwent some relaxation of control, such as the introduction of a more favorable internal settlement rate, retention of foreign exchange earnings, and opening of swap centers to facilitate the adjustment of imbalances, etc. Although the internal settlement rate was abolished on January 1st, 1985 due to its convergence with the official rate (at RMB2.8 each US dollar), the government on the one hand depreciated the RMB several times so as to ease the impact of the high-rising domestic price levels. On the other hand, it allowed the swap market to continue its operation around the country, which created another kind of dual exchange rate system. In the end of 1993, as the official rate was down to RMB5.72 each US dollar, the prevailing swap rate went even lower, at RMB8.72 (Xiao, 2008). By comparing to the fixed official rate, the swap market exchange rate could better demonstrate the real picture of supply and demand. Moreover, it was rather attractive to exporters and helped them realize greater profit margins.

Nevertheless, from a long-term view, the existence of double exchange rates (if counting the black market rate, the number would be three) was undoubtedly a destabilizing factor which caused unfair competition and resource distortion. At the same time, it was also harmful to the absorption of foreign direct investment because investors from abroad would be discouraged to convert their capital into the yuan at official rate and buy foreign exchange at the swap market with a much higher cost.

In an effort to enhance regulation and bring the yuan more approximate to its equilibrium rate, the central leaders initiated a critical undertaking on January 1st, 1994 by transforming the country's exchange regime into a unified managed floating system. Within the following decade, the most remarkable achievements included the replacement of swap centers with a nationwide inter-bank foreign exchange market, full convertibility of the RMB under current account transactions, and permission of opening foreign exchange accounts by domestic enterprises, etc. Very likely, it was due to these preparatory measures that China soon witnessed a rapid growth in both the trade surplus and foreign exchange reserves, which in turn enabled the country to confidently maintain the stability of its currency instead of joining the catastrophic depreciation of its neighboring counterparts throughout the 1997 Asian financial crisis. In this regard, the crisis can be taken as a test of how firmly China could stand against the repercussions caused by external turbulence. At least, based on some key economic indicators for the subsequent years (Table 13), the country had coped rather well. Considering that the crisis started in 1997 and ended in 1999, the table below centers on the three-year period of 1998–2000 to check the impact it had exerted on China. In terms of its GDP, the growth rate had a slight decline of 0.7PCT in 1999 before climbing to 8PCT in the next year.

Behind these movements, what backed the economy were three key pillars, i.e. export, foreign direct investment, and domestic consumption. Understandably, with the official RMB exchange rate remained almost unchanged at RMB8.27 per US dollar while many Asian currencies were dropping sharply, increase in its export could not match the pace of import, thus resulted in a downward slope in the trade surplus. FDI, a measure of foreign investors' confidence in China, plummeted by over USD5 billion in 1999 in the capital actually used, which shows that amid the uncertainties that overshadowed the prospect of a robust future, the wait-and-see

Table 13 Selected indicators of the economy after the 1997 Asian financial crisis, 1998–2000

Year	GDP growth rate (PCT)	Trade surplus (USD billion)	Actually utilized FDI (USD billion)	Growth rate of household consumption expenditures (PCT, at comparable prices)
1998	7.8	43.47	45.46	5.5
1999	7.1	29.23	40.32	7.9
2000	8	24.11	40.72	8.3

Source NBS, 2002

attitude was getting more prevalent. Fortunately, the negative mentality wasn't that contagious and by 2000, a minor recovery appeared showing that the situation was turning for the better. As to the third pillar, i.e. the level of household consumption, it is of no less significance to China, especially given its large population. Calculated by dividing the total amount of consumption by the population, it not only demonstrates the disposable income of the Chinese people; further, it is also reflective of their willingness to spend. In other words, if they are optimistic about the future, they would buy more. Otherwise, they would prefer to keep the money in their wallet. Unlike the other statistics in the table, residents' interest to purchase was not much affected by the Asian crisis, at least from the tendency over these three years, it rose steadily at a pace of more than 7PCT on average. Indeed, no matter under which kind of circumstances, a country should have multiple engines to fuel the economy. If reliant too much on a single contributor and ignore the nurturing of new growth sectors, then it would potentially leave itself vulnerable to external shocks. Conversely, even if the risks are threatening, the country can still expect to make up the losses and rebound by utilizing the advantages of other industry clusters. As an old saying goes: it is not wise to put all the eggs in the same basket, the same principle equally applies to the management of the macro economy.

In addition to the above, one key reason that enabled China to remain relatively unscathed during the severe Asian turmoil was the RMB's peg to the US Dollar, which made it rather stable before 2001. Whereas the yuan's exchange rates were officially determined through trading on China's foreign exchange market, the number of participants in the market was limited by the government. This restrictiveness was deemed appropriate for the central bank to intervene and keep the yuan at the targeted value of RMB8.28 per US dollar. Specifically, to have the goal achieved, what the central bank did was to print more RMB to purchase the increasing foreign exchange earnings from both export and FDI. In order to mitigate the subsequent inflationary pressure, bonds were issued to assimilate the excess supply of the yuan, a method often referred to as sterilization (Wang, 2008).

At that time, the Chinese leaders were not without any worries, especially in view of the ongoing negotiations for the WTO membership, they knew the necessity to abide by its rules. Instead of orchestrating the economic strategies and having them implemented in a top-down way, elements of free market economies should be introduced. At the same time, policymakers from other countries also expressed concerns over the RMB. They unanimously believed that it was due to the undervalued yuan that gave China an unfair advantage in international trade and investment. Thereby, December 11th, 2001, the day when China gained accession to the WTO should be remembered for its twofold meanings: together with the immense opportunities, new obligations were set down as well for the country to cope with. As a fundamental principle, by obliging China to deregulate its market to an extent much more drastic than it would otherwise have done, intervention into the movement of the RMB exchange rates could no longer happen that freely. In essence, this requirement was not contradictory to China's commitment to open its financial sector to foreign competition before 2007 (Zhuang & Wang, 2007). With the entry of foreign banks to conduct domestic currency business, more capital would flow in and out of the country and in turn, this would engage the central leaders to propel the reform of exchange regime onto the national policy agenda.

4.2 Conditions Prepared for the Next Stage of Reform

Starting from February 2002, the strong US dollar began to show signs of weakness against foreign currencies due to the cyclical changes of its economy and major adjustment in the fiscal and monetary policies. The duration lasted for three years and till the end of February 2005, the US dollar/euro exchange rate fell from 0.87:1 to 1.33:1, a devaluation of 52.9PCT, or 18PCT on an annual basis. Regarding its rate against the Japanese yen, it showed the same trend and depreciated from 1:134 to 1:105, or a drop amounting to 22PCT (Zhao, 2008). When the US dollar was heading down, China did not choose to immediately alter its managed floating exchange rate regime, which pegged the yuan to the US dollar. As a result, the competitiveness of the Chinese products in the international market and the policy of encouraging export-oriented FDI created persistent twin surpluses in both its current account and capital & financial account, which led to a continuous increase in the foreign exchange reserves.

The graph below (Graph 7) tells clearly why within a matter of just three years, China's foreign exchange reserves could expand by over 180PCT and hit USD819 billion in 2005. Nonetheless, that pace of accumulation could not last long; otherwise, the very fact that some 70PCT of its reserves were denominated in the US dollars (Yang & Tan, 2007) would make China very vulnerable to the fluctuations in its value. In other words, further decline in the US dollar, if happened, would cause the worth of its reserve assets to shrink tremendously. Moreover, from a diplomatic point of view,

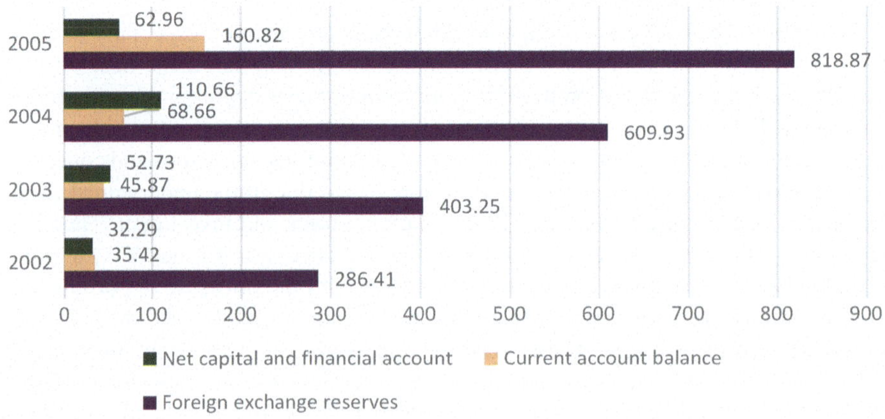

Graph 7 Comparison of Foreign Exchange Reserves and Balance of Payments Performance, USD Billion. *Source* NBS, 2003, 2004, 2005 and 2006

excess current account surplus means deficit for trading partners and once lasted too long, it would easily escalate into tensions or even trade wars, a scenario which is harmful to all. Thereby, toward the year 2005, pressure was mounting both internally and externally for China to revalue its currency so as to adjust the performance of the balance of payments.

Early in October 2003 when the Third Plenary Session of the 16th Central Committee of the CPC was held, the tasks of deepening the financial reform and perfecting the mechanism for shaping the RMB exchange rates were already highlighted among its various priorities concerning the improvement of the socialist market economy. Soon after, the State Council mapped out a working plan in which reform of the financial sector took precedence. In that December, the Pilot State-owned Commercial Bank Overhaul Program was initiated first at the Bank of China (BOC) and China Construction Bank (CCB), with each of them being injected USD22.5 billion of capital to help resolve the problem of non-performing loans and improve their asset quality (Jin, 2007). As another major attempt to enhance the efficiency and corporate governance of Chinese banks, all were encouraged to go public on the stock exchange. In October 2005, the CCB became the first state-owned commercial bank among the "Big Four" (i.e. the ICBC, BOC, CCB, and ABC) to launch its initial public offering (IPO) in Hong Kong (Su, 2005).

While bank restructuring was moving forward smoothly, a special panel was organized by the State Council to design a blueprint for the reform of the RMB exchange rate system. By coincidence, an important seminar on China's foreign exchange rate system took place on May 26th, 2004, after the inaugural ceremony of the Joint China-IMF Training Program (CTP) in Dalian, Liaoning Province (IMF, 2005). Attended by a number of economists as well as the officials from the IMF and the PBoC, the conference provided insightful suggestions and valuable approaches regarding how China should carry out its transition to a basket-based regime. After all these and other preliminary endeavors, 2005 became a year when the preconditions for the reform of the exchange rate mechanism were broadly met. Besides, another favorable aspect was the macro environment of China, which was experiencing both a steady growth and low inflation. Undoubtedly, this strengthened the confidence of the central leaders and facilitated the ultimate implementation of the scheme.

4.3 New Exchange Rate Regime in 2005

The long-expected decision was made finally in the summer of 2005, following the release of the "Public Announcement of the PBoC on Reforming the RMB Exchange Rate Regime". At 7:00 pm of July 21st, 2005, the exchange rate against the US dollar was adjusted to RMB8.11, a 2.1PCT revaluation on the basis of the former RMB8.28 each US dollar. By doing so, the decade-old practice of linking its currency tightly to the US dollar was terminated and as its replacement, the yuan would be floating with reference to a weighted basket of currencies (on August 10th, Zhou Xiaochuan, the governor of the PBoC, claimed that depending on the importance of diverse countries to China's foreign trade, external debt and FDI, etc., the composition of the currency basket was dominated by the US dollar, euro, Japanese yen, and Korean won; plus a smaller proportion made up of the British pound, Singapore dollar, Malaysia Ringgit, Thai baht, Australian dollar, Russian ruble, and Canadian dollar, but the exact weight attached to these currencies in the basket was not disclosed). Also in the announcement, the central bank stressed particularly that although still a managed floating regime, the RMB's pricing mechanism would involve greater flexibility and be based more on the market supply and demand. Like before, the PBoC would continue to publicize the closing price of a foreign currency (like the US dollar) traded against the yuan in the inter-bank foreign exchange market after the closing of the market on each working day and accordingly, this price would be taken as the middle rate for the trading against the yuan on the next working day.

At the outset of the reform, the daily trading price of the US dollar against the yuan was permitted to swing within a band of no more than 0.3PCT from the reference rate set by the PBoC, i.e. RMB8.11 each US dollar. Then on the first trading day, i.e. July 22nd, 2005, the rate could vary between the ceiling of RMB8.0857 and the floor of RMB8.1343. No matter at which level the market closed, it would be automatically taken as the central parity of the second trading day, so on and so forth. Concerning the trading prices of non-US dollar currencies, they would also move against the RMB within a certain range (1.5PCT at that time) fixed by the PBoC. Toward the end of the announcement, the central bank declared that the floating parameter of the RMB would be subject to further modifications in case market development and the overall financial situation made it necessary.

Fairly speaking, the initial step of revaluing the RMB by 2.1PCT was rather moderate and it reflected that the Chinese authorities did not intend to see a dramatic fluctuation in the exchange rates. Moreover, by not unveiling the exact composition of the basket, the central bank could more conveniently intervene the market by changing the currency mix so that the value of the yuan would not move far beyond its expectations. But in the eyes of outsiders, this practice gave rise to the suspicion of currency manipulation, for which China had been criticized on different occasions. Anyhow, although this move could hardly be satisfactory to many foreign policymakers, it still represented a good beginning for the country to introduce free market principles to bring the yuan toward a long-term equilibrium. In the light of its immediate benefit, at least, it could help palliate the discontent of some partners over the growing bilateral trade imbalances, especially that of the United States for its persistent current account deficit with China.

Throughout the remaining months of that year, the RMB exchange rates continued to demonstrate the same trend of gradual revaluation. From RMB8.11 per dollar on July 22nd, it reached RMB8.1 in mid-August and RMB8.09 by mid-September. On the last trading day of 2005, i.e. December 30th, the exchange rate stood at RMB8.0709 (Table 14), which corresponded to a 2.5PCT appreciation from RMB8.2765 each US dollar on July 21st. In contrast to the relative stability of the yuan against the US dollar, there were more fluctuations with respect to other currencies during the same period and the major reason was that the central bank on September 23rd adopted a new band of fluctuation for non-dollar currencies, which

Table 14 Movements in RMB exchange rates against selected currencies, 2005

Date	CNY/USD	CNY/EUR	CNY/JPY100	CNY/HKD
July 21st, 2005	8.2765	9.9914	7.3133	1.0637
December 30th, 2005	8.0709	9.5624	6.8466	1.0405

Source 人民币汇率中间价列表, State Administration of Foreign Exchange. from https://www.safe.gov.cn/wps/portal/sy/tjsj_hlzjj_inquire

doubled the original limit to up to 3PCT around the central parity. Consequently, as compared to the rates on July 21st (Table 14), the yuan (CNY) revalued by 4.3PCT and 6.4PCT respectively against the euro (EUR) and the Japanese yen (JPY) on the last trading day of 2005.

Indeed, successful reform of the exchange regime is not only limited to the establishment of a sound and transparent system; moreover, it is in need of the support of a healthy market in which transactions are conducted with relaxed access conditions and minimum government intervention. Referring to China Foreign Exchange Trading System (CFETS), ever since its operation in April 1994, it has functioned as a unified national inter-bank foreign exchange market for designated foreign exchange banks (members) to square their positions derived from retail business on a daily basis. On this electronic platform, members could make back-to-back (anonymous) quotes through either on-site or distant trading terminals. Although similar to the major foreign exchange markets outside China, it could offer real time matching of orders in an automatic way, the fact that it was an administrative unit of the PBoC largely restrained its efficiency, with very low exposure to competition and loose supervision by the members.

Due to the stringent approval requirements for financial institutions to engage in the business and limited scope of currency products, etc., the development of the CFETS remained rather inhibited. While in the end of 1994, it had 303 members; the figure rose to 366 by June 2005, with market activity concentrated highly among a small number of them. Although 179 of these members were foreign banks (Ji, 2015), it was still the state-owned and joint equity commercial banks which dominated the trading. Apart from this unbalanced distribution, the other noteworthy aspect lied in market access, which was predominantly granted to banks, leaving only two trust and investment companies as the privileged non-bank financial institutions. Therefore, it is not that surprising when comparing to the average daily turnover of the world's major foreign exchange markets in countries like Japan, Germany, Singapore, the UK, and the US, China's inter-bank market appeared very insignificant (Graph 8). Of course, it should still be noticed that over this period, the pace of growth in China has been rather dynamic after the arrival of the new century, which witnessed an expansionexpansion of almost 177PCT in its daily turnover, from USD0.3 billion of 2001 to USD0.83 billion in 2004.

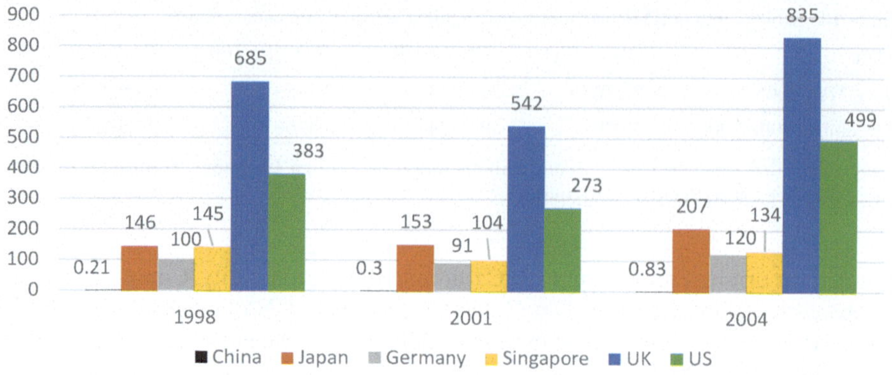

Graph 8 Average Daily Foreign Exchange Market Turnover of Selected Countries, USD Billion. *Note* China's daily turnover for 1998 is calculated by the author by dividing the annual turnover of USD51.96 billion by 252 trading days; for 2001, it is calculated by dividing the annual turnover of USD75.03 billion by 252 trading days; for 2004, it is calculated by dividing the annual turnover of USD209.04 billion by 252 trading days. For China, the volume is based on the entire year and pertains only to inter-bank spot transactions. For markets outside China, daily averages are for the month of April and cover spot, forward and swap transactions. *Source* China: SAFE, 1999, 2002 & 2005; Countries outside China: BIS, 2013

4.4 Establishment of Market Maker System

For the purpose of speeding up the development of such a market and in particular, to make it perform due functions concerning the formation mechanism of the RMB exchange rates, the State Administration of Foreign Exchange (SAFE) decided to introduce the market maker system into the inter-bank foreign exchange market. In general, market makers (dominated by banks) work with customers by telling them both the "bid" (buy) and "ask" (sell) prices for the exchange of foreign currencies; very often, they would also furnish expert information on different finance positions. Standing prepared to enter into transactions with customers at these prices, they are in a position to contribute to market liquidity. Emerged in the over-the-counter securities market of the United States during the 1960s, the services of market makers were not introduced into China until July 2001 when the PBoC approved 9 commercial banks to be bilateral quotation makers ('shuangbian baojia shang') for twenty bond varieties (Liu, 2011). In July 2004 when the name of "market maker" was used by the central bank to replace the original "bilateral quotation maker", the market maker system officially came into being in the country's inter-bank bond market. In terms of the trading of foreign exchange, the prices prior to the 2005 reform were subject to the benchmark quoted by the central bank, which inevitably led to excessive presence of the government and malfunction of the market. With the "Guidelines for Inter-bank Foreign Exchange Market Makers (for Trial Implementation)" released by the SAFE in 2005, qualifications to get the license were simultaneously stipulated, against which 13 banks became eligible providers of the RMB spot trading service

(Wang, 2007). One month later, their names were publicized and among them, the ABN AMRO Bank, Citibank, HSBC, Standard Chartered, and Bank of Montreal were foreign banks, in addition to the four state-owned banks including the ICBC, ABC, BOC and CCB, and four share-holding banks, i.e. Bank of Communications, China CITIC Bank, China Merchants Bank, and Industrial Bank Co., Ltd.

As one further step toward a more market-oriented exchange rate regime, the PBoC released on Jan. 3rd, 2006 the "Announcement on Improving the Inter-bank Spot Foreign Exchange Market". In this No. 1 announcement of the year, it was declared that since January 4th, 2006, over-the-counter transactions (OTC transactions, 'xunjia fangshi') would be brought into the inter-bank spot foreign exchange market while the way of negotiation ('cuohe fangshi') shall still be preserved. At the same time, the system of market makers was to be introduced in order to provide liquidity for the market, thus ending the central bank's role as the sole player in all currency trades. With regard to the formation mechanism of the central parity of the RMB exchange rate against the US dollar, which had been based on the closing quotation in a negotiation mode in the inter-bank foreign exchange market before, it would be calculated instead by taking a weighted average of quotes from market makers. Specifically, every day before the opening of the market, the CFETS would inquire prices from all the market makers for the computation of the central parity. After excluding the highest and the lowest, it would confirm the central parity of the current day by the weighted average of the remaining quotations. The weights for the market makers, although not fully disclosed, were determined by the CFETS in line with the transaction volumes of respective market makers and several other indexes. In terms of the central parity of the RMB rate against euro, Japanese yen and Hong Kong dollar, their calculation was not only to consider the central parity of the RMB-US dollar exchange rate of the current day, the exchange rates of these currencies against the US dollar in the international market at 9:00 am would equally be counted. Then at 9:15 am of each working day, the CFETS would publish the central parity of the RMB against the US dollar, euro, Japanese yen and Hong Kong dollar, which shall be taken as the central parity of the exchange rate for the inter-bank spot foreign exchange market (including OTC transactions and negotiation) and the OTC transactions of the banks on the current day.

According to the timetable set by the PBoC, OTC trading of spot foreign exchange kicked off on Jan. 4th, 2006 when the 13 licensed commercial banks began to exercise their role as market makers. Since they were mandated to trade the yuan at quoted sell and buy prices, the new system limited the extent to which the central bank could intervene in the currency markets. In other words, while it is true that their participation could not immediately remove the control of the central bank, it promised a trend of greater exchange rate flexibility for China. Prompted by the widespread revaluation expectations, the RMB-US dollar exchange rate rose from RMB8.0702 on Jan. 4th (the first trading day of that month) to RMB8.0608 each US dollar on Jan. 27th, 2006 (the last trading day of that month due to the lunar new year which fell on Jan. 29th). Till the end of the first quarter, the yuan appreciated totally by almost 0.66PCT and reached RMB8.017 per US dollar.

4.5 Launch of Foreign Exchange Derivatives

In addition to the above, the new exchange rate regime initiated in 2005 also provided impetus for developing foreign exchange derivatives. With the growing risks caused by frequent variation in the RMB/USD exchange rates, there was a higher demand for hedging instruments. Back in April 1997, 12 branches of the Bank of China became the pioneer in launching on a trial basis forward settlement transactions, an arrangement under which two currencies (one being RMB) are exchanged at an agreed forward rate for delivery on a future date. By prefixing the currency price, this product could help lock costs and revenues for enterprises expecting to pay or receive a given amount of foreign currencies someday in the future. Due to its advantages in risk control, the experiment was later expanded and by 2005, both the four state-owned banks and three joint-stock banks (i.e. Bank of Communications, China CITIC Bank, and China Merchants Bank) had carried out the same business for their customers (Tang, 2007). To a great extent, the shift to the new exchange rate regime on July 21_{st} fastened the liberalization of the RMB derivatives market. Via the "Notice on Relevant Issues for Enlarging the Forward Settlement and Sale of Designated Foreign Exchange Banks to Clients and Launching the RMB Swaps against Foreign Currencies", which was released by the PBoC in August 2005, more banks gained the permission to enter into forward contracts or swap deals with trading enterprises in particular to help them reduce the exposure to exchange rate fluctuations.

Almost at the same time, through another important document entitled the "Notice on Accelerating the Development of Foreign Exchange Market", the central bank not only invited non-financial enterprises and non-bank financial institutions to transact as members of the inter-bank market, it also encouraged the introduction of forward and swap business to broaden the existing scope of activities. Shortly after the issuance of these regulations, inter-bank forward trading started on August 15th, 2005 (Tang, 2007). As displayed in the table below (Table 15), in terms of the number of deals struck and their volume, the growth rate exceeded 99PCT and 59PCT respectively from 2006 to 2007. However, if compared to the size of the world, China's was only an insignificant share. Taking 2007 as an example, in that year, while the average daily turnover of forward contracts in the global foreign exchange market reached USD362 billion, the annual turnover of China was not yet even one tenth of that figure, merely USD22.38 billion (Yang & Chen, 2008).

Table 15 RMB foreign exchange forward and swap transactions, 2006–2007

Year	Number of forward contract	Annual turnover of forward trade (USD billion)	Number of swap contract	Annual turnover of swap trade (USD billion)
2006	1,476	14.06	2,732	50.86
2007	2,945	22.38	15,896	314.61

Source SAFE, 2007 & 2008

Regarding the swap trade (or called foreign exchange swap, 'renminbi waihui diaoqi') which combines a spot and a forward transaction into a single one, it is another form of derivative taking place between two parties to hedge against translation exposure. Usually, they would exchange a certain amount of two currencies at the spot rate in the first place before having them exchanged back after a given time period at the pre-agreed rate. It was in April 2006 that China commenced the RMB foreign exchange swap in the inter-bank market, and the first deal was concluded between the Bank of China and the Export–Import Bank of China (China Exim Bank). Till the end of 2007, the country's turnover registered USD314.61 billion, a phenomenal five-fold rise over the previous year. At the same time, the foreign exchange swaps that happened daily in the world market already averaged USD1,714 billion (Yang & Chen, 2008). Therefore, despite the unprecedented boom of China's foreign exchange market in response to a series of regulatory reforms, it was rather trivial in both breadth and depth once measured against the broader international landscape. For the government authorities, the challenge was how to effectively integrate the norms and practices of foreign countries into their domestic operations so that the gap separating the two sides could be gradually narrowed down.

As a major milestone in the improvement of infrastructure for China's inter-bank foreign exchange market, a brand-new trading system was launched on April 9th, 2007 by the CFETS using the latest technologies. Via this advanced portal featuring automated and programmed quotation, market makers and member banks could trade the yuan electronically against major world currency pairs and foreign exchange derivatives (e.g. forward and foreign exchange swap) in real time. At the initial stage, five currency pairs against the RMB were offered and they were the US dollar, Hong Kong dollar, Japanese yen, euro, and British pound. Facilitated by the revamped currency trading platform, especially its enhanced functionality, one more derivative instrument was shortly put on the market. Based on the PBoC's "Circular on Matters Relevant to the Opening of RMB Swaps against Foreign Currencies in the Inter-Bank Foreign Exchange Market" dated August 17th, 2007, the CFETS was to offer the system for currency swap transactions between the RMB against the US dollar, euro, Japanese yen, Hong Kong dollar, and British pound. Besides, by defining the term "RMB and foreign exchange currency swap" ('renminbi waihui huobi diaoqi') as "a trading agreement on exchanging between a stipulated amount of RMB principal and a stipulated amount of foreign currency principal within the prescribed period of time and exchanging the interests on the two currencies on a regular basis", the Circular also laid out how the principal may change hands between the contracting parties. As to the interest, since permission was given to have it computed either at a fixed or a floating rate, the mechanism of interest rate swap was in fact incorporated into the currency swap business of China.

Since generally, both the counterparties to a swap deal have their own "comparative advantage" in a particular yet different credit market (for example, domestic firms can often receive better rates than a foreign firm), the arrangement of interest rate swap could enable them to fully utilize each other's advantage in one particular market and realize interest rate savings in another market to which access would be otherwise impossible. In other words, a combination of privileged access would help them lower the cost of funding, thus the potential risks arising from the uncertainties in future interest rates are under better control. Because of these benefits, it is rather common to see currency and interest rate swaps used together as financial tools to reduce the cost of raising debt. After the launch of the RMB currency swap business, however, the response of the market was not very active. In 2007 for example, only four contracts were signed and the total value was USD80 million. Following the outbreak of the global financial crisis, the annual turnover for the next year only recorded USD10 million (SAFE, 2009).

4.6 Capital Account Convertibility

From July 21st, 2005 when the basket-peg regime substituted the previous USD-peg regime, the daily trading price of the RMB against the US dollar in the inter-bank spot foreign exchange market was kept at 0.3PCT above and below the central parity announced by the PBoC, while the trading price of non-US dollar currencies such as euro, Japanese yen and Hong Kong dollar against the RMB also moved within a certain range, which had initially been set at ± 1.5PCT before being raised to ± 3PCT in that September. With a view to promoting the flexibility of the RMB exchange rates so that its value could remain at an adaptive and equilibrium level based on market supply and demand, the central bank in May 2007 widened the daily RMB-USD trading band to 0.5PCT around the central parity publicized by the CFETS. Five years later, in view of the fact that China's foreign exchange market was getting more mature and trading entities had achieved greater independence in their pricing and risk management, the trading limit was once again loosened to ± 1PCT after April 2012. As the latest move, the central bank in March 2014 further doubled the band to ± 2PCT, leaving the yuan more volatile to the ups and downs of market forces.

Therefore, if to establish a four-stage timeline based on these five particular days (Table 16), they can vividly demonstrate the gradual relaxation of control over the RMB exchange rates over the two decades. By focusing on the changes in the price of the yuan against the US dollar, it can be found that every time a turning point

Table 16 Four-stage movement of USD/RMB exchange rates, 1994–2014

Date	USD/RMB rate	Revaluation of RMB against USD (PCT)
January 1st, 1994	RMB8.7	–
July 21st, 2005	RMB8.2765	4.87 (stage one)
May 21st, 2007	RMB7.6652	7.39 (stage two)
April 16th, 2012	RMB6.296	17.86 (stage three)
March 17th, 2014	RMB6.1321	2.6 (stage four)

Source 人民币汇率中间价, SAFE. From https://www.safe.gov.cn/wps/portal/sy/tjsj_hlzjj_inquire

occurred, the yuan would grow stronger. In addition, the pace of its appreciation had been accelerating quickly before it slowed down after April 16th, 2012. Taking the entire period as a whole, the RMB totally revalued by almost 30PCT, from RMB8.7 to RMB6.1321 each US dollar.

4.6.1 Stipulations in the IMF Documents

When China began to undertake the obligations of Article VIII under the IMF Articles of Agreement about current account convertibility on December 1st, 1996, the issue of capital account opening was also brought up. Questions were raised in the international community as to when China could provide a specific timetable. Instead of making a quick promise to the world, the policymakers adopted a more carefully sequenced and conservative approach, which was proved sensible following the outset of the Asian financial crisis. Unlike those neighboring countries which were victimized because of their prematurely opened capital account, China's choice to keep its capital account closed buffered the country from the worst of the contagious shocks. Yet despite the caution, the Chinese central leaders were clear on their mind that as part of an apparatus to align credit with development strategies while maintaining financial stability, the capital account policies could exert an irreplaceable role. To them, the decision to move forward had already been made and thereby, the key concern was not if, but when and how the account would be opened.

The Balance of Payments Manual, an authoritative text of the International Monetary Fund, is chiefly on the accounting standards which the member countries (or economies) can refer to when reporting their cross-border economic transactions. Since the publication of its first edition in 1948, the IMF has revised it several times and by far, the latest one is the sixth edition. Entitled the Balance of Payments and International Investment Position Manual (or BPM6), this new version highlights not only transactions, but the capital flow around the world as well, especially the relationship between financial assets and liabilities. According to the interpretation of BPM6, the BOPs of an economy "consists of the goods and services account, the primary income account, the secondary income account, the capital account, and the financial account" (Chapter 2: Overview of the Framework, retrieved from https://www.imf.org/external/pubs/ft/bop/2007/pdf/bpm6.pdf). Regarding the capital account, it shows "nonproduced nonfinancial assets and capital transfers between residents and nonresidents". In other words, it is a record of "acquisitions and disposals of nonproduced nonfinancial assets, such as…, as well as capital transfers, that is, the provision of resources for capital purposes by one party without anything of economic value being supplied as a direct return to that party". In terms of the financial account, it registers "transactions that involve financial assets and liabilities and that take place between residents and nonresidents" (Chapter 8: Financial Account). Usually, these transactions should include "direct investment, portfolio investment, financial derivatives (other than reserves) and employee stock options, and other investment and reserve assets". Here in this book, "capital account" is used to substitute the "capital and financial account" of the BPM6 and describes the subset of BOPs covering all non-current international transactions.

While Article VIII of the IMF Articles of Agreement claims explicitly that "no member shall, without the approval of the Fund, impose restrictions on the making of payments and transfers for current international transactions" (Sect. 2, retrieved from https://www.imf.org/external/pubs/ft/aa/index.htm), the same document does not prohibit the control of capital transfers. Instead, it even allows its members to "exercise such controls as are necessary to regulate international capital movements" (Article VI: Capital Transfers, Sect. 3). However, despite the absence of a constitutional basis for the removal of restrictions on capital mobility, the IMF over the past decade has been working very hard on communicating its approach to capital account liberalization to the member states. For example, to strengthen multilateral surveillance and in particular, financial surveillance of systemic risks, it draws on its empirical analysis through periodical studies such as the Spillover Report and External Sector Report, etc. so that greater attention would be directed to push factors that impact international capital flows. Fairly speaking, capital account liberalization is not necessarily a sure guarantee of long-term economic growth; history does not lack evidence showing that sometimes, opening short-term capital account may even bring serious financial turmoil (like Asia and Latin America in the 1990s). From the experiences and lessons of many countries, if without sound institutions and quality governance in place, liberalizing capital account would only harm growth. Anyhow, the lack of an absolute positive correlation cannot automatically lead to the annihilation of what unrestricted movement of capital may contribute. As a more immediate effect, it can help speed up financial development with increased investment, reduced funding cost, and enhanced efficiency, etc. In turn, given the strong linkage between a nation's financial capability and its economic vitality, capital account liberalization will indirectly but ultimately favor economy.

4.6.2 Three Prerequisites Reviewed

In a broad sense, three critical conditions should be satisfied before moving into capital account convertibility and they are: a strong domestic banking system, relatively well-developed domestic financial market, and an exchange rate that is reasonably close to its underlying equilibrium level. Concerning the Chinese banks during the mid-1990s, they were still heavily reliant on massive government injections of capital to write off the non-performing loans (NPLs) accumulated over years. Due to the extension of excessive policy loans, the outstanding debts of state commercial banks in the end of 1997 was estimated to be about RMB1.5 trillion. If counting the whole banking sector, the magnitude would exceed RMB2.2 trillion (Liu & Xu, 1998). To avoid the dire consequences of insolvency, the government was compelled to adopt different measures to bail out its ailing banks. Most notably, it issued RMB270 billion (about USD32.6 billion) of special T-bonds in 1998 to recapitalize the "Big Four" (Wang, 2006). Moreover, four asset management companies (AMCs) were established in the following year to relieve them of some of their NPLs. By 2000, the AMCs had purchased RMB1.4 trillion (equivalent to USD170 billion) of NPLs from the state banks, upon which they assumed the right to dispose of them on a commercial basis.

In accordance with China's agreement upon its accession to the WTO, the country had to open its banking sector to foreign counterparts before 2007. The tight deadline compelled the government to quicken the pace of restructuring. In December 2003, the Central Huijin Investment Limited, a wholly state-owned investment company, was founded to further consolidate the capital base of the banking sector by writing off the remaining bad loans (Zhao, 2004). To summarize, the process of reshuffling the Chinese banks was in its full swing at the turn of the new century. At that time, their earnings were generated chiefly through deposit taking and lending activities, with the PBoC controlling the benchmark rates of both. Although certain flexibility was allowed for adjustment purposes, interest rates were by no means liberalized, which not only prohibited competition, but also hampered the opening of the country's capital account.

Concerning the second prerequisite, i.e. a relatively mature financial market, its significance is self-evident. While such a market can channel diverse sources of funding for business entities to expand at home and abroad, it also helps stimulate innovation among banks and non-bank institutions so that the overall quality of their services would attain a higher level. By comparison, China has a more developed market for government bonds than enterprise bonds; moreover, issuance has long been dominated by a handful of large state-owned institutions (typically the major banks), which explains why it has been difficult for enterprises, especially the small and privately-owned, to raise capital. Table 17 reports the composition of external financing instruments used by the non-financial sectors of China during the 2003–2005 period. The data suggest that although enterprise bonds was a tool increasingly used to raise funds, bank loans on average were responsible for over

Table 17 Composition of financing instruments by non-financial sectors, 2003–2005

	2003		2004		2005	
	Amount (RMB 100 M)	Share (PCT)	Amount (RMB 100 M)	Share (PCT)	Amount (RMB 100 M)	Share (PCT)
Total	35,154	100	29,023	100	31,507	100
Bank loan	29,936	85.1	24,066	82.9	24,617	78.1
Government bond	3,525	10	3,126	10.8	2,996	9.5
Enterprise bond	336	1	327	1.1	2,010	6.4
Stock	1,357	3.9	1,504	5.2	1,884	6

Note Non-financial sectors include households, enterprises, and public sectors. The flotation of non-financial institutions is not included in the stock. Enterprise bonds mainly consist of short-term financing bill (or commercial paper) and medium-term note. *Source* PBoC, 2005 & 2006

80PCT of external financing. In addition, through 2003 and 2004, the size of the former remained just one tenth of the government bonds issued. Even for 2005 when financing via enterprise bonds experienced a dramatic growth, its portion was still an insignificant one in the entire portfolio.

Apart from the enterprise bond market, the foreign exchange market boomed rapidly after the depegging of the yuan against the US dollar in 2005. With the launch of a number of RMB derivative types such as forwards, foreign exchange swaps, and currency swaps, etc., Chinese importers and exporters could better hedge foreign exchange risks inherent in an environment of increasing RMB volatility. According to the BIS Triennial Central Bank Survey, which is deemed the most comprehensive source of information on the size and structure of global foreign exchange and OTC derivatives markets, the average trading volume of the global foreign exchange markets hit USD5.35 trillion each day in April 2013 (BIS, 2013). Like the ranking of the previous years, the three dominant vehicle currencies were still the US dollar, euro and Japanese yen. On the list of the top ten most traded currencies, there emerged a new member and it was the Chinese yuan. For the first time in history, the RMB was ranked number nine (number four to eight were the British pound, Australian dollar, Swiss franc, Canadian dollar, and Mexican peso, with New Zealand dollar being the tenth most important currency), accounting for 2.2PCT (USD120 billion per day on average in April 2013) in the turnover of the world foreign exchange market, mostly driven by a significant expansion of offshore RMB trading. Together with the increasing status of the yuan, foreign exchange trading in China surged quickly at the same time, reaching USD47.3 billion per day in 2013 (SAFE, 2014), up by 25PCT over the previous year.

In addition to the requirements on banking system and financial market, having a fairly-valued exchange rate is the third major determinant for a country to realize smooth transition to capital account convertibility. Of the different approaches which can help make sure whether the RMB is under- or over-valued, the most common method is to estimate the exchange rate necessary to bring a country's current-account imbalance to a "normal" level. On that basis, the measure of exchange rate deviation is associated with the ratio of the sum of exports and imports to GDP. As a widely accepted criterion for an absence of misalignment between the two, the expected current account balance should share about 3-4PCT of the GDP. In case the trade surplus persistently exceeded that range, then appreciation of the currency would become necessary to balance trade. In other words, the currency is undervalued. On the contrary, the currency is overvalued and a depreciation would be necessary. If referring to the performance of China, its current account surplus has been ballooning ever since the untying of the yuan's peg to the US dollar in 2005. Over the six years up to 2010, it was only in 2009 when the growth rate was a negative 30.27PCT (Table 18). Besides, referring to the magnitude of the foreign exchange reserves which exploded by almost 250PCT to USD2,847 billion in 2010, this was indeed rare in the rest of the world. Behind such a massive build-up, one key contributor was apparently the mounting surpluses on the current account.

Table 18 Current account surplus and foreign exchange reserves, 2005–2010

Year	Current account surplus (USD Billion)	Year-on-year growth rate[1] (PCT)	Foreign exchange reserves (USD Billion)
2005	160.82	134.23	818.87
2006	249.87	55.37	1,066.34
2007	371.83	48.81	1,528.25
2008	426.11	14.6	1,946.03
2009	297.14	– 30.27	2,399.15
2010	305.37	2.77	2,847.34

Note [1]Calculated by the author, with the current account surplus of 2004 at USD68.66 billion
Source 中国统计年鉴 of the selected years, NBS

As a result, the country's current account balance to GDP ratio stayed on average within the range of 4-10PCT throughout the same period, well above the internationally accepted parameter. Therefore, using the remark by Dominique Strauss-Kahn, the former managing director of the IMF, at an annual meeting on Oct. 7th, 2010: "We believe that the renminbi was substantially undervalued and something has to be done to fix this problem over time" (IMF, 2010). For the creation of a healthier economy, China was in need of real price mechanism, not official intervention, to allow its exchange rates to fluctuate in accordance with market forces.

4.6.3 Record of the Developed Economies

After a brief evaluation of how China was prepared for the opening of capital account from the three above-mentioned perspectives, it should be recognized that toward the end of the 2000s, the country was not yet fully ready. Under such circumstances, instead of aggressively pushing forward the process, an incremental model with measures taken in discrete stages would perhaps bring about a more ideal outcome. In particular, given its growing influence across the world, macroeconomic stability is always of the utmost concern to the policymakers. For the creation of spillovers that can exert a constant and positive impact, capital account opening must be carefully timed and coordinated with other reforms, especially the financial sector which should possess the capability of channeling massive cross-border fund flows and the exchange rate regime which needs to be resilient enough to cushion against external shocks.

By referring to the record of several developed economies, it is found rather common that after their current account openness, it would take another fifteen to twenty years to have the capital account liberalized (Table 19). Benchmarking against the US and France, which spent the longest (nearly 30 years) among these five countries, it is reasonable to estimate that China, still a developing economy, may equally use the same amount of time before fulfilling the convertibility of capital account transactions. To be specific, if counting from 1996 when China committed to

Table 19 Time of capital account openness of selected economies

Country	Year of capital account convertibility
The United States	1974
The United Kingdom	1979
Germany	1981
Japan	1991
France	1990

Source Shao, 2014

the IMF that it would bear obligations under Article VIII of its Articles of Agreement, then the prospective liberalization may take place between 2020 and 2025.

Moreover, through a closer look at how these advanced countries have managed the complex task, a number of similarities could be identified. For instance, their road of liberalization mostly followed the same gradual process of phasing out controls, which covered the whole spectrum of capital movements. To counter speculative attacks that may destabilize exchange rates, restrictions on inflows have been mainly applied to short-term capital transactions, especially during the 1960s and the 1970s. Regarding restrictions on outflows, the targets were more oriented to long-term direct investment and foreign equity transactions so that the deficit in the balance of payments could be decreased. Take the United States as an example, from 1963 to 1974, it employed interest equalization tax of up to 15PCT on interests received from foreign borrowers (Qi, 2014). Obviously, this raised the price of foreign securities and made them less lucrative to the domestic investors. As a result, with fewer residents willing to purchase, the decline in capital outflow improved the nation's BOP, which had already endured a worsening deficit since the late 1950s.

4.6.4 Three-Stage Roadmap Outlined

The Annual Report on Exchange Arrangements and Exchange Restrictions (AREAER), a publication of the IMF since 1950, is universally taken as a primary source of information concerning the de jure (legal and policy) controls over the capital account exercised by all its member countries. In the AREAER's post-1996 reporting system (from volume 1997 onward), capital transactions were divided into 7 binary-coded subcategories covering a total number of 40 concrete types. By using a simple 0/1 dummy variable, a country would be considered as having a restricted capital account if the value is "1" whereas it would be coded "0" in case the capital account is open. Thereby, the higher the value, the higher the degree of capital account restrictions. In the AREAER issued for the year 2011, China's capital account performance was displayed. Instead of using the dummy variable, four levels including "not convertible", "partially convertible", "basically convertible" and "fully convertible" were applied to portray in a vivid way the exact extent of restrictions in the country.

From the table below (Table 20), it can be noticed that four items were not convertible, which accounted for 10PCT of the total. Those partially convertible took the

Table 20 Status of capital account liberalization, 2011

Subcategories under capital account transactions	Not convertible	Partially convertible	Basically convertible	Fully convertible	Total
1. Capital and money market instruments	2	10	4		16
2. Derivatives and other instruments	2	2			4
3. Credit operations		1	5		6
4. Direct investment		1	1		2
5. Liquidation of direct investment			1		1
6. Real estate transactions		2	1		3
7. Personal capital transactions		6	2		8
Subtotal	4	22	14		40

Source PBoC, 2012

largest share of 55PCT among the four. With a sum of twenty two, they were mostly concentrated in stocks and bonds transactions, as well as real estate and personal capital transactions. For items that were marked basically convertible, the number registered fourteen and the majority of them were related to credit operations, direct investment, and liquidation of direct investment. However, China at that time did not yet have any item that was graded convertible. In summary of the above, by the end of 2011, 90PCT of all the forty items had become convertible in different degrees. Given the fact that among all the member states of the IMF, almost everyone had certain de jure restrictions and very few were fully-opened in the capital account, the gap between China and the rest of the world was at least not that unbridgeably far.

On February 23rd, 2012, the Statistics and Analysis Department of the PBoC released a policy research report announcing that the conditions for China to facilitate the opening of its capital account were basically mature (PBoC, 2012). After evaluating four major potential risks that may arise from capital account liberalization, namely, assets and liabilities of the commercial banks, the composition of foreign exchange reserves, short-term external debt, as well as the real estate and equity market, the report concluded that they were generally manageable. Therefore, rather than waiting for the complete marketization of interest rates and absolute freedom in exchange rate movements, the country should take concrete actions to loosen capital restrictions, which in turn would also be constructive to the reform of the aforesaid prerequisites. As to how the road map is to be laid out, three stages were suggested and each spanned different lengths of time. To begin with, it was a short-term plan for a period of 1–3 years and the aim was to deregulate outward direct investment by the Chinese companies. Then in the medium run of 3–5 years, the plan was to ease control over commercial credit for trade so as to broaden the channels for inbound RMB flows. Finally, regarding the long-range projection within a time frame of 5–10 years, the focus was on the one hand to consolidate the development of the financial market; at the same time, transactions of real estate, stocks and bonds would be opened with caution, coupled with a gradual substitution of price-based management for quantitative regulations.

4.6.5 Landmark Moves in Policies and Actions

As indicated in the above, capital account is made up of multiple items ranging from capital transfers, acquisition or disposal of non-produced, non-financial assets to direct investment, and portfolio investment, etc. Under each category, there also consists of a wide variety of components. Therefore, opening capital account, or removal of all the barriers that would impede cross-border movements of capital should be country-specific and carefully weighed in the light of both rewards and risks. In view of China's unique conditions as well as the lessons from other countries, its loosening of control has observed a principle covering four dimensions: inflow first, outflow next; long-term transactions first, short-term transactions next; direct investment first, portfolio investment next; and institutional investors first, individual investors next. Guided by this order of priorities, inward foreign direct investment (FDI) has preceded others in its experience of liberalization. Beginning in the early 1980s, the establishment of special economic zones had attracted investors from Hong Kong, Taiwan and South Korea to relocate their factories to the Pearl River Delta. Throughout much of the 1990s, a more massive wave of FDI made the country one of the largest FDI recipients in the world. According to the "World Investment Report 1995" of the United Nations Conference on Trade and Development (UNCTAD), by attracting USD34 billion of direct investment in 1994, i.e. two times higher than that of 1992, China ranked the second largest recipient of FDI in the world, after the United States only (UNCTAD, 1995). Besides, what is even more noteworthy is that the country's outbound FDI during the 1990–1994 period averaged USD2.43 billion per annum, thus making it one of the leading outward investors among developing countries in the 1990s.

In 1993, an important document named the "Decision of the CPC Central Committee on Several Issues Concerning the Establishment of a Socialist Market Economic Structure" was promulgated. It is in this document that China's goal of making the RMB a convertible currency was mentioned officially for the first time. At the outset, it was assumed that 10 years should be enough to accomplish the liberalization of capital account. But the Asian financial crisis in 1997–1998 delayed this process as the Chinese policymakers became more prudent after witnessing the disruptions that unwanted capital inflows had brought to the region. Instead of carrying out the original plan, they switched greater emphasis onto the accumulation of foreign exchange reserves for precautionary purposes. It was only by 2003 that the objective of gradually realizing capital account convertibility was once again declared. In that October, the government indicated in its "Decision on Issues of Perfecting the Socialist Market Economy" that "under the premise of effective risk prevention, restrictions on cross-border capital transactions were to be loosened in a selective and step by step manner". Together with the mission, the significance of maintaining the stability of exchange rates for the RMB so that it could move at a reasonable and equilibrium level was equally highlighted.

Of the various events that led the country to move steadily toward the established target, there are several which should be labeled as landmarks and thus worthy of special attention here. The first major one was the launch of QFII (qualified foreign institutional investor) scheme in 2002. Looking back, it was since 1992 that China's securities market has begun to go international with the first public placement of B shares by Shanghai Vacuum Electronic Equipment Company Limited. In contrast to A shares which were quoted and traded both in the home currency, B shares were quoted in the home currency but traded either in the US dollars at the Shanghai Stock Exchange or in the Hong Kong dollars at the Shenzhen Stock Exchange. From then on, overseas investors could trade B shares directly on the mainland although limits like the number of shares they were allowed to hold remained.

After the turn of the century, with a view to further opening the securities market, China Securities Regulatory Commission (CSRC) and the PBoC jointly released the "Provisional Measures on the Administration of Domestic Securities Investments of Qualified Foreign Institutional Investors" (Decree No. 12) in November 2002, which permitted authorized foreign institutional investors to invest in and trade on the mainland market starting from December 1st of the same year. Based on the definition of the Regulation, these foreign institutional investors included four different types, i.e. fund management institutions, insurance companies, securities companies, and commercial banks. Besides, in order to be eligible for the program, each of them should possess certain qualifications in terms of the years of operation and the securities assets under management. While being granted to invest in RMB-denominated financial instruments such as A shares, treasuries, convertible bonds and enterprise bonds listed in China's stock exchanges, or other financial products approved by the CSRC, each QFII could not hold more than 10PCT of the A shares in one listed company and at the same time, the aggregate shareholdings by all the QFIIs in one single listed company should not surpass 20PCT. On May 23rd, 2003, UBS (Switzerland) and Nomura Securities (Japan) became the first two firms that were awarded the QFII license, with each of them receiving an investment quota of USD790 million and USD350 million respectively by January 2015. Table 21 displays a detailed list of the 12 QFIIs which were approved before the end of 2003.

As first movers entering into the Chinese securities market, they were in a position to take greater advantage of its booming business and expand in an equally impressive way. In the following decade, the number of the group rose sharply as more foreign players applied for the status and by January 30th, 2015, China handed out a record

Table 21 List of the QFIIs approved before the end of 2003

Name of the QFIIs	Place of company registration	Date of approval[1]	Investment quota (USD Million)[2]
UBS AG	Switzerland	May 23rd, 2003	790
Nomura Securities Co., Ltd	Japan	May 23rd, 2003	350
Morgan Stanley & Co. International PLC	United Kingdom	June 5th, 2003	600
Citigroup Global Markets Limited	United Kingdom	June 5th, 2003	550
Goldman Sachs & Co	United States	July 4th, 2003	300
Deutsche Bank Aktiengesellschaft	Germany	July 30th, 2003	600
The Hong Kong and Shanghai Banking Corp	Hong Kong, China	August 4th, 2003	600
ING Bank N.V	Netherlands	Sept. 10th, 2003	210
JPMorgan Chase Bank, National Association	United States	Sept. 30th, 2003	600
Credit Suisse (Hong Kong) Limited	Hong Kong, China	Oct. 24th, 2003	600
Standard Chartered Bank (Hong Kong) Ltd	Hong Kong, China	Dec. 11th, 2003	175
Nikko Asset Management Co., Ltd	Japan	Dec. 11th, 2003	450

Note Figures for investment quota were received by January 30th, 2015
Source [1]CSRC, 2008; [2]SAFE, 2015

of almost USD68 billion of combined quotas to a total of 262 foreign institutions. Among them, UBS was not only the first in getting the license, it also pioneered the trading of A shares (Fan, Hui & Jin, 2005). The transaction took place on July 9th, 2003, within just several minutes, the Swiss bank smoothly consummated its purchase of stakes at four companies, namely, Baosteel Co., Ltd., Shanghai Port Container Co., Ltd. (SPC), Sinotrans Air Transportation Development Co., Ltd. (SINOAIR), and ZTE Corp. Although the exact amount of the deal was not disclosed, its symbolic meaning was more far-reaching than the commercial value itself. Indeed, foreign institutional investment is not only a valuable source of capital for China's indigenous enterprises, its participation can also effectively increase the liquidity and strengthen the governance of the country's securities market.

To a large extent, capital account liberalization is closely related to the convertibility of the Chinese currency. In other words, if the yuan could not be freely exchanged in the international market, it is impossible for capital to flow across national borders in a really unrestricted manner. Therefore, promoting RMB's internationalization has always been an integral part of the process of opening the capital account. As a major effort, the PBoC in early 2005 joined with three other central government agencies (i.e. the Ministry of Finance, the National Development and Reform Commission, and China Securities Regulatory Commission) and published the "Interim Measures for the Administration of the Issuance of Renminbi Bonds by International Development Organizations". In addition to the QFII scheme, it provided one more alternative to help balance capital movement in and out of China. For borrowers that lacked foreign exchange earnings, the arrangement may enable them to reduce the currency mismatches as well. Also named "panda" bonds, they were first issued in October that year by the International Finance Corporation (IFC, the private sector financing arm of the World Bank Group) and Asian Development Bank (ADB). Having the same maturity period of 10 years, the proceeds from the RMB1.13 billion and RMB1 billion bonds were to be used for the funding of private-sector development projects, including health care, infrastructure, and clean energy, etc.

In line with the RMB-denominated bonds issued by non-residents onshore, the offshore RMB bond market emerged two years later. Nicknamed after Hong Kong's favorite dining pastime, the "dim sum" (Cantonese spoken in Hong Kong, 'dian xin' in Mandarin) bond market has played a pivotal role in the internationalization of the RMB and the pricing of its value. Following the "Interim Measures for the Administration of the Issuance of RMB Bonds in Hong Kong Special Administrative Region by Domestic Financial Institutions", a regulatory document published jointly in June 2007 by the PBoC and the NDRC, policy banks and commercial banks based in mainland China could engage in debt financing in Hong Kong where the first offshore RMB deposit center (2004) and the primary offshore settlement center for RMB trade transactions (2009) were established (Li, 2013). Fairly speaking, the timing of the new policy was appropriate because on the one hand, the value of RMB against the US dollar had been rising steadily, from RMB8.19 each US dollar in 2005 to RMB7.6 by 2007, the total revaluation exceeded 7PCT and the trend was still moving in the same direction. On the other hand, the RMB deposits of all the 38 banks conducting RMB business in Hong Kong had reached RMB25.5 billion in the end of April 2007 (Qiu & He, 2008), which represented a potentially large demand for dim sum bonds. Thereby, from the perspective of Hong Kong residents, the upcoming issuance would offer them an investment option and very likely, a higher return in the management of their RMB assets. On June 27th, 2007, China Development Bank (CDB, a core policy bank and transformed into a commercial bank in 2008) became the first issuer of RMB5 billion bond to both retail and institutional investors in Hong Kong (Wang, 2015). Almost three times oversubscribed (reaching RMB14 billion), the debut was symbolic of a good beginning for the subsequent expansion of the offshore RMB bond markets.

Apart from the critical role Hong Kong has played in promoting the international use of the RMB through the sale of the yuan-denominated bonds, the rapid proliferation of the offshore yuan clearing centers in major financial hubs around the world simultaneously facilitated their direct access to China's onshore financial markets. As a result, non-Chinese sovereigns have begun to participate in the issuance of dim sum bonds since 2013. For example, in November that year, the Canadian province of British Colombia initiated the sale of a RMB2.5 billion dim sum bond. Not long

Table 22 QDIIs approved by January 30th, 2015

Type of QDIIs	Number	Investment Quota (USD Billion)
Commercial bank	30	13.49
Securities & Fund Management Company	48	31.85
Insurance Company	40	29.65
Trust Company	11	7.05
Sum	129	82.04

Source SAFE, 2015

later, the British government issued the same bonds worth RMB3 billion in October 2014, just one month ahead of another issuance by Australia's New South Wales government of RMB1 billion dim sum bonds (Hatzvi, Nixon & Wright, 2014). In the nearby future, it is very likely that more sovereigns with RMB clearing centers would also follow suit.

While paving the way for foreign institutions to invest in the Chinese securities, especially the A shares, policymakers were also aware of the growing demand of domestic capital for overseas markets. To enable financial institutions at home to more efficiently allocate their assets across the world, a transitional arrangement which provided such opportunities was available in April 2006 when the PBoC stated through its Announcement No. 5 a series of measures toward a higher level of freedom in capital outflow. Most notably, qualified commercial banks, funds and securities institutions, as well as insurers may invest not only in foreign fixed-income products, but also a portfolio of securities including stocks. Although formal introduction of the QDII (Qualified Domestic Institutional Investor) program occurred one year later, the Announcement symbolized a key step in the creation of a new conduit for Chinese cash to flow abroad. Since the banking sector responded most quickly with a supportive framework guiding the concrete steps, six banks were among the first batch in getting the approval in 2006 to invest overseas on behalf of their customers (Zhou & Chao, 2011); they included the Industrial and Commercial Bank of China (ICBC), Bank of China (BOC), China Construction Bank (CCB), Bank of Communications, Hong Kong and Shanghai Banking Corporation (HSBC), and Bank of East Asia (BEA).

Nevertheless, the subsequent pace of development was largely constrained due to the vagueness on specifics, especially the eligibility criteria and risk control mechanism. In an effort to clarify the regulatory ambiguity so that domestic institutions could more actively engage in the international capital market, "Trial Measures for the Administration of Securities Investment outside the Territory of China by Qualified Domestic Institutional Investors" was promulgated by the CSRC in 2007. Similar to the QFII scheme but representing the opposite direction in two-way capital movement, the QDIIs were chiefly composed of four types of entities, i.e. commercial banks, securities and fund management companies, insurance companies, and trust companies (Table 22). To strengthen supervision, Clause 14 of the Decree stipulated that equity investment by any of the QDIIs should be located in a region or country with which the CSRC had signed a memorandum of understanding (MoU) and maintained an effective surveillance cooperation ever since. According to the Annual Report (2007) of the CSRC, from 1993 till the end of 2007, it had respectively signed 37 Memoranda of Understanding on Supervisory Cooperation with the securities watchdogs of 33 countries and regions in the world, such as the United States, Hong Kong, Singapore, Australia, the United Kingdom, Japan, Malaysia, Brazil, France, and Germany, to name but a few (CSRC, 2008). Among these eligible destinations, Hong Kong was undoubtedly a choice preferred by the majority of the institutional investors based in mainland China. Apart from cultural and geographical reasons, its mature financial infrastructure and sound regulatory system were perhaps the most outstanding characteristics that made it irresistible in the eyes of these QDIIs.

In July 2006, ICBC as China's largest lender launched the first banking QDII product. Fairly speaking, it was not a very good time because on the one hand, the RMB was getting stronger against the US dollars, which was very unfavorable to the investment in USD-denominated assets. At the same time, the domestic A share market was thriving with lucrative returns. By contrast, the yield from the foreign markets was not that satisfactory. Therefore, under the negative influence of these two factors, ICBC only sold less than RMB500 million within two weeks. Originally, the bank was expecting a maximum return of 7PCT on this product, but due to the appreciation of the RMB, the actual gain finally shrank to 2-4PCT (Xiao, 2007). Because of the lower-than-expected performance, Chinese investors were no longer that enthusiastic when in September, Hua An Fund Management initiated the Hua An International Balanced Fund (HAIBF), the first fund QDII product. Against the USD500 million quota approved for this fund, the final subscription only totaled USD197 million. After around five years of unsuccessful operations, especially hit hard by the collapse of its guarantor and paper underwriter Lehman Brothers, the HAIBF was returned to its holders at its original face value when the first investment period ended in November 2011 (Tian, 2011). Even to settle this principal payment alone, Hua An had to spend an extra USD1.76 million to make up the balance. Actually, the failure of the HAIBF was not an isolated case; instead, it reflected a rather common scenario confronting many QDIIs in China. The permit to invest in overseas capital market is not all what it takes to have the goals achieved, it just opened another door through which more opportunities became available. However, behind the door, there were also miscellaneous risks and setbacks. In this regard, the QDIIs were similarly inexperienced as the majority of their domestic customers, they still had a lot to learn. Furthermore, the once-in-a-century global financial crisis happened too abruptly, which not only worsened the prospect of reaping a decent return; to a large extent, it made the price they had to bear dearer.

Foreign direct investment, a key component under the capital account, consists of both inbound and outbound movement of capital that aims to exercise control over assets in the host country. Understandably, China's policy toward the former was much more liberalized than the latter, especially during the 1980s when its foreign exchange reserves were far from enough. For the purpose of accumulating more deposits in foreign currencies, it once exercised very stringent regulations over the use of reserves in making outward investment. As the most typical representatives, the "Procedures for the Administration of Foreign Exchange for Outward Investment" was first released in 1989 by the State Administration of Foreign Exchange (SAFE) before being supplemented with the "Detailed Rules Concerning the Procedures for the Administration of Foreign Exchange for Outward Investment" one year later. In both documents, various provisions were laid out to instruct domestic enterprises the concrete steps they had to observe, from the initial application to the repatriation of profits. As a mandatory requirement, prior to the remittance of capital abroad in additional investment, 5PCT of the total amount should be submitted to a special account to guarantee the repatriation of all the profits that would incur later. Referring to the investment funds, including its source, were made subject to the verification and sanction of the exchange control authorities. Because of these tough conditions, China's outward FDI remained barely noticeable throughout the 1990s, with an annual average of USD2.2–2.4 billion (UNCTAD, 2004).

Anyhow, major policy changes did not happen immediately until after 2000 when the "twin gap" (in domestic savings and foreign exchange reserves) which had persisted since the country's reform and opening up was reversed (Lü, 2006). After several tentative steps to relax foreign exchange restrictions on outward direct investment, like the removal of profit repatriation guarantee (in 2002) and delegation of approval power to lower-level authorities (in 2004), etc.; the quotas imposed on the purchase of foreign exchange for overseas investment was abolished starting from July 2006, which implied that the government would relax the examination of where the investors' foreign exchange was originated. In addition, according to the "Regulations on Foreign Exchange Administration of Outbound Direct Investment by Domestic Institutions" promulgated by the SAFE in 2009, the funding sources of investors were broadened to cover several alternatives, e.g. self-owned foreign exchange (arising from either current account transactions or the capital account deposits of foreign-funded enterprises); foreign exchange borrowed or bought at home using the RMB, intangible assets, and other forms approved by the authorities, etc. In case profits were generated from the project, it could equally be used for re-investment purposes. Further, unlike the prior remittance procedures which had been quite complicated, investors only had to present a license issued by the government agency in charge of investment and a relevant foreign exchange registration certificate to the designated banks for authenticity review before the transfer was made. From limiting outward direct investment to liberalizing it in a progressive manner, Chinese enterprises were among the most immediate beneficiaries of this change. By getting closer to the overseas markets, they could expect to respond more quickly to the local needs. At the same time, the easing control over capital outflow enabled China to absorb valuable experiences while dealing with the uncertainties and turbulence that such exposure may bring; thus making it better prepared for a more profound capital account openness in the future.

Early in 2002, the Chinese policymakers launched the QFII scheme in order to channel more foreign capital into the mainland equity market. Under the arrangement, overseas institutional investors, once obtaining the license and an investment quota, would be permitted to convert their currencies into the RMB to trade A shares. After almost ten years of fruitful operations, the government was very much impressed by the positive impact that the scheme had exerted over the domestic stock exchanges, especially its contributions to the liquidity, risk control, and corporate governance, etc. From a broader perspective, the move also effectively promoted the international use of the yuan. With a view to attracting larger amounts of long-term offshore funds, a mini-QFII scheme named RQFII (Renminbi qualified foreign institutional investor) was launched in the end of 2011. At the initial trial stage, the program targeted at the Hong Kong subsidiaries of mainland-based fund management companies and securities firms. Once being approved of the quotas, they could use the RMB funds raised in Hong Kong and make investment back in the securities exchanges located on the mainland. From March 6th, 2013, the coverage of the scheme was expanded to include not only the aforesaid entities, the Hong Kong subsidiaries of domestic commercial banks, insurance companies, and financial institutions either registered or having their dominant presence in Hong Kong were equally granted the green light to apply for the business.

At the same time, authorized RQFIIs may put up their money in a wider range of financial instruments. In addition to stocks, bonds, and warrants, they were encouraged to trade fixed-income products of the inter-bank bond market, securities investment funds, and stock index futures, etc. Within the approved investment quota, they could equally participate in the issuance of new shares or convertible bonds, etc. By March 26th, 2015, a total number of 111 RQFIIs have received RMB329.8 billion of investment quotas. As can be noticed from the table below (Table 23), although the majority of them were from Hong Kong, more foreign countries have participated in the scheme, implying that with the increasingly active circulation of onshore and offshore RMB funds, global investors are contributing positively to the internationalization of the RMB, which is rather essential for China to ultimately have its financial market integrated with the rest of the world.

To gain some knowledge about the extent of a country's international financial integration (IFI), an indicator often referred to is the international investment position (IIP), which is by nature a balance sheet of cumulative financial flows. Together with trade linkages, foreign assets and liabilities act as another means for countries to

Table 23 RQFIIs approved by March 26th, 2015

Registration Place of RQFIIs	Number	Investment Quota (RMB Billion)
Hong Kong	79	270
Singapore	12	18.6
Great Britain	7	12.2
France	2	6
South Korea	10	17
Germany	1	6
Sum	111	329.8

Source SAFE, 2015

interact with one another. In this regard, the ups and downs that happen constantly can demonstrate in a vivid way how the relationship has evolved. According to the Balance of Payments and International Investment Position Manual (6th edition, BPM6) of the IMF, IIP is defined in Chapter 7 as "a statistical statement that shows at a point in time the value and composition of financial assets of residents of an economy that are claims on nonresidents and gold bullion held as reserve assets, and liabilities of residents of an economy to nonresidents" (IMF, 2009). In general, assets and liabilities are the two categories under the IIP, with each one further broken down into several subcategories. Referring to assets, it includes outbound direct investment, portfolio investment, financial derivatives and reserve assets. In terms of liabilities, it consists of inbound direct investment, portfolio investment, and other investment, etc. If taking the decade of 2006–2015 as an example, the graph below (Graph 9) reflects how exactly the external assets and liabilities of China have increased over these years. In 2015, its reserve assets (including monetary gold, special drawing rights, and foreign exchange reserves, etc.) claimed USD3,406.1 billion, accounting for a dominant 55PCT of the total assets. By referring to the total liabilities, it was the inward direct investments which had the biggest share of 61.5PCT. Most notably, foreign exchange reserves remained the key form of all its reserve assets, which hit USD3,330.4 billion by the end of 2015, or equivalent to almost 98PCT of the aggregate USD3,406.1 billion. In terms of the balance between assets and liabilities, China's net IIP grew almost 150PCT, from USD640 billion in 2006 to USD1,597 billion in 2015. The major driving force that contributed to the dynamic momentum should be the accumulation of its reserve assets, which experienced an equally phenomenal surge.

By comparing the movements of the various components under China's IIP, it is not difficult to find that the government favored long-term direct investments more than short-term portfolio investments since the latter were more vulnerable to speculative attacks. While remaining a net recipient of direct investment, China's net portfolio flows still underwent some twists and turns (Table 24). Prior to 2007, outward portfolio investment kept rising steadily and the trend was reversed because

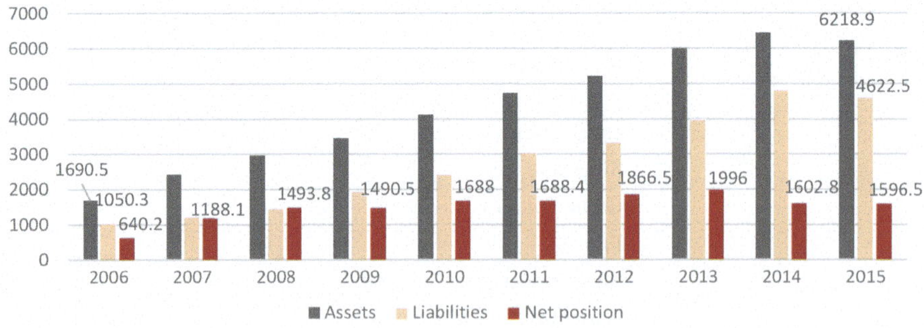

Graph 9 Time-Series Data of International Investment Position, USD Billion. *Note* from the first quarter of 2015, the IIP of China was compiled according to the standard of BPM6 of the IMF. Apart from 2014, those of the previous years were not adjusted. *Source* SAFE, 2016

Table 24 Direct investment and portfolio positions (in USD Billion), 2005–2015

Item	2005	2007	2009	2011	2013	2015
Outward Direct Investment (Assets)	64.5	116	245.8	424.8	660.5	1,129.3
Inward Direct Investment (Liabilities)	471.5	703.7	1,314.8	1,906.9	2,331.2	2,842.3
Net FDI Position[1]	– 407	– 587.7	– 1,069	– 1,482.1	– 1,670.7	– 1,713
Portfolio Investment (Assets)	116.7	284.6	242.8	204.4	258.5	261.3
Portfolio Investment (Liabilities)	76.6	146.6	190	248.5	386.5	810.5
Net Portfolio Investment Position[2]	40.1	138	52.8	– 44.1	– 128	– 549.2

Note [1]calculated by the author by subtracting inward direct investment from outward direct investment; [2]calculated by the author by subtracting portfolio investment liabilities from portfolio investment assets; "+" means net outflow or net asset position while "–" means net inflow or net liability position; From the first quarter of 2015, the IIP of China was compiled according to the standard of BPM6 of the IMF. Apart from 2014, those of the previous years were not adjusted
Source SAFE, 2016

of the 2008 global financial crisis. In May that year, the SAFE suspended the approval of QDII quotas for overseas portfolio investment in order to prevent capital flight and the scheme was resumed until October, 2009. Before 2011, the country's net portfolio investment was persistently positive and this demonstrated that the government had been rather cautious in receiving short-term capital flows from abroad. Prompted by the launch of the RQFII arrangement, the net position from the end of 2011 began to be negative with a larger amount of overseas RMB funds being invested in the mainland securities market.

4.6.6 The Undeniable Gap: A Long Way Ahead

Undoubtedly, the expansion of China's net foreign asset position (i.e. external assets minus liabilities) from USD640 billion of 2006 to USD1,597 billion in 2015 suggests that the country has deepened its financial integration into the global markets. However, a closer look at the breakdown of its international investment position would also disclose the inadequacies that still exist in the openness of the capital account. By relying on trade surplus and inward FDI, China has managed to become the largest holder of foreign exchange reserves in the world, which in turn brings massive reserve assets. Based on the experience of other economies, high-rising reserve assets is often an indicator suggesting that the outward FDI and portfolio investments have been disproportionately low against the rest of the external balance sheet. At the global level, China's outbound portfolio stock is actually insignificant if compared to developed economies such as the US, Japan, and the UK, etc. In

Table 25 International comparison of portfolio investment position against GDP, December 2015

Country	GDP (USD billion)	Portfolio investment assets		Portfolio investment liabilities	
		Amount (USD billion)	Share of GDP[1] (PCT)	Amount (USD billion)	Share of GDP[2] (PCT)
China	11,007.72	261.3	2.37	810.5	7.36
the United States	18,036.65	9,447.72	52.38	10,235.95	56.75
the United Kingdom	2,858	3,778.73	132.22	3,349.14	117.18
Japan	4,123.26	3,511.69	85.17	1,851.98	44.92
Germany	3,363.45	2,905.62	86.39	2,800.7	83.27
France	2,418.84	2,530.04	104.6	2,916.63	120.58

Notes [1,2]calculated by the author. *Source* Figures of China: SAFE, 2016; Figures for other countries: the Coordinated Portfolio Investment Survey (CPIS) by IMF (12 & 13), from https://data.imf.org/?sk=B981B4E3-4E58-467E-9B90-9DE0C3367363&ss=1424963554286; Data on GDP: the World Bank, 2016, from https://databank.worldbank.org/data/download/GDP.pdf

the end of 2015 (Table 25), for instance, the holdings of China was only less than 3PCT of that of the US, which exceeded USD9,447 billion. In terms of the liabilities, the amount was equally small, accounting for 8PCT of that of the latter. Besides, regarding the share of portfolio investment in GDP, China's is again the lowest among the group of countries listed below. Given the fact that China was already the 2nd largest economy in the world in total GDP, the proportion of its portfolio investment appeared to be very asymmetric. To a large extent, such a sharp contrast reflects that the control remained rather tight over non-FDI capital in both directions.

The statistics in the above not only point out the gap that lied between China and the developed world, they too demonstrate the assiduous tasks waiting for China to accomplish in the years ahead. Opening capital account transactions is not just a sure outcome of the reform in foreign exchange regime, it is heavily reliant on the changes that take place in other spheres too, such as the management of interest rates, structure of the export sector, and the profit-making model of financial institutions, etc. At the same time, to reduce the country's dependence on trade surplus and FDI, greater efforts should be directed to the encouragement of domestic consumption. But before expecting any noticeable progress to emerge, the government has to allocate more budget to education, health care and pensions since these have long been the chief concerns that make its people willing to save rather than to spend. Further, as China's economy is getting mature, it will inevitably become more exposed to different types of macroeconomic challenges, both internal and external. In this regard, self-adjustment from the above aspects can enable the country to be better prepared to deal with the impact of increased capital flows. During a globalized era in which nations are closely interconnected with each other, what China does matters a lot to its counterparts. If the process of loosening capital control is successful, it would not only lead to a more balanced and sustainable growth in China; besides, it may also help enhance global liquidity and re-balance demand. But conversely, the international financial system would be destabilized.

Therefore, policymakers should be both discerning and decisive, discerning in making decisions and decisive in taking actions. In particular, they need to know when intervention in the exchange market, as well as the sterilization operations should be curtailed. They are actually prerequisites to push the real effective exchange rates of the RMB to move in the right direction; moreover, they help a lot with the correction of any monetary disequilibrium. Ultimately, like what has been declared in the "Decisions on Major Issues Concerning the Comprehensive Deepening of Reforms" of 2013, the country would be closer to fulfilling three of the primary goals for financial reform, i.e. establishment of a market-based exchange rate formation mechanism for the RMB, interest rate liberalization, and achievement of capital account convertibility.

5 Outward Foreign Direct Investment

Apart from the dynamic pace of inducing foreign capital into a broader range of sectors and regions around the country, the door to some sensitive industries such as telecommunications, securities, media, civil aviation and petroleum, etc. remained largely closed at the turn of the century. Moreover, as an opposite flow demonstrating the confidence of its enterprises in participating in the global economy, outward foreign direct investment remained rather insignificant during the 1980s and even the 1990s.

5.1 Ready for Takeoff

At the initial stage, encouraged by the fifteen economic reform measures issued by the State Council in August 1979 which explicitly allowed the establishment of overseas entities, state-owned corporations specialized in foreign trade and foreign economic & technological cooperation became the first movers heading abroad. In that November, Beijing Friendship Commercial Service Corporation (predecessor of Beijing Foreign Enterprise Service Group) set up a joint venture (JV) in Japan with Tokyo Shoji Co., Ltd. (Tan, 2013). With an aim to introduce advanced food processing equipment & technologies into Beijing and provide experienced professional chefs for restaurants opened in Japan, its formation marked the beginning of transnational operations of Chinese enterprises.

One year later, China State Shipbuilding Corp. (CSSC) and China National Foreign Trade Transportation Corp. (SINOTRANS) co-invested with the Hong Kong-based World-Wide Shipping Group (founded by the famous shipping tycoon Pao Yue-kong) USD50 million in one more JV (Qian, 1994). Headquartered in Bermuda and registered in Hong Kong as well, this project was not only the largest of its kind during that era; more importantly, it created a platform that enabled China's ocean transport industry to access the global market. Besides, it was also in 1980 that the first joint venture in the financial sector — CCIC Finance Ltd. came into being. As a result of partnership between the Bank of China, the First National Bank of Chicago, the Industrial Bank of Japan, and China Resources, Hong Kong was once again selected to host its presence (Liu & Ma, 1987).

By and large, regarding the first wave of OFDI, the dominant players were from the tertiary sector rather than the manufacturing business. Moreover, given the scarcity of foreign exchange reserves, it was unlikely for the central policy to promote outbound investment. Instead, by granting domestic firms limited opportunities to test the water abroad, the ultimate goal was still to channel foreign capital and know-how inward to support the development at home. Toward the end of 1985, China's accumulated stock of OFDI was USD900 million whereas its OFDI flow for that single year hit USD629 million (Pei & Zheng, 2015).

5.2 Growing Presence on the Global Stage

The landmark event initiating the second phase of going global via OFDI should be the release of a document by the State Council in 1987, which approved Sinochem, one of the largest SOEs specialized in the agrichemical and petrochemical industry, to implement the internationalization strategy on a trial basis. One year later, Sinochem entered into an agreement with the Houston-based Coastal Corp. for joint ownership of the latter's Pacific Refining Company. By holding a 50PCT stake in this West Coast refiner, Sinochem was in a position to obtain a long-term outlet for oil resources (Zhang, 2006). At the same time, the joint venture represented the first investment of China in the US energy assets. In fact, Sinochem was by no means the only SOE which pursued this particular route of expansion. Since the mid-1980s, Shougang as another giant from the steel industry has been actively involved in several high-profile acquisition deals. Most prominently, it spent USD3.4 million in 1988 and acquired 70PCT of the Mesta Engineering Company located in Pittsburgh, which greatly enhanced its design and technical level. For the improvement of its mining capabilities, the company in 1992 purchased 98.4PCT shares of Hierro iron mine in Peru for USD118 million and obtained permanent right for exploiting and operating all the mineral resources in its concession area. By the end of 1992, of the 1,363 non-trade enterprises (including equity and cooperative joint ventures, and wholly-owned subsidiaries) established overseas, the capital input by the Chinese side exceeded USD1.59 billion, accounting for almost 40PCT of the total outward investment, which reached USD4 billion that year (Xu, 2003).

In 1992, the 14th National Congress of the Communist Party of China (CPC) affirmed the task of building socialist market economy by facilitating the process of reform and opening up, which boosted the confidence of domestic enterprises in increasing their presence around the globe. Five years later, in the report of the 15th National Congress of the CPC, the government for the first time openly endorsed the outward investment which could utilize the country's comparative advantage. If in China, there is a company whose path of globalization bears the hallmark of this particular era, it should be Haier, the leading supplier of household appliances headquartered in Qingdao, Shandong Province. In 1996, with a view to tapping Indonesia, a market deemed to be of huge potential, it took the initial step of going international by setting up a venture named PT. Haier Sapporo Indonesia (Huang, 2004). Referring to 1997, it was a fruitful year for Haier because three more overseas plants went into operation and they were located in Philippines, Malaysia, and Yugoslavia respectively. By 2000 when its USD30 million refrigerator plant started production in South Carolina, Haier also became the first Chinese company to build a factory in the US. Indeed, the footprint of Haier in the second half of the 1990s was representative of an increasing number of indigenous firms which chose to diversify their business scope and markets through direct investment abroad.

Despite the booming interest among Chinese enterprieses to go international, however, the overall policy environment was not relaxed nor supportive enough. Concerning the approval process, for example, each case remained subject to stringent and comprehensive review by government authorities. Besides, in terms of the knowledge and experience necessary to carry out cross-border investment projects, most mainland companies were still at a learning stage. Consequently, it is not hard to understand why after shooting up to USD4.4 billion in 1993 (Table 26), the pace slowed down quickly and never attained the same height even until the turn of the century. In 2000 in particular, the size of OFDI flow contracted to USD916 million, almost the same level as that of 1991 which stood at USD913 million.

Also for the year 2000, if placing China in a broader picture, it could be found that the share in the world was rather trivial (Table 27), with the outflow and cumulative stock accounting for less than 0.08PCT and 0.38PCT respectively. As compared to those industrialized countries, the gap was apparently tremendous. Even among the

Table 26 Outward FDI flows and stocks, 1985–2002

Year	Outward FDI flows		Outward FDI stock	
	Value (USD million)	Annual growth rate[1] (PCT)	Value (USD million)	Annual growth rate[2] (PCT)
1985	629	369.4	900	232.1
1990	830	6.41	4,455	22.9
1993	4,400	10	13,768	46.97
1996	2,114	5.7	19,882	11.9
1999	1,774	-32.65	26,853	7.08
2002	2,518	-63.43	37,172	7.27

Note [1,2]calculated by the author
Source Foreign direct investment: Inward and outward flows and stock, annual, 1970–2015, at current prices, UNCTAD, from https://unctadstat.unctad.org/wds/TableViewer/tableView.aspx?ReportId=96740

Table 27 Comparison of OFDI flows and stocks with selected countries and the world, 2000

Country	Outward FDI flows (USD Million)	Outward FDI stocks (USD Million)
The United States	142,626	2,694,014
Japan	31,557	278,442
The United Kingdom	232,744	923,367
Germany	56,557	483,946
Brazil	2,282	51,946
The Russian Federation	3,152	19,211
India	514	1,733
China	916	27,768
World	1,163,064	7,436,836

Source Foreign direct investment: Inward and outward flows and stock, annual, 1970–2015, at current prices, UNCTAD, from https://unctadstat.unctad.org/wds/TableViewer/tableView.aspx?ReportId=96740

emerging markets like the BRICs, its flow merely outperformed India; yet to catch up with Brazil and Russia, there was still some distance to go.

5.3 *Accelerated Pace of OFDI*

In the "Outline of the Tenth Five-Year Plan (2001–2005) for National Economic and Social Development" delivered in March 2001, implementation of the "going out" ('zou chu qu') strategy was highlighted as a critical means to the fulfillment of the state-level objectives for Chinese enterprises. Via outward FDI, they could expect to access resources scarce at home, especially technological and intellectual, and optimize the industrial structure. At the same time, considering the challenges from the upcoming WTO membership, a business-support services framework covering finance, foreign exchange, insurance, and entry-exit management, etc. remained to be erected so that these enterprises could expedite the internationalization pace while strengthening their overall competitiveness. As a major step to simplify the project approval system and allow enterprises greater autonomy in making investment abroad, the "Decisions of the State Council on the Reform of the Investment System" was promulgated in 2004. Generally, administrative approval was no longer mandatory for projects not funded by the government; instead, the systems of "authorization" ('he zhun zhi') and "registration and filing" ('bei an zhi') would be adopted where appropriate. When concerning outward FDI, the Decisions stated explicitly that apart from resource exploitation projects involving investment of USD30 million or above and non-resource projects with capital input exceeding USD10 million, which were subject to the authorization of the National Development and Reform Commission (NDRC, a state agency regulating and guiding China's overseas investment), the rest would only need to be filed with the NDRC and the Ministry of Commerce. In case the project was initiated by non-centrally governed enterprises, permission would be extended by the local authorities according to the relevant rules.

In 2005, CNPCI (a wholly-owned subsidiary of China National Petroleum Corporation, the country's leading oil producer) reached an agreement with Canada-registered oil company PetroKazakhstan. With a total spending of USD4.18 billion to acquire the latter, CNPCI's deal broke the national record as the largest single transaction by value (Hai, 2006). Following that deal, a decade-long explosive growth persisted in outbound FDI and among the multiple high-profile cases, the most eye-catching ones included Lenovo's takeover of IBM's PC arm in 2005, Sinopec's purchase of Tanganyika Oil in 2008, Geely's acquisition of Volvo in 2010, and CNOOC's buyout of Nexen in 2013, etc. Together with the rising appetite of Chinese businesses for overseas assets, the volume of its OFDI soared as well. In 2004 (Graph 10), the capital outflow registered some USD5.5 billion, which was merely 0.6PCT of the world's total. By 2014, the number hit USD123 billion, an increase of over 20 fold, or accounting for 9.3PCT of the global volume.

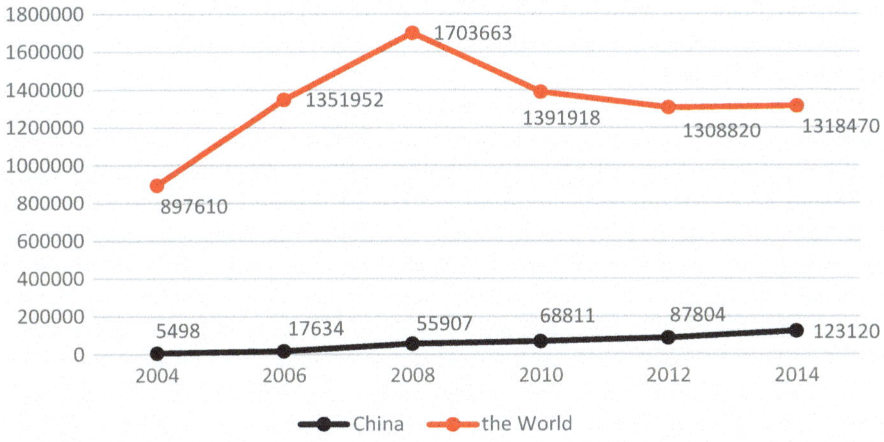

Graph 10 OFDI Flows of China and the World, USD Million. *Source* Foreign direct investment: inward and outward flows and stock, annual, 1970–2015, at current prices, UNCTAD, from https://unctadstat.unctad.org/wds/TableViewer/tableView.aspx?ReportId=96740

5.4 *The Belt and Road Initiative*

With a view to promoting economic cooperation with countries and regions along the ancient Silk Road trade route, the "the "Belt and Road Initiative" ('yidai yilu', namely the Silk Road Economic Belt and the 21st-Century Maritime Silk Road, photo 5–14) was launched as a state strategy in 2013. Consisting of 65 countries across the continents of Asia, Europe and Africa and about 4.4 billion people, the plan also furnished unparalleled investment opportunities for Chinese enterprises to tap new markets as well as resources. In 2015, 49 out of the 65 prospective destinations received capital from China and the amount totaled USD14.82 billion, an increase of 18.2PCT over the previous year (Li, 2016). In the eyes of the Chinese investors, Singapore, Russia and Kazakhstan were among the most favored nations to host their projects.

Given the fact that most countries alongside the "the "Belt and Road" are either emerging economies or developing countries, infrastructure connectivity has been highlighted as a priority in the implementation of the grand initiative. While encouraging domestic enterprises to direct their investment to the construction of transport, energy and communications facilities, etc., supportive measures were adopted simultaneously to deal with the massive funding gap. Among them, the most prominent effort was the establishment of the Asian Infrastructure Investment Bank (AIIB). On the basis of the Memorandum of Understanding (MOU) signed by 22 countries to establish the AIIB in October 2014 and the AIIB Articles of Agreement by 57 Prospective Founding Members (PFMs) before the end of 2015, the China-backed multilateral development bank was finally open on January 16th, 2016, with 57 member states in total.

With registered capital of USD100 billion, the formation of the AIIB provided Chinese infrastructure companies an important platform through which they could finance their investment in the "Belt and Road" countries. Nevertheless, considering that Asia's needs for infrastructure from 2010 to 2020 would amount to a daunting USD8.29 trillion (ADB, 2009), more sources of external financing were needed to fill the funding gap. In November 2014, China pledged to contribute USD40 billion to set up the Silk Road Fund to assist with the infrastructure investment. Shortly after its full operation, the first project was initiated in the next year, which was the construction of an USD1.65-billion Karot hydropower plant on the Jhelum River in northeastern Pakistan (Yang, 2015). The launch of this clean-energy project was not only favorable to the improvement of power supply in Pakistan; in a broader sense, the Fund as a part of the the "Belt and Road" initiative could bring about more financing opportunities to facilitate the development of the China-Pakistan Economic Corridor, a network integrating around 3 billion people from Asia, Europe and Africa.

Apart from infrastructure building, the Silk Road Fund was also committed to the "going out" strategy of Chinese enterprises, especially when the process was impeded by a lack of capital. In June 2015 for example, a cooperative investment agreement was signed by the Fund and China National Chemical Corporation (ChemChina, a dominant SOE in China's chemical sector). By acquiring Italy-based Pirelli, one of the leading tire producers in the world, ChemChina could take advantage of its international marketing channel and become a global leader in the tire industry (SRF, 2015). Moreover, from the perspective of the Fund, this transaction was consistent with its principle of prioritizing the "Belt and Road" initiative by investing in the participating countries. Via equity-holding on a medium and long-term basis, the Fund could be in a position to support the overseas expansion of Chinese enterprises while expediting the industrial upgrading of the domestic high-end manufacturing sector.

On December 14th, 2015, i.e. almost one year after the formation of the Silk Road Fund, it signed the Framework Agreement on the Establishment of China-Kazakhstan Production Capacity Cooperation Fund with KAZNEX INVEST JSC, the national export and investment agency of Kazakhstan. Under this agreement, the Fund would invest USD2 billion to promote production capacity cooperation between the two nations as well as project investment in relevant areas. Already a dominant recipient of China's outbound FDI in central Asia, Kazakhstan had hosted multiple seasoned investors such as China National Petroleum Corp. (CNPC) and China Petrochemical Corp. (Sinopec Group) of the energy sector; Huawei Technologies and ZTE of the telecommunications sector; and the Bank of China specializing in financial services, etc. Among these early entrants, China General Nuclear Power Group (CGN, the nation's top nuclear power supplier) was perhaps the one which first echoed the bilateral production capacity cooperation. Equally on December 14th, 2015, it entered into an agreement with KazAtomProm (the Kazakh national atomic company) to jointly build a nuclear fuel assembly plant and mine uranium deposits in Kazakhstan. In fact, this was by no means their initial cooperation deal. Back in 2009, the two firms had together set up a joint venture (Semizbai-U LLP in Alma-Ata, Kazakhstan) to exploit the abundant uranium resources (Li, 2010). To a great extent, the decision of CGN and its Kazakh counterpart to deepen their collaboration in 2015 was due to the mutually beneficial partnership over the previous years.

In order to better utilize the complementary strengths of the "Belt and Road" countries, the production capacity cooperation between China and Kazakhstan was applied to numerous other partners as well, including Indonesia, Russia, Brazil, and Ethiopia, to name but a few. Fairly speaking, the extension of production chains via such arrangements served as a catalyst that helped mobilize more capital to flow out of China. Although at the current stage, it is largely regarded as a global magnet for inward investment, the robust OFDI signifies that a shift has been taking place and if such a trend continues, the latter is set to eclipse the former soon. In 2015 when its inbound FDI (actually utilized) stood at USD126.27 billion, the non-financial outbound investment registered USD118.02 billion, thus narrowing down the gap further to USD8.25 billion from USD16.67 billion of 2014 (MOC, 2015 & 2016).

If considering the fact that prior to 1979, the concept of FDI was almost non-existent in China, the volume that has been achieved some 35 years later was actually nothing short of a miracle. Looking ahead, what matters most to the country is no longer the numerical year-on-year growth itself; instead, it is the efficiency of fund allocation that deserves an intense concern, especially in case the investment is moving out. By far, Chinese companies don't lack motivation; on the contrary, they have enough of it. Nevertheless, the shortcomings that undermine their overseas performances are not yet fully addressed, such as poor awareness of national disparities, from cultural, technological, to legal; and a shortage of experience in tackling subsequent challenges. As a means to an end, capital inflow and outflow do not necessarily ensure smooth operations; behind it, it is the ability to integrate the best resources available that can ultimately bring about a decent return. China, while in need of improving its environment for foreign investors, should be more prudent and well-prepared when engaging in investment abroad.

6 Agriculture, the Lifeline of the Nation

In view of the fact that China's history as an agrarian society is one of the longest in the world, to gain a comprehensive picture of how this important sector has evolved, it is necessary to look back before having it connected with the present and the future. According to what have been unearthed by modern archeologists in Erlitou (a village of Yanshi county, Henan Province), people during the Xia Dynasty (twenty-first-sixteenth century BC, considered as the earliest recorded state in China) had already acquired the knowledge to make farm implements using stones and bones, or woods occasionally. Moreover, they were rather skillful in the building of irrigation projects. By digging channels and maintaining dikes, crops were grown on a larger scale, chiefly millet, wheat, hemp, and soybeans, etc.

6.1 Situations During the Pre-reform Stage

After thousands of years of cultivation, it has been crystal clear to each generation living on this ancient land that agriculture is fundamental not only to their survival, but also to the stability of the entire country. From the perspective of the rulers, feeding the large population remains a top priority no matter how the time changes. Although in terms of the vast territory as well as its diversified ecological resources, China is without any doubt endowed with much enviable advantages in agriculture. If it comes to food security and sustainable development, however, a critical determinant which should not be underestimated is the available farmland per capita. Also termed arable land, it is defined by the Food and Agriculture Organization of the United Nations (UNFAO) as the land "under temporary crops, temporary meadows for mowing or for pasture, land under market or kitchen gardens, and land temporarily fallow". As demonstrated in Table 28, during the initial years after the founding of the PRC, the arable land area kept increasing and peaked at 111.83 million hectares by 1957. But since then, there was an incessant decline which brought the figure down to 99.39 million hectares in 1978. Since population growth remained rather rapid over this three-decade period, the arable land per capita experienced a fall of over 40PCT, from 0.18 hectares in the beginning to only 0.1 hectares of 1978.

Table 28 Land-population balance, 1949–1978

Year	Arable land[1] (Million Hectare)	Population[2] (Million)	Arable land per capita[3] (Hectare)
1949	97.88	541.67	0.18
1952	107.92	574.82	0.19
1957	111.83	646.53	0.17
1965	103.59	725.38	0.14
1975	99.71	924.2	0.11
1978	99.39	962.59	0.1

Source [1,2]Mao, Zhao & Yang, 2013; [3]calculated by the author by dividing the arable land by the population

Actually, it is not hard to explain the decrease. Early in the 1950s, China launched a land reclamation campaign and even the army was mobilized to participate in the conversion of wasteland into cultivated land. At the same time, in order to make itself militarily stronger and less vulnerable to the pressure from external forces, greater efforts were devoted to the construction of a heavy industrial system. As a result, agriculture became only secondary and its role, apart from the provision of food to cities, was chiefly to support the industrial sector by furnishing the resources needed, from land, materials to funds. Therefore, what happened later was that while the program did contribute some additional land for farming purposes, much more was requisitioned for urban sprawl and the construction of factories, railways, and water reservoirs, etc. (Smil, 1981), thus leading to a shrinkage in the country's farmland starting from 1958.

Based on the above happenings, it is fair to say that the protection of arable land in China prior to 1980 was rather poor. Besides, with priorities given to industrial production, fiscal spending on agriculture has been rather modest against the total expenditure (Table 29), which stayed at about 12PCT toward the end of the 1970s. As to other indicators which can demonstrate the situation of China's agricultural sector at that time, they could be found in the "Decisions of the Central Committee of the

Table 29 State budgetary expenditure for agriculture, 1950–1980

Year	Expenditure for agriculture[1] (RMB100 Million)	Share of the total government expenditure (PCT)
1950	2.74	4.03
1960	90.52	14.06
1970	49.4	7.61
1975	98.96	12.06
1980	149.95	12.2

Note [1]including spending on rural production, capital construction, and technology promotion, etc.
Source NBS, 2001

CPC on Some Questions Concerning the Acceleration of Agricultural Development", a document adopted at the Fourth Plenary Session of the 11th Central Committee of the Party in 1979. According to the Decisions, despite the increase in the yield per unit area and the gross output, the per capita share of grain in 1978 stayed approximately at the same level as that of 1957. In terms of the per capita income of rural residents, it was a bit in excess of RMB70 per year, with around 25PCT of brigade members earning less than RMB50.

6.2 *The Critical Move of Relaxing Grain Circulation*

In recognition of the emergency to revive agriculture, a prerequisite to smoothly carrying out other economic activities, reform measures were introduced in the early 1980s and the dominant one was the re-establishment of a family-based contract system called household responsibility system (HRS). By granting peasants land use rights and linking rewards more closely with their performances, the unprecedentedly high morale boosted production. As a result, grain output rose by over one third, from 305 million tons of 1978 to 407 million tons in 1984. Despite the positive effect, it didn't take long for the limitations of the HRS to emerge; in particular, since land ownership was not possessed by peasants, they could not make decisions, especially long-term decisions for the land contracted. Thus, it was not uncommon to see them behave in a short-sighted and restrained way. Obviously, new incentives were in need to enhance their commitment to the land.

After all, given the deep-rooted top-down approach of management, it was not fresh to witness almost every aspect of the Chinese economy orchestrated by the central planners, including price. Prior to 1978, the leverage function of price was virtually absent and if it had certain roles, it was applied at its best as a tool to ensure that the economy would not derail from the track designed. In 1985, the unified purchase and marketing ('tonggou tongxiao') of grain, a state-monopolized system which had been adopted since 1953, was abolished and from then on, purchase of major crops such as grain and cotton would be subject to a contract signed before the planting season at a set price. As to the output above the contracted quota, peasants were allowed to sell in the market at floating prices. With regard to other agricultural products like vegetables, meat and eggs, their transactions were largely based on the supply and demand in the market. Because of the co-existence of state-guided and market-determined prices, this practice was also known as the two-tier price system ('jiage shuanggui zhi'). Later, with the deepening of the grain circulation reform, government control over the procurement and sale prices was gradually giving place to market forces. By the end of 1993 when deregulation was rather common across the country, the grain rationing system (in the form of ration coupons) which had been implemented since the early 1950s to address food scarcity and required urban & nonagricultural rural dwellers to buy a limited amount of grain at subsidized prices, was brought to an end (Wen, 2012). If in 1978, over 90PCT of agricultural products

Table 30 Grain purchasing price index and the annual output, 1978–1995

Year	Index[1] (Preceding Year = 100)	Grain Output[2] (Million Ton)
1978	100.7	304.77
1981	109.7	325.02
1984	112	407.31
1987	108	402.98
1990	93.2	446.24
1991	93.8	435.29
1992	105.3	442.66
1993	116.7	456.49
1994	146.6	445.1
1995	129	466.62

Note grain mainly includes wheat, paddy rice, corn, sorghum, and soybeans, etc.
Source [1]NBS, 2001. [2]NBS, 1990

were priced by the state, then during the mid-1990s, their proportional share dropped to about 10PCT only.

The ongoing liberalization of China's grain policies, if analyzed from its impact on price changes, was by no means an insignificant move. At the outset, with the government raising the procurement prices for 18 important agricultural products (including grains, edible oils, and live hogs, etc.) in early 1979 and several upward adjustments in the following years, grain prices rose quickly throughout the 1980s (Table 30). Nonetheless, due to the adoption of austerity programs to tackle the alarmingly high inflation (retail price rose by 18.5PCT in 1988 and 17.8PCT in 1989, preceding year = 100), plus problems in grain distribution, the trend moved in the opposite direction during 1990–1991. From 1993 onward, prompted by the resolution of the central planners to expedite the grain marketization process, prices once again picked up in a steady and dynamic manner. Like a chain reaction, these price movements were also accompanied by constant ups and downs in the output, which led to dramatic swings in the grain market over that period.

Although seemingly, these fluctuations were an immediate effect of the multiple price adjustments by the state, they in fact reflected the deficiencies in the mechanism governing grain circulation of China. As long as bureaucratic intervention maintained its dominance, or the channel linking the point of origin with the point of consumption were not well-established, the wait-and-see attitude would continue to influence the mentality of peasants, who may respond with distorted behaviors that challenge the market stability. Given the strategic position of grain in the national economy, policies implemented for this special category were in fact a mirror of the state blueprint for agriculture. Undoubtedly, the climate was getting more relaxed and liberalized, especially concerning the exchange of non-staple farm products; participants ranging from peasants to traders however, were still anticipating even greater autonomy, without which a truly vibrant market could hardly come into being.

According to the "Grain Issue in China", a white paper released by the State Council in 1996, the number of people who still did not have adequate food and clothing by the end of 1995 was 65 million, accounting for about 5PCT of the entire population. Besides, it also estimated that with the gradual change in consumption pattern, food production would become increasingly diversified. To balance the supply and demand of grain, an essential component of traditional Chinese diet for centuries, overreliance on import was obviously not a sensible strategy. Instead, ensuring a high level of self-sufficiency (no less than 95PCT under normal conditions) was not only beneficial to rural employment, but also to the development of a healthy economy. Based on the framework set forth in the white paper, a series of measures have been enacted since 1998 to further improve the grain circulation system. For instance, under the principle of "separating government functions from business operations" ('zhengqi fenkai'), state-owned grain enterprises were required to act as legally independent entities responsible for their own profitability.

Moreover, through reshuffling management and downsizing staff, they as a key player in grain distribution were also assigned the role of stabilizing both the supply and prices of the market. Although it was until 2007 that these enterprises, for the first time since 1961, began to be profit-making (the total profit of that year was RMB167 million), the reform of 1998 enabled them to reduce losses, which had been a fairly huge burden for the state budget, on a gradual basis (Yan & Chen, 2009). In addition, to push forward market-oriented operations of grain purchase and sale, Zhejiang Province was approved by the State Council in 2001 to initiate the experiment. Not long after, the trial was expanded to seven other coastal places which were equally major grain-selling areas, they included Shanghai, Fujian, Guangdong, Hainan, Jiangsu, Beijing, and Tianjin, etc. In 2004, with the release of the "Regulations on the Administration of Grain Circulation", grain trading was officially set free across the nation. Rather notably, by allowing qualified non-state and private entities to participate in the procurement, storage, processing, and transportation of grain, the decree was sending a clear message that the decades-old monopoly by state enterprises was over. Since then, prices would be generally market-driven; unless under special circumstances, the government may only exercise macro control using administrative means.

6.3 Endeavors of Structural Adjustment

Following the resolution to liberalize purchase and sale of grain in 2004, circulation of all agricultural products became regulated by the market, a step consistent with the national goal of building a socialist market economy (Zhuo, 2005). If back in the 1960s and 1970s, the slogan "take grain as the key link" ('yi liang wei gang') was a policy which reflected the most fundamental need of China at that time, it was already obsolete when the changing dietary pattern during the 1980s showed that demand for a wider variety of options like meat, eggs, aquatic products, vegetables, and fruits, etc. was growing fast, a phenomenon resulted from the higher level of per capita income. For policy makers, this represented a pressing need of structural adjustment in agriculture. What's more, given the challenges in securing additional arable land, as well as the great potential of exploiting water, grassland and sloping land resources, the prospect of diversifying non-grain food production was encouraging. Take aquaculture as an example, it was estimated that China in 1999 owned 2.6 million hectares of marine cultivable areas, but what had been cultivated was merely 1.09 million hectares, or about 42PCT of the total.

In a broad sense, agriculture should be composed of four major sectors, i.e. farming, forestry, animal husbandry and fishery. Given the fact that China's policy during the pre-reform era had been heavily tilted toward staple crops, their development was anything but a balanced one. Although the importance of a coordinated growth of the four sectors had been reiterated on many occasions, these statements appeared more symbolic than real. Till 1980 when the gross output value of the four reached RMB192.26 billion, the contribution of farming alone was over 75PCT, at RMB145.41 million. To address the uneven performance of agricultural activities and in particular, as a practical support for non-crop production, the "Report on the Work of the Government" delivered by premier Zhao Ziyang in 1984 pointed out the necessity to establish wholesale institutions nearby agricultural terminals. Very soon, the same year witnessed the emergence of the first vegetable wholesale market in Shouguang (a city nicked named China's vegetable basket) of Shandong Province, as well as some more in provinces like Hubei, Zhejiang, Jiangsu, and Hebei, etc. Since the opening of these markets provided a major channel alternative through which farm produce (chiefly vegetables and fruits at the early stage before diversifying into meat, seafoods, and grains, etc.) from diverse localities could be transacted flexibly across the country, it favored multiple participants like suppliers, processors, traders, and end consumers at large, etc. As a result of rapid expansion, their number rose by almost 70PCT over the 1986–1991 period, from 892 to 1,509, with the total turnover hitting RMB15.3 billion, a 4.4-fold increase over that of 1986 (MOA, 2011).

Although marketized operation of agriculture enabled the Chinese peasants to make input and output decisions less blindly, they were more vulnerable to the risks arising from climate-induced fluctuations or shifts in consumer preferences. Owing to the introduction of household responsibility system, individual families became the main unit of rural production. When facing the immeasurable forces of the market, they often found themselves unable to cope with the uncertainties alone. Furthermore, such a small and fragmented way of production could not generate economies of scale; rather, it only resulted in low efficiency and high transaction cost, which weakened the competitiveness of China's agriculture. Given the existing problems, agricultural industrialization as a practice adopted by many developed countries began to attract greater attention. In order to acquire more advantages, peasants of diverse regions chose to unite with each other by entering into specialized cooperatives. Voluntarily organized and managed, these cooperatives helped pool information and provide technical support that enabled them to capture added value through their produce. Referring to the appearance of various kinds of peasant cooperatives, it happened during the 1980s; toward the late 1990s, their development reached a booming stage. For the nationwide promotion of this special form of rural alliance, the Ministry of Agriculture in 2002 launched a pilot program covering 6 municipalities and 100 peasant cooperatives (Liu, 2004). In terms of the legal framework regulating the operation of these organizations, after Zhejiang Province took the leadership in institutional construction, the "Law of the People's Republic of China on Specialized Peasant Cooperatives" went into effect in 2007, which standardized their establishment and management.

Admittedly, the formation of these cooperatives provided the missing organizational link between peasants and markets. Because of their emergence, agricultural production was arranged in a more reasonable and thus profitable way. However, to have this crucial economic sector industrialized, a task which involves the coordination of numerous business activities like transport, storage, planning, and processing, etc., it was far from enough to simply mobilize peasants. For the attainment of greater efficiency, the mechanisms applied in running a high-performing corporate entity should be introduced. From this perspective, the entire value chain was in need of some key enterprises which could undertake the responsibilities of tapping markets, innovating technologies, and directing farm investment, etc. Then gradually, by cultivating competitive edge in a wider scope of products, the country's agricultural structure may be rationalized.

In 2000, a name list covering the first batch of 151 national leading enterprises for agricultural industrialization was released jointly by the Ministry of Agriculture and seven other ministerial departments. Entrusted with the mission of integrating production, processing and marketing so as to smooth the way for the structural adjustment of the rural economy, these enterprises were entitled to some special privilege such as tax relief and favorable credit terms. Coming from different parts of China, their fields of activities are also quite diversified, ranging from fruits and vegetables, livestock husbandry, to grains and oils, etc. Indeed, the offering of preferential treatments was not only intended to favor the selected enterprises; in an indirect way, they were also designed to serve the interest of a larger number of peasants. For example, as one of the 151-enlisted enterprises, Yili was by then the nation's dominant dairy group based in Inner Mongolia. Among its domestic supply chain partners, individual and household dairy peasants have always remained in a significant position. Through knowledge sharing on how to raise yields and prevent epidemics, as well as the provision of financing guidance, Yili committed itself to turning these upstream partners into professional operators of modern ranches. Till the end of 2014, the number of beneficiaries hit 5 million (Yili, 2015).

What's more, in order to have its own sources of raw milk across the nation, the dairy giant has in recent years tried new models of cooperation, like working with the local animal husbandry companies in the joint operation of pastures. Fairly speaking, the footprint of Yili, especially in the post-2000 period, was not merely a record of how the dairy supplier itself has prospered, it was also a display of the leadership role which an enterprise could play in initiating sectoral adjustment. From the angle of individual peasants, the contractual relationship with Yili greatly boosted their confidence; instead of worrying about sales and payment, they could place a more intense focus on quality and output, thus maximizing the advantages of division of labor. Considering the demonstration effect of leading enterprises for

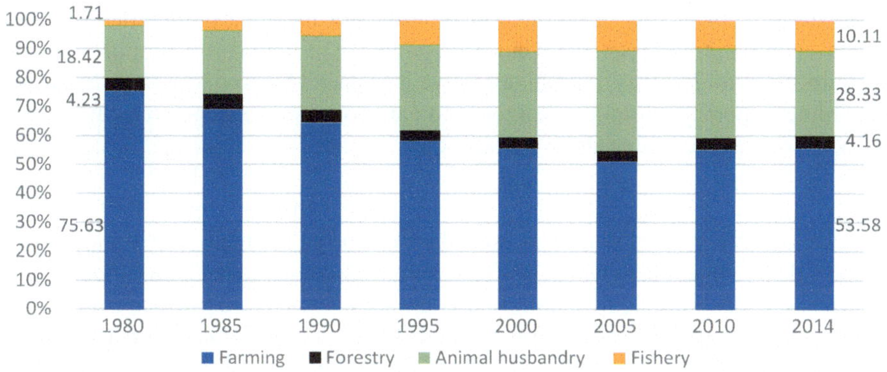

Graph 11 Composition of the Gross Output Value of Agriculture, PCT. *Source* calculated by the author on the basis of China Statistical Yearbook 2015, NBS

the industrialization of agriculture, the same eight agencies by 2011 unveiled four additional name lists and this made the total number of firms reach 1,253.

Given the size of China's rural population which exceeded 795 million, or over 80PCT of the nation's total in 1980, and their low level of education, structural change is hardly an easy job. From the graph below (Graph 11), it can be noticed that for quite a long time, farming maintained its lion's share in agricultural production whereas that of forestry, animal husbandry and fishery combined was incomparable. If during the 1980s, the establishment of a market-oriented circulation system represented an initial trial to improve such an unbalanced structure, then the next landmark stage began after the issuance of the "China Agricultural Development Program for the 1990s" by the State Council in 1993. In its layout for the decade, an integrated crop, livestock, forestry and fishery system was outlined, which highlighted a tailored approach to regional agricultural growth. Together with the adjustment in policy priorities was the allocation of resources. Being increasingly performance-driven, their movement also helped improve the composition of the whole sector. If compared to 1980, the proportion of farming in 2014 declined by over 22PCT. Although forestry did not experience much change, the contribution of animal husbandry and fishery climbed at a similar pace of almost 10PCT, hitting 28.33PCT and 10.11PCT respectively.

6.4 *Growing Reliance on the External Supply*

Usually, the global competitiveness of a country's particular industry sector can be best tested when engaging in the international market. Although today's China is already well-known in the world for its phenomenal trade volume, if dating back to the post-1949 period when the overriding policy was highly protectionist and centralized, there was little awareness of how exchange with foreign countries could adjust the flow of factors of production at home, nor its effect on the identification of one's comparative advantage. Under the guidance of import substitution strategy, the purpose of import was to ultimately have it replaced by products made in China. Regarding export, its dominant role was to earn foreign exchange so as to pay for the needed overseas materials or technologies.

In 1978 when China's import and export volume was merely USD20.64 billion, the share claimed by agricultural goods was USD6.1 billion, almost 30PCT of the total. Since at that time, grain was considered to be of strategic importance to the national development plan which centered overwhelmingly on the heavy industry, all of its transactions were tightly controlled by the state-owned foreign trade companies, chiefly China National Cereals, Oils & Foodstuff Import & Export Corp. (named so after 1961, predecessor of today's COFCO Corp.). In general, rice, soybeans, and corns were among China's main exporting crops whereas wheat belonged to the major crop imported. Prior to 1961, China had remained a net grain exporter; however, the trend was reversed as a result of three consecutive years of output plunge from 1959 to 1961 which turned the country into a net importer (Qu, 2006). While the position as a net exporter was resumed temporarily in 1985 and 1986, shifts continued to occur from 1987 onward. Thanks to the bumper harvest of the mid-1990s, the country's grain export began to surpass import and from 1997 in particular, the surplus persisted until its WTO accession. To gain a better idea of how the fluctuations have occurred, it is somewhat necessary to take a closer look at the performances of two major crops, i.e. soybeans and wheat.

Originated in China, soybeans is not only an important source of dietary protein, it is also the largest single source of edible oil. Before the 1950s, China was still a dominant producer and supplier in the global market. However, due to the shrinkage in the sown area and output, the leadership position was gradually taken over by the US, Brazil and Argentina, etc. According to the statistics of the United Nations (Table 31), China until 1995 remained a net soybean exporter. Ever since 1996 however, its import has begun to soar. In terms of the change in import volume, it accounted for merely 1PCT of the domestic output in 1992. But by 2012, it was almost 3.5 times more than what was produced at home. Accompanying the dramatic expansion, its

Table 31 Soybean production and trade volume, 1992–2012

Year	Domestic output[1] (Tons)	Export[2] (Tons)	Import[3] (Tons)	Net import[4] (Tons)
1992	10,312,562	658,236	120,688	-537,548
1996	13,233,693	191,744	1,107,539	915,795
2000	15,411,495	210,840	10,419,057	10,208,217
2004	17,404,280	334,560	20,229,966	19,895,406
2008	15,542,141	465,143	37,436,262	36,971,119
2012	13,011,059	320,101	58,382,620	58,062,519

Source [1]FAOSTAT, from https://faostat.fao.org/site/567/DesktopDefault.aspx?PageID=567#ancor; [2,3]UN Comtrade database, from https://comtrade.un.org/data/; [4]calculated by the author by subtracting import from export net import underwent an equally accelerated pace of growth, making it the largest consumer of soybeans in the world.

Referring to China's soybean import dependency, a measure of its reliance on import (net import) in relation to domestic consumption, the ratio has been staying at an alarming 80PCT and above since 2011. Actually, this high-rising figure is not unreasonable if an analysis is conducted on the demand side. Because of the booming swine, poultry, and farm-raised aquaculture sector, China has to import unprocessed soybeans with which soybean meal as a protein supplement for feeds is produced. Moreover, given the fact that soya oil is a traditional edible oil for most Chinese; in line with their rising income, consumption has also been pushed up. Furthermore, from the perspective of trade policies, import of soybeans had been subject to very strict quota control since 1996 (Wang, 2010). Under that regime, the out-of-quota tariff rate was set at 180PCT whereas the in-quota tariff was 3PCT. Later, with the gradual abolishment of quota restrictions, a single tariff of 3PCT was applied to all soybean imports in 1999. Stimulated by the lowered duty and stronger domestic demand, imports skyrocketed instantaneously. Within a matter of just one year, China's import volume more than doubled, from 4.32 million tons to over 10.42 million tons by the end of 2000 (UN Comtrade database).

Like a double-edged sword, however, the policy relaxation posed a big threat to the domestic suppliers. Once without the shield of protectionism, their lack of competitiveness against foreign counterparts became self-evident. In terms of the yield per unit area, China back in the 1960s had already fallen behind the US and Brazil, the two largest soybean exporters in the world. Despite some improvements over the following decades, there was still no fundamental change if comparing its position with four major producing nations including the US, Brazil, Argentina, and India at the turn of the century. From 2005 to 2007, in particular, when the global average stood at 2.31 metric tons per hectare, there was an even widened gap which made it less likely for China to catch up (Masudaa & Goldsmith, 2009). By and large, among these four chosen counterparts, it only performed better than India throughout the 1961–2007 period. Additionally, ever since the 2000s, while the harvested area of soybeans in the US and South America moved upward, there was a steady decline in China, from 9.48 million hectares of 2001 to 6.8 million hectares in 2014 (FAOSTAT, https://www.fao.org/faostat/en/#data/QC). Given these disadvantages, plus the fact that the oil extraction rate of domestic soybeans is lower than imports, no wonder the Chinese market has been flooded with overseas players.

Of the various grain crops grown in China, three are regarded as the most important, i.e. rice, corn, and wheat. Before the mid-1990s when the country was still a net exporter of soybeans, its reliance on wheat imports had already been decades-long. Especially within 15 years after its opening to the outside world, the rising standard of living boosted wheat consumption, which climbed from 67.37 million tons of 1980 to 114 million tons in 1997, representing an average annual growth rate of 4.1PCT. Since over the same period, production at home failed to increase at a faster pace, the gap between domestic supply and demand persisted in most of the years (Wang & Sun, 2015). Thereby, the country had to resort to more imports in order to address the imbalance. Fortunately, China's wheat production in the second half of the 1990s

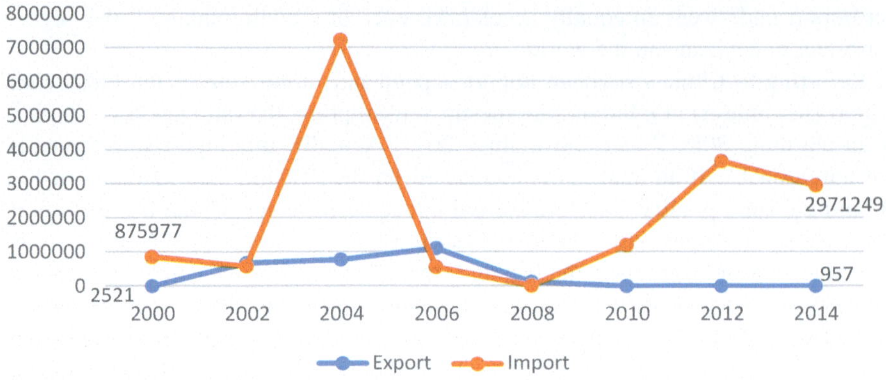

Graph 12 Export and Import of Wheat, Tons. *Source* UN Comtrade database from https://comtrade.un.org/data/

maintained at a high level; in particular, after reaching a historical record of 123.3 million tons in 1997, it became less dependent on import.

After joining the WTO in 2001, China's tariff-rate quota for wheat was increased year on year and since 2004, it has stayed unchanged at 9.636 million tons, with 1PCT in-quota tariff and 65PCT above-quota (most-favored nation) tariff (Qiu, 2006). Considering that 90PCT of the quota is reserved for the state trading companies, much higher than that of rice (50PCT) and corn (60PCT), what it demonstrates is the strategic position of wheat to the nation's food security. In 2002, China for the first time managed to ship more wheat overseas than it brought in, with a net export of over 83,000 tons (Graph 12). Nevertheless, this did not as a result reverse its trade position in the world. Up to 2014, after some irregular movements in both import and export, its role as a net importer remained.

6.5 Concerns Over Food Security

Among various commodities exchanged in international trade, food should be taken as a special category for it is directly related to the issue of national security. In case food insecurity happened to a country, then its overall stability would be at stake. According to the Food and Agriculture Organization (FAO) of the United Nations, "food security exists when all people, at all times, have physical, social and economic access to sufficient, safe and nutritious food which meets their dietary needs and food preferences for an active and healthy life". To have a comprehensive assessment of food insecurity, the FAO has compiled a set of indicators along four major dimensions, i.e. availability, access, utilization and stability. In terms of cereal import dependency ratio which belongs to an indicator of stability, China only in the beginning of the 2000s was a net exporter (Table 32). Later on, its dependence kept

Table 32 Cereal import dependency ratio of selected countries and the world, 2001–2011

Year	China (PCT)	United States (PCT)	India (PCT)	World (PCT)
2001–2003	– 1.7	– 32	– 4.4	– 0.1
2003–2005	0.2	– 28.5	– 4.1	– 0.2
2005–2007	0.4	– 31.3	– 2.1	– 0.2
2007–2009	0.7	– 26.1	– 3.1	– 0.2
2009–2011	2.1	– 24	– 3.1	– 0.2

Note The cereal import dependency ratio tells how much of the available domestic food supply of cereals has been imported and how much comes from the country's own production. It is computed as (cereal imports cereal exports)/(cereal production + cereal imports—cereal exports) × 100. This indicator is calculated in three year averages, it provides a measure of the dependence of a country or region from cereal imports. The greater the indicator, the higher the dependence. Negative values indicate that the country is a net exporter of cereals

Source FAO-Food Security Indicators (Last updated: February 9th, 2016) from https://www.fao.org/hunger/previous-editions/2012/food-security-indicators/en/

rising. By comparison, the US and India have both outperformed the world average, which stood between –0.1PCT to –0.2PCT during the same period.

As another measure of a country's vulnerability to food insecurity, the Global Food Security Index (GFSI), a dynamic quantitative and qualitative benchmarking model, was developed by the Economist Intelligence Unit (EIU) in 2012. By evaluating three categories (i.e. affordability, availability, and quality & safety) of multiple indicators, a ranking is released annually. In the 2016 GFSI overall ranking table, China was No. 42 among the 113 countries selected, scoring 65.5 (0–100 where 100 = most favorable) (EIU, 2016). Like previous years, the top 10 were still dominated by developed countries, with the US scored the highest at 86.6. Indeed, China has achieved some progress if compared to its score of the 2015 index which registered 64.2; however, the very existence of the gap is a reminder that there is still much room to improve its food security. In addition, driven by the dynamic economic growth and enhanced wellbeing, people's dietary preferences have shifted to a more diversified pattern consisting of cereals, meat, eggs and dairy products, which spurs demand for both food and feed grains. Against the rising consumption, the undeniable fact is that several constraints are still standing in the way challenging the agriculture sector.

In 2001, China's rural population shared over 62PCT of the whole country; but starting from 2011, those living in the urban areas were in the majority, accounting for more than 50PCT of the total. Besides, although its arable land in recent years has been staying above 1.8 billion acres (120 million hectares), the minimum line (or known as the red line) set by the state to ensure food security (Table 33); when it comes to the per capita area, it measures only 0.1 hectares, less than a half of the world's average. Moreover, concerning the fertility of soil, one great concern should be the consumption of fertilizers. In fact, Chinese peasants use more than 400 kg per hectare of farmland, far above the global level of 135.3 kg per hectare during the 2011–2013 period (World development indicators: agricultural inputs. Retrieved from https://wdi.worldbank.org/table/3.2). In the long run, excessive fertilizer use not only leads

Table 33 Fertilizer consumption of Arable land, 2010–2014

Year	Arable land[1] (10,000 Hectares)	Total fertilizer consumption[2] (10,000 Tons)	Fertilizer consumption[3] (Kilograms Per Hectare)
2010	13,526.83	5,561.7	411.16
2011	13,523.86	5,704.2	421.79
2012	13,515.85	5,838.8	432
2013	13,516.34	5,911.9	437.39
2014	13,505.73	5,995.9	443.95

Source [1]MLR, 2016; [2]NBS, 2016; [3]calculated by the author by dividing total fertilizer consumption by arable land

to land degradation; besides, it poses a big threat to the environment and food safety as well.

Apart from the above concerns, access to water resources, especially renewable fresh water resources, is equally regarded as an indispensable prerequisite to ensure food security. In 2014, China's per capita renewable fresh water resources was 2,062m^3, only about one third of the world average, which stood at 5,926m^3 (World development indicators: freshwater. Retrieved from https://wdi.worldbank.org/table/3.5). What's more, given the geographic and climatic diversity of the country, another worrisome fact is the uneven distribution of water resources. For instance, areas south of the Yangtze River are in possession of 81PCT of the nation's water and 36.5PCT of its land; but by contrast, regions to the north of the Huai River only have 19PCT of the water yet 63.5PCT of the land (Wang, 2010). Thereby, what often happens in summer is that when the south is dealing with flood, drought is the biggest headache for the north. Nevertheless, due to the steady increase in food consumption, water withdrawal for agricultural purposes from 2010 to 2014 has risen by almost 18 billion cubic meters (Graph 13). In terms of its share in the country's total withdrawal, it remained in the majority of over 60PCT throughout the five-year period. Very likely, the trend is set to continue in the years to come.

To a large extent, the tightening constraints of land and water scarcity signify that China was heading toward its maximum production capacity of food crops. Like several other parts of the world which have confronted the same pressure, improving water use efficiency (WUE) was highlighted as a major solution by the country. In 2012, the State Council issued the "Opinions on the Implementation of the Most Stringent Water Resources Management System". In this important document, "three red lines" were set forth as objectives for the nation to fulfill by 2030. Apart from the water consumption limit of 700 billion cubic meters, as well as a water quality compliance rate of over 95PCT for the control of pollutants discharged into rivers and lakes, the utilization coefficient of irrigation water was targeted to be above 0.6, closer to a globally advanced level of WUE which is 0.7–0.8.

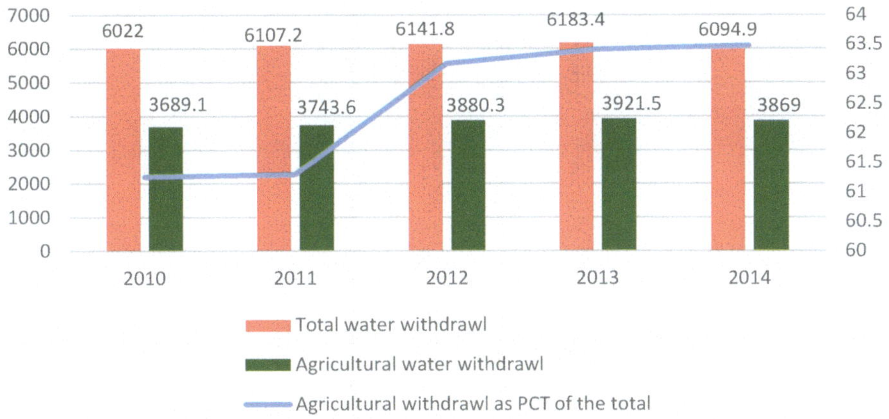

Graph 13 Agricultural Water Withdrawal in Total Water Withdrawal, 100 Million Cubic Meters Per Year. *Note* Agricultural withdrawl as PCT of the total is calculated by the author by dividing agricultural water withdrawl by the total water withdrawl. *Source* NBS, 2016

6.6 *Means to a Sustainable Development*

From a traditional point of view, agricultural output is dependent heavily on the availability of inputs. In other words, an abundant supply of labor, land, and water, etc. is crucial to a bumper harvest. However, once the finiteness of these resources is increasingly recognized as an impediment to higher yield expectations, the former input-based growth model has been shifting toward a new one which is more productivity-driven. Unlike those single-factor indicators such as yield per hectare or value added per worker, total factor productivity (TFP) can provide a comprehensive measure of efficiency in farm production because it takes into account a wider variety of farm inputs, from land, labor, capital, to materials, etc. By analyzing what China has experienced over the 1991–2010 period (Table 34), it is found that despite a slowdown in the growth of agricultural inputs, especially labor and land, improvements in the TFP were not much affected. During the 2000s, its contribution to the growth in agricultural output exceeded four-fifths, outperforming itself a decade before. Regarding the situation outside China, it demonstrated a similar phenomenon, implying that in the future, it is productivity that would set the pace for agricultural development.

In spite of the essential role of productivity, if without constant innovation of science and technologies, its push–pull effect on agriculture could hardly sustain. In 2015, a guideline document entitled the "National Plan for Sustainable Agriculture Development (2015–2030)" was promulgated, which divided China into three zones according to their diversities in factor endowment, environmental capacity, and ecological types, etc. On the basis of such an arrangement, the strategies of the whole sector could be better tailored against local characteristics, thus optimizing the deployment of resources. Besides, of the five priorities outlined for the upcoming years, an innovation-led development model was highlighted as key to promoting the

Table 34 Average annual growth of selected time periods

China	Agriculturaloutput	TFP	Total inputs	Labor	Land	Livestock	Machinery	Fertilizer
1991–2000	0.0511	0.0394	0.0117	– 0.0109	0.009	0.0182	0.0561	0.0341
2000–2010	0.036	0.03	0.006	– 0.0329	0.0068	0.022	0.0789	0.0363
Average Annual Growth of 2000–2010								
Transition Economies	0.0173	0.0204	– 0.0031	– 0.0244	– 0.0030	– 0.0017	– 0.012	0.0393
World	0.0257	0.0177	0.008	– 0.0026	0.0029	0.0146	0.018	0.0205

Note Total inputs include labor, land, livestock, machinery, fertilizer and feed, etc. Source: Agricultural Total Factor Productivity Growth Indices for Regions (Countries Grouped by Income Class), 1961–2013. United States Department of Agriculture, 2016. From https://www.ers.usda.gov/data-products/international-agricultural-productivity.aspx

Table 35 Distribution of population in urban and rural China, 1950–1978

Year	Population in cities & towns (Million)	Share of China's total (PCT)	Population in countryside (Million)	Share of China's total (PCT)
1950	61.69	11.18	490.27	88.82
1957	99.49	15.39	547.04	84.61
1962	116.59	17.33	556.36	82.67
1965	130.45	17.98	594.93	82.02
1970	144.24	17.38	685.68	82.62
1978	172.45	17.92	790.14	82.08

level of farm output. Specifically, the contribution rate of improvement in agricultural science and technologies would grow to more than 60PCT by 2020, in addition to the comprehensive plowing, sowing and harvesting mechanization level which is to surpass 68PCT.

6.7 From "Bringing in" to "Going Out"

In fact, for the fulfillment of these medium-term objectives, numerous efforts had already been put under way prior to 2015. For instance, to encourage the application of advanced technologies and facilities, modern agricultural demonstration parks were established. After the designation of the first batch containing 50 state-level demonstration parks in 2010, their number climbed to 283 by 2015. Moreover, aware of the necessity to borrow the latest know-how from abroad, China has also been working closely with multiple foreign counterparts. Israel, due to its leadership in agricultural R&D, remained for decades a key technology provider and trainer. Early in 1994, a China-Israel demonstration farm had begun its operation in Beijing, with a total investment reaching USD4.7 million (Zhao, 1997). Later on, more similar projects were materialized between the two parties, with locations distributed in Ningxia Hui Autonomous Region, Tianjin, and Zhejiang Province, etc. If reckoning the most comprehensive one which incorporated not only the full suite of cutting-edge technologies of Israel, but also a wide scope of activities from production, training, research, to innovation, etc., it should be the Fujian-based Sino-Israeli Demonstration Farm set up in 2014. Through cooperation in aquaculture production, poultry raising, and planation of horticultural crops, China could expect to access technologies more environmentally-friendly and raise the standards of its agricultural produce.

If from Israel, what China has mainly learned are the approaches to ecologically sustainable farming, then its partnership with Germany was characterized by the introduction of modern machinery and equipment. Initiated in 2009, the German-Chinese Ganhe (in Inner Mongolia) Demonstration Farm was projected for a duration of five years. Of the €2.2 million invested in the joint venture, €1 million was spent on German equipment such as combine harvesters, tractors, and fertilizer spreaders, etc. Toward 2014 when the contractual term was drawing to an end, yield improvements for crops like wheat and soybeans had already been encouraging. On the one hand, such a phenomenon was reflective of enhanced efficiency in land use; on the other hand, it was due largely to the imported machinery that made the change happen. As a successive endeavor to consolidate their fruitful collaboration, 2015 witnessed the inauguration of the Sino-German Crop Production and Agrotechnology Demonstration Park in Huanghai state farm of northern Jiangsu Province. Similar to the Ganhe project, equipment was still provided by the German partners, together with other inputs and training programs. Besides, given the problem of soil degradation along the Yangtze River Valley, namely, soil compaction and nutrient depletion, trials would be launched to replace the conventional wheat-rice rotation cropping on paddy fields with wheat-soybean or wheat–maize intercropping in dry lands, an agronomical practice beneficial to erosion control and intensification of crop production.

For a developing country like China, borrowing foreign expertise and experiences is indeed an efficient alternative to enable its agricultural sector to be transformed in a way that is more economically viable and ecologically sound. Meanwhile, in view of the fact that its low per capita arable land has remained a hard constraint prohibiting strong output expansion, the "going out" strategy was also adopted to deal with the concern over food security. Nicknamed "granary of China", the northeast province of Heilongjiang is endowed with highly fertile black soil. Unfortunately, due to overexploitation and inappropriate land use, losses in nutrients and top soil posed a big challenge to maintaining its grain yield. As a result, together with the numerous preservation efforts implemented by the local authorities to ease the retrogression, renting land abroad was increasingly a feasible option among enterprises. For instance, Dongning Huaxin Industry and Trade Group in 2004 set up Armada, a joint venture, in Russia's Primorye krai (or the Primorsky region), which borders China to the west. According to its agreement with the host government, the company was in a position to cultivate crops and raise livestock on 40,000 hectares of land under a 49-year lease. After a decade-long development, Armada has evolved into the biggest agricultural cooperative project between China and Russia. By the end of 2014 when its arable land amounted to 68,000 hectares (equivalent to 1.02 million acres), the total investment hit USD120 million. As an official recognition of Huaxin's model, its cooperative farm in Primorye krai became the first national-level agricultural industrial zone outside China in 2015 (Huaxin, 2015).

Historically celebrated for their abundant agricultural resources and in particular, the huge amount of arable land, South America has also been a favored destination for Chinese investors. Referring to Chongqing Grain Group (CGG), a leading state-owned grain company based in the southwest, it gained the approval of the NDRC (National Development and Reform Commission) in 2010 to establish a soybean production base in Brazil. One year later, the first shipment carrying 65,000 tons of soybeans originated in Brazil arrived at Nantong port (Jiangsu Province). After being crushed into cooking oil, the product was sold in the supermarkets of Chongqing. As a matter of fact, there was yet another Chinese company which had conducted its operations in Brazil earlier than the CGG. By building two farms on an area covering over 16,800 hectares, Zhejiang Fudi Agriculture Group started to grow soybeans and upland rice in 2008 (Hu, 2011).

Together with China's growing interest in the farmland of Russia and South America, there has been a simultaneous expansion of its physical presence to other parts of the world, like Africa, Oceania, and Southeast Asia, etc. Moreover, instead of being confined to the cropping business, there demonstrates a broadened spectrum of activities ranging from animal husbandry, fishery, to forestry. Nevertheless, since land is such a critical resource to every nation state, the move of China around the globe has provoked some controversies and restrictions, even if the deal is only under concession. Apart from the obstacles against foreign access to agricultural land, the other major concern China has to deal with is how to realize integration of the whole value chain. From a long-term perspective, rather than focusing predominantly on the upstream, ownership of downstream assets is more critical to seizing the initiative in food supply. In October 2014, a deal was finalized between COFCO, China's leading company of agriproducts & foodstuffs, and the Dutch-based grain trader Nidera. By holding a 51PCT controlling stake of the latter with a consortium of international investors, COFCO could take advantage of Nidera's worldwide network which incorporated a complete set of functions, i.e. production, collection, processing, and distribution, etc. (Lü, 2014). Via this platform, the Chinese food giant may further consolidate its overseas logistics facilities and build a high-performing channel connecting the place of origin with the place of consumption internationally.

As a matter of fact, the transaction of COFCO provided the agribusinesses of China a fresh way of thinking when planning cross-border acquisitions. In particular, given the complexities of securing arable land abroad, as well as the unmeasurable opportunity cost arising from policy shifts, alliance with complementary partners should be a fairly viable approach since the synergy effect generated could enable Chinese players to access target resources in a time-efficient way. Further, backed by the mutually-favorable relationship, a stable chain of supply would come into being, which can better assure food security for the country.

7 Urbanization and the Fate of Migrant Workers

Universally, the emergence of towns and cities is regarded as a symbol of civilization. Representative not only of a higher level of architecture, their construction also marks a demand for enhanced security to protect the rising wealth. Based on the discovery of archeologists in Henan Province (namely, the Xinzhai Ruins and Erlitou Ruins), cities with large buildings, defensive moats, as well as rammed-earth walls, etc. had already existed since Xia (circa 2070–1600 BC), the first dynasty in China's recorded history.

Thousands of years later, benefiting from the booming industrial and commercial activities, the Song Dynasty (960–1279, divided into the Northern Song and Southern Song) witnessed an unprecedented relocation of the rural population which greatly pushed up its urbanization rate. During the end of the Southern Song Dynasty, in particular, the capital city Lin'an (today's Hangzhou, Zhejiang Province) was home to over 1.2 million people (Lin, 1979). If compared to Venice, the largest and most prosperous city of Europe in the same period of time, the inhabitants were just about 100,000. Fairly speaking, the relaxed household registration (also known as "hukou") system of the Song was a key factor that facilitated occupational mobility. When an increasing number of peasants poured into cities for a better life, many of them opened their own stalls and shops selling a diverse assortment of commodities, from farm produce to handicrafts, etc. In turn, such a dynamic business environment, while contributing to the economic boom, helped with the expansion of cities. Similar to Lin'an, the Northern Song capital Bianjing (today's Kaifeng, Henan Province) also boasted over one million residents.

7.1 "Hukou" System, a Constraint on Labor Mobility

Unfortunately, the impressive pace of urbanization achieved by the Song was no longer repeated over its succeeding dynasties. At the initial stage after the founding of the PRC, rural–urban migration was basically unrestricted, which led to the establishment of more cities whose number rose from 132 of 1949 to 176 in 1957. Simultaneously, their population underwent an expansion of 80PCT, reaching 70.77 million by 1957 (NBS, 2009). Confronting the over-rapid pace of demographic explosion, job creation became a dominant headache among the series of problems emerged in urban China.

In order to curb the irrational and senseless outflow of rural labor into cities, the "Regulations of the People's Republic of China on Household Registration" was promulgated in 1958. By linking entitlement to public services like health care, housing, and education, and certain privileges such as state-subsidized food ration, to the place where a person's hukou is registered, the new institution marked the formation of a two-tier system which strictly separated rural residents from those living in the urban area (Wang, 2011). Although it was until 1975 that migration freedom enjoyed by Chinese citizens was officially removed from the constitution, the 1958 arrangements had in essence erected a barrier discouraging geographic mobility from the countryside to cities. In addition, several other stringent rules were released prior to 1978, both without exception aimed to control the conversion of hukou status from the agricultural to the non-agricultural one (named 'nong zhuan fei'). As a result of these tightening constraints, China's urbanization process almost stalled after stepping into the 1960s (Table 5.35), with its rate stayed below 20PCT toward the end of the 1970s.

Source NBS, 1999 & 2016.

7.2 *ID Card: "Passport" to Liberalized Migration*

Under the impact of the nationwide economic reform and opening up, the overall policy environment in China became increasingly liberalized. Concerning the agricultural sector, the implementation of the "Household Responsibility System" since the early 1980s has granted peasants greater autonomy. Instead of reaping revenues solely out of the land, more chose to tap new opportunities by heading out to nearby towns or cities farther apart where they began to engage in some industrial and commercial activities. In recognition of this spontaneous movement and to attract a larger number of skilled peasants to participate in township development, the State Council in 1984 issued a notice which gave them permanent residence in towns. Dissimilar from the other urban residents, however, these new holders of "non-agricultural hukou" were denied access to public provisioning of subsidized foods. Strictly speaking, the concept of personal identity at that time was almost nonexistent in China. Even in case a proof was needed, the household registration book ('hukou bu') or an introduction letter with the official seal of the work unit ('danwei jieshaoxin') would be sufficient enough.

Nevertheless, given the increasingly mobile population, such a practice was by no means a long-term solution. From 1984 to October 1991, after the passage of the "Provisional Regulations of the PRC Concerning the Resident Identity Card", some 755 million first-generation ID cards were issued to citizens reaching 16 years old. Although a modern computerized management system was not that quickly established, these cards enabled holders to move around the country with fewer restrictions. More significantly, their issuance smoothed the way for enhanced freedom of employment across the rural and urban regions.

Benefiting from the preferential policies of reform and opening-up, the economic vibrancy of China's Pearl River Delta has made it the most favored destination for job seekers nationwide since the mid-1980s. In particular, with regard to cities like Shenzhen, Guangzhou, and Zhuhai, etc., their leadership in hosting foreign direct investment attracted soaring numbers of rural labor force to search for good fortune. Contemptuously referred to as "blind drifters" ('mang liu') at that time, which implied a kind of irrational movement without specific plans, this group of people not only worked hard to generate wealth for themselves; moreover, their assiduousness has also contributed a lot to the nation's miraculous development over the subsequent decades.

Concerning the formation of the first wave of "migrant workers" ('nongmin gong') in China, it was not comprehensively documented. Nevertheless, after several unanimous warnings by major transit hubs (e.g. Guangzhou, Haikou, Wuhan and Shanghai, etc.) during the 1989 Spring Festival, which pointed to an unprecedented burden on their capacities, the press began to use "Spring Festival rush" ('chun yun', a special period of about 40 days when China faces an extremely high traffic load because of the Lunar New Year holiday) to describe the phenomenal "tide of rural exodus" ('mingong chao', photo 5–23). If compared to the early 1980s when there were approximately 2 million migrant workers who had left the countryside, the number climbed to some 30 million in 1989 (Guo & Wang, 2012).

7.3 *Headaches Following the Designation of New Towns and Cities*

Apart from the shift of rural labor force, what can equally represent the ongoing urbanization in China should be the construction of small towns. In this regard, a major move that accelerated its pace of development occurred in 1984 when the criteria for designated towns ('jian zhi zhen', meaning the officially approved towns) were lowered. In general, all the seats of county-level government agencies would qualify for the title. Besides, regarding the townships ('xiang') of fewer than 20,000 people, if the location of the government was inhabited by over 2,000 non-agricultural population, they may also be granted the same status. Meanwhile, considering that the segregated distribution of towns ('zhen') and villages ('cun') in certain areas had adversely affected their management efficiency, all the townships eligible for the shift were mandated to implement the mechanism of "placing villages under the governance of towns" ('zhen guan cun'). Triggered by the decline in threshold, there was a rapid boom of designated towns, whose number more than quintupled from 2,176 of 1978 to 11,481 in 1988 (Peng & Huang, 2012).

Not long after the relaxed standards for the officially recognized towns, the definition for cities was also adjusted to help boost urban expansion. In a notice issued by the State Council in 1986, numerous conditions were laid out for the establishment of cities. For instance, towns would be granted city status in case they were regional economic centers with non-agricultural population exceeding 60,000 and the annual gross national product (GNP) surpassing RMB200 million. Besides, for counties of less than 500,000 people, as long as the seat was based in a town of over 100,000 non-agricultural population, their rural residents accounted for no more than 40PCT of the total, and the GNP per annum was in excess of RMB300 million, they too could be designated as cities. Once the conversion was accomplished, the townships and towns administered formerly by counties would be put under the governance of cities. During the course of implementation, however, some inadequacies were detected and the primary one was the failure of the new policy to look after regional disparities, which gave rise to application bottlenecks. Therefore, further amendments were made in 1993, including an additional criterion for prefectural cities ('di ji shi'). Ever since the release of these regulations, officially-designated cities mounted steadily year on year. By 1997, they peaked at a record high of 668, a level hardly surpassed in the following decade (Zhu, 1998).

Driven by the rapid development of towns and cities, China's urban population hit 459 million in 2000, accounting for 36.22PCT of the total, over 18PCT higher than that of 1978. On the one hand, it was urbanization that has enabled the workforce of the countryside to live in a way different from their forefathers. More importantly,

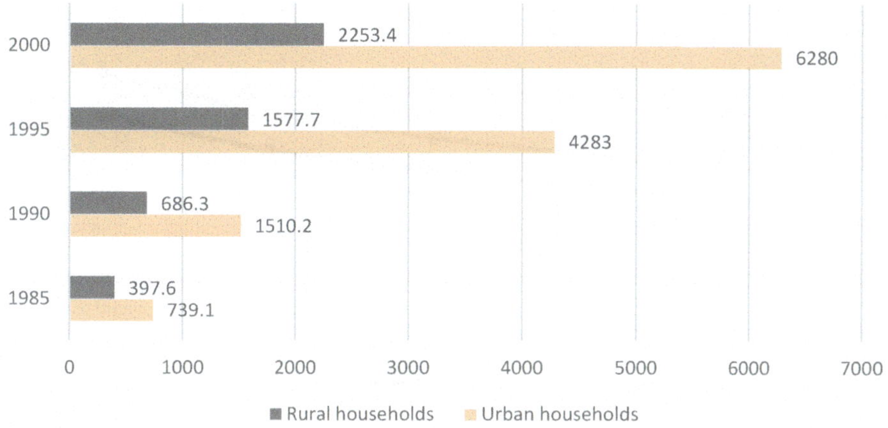

Graph 14 Per Capita Income of Urban and Rural Households, RMB/Month. *Note* figures for rural households are the per capita net income whereas those for urban households are the per capita disposable income. *Source* NBS, 2001

it broadened their vision and offered them bigger opportunities to have the goals fulfilled. But similar to a double-edged sword, the downside was the diminishing attractiveness of the rural areas, a phenomenon accompanied by the widening urban–rural income gap since the mid-1980s. In 1985, for instance, the ratio between urban and rural per capita income stayed at 1.86:1 (Graph 14). Fifteen years later, it picked up to 2.79:1, implying that the per capita income of urban residents was almost 2.8 times that of their rural counterparts. Fairly speaking, the enlarged gap was not a result of stagnant rural income; rather, the reason lied in the faster pace of urban income growth. From a long-term perspective, if the inequality could not be reversed, not only the rural economy, the national economy too, would be dragged backward.

As a matter of fact, the disparities between urban and rural China were not merely limited to the income distribution, they existed simultaneously in several other aspects such as education, health care, housing, employment, and consumption pattern, etc. In terms of education, spending directed to the rural has always fallen behind the national average. Take the elementary schools as an example, from 1996 to 2000, the recurrent expenditure for each rural student remained at about 80PCT of the nation's average (Graph 15). According to a report (i.e. "Social Mobility in Contemporary China", 'Dangdai Zhongguo Shehui Liudong') published by the Chinese Academy of Social Sciences, of the RMB580 billion aggregate investment in education for 2002, the rural area which was inhabited by more than 60PCT of the total population received 23PCT only (He, 2007). If looking around the country, such a disproportionate allocation of resources was not uncommon. Rather, it was characteristic of its dual urban–rural economic structure, a long-standing hurdle impeding coordinated development. Moreover, given the exacerbated polarization between the two sides, the distributional bias in favor of the urbanites should undeniably be regarded as its root cause.

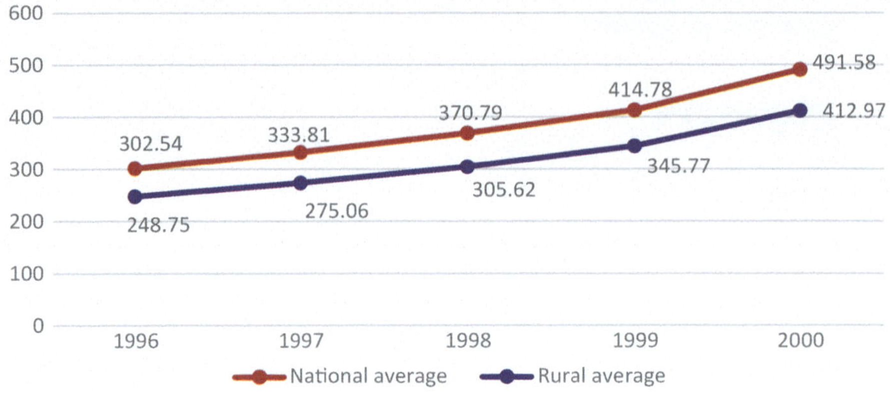

Graph 15 Budgetary appropriation for recurrent expenditure per student of elementary schools, RMB. *Source* MOE, 1998, 1999, 2000 & 2001

7.4 "Secrets" Behind Export Miracle

Almost two decades after the introduction of the ID system, the "Law of the People's Republic of China on Resident Identity Cards" went into effect in 2004, which laid greater emphasis on the protection of holders' rights. In that same year, the second-generation ID cards with embedded smart chips were also issued to gradually replace the old ones. Like many foreign countries in the world, using modern technologies to upgrade ID cards could of course improve the efficiency of China in managing its large population. Additionally, these arrangements demonstrated from another angle the effect of urbanization, i.e. with fewer people willing to make their ends meet through agricultural works only, there has been a surge in those heading to cities since the beginning of the new millennium. From 1995 to 2000, migrant workers in China had risen from 70 million to 78.49 million, representing an average annual increase of some 1.7 million. Over the next two years, their number leaped further to 83.99 million and 104.7 million, a dramatic growth of 5.5 million and 20.71 million respectively (Wei & Su, 2013).

Starting from the early 2000s, China was often referred to as the "workshop of the world" by the overseas media. While this label symbolized a recognition of the country's growing importance in international trade, if without the massive labor input of its rural workforce, it would be unlikely for huge volumes of "Made-in-China" products to be sold around the globe. In 2002 when migrant workers amounted to 104.7 million, those employed in the manufacturing industry shared 22PCT. Over the following years, the same sector continued to have the highest concentration of migrant workers, whose proportion rose to 37.2PCT of the total 225.42 million by 2008 (NBS, 2013). Besides, another critical factor contributing to the competitiveness of the Chinese manufactured goods should be the income of these workers, which stayed at a rather low level if compared to that of the urban

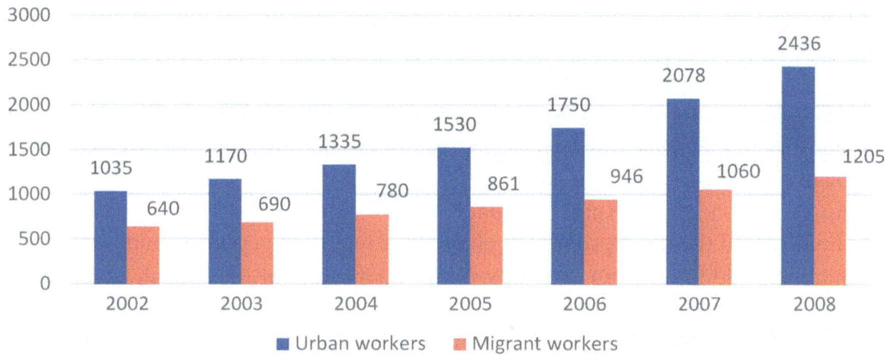

Graph 16 Comparison of Average Salaries between Urban and Migrant Workers, RMB/Month. *Source* Salary of urban workers is calculated by the author on the basis of the average annual salaries of employees working in China's cities and towns. NBS, 2010. Salary of migrant workers: Lu, 2012

workers. From 2002 to 2008 (Graph 16), their salary gap kept widening at a speed faster than the pay rise of migrant workers year on year.

To a certain extent, it was the existence of such a gap that has enabled China to realize a quick expansion of trade surplus. During the 7-year period, it grew by almost 900PCT from USD30.43 billion of 2002 to USD298.13 billion in 2008. As an economy whose development has been largely powered by export, the miracle of a double-digit average growth (at 21.9PCT per annum) in the 2000s was without doubt attributable to the dynamics arising from countless migrant workers. Toiling in obscurity and earning wages at discriminatory levels, their role in China's urbanization and industrialization was irreplaceable. Although it is true that by moving into cities, they could more easily share the fruits of a transforming society; the very fact they had to confront was that like a marginalized group, it was rather hard, if not impossible, to integrate with the local residents holding the urban *hukou*.

7.5 Citizenization of Migrant Workers

In general, a nation's degree of urbanization is measured either by the percentage of its urban population or the rate of change in the size of the urban population. While both two are fairly informative indicators, they do not reflect in a qualitative manner the actual status of city dwellers, especially the newly-settled. In view of China's gigantic scale of rural-to-urban migration, and the profound socio-economic impact it can exert, greater attention has been directed to the citizenization ("*shi min hua*") of the incoming workforce. More than just a number, it is a comprehensive index describing to which extent migrant workers as well as their families share the rights enjoyed by the permanent urban residents. Specifically, the benchmarking criteria of citizenization involve fair employment and access to basic public services like children's education, housing, health care, and pension benefits, etc.

From a long-term point of view, if China expects to promote urbanization smoothly, greater emphasis should be laid on the interests of migrant workers so as to improve their social and emotional wellbeing. As a major institutional arrangement to eliminate inequalities of treatment, the "Opinions of the State Council on Resolving the Problems concerning Rural Migrant Workers" was released in 2006, which not only highlighted the most prominent challenges facing the country, approaches for the creation of a fair and more friendly environment were also outlined. Concerning the issue of pay and pay equity, the provincial-level governments were required to apply minimum wage systems strictly to all businesses and workplaces. Further, their lowest wage rates should be adjusted moderately to ensure a steady increase of earnings for migrant workers.

In addition to the above, for the eradication of wage arrears, a phenomenon which had been rather prevalent in the construction sector hiring millions of migrant workers, the Opinions put forward a guarantee scheme composed of several key measures. In normal conditions, salary payment would be put under supervision; once default were detected, the employer would face severe punishment in addition to mandatory wage deposit ahead of the payday. According to the Ministry of Labor & Social Security (today's Ministry of Human Resources & Social Security), from 2004 to July 2007, RMB43.32 billion of deferred wages have been reclaimed across the country (Fan, 2007). Furthermore, in 2008, the share of migrant workers in need of demanding overdue wages stood at 4.1PCT. As a result of tightened control by regulatory authorities, it fell to 1PCT in 2015 (NBS, 2016).

For the urban residents of China, they often take it for granted that the benefits offered by the employers are inclusive of a social insurance scheme. Indeed, ever since the enactment of the "Labor Insurance Regulations of the People's Republic of China" in 1951, which marked the initiation the country's social security system, participants have largely been the workforce living in cities and towns. In other words, given the coexistence of agricultural and non-agricultural hukou holders, there was also a dual structure in their welfare entitlements. Despite several reforms during the 1980s and 1990s, the interest of the rural population still didn't gain equal attention. As to the first time migrant workers were integrated into the urban pension system, it happened in 2010 after the implementation of a notice (i.e. the "Interim Measures for the Transfer and Continuation of the Basic Pension Insurance Relations of Urban Employees") from the State Council. With provisions pointing out explicitly that the same practice would apply to migrant workers, the notice was an improvement in that it lowered the barriers against free labor movement from the countryside into cities.

One year later, the long-awaited "Social Insurance Law of the People's Republic of China" went into effect. Although it did not address at a regional level how the rural labor should participate in the social security system when recruited by urban employers, the law specified separately in Article No. 95 the necessity of their involvement. What's more, given its inclusion of all the five categories of insurance that made up China's social insurance system, namely, pension, medical, occupational injury, unemployment, and maternity insurance, etc., the comprehensive law provided a solid basis for all citizens, especially the disadvantaged migrant workers, to better safeguard their interests. Over the 2008–2014 period, there was a gradual increase in the migrant workers covered by the social insurance scheme (Graph 17). However, as compared to those not yet granted the same treatment, they were still in the minority.

To enable all the migrant workers to benefit from the system, further improvements were without doubt necessary. At the same time, what should also be noted is that the phenomenon was by no means a mere accident; in fact, its occurrence was largely due to an institutional flaw deep-rooted in China, i.e. the dual household registration system. Kicked off in 1958, the system from then on erected an invisible wall dividing the urban from the rural. Accordingly, the entire population was classified into two groups, based on which their employment as well as the entitlement to almost all the public services like education, medical care, and social security, etc. became divergent. Besides, with the state priorities oriented to the development of heavy industries, more resources flowed into cities, thus making its residents far better off than their rural compatriots. Despite the fact that triggered by the reform of 1978, barriers prohibiting urban-bound migration were relaxed step by step to cope with the ongoing process of urbanization and industrialization, the domicile management system of China remained virtually intact. In a society characterized by high population mobility and widening wealth gap, such a rigid mechanism could no longer fit. For the restoration of fairness, eradication of urban–rural dualism was a task not only crucial, but also imminent.

After more than 50 years of implementation, the regime separating agricultural and non-agricultural hukou was finally abolished following the issuance of the "Opinions on Further Promoting the Reform of Household Registration System" in 2014. Since

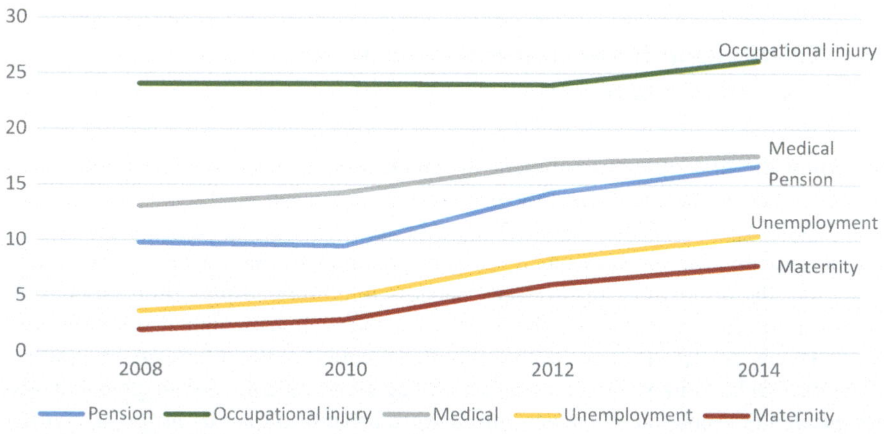

Graph 17 Proportion of Migrant Workers Participating in Social Insurance Program, PCT. *Source* NBS, 2014 & 2015

its release coincided with the announcement of the "National New-Type Urbanization Plan (2014–2020)" in the same year, establishment of a unified "residence permit system" ('juzhuzheng zhidu') was projected as the ultimate goal to adapt to the differentiated settlement policies laid out in the plan. Specifically, for a better alignment between urbanization and transfer of hukou, cities of different sizes should observe their own principles in rural labor absorption. Regarding the designated towns ("jian zhi zhen") and small cities, they were fully open to incomers; as to the medium-sized cities (with population of over 500,000 but under 1,000,000) and large cities (with one to three million people), their openness was subject to certain conditions. In case of megacities whose population was in excess of five million, the scale would be put under strict control.

Actually, the unification of household registration system should be considered as a decisive step to the ultimate removal of urban–rural distinctions that have stratified the society. Given the complexities behind, particularly the arduous challenge of how to detach the entrenched interests from one's hukou, what China has done in 2014 was just a beginning. If the late 1980s witnessed the first wave of rural migrant workers pouring into cities, then many of them were already in their 40 s and even 60 s. Based on the "2015 Nationwide Monitoring Survey Report on Migrant Workers" issued by the National Bureau of Statistics, of the total 277.47 million migrant workers in the end of the year, 17.9PCT or almost 50 million were over 50 s, a rather massive group. Considering the average retirement age of the country which is around 60, this is a stage when the biggest concerns are centered on pension and health care. What's more, within another two to three decades, the second generation migrant workers who were generally the post-80 s (born in the 1980s) would also be aging. Therefore, in view of the tremendous pressure ahead, as well as the limited amount of time, the government right now does not have much choice but to call for a faster pace of reform aimed at promoting equal opportunity and fair share of social resources.

7.6 *Relationship Between the Service Sector and Urbanization*

Regarding the first official document in which urbanization was proclaimed as a strategy to harmonize the development of China's urban and rural economy, it should be the tenth Five-Year Plan (2001–2005) released at the outset of the new century. In this nationwide program covering a series of priorities for the upcoming five years, issues like the removal of institutional barriers inhibiting surplus rural labor from moving into cities and the establishment of a rationally-distributed urban system were taken as the determinants to the smooth execution of the urbanization strategy. Given the fact that industrialization as a major catalyst could not only trigger, but also precipitate the transition of society into a more urbanized one, its progress is often used to mirror the pace of urbanization. Among the numerous methods to calculate the level of industrialization, a frequently adopted one is the value added to GDP by

Table 36 Comparison of urbanization rate and the level of industrialization, 2000–2010

Year	Urbanization rate[1] (PCT of the total population)	Industry, value added[2] (PCT of GDP)	Ratio between 1 & 2[3]
2000	36.22	45.4	0.80
2002	39.09	44.3	0.88
2004	41.76	45.8	0.91
2006	44.34	47.4	0.94
2008	46.99	46.8	1.00
2010	49.95	46.2	1.08

Note Urbanization rate is measured by the urban population as a percentage of the total population; level of industrialization is measured by the value added to the GDP by industry as a percentage
Source [1]NBS. 2011; [2]World development indicators of the World Bank, from https://data.un.org/Data.aspx?d=WDI&f=Indicator_Code%3aNV.IND.TOTL.ZS; [3]calculated by the author

industry as a percentage. Based on global experiences, a country's urbanization rate would often surpass its level of industrialization. Besides, it is considered normal in case their ratio, an indicator suggesting how rationally the two forces interact with each other, falls within the range between 1.4 and 2.5 (Ma & Hu, 2010).

For some developed countries like the US, France, and the Great Britain, etc., their number was already in excess of four in 2010 (Zhou, 2012). If using the same approach to evaluate China's urbanization, it can be found that the momentum has severely fallen behind industrialization. During the 2000–2010 period for example, while the ratio kept rising in a steady way (Table 36), the gap with the rest of the world was still significant, which averaged 1.95 in 2010.

Although it is true that the dynamism of urbanization in China was incommensurate with its growth of industrialization, the disharmony only represents a part of the full picture. To a large extent, the phenomenon shows the existence of a more profound relationship between urbanization and the sectoral composition of the economy. As a byproduct of industrialization, urbanization inevitably bears the hallmark of structural shifts that have taken place in a country. For China, the reason why its secondary sector could maintain its dominance for several decades is attributable to the persistent lack of vibrancy in the tertiary activities. By comparing to countries whose gross national income (GNI) of 2010 stood at similar levels (Table 37), the weight of services in China's GDP ranked at the bottom. Even if compared against the low-income countries, China was still about 3PCT below their average.

Generally, a nation's reliance on the service sector would increase as its economy matures. This explains why in most developed countries, it is the service sector which employs the majority of the workforce. Due to the same reason, their society is often characterized by a high level of urbanization. Although China is still a developing country, its track record demonstrates a similar pattern of structural change. In 1978, the primary sector (agriculture) contributed 27.7PCT to the GDP whereas that of the secondary (manufacturing and construction) and tertiary sector (service) accounted for 47.7PCT and 24.6PCT respectively. By 2010, the breakdown of the three main

Table 37 Comparison of China's service sector with selected countries and income groups, 2010

Country or income groups	GNI per capita, PPP[1] (Current International USD)	Services, etc., value added[2] (PCT of GDP)
China	9,200	44.2
Colombia	10,260	57.9
Dominica	9,830	71.9
Ecuador	9,030	53.5
Jordan	10,150	65.9
Maldives	8,920	80.1
Low-Income	1,293.6	47.1
Middle-Income	8,137.5	53.4
High-Income	39,151	73.4
World	12,755.3	67.5

Source [1]World development indicators of the World Bank, from https://data.un.org/Data.aspx?d=WDI&f=Indicator_Code%3aNY.GNP.PCAP.PP.CD; [2]World development indicators of the World Bank, from https://data.un.org/Data.aspx?d=WDI&f=Indicator_Code%3aNV.SRV.TETC.ZSs

sectors turned out to be 9.5PCT, 46.4PCT, and 44.1PCT (NBS, 2016). With the shrinking share of agriculture, China's economic output has become more dependent on services. Accompanying the trend, there were also changes in the composition of employment. While the workforce employed in the service sector rose from 12.2PCT of the total in 1978 to 34.6PCT by 2010, the proportion of the primary sector dropped from 70.5PCT to 36.7PCT over the same period.

If the development of industrialization can be divided into three stages, i.e. the incipient, intermediate, and advanced stage, then China should have stepped into the third stage since its 12th Five-Year Plan period (2011–2015), with the composite index of industrialization standing at 83.69 in 2014 (Huang, 2015). As a typical feature of this phase, growth in the secondary sector tends to slow down before being overtaken by the tertiary sector. In other words, the latter is to exert a crucial role in powering the economy. Besides, following the progress in technologies and application of modern means of production, the ability of the secondary sector to absorb new labor force entrants would fall. By contrast, the job creating potential of the service industry is rather immense. In terms of their employment elasticity, a labor market indicator measured by the ratio between percentage change in the number of employed people and the growth rate of GDP, it is the service sector which has exhibited a relatively higher intensity, suggesting better employment performance in response to each one percent rise of economic output.

In view of the above, if China wishes to fulfill its goals on urbanization, it should not simply promote a transformation of industries that is driven by innovation, support for the service sector is of no less importance. For the time being, among the municipalities whose tertiary sector is dominant in their local economy, the performance of Beijing is perhaps the most outstanding. As the state capital, its attraction to migrant workers has also remained unmatchable. In 2010, of the 19.62 million permanent

Table 38 Employment elasticity of Beijing municipality, 2001–2010

Period	Overall employment elasticity	Primary sector	Secondary sector	Tertiary sector
2001–2010	0.33	– 0.35	– 0.01	0.49
2001–2005	0.44	– 1.36	0.15	0.65
2006–2010	0.21	– 0.03	– 0.23	0.33

Source Li, Zhang, Lu & Qin, 2013

residents living in Beijing, those of the urban area hit 16.86 million, sharing 86PCT of the total. Together with the high rate of urbanization, the service sector in the same year claimed over 75PCT of the GDP (BMBS, 2016). Fairly speaking, such an occurrence is not coincident and to some extent, it is a chain reaction reflecting how the sectoral employment elasticity has evolved.

During the 2001–2010 period (Table 38), both the primary and secondary sector had a negative elasticity, which demonstrates that due to the enhanced level of productivity and mechanization, there has been an accumulation of excess labor. Instead of creating more jobs, the actual employment fell. Referring to the tertiary sector, however, it stayed rather elastic over the decade. With a high average coefficient of 0.49, the sector's pull effect on employment has enabled Beijing to absorb significant amounts of workforce. Their settlement, in turn, also helped accelerate the pace of urbanization. Besides, if compared to the first half of the decade, elasticity for the second half dropped to 0.33, a phenomenon reflecting the on-going structural optimization and upgrading in the service industry.

What has happened to Beijing is not an exceptional case; actually, it is an experience shared by many other countries. In particular, after going through changes in the model of economic growth, or the restructuring of industries, employment elasticity would move downward, which in turn poses a direct challenge to urbanization. Although urbanization is not equivalent to job creation, the constant availability of new vacancies is one major catalyst for the former to proceed in a vigorous way. In this consideration, since the service sector features a brighter outlook for job hunters, the necessity to prioritize its development is self-evident.

7.7 *Key to Sustainable Urbanization*

To explore a model replicable in different parts of China, the release of the "National New-Type Urbanization Plan (2014–2020)" in 2014 was shortly followed by a comprehensive pilot program. At the initial stage, 2 provinces (i.e. Jiangsu and Anhui Province) and 62 cities or towns (i.e. Ningbo, Dalian, Qingdao, and Wuhan, etc.) were selected to participate. While accomplishing the tasks laid out in the scheme, they were also required to accumulate experiences that could be shared elsewhere before the end of 2017 so that from 2018 to 2020, these valuable gains may benefit the rest of the country (NDRC, 2014). Even though the five highlighted tasks looked after different aspects of urbanization, such as the establishment of a cost-sharing mechanism to "citizenize" the rural population, formation of a diversified funding system for urban utilities, and the initiation of institutional reform, etc., their motive was without exception to urbanize the Chinese society in a sustainable pattern.

In view of the regional disparities and diverse locational characteristics, each participant tailored a plan on the basis of its unique conditions. Take Jiangsu Province as an example, located on the east coast of China, its urban residents in 2013 reached 50.9 million, or 64PCT of the total 79.4 million permanent population. For 2017 and 2020, it aimed to transfer an additional 4 million and 8 million people from rural to urban areas respectively, which would not only push up the proportion of permanent urban residents, but also the share of residents with urban hukou (household registration) in the total population (Graph 18).

Since alongside the expansion of cities, there is simultaneously renovation of infrastructures and upgrading of public services, which necessitate huge fiscal inputs. If the government remained the sole investor as before, it would be incapable of bearing the burden, nor could it handle all the complexities involved. For the assurance of an inexhaustible supply of funds and a reallocation of risks, public–private partnerships (PPP) was adopted by Jiangsu Province in its financing of multiple urban projects, such as wastewater treatment, rebuilding of shantytowns, and construction of expressways, etc. (Lan, 2015). By enabling the private sector to participate in the provision of public goods, government agencies can take advantage of its expertise and experiences, through which the operation would become more viable and market-oriented. From the perspective of the private sector, via the opportunity to access the formerly prohibited area of activities, it could expect to have a diversified stream of revenues. In addition, given the long-term nature of contracts, suppliers

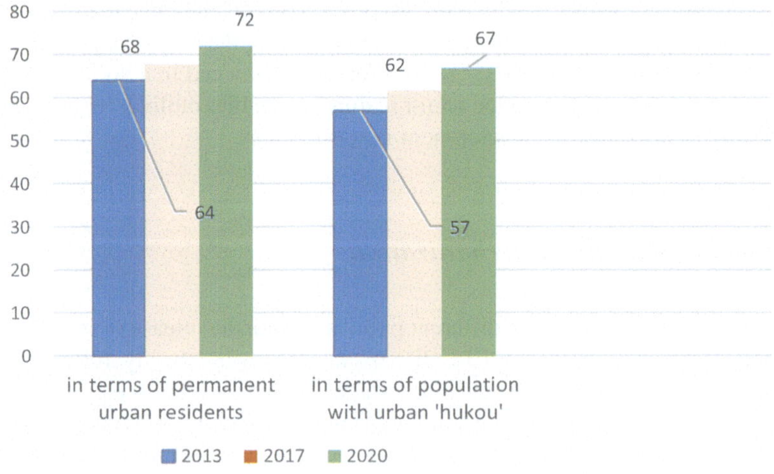

Graph 18 Urbanization Rate of Jiangsu Province in 2013 and Targets for 2017 & 2020, PCT. *Source* 江苏省国家新型城镇化综合试点工作方案要点, 2014. From https://www.gov.cn/xinwen/site1/20150204/40201423027629790.pdf

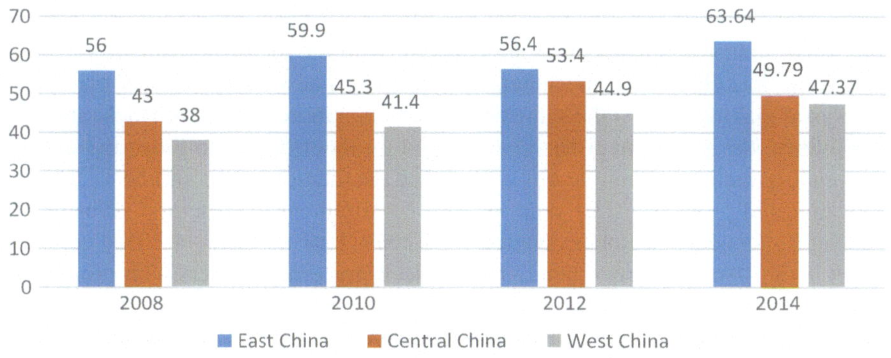

Graph 19 Regional Comparison of Urbanization Rate, 2008–2014, PCT. *Note* According to the National Bureau of Statistics, the three parts of China are divided as follows: East China include 11 provinces (including municipalities directly under the central government), i.e. Beijing, Tianjin, Hebei, Liaoning, Shanghai, Jiangsu, Zhejiang, Fujian, Shandong, Guangdong, and Hainan; Central China include 8 provinces, i.e. Shanxi, Jilin, Heilongjiang, Anhui, Jiangxi, Henan, Hubei, and Hunan; West China include 12 provinces (including municipalities directly under the central government, autonomous regions), i.e. Inner Mongolia, Guangxi, Chongqing, Sichuan, Guizhou, Yunnan, Tibet, Shaanxi, Gansu, Qinghai, Ningxia, and Xinjiang. Source: classification of the three parts of China: https://www.stats.gov.cn/tjsj/zxfb/201604/t20160428_1349713.html; 2008 & 2010: http://www.gov.cn/zhengce/2014-03/13/content_2637871.htm; 2012: http://www.chinacity.org.cn/cstj/zxgg/125672.html; 2014: http://chinareform.org.cn/area/city/Practice/201604/t20160414_246899.htm

have more time to optimize their cost structure. Driven by profit motives, they would lay greater emphasis on innovation and efficiency, which helps enhance their potential for further growth.

In terms of rural labor absorption, not only Jiangsu Province, East China as a whole has also outperformed the rest of the country because of its location advantage. From 2008 to 2014 for example, since the urbanization rate of Central and West China proceeded at a pace similar to that of the East, their gap didn't change much (Graph 19). Fairly speaking, this is not just a mirror reflecting regional attractiveness; at a deeper level, it also shows how these areas differ from each other in industrial competitiveness. Very often, there exists a synergistic relationship between urbanization and the evolution of sectoral structure. On the one hand, it would be hard to expedite urbanization if without the support of reasonably-developed industries; on the other hand, driven by the acceleration of urbanization, geographical distribution of industries would become optimized. Concerning the reasons why the urbanization of Central and West China has fallen behind the East, economic weaknesses should be taken as the primary one. Specifically, they both lack a well-tailored industrial plan which enables them to maximize gains from the resources available in their particular localities.

Of the 62 cities and towns chosen in 2014 to pioneer the national experiment of new-type urbanization, Yicheng is a county-level city of Central China's Hubei Province. Aware of the fact that the model of economic growth has significant impact on the promotion of urbanization, its priorities have been directed to the formation of five industrial clusters that are coherent with the local endowment, i.e. agro processing, fine chemicals, machinery & electronics, new energy & new materials, and crystal making, etc. At the same time, to channel more capital into these spheres of activities, the government has also stepped up its efforts to improve the investment environment, making the city a preferred destination that could host multiple innovation-led projects. After years of firm commitment to structural adjustment, Yicheng's secondary sector accounted for 57.6PCT of its GDP in 2015, up from 50.6PCT of 2010 (Wang & Chen, 2016). Indeed, fostering clusters with prominent regional features is crucial since it helps create a decent number of jobs and thus can attract more workforce to relocate out of the countryside. However, when it comes to the retention of rural labor, especially the highly-skilled, additional incentives are of equal significance. Toward the end of 2015, Yicheng has managed to provide compulsory education to all the children of migrant workers. Besides, with regard to the permanent urban residents covered by basic pension insurance and medical insurance, they accounted for 99.92PCT and 99CT of the total respectively (Zhang, 2016). In terms of the expenditures on the public sector, like health care, education, transport, social security, and employment, etc., the year-on-year growth rate of Yicheng averaged 28.3PCT throughout the 2010–2015 period (Wang & Chen, 2016), which from a fiscal perspective assured quality improvement of public services.

Referring to China's plan for a new model of urbanization 2014–2020, it contained numerous initiatives and they were almost without exception people-oriented. Based on such a common ground, it can be inferred that over the six-year period, wellbeing enhancement would be taken as the priority of the country's urbanization drive. Unlike the initial stage when the emphasis was laid more heavily on the expansion of cities and towns, and the construction of high-rising buildings, the scheme represented a major switch in the focus, which may better ensure that the nationwide campaign would not lose its momentum for lack of inherent driving force. Undeniably, the majority of migrant workers in China still belong to the low-income group whereas the role they play is rather crucial to the accomplishment of the giant task, making them better off so that they are no longer in a disadvantaged position is a task both critical and challenging. In this regard, the practice of Yicheng is worthy of promotion because it was not shortsightedly obsessed with quantifiable results; instead, attainment of a secure and sustained livelihood has been the centerpiece of its ambitions.

Although around the world, urbanization is not a phenomenon exclusive to any single country, the hallmarks they bear still differ from one to another. In view of China's unprecedented magnitude of labor transfer from agriculture to industry, which started in the late 1980s, integration of migrant workers into cities so as to let them enjoy the same rights and opportunities as urbanites becomes the key performance indicator of its urbanization. Put another way, the endeavor would be considered a failure if ultimately, they were not among the primary beneficiaries. According to a report of the National Bureau of Statistics, in 2015, China's rural migrant workers reached 277.47 million, accounting for around 20PCT of the total population. However, given the fact that the proportion of the workers with employment contracts was only 36.2PCT, a decrease of 1.8PCT over the previous year, those who could not get punctually paid climbed to 1PCT and on average, the wage arrears amounted to RMB9,788 per person (NBS, 2016). Moreover, despite an income rise of 7.2PCT as compared to 2014, the growth rate fell by 2.6PCT.

In view of the above facts and figures, which demonstrate at least partially the current conditions of the Chinese migrant workers, it is fair to say that in contrast with their remarkable contributions to the national economy, what they have gained is disproportionately meagre. To eliminate this effort-reward imbalance, a relaxed control over urban residency is far from enough. If the status were not backed by corresponding entitlement to citizenship, such an inequity could not be fully reversed. Therefore, since it has already been clarified that a sustainable urbanization is people-centered whereas the surplus agricultural labor in China has and will continue to dominate the population shift from rural to urban areas, as long as their identity remains a barrier to accessing public services, and a sense of rootlessness persists no matter in which cities they are employed, the stumbling block to the urbanization process would pose a constant threat prohibiting not only the fulfillment of the goals pertinent to the course itself; moreover, the nation's economic transformation could hardly hit the target.

References

Beijing Municipality Bureau of Statistics (BMBS). (2016). *Beijing statistical yearbook 2015*. Beijing: China Statistics Press.

Cai, L. (2013). New "Third Board" serving the development of small and medium-sized enterprises. *Investment in Beijing, 5,* 88–89.

CGSDTC. (2006). 2005 annual analysis report of China's bond market. Retrieved January 2, 2017, from https://www.chinabond.com.cn/cb/cn/yjfx/zzfx/nb/20080920/920320.shtml.

CGSDTC. (2007). 2006 annual analysis report of China's bond market. Retrieved January 2, 2017, from https://www.chinabond.com.cn/Info/920272.

CGSDTC. (2010). 2009 annual analysis report of China's bond market. Retrieved January 2, 2017, from https://www.chinabond.com.cn/Info/5002944.

Chen, H. L., & Yi, M. (2004). A probe into risk prevention of convertible bond financing. *Commercial Accounting, 2,* 43–44.

Chen, J. D. (2006). A brief discussion on the road to the reform of state-owned foreign trade enterprises: Also an analysis of the reform practice of Zhongda Group's foreign trade enterprise system. *Enterprise World, 8,* 10–11.

China Securities Regulatory Commission (CSRC). (2007). Introduction to China's securities and futures market in 2007. Retrieved January 5, 2017, from https://www.csrc.gov.cn/pub/newsite/gjb/cbwxz/.

Chu, J. (2005). What problems does split-share structure reform resolve? *China Petroleum and Chemical Industry, 6,* 52–54.

CSRC. (2008). Statistical table of securities market from January to October 2008. Retrieved January 5, 2017, from https://www.csrc.gov.cn/pub/zjhpublic/G00306204/zqscyb/200811/t20081120_108740.htm.

CSRC. (2008). China Securities Regulatory Commission annual report. Retrieved January 5, 2017, from https://www.csrc.gov.cn/pub/newsite/zjhjs/zjhnb/.

CSRC. (2009). Statistics of the stock market in August 2009. Retrieved January 5, 2017, from https://www.csrc.gov.cn/pub/zjhpublic/G00306204/zqscyb/200909/t20090910_163956.htm.

CSRC. (2016). Stock market monthly report. Retrieved January 5, 2017, from https://www.csrc.gov.cn/pub/newsite/sjtj/zqscyb/index_1.html.

Ding, X. Y. (1999). Enactment of Securities Law and securities market management. *Shanghai Finance and Taxation, 3*, 24–25.

Economist Intelligence Unit (EIU). (2016). Global food security index 2016: An annual measure of the state of global food security. The Economist Intelligence Unit. Retrieved January 5, 2017, from https://foodsecurityindex.eiu.com/.

Fan, K., et al. (2005). Impact of introducing QFII on China's securities market: From UBS's stock selection strategy. *Special Zone Economy, 12*, 83–84.

Fan, P. 2007 Chinese farmer development report: New development, new problems, new challenges. Ru X. et al. (Eds.). (2007). Analysis and forecast of China's social situation in 2008. Beijing: Social Sciences Literature Press.

Fang, M., & Liu, N. N. (2004). Silicon Valley venture capital favors China. *China Investment, 8*, 116–118.

Gong, X. P. (Ed.). (1999). *Shanghai yearbook 1999*. Shanghai: Shanghai Yearbook Press.

Groh, A. et al. (2011). The global venture capital and private equity country attractiveness index 2011 annual. IESE Business School. Retrieved January 12, 2017, from https://www.iese.edu/research/pdfs/ESTUDIO-143-E.pdf.

Groh, A. et al. (2016). The venture capital and private equity country attractiveness index 2016 annual. IESE Business School. Retrieved January 12, 2017, from https://blog.iese.edu/vcpeindex/files/2016/06/annual.pdf.

Gu, L. M. (2006). The "Third Board" market will bring phoenix to nirvana. *Financial Economy, 3*, 37–38.

Guo, L., & Yang, P. (2015). Development of the bond market should be dominated by the inter-bank market. *Financial Development Review, 7*, 54–57.

Guo, Y. C., & Wang, Y. T. (2012). A probe into the effective path of migrant workers' citizenization. *Agricultural Economy, 12*, 84–85.

Hai, S. (2006). CNPC's successful acquisition of PK sets a new record for Chinese companies' overseas mergers and acquisitions. *International Petroleum Economy, 1*, 4–5.

Hatzvi, E., et al. (2014). The offshore Renminbi market and Australia. *Reserve Bank of Australia Bulletin, 12*, 53–62.

He, Y. S. (2007). Legislative thinking on accelerating the enactment of Education Investment Law. *Fujian Theory Study, 4*, 40–42.

Hu, J. (2003). On deepening the reform of state-owned assets management system. *Fujian Forum (Humanities and Social Sciences Edition), 4*, 2–8.

Hu, J. H. (2011). COFCO grows soybeans in Brazil. *Agricultural Market Weekly, 14*, 28–29.

Hu, Y. M. (1997). On convertible bonds issued by Chinese companies. *China Economic Issues, 5*, 58–61.

Huaxin. (2015). Agricultural cooperative zone being promoted to national-level overseas agricultural industry cooperative zone. Retrieved January 10, 2017, from https://www.huaxin-agri.com/cn/news_view.asp?id=444.

Huang, Q. H. (2015). *Blue book of industrialization: Report on the industrialization process of countries along the Belt and Road*. Beijing: Social Sciences Literature Press.

Huang, W. (2004). Product internationalization strategy and tactical innovation of Haier's road of multinational operations. *Group Economic Research, 8*, 142–143.

IMF. (2005). The joint China-IMF training program in Dalian begins operation. Retrieved January 10, 2017, from https://www.imf.org/External/NP/INS/english/pdf/courv80305.pdf.

IMF. (2009). Balance of payments and international investment position manual (6th edition, BPM6). Washington D.C.: IMF. Retrieved January 10, 2017, from https://www.imf.org/external/pubs/ft/bop/2007/pdf/BPM6.pdf.

IMF. (2010). Transcript of a press conference by International Monetary Fund managing director Dominique Strauss-Kahn with first deputy managing director John Lipsky, and external relations director Caroline Atkinson. Retrieved January 10, 2017, from https://www.imf.org/en/News/Articles/2015/09/28/04/54/tr100710.

Ji, L. T. (2015). Research on RMB inter-bank foreign exchange market. *Jiangsu Business Review, 15,* 249–250.

Jiang, X., & Li, Q. (2010). Analysis of the phenomenon of over-subscription of ChiNext. *China Finance, 2,* 47–49.

Jin, Z. H. (2007). On the current situation, resistance and countermeasures of the reform of state-owned commercial banks in China. *Financial Economy: Theory Edition, 16,* 128–129.

Lan, A. & Tang Z. L. (2008). China's first stock: Shen Baoan. Shenzhen Special Zone News. Retrieved January 10, 2017, from https://sztqb.sznews.com/html/2008-12/04/content_439141.htm.

Lan, L. (2015). Analysis of Jiangsu Agricultural Bank's participation in PPP project financing model. *Modern Finance, 9,* 30–32.

Leng, Z. S. (2013). A summary of the main disagreements over "state advances, private sector retreats." *Red Flag Manuscript, 1,* 17–20.

Li, C., et al. (2013). The interactive relationship between population control and industrial structure optimization in Beijing. *Urban Issues, 8,* 2–6.

Li, C. F. (2015). Reflections on the development of mixed ownership economy to promote the transformation and upgrading of evaluation industry. *China Asset Evaluation, 1,* 20–22.

Li, D. M. (1998). International comparison of convertible bonds. *Capital Markets, 3,* 44–47.

Li, K. (2006). WTO and protection of intellectual property in China. *Theoretical Study and Exploration, 5,* 68–69.

Li, L. & Pang R. F. (2005). Standing at a new starting point: Six years of great changes in the Chinese stock market. Southern Weekend. Retrieved January 15, 2017, from https://www.southcn.com/weekend/commend/200506020002.htm.

Li, N. (2010). Kazakhstan's diversified international cooperation in nuclear energy and its enlightenment. *Natural Resource Economics of China, 11,* 40–44.

Li, Q. (2016). Overseas investment cannot avoid these things. *Import and Export Manager, 4,* 37–39.

Li, W. Z. (2013). Ways to consolidate Hong Kong's position as offshore RMB center. *Financial World, 3,* 99.

Lin, Y. (1997). Pilot of Sogo Shosha in China: Difficulties and choices. *International Economic Cooperation, 1,* 21–22.

Lin, Z. Q. (1979). A survey of the population of Lin'an, capital of the Southern Song dynasty. *Journal of Hangzhou University (Philosophy and Social Sciences Edition), Z1,* 147–149.

Liu, D. G. (2004). Pilot demonstration and guidance by models to actively support the development of farmers' professional cooperative economic organizations. *Rural Management, 3,* 26–28.

Liu, H. (2011). Further improvement of market maker transaction system in the inter-bank bond market. *Southwest Finance, 12,* 74–76.

Liu, T. S., & Xu, C. S. (1998). Countermeasures to prevent and resolve non-performing loans of state-owned commercial banks. *Hubei Rural Finance Research, 6,* 35.

Liu, X. (2013). Process and impact of interest rate marketization reform. *Economist, 11,* 35–36.

Liu, Z. B., & Ma, N. S. (1987). Rise and development of overseas investment companies in China. *International Economic Cooperation, 8,* 25.

Long, Y. T. (2004). Statement by Mr. Long Yongtu, assistant minister of MOFTEC, at the first meeting of the working party on China's accession to WTO (March 22nd, 1996, Geneva), permanent mission of the People's Republic of China to the United Nations at Geneva and other international organizations in Switzerland. Retrieved January 13, 2017, from https://www.china-un.ch/eng/qtzz/wtothsm/t85617.htm.

Lu, F. (2012). Wage trends of Chinese migrant workers: 1979–2010. *Social Sciences in China, 7,* 47–67.

Lu, L. R. (2007). Shenzhen: High-technology property exchange builds a private equity investment and financing platform. *Property Rights Guide, 11,* 56–58.
Lü, H. B. (2006). From "double gap" to "double overflow": Analysis of the current situation of China's foreign investment and countermeasures. *Journal of Northeast University of Finance and Economics, 4,* 13–17.
Lü, T. (2014). COFCO completes the largest overseas merger and acquisition, ranking among world-class grain merchants. *China Food, 22,* 100–101.
Lü, W. L. (2010). Beijing, Shanghai, Shenzhen, Tianjin, Chongqing and Ningbo competing for "national equity investment center." *Internet Weekly, 5,* 14.
Ma, X. H., & Hu, Y. J. (2010). China's urbanization process, problems and its overall layout. *Reform, 10,* 30–45.
Ma, Y., & Li, J. B. (2007). From import substitution to export orientation: A comparison of trade development strategies between the mainland and Taiwan. *Asia Pacific Economy, 3,* 78–82.
Mao, Y. S., et al. (2013). *Food security and farm land protection in China.* Singapore: World Scientific Publishing.
Masudaa, T. & Goldsmith, P. D. World soybean production: Area harvested, yield, and long-term projections. International Food and Agribusiness Management Review, 4, 143–162.
Ministry of Land and Resources (MLR). (2016). Bulletin of China land and resources 2015. Retrieved January 18, 2017, from https://www.mlr.gov.cn/zwgk/tjxx/201604/P020160421532279160618.pdf.
Ministry of Agriculture (MOA). (2011). Report on the development of wholesale market for China's agricultural products. Retrieved January 18, 2017, from https://www.moa.gov.cn/sjzz/scs/sclt/201106/t20110606_2008211.htm.
MOC. (2004). China's foreign trade development status in 2002. Retrieved January 18, 2017, from https://zhs.mofcom.gov.cn/aarticle/Nocategory/200405/20040500221430.html.
MOC. (2014). Data briefing: China has signed free trade agreements with 20 countries and regions. Retrieved January 18, 2017, from https://tradeinservices.mofcom.gov.cn/local/2014-07-03/245035.shtml.
MOC. (2015). Shanghai's foreign trade increased by 4.6% in 2014. Retrieved January 18, 2017, from https://www.mofcom.gov.cn/article/resume/n/201501/20150100875080.shtml.
MOC. (2015 & 2016). Ministry of Commerce notified business operations in 2014 & 2015. Retrieved January 18, 2017, from https://www.scio.gov.cn/xwfbh/gbwxwfbh/xwfbh/swb/index_1.htm.
MOC. (2016). China's foreign trade development in 2015. Retrieved January 18, 2017, from https://zhs.mofcom.gov.cn/article/Nocategory/201605/20160501314688.shtml.
MOC. (2016). China service trade statistics 2015. Retrieved January 18, 2017, from https://tradeinservices.mofcom.gov.cn/c/2016-01-26/284930.shtml.
Ministry of Education (MOE). (1998–2001). Statistical bulletin on the implementation of national education funds 1997, 1998, 1999 & 2000. Retrieved January 18, 2017, from https://www.moe.gov.cn/s78/A05/cws_left/s3040/.
Ministry of Finance (MOF). (2012). Performing obligations and safeguarding rights and interests: Review of the 10th anniversary of China's accession to the WTO. Retrieved January 18, 2017, from https://gss.mof.gov.cn/zhengwuxinxi/gongzuodongtai/201201/t20120116_623584.html.
NBS. (2009). Urban development. Retrieved January 20, 2017, from https://www.gov.cn/test/2009-09/22/content_1423390.htm.
NBS. (2013). National survey report on migrant workers in 2012. Retrieved January 20, 2017, from https://www.stats.gov.cn/tjsj/zxfb/201305/t20130527_12978.html.
NBS. (2014). National survey report on migrant workers in 2013. Retrieved January 20, 2017, from https://www.stats.gov.cn/tjsj/zxfb/201405/t20140512_551585.html.
NBS. (2015). National survey report on migrant workers in 2014. Retrieved January 20, 2017, from https://www.stats.gov.cn/tjsj/zxfb/201504/t20150429_797821.html.
NBS. (2016). China statistical yearbook 2015. Beijing: China Statistics Press. Retrieved January 20, 2017, from https://www.stats.gov.cn/tjsj/ndsj/.

NBS. (2016). 2015 nasstional economic and social development statistical bulletin. Retrieved January 20, 2017, from https://www.stats.gov.cn/tjsj/zxfb/201602/t20160229_1323991.html.
NBS. (2016). Survey report of migrant workers in 2015. Retrieved January 20, 2017, from https://www.stats.gov.cn/tjsj/zxfb/201604/t20160428_1349713.html.
National Development and Reform Commission (NDRC). (2014). National comprehensive pilot program for new urbanization. Retrieved January 20, 2017, from https://www.gov.cn/xinwen/2015-02/04/content_2814341.htm.
National Equities Exchange and Quotations (NEEQ). (2015). Statistical express of national SMEs equity transfer system 2015. Retrieved January 20, 2017, from https://www.gscm.org.cn/data/6678.html.
PBoC. (2012). Annual data and structure of social financing scale since 2002. Retrieved January 20, 2017, from https://www.pbc.gov.cn/diaochatongjisi/116219/116225/2863552/index.html.
PBoC. (2005 & 2006). China monetary policy implementation report, fourth quarter of 2004 and fourth quarter of 2005. Retrieved January 20, 2017, from https://www.pbc.gov.cn/zhengcehuobisi/125207/125227/125957/index.html.
PBoC. (2015). China monetary policy implementation report: Fourth quarter of 2014. Retrieved January 20, 2017, from https://www.gov.cn/foot/site1/20150210/48111423567940903.pdf.
PBoC. (2016). China monetary policy implementation report: Fourth quarter of 2015. Retrieved January 21, 2017, from https://www.chinabond.com.cn/Info/22938958.
PBoC. (2016). Financial market operation in 2015. Retrieved January 21, 2017, from https://www.pbc.gov.cn/goutongjiaoliu/113456/113469/3009101/2016012516493935858.pdf.
PBoC. (2016). Statistical report on the increment of social financing scale in 2015. Retrieved January 19, 2017, from https://www.pbc.gov.cn/goutongjiaoliu/113456/113469/3004957/index.html.
PBoC. (2012). Conditions for accelerating capital account opening in China are basically mature. Retrieved January 17, 2017, from https://www.pbc.gov.cn/diaochatongjisi/116219/116221/116241/1044593/index.html.
PBoC. (2016). Operation and characteristics of China's inter-bank bond market in 2015. Bonds, 3, 21-26.
Pei, C. H., & Zheng, W. (2015). *China's outbound foreign direct investment promotion system.* Berlin: Springer-Verlag.
Peng, L. L., & Huang, J. L. (2012). Structural changes in social practice and reconstruction of urban grassroots communities: Chinese experience of community construction from the perspective of sociology (1986–2012). *Learning and Practice, 9,* 56–65.
Preqin. (2014). Private equity industry raises largest amount of capital since global financial crisis. Preqin press release. Retrieved January 6, 2017, from https://www.preqin.com/docs/press/Private_Equity_Q4_2013.pdf.
Qi, X. L. (2014). American interest equalization tax and its effect and impact (1963–1974). *Historical Research in Anhui, 5,* 108–114.
Qian, S. W., et al. (2009). An empirical study of the corporate capital structure of seven cities in China. *Finance and Economics: Academic, 11,* 56–57.
Qian, Y. W. (1994). Welcoming foreign investment in China's shipbuilding industry: Talks by the general manager Wang Rongsheng of China state shipbuilding corporation. *China Foreign Trade, 10,* 9–10.
Qiu, Y. (2006). Impact of the establishment of China-Australia Free Trade Zone on China's wheat. In: Cheng, K. et al. (Eds.). (2006). New rural construction and the three rural issues: Proceedings of the 2006 national annual conference of young and middle-aged agricultural economists. Beijing: China Agricultural Press.
Qiu, Z. X., & He, L. F. (2008). Current feasibility of RMB regionalization. *China Finance, 10,* 46–47.
Qu, S. (2006). A historical analysis of the international trade and nature of China's grain. *Chinese Economic History Research, 3,* 20–28.
Ren, Z. L. (2008). Estimation of the fair value of RMB interest rate swaps based on SHIBOR. *Finance and Accounting Monthly, 18,* 53–54.

SAFE. (1999, 2002 & 2005). China foreign exchange annual report 1998, 2001 & 2004. Retrieved January 5, 2017, from https://www.safe.gov.cn/wps/portal/sy/cbw_whglnb.
SAFE. (2007 & 2008). China's balance of payments report 2006 & 2007. Retrieved January 5, 2017, from https://www.safe.gov.cn/wps/portal/sy/cbw_gjszbg.
SAFE. (2009). China's balance of payments report 2008. Retrieved January 5, 2017, from https://www.safe.gov.cn/wps/portal/sy/cbw_gjszbg.
SAFE. (2014). China's balance of payments report 2013. Retrieved January 5, 2017, from https://www.safe.gov.cn/wps/portal/sy/cbw_gjszbg.
SAFE. (2014). Qualified foreign institutional investor (QFII) investment quota approval form, deadline: January 30th, 2015. Retrieved January 5, 2017, from https://www.chinaforex.com.cn/attachment/cms/item/2015_02/02_08/097d97cc34daa960.pdf.
SAFE. (2014). Qualified domestic institutional investor (QDII) investment quota approval form, deadline: January 30th, 2015. Retrieved January 5, 2017, from https://www.chinaforex.com.cn/attachment/cms/item/2015_02/02_09/7502fd3a853d893d.pdf.
SAFE. (2014). RMB qualified foreign institutional investor (RQFII) investment quota approval form, deadline: March 26th, 2015.
SAFE. (2016). China international investment position table (time series data). Retrieved January 5, 2017, from https://www.safe.gov.cn/wps/portal/sy/tjsj_tzctb.
Shao, M. (2014). Lessons and inspirations from capital account opening in advanced economies. *Southern Finance, 1,* 54–58.
Silk Road Fund (SRF). (2015). Silk Road Fund joined with ChemChina in investment in Pirelli. Retrieved January 15, 2017, from https://www.silkroadfund.com.cn/cnweb/19930/19938/20115/index.html.
Sinochem. (2016). Sinochem group ranked 9th in "China's top 500 foreign trade companies" list. Retrieved January 15, 2017, from https://www.sinochem.com/s/1375-4608-19987.html.
Sinopec. (2014). Sinopec announces list of investment introduction by sales. Retrieved January 4, 2017, from https://www.sinopecgroup.com/group/xwzx/gsyw/20140914/news_20140914_674115581102.shtml.
Smil, V. (1981). Land use and management in the people's republic of China. *Environmental Management, 4,* 301–311.
Su, S. S. (2005). Lsting of state-owned commercial banks: From government ownership to public companies. *Western Forum, 12,* 52–55.
Sun, Z. Y. (2011). Retrospect and prospect of the 10th anniversary of China's accession to the WTO. *International Economic Review, 4,* 114–123.
Tan, X. M. (2013). China's overseas investment in the energy/resources sector: Its scale, drivers, challenges and implications. *Energy Economics, 36,* 750–758.
Tang, J. (2013). The deep meaning behind the IPO restart. *China Economic Weekly, 47,* 85.
Tang, X. L. (2007). Analysis of the problems and development strategies of China's foreign exchange derivatives market. *Business Modernization, 16,* 15–16.
Tian, L. (2011). QDII fund's overseas investment is a bittersweet picture. *Legal Person, 10,* 33.
UNCTAD. (1995). World investment report 1995. Retrieved January 6, 2017, from https://unctad.org/en/Docs/wir1995_en.pdf.
UNCTAD. (2004). FDI from developing countries takes off, is a new geography of investment emerging? Retrieved January 6, 2017, from https://unctad.org/en/pages/PressReleaseArchive.aspx?ReferenceDocId=5185.
Wan, Y. (2013). Analysis of the financial effect of share repurchase of Yinji development. *Science and Technology Square, 4,* 28–30.
Wang, B. J. (2007). Market maker system and the development of China's foreign exchange market. *Science and Technology, Economy, Market, 4,* 246–247.
Wang, C. (2015). Enterprises praise the new customs clearance policy of Shanghai Free Trade Zone. *Shanghai-Hong Kong Economy, 12,* 32–35.
Wang, D. N. (2006). The current status of China's commercial banks' capital adequacy ratio and complementary approaches. *Economic Forum, 13,* 110–112.

Wang, H. G. (2011). Formation of urban-rural dual household registration system. *Annals Yellow Emperor, 12*, 6–14.
Wang, J. (2001). Institutional conflicts of interest of Chinese listed companies. *Peking University Law Review, 1*, 82–117.
Wang, Q. X., & Chen, R. (2002). On the choice of venture capital organization. *Modern Finance: Journal of Tianjin University of Finance and Economics, 10*, 49–53.
Wang, R. W. (2006). Analysis of the newly revised securities law. *Cooperative Economy and Technology, 22*, 46–47.
Wang, S. C. (2010). Problems and countermeasures of water resources security in China. *Geography Teaching, 1*, 4–7.
Wang, S. S., & Ji, Y. F. (2005). Analysis of the factors that restrict the current rise in A-share prices. *Financial Economy, 16*, 11–12.
Wang, W. P. (2008). An empirical analysis of the monetary sterilization operation of the central bank of China: 1994–2007. *Finance and Economics Theory and Practice, 5*, 14–17.
Wang, X. (2015). Cumulative financing of SME board exceeds 900 billion yuan. Shenzhen Special Zone Daily. Retrieved January 7, 2017, from https://sztqb.sznews.com/html/2015-05/22/content_3231234.htm.
Wang, X. P. (2015). The development status, problems and suggestions of the RMB bond market in Hong Kong. *Bonds, 5*, 44–49.
Wang, X. L., & Sun, J. M. (2015). Analysis and prospect of wheat consumption in China. *Journal of Wheat Crops, 5*, 655–661.
Wang, X. J. (2010). Crisis and countermeasures of China's soybean industry. *Economic Problems, 1*, 81–86.
Wang, Z. H., & Chen D. G. (2016). Economic and social development of Yicheng during the Twelfth Five-Year Plan period was brilliant. Yicheng Statistics Bureau. Retrieved January 7, 2017, from https://www.yichengnews.com/2016/0510/521830.shtml.
Wei, H. K., & Su, H. J. (2013). Research on the process of citizenization of Chinese agricultural migration population. *Chinese Population Science, 5*, 21–29.
Wen, R. (2012). Emergence and abolishment of food stamp system. *Communist Party Members, 10*, 46.
WTO. (2016). Trade growth to remain subdued in 2016 as uncertainties weigh on global demand. Retrieved January 7, 2017, from https://www.wto.org/english/news_e/pres16_e/pr768_e.htm.
Wu, L. (2014). Current problems and suggestions in the production and operation of micro, small, and medium enterprises. *Decision Exploration Monthly, 9*, 61–62.
Wu, L. H. (2014). Implementation of the "strictest in history" delisting system, 18 listed companies are hanging on the front line. Economic Reference News. Retrieved January 7, 2017, from https://news.xinhuanet.com/fortune/2014-11/17/c_1113270154.htm.
Wu, X. W., & Wu, W. B. (2014). Empirical research on benchmark interest rate selection. *China Finance, 18*, 79.
Xia, W. W. (2001). International financing practices of Chinese enterprises. *Journal of Jiangxi University of Science and Technology, 6*, 106–108.
Xiao, F. J. (2008). Review and prospect of China's foreign exchange management system reform. *International Trade, 7*, 51–55.
Xiao, X. (2007). QDII: Finding a professional to help manage your assets overseas. *Accounting Newsletter: Financial Management Edition, 9*, 9–10.
Xin, Y. (2014). Mixed ownership reform staggers forward. *Legal Person, 11*, 22–27.
Xu, D. W. (2009). Application of option theory of securities liquidity discount in restricted shares valuation. *China Asset Valuation, 3*, 11–13.
Xu, X. (2001). Limited partnership enterprise system and the choice of China's venture capital enterprise model. *Social Sciences, 7*, 64–68.
Xu, X. H. (2003). Current status and characteristics of Chinese companies' direct overseas investment. *Economic System Reform, 6*, 98–101.

Xu, Z. Y., & Hu, L. (2014). The impact of private equity M&A on the value of company: Taking new bridge capital's acquisition of Shenzhen development bank as an example. *East China Economic Management, 12,* 151–156.

Yan, B., & Chen, Y. Z. (2009). 30 Years' reform of grain circulation system. *China Grain Economy, 3,* 18–25.

Yang, R., & Chen, J. (2008). Development of China's foreign exchange market since exchange rate reform. *Banker, 11,* 80–81.

Yang, S. G., & Tan, Z. (2007). Research on the currency structure management of China's foreign exchange reserves based on AHP. *Finance Theory and Practice, 3,* 2–7.

Yang, X. X. (2015). Silk road fund enters the blue ocean. *Chinese Financiers, 6,* 48–49.

Yili Group. (2015). Power of quality: Corporate citizenship report of Yili Group 2012–2014. Retrieved January 3, 2017, from https://image.yili.com/upload/usrFiles/20160831182113294.pdf.

Yuan, M. (2001). Commitments China should fulfill after joining the WTO. *Popular Science and Technology, 12,* 37.

Yue, Q. Z. (2014). Opportunities and risks of PE under the wave of state-owned enterprise reform. *Modern State-Owned Enterprise Research, 6,* 63–66.

Zero2IPO Research Center. (2015). A review of Chinese equity investment market in 2014. Retrieved January 3, 2017, from https://www.zero2ipo.com.cn/promotion/survey/2015/0209/20150209.pdf.

Zhang, D., & Guo, Y. J. (2012). Expansion of the New Third Board. *Financial World, 9,* 76–77.

Zhang, H. (2016). Bold exploration in the new urbanization of Yicheng, Hubei province, with farmers entering the city can enjoy the same treatment as local residents. Changjiang Commercial Daily. Retrieved January 3, 2017, from https://www.changjiangtimes.com/szb/20160509/a07.html.

Zhang, J. (2006). RMB interest rate swaps surfaced. *Shanghai and Hong Kong Economy, 4,* 30–31.

Zhang, M. (2016). Banks tightening loans for excess capacity to mitigate risks. *Financial World, 3,* 66–67.

Zhang, N., & Xu, Y. B. (2005). Investment strategy under the pilot reform of split share structure. *Reform Open up, 6,* 39–40.

Zhang, Z. L. (2006). Current situation and improvement measures of Chinese companies' cross-border mergers and acquisitions. *Science and Technology Achievements, 4,* 26–27.

Zhao, W. M. (1997). Rapid development of China-Israel economic and technological relations (Part 2). *International Outlook, 5,* 13–14.

Zhao, X. F. (2008). Depreciation of the U.S. dollar and its situation: Interview with Bi Jiyao, deputy director of the foreign economic research institute of the national development and reform commission. *China Finance, 3,* 17–19.

Zhao, Y. (2004). Does "last supper" become "free lunch" again? A rational analysis of the establishment of Huijin. *China Economic Information, 16,* 66–67.

Zhou, Q. R. (2012). Industrialization ahead and urbanization behind. *China Foreign Trade, 5,* 37.

Zhou, R. F. (2014). Reform and innovation: The main theme of the development of intersbank bond market. Financial Times. Retrieved January 19, 2017, from https://www.chinabond.com.cn/Info/18729328.

Zhou, Y. J., & Chao, K. T. (2011). Research on overseas investment policies of China's financial industry. *Financial Theory Research, 1,* 57–62.

Zhu, C. H., & Li, F. (2016). Analysis of the main achievements and problems of the construction of Shanghai free trade zone. *Asia-Pacific Economy, 1,* 107–111.

Zhu, W. H. (1998). Development trend of Chinese urban planning from 1997 to 1998. *Journal of Urban Planning, 4,* 3–11.

Zhuang, Q. S., & Wang, J. (2007). Test of the role of China's WTO accession commitment concerning financial service trade in the post-WTO Era. *World Economic and Political Forum, 2*, 30–34.

Zhuo, L. (2005). 2004: Accomplishment of agriculture's soft landing from planned system to market track. *China Cooperative Economy, 1*, 25.

Chapter 6
Conclusion

Throughout the world history, economy has been commonly referred to as a key measure reflecting the hard power of a country. Nevertheless, if to break it down into distinct segments for an in-depth examination, what they can mirror are rather multifaceted, from institutional construction, governance capacity, to entrepreneurial and innovative spirit, etc., which in fact makes it a pointer to the soft power of the state. With regard to the footsteps of China over the past decades in developing its economy, while there were no lack of twists and turns, the journey was also intertwined with constant trials and adjustments. To a large extent, it is because of the contagious nature of these dynamics that other spheres of the society have been mobilized as well, which makes the country a prodivder of immense opportunities and possibilities.

From a macro perspective, given the increasing interconnectedness of the global economy, China's performance matters a lot. In particular, viewing the fact that in 2015, its GDP exceeded USD11 trillion, accounting for some 15PCT of the world's total, which was USD73.9 trillion (the World Bank, from https://databank.worldbank.org/data/download/GDP.pdf), the responsibilities to shoulder are self-evident. Put another way, China's ongoing process of reform and opening up has impact not just on the inside; furthermore, it would spread beyond its border via different channels, causing effects that are not entirely predictable. Thereby, this requires the policymakers to be more prudent in every major decision they take so as to avoid subsequent harms. Besides, at a micro level, since the transition in China has been a rather profound one whereas the ultimate success relies heavily on the mobilization of the entire population; to ensure that they act in a cohesive way, systemic fairness is an essential determinant. Specifically, along with the process, there necessitates a growing perception of enhanced justice in the distribution of outcomes, a prerequisite which brings about enduring satisfaction. In this consideration, it doesn't pay to chase faster speed unless the sense of well-being among the majority Chinese could simultaneously get stronger.

Looking back, the evolvement of China's economy is accompanied by numerous rounds of self-correction and self-improvement. At the outset when the country

C. Yu, *China's Economy: Towards 2049*,
https://doi.org/10.1007/978-981-15-9227-0_6

Table 1 GDP of China and the World, 1–1950 AD (Million 1990 International Geary-Khamis Dollars)

Year	1	1000	1500	1600	1700	1820	1913	1950
China	26,820	27,494	61,800	96,000	82,800	228,600	241,431	244,985
World	105,402	121,208	248,321	331,344	371,058	693,502	2,733,190	5,335,860
PCT of the world[1]	25.45	22.68	24.89	28.97	22.31	32.96	8.83	4.59

Note China was under the rule of the Western Han Dynasty in 1 AD; Song Dynasty in 1000 AD; Ming Dynasty in 1500 & 1600 AD; and Qing Dynasty during 1700–1912 AD; between 1912 and 1949, the state name became the Republic of China; after Oct. 1st, 1949, it was succeeded by the People's Republic of China. 1: calculated by the author by dividing China's GDP by the world total.
Source Maddison, 2010

was newly founded in 1949, the legacy it inherited was a blend of both amazing achievements and unlearned lessons. As one of the earliest civilizations in the world, its outstanding performance in economy, especially the openness, had made it a hub for international exchange during the Han, Tang, Song, and Yuan dynasties, etc. However, due to the close-door policy of the subsequent Ming and Qing rulers, the nation was not only threatened by external military forces; the economic strength kept diminishing as well. Although until 1820, i.e. the mid-to-late Qing period, China's GDP still accounted for almost one third of the world's total (Table 1), the increasing occurrence of natural disasters, civil uprisings, and foreign invasions, etc. caused serious depletion of resources. While the Second Industrial Revolution in Europe and America was bringing dramatic advances in productivity and technology, the Qing court was preoccupied with the imperative of stabilizing the incessant turbulences at home. Despite the initiation of some institutional reforms like the Self-strengthening Movement (also known as the Westernization Movement, or '*yangwu yundong*') in the second half of the nineteenth century, the full-fledged downturn was even more overwhelming. Economically, shrinkage became an overriding theme and after being overtaken by the US in the 1890s, its GDP in the world was getting less and less significant. In 1913, i.e. one year after the collapse of the Qing Empire, the share plunged to 8.83PCT (Table 1). For lack of political unity in the post-1912 China, the situation was deteriorated by a series of upheavals, including the inception of warlordism, the intrusion of the Japanese troops, and the outbreak of the civil war, etc., all without exception dampened the already fragile economy. In 1950, it merely contributed 4.59PCT to the global GDP, a level unbelievable if taking into consideration the entire timeline since 1 AD.

When stepping into the 1950s, the footprints China left behind were a collection of the highs and lows it had gone through. At this fresh starting point, the Soviet-style command economy was applied as a mechanism to coordinate the development of diverse sectors. With regard to agriculture, collective farming replaced the former household-based production, which brought almost all peasants under the administration of rural cooperatives and people's communes. Besides, by launching the socialist transformation of industry and commerce, public ownership of non-state

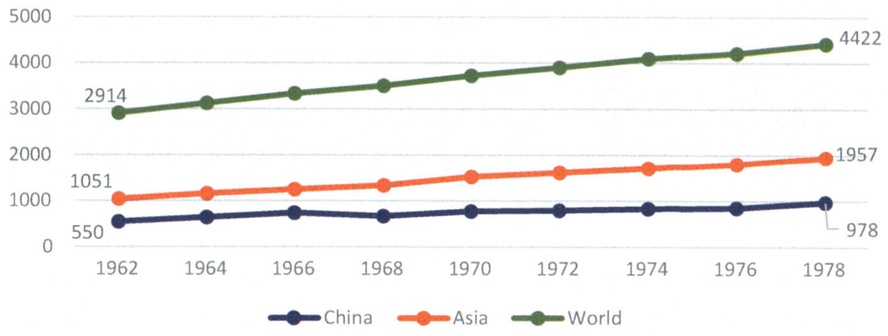

Graph 1 Per Capita GDP of China, Asia and the World, 1990 International Geary-Khamis Dollars. *Source* Maddison, 2010

enterprises was consolidated. These two moves, while facilitating the elimination of market forces, enabled the government to direct massive inputs to support the national strategy centered on heavy industries. To achieve a faster pace of growth, objectives impossible to accomplish were set forth in the movement called the Great Leap Forward. Ironically, instead of leaping forward, the blind pursuit ended up with three years of famine from 1959 to 1961, which took the life of millions. In addition, before the economy regained its footing in the aftermath, a decade-long Cultural Revolution (1966–1976) further exacerbated the shaky situation, pulling the country into another cycle of craziness.

From a comparison of China's per capita GDP with Asia and the world during that special era, the most noticeable trend was the persistently expanding gap (Graph 1). In particular, over the ten-year catastrophe (as the Cultural Revolution is often referred to), the per capita GDP of China only rose by around 14PCT whereas that of Asia and the world climbed almost 45PCT and 27PCT respectively. Based on the sharp contrast, it is not hard to understand why two years after the Revolution, policymakers in China were so determined to transform the economic system. Otherwise, the rigid central control would only result in heavier losses and once that happend, it would be even more unlikely to have the situation turned around.

Thereby, the decision of 1978 to explore an alternative development model was partially motivated by the compelling need to catch up. Above all, facing some twenty years of missed opportunities, the paramount task of China at that moment was nothing but to strive forward. If the introduction of the household responsibility system (HRS) in the rural area unveiled the strategy of reform, establishment of special economic zones in the coastal regions marked the first step of opening up. As China's international cooperation was flourishing on multiple fronts, the goal of setting up a socialist market economy became affirmative, which further strengthened its resolve to join the World Trade Organization (WTO). Fairly speaking, accession to the WTO in 2001 was a watershed event since afterwards, the country had to align itself with a variety of international rules and practices. Unlike the adjustment which had been conducted over the previous decades, the upcoming one was no longer a pure domestic affair. Given the involvement of universal norms, it called for another wave of reform and opening up with bolder steps. Although to a large extent, the impetus this time was mainly derived from the outside, it pushed China to move on without missing the right direction. Most notably, in the course of fulfilling its pre-entry commitment, transparency of the legal system was increased, thus enhancing the predictability of the economic environment. Besides, thanks to the growth of foreign trade and investment, there were also major improvements in the structural composition of industries, as well as their efficiency of operation. In addition, guided by the WTO's central tenet of securing a level playing field for all the member states, government interference was subject to more restraints, which led to fairer competition between businesses of different types.

Admittedly, these changes have both touched the fundamental aspects of the Chinese economy and in the foreseeable future, they are set to proceed in a more profound manner. At the same time, through a closer integration with the rest of the world, China has gained a much broadened vision, a standpoint that encompasses not only the wellbeing of itself, but also the interaction with other countries. In a globalized era featured by a higher degree of interdependence, the responsibilities that fall on each nation are on the rise too. From this perspective, the transition that has and will continue to take place in China, plus the international repercussions, are of equal significance to policymakers. According to what the celebrated Chinese philosopher Mencius (circa 372–289 BC) has written in his masterpiece *The Works of Mencius*, in a battle, "opportunities of time vouchsafed by Heaven are not equal to advantages of situation afforded by the Earth, and advantages of situation afforded by the Earth are not equal to the union arising from the accord of Men" (Yu, 2012); if China expects to fulfill its reform objectives smoothly, the "accord of Men", i.e. a harmonious multilateral relationship is indispensable. In particular, since the country at the current stage is seeking a balanced model of development which centers on the efficient utilization of resources and redistribution of wealth, strong coalition with foreign countries should be taken as an important strategy. On the one hand, this can help draw experiences and avoid their wrong turns; on the other hand, it may also create a favorable external environment for China to engage more intently in the aggressive agenda.

Victor Hugo once said: "What is history? An echo of the past in the future; a reflex from the future on the past". Looking back at the thousands of years of the Chinese history, although it had once remained at its zenith for quite a long period, the stage when it slumped to the nadir was an equally indelible episode. While the former is reminiscent of something glorious, the latter serves as a vivid reminder of the lessons from the past. Considering that China still has some way to go before claiming itself a full market economy, these twists are indeed valuable heritage for the forthcoming generations to take warning. Furthermore, like other peoples around the globe, the Chinese are also blessed with remarkable wisdom and creativity; by relying on these two important traits, they can manage to achieve growth through learning.

According to the 13th Five-Year Plan (2016–2020) on National Economic and Social Development, China's goal at this particular phase is to build a moderately prosperous society ('*xiaokang shehui*'). For the fulfillment of this ambition, five tenets were expounded too in the Plan and they included innovation ('*chuang xin*'), coordination ('*xie tiao*'), green development ('*lü se*'), openness ('*kai fang*'), and inclusiveness ('*gong xiang*'), etc. By setting the country's annual GDP growth rate at no less than 6.5PCT for the next five years, the so-called "new normal" of the economy is no longer focused on the fast speed, but a high-quality growth pattern that is both environmentally-friendly and beneficial to the entire population. Through this blueprint, China's vision for the future reforms is unveiled and in view of the five underlying principles, the vision is also consistent with the trend of the contemporary era. On top of the disparities and frictions between nations, the world today has a stronger sense of shared fate, which makes it more united in tackling diverse affairs, especially challenges.

"When the Grand course was pursued, a public and common spirit ruled all under the sky" ('*Dadao zhixing ye, tianxia weigong*', Confucius, *The Book of Rites* or '*Li Ji*') (Müller, 1885). This benevolent concept, although coined over two thousand years ago, pictures accurately the ultimate ideal of the humanity. At the core, what sustains the global civilization is not just material abundance, but harmony based on the promotion of public good. Economy, like politics and culture, serves as a means to help realize public ends. Out of deference to the teachings of the ancient sage, and to better perform its citizenry obligations in the twenty-first century, China is in need of a strengthened partnership with the international community. Back in the Han Dynasty, i.e. around the second century BC, the "Silk Road" was established linking China and the Mediterranean. In 2013, an initiative named "One Belt and One Road" (OBOR) opened up the new "Silk Road". Covering four continents (i.e. Asia, Europe, Oceania, and Africa) and three oceans (i.e. the Pacific Ocean, the Atlantic Ocean and the Indian Ocean), the route is to be extended further over the upcoming years. Till then, together with a closer economic connectivity, cross-border exchanges on multiple fronts are also expected to flourish, which would enable a greater number of participants to reap fruits via the bridge.

References

Müller, F. M. (1885). *The sacred books of the east translated by various oriental scholars*. Vol. XXVIII: The sacred books of China. The texts of Confucianism, translated by James Legge. Part IV. The Li Ki, XI-XLVI. Oxford: Clarendon Press. Retrieved October 20, 2015, from https://lf-oll.s3.amazonaws.com/titles/2014/Muller_1345-28_EBk_v6.0.pdf.

Yu, F. T. (2012). *Entrepreneurship and Taiwan's economic dynamics*. Berlin: Springer-Verlag.

The manufacturer's authorised representative in the EU is Springer Nature Customer Service Centre GmbH, Europaplatz 3, 69115 Heidelberg, Germany. If you have any concerns regarding our products, please contact ProductSafety@springernature.com

Printed and bound by CPI Group (UK) Ltd, Croydon, CR0 4YY
30/09/2026
02225452-0016